Saint and singer

D0075329

Definition of a type. Autograph page from Edward Taylor's *Upon the Types of the Old Testament*. Courtesy of Charles W. Mignon, the Archives of Love Library, University of Nebraska-Lincoln, and the University of Nebraska Press.

Saint and singer

Edward Taylor's typology and the poetics of meditation

KAREN E. ROWE
University of California, Los Angeles

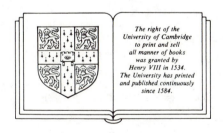

The right of the
University of Cambridge
to print and sell
all manner of books
was granted by
Henry VIII in 1534.
The University has printed
and published continuously
since 1584.

CAMBRIDGE UNIVERSITY PRESS

Cambridge
London   New York   New Rochelle
Melbourne   Sydney

Published by the Press Syndicate of the University of Cambridge
The Pitt Building, Trumpington Street, Cambridge CB2 1RP
32 East 57th Street, New York, NY 10022, USA
10 Stamford Road, Oakleigh, Melbourne 3166, Australia

First published 1986

Printed in the United States of America

Library of Congress Cataloging in Publication Data

Rowe, Karen E.

Saint and singer.

(Cambridge studies in American literature and culture)

Bibliography: p.

Includes index.

1. Taylor, Edward, 1642–1729 – Criticism and
interpretation.   2. Christian poetry, American –
History and criticism.   3. Typology (Theology) in
literature.   4. Theology, Puritan, in literature.
I. Title.   II. Series.
PS850.T2Z78   1986   811′1   85–11316
ISBN 0 521 30865 8

British Library Cataloging-in-Publication applied for

The following publishers have generously given permission to use quotations from copy-
righted works: From *Upon the Types of the Old Testament* by Edward Taylor. By courtesy
of Charles W. Mignon, the Archives of Love Library, University of Nebraska-Lincoln,
and the University of Nebraska Press. From *Edward Taylor's Treatise Concerning the Lord's
Supper,* ed. Norman S. Grabo. Reprinted by permission of the publishers, Michigan State
University Press. From *The Unpublished Writings of Edward Taylor,* 3 vols., ed. Thomas
M. and Virginia L. Davis. Reprinted by permission of the publishers, Twayne Publishers
(a division of G. K. Hall & Co.). From *Edward Taylor's Christographia,* ed. Norman S.
Grabo. Reprinted by permission of the publishers, Yale University Press. From *The Poems
of Edward Taylor,* ed. Donald E. Stanford, Yale University Press. Reprinted by permission of Donald E. Stanford.

To my parents,
Earnest and Elizabeth Rowe,
my grandmother "Am,"
Irene I. Leng,
and my grandmother
Mabel E. Rowe, in her 100th year,
for their love and faith

Contents

Preface   *page* ix

A note on the text   xvii

1 The heritage of Puritan typology   1

2 Prophets and poets: typology as illumination   24

3 Of prophets, priests, and kings: personalizing the types   53

4 Edward Taylor's Puritan "Worship-mould"   90

5 New England's saints delivered   131

6 Sacramental types: seals to the Covenant   165

7 Preparing for the wedding feast   196

8 The artistry of types   229

Appendixes   277

1 Comparative analysis of Edward Taylor's typological
   sermons and meditations   278

2 Thomas Taylor's *Christ Revealed:* organization   282

vii

3   Samuel Mather's *The Figures or Types:* organization   283

4   Edward Taylor's *Preparatory Meditations* and *Upon the
    Types of the Old Testament:* organization   287

5   The Stoddardean controversy concerning the Lord's
    Supper: a calendar of significant events and documents   289

    Notes   294

    Index   333

Preface

When Perry Miller first noted the centrality of typology for Jonathan Edwards's *Images or Shadows of Divine Things* (1948), he could hardly have anticipated the explosion of scholarship that would irradiate his nascent insight. Miller's introduction pointed to the narrower significance of figuralism as an ancient form of biblical exegesis, but it remained for later critics to rediscover in it the genesis of the Puritan imagination. Led by Sacvan Bercovitch's pioneering work "Horologicals to Chronometricals" (1970; rev. *The American Jeremiad,* 1978), scholars began to delineate the impact of typology on colonial American sermons and histories. In need of a mythology to sanctify their errand, chroniclers, such as William Bradford and Cotton Mather, adopted the sacred exemplum of the Israelites, who once freed from Egyptian slavery were guided by Moses through the wilderness to a promised land flowing with milk and honey. Essays by Jesper Rosenmeier and Mason I. Lowance, Jr., in *Typology and Early American Literature* (1972), edited by Sacvan Bercovitch, together with Bercovitch's *The Puritan Origins of the American Self* (1975), established how biblical patterns of prophecy and fulfillment gave rise to Puritan myths of a New England Canaan and millennial hopes of Christ's Second Coming. The 1972 collection of essays heralded the arrival of Puritan typology as a critical perspective from which to survey the visionary designs out of which America rose majestic.

To focus primarily upon the communal myths of Puritan historiographers, however, was to overlook more exegetical and devotional uses of types. Ursula Brumm in *American Thought and Religious Typology* (1963; English trans., 1970) recognized early that Edward Taylor and Jonathan Edwards helped to convert the strict form of typological exegesis in which prefiguration and fulfillment remain real historical phenomena into more pliable forms of symbolic thought. Brumm's ideas took root and flowered in Earl Miner's Princeton seminar (1974) and the collected papers *Literary Uses of Typology from the Late Middle Ages to the Present* (1977), in which prominent scholars defined how biblical types as image and strategy distinctively shaped literary esthetics in England and America. Whereas Barbara Lewalski perceived typological symbolism in the personal spiritual lives recorded by meditative poets from Donne to Milton, Stephen Zwicker pointed to Dryden's and Pope's later applications in partisan political poetry. Most recently, in *Typologies in England 1650–1820* (1982) Paul J. Korshin defined a concept of abstracted typology and delineated its use in novels, satires, and everyday life throughout the eighteenth century. Across the ocean, Jonathan Edwards, according to Lowance and Karl Keller, prepared the way for American transcendentalism by first mingling Old Testament types with nature's shadows of divine truths. Drawn upon to serve diverse literary purposes, types entered into American culture as both historical prefiguration and literary metaphors, thereby blurring a fine distinction between God-ordained prophetic acts fulfilled in Christ and His church and biblical images adopted to signify human experiences. In *The Language of Canaan* (1980) Mason Lowance traced the development of a Puritan figural imagination from its germ in Reformation exegesis to its fruition in Joel Barlow's vision of America's rising glory and the transcendentalism of Thoreau and Emerson. Examinations of typology as exegetical method, mythic history, and literary metaphor have so flourished over the last decade that it has become a concept crucial for understanding colonial American thought and for reassessing seventeenth-century religious poetry.

Edward Taylor (1642–1729) has often been absorbed into these broader historical and literary movements largely, one suspects, because he arrived so late to the canon of American literature. Thomas H. Johnson's discovery in 1937 of a lyric sequence, *Gods Determinations touching his Elect,* and extended poetic series, selectively edited as *Sacramental Meditations* (1939), catapulted Taylor into preeminence as America's finest colonial poet. Early critics rushed to align him with predetermined poetic modes by labeling him an American metaphysical, Roman Catholic baroque, or Cambridge Platonist. When fully edited by Donald E. Stanford as the *Preparatory Meditations* (1960), these 217 poems established Taylor as a colonial descendant from the English meditative poets. With new discoveries, most notably Norman S. Grabo's edition of the *Christographia* sermons (1962) and *Treatise Concerning the Lord's Supper* (1965), Taylor's reputation as covenant theologian further escalated. Our assessments of his reputation as a poet and theologian continue to change, most recently because of the publication by Thomas and Virginia Davis of three additional volumes of his writings: *Edward Taylor's "Church Records" and Related Sermons; Edward Taylor vs. Solomon Stoddard: The Nature of the Lord's Supper;* and *Edward Taylor's Minor Poetry* (1981).

Edward Taylor has continued to defy ready assimilation into single categories. Neither a continental metaphysical nor simply a provincial versifier, neither published historian nor natural philosopher, he yet toiled within the same Christian vineyard as George Herbert and Anne Bradstreet, Cotton Mather and Jonathan Edwards. Precisely because his Puritan hermeneutics, sacramental dispute with Solomon Stoddard, and meditative poetry locate him at the nexus of so many traditions, Taylor raises issues as fascinating as they are problematic. As a dissenter and immigrant, how does he envision New England's errand into the wilderness? What is the relationship between his sermons and meditations? between the meticulous intellect that craves ramistic order in homilies, yet unleashes the soul's agons in poetic art? For Taylor, in comparison with Herbert and Vaughan, where does one draw the line between sacred figures as prophetic signs and as personal metaphors? How does exegesis transmute into art? In order to address these issues, my study delineates Edward Taylor's place in the history of Puritan typological exegesis. Much as it stimulated reevaluations of colonial American history and literature, typology also provides one of the most fruitful contexts within which to assess the creativity of Taylor as both public preacher and private poet.

The ancient lineage of figural hermeneutics from the New Testament authors to the Protestant Reformers, which I survey initially, established a genealogy within which Puritan historians and covenant theologians served as latter-day disciples. Expositors within this reformed tradition, such as William Guild (*Moses Unvailed* 1620) and Thomas Taylor (*Christ Revealed* 1635), explicated Old Testament types well before Samuel Mather preached his sermons in Dublin (1667–9), published posthumously as *The Figures or Types of the Old Testament* (1683), to reaffirm the fundamentals of Puritan theology and ecclesiology. A dissenting minister, educated at Cambridge and Harvard, Edward Taylor immigrated in 1668 to Boston rather than submit to the Act of Uniformity. Yet, as Chapter 2 examines, even though he became a contemporary of prominent colonial chroniclers, including Cotton Mather, Taylor eschewed historical applications of typology and preferred instead to pen his sermons *Upon the Types of the Old Testament* (1683–1706) as a New England companion to Thomas Taylor's and Samuel Mather's compendiums.

Like many other clerics who gathered sermons into instructive biblical commentaries, Taylor handbound but did not publish his thirty-six homilies. We did not retrieve this manuscript, as has often been the history of Taylor scholarship, until family descendants donated their holdings to the University of Nebraska in fall 1977. The *Preparatory Medita-*

tions indicates, however, that Taylor dabbled with the figures of the golden "Shew-Bread Table" and "Died Robes from Bozrah," Christ's antitypal "Treasures of Wisdom," and the types of priests, prophets, and kings as early as 1685–6 in the first series, Meditations 11–17. He then initiated his second series of meditations with a lengthy consecutive analysis of sacred figures (II. 1–30) from 1693 to 1699, sporadically returning to this topic again during 1703–4 (II. 58–61) and 1706 (II. 70–71). The discovery of *Upon the Types of the Old Testament* establishes striking correlations between the sermons and meditations and illuminates the imaginative processes by which Taylor transformed reasoned doctrine into personalized lyrics. The sermons confirm his adoption of *Christ Revealed* and *The Figures or Types* as primary models for his own typal theories, structures, and analogies. Moreover, the rhetoric of types, appeals for a divinely illumined "mentall Eye" and "Visive Spirits" to pierce dark mysteries, and recasting of the "rude Draught" metaphor testify to Taylor's lineal descent from Christian exegetical forefathers.

Within Taylor's typological series, Sermons and Meditations II. 1–2 serve as complementary introductions, because they balance the Old Testament focus on prophetic "Shaddows" with the New Testament proclamations of Christ's "Sparkling" revelations. Taylor imitates prior schemas for the types when he next explicates Old Testament persons from Adam to Jonah and sacred ranks (II. 3–15, 30) as foreshadowings of Christ's glories as antitypal prophet, priest, and King and *exemplum exemplorum* for New Testament believers. As Chapter 3 enunciates, Taylor rejects the use of personal types as *exempla fidei* for contemporary magistrates and pursues instead more circumscribed exegetical interpretations. He instructs his Westfield parishioners not to look outward for leaders and frontier utopias but, as his poetic exhortation later counsels, to pass through this world's "Wilderness of Sin," an "interchanging Course, like miracles," where "works must goe / Of Providences, Honycombs and Stings" until "here *within* Celestiall Canaan sings" (II. 58. 113, 117–20). The church militant in New England seems less substantial, more ephemeral to Taylor's introspective imagination than the church triumphant, wherein each saint as a Bride would be wed to Christ the Bridegroom for eternity – a nuptial that his final meditations (1713–25) on Canticles joyfully celebrate.

Though his devotional concern for the soul's spiritual journey to "Celestiall Canaan" subsumes a focus on New England's historical progress, nonetheless, Taylor does apply types polemically to defend the principles of Puritan covenant worship. Opposed to resurgent Socinian and Quaker "heresies" and unable to tolerate Catholic and Anglican abuses of church altars and crosses, feast days, priests and saints, and sacraments, he preaches the abrogation of all Mosaic legal ceremonies under

Christ's superior gospel institutes. Taylor's sermons reveal his penchant for subdivisions and ramistic arguments, as he methodically explicates the Old Testament church (II.16), temple sacrifices and altars (II.17–20), sacred seasonal feasts (II.21–25), and purification rites (II.26–28). But whereas *Upon the Types* rigorously exposes minute analogies and schemas for ceremonial law, the meditations record Taylor's personal attempts to strengthen the "Worship-mould" within his own heart's temple. Chapter 4, therefore, illustrates how Taylor transformed homiletic teaching into meditative praxis and consequently crossed the boundary from rational exegete to poetic singer. But his concern is not simply for the saint's earthly worship, but also for the deliverance from sin which liberates the soul finally into an eschatological paradise. In the sermons and meditations on purifications, Taylor begins an exploration of the Puritan morphology of conversion, a progress that leads from the mortifying of sins, to the deliverance as prefigured by Noah's ark and Israel's flight from Egypt, to the celebration of the church fellowship, signified under the Old Testament by God's providential care of his chosen people. As Chapter 5 suggests, Taylor traces the saint's spiritual deliverance and reaffirms the need for the Lord's Supper's manna and wine, the sacramental seals of man's new evangelical covenant with Christ as they were the signs of God's favor to the Israelites.

My study of Taylor's typology is not restricted to his major treatise and related poems, because figuralism also substantially influenced his other writings, including the *Christographia* (1701–3). More importantly, during his ministry Taylor became embroiled in debates between Solomon Stoddard and Increase Mather over the Lord's Supper as a converting ordinance. In this dispute figural analysis of circumcision (II.70), Passover (II.22 and II.71), God's wilderness dispensations (II.29, 58–61), and the Sacrament itself (II.102–111) became integral to doctrinal reasoning and rhetoric (Chapter 6). Taylor wields typological arguments with persuasive clarity in his then unpublished *Treatise Concerning the Lord's Supper* (1693–4) and later rebuttal to Stoddard "The *Appeale* Tried" (1709–11) specifically on the Supper in which Passover appears as a dominant ceremonial type. Both the habitual praxis of his meditations and sacramental doctrine, moreover, emphasize preparation of the heart for effectual conversion, that is, the receipt of saving grace whereupon church membership and admission to the Supper would be granted (Chapter 7). As Taylor's full title specifies, his regular meditations *before my Approach to the Lords Supper. Chiefly upon the Doctrin preached upon the Day of administration* are preparatory self-examinations. Here too, Mosaic tabernacle worship merely foreshadows a superior new gospel preparation which robes the partaker in "Wedden" finery of spiritual graces to attend the eucharistic banquet. Whether employed for exegetical, devotional, or polemic purposes, typology remains a lifelong method which permeates Taylor's homiletic treatises and *Preparatory Meditations,* in which he becomes a New England imitator of David and Solomon petitioning God with poetic psalms and epithalamiums.

Because his spiritual insights take form in ritualistic, personalized meditations, Edward Taylor imaginatively moves beyond exegetical and polemical to devotional uses of typology. My study, therefore, adopts an approach comparable to Barbara Lewalski's in *Protestant Poetics and the Seventeenth-Century Religious Lyric* (1979), in which she delineates a biblical esthetic, derived from commentaries on types, Psalms, and Canticles, and its influence on Donne, Herbert, Vaughan, Traherne, and Edward Taylor. Although these poets share a common Protestant esthetic, their poetic individualism accounts for finer variations in the use of divine types as literary metaphors. For example, all aspects of church architecture, liturgy, ceremonies, and history are recapitulated in the speaker's spiritual experience as particular priest and Christian Everyman of Herbert's *The Temple* (1633). Even though the heart becomes primary antitype for all Old Testament figures, including the altar of unhewn stones, still Herbert's fascination with God as "Architect" and the temple as structure (literal and poetic) – its floors, windows, porches, music, and monuments – bespeaks his Anglicanism. In contrast, Edward Taylor rejects any "Paintery" of the church as artifact and type for human religious virtues and in his *Preparatory Meditations* praises Christ alone as *forma perfectior,* a "Tabernacle, Temple right," "Medium of Worship," and "Saints Paradise" (II.20.30, 43, 50, 54). Though he too preaches a new worship within each human heart, the Old Testament unhewn altar signifies primarily Christ's "Deity" and "Manhood, on't my sacrifice. / For mine Atonement" (II.18.55, 56–7). As this example and Chapter 8 on his artistry illustrate, Taylor may be consonant but not identical with other seventeenth-century poets. Even though they share a typological heritage and Protestant orientation to poetics, none of these other poets create meditations so consistently linked to sermons. Nor do they envision each poem as part of a preparationist morphology essential to the Puritan who would approach the Lord's Supper. Nor do these poets undertake so habitually the act of meditation which enables us to trace Taylor's development from Puritan typologist to expositor of the allegorical Canticles. As Albert Gelpi maintains in *The Tenth Muse: The Psyche of the American Poet* (1975), Taylor's typological vision is at the very heart of his poetic creativity, thereby distinguishing him from tropological poets and establishing him as the progenitor of an American lineage that descends through Emerson and Whitman to Pound and Williams. Hence, Taylor's singular applications of figural hermeneutics deserve extensive study before we can judiciously locate him within the broader contexts of English Protestant poetics and an American literary culture.

My version of Taylor as Puritan typologist and polemicist, a poetic diarist of his quest for salvation, a meditative preparationist for the Lord's Supper, at once penitent sinner on earth and heaven-bound spiritual pilgrim, does not exhaust the complexities of his theology or his art. But rooted in a typological tradition from St. Paul to Samuel Mather, Taylor's adaptations of figural persons, events, and ceremonies become crucial for evaluating his exemplary life as preacher to New England's Israelites and his inward journey as elect saint. Just as ancient exegetes sought an inspired vision to penetrate biblical prophecies and allegories, so I have often desired the "mentall Eye" and "Visive Spirits" to pierce the religio-poetic meditations left as Edward Taylor's legacy to future generations. In *Saint and Singer* I have undertaken a modest mission to shed some light on the shadows of divine things in Edward Taylor's works, so that an understanding of his Puritan hermeneutics and poetics of meditation might fulfill the promise of his contribution to American literature.

This work would not have been possible without the early encouragement of Professor Ben Reid, who found in my approach to Meditation II.27's biblical typology deeper insights into Taylor's poetry. The generosity and knowledge of later mentors, especially Mary Rountree, Josephine K. Piercy, and Wallace E. Williams, reinforced the value of my methodology, because as teachers they learned from my work. To Thomas M. Davis and Mason I. Lowance, Jr., I owe more than can be acknowledged, Thomas for his meticulous scrutiny of chapters and his immensely learned and dedicated retrieval of Taylor's manuscripts. The collegial relationship with Mason has enabled us to define our separate pursuits, yet to find in rare hours of conversation the excitement of a shared scholarly endeavor. To Norman S. Grabo for editing Taylor's sermons in the *Christographia* and *Treatise Concerning the Lord's Supper* and for reading this book in manuscript, I am also grateful. That I have been permitted to use and to publish excerpts from the manuscript of *Upon the Types of the Old Testament,* I owe entirely to the generosity of Taylor's descendants and patient mediation of Professor Charles W. Mignon, as well as to the University of Nebraska Special Collections. Without stinting, Charles has given of the materials that form the core of my analysis, and with his forthcoming edition in hand, future scholars will possess the data and directions to read Taylor aright. Special thanks are due Everett Emerson, Karl Keller, Sacvan Bercovitch, and Albert Gelpi for their unflagging support and balanced editorial suggestions. The meticulous research and editorial assistance of Christy Desmet, Geraldine Moyle, Jean Toll, and Renée Gernand made the final stages of manuscript preparation and book production far smoother.
My work has been supported by grants from the Woodrow Wilson

Foundation, the Academic Senate Committee on Research at the University of California, Los Angeles, and the award of two Humanities Institute Summer Fellowships from UCLA. I gratefully acknowledge the assistance of librarians from the American Antiquarian Society, Andover-Harvard Theological Library, Boston Public Library, Congregational Christian Historical Society, Henry E. Huntington Library, John Carter Brown Library, Boston Athenaeum, Lilly Rare Book Library at Indiana University, Massachusetts Historical Society, McAlpin Collection of the Union Theological Seminary, New England Historic Genealogical Society, Simmons College, University of Iowa, Westfield Athenaeum, Westminster Theological Seminary, and William Andrews Clark Memorial Library. I owe particular debts to the Krauth Memorial Library of the Lutheran Theological Seminary, Presbyterian Historical Society, Beinecke Rare Book and Manuscript Library at Yale University, Harvard's Houghton Library, and the University of Nebraska for providing microfilms, copies and photographs of manuscripts and rare editions essential for this study.

A note on the text

In transcribing excerpts from the holograph manuscript, "Upon the Types of the Old Testament," I adhere to principles established by Thomas M. Davis and Norman S. Grabo in their previous editions of Edward Taylor's works. In general, I let stand Taylor's capitalization and spelling, even with their inconsistencies, and his use of the ampersand. Differences between Taylor's capital *S* (S) and lower case *s* (ʃ) often seem unclear, though I agree with professors Davis and Grabo that a capital should be rendered when the down stroke stops at the line, turns upward, and curls round for its termination. I silently correct a few scribal errors (e.g., "Prists" for "Priests"), regularize the use of & for etc., and where Taylor uses *v* initially and *u* medially, I modernize.

I spell out habitual contractions (*y^e* for the, *y^t* for that, *y^ir* for their, and so forth) and also his favorite abbreviations, such as *Chch, bec, o^r, w:^ch, w:^th, sd, D^ctr,* and *Coven:^nt* for Church, because, our, which, with, said, Doctor, and Covenant, and related variations. Taylor's *tho'* or *thô, thro'* or *thrô,* and *altho'* remain as such, but I convert the circumflex to the double consonant, as in *Comunion* for Communion or *glimering* for glimmering. Punctuation reflects Taylor's practices, even with the interchanging of colons, commas, and periods, but I occasionally provide terminal punctuation and initial capitals to avoid confusion. Where blurred or partially missing words can be supplied with certainty, I have done so in brackets; where manuscript deterioration prevents conjectural emendations, I indicate lacunas with bracketed ellipses.

As I was writing *Saint and Singer,* I transcribed parts of the *Types* manuscript at the same time as Charles W. Mignon, who is editing the complete typological sermons, and I have confirmed all of my readings with him. Because of a complete lack of order in Taylor's manuscript, Mignon has made a new sequence of pagination that corresponds to the actual sequence of leaves of writing bound in the manuscript. I have adopted his pagination, since it will be most useful for anyone wishing to consult the edition. I deeply appreciate Charles Mignon's generous efforts in double-checking my transcriptions and puzzling out semiobscured or uncommon words and interlinear substitutions in Taylor's manuscript.

1

The Heritage of Puritan Typology

Then lead me, Lord, through all this Wilderness
  By this Choice shining Pillar Cloud and Fire.
By Day, and Night I shall not then digress.
  If thou wilt lead, I shall not lag nor tire
  But as to Cana'n I am journeying
  I shall thy praise under this Shadow sing.[1]

Astray in the wilderness of Westfield, deep amid the Connecticut Valley, in the year 1703, Edward Taylor composed his poetic plea for guidance from God. From Virgil to Dante and Spenser, the heroic search for supernatural guidance had been figured as a perilous journey. Preserved by miraculous signs and a superior guardian, the wandering human battled natural forces of confusion and darkness in pursuit of the narrow spiritual way to the promised paradise. By adopting the archetypal symbolism, Edward Taylor recreated the same experience of human striving, trust in a divine protector, and hope of ultimate security in a literal or spiritual destination. The fundamental needs and the universal symbolism remained as germane for Taylor as for previous poets and religious visionaries.

Despite the universality, however, particularities of the metaphor and its usage decisively locate Taylor in Puritan New England of the late seventeenth century. When Taylor adopts the images of "Wilderness," the "Pillar Cloud and Fire," and "Cana'n," he employs a distinctly Christian framework. Specifically, he relies upon a typological schema which relates the Old Testament accounts of the Israelites to the New Testament teachings of Christ and he applies the perceived moral truths or correspondences to himself, a seventeenth-century Puritan operating under the gospel. In this poem he selects a metaphor, or more accurately "biblical type," which arouses as well singular connotations for the Puritan of New England. Edward Taylor is not only a pilgrim in search of a guide and a home, a poet in quest of higher knowledge, and a Christian in pursuit of the paradisiacal kingdom. He is also a minister in the New England wilderness who requires God's strength to guide his congregation of elect saints and himself in the founding of a New Canaan which will be a godly nation on earth and a foreshadowing of the heavenly kingdom to come.

New England theologians inherited the method of reading Scripture typologically from an impressive lineage of biblical exegetes, descending from Paul and the Church Fathers through medieval allegorists to the Protestant Reformers. In their applications of typology seventeenth-century American Puritans reaffirmed the purity of this well-established exegetical tradition, yet also modified the basic concept in order to justify their role in religious history. Typology provided them with the Exodus as an ancient model for their own mission into the wilderness and strengthened the warp of covenant theology. What distinguishes Edward Taylor from other Puritans of New England is not, therefore, his adoption of typology, but his serious explication of biblical types in poetic meditations written over a period of thirty-two years. He participated in the heritage of both Christian typology and poetry. His knowledge of previous literary traditions is apparent in the universality of his metaphors. But Taylor's Puritan theology and his poetic achievement can be discriminated only by first understanding the historical and contemporary concepts of typology that informed his milieu, his sermons *Upon the Types of the Old Testament,* and the *Preparatory Meditations.*

The Principles of Typology

The principles of typology, whether used by Paul in the first century to convert the Jews or by Puritans in the seventeenth century to denounce Catholic exegetical extravagances, remain fundamentally the same.[2] Typology presumes a providential concept of history in which God directly manipulates human affairs to conform to His eternal design for redemption. In accord with this historical viewpoint, typologists perceive the Old Testament events, persons, and ceremonies as channels through which Yahweh communicates his divine intentions. Every Old Testament type, therefore, possesses a vertical significance. Since it originated with God, the type signifies His willing intercourse with man and partially reveals God's omniscient plan for salvation. Although types continually direct attention to this overarching redemptive design, they also participate in the horizontal plane of temporal life. Moses and the Exodus are a historically verifiable man and event, not merely symbols. And their factualness in part validates them as types. More important, as Walther Eichrodt observes, is their "theological significance in the historical revelation of the Old Testament," which "gives to them their significance as divinely established prerepresentations of important elements in the salvation manifested in Christ."[3] In the development of

Christian exegesis, this insistence upon the historicity of Old Testament types consistently differentiates typology from other exegetical theories.

In his essay on "Figura," Erich Auerbach not only emphasizes the historical reality of divine figures, he also clarifies their function as prophecies and the necessary bipolarity of typology:

> Figural interpretation establishes a connection between two events or persons [or ceremonies], the first of which signifies not only itself but also the second, while the second encompasses or fulfills the first. The two poles of the figures are separate in time, but both, being real events or figures, are within time, within the stream of historical life. Only the understanding of the two persons or events is a spiritual act, but this spiritual act deals with concrete events whether past, present, or future . . . since promise and fulfillment are real historical events, which have either happened in the incarnation of the Word, or will happen in the second coming.[4]

Old Testament persons, events, and ceremonies prefigure the New Testament fulfillments in Christ's person, deeds, and teachings. Moses and Joshua leading the Israelites out of the wilderness into Canaan foreshadows Christ's spiritual deliverance of all Christians from a sinful world into heaven. In scope and nature typology differs from Old Testament prophecy, because the prophets proclaim the Messiah through a haze of uncertainty about the form of His coming; they merely project the future fulfillment. In contrast, typology denotes a bipolar concept which presumes knowledge of both the historical prophecy and its fulfillment, the type *and* the antitype. Through Christ the shadowy types find visible embodiment, the messianic promises are discharged, and God's omnipotent design becomes more clearly manifest. Possessing knowledge of Christ and His deeds, typologists perceive the resemblances and differences between the New Testament fulfillment and the Old Testament adumbration. For example, Moses' mediatorial role imperfectly foreshadows Christ's new mediation between God and man and the superior means of achieving salvation through grace, not law. Thus, typology designates a total complex of Old Testament adumbration, New Testament fulfillment, and an interpreted spiritual relationship between two historical occurrences.

In opposition to other exegetical theories, the uniqueness of typology also derives from its Christocentricity.[5] By asserting Christ's fulfillment of Old Testament types and messianic prophecies, Paul and the author of Hebrews maintain the value of Jewish history but redefine its primary function as prefigurative history. These epistles and the Gospels elaborate the doctrine of grace and faith to accentuate Christ's spiritual preeminence over types and His annulment of Judaic law. The New Testament typologists stress the repetitive configurations of situations, such as Israel's forty years in the wilderness and Christ's forty-day temptation, which link Old and New Testament accounts. But the superficial correspondences only point to less accidental correlations. Christ's life as a pattern for mankind's salvation parallels Yahweh's earlier model in the Exodus for His chosen people. Christ as the obedient figure of "Thy will be done" perfects the obedience demanded of Israel by Yahweh. In one sense Jesus and His mission climax the succession of historical events that begins with God's declaration of future grace to Abraham, the visible mercy to Israel in the Exodus, and promises of a Messiah. However, Christ's fulfillment is twofold, not only temporal but also spiritual, not only a perfecting of Israel's vocation but also of God's role, both human and divine. Christ incarnates God's Word and mercy and offers the possibility of eternal life to man by sacrificing His life to satisfy God's justice. He inaugurates a New Testament covenant of love between God and man which abrogates the Old Testament covenant of law. His humanity enables Christ to fulfill the mortal responsibilities and historical prophecies, whereas His divinity permits Him to transcend the temporal and institute a superior new spiritual order.

For most exegetes, including the New Testament authors, the Christocentrism of typology is broad and flexible. Old Testament persons and events variously type Christ and His immediate deeds and teachings, but they also foreshadow the nature of the church, its continuing relationship with Christ after His death, and the pattern of Christian spiritual experience. Beyond these fulfillments directly by Christ or associated with Him, typologists also point to eschatological consummations yet to come. The Judaic law and history initially act as prophetic *figurae,* but Christ institutes a new series of *figurae* in the promises of a millennial kingdom, the end of the world, and the Last Judgment. Only the final judgment of damnation or salvation eternally consummates and fully actualizes God's providential design.

The antiquated terminology and modern distaste for biblical allegory make it easy to dismiss typology as a mythical scheme or mechanical methodology and to obscure the fundamental passion of belief. For the early Christians and for Puritans in seventeenth-century England and America, typology demanded a commitment of faith and a resolution to imitate the pattern of Christ's obedience and life. Because typology necessitated this commitment of faith, it was a vital, not a static system of ethics or a dead mythology. "The intellectual claim of typology," according to A. C. Charity, "is nothing without the existential claim, and demand, which accompany it. The proposition 'Jesus Christ is history's fulfillment, to which all history is related in as much as in him it finds its norm, its perfector and judge,' is not a proposition to which one

can assent without affirming also 'Christ is my perfector and my judge.' "[6]
For the authors of the New Testament and for Puritan theologians this
commitment of faith was a priori to their writing and preaching of typology. With its emphasis on a providential *Heilsgeschichte,* the mutual historicity of Old and New Testament events, persons, and ceremonies, the
bipolarity of type and antitype, and the Christological fulfillment and
abrogation, typology contributed to the spread of Christianity, to an
evolving New Testament theology, and to later Puritan beliefs.

Typology Versus Allegory: The History of Biblical Exegesis

In the development of biblical exegesis a second tradition gradually infiltrated scriptural interpretations by the Church Fathers, medieval exegetes, and sixteenth-century Catholic theologians.[7] In contrast to
the Hebraic origins of Pauline typology, Alexandrian exegesis took root
from Hellenistic allegorizing of classical literary texts, such as Homer.[8]
Philo Judaeus (c. 20 B.C.–A.D. 40), for example, then adapted this method
to religious texts and allegorized all Scripture into statements about psychology and morals. Philo postulates a Platonic creation in which God
(pure Being and *Logos*) conceives models for parts of the universe, then
constructs archetypes discernible only by the mind, and finally, with these
as patterns, creates the world perceptible to the senses. Philo uses the
term "type" to designate the archetypal patterns or models in the ideal
world, perceptible to the mind, of which the embodiments in the phenomenal world are mere copies or shadows.

Because of its Platonic assumptions, Philonic exegesis differs in three
respects from Christian typology. First, whereas Pauline typology asserts
the historicity of events, persons, and ceremonies, allegory stresses instead
their vertical or symbolic meanings. In his explications Philo frequently
downplays historical realities in order to pursue archetypal truths. Samuel may have been a historical personage, but for Philo he represents the
mind that rejoices in the worship and service of God alone. Second,
typological exegesis establishes meaningful correspondences between
historical prefigurations and fulfillments recorded in the literal text. In
contrast, allegorism extracts secondary and hidden meanings underlying
the primary textual sense; literal meanings function only as the body to
the soul, the perceptible type to the archetype. Old Testament figures
are not historical precursors of Christ, in Philo's view, but paradigms of
particular virtues – Moses of intelligence, Aaron of speech, and Noah of
righteousness, for example. Third, Pauline and Puritan theology hinges
on the belief that God's redemptive design becomes visibly manifest in
Christ. For New Testament writers biblical exegesis and Christian teach-

ing reveal how all threads woven together in the fabric of history picture God's design for man's salvation. In allegorical exegesis the individual creates his own patterns of symbolic meaning rather than attempts to discover God's already woven pattern. Philo ignores almost entirely the messianic prophecies and seeks what he considers to be truer and more profound meanings in Scripture. His exegesis produces philosophical statements that are shaped by his individual composite of Platonism, Stoicism, and Judaism. Hence, motivated by a desire to read various Greek philosophies into the given text, Philonic and later Alexandrian allegory tends to be anhistorical, knows little of typology or messianic expectation, and allows for divergent subjective analyses of the same event by each expositor.

In pre-Augustinian exegesis commentators gradually subordinated typological to subjective allegorical interpretations and multiplied the spiritual levels of meaning. In *Contra Celsum* (c. A.D. 248) and *De Principiis* Origen uses the division of man into body, soul, and spirit to justify a threefold literal, moral, and spiritual reading.[9] Although he does not deny literal and historical senses, Origen somewhat scornfully associates them with unintelligent readers and simpler Judaistic tendencies. In practice he rarely comments upon historical meanings except to establish arbitrary connections between the literal and spiritual senses. He theoretically proposes a moral sense similar to Philo's ethical statements about the pious conduct of the ordinary Christian life, but pragmatically cannot maintain distinctions between the moral and spiritual senses. Origen allows the spiritual sense to absorb the moral in his pursuit of secret "mysteries" of God which coincide with his speculative theology. Traditional Christian typology exists, but only "like the bones of his exegetical skeleton hidden beneath the flesh of allegorical elaboration," as Origen conflates his declared three senses of Scripture into the omnipresent "spiritual" reading.[10] Although later exegetes (Jerome, Augustine, and the Antiochenes) sometimes bitterly attacked Origen, his subjectivity, wholesale application of symbolic methods of Hellenistic origins, and three graduated levels of understanding Scripture decisively altered later commentary. Even while they used him repeatedly, Puritans still criticized Origen as a proponent of the allegorical tradition because of his antiliteralism and seemingly arbitrary spiritualizing.

Although Jerome originally attached the term *tropologiam* restrictively to moral significations and introduced a fourth or anagogical level, Augustine in *Contra Faustum* (397–8) and *De Doctrina Christiana* (397) implemented and Cassian (5th century) codified the embryonic four senses of Scripture. The *sensus historicus* or *literalis* simply explains the words of the text; the *sensus tropologicus* looks to the correction of morals; the *sensus allegoricus* renders an exposition by a sense other than the literal (i.e., symbolic); and the *sensus anagogicus* stirs the mind by mystical revelations to the contemplation of heavenly things.[11] However, Augustine's attitudes toward scriptural exegesis are complicated. In an effort to reconcile the tradition of literal and typological interpretations with Origen's symbolism, Augustine elucidates another fourfold scheme. The Scripture should be read according to history, etiology which explains the causes behind actions and words, analogy which adjusts the meaning of the Old Testament to the broader intent of all Scripture, and allegory which interprets the meaning of figures. Since the first levels all require close attention to literal and historical meanings, the scheme encourages typological readings. But Augustine also incorporates the Platonic assumptions of Origen by flexibly defining the literal meaning as "not simply the word (or letter), but the act or thought or thing of which the word was a sign."[12] Emphasis on the symbolic significances ultimately converts all objects and historical events into hieroglyphs of God. The renewed insistence on historicity and the letter coupled with Origen's assumptions and methods of symbolism creates a prevailing tension in Augustine's exegesis; the letter never wholly accounts for the meaning of the figure, but the spiritual or allegorical world never totally subsumes the phenomenal world. Both this tension and Augustine's tendency to glide from strict typological correspondences to elaborate allegorical readings characterized Christian exegesis for the next one thousand years.

Depending upon the political and exegetical climate, the emphasis on historicity or symbolism and on multiple levels of meaning diverged widely during the Middle Ages.[13] A renewed interest in original Hebrew texts led the Victorines, monks of Saint Victor's monastery in Paris (1150–1300), to study Scripture closely through etymological and literal analyses. In this same period St. Thomas Aquinas coordinated his version of Augustinian allegorical exegesis with Aristotelian terminology, and St. Bonaventure used it to defend mystical illumination. Similar tensions and collations of philosophic and exegetical belief influenced medieval art.[14] In stained glass windows, manuscript illuminations, and cathedral statuary, artists of the thirteenth through fifteenth centuries juxtaposed Old Testament typal events with scenes from the Gospels to represent symbolically moral conflicts between vices and virtues, the ladder of mystical ascent and genealogical tree of evil and good, and allegorical meanings of events in Christ's life. Even if one sets aside the rhetoric and antimedieval, antipopish biases of sixteenth- and seventeenth-century Protestant commentators, it seems accurate to conclude that allegorical interpretations overshadowed limited typological analyses and that exegetical systems from the Church Fathers through the medievalists became progressively more cumbersome and individually subjective.[15] Allegory so centrally entered into church tradition that by the sixteenth century it coexisted with Scripture as the basis of orthodox Catholic doctrine.

The Reformation: Puritan Definitions of Typology in the Seventeenth Century

Before the Reformation only Antiochene theologians of the first four centuries, among them Eusebius of Caesarea, St. Basil, Cyril of Jerusalem, and Chrysostom, consistently viewed typology as a limited analysis of historical and spiritual meanings. Despite Augustine's early attempt to reconcile the different modes and cautions by the Victorines, it was the religious upheaval of the Reformation that enabled a genuine revival of pure typological exegesis.[16] In promulgating the concept of justification by faith not works, Luther and other Reformers rejected the validity of church tradition and ecclesiastical authority as a basis for doctrine. Because of demands for vernacular translations of the Bible, leading humanists studied Hebrew and Greek texts and the historical contexts and aims of Scripture. As a result, Luther, Melancthon, Calvin, Ramus, Bèza, and Tyndale launched full-scale criticisms of Alexandrian and medieval allegory. Tyndale ridiculed patristic and scholastic distortions: "Then came our sophisters with their anagogical and chopological sense, and with an antitheme of half an inch, out of which some of them draw a thread of nine days long."[17] In terms similar to those of the Antiochenes, the Reformers insisted that Scripture is God's Word spoken historically and demanded *ad fontes,* a return to scriptural foundations of doctrine. These assertions of the primacy of a literal sense contributed to a resurrection of typology as the dominant method of biblical exegesis.

Although typology permeated earlier treatises by the Reformers, Protestant and Puritan works devoted solely to the identification of typal parallels first appeared in 1620 with William Guild's *Moses Unvailed: Or, those Figures Which Served unto the patterne and shaddow of heavenly things pointing out the Messiah Jesus Christ.*[18] Following Guild's example, theologians published typological guides throughout the seventeenth century, including Thomas Taylor's *Christ Revealed; or the Old Testament Explained* (1635), Henry Vertue's *Christ and the Church: or Parallels* (1659), Samuel Mather's *The Figures or Types of the Old Testament by which Christ and the Heavenly Things of the Gospel were Preached and Shadowed to the People of God of Old* (1683; 2d ed. 1705), and Benjamin Keach's *Tropologia: A Key To Open Scripture-Metaphors* (1681).[19] These treatises all contain remarkably homogeneous typal parallels and reflect consistent reformed attitudes. But with its Puritan theological assumptions and elaborate systems of correspondences, Samuel Mather's *apologia* constitutes the *summa* of Puritan typology and Benjamin Keach's introduction yields an illuminating gloss.

Both Mather and Keach condemn what they call the fanciful mental cobwebs of Catholic and scholastic allegorists. Mather exhorts: "But for Men to set their Fancies a Work to extract Allegories out of every Scripture-history, as the Popish Interpreters use to do, is not safe nor becoming a judicious Interpreter. *Luther* called such Allegories *Spumam Scripturae,* they beat the Scriptures into Froth by allegorizing all things" (*FT,* pp. 129–30). Mather censures the allegorists who presume to rival God by creating divine meanings and so entirely disregard literal meanings of Scripture. Puritan typologists reaffirm apostolic and Antiochene insistence on historicity whereas allegorists subordinate or cast it off. *"There is an Historical Verity in all those typical Histories of the Old Testament. . . .* They are a true Narration of Things really existent and acted in the World, and are literally and historically to be understood,"* declares Mather (*FT,* p. 128).

In further contrast to Alexandrian allegory, which presumes symbolic meaning in all Old Testament details, Keach designates only some typical things, persons, and events, and Mather formulates strict guidelines for determining legitimate types. We may know a type, Mather says,

> 1. When there is express Scripture for it. As *Adam* here in the Text [Rom. 5:14] is called *a Type of him that was to come:* So the Whole Ceremonial Law is said *to have a Shadow of the good things to come* under the Gospel, *Heb.* 10. 1. . . .
>
> 2. When there is a *permutation of Names* between the *Type* and the *Antitype,* this is a clear Indication of the Mind of God. . . . so Christ is called *Adam, the second Adam, Cor.* 15. 45. . . .
>
> 3. When by comparing several Scriptures together, there doth appear *an evident and manifest* Analogy *and parallel between Things under the Law, and things under the Gospel,* we may conclude, that such legal Dispensations were intended as *Types* of those Gospel Mysteries whose Image they bear. . . . As the Deliverance out of *Egypt* and *Babylon,* if we read the History thereof in the Old Testament, and compare it with the Prophesies in the New Testament, concerning the Churches Deliverance from Anti-christian Bondage, we shall clearly see, that it was a Type thereof. (*FT,* pp. 53–4)

Mather's requirement of verbal, etymological, and analogical criteria testifies to the importance of the literal text. He also upholds typology's bipolarity with its emphasis on evident parallels between type and antitype; the kinship is verifiable only by the presence of and fulfillment in the antitype. Mather's third guideline seems to open the door to individualistic allegorical interpretations, for he suggests that the discovery of types necessitates a spiritually illuminated reader. He later concludes that "the meaning of the Types is seldom fully and explicitly declared and held forth, but for the most part briefly and obscurely hinted, and so left by God to be collected by the Christian Wisdom and Industry of his People" (FT, p. 480). But in actual scriptural analysis this apparent open-door policy is constantly narrowed by the emphasis on literally manifest associations between Old Testament types and New Testament anti-types. The judicious balance of interpreter's license with restricted material and guidelines and Mather's continual attention to historical readings as a basis for spiritual meanings preclude indiscriminate allegorizations of all types.

Having asserted the historical verity of types and counseled a careful inspection of literal meanings to determine their legitimacy, Puritan typologists specify the function of types with equal rigor. Although Mather adopts patristic terms and metaphors, the thrust of his definition remains historical and Christological, not symbolic:

> 2. There is the *thing shadowed* or represented by the *Type,* And what is that? *Things to come,* saith the Apostle, *Col.* 2. 17. and *good things to come, Heb.* 10. 1. The good things of the Gospel, *Christ and his Benefits; but the Body is of Christ,* as *Col.* 2. 17. This we call the *Correlate,* or the *Antitype;* the other is the *Shadow,* this the *Substance:* The *Type* is the Shell, this the Kernel; the *Type* is the Letter, this the Spirit and Mystery of the *Type.* . . .
> [3] But what is this *shadowing?* And *how* do *Types* shadow?
> It is a metaphorical expression. A shadow represents the proportion of the Body, with its actions and motions; though it doth it but obscurely and darkly. So the Types had some dark resemblance of Christ and his Benefits, and did some way adumbrate and represent them, and hold them forth unto his People, to enlighten and inform their Understandings, and to strengthen and confirm their Faith in him. (FT, p. 52)

The terms "Letter" and "Shell" refer to outwardly visible signs and words, specifically to Old Testament earthly foreshadowings and prophecies of yet invisible future events. The term "Shadow" (σκία) describes the *function* of the type as a "dark resemblance" or adumbration that will be clarified at a future date in history. The terms "Correlate," "Kernel," and "Anti-type" all designate specific *"Things to come"*: the good news of Christ and His benefits, His life, and His teachings. Typological correspondences, therefore, demonstrate the unity of the Bible. Both the Old Testament and New reveal the gospel of Christ, but in diverse manners, the former through promises and shadowy types, the latter through actual fulfillment. Puritan typologists further stress the New Testament's superiority, since Christ's advent and teachings abrogate the Old Testament types, including the ceremonial laws propounded by Moses. Unlike the allegorists who construct links between earthly signs and a Platonic idea or virtue to support mystical doctrines, Puritans restrict their exegesis to demonstrable correspondences between historical facts to explicate the Christocentricity of all Scripture.

Denouncing the allegorists' "mystical" senses, that is, the tropological and anagogical meanings, Puritan typologists endorse instead a simple twofold meaning. Puritan interpretations usually open by explicating the historical importance of the Old Testament type and by defending its legitimacy as a prefiguration. The analysis then exposes the doctrine or spiritual level of meaning by establishing similarities and disparities between the type and its fulfillment in Christ and in the gospel message. Although they reject the allegorists' tropological level as twice removed from the literal text, Puritan exegetes do not entirely negate the moral equity of types.[20] Spiritual meanings often possess moral and eschatological implications, but ones firmly derived from the scriptural text, not manufactured by the expositor to sanction his doctrinal predilections. Whereas Origen represents the Exodus journey as a moral allegory of the conflict between the flesh and spirit in a baptismal candidate, Samuel Mather, for example, simply instructs his reader to "Trust God and follow the Lord fully, when he leads you into dangers and difficulties, as deep as the Bottom of the Sea" (FT, p. 158). In the tripartite structure of sermons, Puritan ministers often translate the typological teachings into similar moral exhortations under the heading of "Uses." Samuel Mather, who asserts the value of types for *"outward and temporal Good"* and for "Instructions in Moral Duties, as indeed all Providences are," staunchly defends the basic literal meanings, defines their primary function as *"typical Adumbration of Christ and Gospel-mysteries,"* and constructs a twofold, not threefold, explication (FT, p. 129).

Despite their denunciations of allegorism, Puritan commentators do acknowledge and interpret the infrequent allegorical portions of Scripture. Benjamin Keach captures the essential distinction between Puritan concepts of allegorical Scripture and patristic allegory: "There is a great difference betwixt an *Allegorick* Exposition of Scripture, and an Exposition of *Allegorick* Scripture: The first is that which the Fathers and School men fail in, *i.e.* when they allegorize plain Scriptures and Histories, seeking to draw out some secret meaning, other than appears in the Words."[21] Puritans thus allow an "Exposition of *Allegorick* Scripture," such as Canticles and Revelation. Likewise, in preaching and exegesis, figurative biblical texts and similitudes sometimes usefully clarify the Scripture's literal sense, but they prove nothing, as Tyndale had argued, when divorced entirely from the literal meaning or when used as sole doctrinal proofs. Inevitably, because of the Puritan scholars' familiarity with patristic, medieval, and Catholic treatises, remnants of allegorizations may appear in the typological explications of even conservative exegetes. But Puritan interpretations of allegorical Scripture and their infrequent recourse to figurative illustrations never resemble the complex fantasies or so-called foolishnesses of Philo, Origen, the Alexandrians, Bonaventure, Aquinas, or contemporary Catholic theologians. Puritan divines generally confine typology to historical parallels manifest in literal, easily intelligible ways in Scripture, relate shadowy Old Testament types to substantial New Testament realities in Christ, and reiterate their faith in a God-created redemptive scheme working through temporal events.

Typology and the Puritans of New England

The prevalence of typology in historical chronicles, theological treatises, and sermons testifies to its crucial function in American Puritan historiography and covenant theology. Although aware of the narrow principles of typology outlined in the guides, New England Puritans did not restrict themselves simply to devotional or hermeneutic explications of Scripture. Departing from traditional Puritan insistence upon gospel fulfillments, historians utilized biblical personages and patterns, whether as metaphors or prophetic types, to justify their errand into the New World and to defend their claim to national election. In an effort to clarify the critical terminology, Mason Lowance in *The Language of Canaan* adapts Paul Hunter's term "broadened" as "developmental" typology to signify the means by which Puritan theologians " 'extended to contemporary history the principle of reading one time in terms of another: biblical objects or events now might not only prefigure other biblical events or concepts but also the events of later history.' "[22] As the initial fervor of the Great Migration and the need to establish God's providential care of this new separatist community gave way in the late seventeenth and eighteenth centuries to millennial expectations, biblical types as well as prophecies of the apocalypse and Second Coming were applied not only to contemporary events in Puritan New England but also to anticipated future events. Lowance observes:

> In millennial writing the figures and types follow a pattern of developmental typology, recapitulating the experience of past historical episodes as prophetic synecdoches of future fulfillment. Recapitulative typology is thus not a new departure in exegetical reasoning; rather, it is an extension of the principles of developmental typology so that human history from the incarnation to the judgement looks forward – through revealed and instituted figures – to the Second Coming of the eternal antitype.[23]

Within the American tradition, developmental or recapitulative typology (by way of hagiographic exempla, extended parallels or claims of antitypal accomplishment) increasingly diverged from the stricter tenets of reformed exegesis which emphasized the self-contained nature of Scripture and the correspondences that linked Old Testament figures to Christ's gospel fulfillments, a tradition that Edward Taylor and Samuel Mather upheld, even as their contemporaries created the vision of New England as the New Canaan and seat of the New Jerusalem.

Puritan historians fluctuated between applying the types as parallels or models for contemporary events and outright claims of New England's antitypal fulfillments despite an acknowledgment of Christ's antitypal abrogations. Cotton Mather in the *Magnalia Christi Americana* (1702) primarily establishes illustrative correspondences between New England and Israel, as in his classic portrayal of John Winthrop:

> Accordingly when the *Noble Design* of carrying a Colony of *Chosen People* into an American Wilderness, was by *some* Eminent Persons undertaken, *This* Eminent Person was, by the Consent of all, *Chosen* for the *Moses*, who must be the Leader of so great an Undertaking: And indeed nothing but a *Mosaic Spirit* could have carried him through the *Temptations*, to which either his *Farewel* to his *own Land*, or his *Travel* in a *Strange Land*, must needs expose a Gentleman of his *Education*.[24]

Although parallels between Old Testament figures and New England divines became staple metaphors in funeral orations as well as chronicles of the migration, scrupulous historians, such as Cotton Mather, used them as hagiographic exemplars rather than precise typological analogies.[25]

From the earliest promotions of the New Canaan to the later millennial sermons prophesying Christ's Second Coming to this New Jerusalem, other Puritan theologians virtually envisioned contemporary trials and triumphs as fulfilling Old Testament types. As descendants of Israel, New England Puritans must experience "Contrition and Humiliation before the Lord comes to take possession," according to Thomas Hooker, for "this was typified in the passage of the Children of Israel towards the promised Land; they must come into, and go through a vast and a roaring Wilderness, where they must be bruised with many pressures, humbled under many overbearing difficulties . . . before they could possess that good Land which abounded with all prosperity, flowed with Milk and Honey."[26] As early as 1643, Richard Mather adopted Israel's freedom from Babylon as a type for the destiny of New England's chosen people: "Although that which is foretold . . . was in part fulfilled when the people of God returned from Captivitie in *Babylon* at the end of seventie yeares: yet we must not limit the place to that time onely. . . . Many things that literally concerned the Jewes were types and figures signifying the like things concerning the people of God in these latter dayes."[27] Later, millennial enthusiasms so shaped the Puritan vision that even Cotton Mather invested biblical types with prophetic intent to predict confidently New England as the site of the New Jerusalem, since the Lord's Second Coming was not "a Metaphor," but "the Next Thing that is to be Look'd for."[28] Historical analogies, as a rhetorical strategy for identifying New England Puritans with Old Testament Israelites, often shaded thus imperceptibly into overt recapitulative claims for progressive historical dispensations in which the ancient prophecies (Old Testament and Revelation) and fulfillments recurred.

To allay the fears of uprooted colonists or later to sublimate anxious disillusionments, these imaginative visions of the New England migration grew out of scriptural prophecies.[29] By creating pervasive typal or metaphoric correspondences between their history and Old Testament types, the Puritans implicitly sanctioned their mission with biblical authority and asserted their recapitulative participation in religious history under God's direct providential guidance. They regularly equated their journey and habitation of New England with Israel's Exodus, crossing the Red Sea, wilderness wanderings, and settlement of Canaan. In a lavish glorification of God's benevolence to New England, Urian Oakes exclaims:

> As you are a people of many Mercies and Priviledges, so I may well parallel you with *Israel*. . . . The Lord hath brought you over the *great Ocean* from your Native Land, the Land of your Progenitors, to *a place of Rest,* where you have enjoyed singular mercies. . . . This *wilderness* was the place which God decreed to make a *Canaan* to you: and *what he thought in his heart, he hath fulfilled with his hand, in bringing you to this good Land.* . . . *You have had Moses,* Men, I mean, of the same spirit, *to lead and go before you.* . . .God hath instructed us, as he did *Israel* in the Wilderness, Deut. 23. 10 you have been provided of all helps and advantages for the edification of your souls and a rich Blessing upon them. This is the Milk and Honey with which this *Canaan* though a Wilderness flows. . . . So that God hath made this Wilderness *to be glad for his People,* and this Desert *to rejoyce and blossome as a Rose,* Isai. 35. 1.[30]

Similarly, the historians adopted Old Testament accounts of Israel's release from Babylonian captivity and reconstruction of Jerusalem and Revelation's apocalyptic vision of Christ's Second Coming, the Millennium, and the eternal New Jerusalem as adumbrations of the American Puritan experience.[31] John Winthrop cherishes a vision of the New Jerusalem to be founded in America: "For wee must Consider that wee shall be as a Citty vpon a Hill, the eies of all people are vppon us."[32] Transmuting second-generation tribulations, which made New England seem more like Babylon itself than Jerusalem, into a millennial utopianism,

Cotton Mather in 1692–3 assuages personal as well as communal anxieties:

> Good News for the *Israel* of God, and particularly for his *New-English Israel*. . . . Surely we are not a *thousand years* distant from those happy *thousand years* of rest and peace, and . . . *Holiness* reserved for the People of God in the latter days . . . there is cause to think that we are not an *hundred*. . . . Shortly, didst thou say, dearest Lord! O gladsome word! . . . Alas, I may sigh over *this* Wilderness, as *Moses* did over *his* . . . when I consider the declining state of the *Power of Godliness* in our Churches. . . . Our *New-England* has then . . . done all that it was erected for. But if God have a purpose to make here a seat for any of *those glorious things which are spoken of thee, O thou City of God,* then even thou, O *New-England,* art within a very little while of better days than ever yet have dawn'd upon thee. . . . and the *Frown* of Heaven which has hitherto been upon Attempts of better Gospellizing the Plantations, considered, will but increase the Dawn.[33]

The Wonders of the Invisible World illustrates Mather's desperate need to transform the period of declension into a predictive sign of Christ's imminent return to establish the millennial kingdom. So too in the building of the second temple at Jerusalem, historians found a fitting antecedent for their own construction of a godly center of worship in New England, where the bright dawning of the glorious "thousand years" would originate.[34] Despite their professed exegetical caution, Puritan chroniclers thus often suppressed the New Testament antitypal and Christological focus of typology. They supplanted traditional correspondences between the Old and New Testaments with Old Testament to New England correlations and wrenched typology to accommodate immediate historical needs.

Puritan historians considered their Great Migration not only a historical act but also a significant spiritual departure from sin and progress toward redemption. In typology they discovered an authoritative method which defined both the temporal *and* eternal, the material *and* spiritual meanings of historical events in Scripture and which was compatible with their dualistic approach to contemporary experience itself.[35] Identifications of their mission with the exodus from Babylon and building of the New Jerusalem illustrate precisely this dual emphasis on temporal and spiritual enactments. On the one hand, the Puritans constitute an elect nation or chosen remnant in literal flight from the actual Babylonian captivity, under first Catholic and then English episcopal demands for conformity. They formed a vanguard migration directed by God to erect a new model covenant community, a historical illustration, a "Citty vpon a Hill" for the "eies of all people." This harmonious society, knit together by authority and reasoned consent, would become the New Jerusalem, an identifiable locale and nation readied for the Second Coming. Implicit in this application of Old and New Testament prophecies was the typological premise that all types and antitypes are real historical events; the Puritans believed that they historically and temporally were to construct a new Holy City.

On the other hand, the emigrants interpreted their flight also as a spiritual separation:

> Now as the people of God in old time, were called out of Babylon civil, the place of their bodily bondage; and were to come to Jerusalem, and there to build anew the Lord's temple, or tabernacle . . . so are the people of God, now to go out of Babylon spiritual, to Jerusalem . . . to build up themselves as lively stones into a spiritual house, or temple for the Lord to dwell in, leaving Babylon to that destruction and desolation, yea furthering the same, to which she is devoted by the Lord.[36]

Rather than emphasize the specific political purposes of New Jerusalem–New England, John Robinson's separatist viewpoint stressed the spirituality of the collective Elect who fled from sin and formed a sanctified temple for the Lord. Puritan historians entertained both interpretations simultaneously. They used the typological premise of historical and spiritual fulfillment to claim their joint material *and* spiritual consummation of the Old and New Testament prophecies respecting Babylon and the New Jerusalem. And because typology subsumed all temporal events within a framework of *Heilsgeschichte,* Puritan historians proclaimed the individual saint's and New England's corporate participation in a providential progress toward redemption.

In addition to adopting types as prefigurations of contemporary experience and coordinating a historical with a typological synthesis of the temporal and eternal, Puritans also appropriated the proposition of superior fulfillment into their chronicles. Collectively these three typological assumptions contributed to a Puritan doctrine of historical and religious progressivism. Because Christ fulfills the messianic prophecies and institutes the New Testament dispensation, each subsequent historical event reveals with greater spiritual clarity the meaning of Old Testament types. Puritan history, then, does not merely repeat the pattern of the Exodus; instead, contemporary events recapitulatively participate in a history of advancing dispensations from Israel under Solomon through Jerusalem under Nehemiah to New England under the founding fathers.[37] John Norton calls upon the types of Moses, Solomon, and David as leaders of Israel under the old dispensation to counsel his new dispensation generation to take up their gospel duties:

> And as *David* said to *Solomon,* I. *Chron.* 28. 10, 11. *I give unto thee the patern of the House of God, & c.* what God will do with us he knows best;

David lived not to build the Temple himself, but he left the patern thereof to his Son *Solomon:* And lo we have the patern, only this is complained of, that it is not practised, though we have had it many years ago; now practice is the end of Doctrine. . . . we are all concerned in this service, I mean in setting up the Throne of Christ. *Moses* is concerned, and it is his commendation that he was a man of God, who erected the Tabernacle, and set up the Worship of God according to the Patern in the Mount: and so *David* and *Solomon* & c. *Thou Solomon my Son, if thou doest bold here, the Lord will be with thee* and let the Churches look to it, we are all concerned herein, our Fidelity in this cause is our Crown; see that it be not taken from us.[38]

Following the pattern of these illustrious leaders, New England's ministers also must build the gospel temple in New England. Not merely to institute, they must then also insure the practice of a purified *"Order of the Gospel"* which supersedes patterns of worship handed down from Moses.[39] An inward, spiritually, *"compleat walking in the Faith of the Gospel,"* not in the episcopal or *"Presbyterian way,"* but in the "way Congregational," is the service God now requires and for which He rewards elect saints with crowns of eternal life.[40]

Initially optimistic, historians exalted New England's mission as the last dispensation to manifest most fully God's will before the Second Coming. This theory of historical progressivism increased the certainty of some theologians that New England would be the earthly seat of Christ's millennial kingdom and, therefore, encouraged eschatological predictions. Hearing the trumpets of the apocalypse not far off, Cotton Mather presages that "this at last is the Spot of *Earth,* which the God of Heaven *Spied out* for the Seat of such *Evangelical,* and *Ecclesiastical,* and very remarkable Transactions" and *"here* 'twas that our Blessed JESUS intended a *Resting-place"* among the "glorified Saints of the *New Jerusalem.'"*[41] By definition typology promoted the foretelling of future events based upon analogies with events in earlier times. Just as New England fulfilled and surpassed the Old Testament types of Canaan and Jerusalem, it in turn prefigured first Christ's millennial kingdom on earth and then the eternal heaven and New Jerusalem beyond. At once like the typology advocated by the New Testament authors and seventeenth-century devotional guides, the Puritan developmental typology yet significantly deviated from conservative definitions and usages.[42]

The avant-garde development of recapitulative typology to defend their participation in sacred history represents only one distinctive application of typology by American Puritans. Combining typological exegesis with ramistic logic, Puritan theologians elaborated the doctrine of the Covenant of Grace and the corollary covenants for civil government and church polity in New England.[43] Originated by English and continental Calvinists to counteract weaknesses in the creed and to combat Antinomian and Arminian heresies, the covenant or federal theology was transmitted through the leaders of the Great Migration. By 1650 New England Puritans had so extended the federal theology that they constituted an isolated faction, different not only from the Anglicans but also from other Puritan sects (Presbyterians) and European Calvinists. Whatever the contributing factors (common law, new theories of government and church polity, political exigency) that stimulated the growth of covenant theology, Puritan theologians steadfastly cited biblical sanctions for the scheme. Because typology supplied appropriate presuppositions about the unity of all Scripture as a revelation of God's divine pattern for salvation and about the differences between the Old and New Testament dispensations, it supported the Puritan concept of a Covenant of Grace.

The Covenant of Grace defines man's relationship with God as a contract in which two consenting parties voluntarily swear to fulfill specified obligations. Initially, God plights a Covenant of Works with Adam, stipulating that in return for Adam's obedience to certain moral laws (symbolized by not eating of the fruit of the tree of knowledge), God will grant him eternal life. When Adam and Eve violate this first covenant and incur God's just punishment of death, God graciously institutes a second covenant. In the new Covenant of Grace God promises forgiveness of sins, reconciliation, and eternal life through Christ, the seed of woman who will bruise the serpent's head (Gen. 3:15). In return he requires man's voluntary submission to the covenant and belief (not deeds) in the promises (Old Testament) and then in the incarnate Messiah (New Testament). God voluntarily moderates His divine right to enforce obedience and His requirements in order to institute terms that natural and rational man can reasonably fulfill. By emphasizing the effectiveness of faith alone for salvation and the predestination of the Elect, Calvinism had potentially negated the need for man's obedience to moral laws and postulated an omnipotent God who arbitrarily distributes mercy. Covenant theology subtly reorients the nature of grace from a "gift" to a "covenant" which promises future good, but not without moral responsibility. Rather than entirely deny visible goodness, covenant theologians might be said to incorporate the Covenant of Works so that obedience to moral laws manifested in deeds becomes an evidence of sanctification. Rather than stress the impotence of the believer who is subject to predestination, covenant theology encourages assurance by accentuating the free will with which man participates in the contract.

In order to defend their theory of covenanting, Puritan theologians, as might be expected, employed typological readings of Scripture, assuming first the perpetual revelation of God's grace in both Testaments. Since God inaugurates the Covenant of Grace through his promise to Adam and Abraham, study of the Old Testament as well as the New reveals the truths of the covenant relationship. *A Confession of Faith* (1680) of the New England churches reminds the believer of the gospel unity in Scripture and specifically of Old Testament types, promises, and sacrifices that prefigure Christ and his work of redemption:

> VI. Altho' the *Work* of *Redemption* was not actually wrought by Christ, till after his Incarnation, yet the Virtue, Efficacy and Benefits thereof, were communicated unto the Elect in all Ages successively from the beginning of the World, in and by those Promises, Types and Sacrifices, wherein he was revealed and signified to be the Seed of the Woman, which should bruise the Serpent's Head, and the Lamb slain from the beginning of the World, being yesterday and to day the same, and for ever.[44]

In his systematic introduction, Samuel Mather cites the texts and dispensations under which God in the Old Testament reveals the covenant. To reaffirm his promises to Adam, God renewed *"his Covenant with . . . Noah and all his Seed, even all mankind; and gave them the Rainbow for an outward Sign and Pledge thereof, Gen.* 9. 8, 9, 12. to 18. This is the first instance where the word *Covenant* is used concerning the Transactions between God and Men"* (*FT*, p. 27). The Old Testament's literal and historical usage of the term "covenant" provides one Puritan justification for the rational and contractual nature of the Covenant of Grace. For Mather, the covenant with Noah forms, however, only the second of seven Old Testament dispensations from Adam to Israel's return from Babylon and building of the second temple. In each dispensation God reveals "further, clearer, and more plentiful beamings forth of Gospel-light upon the Church, above what had been before" (*FT*, p. 34). By citing Old Testament institutions and dispensations, theologians affirmed God's willing participation in a Covenant of Grace, His accommodation to man's understanding through gradual unveilings, and His preparation for the fulfillment in Christ.

God formulates His covenant with Moses as a legalistic contract which specifies man's obligatory obedience to *"Moral, Judicial* and *Ceremonial* Law" and in return promises spiritual redemption to the descendants of Israel (*FT*, p. 37). But according to covenant theology and typology, Christ's evangelical teachings fulfill and surpass the prefigurative Mosaical dispensation: *"Moses* delivered *Law* that is, *Shadows* and *Ceremonies,* which were but legal, and dark and rigorous: But *Christ* brought in *Grace* and *Truth,* that is, the real and sweet *Accomplishment* and *Performance,* of all the good, that *Moses* had promised . . . *the Law hath the Shadow, but not the very Image of the Things themselves"* (*FT*, pp. 167–8). As an antitypal fulfillment of Adam and Moses, Christ institutes a new covenant in which the contractual nature of grace persists; however, requisite duties become entirely spiritual declarations of faith, love, and obedience to moral injunctions in return for eternal salvation. This New Testament Covenant of Grace surpasses, indeed abrogates, the previous Covenant of Law.

Samuel Mather stresses the typological and covenantal concept of abrogation in the three cardinal reminders that conclude his treatise:

> 1. *That all this typical Dispensation is expired and abolished by the exhibition of Jesus Christ the Truth and Substance and Scope of all:* These shadows are vanished away by the rising of that Sun of Righteousness. . . .
> 2. *The Gospel-Dispensation doth succeed, and is substituted.* . . . instead of the Law and the Prophets, we have the Gospel and Evangelists, who give us an History instead of Prophesy. . . .
> 3. *This Gospel-Dispensation is far more glorious then that old Legal Dispensation.* For is not the Substance better then the Shadows. . . . The Spirit is better then the Letter, 2 *Cor.* 3. 6 to *Vers.* 11. The Letter there is not the *written Word*, and the Spirit the *Enthusiasms* of a deluded Fancy, (as some have understood it;) but the Letter is the *Law*, and the Spirit is the *Gospel*, as the whole Context shews. (*FT*, pp. 539–40)

The concept of abrogation for both covenant theology and typology acknowledges the Old Testament's legal efficacy, *because* it serves a typal function. But this principle also provides the basis upon which Puritans counter popish and Anglican insistence on ceremonies, music, and priestly garb within the church. With Christ's advocacy of a new spiritual and internalized covenant between man and God, the need for Mosaic judicial and ceremonial laws disappears, while the moral laws retain their validity. Similarly, by citing the Old Testament typal signs (circumcision, crossing the Red Sea) and marking only the sacraments of Baptism and the Lord's Supper as gospel fulfillments, Puritan covenant theologians designate these observances alone as seals of the Covenant of Grace.

Typology was not, therefore, merely a gratuitous addition to Puritan doctrine but an integral part of covenant theology. Typological insistence upon Old Testament historical sanctions, prefigurations, and fulfillments, and abrogation of types through Christ provided a substantial exegetical method by which federal theologians read the Bible, justified their covenant concept of grace, defended the two sacraments as seals, and advocated the purification of ceremonies. Once federal theologians established the Covenant of Grace as a contractual agreement between man and God instituted in the Bible, they then used further typological correspondences and ramistic logic to erect the social and congregational covenants. As part of the Covenant of Grace, God required that men openly profess their faith and perform duties for other men as well as for Himself. When these regenerate men operating individually under the

Covenant of Grace compacted together, they created a church covenant, a communion of saints analogous to the Old Testament congregation of the Israelites. In New England this theory of church covenant dictated the congregational polity that differentiated New England Puritans from Presbyterians and Anglicans. Although it is unclear whether the social covenant stimulated or derived from the Covenant of Grace, it is certain that in New England the social and religious covenants became one. In the theocratic commonwealth the compacting of the Elect became the basis for political incorporation, and the duties of civil obedience duplicated the covenant terms for salvation and Christian worship. As both historians and theologians took pains to illustrate, New England constituted a unified church and nation of the Elect, spiritual inheritors of the Israelites, and participants as individuals and a community in the perpetual Covenant of Grace. Typology contributed the fundamental exegetical method, authoritative principles for relating successive dispensations in religious history, and biblical examples crucial to these historical and theological defenses of the New England Way.

Within this milieu Edward Taylor preached his sermons and created his poetry. Having fled the Babylonian captivity of conformity in England, he arrived in New England on July 5, 1668.[45] After three years at Harvard he traveled westward a hundred miles into the wilderness on a "tedious & hazzardous journey, the snow being about Mid-leg deepe, the way unbeaten, or the track filled up againe, and over rocks and mountains . . . [on] the desperatest journey that ever Connecticut men undertooke."[46] Within twenty-four hours of his arrival at Westfield, where he lived and ministered until his death in 1729 at the age of eighty-seven, he preached his first Sunday sermon. Like so many immigrants before him, Taylor sensed the hazards and desperation of not only the physical trek, but also the personal and communal trials of the spirit in the wilderness. Some thirty years later, the immediacy of this first confrontation with the harsh New England environment lingered in Taylor's plea, "Then lead me, Lord, through all this Wilderness" (II.59.31).

Urian Oakes could well have included Taylor among those "Worthies" to whom God stretched out a "mighty hand" and "sweetned their wilderness condition to them, conducted them as with the *Pillar of Cloud and Fire,* protected them from the many dangers that threatned them, and directed them (being *a Sun as well as a shield unto them.* Psal. 84. 11.) in the happy settlement of Church and State."[47] Although undoubtedly aware of such recapitulative correlations between the Israelites and the New England settlers, Taylor elects at once a more personal and a more universal use of devotional typology in his poetry. "Lead *me,*" "*I* shall not lag nor tire," "to Cana'n *I* am journeying," he declares (II. 59.31, 34, 35). These personal requests and dedications reflect Taylor's aching susceptibility to sin, tenacious search for the way of salvation, and his optimistic anticipation of the eschatological New Canaan. For Taylor, covenant theologian and Puritan typologist, the means to that salvation are through Christ alone:

> Christ in this Pillar, Godhead-Man'd doth rise
>   The Churches King, to guid, support, Defend.
> Her Priest to Cleanse her: in the Cloud to baptize.
>   And Reconcile with Incense that ascends.
> Her Prophet too that Lights her in her way
> By Night With Lanthorn Fire. With Cloud by day.
>   (II. 59.25–30)

In His nature as true prophet, priest, and King to the new covenant church, Christ fulfills all the guiding functions symbolized by the miraculous types, such as the pillar of cloud and fire. By drawing upon the typological associations from centuries of biblical exegesis, Taylor makes the plea for guidance not merely personal but representative. Within God's design for salvation each lonely soul traverses the wilderness of sin, pursues Christ the antitypal fulfillment, and journeys finally to the promised paradise. In the church under a New Testament Covenant of Grace, the saint enjoys the certainty of future redemption.

Even this brief example illustrates Edward Taylor's alignment with the more conservative typologists among Puritan covenant theologians. A man of his time and culture who is not unaware of the external wilderness, Taylor yet foregoes an overtly developmental or recapitulative use of types in his poetry. Most poems relate to a sacrament Sunday sermon, as the full title, *Preparatory Meditations before my approach to the Lords Supper. Chiefly upon the Doctrin preached upon the Day of administration,* indicates. Both these poems and the sermons of *Upon the Types of the Old Testament* share the ramistic rigor, moral and devotional focus, and conservatism of Samuel Mather's, Thomas Taylor's, or other Puritan treatises. Conservative in his use of typology for hermeneutics and meditation, Edward Taylor is yet a "radical" among New England Puritans because he chooses to write the autobiography of his soul in a series of poems. Taylor accepts the protecting covenant grace of God shadowed under the typal "Pillar Cloud and Fire," when he promises, "I shall thy praise under this Shadow sing" (II. 59.32, 36). He praises the efficacy of Old Testament types as figures of the New Testament dispensation and as moral examples for the seventeenth-century Christian. But for Taylor the types become also poetic shadows or images of personal spiritual realities and intimate fears, desires, or consecrations. In his poetic meditations he seeks assurances of personal sanctification and fulfills a self-imposed covenant responsibility to examine his conscience and to sing God's praises. To the vitality of typology as a theological concept which was centuries' old and crucial to New England Puritanism, Edward Taylor adds the intensity of personal belief and the dynamism of artistic inspiration.

2

Prophets and Poets: Typology as Illumination

Oh! that I had but halfe an eye to view
  This excellence of thine, undazled: so
Therewith to give my heart a touch anew
  Untill I quickned am, and made to glow.

                    (II.1.25–8)

Edward Taylor's intellectual stature and orthodoxy as a Puritan theologian go unchallenged. In public ceremonies on August 26, 1679, he presided over Westfield's formal entrance into a church covenant according to the strict dictates of federal theology and the New England congregational polity.[1] He brought to his ministry an education at Cambridge and Harvard, a command of Latin, Greek, and Hebrew, and a learning that was admirable even among seventeenth-century divines.[2] In his extensive library he accumulated standard theological texts, including writings by major English and American covenant theologians and works on medicine, cosmography, history, metallurgy, cometography, philosophy, angelography, rhetoric, and poetry.[3] The extent and diversity of his holdings reflect Taylor's intellectual curiosity, and even the few extant remnants of his own works attest to his prodigious output and literary experimentation.[4]

Taylor represented the conservative faction of late-century Puritanism in New England, and he actively employed his considerable erudition by undertaking a "Harmony of the Gospels" organized according to ramistic principles and by translating Origen's *De Principiis* and *Contra Celsum* from Greek into English.[5] He also combined extracts from previous authors with personal observations in a "Metallographia" and "Dispensatory," compendiums about metals and medicinal herbs useful for the frontier minister who also served as a physician.[6] Besides notes on theology, business letters, and accounts of current events found in one "Commonplace Book," a peculiar fascination with China and with bizarre monstrosities and remarkable providences appeared in his "China's

Description and Commonplace Book."[7] Early experiments with elegies, acrostics, love poems, metrical paraphrases of Job and the Psalms, and religious lyrics eventually culminated in three major poetic works: a twenty-one-thousand-line narrative in decasyllabic couplets of *A Metrical History of Christianity* (1690–1710), *Gods Determinations touching his Elect,* and the *Preparatory Meditations* (1682–1725).[8] These extant manuscripts represent, however, only a portion of the "many . . . smaller ones . . . of his own composition," which were, according to his descendant Henry Wyllys Taylor (1851), among the "more than a hundred volumes" which "tradition says he left, at his death."[9] A defiant intellectual in the Westfield wilderness, Edward Taylor upheld a seventeenth-century tradition of ecclesiastical scholarship and literary achievement, while he defended the tenets of covenant theology.

From this orthodox Puritan who cultivated the art of poetic devotion, the second series of *Preparatory Meditations* on typology (II.1–30, 58–61, 70–71) and the allegory of Canticles (II.115–165) seems a not unlikely creation. Taylor's full title, *Preparatory Meditations before my Approach to the Lords Supper. Chiefly upon the Doctrin preached upon the Day of administration,* suggests just how intimately these poems developed from his immediate hermeneutic concerns.[10] Between 1693 and 1706 Edward Taylor composed as well the typological sermons *Upon the Types of the Old Testament,* his *Treatise Concerning the Lord's Supper,* and the fourteen *Christographia* sermons. During these years, theological disputes raged in the Connecticut Valley when Solomon Stoddard admitted all believers to the Supper and advocated the use of the Sacrament as a converting ordinance. Appalled by the shift in church polity and Stoddard's liberalism, Edward Taylor, most notably in the *Treatise,* defended the traditional Puritan concept of the Eucharist as a confirming sign of church membership.[11] His attempts to stem a liberalizing trend significantly paralleled Samuel Mather's motives for an earlier crusade in Dublin against the encroachment of Anglican and Catholic ceremonies. Like the English Reformers before him, Edward Taylor found in typology a doctrine fundamental to reestablishing strict principles for reading Scripture and reaffirming the purity of covenant theology.

As early as 1685–6, Taylor had dabbled in the types with six meditations (sermons not extant) on the Old Testament "Shew-Bread Table" (I.11), "Robes from Bozrah" (I.12), Christ the "Choicest Cabbinet" of "All Wisdom" (I.13), and on the high priest (I.14/15), prophets (I.16), and kings (I.17). Although these poems anticipated the images and themes of Taylor's later series on types, his early poetic method tended more toward metaphoric allusion than elaborate conceits. Including these six, Taylor had already transcribed forty-nine meditations into the "Poetical Works" manuscript when in 1693 he abruptly began renumbering his poems. Meditation II.1 proclaimed a renewed exegetical and poetic fascination with those divine figures that adumbrated Christ's excelling glory:

> The glory of the world slickt up in types
>   In all Choise things chosen to typify,
> His glory upon whom the worke doth light,
>   To thine's a Shaddow, or a butterfly.
>   How glorious then, my Lord, art thou to mee
>   Seing to cleanse me, 's worke alone for thee.
>
> The glory of all Types doth meet in thee.
>   Thy glory doth their glory quite excell:
> More than the Sun excells in its bright glee
>   A nat, an Earewig, Weevill, Snaile, or Shell.
>
> (II.1.13–22)

Composed over the next six years (1693–9), Meditations II.1–30 executed Taylor's ambition of cataloging Old Testament persons, events, and ceremonies that prefigured Christ's antitypal supremacy. Not merely fulfilled but surpassed by the advent of this Son/Sun, the ancient persons and ceremonies foreshadowed Christ and His mission in providential history. Taylor's absorption with typology surfaced as well in the *Treatise,* written in the same period (1693–4) as Meditations II.4–5, in which he counterattacked Stoddard by analyzing figural correspondences that linked the Old Testament circumcision and Passover to the New Testament Lord's Supper.[12] This *Treatise* and the later *Christographia* (1701–3) established Taylor's predilection for collecting sermons in order to expose key doctrines, and the deliberate reorientation of the *Preparatory Meditations* in 1693 made it yet more likely that he had also preached a series on Old Testament figures.

But it was not until fall 1977 that a holograph, vellum-bound manuscript, entitled "Vpon yᵉ Types of yᵉ Old Testament," was placed for assessment with a bookseller in Lincoln, Nebraska.[13] Subsequently identified by Professor Charles W. Mignon as Edward Taylor's work, this 844-page manuscript had passed down through generations of Taylor's lineal descendants from "Ezra Stiles 1782," as the marginalia confirms (*UTOT*, p. 397), to Judge Henry Wyllys Taylor, whose inscription "By the Rev.ᵈ Edward Taylor of Westfield" appears beneath the title. *Upon the Types of the Old Testament* contained twenty-nine homilies dating from May 1693 to February 1698/9 and corresponding almost exactly with *Preparatory Meditations* II.1–30. In addition Taylor bound in this volume five sermons, dated December 1703 to July 1704, on occasional types from Israel's wilderness journey identical to Meditations II.58–61 and a dyad from October and November 1706 that paralleled II.70–71 (Appendix 1).[14] According to express rationales in the sermons, Taylor divided his initial thirty meditations into two major categories – typical persons, both individuals (II.3–13, 30) and ranks (II.14–15), and real things, including Old Testament sacrifices, the temple, feasts, and purifications (II.16–28). Sermon and Meditation II.29 ushered in the occasional providential guidances (II.29, 58–61) given by Yahweh during Israel's flight from Egypt (Appendix 4). What this homiletic treatise offered to scholars was added testimony to Edward Taylor's exceptional ministerial diligence and poetic creativity and to his participation in a Puritan typological tradition which germinated in seventeenth-century England but flowered in New World America.

As discussed earlier, in sixteenth-century Europe and England, a sweeping tide of Reformers had demanded a return to the literal Word of God, away from the multiple allegorical senses of Scripture so proliferated by Catholic expositors and toward renewed adherence to the Old Testament's historical reality. Although the tradition threaded back to St. Paul, Augustine, and the Antiochenes, the *figurae* of David, the Exodus, and the sacraments reappeared prominently in homiletic writings by Luther, Calvin, Tyndale, and Whitaker (among others). It was during the seventeenth century that handbooks on the biblical types flourished. Works by William Guild (*Moses Unvailed* 1620), Thomas Taylor (*Christ Revealed* 1635), Henry Vertue (*Christ and the Church: Or Parallels* 1659), Benjamin Keach (*Tropologia* 1681), and Samuel Mather (*The Figures or Types* 1683) emphasized, in keeping with Protestant theory, that typological significations were an integral dimension of the literal text and that the prophetic signs instituted by God through Old Testament events were exhibited openly by Christ under the New Testament dispensation. Whatever their ecclesiastical leanings, figural categories, or distinctions between metaphors and types, these writers, who belonged to the Protestant mainstream, insisted upon the primacy of Scripture as the repository of all divine knowledge. As Edward Taylor's annotations in *Upon the Types of the Old Testament* evidence, he drew heavily upon the broad range of theologians from the Church Fathers, Augustine, and Origen to the Reformers, including Calvin, Bèza, Ainsworth, Weemse, and Ames. Although no doubt aware of other typological resources, whose influences cannot be discounted, nonetheless, Taylor more regularly turned to those handbooks, namely, Thomas Taylor's *Christ Revealed* (1635) and Samuel Mather's *The Figures or Types* (1683), that would have been most compatible for a Calvinist covenanting theologian in New England.

In *Christ Revealed* Thomas Taylor assumed the schoolmaster's role. He offered the reader an abundance of figural comparisons and devotional applications, primarily of the personal (Adam through Jonah) and sacramental types (circumcision, Passover, the Exodus). Echoing the typological postulates of other Reformers, Taylor affirmed the continuity of Scripture, allowed the efficacy of Jewish ceremonies for educating the "rude and dull" tribes of Israel and for shadowing "the glory of Christs Kingdome," and praised the gospel's greater "light at noonday" compared with the "light in the dawning" of the Mosaic law (*CR*, pp. 201–2, 3). Although silenced himself for preaching against the harsh treatment of Puritans, Thomas Taylor chose not to enflame ecclesiastical debates but to provide a typological primer, replete with the devotionalism to which readers might turn for instruction and reassurance.[15] By contrast, Samuel Mather wrote his treatise in direct response to political and theological upheavals. He initially preached two sermons, collectively printed as *A Testimony from the Scripture against Idolatry & superstition* (1670 ?), in which he invoked the doctrine of types to inveigh against the renewal after the Restoration (1660) of Anglican and Catholic ceremonies, priestly garments, and music in church worship.[16] Prompted by other "*Non-Conformist* Ministers," continuing persecutions, and disputes between covenanting theologians and English Anglicans, Mather compiled an extended homiletic series (March 23, 1666/7–February 28, 1668/9) on the types for his Dublin congregation, which was published posthumously as *The Figures or Types of the Old Testament* (1683). Mather's polemical rather than devotional purposes transformed his study into an *apologia* for Puritan methods of reading Scripture and for covenant theology as well as an erudite attack on Catholic and Anglican polity and theology. He presented a thoroughly conservative analysis, emphasizing repeatedly the abrogation of Old Testament figures by the new dispensation of grace as preached by and embodied in Christ to counter the uses of ancient ceremonies. But he refrained from Puritan recapitulative applications of types as prefigurations for contemporary historical events and, therefore, as justifications for the colonizing of New England, for jeremiad predictions of doom in the imminent "Last Days," or for millenarian optimism. Mather's fascination with hermeneutics, a penchant for ramistic distinctions, and his scholarly grasp of covenant theology made *The Figures or Types* the most widely reprinted and circulated typal treatise in England and America.[17]

When inventoried at his death, Edward Taylor's library contained neither typological guide. Nevertheless, Gordon Slethaug's discovery at Yale of Taylor's copy of *Christ Revealed* demonstrates his possession of it, as do the scattered annotations in Taylor's hand on Adam, Joseph, and the Red Sea that confirm his close reading.[18] Not only numerous parallels evidence Taylor's use of this treatise in his meditations, but as well on seven occasions in *Upon the Types of the Old Testament,* he directly refers to Thomas Taylor on the types (*UTOT*, pp. 219, 472, 558, 598, 600, 831, 832). Similarly, Taylor also cites Mather on the types of David, the burnt, sin, and meat offerings and substantially incorporates his theories and structures (*UTOT*, pp. 219, 365, 370, 382). Exchanges of pertinent theological works with other New England divines, early distribution of his library to relatives, or the possible loss of 85 percent of Taylor's personal transcriptions and writings may explain the absence from his library, yet he was obviously familiar with *The Figures or Types* as early as 1685 and no later than 1693–9.[19]

Although he probably consulted both sources contemporaneously, textual evidence suggests that Edward Taylor more consistently adopted Mather's typological divisions and imagery into his own sermons and *Preparatory Meditations*. Even in such an unlikely spot as the marginalia of *Christ Revealed*, Taylor sketches a diagram, bisecting Adam's "Influences" and "Headship" and designating Christ's "Mediatoriall" function by which "he is made a Coven^{ntr} on ye account of all mankinde."[20] No such distinction appears in Thomas Taylor's analysis, whereas Mather proclaims boldly that Adam resembles Christ "chiefly in regard of his *Headship and Influence*" and as "the Covenant Root and Head of all Mankind" (*FT*, p. 64). Adhering to his diagram, Edward Taylor then preaches in Sermon II.3 on Adam's "Influences" and "Mediatoriall Headship of the first Covenant" (*UTOT*, p. 39), developing themes and images that are echoed in Meditation II.3's praises of Christ's "mediatoriall glory in the shine/ Out Spouted so from Adam's typick streame" (II.3.8–9).[21] In a fashion common among exegetes, Mather had incorporated premises, organizations, and details from earlier guides, most notably *Christ Revealed*. Mather's reliance on Thomas Taylor opened the way for Edward Taylor to absorb figural correlations not only from direct readings of *Christ Revealed*, but ones also reinforced through Mather's extensive redactions. Thomas Taylor, for instance, provides the seminal concept that by *"Adams sinne we are all driven out of Paradise"* (*CR*, p. 10). Mather characterizes Eden's "Garden of Pleasure" as a *"Type of Heaven"* over which Christ will reign, since *"Adam's Dominion over the Creatures"* shadows forth *"Christ's Dominion and Kingdom"* (*FT*, pp. 66, 65). Paradise preoccupies both expositors; the term "Dominion" appears only in Mather's treatment. Edward Taylor's Sermon II.3 cites both "this Garden in Paradise" as "a type of Heaven" and also Adam's "Dominion over the Creatures. . . . Which Dominion being lost in Adam is given unto Christ in the Covenant" (*UTOT*, pp. 36–7).[22]

When Taylor composed his typological sermons and meditations, Mather's *Figures or Types*, it would seem, became more than a duplicate desk-side companion with *Christ Revealed* – indeed, it became an essential resource. Taylor's preference for Mather apparently stemmed from congeniality in their motives and form, for both theologians shared a need for polemical defenses and were schooled at Harvard in ramistic proofs. Sophisticated theoretical points, shared anti-Catholic sentiments, striking overlaps in typal orderings and images, deliberate choices to cre-

ate homilis – these features differentiated the works of both later theologians from Thomas Taylor's noncontroversial schemes, William Guild's
perfunctory catalogs in *Moses Unvailed* (1620), and Henry Vertue's listing
of personal types and metaphors in *Christ and the Church* (1659). Imitating
Mather, who initially preached his sermons for a Dublin congregation,
Edward Taylor also designed his collection as a "key" to unlock mysteries of the Word for his Westfield gathering of the Elect and as a fitting
scholarly defense of covenant theology. By explicating Old Testament
types, Taylor sought to preach Christ's superseding excellencies, defend
gospel worship, and refute Stoddard's liberalizing sacramental practices.
But Taylor's *Upon the Types of the Old Testament* became more than a
derivative imitation; it recast biblical figures into patterns and preachments uniquely his own and deserving of recognition, however belat-
edly, as the last major typological guide of the Protestant Reformation.

Taylor begins *Upon the Types of the Old Testament* by citing Paul's
opposition in Colossians 2:17 to the "infection of Heathenish Philosophy" and "Jewish Ceremonies," since such rites merely presignify "all
the Speciall Gospell Concerns carried on by Christ" (*UTOT*, pp. 1, 2).
Like Mather, Taylor pauses to inquire, "What is a Type?" and, citing its
etymology from the Greek "Τύπτω" meaning "to smite," he sets
forth a definition: "A type is a Certain thing Standing with a Sacred
impression set upon it by God to Signify Some good to come as Christ,
or the Gospell Concerns in this Life" (*UTOT*, p. 3). He then hastens
toward his main doctrinal design to demonstrate the Savior "whose
Excellency doth as far Exceed" shadowy types "as the body of the glorious Sun the Shade thereof" (*UTOT*, p. 3). In a characteristic burst of
imagery, he extends the analogy by comparing types "with the moon;
whose light is said to be a borrowd Light, that she hath no light, but
what the Rayes of the Sun give her, & therefore when out of those rayes
she never gives light," just as Old Testament figures possess no efficacy
without the Son's irradiating presence (*UTOT*, p. 8). Having established
Christ's superior excellence, Taylor concludes with some "briefe
Improovment" or "Uses," linking this revelation to the progress of man's
redemption, the need for gospel worship, and the salutary truths gleaned
from studying types. Ruined by sin, man must turn to the redeemer,
Christ. In order to understand the Savior's true efficacy, the Westfield
parishioner need only heed the lessons taught by Old Testament figures:

> Now the Grace of God having provided Christ as the onely reliefe of
> poore Sinners, & knowing how Sin had besotted, & dulld man that he
> decerns not what is Spiritually excellent, nor mooves after it, doth set
> him forth thus transcendently Excellent by all the Luster of the Types,
> & glory of the Metaphors used to represent him as most excellent that
> the beaming glory of his Excellency shining upon our Souls might stir

our desires to set them in motion after him & so to stir our Endeavours
to Seek him. (*UTOT*, p. 13)

In this way Taylor joins together the extended lessons on the types in his
subsequent thirty-five sermons and the purposes of his preaching – to
promote "the Greate worke of Divine Grace in the Dispensation of the
Gospell" and to "bring persons out of a State of Sin, unto Christ Jesus"
(*UTOT*, p. 1). Like his exegetical ancestors from Paul to Mather, Edward
Taylor reconfirms the basic tenets of typology itself – the continuity (yet
different manner) of the old legal and new evangelical dispensation of
grace, the Christocentricity of God's plan for redemption, and the Puritan repudiation of Jewish ceremonies (and Catholic or Anglican imitations) in favor of a spiritual worship, one capable of sustaining the kingdom of the Elect in the New Canaan of an American wilderness.

Though Sermon II.1 first formulates Taylor's Puritan theory of types,
it is his later Sermon IX (December 1702) from the *Christographia* that
strikingly demonstrates the centrality of types for covenant theology.
The *Christographia* sermons focus thematically on the Savior's merciful
mediation in the history of man's salvation, and in Sermon IX Taylor
preaches on the fullness of truth in all "Prophesies, Promises, and Types"
which "lodges in Christ" (*CHR*, p. 270). He offers a use by way of
inference for his congregation's improvement:

> That the Faith of the Old Testament Church, and of the Church of the
> New Testament is set on the Same Object: That Christ was as truely
> the Object of old testament faith as of the New. That the old Testament
> believer did as truelie believe in Christ, as the New doth. Christ is the
> Same Christ to both: that the faith in Christ was the Same faith to both:
> that they are both Saved by the Same Faith, as the means: by the Same
> Christ, as the Cause of Salvation, the one as the other. For in that
> the one Was under Christ in the Promise, Prophesy and Type, and the
> other under Christ dispensed in the Substance, Spirit, and Power of the
> Gospell: they both Sit under the Exhibition of the Same Christ, of the
> Same Grace, and in the Exercise of the Same faith; onely there is a
> difference as to the manner of the Dispensing the Same. They had Christ
> dispensed in Promises and Types, as a Mediator to Come. We have him
> dispensed in a Cleare, and Manifest way as Come already. But the dif-
> ferent manner of dispensing of the Messiah, doth not produce, a Dif-
> ferent Christ, nor a different Faith on Christ. . . . Now in that Christ
> hath the fulness of Propheticall, Promisive, and Typicall Truth in him:
> He is the Kirnell of this Way of Discovery, for those under it to feed
> upon, and the New Testament Dispensasion is the Divine Hammer that
> breakes this Shell, and brings forth the Kirnell and feeds the Gospell
> believer therewith. . . . Now to use the type is to say, the Shadow is
> better than the Substance, and to deny that the thing typified is come.
> (*CHR*, pp. 287–8)

Taylor clearly uses typology to buttress the doctrine of the Old and New
Testament dispensations of grace. Scripture records historical adumbrations of the Messiah whether in promises, prophecies, or types, and subsequently presents Christ as the antitypal fulfillment, agent of grace, and
object of faith. He also acknowledges a historical continuum by distinguishing the Old Testament foreshadowing of future events and a
"Mediator to Come" from Christ the antitype who is "Come already"
to effect the prophecy. He emphasizes the continuing essence of the gospel message that preaches the "Same Christ," the "Same Grace," and the
"Same faith," but he differentiates the old and new manners of its dispensation. Imagistically, by setting the shadow against the substance,
kernel against the shell, Taylor distinguishes the legal from the evangelical testament, and he dramatizes the coming of the new dispensation as
a violent action. Animated to become a "Divine Hammer," the New
Testament "breaks this Shell" of divine truth which spiritually "feeds
the Gospell believer."[23] Elaborating upon these differing dispensations
in Sermon Xth, he contends that God "change the Nature of the Obedience from Legall, to Evangelicall, because the Qualifications fitting and
inabling thereunto, are wholy New–Covenant Guifts: and the Condition, Nature and Use of the Same wholy Evangelicall" (*CHR,* pp. 314–
15). Thus, Edward Taylor uses typology as a substantial proof of God's
providential salvation, His prudent establishment of progressive historical dispensations, and the importance of Christ's grace and mediation for
redemption.

Traditionally, from St. Paul through Augustine to Samuel Mather and
Edward Taylor, typology also provided a method of reading Scripture
that closed the gap between Christian and Jew by asserting the reciprocal
functions of both testaments. In his attempt to convert the Jews, Paul
reinterpreted the Old Testament to stress its anticipation of the Messiah
and then defined Christ's adherence to Jewish law as an example of his
messianic obedience and fulfillment of prophecy. But Paul and the evangelists also claimed that Christ's fulfillment abrogated the law and sub-
stituted a new reign of spiritual worship. Puritan theologians accentuated
the concept of abrogation, more perhaps than the Church Fathers and
medieval exegetes, in order to reclaim the supremacy of spiritual worship from Catholic distortions of ceremonies. Sensitive to the contemporary controversies, Edward Taylor exhibits a Puritan certitude when,
in Sermon II.1 from *Upon the Types,* he proclaims, "All the Ceremonies
of the Law were shadows of Good things to come" and "being but Shadows they must Cease, when Christ the Substance of them is come," for
the "Apostle comprehends them all in that term the Law Heb. 10.1 &
asserts its Excellency to be but a Shadow, & not the Image of the things"
(*UTOT,* pp. 2, 3). Even more zealously in the later figural sermons and

Christographia, Taylor reiterates Christ's abolition of legal types, since "in the New Testament Exhibition of Christ a Ceremoniall Worship is unlawfull, and not to be admitted. Christ having the truth of the types in him, as fulfilling of them, all the Ceremoniall Worship is accomplished, and it hath by the authority of the Spirit of God been utterly laid aside, and never did appear in the Gospell Worship" (*CHR,* p. 288). Based upon irrefutable scriptural proof of Christ's abrogation of ceremonies, Edward Taylor thus condemns those who worship "as the Jews by the type and Shadow," since "such things of the Jewish Customs, and rites of things to come are dissolved" (*CHR,* p. 288).

In Taylor's *Upon the Types of the Old Testament* and the *Christographia,* repeated explications of Christ's fulfilling and abrogating of ceremonial law fuel Puritan attacks on Catholic and Anglican perpetuations of Old Testament rituals. Not sharing quite the dark humor of Mather, who claims that "to reintroduce these old legal Ceremonies, and to talk of literal Sacrifices under the Gospel, is to dig *Moses* out of his Grave, and *to deny Jesus Christ*" (*FT,* p. 277), Edward Taylor yet argues with equal force. The doctrine of Christ's abrogation, he pronounces, convicts of error "Such as Carry on a Ceremoniall Worship under the Gospel dispensation. As the Papists, and Prelates," for "to use the type is to say, the Shadow is better than the Substance, and to denie that the thing typified is come" (*CHR,* pp. 290, 288). He erupts with Puritan dismay, even hostility, for the "Idolatrous Papist. . . . these know Christ to be the Onely Mediator: and yet doe they sett up Saints of their own Canonizing to be their Advocates to pray to, and to mediate for them. Yea they are more frequently at their Ave Maria's than at their prayers to God in the name of Christ. . . . But, oh! what Superstition is here?" (*CHR,* p. 429). In Taylor's opinion the "Idolatrous Papist" who erects self-devised ceremonies and saints defies the new evangelical faith and dilutes Christ's office as sole mediator for man.

Such theological truculence stems not only from the traditional dialectic between Jew and Christian, Catholic and Puritan, but from absolute belief in Christ's fulfillment and abrogation of ceremonial law as an essential cornerstone of covenant theology and polity. The external purifications, festivals, sacrifices, and temple worship manifest the Old Testament believer's contractual relationship with Yahweh. But the New Testament preaches an internalized alliance between individual souls within the church and Christ. For Edward Taylor the continuance of ceremonies, priestly garments, and church music justified by appeal to the Old Testament undercuts new gospel teachings. Moreover, he appreciates the dangers of a facile literalism; when man can find an easy pathway to God through strict adherence to mere law and works, then he believes in "Shadows" and neglects to cultivate the spirit. Heeding Anglican and

Catholic mandates, man expends more in obedience to carnal visible authorities and practices and diverts intensity from the inner seeking for salvation through a spiritual union with Christ. Religion becomes a matter of rules not faith.

In addition, the Jew's clinging to and the Catholic's imitation of Mosaic ceremonies constitute serious breaches of exegetical principles by blatantly disregarding scriptural unities and Christ's terminal fulfillment of messianic prophecies and types. Taylor imagistically vivifies the Puritan typal doctrine when he proclaims, "Christ said, the Hour now is, that the true Worshipers shall worship the Father, (not with Types, and Shadows:) but in Spirit and in truth. We may here say With Bernard, the Promises are the Seed, the Types are the Blossoms and Christ is the ripe fruite. And hence Ceremonies go no further. There is no fruite founde on them when used after the accomplishment of them" (*CHR*, p. 290). Although Taylor stresses the abolition of types for polemical purposes, he does not entirely deny the value of studying ceremonial law. Recall that Mather devoted three-fifths of his treatise to Old Testament festivals, offerings, and priests, and so also Taylor dedicates one-third of his typological sermons and poems to the topic (II.16–28). Rather than dismiss ceremonial law as invalid (a theologically indefensible position, since it would countermand God's scriptural patterns), both exegetes illustrate judicious Puritan methods of reading the Old and New Testaments typologically. The focus remains decidedly anti-Catholic, because they use Christ's abrogation of all ceremonial types to argue against non-Puritan worship practices. A self-conscious theoretician, Edward Taylor thus reaffirms orthodox Puritan principles – the historicity, bipolarity, and Christocentricity of typology and its intimate relationship to covenant theology. Determinedly Pauline and Christological, he denies any intrinsic or perpetual value in Old Testament law. But he accepts it as prefiguring and preparing man for the superior gospel dispensation under Christ and as revealing the unity of God's evangelical promises throughout all Scripture.

In organization as in the theory of types, Taylor turns to traditional Protestant systems of biblical types.[24] For Edward Taylor the appeal of carefully delineated categories did not stem solely from personal penchant, his Harvard education, or the shepherd's solicitude for his flock's memories. Structural clarity also underscored for his parishioners a fundamental typological dictum: God's patterns prevail in Scripture and are available for Christian believers to discover and decipher. First in shadows, then in Christ's clear light shining forth in the Gospel, the Bible reveals God's providential plan, the truth of messianic fulfillments, and the design for man's redemption. As an accomplished exegete, he uses his structural principles to preach the right reading of Scripture, a Pauline restraint in correspondences, and a correction of prelatical and papist distortions of the ceremonial types.

Inserted on a half sheet preceding the collection *Upon the Types of the Old Testament,* Taylor writes in a faint, aged hand that "Types are either

$$
\left\{
\begin{array}{l}
\text{Parsonall} \\
\\
\text{Not Personall}
\end{array}
\right.
$$

," crediting those "other learned learned *[sic]* men," such as

Thomas Taylor and Samuel Mather, who "Touching the Personall" presented "very lean Scriptu[re] proof confirming their typicall Relation." Restating this distinction in Sermon II.3 on Adam, Taylor then bisects his groups again, since

individual types are "
$$
\left\{
\begin{array}{l}
\text{Single persons} \\
\\
\text{Personall Ranks}
\end{array}
\right.
$$
," while those "Not Personall" are

$$
\left\{
\begin{array}{l}
\text{Providentiall} \\
\\
\text{Reall}
\end{array}
\right.
$$
" (*UTOT,* p. 33). In keeping with his designs, Taylor in Sermons

and Meditations II.3–13 focuses first on personal types from Adam, the first man and mediator with God, to Solomon, the builder of the temple and earthly paragon of kingship, and all those intervening patriarchs who prefigure Christ, the perfect mediator and King. Although located as II.30 in the meditations, Jonah is appropriately relodged in the homilies as a personal type after Solomon. Adhering to the distinction between individual figures and ranks, Taylor then switches in Sermon and Meditation II.14 to prophets, priests, and kings, Nazarites (II.15), and the house of Jacob (II.16), the last serving doubly as a transition into the "Reall" or ceremonial types. Because he shares with Samuel Mather the need to defend Puritan worship, Edward Taylor includes Sermons and Meditations II.16–28, on perpetual ceremonial laws, including those on sacrifices and altars (II.17–19), temple worship (II.20), festivals (II.21–25), and purifications (II.26–28). He adopts the ark as a type of universal deliverances in Sermon and Meditation II.29 to inaugurate the extraordinary events, but not until four years later (1703–4) does he pick up the remaining occasional types from Israel's wanderings (II.58–61). These providential types on Israel's deliverance from Egypt (II.58), the pillar of cloud and fire (II.59), manna (II.60A), water from the rock (II.60B), and brazen serpent (II.61) had appeared as prefigurations of the sacraments in *Christ Revealed* but as types of mankind's spiritual journey in *The Figures or Types* – exegetical emphases that Edward Taylor elects to combine. Called forth probably by Stoddard's inroads into administering the Lord's Supper as a converting ordinance, both circumcision and Passover emerge as central types in Sermons and Meditations II.70–71 and subsequently in an extended series of sacramental meditations II.102–111 (1711–12) for which sermons are not extant. By adopting codifications from his predecessors, Taylor committed himself to the mainstream of Puritan exegesis, but as an independent theoretician and a ramistic structuralist, he also impressed upon this tradition the stamp of his own ministerial and devotional needs.

Perhaps modeling themselves on great Old Testament prophets, Thomas Taylor, Samuel Mather, and Edward Taylor all sensed their mission in this earth's wilderness – not to lead New Israelites to a literal Canaan, but to translate God's law into human terms by guiding believers in seeking gospel truths. Thomas Taylor viewed himself as a patient schoolmaster, instructing his flock in typal correspondences. Samuel Mather saw his role as a Puritan Jeremiah, warning against mid-century backslidings that threatened to lead saints astray into popish or Anglican idolatries and laying down exegetical principles to defend the Puritan vision of Christ's New Testament covenant. A descendant of this ministerial tradition, Edward Taylor in his *Upon the Types of the Old Testament* emulated both the Old Testament Moses and the New Testament Paul. He pleaded for Moses' prophetic vision, "Thy Looking-glass give mee./ And let thy Spirit wipe my Watry eyes," so "That I may see his [Christ's] flashing glory darte/ Like Lightening quick till it infire my heart," to pierce beyond literal to spiritual meanings and then for the Word's power to transmit gospel truths (II.9.51–4). Like Paul he wanted his parishioners to appreciate Christ's personhood figured by individual types and ranks – all surpassed by the Savior's incarnation. Beyond the focus on Christ's person, however, Taylor exhibited the passion of a devoted biblical scholar and seventeenth-century polemicist for Mosaic rituals. Properly interpreted, ceremonial law not only refuted papist and prelatical abuses, it also pointed to a purified New Testament worship within the temple of human hearts. A latter-day Puritan disciple, he thus preached typology to confirm the faithful in their covenant bond and to bring saints to a proper understanding of Old Testament persons and ceremonies as God's ordained prefigurations of His Son.

Although Taylor relied upon his sources and the Bible for typological subjects, he nonetheless set forth gospel truths in a manner uniquely different from either messianic prophets of old or new Puritan seers. Whereas the pulpit and congregational meetings provided a public forum, the *Preparatory Meditations* became his finest medium of worship, because they affirmed his private sainthood and covenant with Christ. By transmuting rational explications of types into imaginative poetic visions, Taylor undertook a task consistent with his previous habits of meditation but strikingly original among seventeenth-century poets. Building upon those prose treatises that generated the rational inspiration and images for his sermons and poesy, Taylor found in divine figures and the antitype Christ spiritual stimuli that unleashed a flood of agonizing self-examinations and metaphoric searches for the quickening truth of God's grace. An intermingling of the homiletic and contemplative creates in the meditations on types a peculiar mélange of the public and private voices. Resounding with the ardent intellectualism of his sermons, yet fraught with personal anxieties and ecstasies, the meditations project for us a vision of Taylor's divided role as both Puritan preacher and poet. From his immersion in a conservative tradition of Puritan exegesis paradoxically sprang the spiritual motivations and metaphoric resonances that most distinguish his lyric meditations.

Taylor shared with other exegetes a repertoire of metaphors to depict the figural relationship of the Old and New Testaments, and he acknowledges the Pauline origins by adopting as his text for Sermon and Meditation II.1 the *locus classicus* from Colossians 2:17: "Which are Shaddows of things to come and the body is Christs." Writing sixteen hundred years after Paul, Thomas Taylor had elaborated the metaphors for types, declaring that the "Ministery of the old Testament in rites and Ceremonies, is a darke representation of the body, namely Christ and his spirituall worship," which "as the body is solid, firme, and of continuance" (*CR*, p. 4). Oppositions between the ephemeral shadow and substantial body, the dark or "obscure resemblance" and Christ's spiritual illumination took on yet greater rhetorical force in Samuel Mather's definitions. Starting too with Paul's epistle, he compounded the traditional metaphors by piling term upon term to distinguish ancient ceremonies from Christ's new gospel: "*Christ and his Benefits; but the Body is of Christ, as Col. 2. 17. This we call the Correlate, or the Antitype; the other is the Shadow, this the Substance: The Type is the Shell, this the Kernel; the Type is the Letter, this the Spirit and Mystery of the Type*" (*FT*, p. 52). In his sermons Edward Taylor also borrowed the conventional metaphors, characterizing a type as "a Shadow" which "onely gives a darke draught of the thing as to its externall Shape," a "very incompleate thing," and an "obscure, & dark Representing" (*UTOT*, p. 4).[25] Not being "Durable," the "Ceremonies of the Law were Shadows" and "not to be imbraced" when "Christ & all the Speciall Gospell Concerns" prevail (*UTOT*, p. 2). With the moralizing tone of a homespun fabulist, Taylor warns that "Seing they are Shadows of things to Come, & the body, Substance or the truth Signified by them is of Christ . . . who is now Come . . . to Catch at the Shadow now will be to lose the Substance as

Esop Signified by the Dog" (*UTOT*, p. 2). As he shifts toward exclamatory appeals in his uses, Taylor heightens the doctrine with loftier images and praises:

> For the Chief Excellency in the Creation, in one type or metaphor or other is used to intimate, & adumbrate to us the Excellency of the Lord Jesus . . . & that Excellency in Christ Signifyed hereby, which as far excells this as any lively Glorious body doth the darke Shadow that Falls from it, upon this worke of redemption of Sinners . . . oh, what Excellency is here imployed? . . . there are in Christ their Redeemer such Excellencies as do so far out Shine the Excellencies of the Types, that they are but as darke Shadows thereof. (*UTOT*, pp. 10–11)

Nevertheless, the doctrinal applications of Sermon 1 seem uninspired when compared with the unleashed hyperboles of Christ's antitypal glory in the corresponding meditation. Paul supplies appropriate biblical justification of types and Thomas Taylor's reasoned discourse influences the cogitative comparisons, but Samuel Mather's metaphors spark the meditative imagination. Though predicated upon homiletic themes and images, Edward Taylor's own spiritual yearnings for an awakened vision and newly quickened heart finally burst forth in this intensely personal call:

> My Stains are such, and sinke so deep, that all
>   The Excellency in Created Shells
> Too low, and little is to make it fall
>   Out of my leather Coate wherein it dwells.
>   This Excellence is but a Shade to that
>   Which is enough to make my Stains go back.
>
> The glory of the world slickt up in types
>   In all Choise things chosen to typify,
> His glory upon whom the worke doth light,
>   To thine's a Shaddow, or a butterfly.
>   How glorious then, my Lord, art thou to mee
>   Seing to cleanse me, 's worke alone for thee.
>
> The glory of all Types doth meet in thee.
>   Thy glory doth their glory quite excell:
> More than the Sun excells in its bright glee
>   A nat, an Earewig, Weevill, Snaile, or Shell.
>   Wonders in Crowds start up; your eyes may strut
>   Viewing his Excellence, and's bleeding cut.
>
> Oh! that I had but halfe an eye to view
>   This excellence of thine, undazled: so
> Therewith to give my heart a touch anew
>   Untill I quickned am, and made to glow.
>   (II.1.7–28)

Although this poem is often cited as the link between Taylor's typology and Jonathan Edwards's later perception of *Images or Shadows of Divine Things* within the created world of nature, Taylor in fact uses Meditation II.1 to introduce his more traditional Pauline and Puritan reading of biblical types.[26] Adopting Mather's metaphors, Taylor argues for the inferiority of "Created Shells," whether they be natural objects or Old Testament types. Both the "glory of the world" and the "glory of all Types" become mere "Shade" or "Shaddow" in comparison to Christ's "glory upon whom the worke doth light." Through observation, Taylor discovers that in nature the sun "in its bright glee" overpowers smaller, lowlier creatures that cower in darkness like the "Snaile" beneath a protecting "Shell." Similarly in the spiritual realm, Taylor reasons that the divine Son (pun intended) excells in His "bright glee," "glory," and "light" the apparently glorious but actually shadowy biblical "Types." Sermon II.1 makes plain the condensed poetic simile: "So here the Excellency of the types put all together, must needs represent Christ yet but as a Shadow of his Excellency, whose Excellency doth as far Exceed theirs as the body of the glorious Sun the Shade thereof" (*UTOT,* p. 3). Far from anticipating Edwards or Emerson by a belief in divine effulgences in nature itself, Taylor uses this humanly accessible *example* as an analogy to clarify the relationship between Old Testament types, shadows, or "shells" and Christ's antitypal glory. Not a sign of Taylor's prescient transcendentalism, this poem condemns the natural creation as too shadowy, lowly, and inadequate for moving the heart from sin to grace.

Taylor grants more efficacy to biblical types, but he finds even them mere "shades" and "shells" compared with the light shed by Christ, who is the substantial body and kernel of glory. Infusing this meditation as well as the sermon is Taylor's fascination with the mystery of Christ's "theanthropie." The Son debases himself by taking on the human form in order to effect the world's salvation. Just as types are lowly shells which remain earthbound and historical, although they prefigure spiritual truth incarnate in Christ, so too Jesus puts on the human "Created Shell" (consigning himself to time and space) in order paradoxically to shade and reveal to mankind his excelling divinity. Uniting the "Humane nature to the Divine argues the Perfection of the Humane," Taylor opines in Sermon II.1, and he affirms Christ to "be the Perfectst piece of Excellency, & the most Complete piece of beauty that ever trod upon the face of the Earth, or that ever the Sun shone upon" (*UTOT,* pp. 5, 6). No agency in nature itself ("The Excellency in Created Shells/ Too low, and little is"), but only this divine agent, "as Theandrick, & the Mediator between God & man" (*UTOT,* p. 7) has power "to make my Stains" of original sin "go back." Or as Taylor's internal rhyming underscores in the homily, "His Excellency is Efficatious against Sin: against the *reign* of it: it destroyes it . . . against the *stain* of it: it cleanseth it away . . . & against the *baine* of it it doth away the guilt of Sin" (*UTOT*, p. 7; my emphasis).

Extending his imagery of "shells" in the meditation, Taylor also decries man's innate depravity, emblemized by the "stains" that "sinke so deep" and corrupt the "leather Coate" of man's body (another variant of the "Created Shell"). Only Christ, who is the earthly embodiment of godhead "upon whom the worke doth light," can "cleanse" sins. Beyond purification of human sin, however, another wonder appears in Christ's incarnation and crucifixion. Through his "Excellence, and's bleeding cut," Christ grants the human "heart a touch anew," thus quickening man into a life born of the spirit (not nature) until he glows from within. Taylor argues that, because Christ comes as the light that irradiates the shadowy shells of insufficient natural and biblical types, he brings to man an analogous possibility for spiritual illumination: that glow of inner faith eradicates the body's "Stains." Furthermore, Christ incarnate bestows not only hope for a newly vivified inner spirit, but the future promise of shedding forever the "leather Coate" for a heavenly "wedden garment." Taylor's carefully crafted images of "Created Shells" and a "leather Coate," give body to the more abstruse vocabulary of typology itself (shade, shadow, typify). And the repetition of "Excellence" and "excell," "glory" and "glorious," "Choise" and "chosen" heighten Christ's spiritual capacity as God's anointed Son/Sun to irradiate types, the world, and the human soul. The metaphoric oppositions of stains and cleansing, and of lowly creatures (man and "nat") and the Godhead, the created world and the godly realm increate intrinsically remind us of Christ's redemptive sacrifice, a messianic salvation adumbrated darkly in types and fulfilled luminescently in Christ's incarnation. By building upon the more prosaic exordiums of Taylor and Mather and upon Paul's doctrine, Edward Taylor thus develops a multilayered poetic defense of types.

Figures help Christian scholars and believers to discover sublime spiritual truths, but they remain inferior to direct revelations from Christ the antitype. Hence, Taylor again adopts a Pauline text and numerous analogies from *Christ Revealed* for Sermon and Meditation II.2 when he lauds "the Excellency of the Lord Christ that he is the Antitype of, or what was typified by the Typicall First Born" both before and under the law (*UTOT*, p. 17). He elaborates parallels to prove that Christ "was the First that ever was Constituted of the Womans Seed without the Seed of man that ever was born of a virgin," the "first that ever was born without Sin," hence "Gods First Born, & Onely Born Son . . . heir to all God the Fathers Revenues Heaven, Earth, Saints, Angells, Grace Glory" (*UTOT*, pp. 18, 20). The apostle Paul had preached the preeminence of

Christ, "Who is the image of the invisible God, the first-born of all creation" (Col. 1:15) to counter threats from Gnostics. In Sermon II.2's use
"by way of Reproofe," Edward Taylor similarly perceives himself as a
preacher in the wilderness of New England who, like Paul in the Roman
Empire, refutes ancient heresies of the Sabellians, Arians, and Socinians.
To refute these heresies, Taylor expands upon Paul's exaltation of Christ
as God's firstborn Son and heir come in the flesh to fulfill Old Testament
prophecies:

> First Born of e'ry Being: hence a Son
>   Begot o'th'First: Gods onely Son begot.
> Hence Deity all ore. Gods nature run
>   Into a Filiall Mould: Eternall knot.
>   A Father then, and Son: persons distinct.
>   Though them Sabellians contrar'ly inckt.
>
> This mall of Steell falls hard upon those foes
>   Of truth, who make the Holy Trinity
> Into One Person: Arrians too and those
>   Socinians calld, who do Christs Deity
>   Bark out against. But Will they, nill they, they
>   Shall finde this Mall to split their brains away.
>
> Come shine, Deare Lord, out in my heart indeed
>   First Born; in truth before thee there was none
> First Born, as man, born of a Virgin's seed:
>   Before or after thee such up ne'er sprung.
>   Hence Heir of all things lockt in natures Chest:
>   And in thy Fathers too: extreamly best.
>
> Thou Object of Gods boundless brightest Love,
>   Invested with all sparkling rayes of Light
>
> . . . .
>
> Oh! that my Soul was all enamored
>   With this First Born enough: a Lump of Love
> Son of Eternall Father, Chambered
> Once in a Virgins Womb, dropt from above.
> All Humane royalty hereby Divin'de.
> The First Born's Antitype: in whom they're shrin'de.
>   (II.2.7–26, 31–6)

Accentuating His deity and the mystery of His incarnation, Taylor extols
Christ as the perfect antitype, *alpha* and *omega* of all lesser born creatures,
even those firstborn consecrated to God in the Old Testament. He invokes
images of enclosure ("Mould," "lockt in natures Chest," "Chambered/
Once in a Virgins Womb," "shrin'de") and of light ("Thou Object of
Gods boundless brightest Love,/ Invested with all sparkling rayes of
Light") to remind himself that through Christ's embodiment His radiant

divinity shines forth. Christ, "the Golden Rose! Oh. Glittering Lilly White," is so "spic'd o're With heavens File divine," that "Rayes/ Fly forth whose Shine doth Wrack the strongest Sight/ That Wonders Eye is tent of," for the luminescent Savior's "Swaddle Bonde's Eternity./ And Sparkling Cradle is Rich Deity" (II.2.1–6). The graphic images of a human "Virgin's seed" and "Womb" and "Swaddle Bonde's" only set the stage for the yet more miraculous paternity by which "Gods nature run[s]/ Into a Filiall Mould," creating thereby an "Eternall knot" between Father and Son that makes Christ sole "Heir" to two kingdoms "of all things lockt in natures Chest:/ And in thy Fathers too" (II.2.9–10, 23–4).

The poetic evocations of Christ's preeminent fullness as deity, His status as the "First Born of e'ry Being," and his dazzling essence balance the previous meditation's focus on the world's "Created Shells," mankind's sinful stains, and shadowy types. In *Upon the Types* Taylor deliberately relocates the "First Born" from the typical ranks (as specified by Thomas Taylor and Mather) to complement II.1's general definition and facilitate the transition to "Particular Types" (*UTOT*, p. 16). Meditation II.1 enunciates the typological method; Meditation II.2 affirms the goal – to perceive within those shells Christ's wondrous glory as the antitype. As companion pieces, therefore, these meditations set forth the typological doctrine that becomes Taylor's consuming poetic theme in the next twenty-eight lyrics.

However, as "prefigurations" themselves of later poetic treatments, Meditations II.1 and II.2 seem both predictive and unusual. Though clearly steeped in Pauline doctrine, Thomas Taylor's comparisons, and Samuel Mather's metaphors, Edward Taylor departs radically into flights of exulting imagery which frame a series often more restrained and exegetical. He launches his new series with a novitiate's fervor, designed to raise his mind and heart to the arduous yet illuminating meditative unveiling of mysterious types. But despite vivifying bursts of praise and imaginative extrapolations of figural images, the later meditations frequently reflect more the erudite rationality of the coordinated sermons. Nonetheless, the terms that appear in these initial sermons and poems recur throughout Taylor's series as reminders of the basic contrasts between typal shadows and divine light. He habitually adopts images of "Shine," "sparkling rayes of Light," the "Sun of Righteousness," and excelling "Glory" to portray Christ's superiority over veiled "shaddows," a "fleeting Sparke in th'Smoke," or the clouded yet still "blazing Star," "Beam," or "Shine" of inferior historical types. Centuries old, these terms and images, derived from Paul's epistles, the Church Fathers, among whom Taylor often cites Origen, Augustine, and the medieval Theophylact, and Protestant contemporaries.[27]

Another metaphoric exemplum, one closely allied with the images of shadow and shine, also prevailed among purist expositors from St. Paul to the Antiochenes and Puritans. St. Chrysostom in his fourth-century commentary on 1 Corinthians 10, specifically on the Red Sea as a type of Baptism, first invoked the image of an artist's rough sketch in contrast to a final painting as an aid in defining types:

> Let us take the example of a picture. You have often seen the portrait of a King, sketched in black; the painter fills in the outlines showing the King, the royal theme, horses, bodyguards at his side, his enemies in chains at his feet. From what you see portrayed you cannot know everything, and yet you are not entirely ignorant. You know in a general way that it is about a King and a horse. but who the King is, and who is his enemy, you do not know with any certainty until the colouring itself makes the outlines more clear and distinct. Now, just as in the case of the picture you do not expect to grasp everything before the colours are filled in, though even if you have only a general idea of what it is all about you think the outline sufficiently accurate, so, I say, should you think on the subject of the Old and New Testaments, and not demand of the type all the exactness of the reality.[28]

Chrysostom appropriately selects the example of a king's portrait to differentiate types from Christ's fulfillment. He sets the basic metaphoric contrast by first identifying Old Testament types as "outlines" or "sketches" which leave us not entirely ignorant, because as prophetic foreshadowings they herald the real king yet to come. But certain knowledge comes only with the "colouring" filled in, bringing into "clear and distinct" relief the nature of Christ's monarchy under the New Testament. Some one thousand years later, Calvin not only lauds "golden Chrysostom" in his *Institutes,* but also paraphrases this very example in the *Commentary on Colossians* and emphasizes the fact that Christ brings typical sketches into "life": "As painters . . . in the first instance draw rude and obscure lines, so the representation of Christ under the law was unpolished – a first sketch, but in our sacraments it is seen drawn out to the life."[29]

No doubt through Calvin the exemplum entered into mainstream Puritan exegesis of figures, for first Thomas Taylor then Samuel Mather also reiterate this distinction. Attributing his inspiration in part to Hebrews 10:1, Thomas Taylor in *Christ Revealed* glosses the text: "that is, It had a rude and darke delineation of good things to come, as a draught made by a painter with a coale; but the Gospel exhibits the picture it selfe in the flourish and beauty; that is, the truth and being of it" (*CR,* p. 4). Obviously a popular analogy to enliven theoretical discussions of typology, the exemplum receives new "flourishes" from each exegete. Taylor here introduces the "coale" to underscore implicitly the shadowy or fuzzy draft in contrast to Christ's "beauty," which is, however, spiritual rather than physical in its "truth and being."

Borrowing from Calvin (as he notes), Mather may also recollect Thomas Taylor when setting forth his similar illustration in *The Figures or Types* to distinguish legal shadows from the gospel's lively image of the Savior. His version identifies Colossians 2:17 as the inspiration for Calvin's exemplum:

> In a Word, a Shadow here, is a dark and weak resemblance and repre-sentation of Things. But the very Image of the Things themselves, is a clearer and better Representation of them. The Apostle useth this *Met-aphor* of a Shadow, concerning the *Mosaical Ceremonies,* Col. 2. 17. In Opposition to *Christ* the Body and Substance thereof. Here he opposeth σχια and ἀχῶν [sic]. Alluding (as it seemeth) to the rude Draught and first delineation of a Picture by the Painter, and to the full Perfection thereof, when drawn forth in all its Lineaments and Colours and whole Proportion. So the Shadow is the first rude Draught: But the Image is a more lively and exact Representation. So the dark Shadow is ascribed to the *Law*. The more lively Image to the *Gospel*. The Things them-selves are in Heaven. So some Interpreters carry it, *Vide* Mayer. Calvin *in loc. (FT,* p. 169)

Mather stresses the shadowy weakness or inadequacy of Mosaic cere-monies in particular, perhaps developing Calvin's reference to the sacra-ments when he cites the superior "Body and Substance" of Christ. But he also appends a distinction that should be kept in mind, though it imposes a curious Platonic overlay upon Puritan concepts of a historical contin-uum of types. If the "Shadow" under the Old Testament is the "first rude Draught," Mather designates Christ and his instituted ceremonies under the New Testament as a "more lively Image and Portraiture" (*FT,* p. 170) but, envisioning the eschatological realities or truths, he locates the "Things themselves" in "Heaven." Mather thus transforms a com-parative exemplum into a metaphor for the progressively more perfect three dispensations under God's providential plan – the Mosaic, the New Testament, and the millennial or eternal. Or perceived as a Platonic scheme, he differentiates three levels of reality with the historical law (shadow), the spiritual fulfillment in the gospel (a portraiture), and the divine pat-tern or truth (thing itself).

Edward Taylor also finds this exemplum compelling when he intro-duces *Upon the Types of the Old Testament*. To differentiate "Types" as "Shadows" from Christ the "precious Orient Pearle," he recollects Thomas Taylor's version: "Some take the Word Shadow, to be in allusion to the first drawght of a Picture which is pensild out with a Coale, or black Lead. & as such is calld the Shadow: but after its compleated with fair

Colours" (*UTOT,* p. 4). Ornamenting this theme later in Sermon II.1's uses, Taylor echoes Mather in finding even the most exquisitely drawn portrait inferior to the living object:

> Suppose a Picture of a thorowly accomplisht Person was drawn to the Life of the most Exquisit art in the most Sparkling Colours in all the World, adornd with richest orient Gems that are to be found in all the Creation of God. What should wee think of this draught? Oh! the Vivid beautiousness of this Piece! but now this being presented you, you should have it thus flowerisht over: Well thô this is so glorious: yet its but a dull Shadow, & Smutty Lineament of the person it represents. Would not this be an high Encomium of the Beauty of that person whose Portraiture it is: But all this is to be found & more abundantly before us in the present Case. Oh then the Beauty of this glorious Object! What a Lovely one then is Christ Jesus, that is here presented you for you to set your Love upon! (*UTOT,* p. 12)

Neither types which "shadow" in "Coale, or black Lead," nor the gospel's picture in most "Sparkling Colours"-ultimately capture Christ's beauty. Drawn further from mere exegetical motives for this exemplum, Taylor seems exhilarated by the images themselves, enamored of comparisons between art and life.[30] Even as he accumulates poetic flourishes to inspire awe of Christ's loveliness, a doubt lurks implicitly that such verbal encomiums like "Smutty Lineaments" also only approximate the ineffable "Beauty of this glorious Object!" Nevertheless, to adorn in "richest orient Gems," to visualize with "most Exquisit art" the Savior's divine perfection becomes the preacher's duty, the meditator's pursuit, and the artist/poet's dream.

As often happens in the transition from Sermons to the *Preparatory Meditations,* the exemplum takes on more various resonances. Opening his meditation on Samson, for instance, Taylor addresses the Lord who is "portrai'd . . . in Colours bright, that stick/ Their Glory on the Choicest Saints, Whereby/ They are thy Pictures made" (II.11.3–5). Intrigued by the concept of a sketch or "rude Draught," Taylor in Meditation II.7 on Joseph also queries Christ (or God) as the omnipotent artist: "How hast thou pensild out, my Lord, most bright/ Thy glorious Image here, on Josephs Light" (II.7.35–36). Self-conscious about his artistic inferiority to the divine, Taylor begins this same meditation by discovering once again that "my inke is dim,/ My pensill blunt," only sufficient to draw out a crude draft of gospel truths (II.7.4–5). Nevertheless, just as the very types are bound in history, yet point to a spiritual completion under the gospel, so too Taylor as earthbound artist hopes that the "Lord" might "lay thy brightsome Colours on me" (II.7.39). Under the tutelage of Christ's example and shining grace, Taylor himself might become a more lively imitation – a quickened spirit. Despite Tay-

lor's presumption in identifying with the divine "painter," he remains
within Puritan bounds by making Christ a tutor or muse who grants a
measure of his vitalizing "colours" to saintly poets that they too might
portray or "represent" spiritual truths in a verbal rather than visual
medium.

Thus, spanning a thousand years from Chrysostom to Edward Taylor
the seventeenth-century Puritan, the essential terms and meanings of this
exemplum remain identical. A rude sketch or draft corresponds to types,
those shadowy personages and ceremonies under the Old Testament. By
contrast, the New Testament represents a fully colored portrait of Christ's
incarnate perfection, as he temporarily manifests his kingship on earth.
But even the New Testament cannot recreate the living reality that is
Christ who in divine radiance resides eternally in heaven. Even though
the metaphors appear scattered among Taylor's typological meditations,
they undergo more impressive metamorphosis in Meditation II. 50:

> The Artist Hand more gloriously bright,
>   Than is the Sun itselfe, in'ts shining glory
> Wrought with a stone axe made of Pearle, as light
>   As light itselfe, out of a Rock all flory
>   Of Precious Pearle, a Box most lively made
>   More rich than gold Brimfull of Truth enlaid.
>
> Which Box should forth a race of boxes send
>   Teemd from its Womb such as itselfe, to run
> Down from the Worlds beginning to its end.
>   But, o! this box of Pearle Fell, Broke, undone.
>   Truth from it flew: It lost Smaragdine Glory:
>   Was filld with Falshood: Boxes teemd of Sory.
>
> The Artist puts his glorious hand again
>   Out to the Worke: His Skill out flames more bright
> Now than before. The worke he goes to gain,
>   He did portray in flaming Rayes of light.
>   A Box of Pearle shall from this Sory, pass
>   More rich than that Smaragdine Truth-Box was.
>
> Which Box, four thousand yeares, o'r ere 'twas made,
>   In golden Scutchons lay'd in inke Divine
> Of Promises, of a Prophetick Shade,
>   And in embellishments of Types that shine.
>   Whose Beames in this Choice pearle-made-Box all meet
>   And bedded in't their glorious Truth to keep.
>
> But now, my Lord, thy Humane Nature, I
>   Doe by the Rayes this Scutcheon sends out, finde
> Is this Smaragdine Box where Truth doth ly
>   Of Types, and Promises, that thee out lin'de.

Their Truth they finde in thee: this makes them shine.
Their Shine on thee makes thee appeare Divine.

                                               (II. 50. 1–30)

Taylor's reanimation of the "artist" exemplum transforms the metaphor in several ways. In the prose commentaries the image of the painter functions subordinately to prove a point by an apt illustration, thus making convoluted theories more accessible. But in the poem, the recurrent and ornamented images enable Taylor to transcend merely rational understandings and experience an emotional or spiritual crystallization. Moreover, Taylor only begins with the raw material from the commonplace metaphor of a dark draft, for in this poem he lays out the panorama of salvation history over which God presides with the "Artists Hand more gloriously bright" of perfect, omnipotent creativity. He locates the "rude Draught" of all types within the overarching context of God's providential design for man's redemption. Instituted only after man's original fall from "Smaragdine Glory" into "Falshood," the "Promises, of a Prophetick Shade" become mere preludes to that "Smaragdine Truth-Box" of Christ. The ancient oppositions still obtain between "falsehood" and "truth," the "Types, and Promises, that thee out lin'de" and the "Truth" in Christ which "makes them shine."

Two variations on the previous metaphors deserve special note because they suggest a strikingly imaginative adaptation by Taylor. Substituting for the usual metaphor of a portrait, Taylor adopts the "Scutchons lay'd in inke Divine," alluding to an ancient shield used both as a protection and as an area on which armorial bearings can be displayed. Comparable to a sketch that crudely limns out the Savior, yet leaves the perceiver in some shadow, the "Scutcheon sends out" rays that adumbrate the "Smaragdine Box where Truth doth ly"; that is, it reflects but cannot match the reality of Christ's presence in the flesh. Furthermore, the whole concept of "boxes" which threads throughout Taylor's meditation subtly reminds us of distinctions between the external body, shadow, or enclosure and the dazzling light or truth contained therein. Hence, the "Promises, of a Prophetick Shade" foretell, but the ultimate "Beames in this Choice pearle-made-Box all meet," reminding us too of Sermon II.1's claim that "every Truth of Christ is like unto a Jewellers Cabbinet; if it be opened, it discovers itselfe full of Costly Pearles" (*UTOT*, p. 9). Even in his incarnation, however, Christ comes as a "pearle-*made*-Box" or "Smaragdine Box" which is His "Humane Nature." Within the human form as in a box (no matter how richly ornamented the outside), the "true Messiah shin'st" in his divine beauty and glory (II.50.34). Compared to the two-dimensional representations that preceding exegetes emphasize, the three-dimensional image of a "box" marvelously captures two truths: Christ as the "Jewellers Cabbinet" which holds all truths, foreshadowed in the prophecies, promises, and types, and Christ as incarnate Deity, born of the womb, yet enclosed momentarily in a human body.

The ingenious redesigning of these age-old images also brings about a change of perspective from the original exemplum. Used by previous theologians, the painter exemplum underscored the interpreter's point of view as he struggled to decipher in the product or portraiture the colors of gospel truths and Christ. But Taylor's meditation shifts this focus to capture God's point of view as the supreme artist, the archetypal creator at work fashioning the means to convey His grace to man. The poem recreates action rather than observation, involvement rather than detached illustration. In accord with the aims of all his meditations, this poem is designed by Taylor to engage himself actively in pursuit of typological truths, so that he can then turn to God with an intimate prayer:

> Hence thou art full of Truth, and full dost stand,
>   Of Promises, of Prophesies, and Types.
> But that's not all: All truth is in thy hand,
>   Thy lips drop onely Truth, give Falshood gripes.
>   Leade through the World to glory, that ne'er ends
>   By Truth's bright Hand all such as Grace befriends.
>
> O! Box of Truth! tenent my Credence in
>   The mortase of thy Truth: and Thou in Mee.
> These Mortases, and Tenents make so trim,
>   That They and Thou, and I n'eer severd bee.
>   Embox my Faith, Lord, in thy Truth a part
>   And I'st by Faith embox thee in my heart.
>   (II.50.37–48)

As an enflamed Puritan, Taylor desires to be one whom "Grace befriends," to receive a part of Christ's "Truth," and by "Faith" to "embox" the Savior in his own heart. Taylor's ingenious appeal to the carpenter's craft mimetically underscores the humility with which he seeks to insert the tenon (a projection in a piece of wood) of his belief or faith into the mortise (hole or groove in a piece of timber to receive a tenon) of Christ's truth, so trimly that the jointure can "ne'er severd bee." But the frail human "box" that Taylor seeks so craftily to construct (his union with God *and* his poem) remains rough-hewn compared with God's "Choice pearle-made-Box" carved by the "Artists Hand." Only Christ, a carpenter's son who extends "Truth's bright Hand" can lead "all such as Grace befriends" to eternal glory. Lest Taylor's clever wordplay go unappreciated, we might recall that "Credence" signifies not only beliefs, but also credentials (those of faith) and a small table where the bread and wine rest before consecration – the very act in the Lord's Supper that Taylor anticipates in all his *Preparatory Meditations* and for which he must spiritually "mortase" himself with the divine architect of salvation. Far more personal than the exegetical detachment of previous expositors' or even his own homiletic uses in the *Christographia* Sermon IX which accompanies Meditation II.50, the poetic transmutation endows the exemplum with added imagistic "colours" and spiritual import. No longer illustrative allusions suitable for hermeneutic debates, the images of sketches and portraits, escutcheons and realities, shades and light, emboxment and pearls (like kernels) of truth, cabinetry and creation contribute to the drama of spiritual catharsis. The rational truths gained from studying types are here illuminated, not merely because Taylor possesses the exegete's discerning eye, but because he also cultivates a poet's vision.

Works from the apostles to the Protestant typologists are permeated by the concept of the expositor as a seer, someone blessed with divine inspiration to see spiritual meanings in literal Scripture and to transmit truths. Accordingly, the perception of typal significances necessitates an inspired vision sustained by the interpreter's faith. Taylor adopts a commonplace Renaissance analogy between physical sight and spiritual insight when he opens his typological series by confessing his human insufficiency to gaze upon God's splendor: "Oh! that I had but halfe an eye to view/ This excellence of thine, undazled" (II.1.25–6). Lacking an immediate vision of Christ, that reserved for saints in eternity, Taylor struggles in sermons and poems for shadowy, half-visions. He scans the typal prefigurations of Old Testament persons, events, and ceremonies for glimpses of Christ's antitypal excellences and the gospel doctrine of salvation. Repeatedly in these meditations, he echoes the initial refrain: "Christen mine Eyeballs with thine Eye Salve" and "enoculate within mine Eye/ Thy Image bright, My Lord" (II.58.13; II.59.1–2). And in Meditation II.9 on Moses, he gives fullest expression to his yearnings for an insight inspired by faith:

> Lord, let thy Dazzling Shine refracted fan'de
>   In this bright Looking Glass, its favour lay
> Upon mine Eyes that oculated stand
>   And peep thereat, in button moulds of clay.
>   Whose glory otherwise that Courts mine eye
>   Will all its sparkling family destroy.
>
> Yea let thy Beams, better ten thousand times
>   Than brightest Eyebright, cherishing revive
> The Houshold that possesseth all the Shrines
>   In Visions Palace, that it well may thrive.

> Moses is made the Looking glass: in which
> Mine Eyes to spie thee in this Type I pitch.
>
> (II.9.1–12)

Without God's graciously given beams of illumination, Taylor's eyes, those "button moulds of clay," would endure the chronic "peephole" vision of mere physical sight. Insufficient to pierce through even typical "shadows," much less tolerate the brilliant shine that emanates from the antitype Christ himself, Taylor's earthbound vision is by nature virtually blind, certainly clouded with sin. But endowed with divine "Beams, better ten thousand times/ Than brightest Eyebright," the exegete gains sufficient power to perceive both figural reflections and Christ's originating Son "Shine."

In part, the view Taylor seeks resembles Christ's "Created Wisdom" which "is that light that is Seated in the Intellectuall Faculty filling the Eye of the Soul with a Cleare Sight into all things that are the proper Objects thereof," including Old Testament figures (CHR, p. 122). More important than this intellectual light which enables Taylor as an expositor to delineate figural correspondences is the superior mystical insight derived from faith. Taking as a type the windows of the temple, Samuel Mather draws a distinction applicable to both ministers and saints: "As the Eyes are the Windows of the Body . . . So the Eyes and Windows of the Soul are the Faculty of the Understanding elevated and sanctified by the Holy Ghost, whereby it receives the Light of the Gospel. There is in the Saints a spiritual visive Faculty, those Eyes of the Soul, whereby it receives the Light of the Sun of Righteousness darting in his Beams of spiritual Light into the Soul" (FT, p. 348). Rational insights allow the preacher to speak of the truth, but only the God-given "visive Faculty" fills him with spiritual illuminations and belief in those truths. Hence, when Edward Taylor prays to God to "let thy Spirit wipe my Watry eyes," he wants an infusion of grace that will "wipe" away tears of remorse for his sins, then cleanse or "salve" his eyeballs, and ultimately dilate and clarify his spiritual vision (II.9.52). Through these cleansed windows or eyes of the soul Christ's "flashing glory" will "darte/ Like Lightening quick till it infire my heart" (II.9.53–4).

Once gifted with a saintly expositor's insights, Taylor can comprehend the refracted shine of Christ which appears in the "Looking Glass" of his types. Using Moses as his example in Sermon II.9, Taylor comments upon the process by which "Moses sets himselfe before them with Christs Effigies drawn out upon him," thereby "presenting himselfe as a Cleare Glass thus of this Prophet" so that "Gods people may see Christs Glory Shine forth" (UTOT, p. 145). Not reserved for Moses alone, the image applies also in Meditation II.60A to manna, as "a Shining Glass, wherein thy face/ My Lord, as Bread of Life, is clearly seen" (II.60A.25–

6). For Meditations II.9 and II.60A, Taylor adopts this provocative metaphor from 1 Corinthians 13:12, in which Paul prophesies, "For now we see through a glass, darkly; but then, face to face, now I know in part, but then shall I know even as also I am known." Echoing earlier glosses by Calvin, William Guild in *Moses Unvailed,* and Thomas Taylor, Samuel Mather summarizes the familiar typological application and links it with his preceding concept of the "Draught": "And the Apostle hath some Expressions looking that way in other Scriptures; as when he saith, that *here we see but in a Glass darkly,* that is, the Glass of Gospel-Administrations, wherein we see the lively Image and Picture (as it were) of Christ crucified, *Gal.* 3. 1. 2 *Cor.* 3. 18. *see as in a Glass.* He is there comparing the Law and the Gospel, *But in Heaven we shall see Face to Face,* see I *Cor.* 13. 12. Under the Law they had no more but the *Shadow;* but now under the Gospel we have the *very Image,* we see Things *as in a Glass;* but in Heaven we have *the Things themselves" (FT,* pp. 169–70). Both exegetes have in mind looking glasses of polished brass, as defined in Exodus 38:8. But whereas Mather identifies the glass strictly with "Gospel-Administrations," Edward Taylor first attributes the image to Moses, who "refracted" Christ's "Dazzling Shine," then later requests God to "make thy Son to shine" and as "Thy Looking-glass give mee" (II.9.1, 50, 51).

Applied, therefore, as an image for types, the "mirror" metaphor sets off two interrelated notions. First, by studying the typical ceremonies and events, we see Christ but darkly, because figures act as a necessary medium to filter the direct glory of the Son and make it bearable to limited human vision, particularly under the Old Testament dispensation. However, when Christ comes in person to disperse the shadows by fulfilling typological promises, He confronts man face to face. To the saint who lives under the New Testament dispensation, faith so inoculates his eyes that he can perceive the spiritual shine from Christ the antitype. No longer in search of prefigural beams in imperfect typal shadows (or "Looking-glass"), the believer "sees" the "Lovely Beauty, Lord, set out/ In Dazzling Shining Flashes 'fore mine Eye," sufficient to "Enchant my heart . . . till't spout/ Out streames of Love refin'd" (II.12.19–22).

However, Mather adds a second codicil, specifying that Christ too as portrayed under the gospel administration is merely a "lively Image and Picture" of the Deity in heaven. Capturing this distinction later in Meditation II.72, Taylor not only echoes the very language of Mather's two kinds of vision but also expresses his personal eschatological anticipations:

> Enoculate into my mentall Eye
> The Visive Spirits of the Holy Ghost

My Lord, that I may see the Dignity
   Of thy bright Honour in thy heavenly Coast
   Thou art deckt with as Sunshine bright displaid
   That makes bright Angells in it, cast a Shade.
Enrich my Phansy with Seraphick Life,
   Enquicknd nimbly to catch the Beams
Thy Honour flurs abroad: in joyous Strife
   To make sweet Musick on such Happy Themes.
   That in such Raptures, and Transports of joy,
   To Honour kings I may my Phansy 'ploy.
                    (II.72.1–12)

Moving one further step beyond the exegesis of his mentors, whether Chrysostom the ancient father or Mather the contemporary Puritan, Taylor requests not just the "mentall Eye" and "Visive Spirits" with which to see through the types to the "Sunshine bright" of Christ both under the Gospel and enshrined in heaven. These men are prophets and seers in a typological tradition that remains fundamentally homiletic and expository in form. But Edward Taylor seeks an added quickening of the "Phansy," virtually an infusion of "Seraphick Life," so that he can create "sweet Musick" of visionary poetry. In the sermons *Upon the Types of the Old Testament* and the companion *Preparatory Meditations,* he employs the "mentall Eye" to work through the "Looking Glass" of types and the "Visive Spirits" to perceive the Son's fulfillments. But the ultimate results are both meditative and poetic "Raptures, and Transports of joy,/ To Honour" Christ's eternal kingship.

3

Of Prophets, Priests, and Kings: Personalizing the Types

Make mee thy Nazarite by imitation
Not of the Ceremony, but thy selfe.
  In Holiness of Heart, and Conversation.
  Then I shall weare thy Nazarite like Crown
  In Glory bright with Songs of thy Renown.
                                                (II.15.38–42)

The eulogizing of magistrates and ministers in New England, whether as Moses, Joshua, or Nehemiah, played an important role in the formation of American culture. Initially an effort to consecrate the leaders of the mission into the wilderness, attributions of biblical identities together with qualities peculiar to that figure enhanced the confidence of Puritan followers. Visualizing a journey over a treacherous ocean to a reputedly uninviting land might overwhelm the most stalwart separatist, were it not for his faith in God's providential care, that is, an unshakable belief in the chosenness of this New Israel. But that trust also derived from a further perception of Puritan leaders, such as John Winthrop and John Cotton, as designated emissaries – men who like prophets and priests in the Old Testament had received their visions from God. Anointed by God, they would appear invulnerable, their strength not subject to geographical accidents or obstacles. Much like Washington, Lincoln, Kennedy, and King, who became the secular visionaries and heroes of later American epochs, these colonizing fathers achieved the status of folk heroes. But the folk were the small band of Puritan Elect, and the heroes were heralded as historical descendants, if not antitypes, of the Old Testament prophets, priests, and kings.

In the chronicles of New England the adoption of biblical patriarchs to provide contemporary leaders with an aura of God-given authority primarily illustrates the use of types as historical exempla or archetypes. Although historians might rhetorically proclaim a minister, such as John Cotton, the antitypal fulfillment of Moses, the chronicler often recognized that biblical types do not strictly prefigure, do not later proselytizing divines (as opposed to Christ) literally fulfill those ancient figures.

Nevertheless, the extensive identifications suggest not only a desire to immortalize the dead, but a longing to keep alive faith in the destiny of the New English Israel. Because they applied to themselves the promise of Christ's perpetual benefits under the New Testament, Puritan chroniclers often translated Old Testament types into models, for as John Wilson claims in his *Song of Deliverance* (1680), "what is there to Israel committed,/ Hath a more large and general extent,/ And to our present times may well be fitted."[1] Wilson's preface portrays the poet as a latter-day Moses, charged like "that holy Shepherd, Isrells guide" to write a song, warning the "Isralytish fry" of God's stern judgments as well as mercy toward New England's Canaanites.[2] Particularly in Israel's deliverance from Egyptian bondage, God's guidance through the wilderness, Moses' vision of Canaan, and Joshua's founding of the church in the promised land, the English emigrants found an inspirational pattern for their own sacred mission and the continuity of its leadership.

It seems not surprising that in later years the types invoked became less often Moses and Joshua and more often David, Solomon, and Nehemiah, who respectively ruled over the settled but embattled kingdom, supervised the building of the temple, and delivered Israel from Babylon to a New Jerusalem. In the period of second-and third-generation declension, as Cotton Mather portrays in his *Magnalia Christi Americana* (1702), using typal persons as historical models for New England's leaders became an effective device for calling wayward New Israelites back into the fold. Recounting the death of "Nehemias Americanus" John Winthrop, Mather depicted typal parallels that made this ten-times elected magistrate the very epitome of Christian political service: "having, like *Jacob,* first left his *Council* and *Blessing* with his Children gathered about his Bed side; and, like *David, served his Generation by the Will of God,* he *Gave up the Ghost,* and *fell asleep* on *March* 26. 1649. . . . The Words of *Josephus* about *Nehemiah,* the Governour of *Israel,* will now use upon this Governour of *New-England,* as his EPITAPH."[3] As the dimming visions of second-generation sons gave way to disillusion and despair, the evocation of biblical patriarchs as historical exempla served to challenge the youth to return to the faith and strength of the founding fathers. In a direct lineage from Abraham to whom God promised grace, the latter-day fathers in America would be builders and perpetuators rather than journeyers and founders of the New England settlement.

Not entirely immune to the surrounding cultural milieu, Edward Taylor in his 1671 elegy on the Reverend Zecharia Symmes invoked Moses as the type to whom God entrusts specifications for the tabernacle:

> [Deprive]d of his abundant Grace, & Care
> [They in t]he Wilderness them place prepare.

[He in t]he Wilderness alures apart
[Deep the]n in bowells speakes unto their heart
[He'd have] them build his house compleate, compact,
[Measures the]n gave them on the mount exact.
[The whic]h they tended. & this Sims (alass
[He ha]th laid down his Square) a Builder was
[As well as] Pillar, & a Builder who
[Both built], & long up[held] the building too.[4]

Like the historians, Taylor models his eulogistic portrait of Symmes on
Moses, stressing not only this contemporary divine's call into the wilderness, but also his building and upholding of the church in New England-
Israel. Comparable to developmental uses of types that appeared regularly in elegies by John Wilson, John Danforth, and Benjamin Tompson,
Taylor's poem assumes a communal knowledge of the parallels between
Old Testament patriarchs and New England ministers. This investiture
of authority, based on deliberately evoked correspondences by way of
qualities, life, duties, death, surrounded the Puritan minister with an aura
of reflected sainthood, earned in life but bestowed more often in death.

Despite this singular elegy and the plethora of similar contemporary
recapitulative uses of biblical types, in *Upon the Types of the Old Testament*
and the *Preparatory Meditations* Taylor's mode is not one of cultural identification, but a more exegetically stringent and devotional approach. He
does not range far beyond the Old-to-New Testament correspondences,
nor in Meditations II.2–15 and 30 does he overtly use biblical persons as
historical exempla for his Puritan colleagues. Instead, the sermons and
meditations take an exegetically conservative turn toward a schematic
examination of the major biblical types, chronologically distributed from
Adam through Moses and Joshua onward to David and Solomon.[5] Modeling his selected types on the scriptural order of their descent, Taylor
views all Old Testament fathers as foreshadowers of the ultimate Son in
Christ. Thus, the Christological emphasis, which so often disappears or
remains implicit in historical chronicles and elegies, retains center stage
in Taylor's poetry. In part, this exegetical rather than historical bias is
determined by Taylor's close reliance on equally Christocentric sources,
Christ Revealed and *The Figures or Types*. Neither Thomas Taylor nor
Samuel Mather indulge in wholesale historical applications of types; indeed,
Mather may have been the catalyst to bring his errant brother Increase
Mather back from the extravagances of recapitulative typology which
permeated his jeremiads of the seventies.[6] But the predilection for a
Christocentric typology seems also to grow out of Edward Taylor's own
personality and his homiletic and meditative aims. Less willing, after the
Harvard elegies, to envision himself or his contemporaries as a leader,
antitype, or cultural hero, Taylor turns to devotional rather than histor-

ical applications. Whereas Cotton Mather focuses upon geographical and temporal realities, Taylor concentrates on moral and spiritual patterns of the Christian life, prefigured by Old Testament priests and prophets but epitomized by Christ's life. Consequently, the meditations reflect his exegetical approach and often mirror the rational explications of his sermons. But just as one would expect homiletic doctrine to culminate in moral improvements, so too the meditations repeatedly close with Taylor's personal requests for guidance – that he might imitate the typal personages in his spiritual strivings. Although he ultimately seeks inspiration from the lives of these patriarchs, Taylor travels by way of the figural parallels set forth so intellectually in his sermons *Upon the Types of the Old Testament.*

Longstanding patristic and Protestant tradition had designated prominent Old Testament persons as types because their names, deeds, and prophecies adumbrated Jesus Christ, his person, offices, and those gospel truths revealed by him, as distinct from foreshadowing events and things that might equally apply to Christ's mission, the church, or worship forms. So commonplace is the distinction between personal and real types, or holy persons and things, that Taylor introduces it with a few graphic bilateralisms: "Types are either

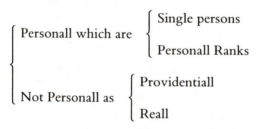

We are Now upon the Single Personall Types of which I shall Single out Some few as Eminent Types of Christ as Mediator thô not onely as a Mediator. & here I begin with Adam" (*UTOT*, p. 33). From the Church Fathers to the seventeenth-century Puritans, the chronological ordering had remained relatively constant, although interpreters might create elaborate allegories or succinct catalogs. In keeping with his strict rules for identifying types as a counterbalance to medieval and Catholic extravagances, Edward Taylor prefers not to "burden the Faith of Gods People with Presumptions drawn from very dim or Curious Allusions" which prove more as "Simile or illustrations, than by way of Argument fortifying any truth, drawn from any Typicall face" (*UTOT*, p. 42). He omits such dubious figures as "Abel, Seth, Enoch, Methuselah, Lamech," and "Severall others" that more lavish expositors, such as Henry Vertue, might compile (*UTOT*, p. 42). Instead, his Puritan selectivity results in a basic list similar to Samuel Mather's and Thomas Taylor's, of Adam, Noah, Abraham, Isaac, Jacob, Joseph, Moses, Joshua, Samson, David, Solomon, and Jonah (Appendixes 2, 3, 4). Less innovative than imitative in his choice of personal types, Taylor remains securely within the bounds of orthodox Protestant tradition.

Nonetheless, it is worth noting some quirks in the sermons and *Preparatory Meditations* that paradoxically confirm Taylor's dependence upon preceding treatises, yet also point to his independence – sufficient to design a structure compatible with his own concepts of figuralism. Melchizedek, for instance, does not appear in Meditation II.3. But considered among the holy eminents by Thomas Taylor and Samuel Mather, this patriarch is explicated in Sermon II.3 as a type endowed with "Priestly & Kingly dignity" who adumbrates both Christ's "Eternall Mediation" and His reign as "King of Righteousness" and "Peace" (*UTOT*, pp. 48, 46, 47). Taylor may have found Melchizedek an unwieldy rhyme, or in the less doctrinally complex meditation found his psychic need for Christ, "a Mediator unto God for mee" more compelling than a catalog of all mediatorial figures (II.3.22). Later in the series, Taylor also clearly incorporates Abraham (II.4) and Jacob (II.6), figures omitted from *Christ Revealed* but prominently displayed in Mather's *The Figures or Types*. Edward Taylor sees in Abraham and his two wives, Hagar and Sarah, a fitting allegory for the two Covenants of Works and Grace, of man's bondage unto nature and freedom within faith, and like Mather he pursues the striking trilogy of Abraham, Isaac, and Jacob as transmitters of the "Promised Seed" who is Christ Himself (II.5.2). In his subsequent sermons Taylor takes note of Mather's other "conglobations" by admitting that "many more I might have gone over. As Job. Barack, Gideon, etc Samuel, Elijah, Elisha, Joshua, & Zerubbabel," but he refrains, since "I have been long already in what I have done. & shall not go any further on with them" (*UTOT*, pp. 278–9). Having surveyed the major figures before the law (Adam, Noah, Melchizedek, Abraham, Isaac, Jacob, and Joseph) and under the law (Moses, Joshua, Samson, David, Solomon), Taylor completes the single persons with Jonah. Compared with its placement in other treatises, Meditation II.30 on Jonah might seem curiously detached from the other personal types, mainly because the date of composition, April 1699, places it as the last of Taylor's initial thirty figural poems. According to *Upon the Types of the Old Testament,* however, this type resumes its place among the other personal types immediately after Sermon II.13 on Solomon. Taylor explicates how aptly Jonah's deliverance from the whale's belly prefigures Christ's resurrection after "three dayes, & three nights in the heart of the Earth" (*UTOT*, p. 255). This relocation (among other details) suggests that Taylor may have considered publishing the sermons and taken pains to rearrange his col-

lection according to figural logic rather than a strict chronology of composition. That possibility might also be supported by Taylor's deliberate
adaptation of the firstborn, usually included as a typical rank, but used
by Taylor in Sermon and Meditation II.2 to introduce Christ's "Excellency as it shines forth in Particular Types" and to create a companion
piece for Sermon and Meditation II.1's exploration of "the accomplishment of the Types in Generall" (*UTOT*, p. 16).

In order to prove the legitimacy of each type, Taylor frequently invokes
the same telling denominators established as criteria by earlier Puritan
exegetes. In Samuel Mather's words, an expositor may safely judge a
type when there is "express Scripture," a *"permutation of Names,"* or *"an
evident and manifest* Analogy *and parallel between Things under the Law, and
things under the Gospel"* (*FT*, pp. 53, 54). Edward Taylor routinely explicates his chosen Scripture before enunciating the sermon's doctrine, and
he seeks to justify each person as a reputable type by citing previous
authorities, dissecting biblical words and phrasings, responding to
interpretive objections, and accumulating additional scriptural proofs. He
chooses Romans 5:14, for example, to establish how the "Mediatoriall
glory in the shine/ Out Spouted so from Adams typick streame," from
"Noahs pollisht shrine," and from illustrious Melchizedek (II.3.8–9, 10).
He also initiates his exposition of single persons under the law with Romans
5:14, because this passage (a common one among figuralists) expressly
delineates the figural process: "Nevertheless, death reigned from Adam
to Moses, even over them that had not sinned after the similitude of
Adam's transgression, who is the figure of him that was to come." Similarly, despite Catholic and Puritan controversies over the meaning of
allegoria, Taylor cites Galatians 4:24 in Sermon and Meditation II.4 to
designate "Abraham & his two Sons Ismael & Isaac or two Wives Sarah
& Hagar. . . . Which things are an Allegory" of "the two Covenants"
(*UTOT*, pp. 57, 58). Six and eleven of Taylor's head texts for his meditations on typical persons and ranks correspond with those set in *Christ
Revealed* and *The Figures or Types* respectively, although many of the
passages were commonplace in theological and biblical glosses from the
Church Fathers to the Protestant Reformers.

Equally conventional were the proofs by permutations in names (Christ
as Adam or David, and the church as Jerusalem and Israel), though the
permutations might gradually slide from names proper (Christ the second Adam) to epithets (the paschal lamb, sun of righteousness, King of
Israel) to metaphors (bright and morning star, pearl of great price, a
wedding garment). Unlike Henry Vertue in *Christ and the Church: Or
Parallels* (1659) or Benjamin Keach in *Tropologia: A Key to Open Scripture-
Metaphors* (1681) who amply analyzed metaphors, Taylor plumbed a type's
validity with etymological zeal, in part because of his Puritan respect for

Scripture's literal sense. Schooled in Latin, Greek, and Hebrew, Taylor selects Acts 7:45 as the text for Sermon and Meditation II.10 in order to prove Joshua's typal efficacy: "In his Name. There is the very name our Lord hath as his own proper Name given to him. Here in our text he is called by Christ's own Name: Jesus. So Nehe. 8. 17. Jesua. If we write the Name Jesus in Hebrew it is written Jesua. Hence his Name is Typical of Christ. Both have the Name Jesus" (*UTOT*, p. 163). In a more elaborate proof in which Hebrew names translate into congruent English epithets, Taylor classifies Melchizedek as "Typicall

$$\&\ \text{this as to the Name of his} \left\{ \begin{array}{l} \text{Person} \\ \\ \text{Kingdom} \end{array} \right. ,"\ \text{for "the Name of his Person which is}$$

Melchizedeck. the Apostle tells you Heb. 7. 2. it is being interpreted King of Righteousness. . . . & so a fit Emblem of Christ whose name is Jer. 23. 6. יהוה צדקנו the Lord our Righteousness" (*UTOT*, pp. 46–7). The same process of declension applies to the "Name of his Kingdom which is Salem. King of Salem that is King of Peace. . . . Hereby rightly delineating the Lord Jesus in his Mediatoriall title who is Stiled by the Prophet שר שלום Isai. 6.9 Prince of Peace" (*UTOT*, p. 47). For personal types the argument from parallel names is often the exegete's first major category to be followed by links between type and antitype by virtue of their offices, whether Joshua as the savior or Melchizedek as mediator, Salem's king, and priest. Names achieved an almost talismanic power when Puritan historians and elegists invoked them to transfer to New Israel's magistrates and ministers the lustrous qualities and offices of Old Testament patriarchs. Behind the seemingly casual transference rose the whole edifice of typological readings from the apostles to the Puritan divines, and it was that heritage which invested recapitulative applications with more than just a metaphoric dimension. Edward Taylor's exegetical commitment, as revealed by *Upon the Types,* was to reconstruct the very foundations of typology and, by rooting figural correspondences in Scripture, to teach his congregation that Christ alone is the supreme spiritual guide. Even in the devotionalism of his meditations, Taylor never neglects Christ's fulfillment, since "Joshua's but a Beam/ Of thy bright Sun, my Lord" (II.10.49–50) and "Christ's Antitype Isaac his Type up spires" (II.5.7).

Laying the foundation meant also surveying the manifold parallels between persons under the law and Christ's life, ministry, and redemptive sacrifice under the gospel. For Mather *"evident and manifest Analogy"* denoted a process firmly based on Scripture, "for the *Type* must be made like the *Antitype,* as the Apostle speaks of that illustrious Type *Melchise-*

dec, Hebr. 7. 3. *he was made like unto the Son of God"* or as *"Samson* a Type of Christ" for whom "there is such a fair and full Analogy in sundry particulars of his Life and Death between him and Christ" (*FT,* pp. 54–5). By the seventeenth century this principle had calcified into a methodology by which theologians *made* manifest and evident the parallels. For William Guild and Benjamin Keach, the method resulted in neat columns or lists of congruities; for Thomas Taylor, the format became categorical, a declaring of "Salomon *a type of Christ: in 6. things"* or Samson in four ways, according to person, actions, suffering, and victory (*CR,* p. 77). In Mather's treatise, the familiar sermon structure (explication of text, analysis of doctrine, applications) erected yet another framework around numerous correspondences and categories. For his sermons Edward Taylor not only adopted these methods, he also superimposed ramistic divisions and subdivisions, careful delineations sermon by sermon of his place in the survey of types (arranged by categories), and more developed uses by way of trial, reproof, information, and exhortation. Despite Taylor's attempts to orient his audience and to clarify figural doctrines, at times the proliferating of frameworks threatens to obscure meanings. Still the substance of each sermon emerges as a thorough, almost painstaking analysis of congruities between types and the antitype. What appears in the meditations is an embossed impression or skeletal shadow of the sermons' complicated didactic analyses out of which Taylor creates flourishes of metaphors and conceits to capture his personal internalization of rational truths.

In Sermon and Meditation II.4, for example, Taylor adopts Galatians 4:24 as his text and Abraham as the type in order to defend covenant doctrine. He begins by defining "Allegory" as signifying things that contain "a Speciall meaning in them of Some Spirituall Mystery, as Figures, Tropes, Types," or as "Tropus multiplicatus. in diversis dictionibus" (*UTOT,* p. 58). Paul's epistle enables Taylor to constrain allegorical interpretations to the narrower sense of figural, as determined by the Puritans, that is, to show that "Abraham in Relation to Hagar & Sarah with their two Sons is a Type of Christ Mysticall, as He Stands incorporated in the Body of his Visible Church or as Head & Members in one body" (*UTOT,* pp. 58–9). Thus, the sermon uses both express Scripture and evident analogies (from Gal. 4:19–31) to establish Abraham's typical efficacy. Although it echoes the key terms, the companion poem showers the antitype Christ with exulting praises and metaphors which evoke (rather than preach) figural parallels and antitypal supremacy:

> O Glorious One, the gloriou'st thought I thincke
> Of thee falls black as Inck upon thy Glory.
> The brightest Saints that rose, do Star like, pinck.

> Nay, Abrams Shine to thee's an Allegory,
> Of fleeting Sparke in th'Smoke, to typify
> Thee, and thy Glorious Selfe in mystery.
>
> Should all the Sparks in heaven, the Stars there dance
>   A Galliard, Round about the Sun, and stay
> His Servants (while on Easter morn his prance
>   Is o're, which old wives prate of) O brave Play.
>   Thy glorious Saints thus boss thee round, which stand
>   Holding thy glorious Types out in their hand.
>   (II.4.7–18)

In familiar images Taylor contrasts the "fleeting Sparke in th'Smoke" of "Abrams Shine" with the far surpassing "Glorious Selfe in mystery" of Christ. Ephemeral, multiple, darkened by human liabilities, neither man's vivid imaginings, nor the "brightest Saints," nor illuminating types hold a candle to the mystical radiation from the "Glorious One." Taylor's associative imagination leads him, however, to ornament even this plain poetic declaration with an extended comparison that blends astronomy, dance, bookbinding, architecture, and typology itself. From the mere notation of "fleeting Sparke" and "Star like," he envisions the multitudinous stars circling the radiant sun in a Renaissance "Galliard"; so likewise the Old Testament saints, embossed in almost iconographical poses, surround Christ, holding "thy glorious Types out in their hand." The compounded metaphoric references exude cleverness. But Taylor also clumsily digresses into the old wives' tales and "brave Play," though Easter morn reminds one of Christ's necessary descent into the darkness of a grave, only to rise again more radiantly bright than sun, stars, or saints. Hermeneutic proofs by way of rational dissection and authority (Calvin, Chrysostom, and Origen) give place to distillations of belief, the rhetoric of defense and argument to faith-affirming poesy.

In order to fit the doctrine for his congregation's "Improovment," Taylor in Sermon II.4 creates a series of interlocking ramistic subdivisions. "I shall

$$\left\{ \begin{array}{l} \text{Explain it} \\ \\ \text{Confirm it} \end{array} \right.$$
," he proclaims, and "In Explaining it I shall Evince it by Abraham

as he is a $\left\{ \begin{array}{l} \text{Simple, \&} \\ \\ \text{Compound} \end{array} \right\}$ Type" (*UTOT*, p. 59). As a "Simple Type," meaning

"Abraham in his own person," he foreshadows both " $\left\{ \begin{array}{l} \text{Christ} \\ \\ \text{Christians} \end{array} \right\}$," and as a "Type of Christ Singly Considered," Abraham adumbrates the Savior as to His

$$\left\{\begin{array}{l} \text{Betrustment} \\ \text{\qquad\qquad " } (UTOT, \text{ p. 59). For "Betrustments," Taylor adopts a categorical} \\ \text{Performance} \end{array}\right.$$

approach and lists them one, two, three, according to the "Promises . . . respecting the people of God," Abraham as an "Arch Father: a Prime Patriarch," and "that in him God Changed the Dispensation of the Covenant of Grace" (UTOT, pp. 59, 60). As "Head Receiver of the Promises" from God and "Heade Father," Abraham presides over the change in Israel's dispensation from private to public, domestic to national (UTOT, p. 59). Furthermore, as God's designate in his "Performance" or offices, Abraham inaugurates the "Seale of the Covenant of Grace in Circumcision" and serves triply as "Priest Prophet, & King" (UTOT, p. 61). But as Taylor had indicated in his initial bifurcations, "Abraham Singly Considered" is not only a type of Christ but also of all "Christians: & of Every Childe of God," and that in four ways: "1. In his being Brought to his Excellent Estate by Grace"; "2. In His Call . . . the Effectuall call . . . out of a State of Sin unto a State of Grace"; "3. In his Obedience"; and "4. In his Justifying Faith" (UTOT, p. 62). These elaborate breakdowns may burden a modern reader, but they reflect Taylor's assimilation of ramistic logic, of methods common in figural treatises, and of sermon forms his congregation would expect. For a Sunday sermon, the denoting, dividing, and numbering of points would have assisted a dutiful scribbler attentively listening to intricate typal analogies.

Not simply adumbrating the *person* of Christ, Abraham also figures forth the evangelical covenant's superiority to the Old Testament legal covenant. In this respect, explications of Paul's epistle to the Galatians had appeared in theological tracts from the Church Fathers to the contemporary Puritans. Hence, Edward Taylor preaches that Abraham is a "Compound Type . . . whose typicall nature is produced, constituted, educed, or emanates from the Relation it Stands in unto another thing," as here "Abrahams Relation to these two Sons by these two women (which the Spirit of God interprets, to import the two Covenants)" (UTOT, p. 63). Taylor distinguishes between Abraham with "Respect unto the Bondwoman" Hagar who signifies "Such as are under a Covenant of works State" and unto Sarah "the Free Woman," who typifies "Christ in relation to the Saints his Body" under a state of grace (UTOT, pp. 63–4). Taylor's intepretation clearly upholds Abraham in this typical relation as a *prophetic* symbol, differentiating those bound by an Old Testament Covenant of Works (or law) from those spiritually liberated by

Christ's New Testament dispensation. Sustaining this Puritan emphasis on linear prophecy and fulfillment (unlike the Platonic allegorism of the Middle Ages), he conceives of his Westfield Elect as under a "New Covenant Relation," a fulfillment of the promise set forth in Sarah and Jacob.

But Taylor takes the analysis one step further by calling each parishioner to examine the self within, which may be bound to earthly desires (an "Old Covenant State"), yet seeking a new faith to free the spirit. Consequently, the sermon's uses by trial and exhortation list properties for the bond and free soul; Taylor urges his flock to "labour in this matter, that we antitype not, that held out in the Bondwoman, & her Son: but that Constituted by the Relation unto the freewoman, & her Son" (*UTOT*, p. 71). In Meditation II.4 Taylor translates these uses into a personal prayer, as he heeds Paul's warning: "Then, my Blesst Lord, let not the Bondmaids type/ Take place in mee. But thy blesst Promisd Seed" (II.4.25–6). Fearing that he, like other weak-willed men, might succumb to Hagar's fleshly bondage, Taylor desires to be born again, as figured by Sarah who brings forth Isaac, the promised seed: "Distill thy Spirit through thy royall Pipe/ Into my Soule, and so my Spirits feed" (II.4.27–8). The meditation does not detail other typal analogies but rather crystallizes and personalizes the essential truth, that belief in works under the law binds one everlastingly to sin, but faith in promised salvation inaugurates an eternal liberty within Christ's Covenant of Grace. And Taylor's interpretation illustrates how, within a covenant theology, Puritans saw in the macrocosmic patterns of Old Testament prophecy and New Testament fulfillment the microcosmic pattern for each saint's spiritual progress toward salvation.

The analysis of Abraham thus reveals the several levels at which Taylor, in both homilies and poems, unfolds scriptural meanings. Extracting his raw matter from the Bible and traditional glosses, Taylor perceives Abraham as a type of two different orders, from one perspective adumbrating Christ's relationship with His church as a historical phenomenon and a mystical relationship. Hence, Abraham's paternity of his flock and transmittal of God's promises foreshadow Christ's mission, in which He assumes a mystical headship of the body which is the church of all believers. But the exegesis holds implications not only for the collective church but also for each individual saint, defined as one who renounces works for Christ's saving grace. Taylor thus exegetically construes Abraham in this double way, as a prophetic figure for a later historical dispensation and for an ongoing spiritual process. Once, however, he sets the scriptural explication within the context of a publicly preached sermon, he implicitly acknowledges a further historical continuum which makes the New Testament church mystical one and the same with his Westfield congregation, to whom Jesus' promises are as spiritually as they were literally real to the apostles. Unlike Cotton Mather or contemporary historians, Taylor does not elaborate these connections into a recapitulative typology, because he seeks not so much to sustain the glorious emigration as to preach an enduring inward journey. His homiletic applications speak immediately to the troubled saint who seeks freedom from Hagar's curse of bond-slavery and craves nurture instead from a spiritual fount, represented by Sarah's promise through Isaac that the Savior will deliver men from sin. Removed one step further from the pulpit's public oratory, Edward Taylor delves yet more deeply into the personal by making his meditation an example of incorporation, of Abraham's figural prophecies and Christ's fulfillment absorbed by his own soul. In Meditation II.4 covenant theology becomes realized not as a theory of the chosen nation in New England, but rather as a repeated act of internalized belief essential to support Taylor, the elect saint, in his worldly progress. Taylor both stands so removed from the contingencies of temporal life that historical recapitulations become irrelevant, and yet strikes so close to the heart of figural meaning (one saint rather than a nation, a gospel covenant to supersede the Old Testament, grace not works) that his poem embodies the essence of what Allan Charity calls typology's existential claim of faith.

Taylor's personal engagement may explain why he metaphorically elaborates the concept of a "promisd Seed" to link Abraham, Isaac, and Jacob in his figural treatise and poems. But it is equally true that earlier groupings of types (as in Mather), Taylor's penchant for order, and a need to reinforce a sense of Scripture's coherence for his congregation may call forth the conjugation. In Sermon II.5 on Isaac, Taylor writes: "But yet we find Isaac Expresst by name in Gods Promise to Abraham. . . . Wherefore it must be granted that, as Isaac was a Promised Seed, he was wholy typicall & so not the Onely promised Seed; but given in the Promise wholy with respect unto the Lord Christ the alone Single Promised Seed" (*UTOT*, p. 74).[7] Taylor reinvokes this image in his head text, Galatians 3:16, and in the queries that open Meditation II.5 on Isaac:

> Art thou, Lord, Abraham's Seed, and Isaac too?
>   His Promisd Seed? That One and Only Seed?
> How can this bee? Paul certainly saith true
>   But one Seed promisd. Sir this Riddle read.
>   Christ is the Metall: Isaack is the Oar.
>   Christ is the Pearle, in Abraham's tread therefore.
>
> (II.5.1–6)

In neither Sermon nor Meditation II.4 on Abraham had Taylor explored the means by which Christ would assume headship of the church or effect mankind's promised salvation. But in analyzing Isaac, he focuses on Abraham's intended sacrifice of his son and the ram's substitution as a figure of Christ's hypostatic union and resurrection. In Sermon II.5 Taylor claims that "Isaac & the Ram united in one Offering" are "a type of the Divine, & Humane Natures of Christ united in one Person" (*UTOT*, p. 76), a claim echoed in Meditation II.5 in which Isaac types "Christs Person, all Divine, joynd whereto's . . . / Unperson'd Manhood" (II.5.11–12). Taylor obeys the "Godly Learned," including Origen and Augustine, when he emphasizes the ram's sacrifice in lieu of Isaac: "he that shall Secure man from Sin, must consist of two Natures one Mortall one Immortall: one Humane, & one Divine. the one to tender the price the other to render the Price sufficiently pretious to Satisfy, & purchase the one to Die, the other to render the Death Efficacious. Both must bee laid upon the Altar, the one burnt in the Fire of Gods justice for a burnt offering" (*UTOT*, p. 86). Taylor recasts the sacrifice in the dramatic scenario of Meditation II.5 in which "Under the Knife" the ram suffers death, thereby figuring forth that Christ must submit to "manhoods Death, and Groan," but "Isaac's leaping from the Altar's bed,/ Foretold its glorious rising from the Dead" (II.5.16–18). That is, the conjoining of Isaac and the ram not only foreshadows Christ's human death, as a scapegoat and burnt offering for man's sins, it also prophesies the Savior's divine resurrection for man's salvation. In respect to his person, linkage with the ram, and enacted death and resurrection, Isaac thus typifies Christ the promised seed and perfect redeemer.

Abraham and Isaac comprise only two persons, however, in an illuminating trilogy of personal types which includes Jacob. Edward Taylor does not, as one might expect, highlight Mather's trinitarian reading (Father, Son, Holy Spirit), but instead links these types to Christ's progressive acts:

> Abraham considered in relation to his posterity by Sarah, & Hagar typified Christ, & his Church under a generall Profession, of good & bad. That Isaac was an Eminent Type typifying especially what it would cost Christ to effect Salvation for his People, He must be their Sacrifice to make attonement for them. And now I am come to Jacob who is a Type especially Emblemizing the multiplying of Christs Intrest after his being Sacrificed for them, by his Apostles as answering to the twelve trybes of Israel, & that Erected his Church of Jews, & Gentiles. (*UTOT*, p. 91)

In Meditation II.6 he eschews doctrinal schemas for metaphoric evocations. Echoing the earlier meditation on Abraham in which "glorious Saints thus boss thee round" (II.4.17), Taylor again spies Christ "as Golden Bosses fixt/ On Bible Covers," shining "in Types out bright,/ Of Abraham, Isaac, Jacob" (II.6.7–8, 8–9). To praise the illustrious trio's typal functions, he fills the poem on Jacob with images of "shine," "bright," and "streaming Beames of Christ displaying Light" (II.6.10). And further to verify Jacob's figural stature, Taylor underscores the significance of his alternate name: "The Name of Israel in Scutcheons shows/ Thou art Gods Prince to batter down his Foes" (II.6.17–18).

Rarely can we appreciate more clearly than in this poem the process by which Taylor first constructs the categories of his sermons, then transforms them into the narrative skeleton of a meditation. In Sermon II.6 he traces the "Circumstances" by which Jacob types Christ, both "Singly" and "Relatively" (*UTOT*, p. 92). Singly, Jacob "hath his Fathers Blessing," "is a man of Sorrows, & acquainted with griefs . . . most afflicted man of any Saint in Scripture, Job only excepted," and "is carryed down into Egypt by Joseph" (*UTOT*, pp. 92, 93, 94). "Sent by his Father" into a "far Countrey to seek a wife," Jacob also relatively types the conjugal state between Christ and His church, "Consisting of Jews & Gentiles," from which springs "twelve Stems" or "Apostles" to establish the visible "Kingdom on Earth" (*UTOT*, pp. 95, 96). Allowing for biblical interpolations and rearrangements to suit his usual iambic pentameter, six-line stanza, Taylor's poetic rendering virtually glosses the related preachment:

> His Fathers blessing him, shews thou camest down
> Full of thy Fathers blessing: and his Griefe
> That thou shouldst be a man of Grief: A Crown
> Of Thorns thou wer'st to purchase us reliefe.
> Isr'el by Joseph's had to Egypt, and
> Joseph thee thither, and from thence did hand.
>
> Jacob doth from his Father go and seek
> A Spouse and purchased by his service two.
> Thou from thy Father came'st thy Spouse most meek
> Of Jews, and Gentiles down to purchase, Wooe
> And gain, and as Twelve Stems did from him bud
> Thou twelve Apostles sentst, the Church to stud.
> (II.6.19–30)

Taylor fleshes out typal meanings with additional details, accentuating the "Fathers blessing," Jacob's "Griefe," and the "Twelve Stems" as emblems of Christ's divine origins, his sacrificial suffering to "purchase us reliefe," and the apostolic founding of the church. The specific allusion to Joseph, use of "purchase," and focus on Jacob's double espousals link Taylor's meditation to Mather's reading and to the ancient typologists. But what the meditation makes yet more apparent is the typological method, a pairing of ancient prophecies and Christological completions, an almost schematic balancing of Jacob's life with Christ's. Although the cataloging of similarities appears in the sermons, the meditation's alternation from "Jacob" to "thou" more emphatically expresses the bipolarity of figuralism. Jacob's filial obedience, his griefs, and marriage derive their prophetic force not from an intrinsic meaning, but only insofar as they foreshadow Christ's life and ministry.

Taylor's analysis of Abraham exemplifies his exegetical scaffolding, that is, the multiple frames that structure the sermons, yet just as inevitably lead from rational understandings toward exhortatory applications and finally to intensely felt prayers in the meditations. Isaac reveals Taylor's search for connections, whether through imagistic associations (promised seed), biblical "begats" as sons succeed their fathers, or conglobations, either traditional or newly created by Taylor, which place the personal figures in an overarching schema. Although Taylor presents these patterns as inherent in Scripture and reflective of God's prophetic intentions, we cannot escape the sense that the categories (mediator, mystical headship, promised seed, Christ's progress) become occasionally artificial, though admittedly of service to the exegete, preacher, and audience.[8] Jacob also illustrates the extent to which Taylor, like other seventeenth-century figuralists, relies upon *manifest* analogies between the Old and New Testaments, thereby mirroring in method the fundamental principles of Puritan typology – its historicity, pattern of prophecy and fulfillment, and celebration of Christ's superiority *forma perfectior* over ancient persons. Because of the close relationship between sermons and poems, Taylor's exegetical methods inevitably influence the structure of his meditations. But the meditations also reveal Taylor's fascination with imagery, with his personal need to translate didactic teaching into felt learning, and with a poetic medium in which the private man speaks directly to his God.

In the typological series, Meditation II.8 seems superficially digressive, a poem that breaks the flow of personal types by setting no historical figure as its topic.[9] This lack of a personage may explain the absence of a sermon in *Upon the Types,* even though the meditation's date (October 14, 1694) suggests that Taylor may have composed a corresponding homily only to eliminate it later. However, it is equally possible that he created two meditations, both inspired by Moses' typal functions. Samuel Mather offers a precedent and model when he argues that Moses served a twofold function: as *"a Type of Christ,"* if "we consider him in his own Person" as a prophet, and as a *"Type of the Law"* to "adumbrate and shadow forth the Covenant of Works" (*FT,* pp. 95, 93).[10] Under a Mosaic dispensation, "the Strength of the Law" exerts "its condemning Power over Sinners . . . the Power whereof decayeth not in the Conscience of Sinners by number of Days or multitude of Works, till God take it away, and abolish it by Grace in Christ" (*FT,* p. 94). Before Christ can, however, abolish the old covenant law and bring forth his new covenant promise of mercy, God requires His crucifixion to satisfy the letter of the law and atone for mankind's sin. Neither can man escape death or the law until he receives saving grace through Christ. In *Upon the Types of the Old Testament,* Edward Taylor combines Mather's two focuses into one unusually long sermon. Within his exegesis of Moses' public actions or services, Taylor surveys his work as a prophet, specifically the "Delivering the Morall Law unto them from God writt by God himselfe in tables of Stone" (*UTOT,* p. 137). In support, Taylor recounts the saga of man's fall, since the natural "Law being broken by Adam, we are all made Sinners by it, & so fall Short of the Fruite of it, which otherwise had been Life, & Eternal Glory. Yet God hath given it in Grace unto us by Moses, as Moses is a Type of Christ" (*UTOT,* p. 138). Drawing also upon passages in Romans, Taylor deplores man's "State of Sin Curse, & Damnation. Rom. 7," while he encourages parishioners to "Get a righteousness" and heed the "Rule of Obedience" first writ by Moses, then epitomized by Christ's sacrifice (*UTOT,* p. 138).

Reread against this doctrinal background, Meditation II.8 assumes the same purpose as Mather's discourse on Moses as a type of the law and forms a companion piece for Meditation II.9 on Moses as a personal type of Christ. Initially in II.8 Taylor agonizes over man's "Curse" of sin which alienates him from God's love and dooms him to divine wrath and "to dust":

> Poore sinfull man lay grovling on the ground.
>   Thy wrath, and Curse to dust lay grinding him.
> And Sin, that banisht Love out of these bounds
>   Hath stufft the world with curses to the brim.
>   Gods Love thus Caskt in Heaven, none can tap
>   Or breake its truss hoops, or attain a Scrap.
>   (II.8.7–12)

The head text, "God commends his Love unto us, in that while we were yet sinners, Christ died for us" (Rom. 5:8), and Mather's assertion of the law's perpetual "condemning Power over Sinners" may provide germinal images for this drama of human deprivation (*FT,* p. 94). But Taylor's homespun metaphors solidify the "grounded" condition of man, who is "grovling" in the dust, bound within a world "stufft . . . with curses," and forbidden soothing liquid relief from "Gods Love thus Caskt in Heaven." A gristmill to process meal and a wine cask with "truss hoops" signify man's suffering beneath God's denial of divine sustenance. Yet, these images implicitly forecast the possibility of a changed estate, when ground meal and wine will transmute into elements of the Lord's Supper. Instituted by Christ, this banquet commemorates God's forgiveness of sin which countermands his punitive wrath. Incorporating ideas from Romans 5:12 and 14, "by one man sin entered into the world" and so "death reigned from Adam to Moses," Taylor imagistically alludes to Adam's original sin which provokes God's ire, the withdrawal of "Love out of these bounds" (the garden of the world), and his death sentence. Representing all instances of sin, Taylor depicts its earthly perpetuity, since sin inclusively afflicts the apostate Israelites, the unredeemed Puritan, even the poetic speaker himself. Sin and death are not simply facts in history but the existential condition of mankind for all time, prevailing under the law and mitigated only by a new dispensation of grace.

While asserting Christ's preaching of faith to replace the Mosaic covenant, Taylor still recognizes the law's efficacy as preparation. He reaffirms the legal mandate upon mankind as "essentiall to his nature," for it is "as a Schoolmaster . . . to bring us to Christ. for Shewing of us in Cursed State by Sin," and it turns us to Christ who "is the End of the Law for Righteousness Sake to every one that believes" (*UTOT*, pp. 138–9). Through his figural images in Meditation II.8, Taylor thus sustains a vision of Mosaic law, while he also contemplates Christ's fulfillment and surpassing of the old covenant:

> Like as a flock of Doves with feathers washt,
>   All o're with yellow gold, fly all away
> At one Gun crack: so Lord thy Love Sin quasht
>   And Chased hence to heaven (Darksom day).
>   It nestles there: And Graces Bird did hatch
>   Which in dim types we first Pen feather'd catch.
>
> God takes his Son stows in him all his Love,
>   (Oh Lovely One), him Lovely thus down sends
> His rich Love Letter to us from above
>   And chiefly in his Death his Love Commends,
>   Writ all in Love from top to toe, and told
>   Out Love more rich, and shining far than gold.
>
> For e'ry Grain stands bellisht ore with Love,
>   Each Letter, Syllable, Word, Action sounde
> Gods Commendations to us from above,
>   But yet Loves Emphasis most cleare is found
>   Engrav'd upon his Grave Stone in his blood
>   He shed for Sinners, Lord what Love? How good?
>
> It rent the Heavens ope that seald up were
>   Against poore Sinners: rend the very Skie
> And rout the Curse, Sin, Divell, Hell (Oh Deare,)
>   And brake Deaths jaw bones, and its Sting destroy.
>   Will search its Coffers: fetch from thence the Dust
>   Of Saints, and it attend to glory just.
>   (II.8.13–36)

Hatched from God's heavenly love, "Graces Bird" or Christ descends to shed his blood, rout "the Curse, Sin, Divell, Hell," and redeem mankind from "Dust," to "glory just." Masterfully punning, Taylor substitutes "Pen feather'd" for "pinfeathered" to effect an elegant comparison and shift in metaphors. Just as fledglings sprout pinfeathers which anticipate their adult plumage, so the "Pen feather'd" Mosaic law dimly predicts the glorious messianic revelation of grace. Taylor also cleverly shifts the basic metaphor from Christ as descending spiritual dove to Christ as God's "rich Love Letter to us from above." Simultaneously exploring both type and antitype, he alludes to "Gods Commendations," meaning the ten commandments or Old Testament legal types in which "e'ry Grain stands bellisht ore with Love,/ Each Letter, Syllable, Word, Action." To exemplify the commandments and set aside the commands of the prefigurative "Letter" of Mosaic law, God "Commends" Christ to us "Writ all in Love from top to toe" through the incarnation. Subsequently, Christ's "Grave Stone in his blood/ He shed for Sinners" signifies the Son's sacrificial atonement and displays as well "Loves Emphasis most cleare" by which God forgives and opens heaven once again to "poore Sinners." Christ's fulfillment through His blood and death abrogates the functions of the Mosaic law to restrain and punish miscreants, and the New Testament spirit of love supersedes the Old Testament letter of the law. The commandment of faith graven within the heart of gospel believers supplants Yahweh's commandments to Moses engraved in tablets of stone. Within this poetically recreated history of man's sin and salvation, Taylor thus embeds his typological argument.

Though the meditation abounds with original metaphors and puns, many of Taylor's images derive from a curious digression in Sermon II.9, in which he defends the theory that Moses was the first man to write, specifically to transcribe both the "Morall law writ by God in tables of Stone. & so a type of Christ, who writes the Law by the finger of God upon the fleshly tables of the Heart Heb. 8" and the "Ordinances appertaining unto the Worship of the Tabernacle" also written "Down by the Pen of Gods Spirit" (*UTOT*, pp. 137-8, 139). Though it is a theological commonplace to discriminate between tables of stone and the human heart, it is Taylor's fascination with language that motivates his extended analysis. Taking a hint from Mather, who also attributes the invention of writing to Moses' time (*FT*, pp. 37–8), Taylor revels in the "Invention of Consonants, & Vowells that will give the Sound of Every Such Article, or Syllable" and "Then putting together the Syllables, & Articles of any word so made of Letters, to make the Word" (*UTOT*, p. 140). Even if embedded in Sermon II.9, the references to graven tables, the "Pen of Gods Spirit," and the art of writing clearly inspired Taylor's Meditation II.8 on the law and Christ's love, in which he restates the basic premises of covenant theology and typology. As we have seen, Taylor's Sermon II.9 conjoins Moses' dual functions as a type of the law and of Christ. But in the *Preparatory Meditations* he acknowledges these different roles by coupling Meditation II.8, touching upon the Mosaic dispensation of the law and commandments, with Meditation II.9 which proclaims from "Deut. 18.[15] The Lord thy God will raise up unto thee a Prophet – like unto mee."

Meditation II.8 also signals a major transition from Old Testament personal types before the law, according to Mather *"Adam, Enoch, Noah, Melchizedek, Abraham, Isaac Jacob,* and *Joseph,"* to those under the law, including Moses, Joshua, Samson, David, Solomon, and Jonah (*FT,* p. 64). Despite his disavowal of many figures who make up Mather's conglobations, nonetheless, Edward Taylor imitates the groupings by yoking Moses and Joshua as leaders of Israel, David and Solomon as famous kings, and Samson as a judge and deliverer. He emphasizes each patriarch's contribution to Israel's history as it foreshadows Christ's building of the gospel church:

> We have heard Christ typified as Erecting his Gospell Worship in a Visible Church State by Moses: In his Giving his Church a Settled possession of Gospell Worship, Conquoring the Gentile World; by Joshuah. In his Delivering his Church thus Settled, from their adversaries that Seek its molestation, & inthralldom, as begun, by Samson: & as Compleated, by David. & now I come to Consider him, as to the Prosperity Peace, & Glory that he brings to his Church, by Solomon. (*UTOT,* p. 237)

In the *Preparatory Meditations* he similarly clusters the types, beginning in II.9 by lauding Moses who did "Gods Israel from Egypt through/ The Red Sea lead, into the Wilderness" even unto the "border of God's Land" (II.9.25–6, 43). Meditation II.10 then links Moses with Joshua, who finally "brings the Church into the Promisd Coast" of Canaan (II.10.13). Samson, who delivers his people from thralldom, appears in Mediation II.11, typifying Christ, because he "Dies freely with great sinners" and "With arms stretcht greatly out,/ Slew more by death, than in his Life he slew" (II.11.27, 28–9). Praising David's virtues who "in all his gallantry now comes,/ Bringing to tende thy Shrine, his Royall Glory," Taylor further hails his "Rich Prowess, Prudence, Victories, Sweet Songs,/ and Piety to Pensill out thy Story" (II.12.13–14, 15–16). Thematically and typally linked with David, Solomon epitomizes kingliness as his pacifism and wisdom foreshadow Christ the King of Kings:

> Was He a bud of Davids stock? So thou.
>   Was he a King? Thou art a King of Kings.
> Was He a Make-peace King? Thy royall brow

Doth weare a Crown which peace Eternall brings.
Did He Excell in Wisdome? Thine doth flame.
And thou art Wisdom's Storehouse whence his came.

(II.13.13–18)

Although both the poem and sermon on Jonah are dated 1699, Taylor locates Meditation II.30 at the end of his figural series, but in the sermons he relocates it immediately after II.13 on Solomon composed in 1695.[11] Mather's alignment of Jonah with prophets and Thomas Taylor's analogies clearly gave Taylor warrant for including Jonah among the personal types, specifically as a figure of Christ's death and resurrection: "As Jonas was three days & three nights in the Whales belly: So shall the Son of Man be three dayes, & three nights in the Heart of the Earth" (*UTOT*, p. 260). Saltier than most meditations in its boisterous imagery, Meditation II.30 reads like a seafaring tale, despite the carefully wrought typal parallels. It is "A Mighty Whale nam'd Neptunes Dog" that "doth skip/ At such a Boon, Whose greedy gorge can't kill" though "its Chest/ Became the Prophets Coffin" (II.30.27–8, 29–30). Yet, much as Jonah "Prooves working Physick in the Fishes Crop" and is vomited "alive out on the Land," so "swallow'd down" by the grave, Christ is a "Working Physick full of Virtue which/ Doth purge Death's Constitution of its ill," before "out hee comes Cast up, rais'd up thereby" (II.30.32, 35, 55, 56–7, 60). Though Taylor frames his meditation on Jonah with a predictably methodical pairing of figural episodes with antitypal events, he also adopts a coarser, more colloquial vocabulary of the sea and sin-sickness. Drowning in the "fiery storm" that "tempestiously doth spend/ The Vessill," the seamen's "Spirits faile," and they "Bestir their stumps, and at wits end do weep," until Jonah (a type of Jesus who will rescue sinners) sacrifices himself to the whale's deadly and "greedy gorge" (II.30.45, 45–6, 46, 22, 28). But the whale "puking falls" and "vomits him alive out on the Land"; hence, Jonah becomes beneficiary and exemplar of God's "Sweet Sweet Providence" (II.30.34, 35, 41). In a startling, but convincing jointure of seafaring tall-tale with pharmaceutical prescription, Taylor likens the whale to the grave, Jonah to Christ, and both to a "rich Pill/ Of Working Physic" that "Doth purge Death's Constitution of its ill./ And womble-Crops her stomach where it sticks" (II.30.55–6, 57–8). "Celestiall Dews" replace torrential rains, Christ's "sweet sweet breath" of grace perfumes the sour stench of sin, and Christ (like Jonah) once sunk in darkness rises on "Dovy wings" (II.30.76, 69, 74). Blunt and blustery, Taylor seems virtually recast as a tale-spinning sailor, whose saga, however, carries a didactic moral to all latter-day "Jonahs," who must repentantly seek "rich Atonement in thy [Christ's] Death" (II.30.67). Meditation II.30 thus illustrates the potential, not always realized in Taylor's poems on personal types, to encapsulate sterile catalogs of figural parallels within an engagingly homespun narrative, one that yet repeats the timeless tale of sin and salvation.

Taylor does not specify a rationale for the positioning of Jonah, neither for the poem's location among God's miraculous deliverances as emblemized by Noah's ark (II.29) and Israel's liberation from Egypt (II.58), nor for the traditional position after Solomon, as the sermon now appears in *Upon the Types*. But it is perhaps appropriate that Christ's glorious arrival, prophesied in David and Solomon's reigns of peace and wisdom, should be followed by a more earthbound reminder of the price paid for that kingship and man's salvation. Jonah speaks to Christ's humanness, His suffering and death, which are the only vehicles by which man can be reconciled with God and the resurrection of souls instituted. We might recall that the Old Testament prophets, such as Isaiah, anticipated the King's advent in royal splendor, but the New Testament transforms that promise into an eternal kingship by which Christ rules only after His temporal sojourn, death, and resurrection. As well, in Jonah, the man who first seeks to flee from God's calling, then through his tribulations is redeemed, Taylor captures the humanness of every man's dilemma and the need for spiritual deliverance. "Here is my rich Atonement in thy Death,/ My Lord," he proclaims, for "thy Rising up o're bosst/ My Soule with Hope seeing acquittance in't/ That all my sins are kill'd, that did mee sinke" (II.30.67–8, 70–2). The universal and personal significances coalesce in the poem's final stanza, in which Taylor renders thanks for Christ whose "death hath deadned quite/ The Dreadfull Tempest" of God's wrath, thereby providing for each saint the possibility of grace and heavenly ascension: "Let thy Dovy wings/ Oreshadow me, and all my Faults benight/ And with Celestiall Dews my soule besprindge./ In Angells Quires I'le then my Michtams sing" (II.30.74–7). Ranging thus from instructive parallels in Meditation II.9 on Moses to this lustier saga of Jonah, the meditations on persons under the law reveal Taylor's penchant for figural clusters, but as well they suggest his skill at transmuting doctrine into poetic conceits, often ones (like those in II.8 and II.30) startlingly ingenious despite the strictures of Puritan typological methods.

Traditionally, typologists had lauded Solomon and David as kings, Elijah, Elisha, and Jonah as prophets, and they might add various examples of high priests as Mather does with Jehoshua and Aaron.[12] Thomas Taylor identified those men "separated and set apart from others," including high priests, kings, and Nazarites, "By which order the Lord would have the eminent sanctity of Jesus Christ to bee typified, as well as his sacrifice and kingly Office by Priests and Kings" (*CR*, p. 151). Samuel Mather repeatedly stressed the prophetic, priestly, and kingly foreshadowings by typical persons and carried his theme further into the typical ranks by setting aside three distinct orders of *"Prophets,"* the *"Priest hood,"* and the *"Kings of the House of David"* (*FT*, pp. 123, 124). Invoking the oft-repeated metaphor of starlight versus sunshine, Mather also concludes his survey of personal types by exhorting readers to

> *See the Glory of the Antitype in whom all these meet in one;* all the *individual personal Types* before-mentioned, and all these *religious Orders* now opened. He is the *true Israel,* and the *First-born,* he is *the true Nazarite;* he is *our Prophet, Priest and King.* They were but *Stars* that shone in the Night, he is *the Sun of Righteousness.* (*FT*, p. 126)

He calls upon them to "bear your Testimony to him," because "ye are the *Lord's Witnesses and Prophets"*; to "offer the Sacrifices of Praise and Thanksgiving," for "Ye are also *Priests unto God"*; and "to rule over your own Lusts," for "remember ye are *Kings"* (*FT*, p. 126). Mather's enthusiasm culminates in this exhortation, encouraging his parishioners to become living, evangelical prophets and priests and kings in grace.

With Meditation II.14 on "Prophets, Priests, and Kings," Edward Taylor not only climaxes his study of individual types, he also introduces the typical ranks of men into his figural series.[13] This sermon and meditation were not, however, the poet's first attempt to grasp the mysteries of these figural orders. A decade earlier in 1685 in the first series of *Preparatory Meditations,* for which no sermons remain extant, Taylor celebrated Christ's antitypal supremacy as "A Great High Priest" (I.14/15), "A Greate Prophet" (I.16), and "King of Kings" (I.17). Evoking repeated images of the priest's garments, for instance, Taylor pleads, "Be thou my High Priest, Lord; and let my name/ Ly in some Grave dug in these Pearly rocks/ Upon thy Ephods Shoulder piece," for "Thou'lt then me beare before thy Fathers Throne" (I.14/15.49-51, 53). He yearns for the "Grace then Conceald in God himselfe" which now "nestles all its beams buncht in thy Soule/ My Lord, that sparkle in Prophetick Lines" to outfit himself for the "Celestiall Day" (I.16.13, 15–16, 24). Piling together the words "king," "crown," and "glory," he seeks to have his name inscribed in the "Record" of saints: "Thou art my king: let me not be thy Shame./ Thy Law my Rule: my Life thy Life in Mee./ Thy Grace my Badge: my Glory bright thy Name" (I.17.41, 37–9). Rich with the rapid flashes of jewel-bedecked robes, bright "Golden Beams" of "heavenly Light," and "Sparkling Crowns" of kingly righteousness and grace, these poems reveal Taylor as a poet willingly abandoned to imagistic exuberance, a measure of his spiritual ecstasy as he contemplates the wealth of Christ's fulfillment. These meditations also point to Taylor's early enthusiasm for typology, perhaps stimulated by the 1685 reissue of Samuel Mather's *The Figures or Types.* Taylor's poetic prayers read like antiphonal responses to Mather's exhortations, reminding saints to partake of Christ's functions as prophet, priest, and King. But his humility prevents him from claiming equal stature, for a mere gem from Christ's breast plate, a glance from the "Lightning Eye," a touch of the King's "flaming Swords" will suffice to bring Taylor into the heavenly realm.

In the first series Taylor also prefaces his meditations with a collective contemplation, based on Colossians 2:3, entitled "All the Treasures of Wisdom" (I.13). And it is not surprising that composing Meditation II.14 some ten years later on a similar topic Taylor reverts to this biblical passage as his text. As if inspired by the uses of his own sermon, Taylor exalts the enlightening wisdom and curative power of Christ which "these Pointers type":

> Shall not that Wisdom horded up in thee
>   (One key whereof is Sacerdotall Types)
> Provide a Cure for all this griefe in mee
>   And in the Court of Justice save from Stripes,
>   And purge away all Filth and Guilt, and bring
>   A Cure to my Consumption as a King?
>
> Shall not that Wisdom horded in thee (which
>   Prophetick Types enucleate) forth shine
> With Light enough a Saving Light to fix
>   On my Poore Taper? And a Flame Divine?
>   Making my Soule thy Candle and its Flame
>   Thy Light to guide mee, till I Glory gain?
>
> Shall not that Wisdom horded in thee up
>   (Which Kingly Types do shine upon in thee)
> Mee with its Chrystall Cupping Glasses cup
>   And draine ill Humours wholy out of mee?
>   Ore come my Sin? And mee adorn with Grace
>   And fit me for thy Service, and thy Face?
>
> How do these Pointers type thee out most right
>   As Graces Officine of Wisdom pure
> The fingers Salves and Medicines so right
>   That never faile, when usd, to worke a Cure?
>   Oh! that it would my Wasted lungs recrute.
>   And make my feeble Spirits upward shute.
>
> How Glorious art thou, Lord? Cloathd with the Glory
>   Of Prophets, Priests, and Kings? Nay all Types come
> To lay their Glory on thee. (Brightsome Story).
>   Their Rayes attend thee, as Sun Beams the Sun.
>   And shall my Ulcer'd Soule have such reliefe?
>   Such glorious Cure? Lord strengthen my beliefe.
>   (II.14.7–36)

Edward Taylor applies to himself these typal illuminations from the prophets, priests, and kings by accumulating poetic images of disease and cure. Suffering "Consumption" which leaves him a "Shell" with "Wasted lungs" and "Halfe Dead: and rotten at the Coare," he deplores his susceptibility to the sensuality of "Sent and Smell" and immersion thereby in "Guilt and Filth" (II.14.12, 5, 2, 1, 6). Beset with fleshly ills, Taylor seeks the master's health-restoring ordinances. He prays for the "Saving Light to fix" and "to guide mee, till I Glory gain"; he yearns for "Grace" which will fit him "for thy Service, and thy Face"; and he requests the medicinal salve from "Graces Officine of Wisdom pure" to make his "feeble Spirits upward shute." Maintaining his hope for an apocalyptic reunion with Christ, he promises to cultivate his earthly role as poetic prophet and priest who tunes "thy Praise with holy Breath" (II.14.48). As Mather had directed, Taylor aspires to "reign with him [Christ] as *Kings in Grace here,*" so that he "shall reign with him *in Glory for ever*" (*FT*, p. 126). Taylor creates his unifying theme from Colossians 2:3 which focuses on Christ's antitypal virtues, "In whom are hid all the Treasures of Wisdom, and Knowledge"; but he allies himself with previous typologists in pursuing the personal benefits of the prophetic, priestly, and kingly types. Enlightened by these Old Testament types, which act as keys, lights, and enucleations of Christ, the sinner agonizes more acutely over his captivity to spiritual diseases and fleshly temptations. Yet, the "Ulcer'd Soule" extracts hope from contemplating the types, because they also prefigure the Savior's restorative wisdom, grace, and glory.

Meditation II.14 concludes Taylor's poetic overview of individual types before and under the law, as he passionately declares, "How Glorious art thou, Lord? Cloathd with the Glory/ Of Prophets, Priests, and Kings? Nay all Types" which "come/ To lay their Glory on thee" (II.14.31–3). He adopts the recurrent biblical metaphor of the "Sun of Righteousness" to exalt these types which tell a "Brightsome Story" of salvation, since all figures, whether persons or ranks, "Their Rayes attend thee, as Sun Beams the Sun" (II.14.33–4). Taylor returns to the triumvirate and the same metaphors six to eight years later in the *Christographia* sermons and poems. Heralding Christ's "Propheticall" and "Kingly" offices in Sermon II, he resurrects the images of light: "Other Prophets are, as Candles, that received all their light at his flame, but their Wicks could hold but a little of his light. . . . Not so much, as a Candle amounts to, compared with the Sun. This Sun of righteousness makes daylight where ever he Shines" (*CHR*, p. 59). Invoking the figure of Moses, Sermon IV lauds Christ, Who contains "all Propheticall Wisdom in him as a Prophet. He was foretold to arise as a Prophet by Moses Deut. 18. 15. 18, and hence had all Propheticall Light in him. . . . and so the Wisdom of the Law is treasured up in him. And so the Accomplishment of all Prophesies lies in him" (*CHR*, p. 123). In the accompanying Meditation II.45 (the third instance in which Taylor adopts Col. 2:3 to proclaim "all the

Treasures of Wisdom"), he captures the figural dimness of prophets in contrast to Christ's antitypal brilliance of both intellect and spirituality by accumulating images of jewels and light: a "Sparkling Treasury," "richer than Corinthian Amber tills/ And Shelves of Emralds," "Like to a Sparkling Carbuncle up Caskt/ Within a Globe of Chrystall glass most cleare," or "as the Sun within its Azure bowre/ That guilds its Chrystall Walls with golden rayes," so also Christ's wisdom flames out upon mankind (II.45.13, 20–1, 25–6, 31–2). In these fourteen *Christographia* sermons as in his earlier figural sermons and meditations Taylor prominently proclaims Christ's kingly and priestly offices, and in Sermon XII a flowery array of images adorns a synopsis of the typological theme:

> Christ as to his Priesthood riseth up as the Pillar of Frankincense in a perfuming vapour, that Quencheth the fiery beams of Gods Wrath, and doth Sweetly perfume and delight the minde of God pacifying him, and purchasing all things for his people. As to his Propheticall Office, he is as a Golden Window, thro' which there shines forth upon us the glorious Sunshine of the Holy Will of God, and thro' which we may looke upon what lies in the very heart of God so far as is meet to be beheld. And as to his Kingly Office, he is a Golden Wall of Burning Fire rounde about them. Upon whose Turrits Stand the Golden head of Celestiall influences Conveighing, as through its Royall Gates, all the Gifts, and Graces of the Spirit, and Spirituall and Gracious Benefits to his people, and by whose Strength he gives Secure defence against all, and all Sorts of Enemies. (*CHR*, p. 367)

By adding his personal elaborations of images to the prosaic accounts of his predecessors, Taylor in Meditations I.13–17, Sermon and Meditation II.14, and the *Christographia* sermons compellingly testifies to the potency of these typical ranks and their centrality for delineating Christ's mission on earth.

But Taylor also makes prophets, priests, and kings the thematic bridge between individuals and the typical ranks in *Upon the Types* and the meditations. In Sermon II.14 he announces that "leaving the Personall Types, [I] do come to Typicall Ranks or Orders of men," which he then pursues in Sermon II.15 on Nazarites and Sermon II.16 on the house of Jacob (*UTOT*, p. 279). Among earlier exegetes, Thomas Taylor had announced his criteria for holy orders as those "men, sanctified and specially seperated to the Lord" and forged four classifications out of seemingly disparate groups: "the first-borne" by birth, "Priests" by office, the "Nazarites" by vow, and by ceremony those "cleane persons, legally cleansed" (*CR*, p. 92). Acknowledging the *"mixt* Nature" of "some of these Orders," Mather creates a variant sixfold categorization which includes the "whole Nation and People of *Israel*," "First-born," *"Nazarites,"* "Prophets,"

"Priests," and "Kings" (*FT*, pp. 125, 118). Although Mather applauds the continuing moral efficacy of some ranks, he insists upon Christ's fulfillment and abrogation of any strictly ceremonial observances, particularly those "Religious Orders" of the *"Nazariteship, and the Priesthood"* (*FT*, p. 126). Angered by Catholic and Anglican appropriations of Old Testament rituals to justify segregated orders discrete from the fellowship of all believers, Mather locates unclean persons and the priesthood within an extended consideration of the ceremonial law. Edward Taylor also postulates six religious orders – the firstborn (II.2), prophets, priests, and kings (II.14), the Nazarites (II.15), and the house of Jacob (II.16). Like Mather he excludes ceremonial uncleanness (II.26–27) and the Aaronic priesthood (II.23) from these religious orders, incorporating both within his examination of Old Testament legal rites. But Taylor also superimposes his own framework by dividing the "Typicall Ranks" first into those "Naturall" as the "First Born of Which we have already had an account" and the "Israelitish Nation" which he briefly explicates in II.14, then develops fully in Sermon II.16 as "both a Type of Christ, & of the Church of Christ under the Gospell" (*UTOT*, p. 279). The second kind, "typicall Ranks of an Instituted nature" are such either by "Office" or "Vow" (terms borrowed from *Christ Revealed*) by which he distinguishes the prophets, priests, and kings (II.14) from the Nazarites (II.15) respectively (*UTOT*, p. 280).

In much the same way that Taylor adopts prophets, priests, and kings to create a bridge between individual types and the ranks, so also he later redesigns the Israelite nation into a suitable transition to the ceremonial law, for the house of Jacob foreshadows Christ's kingdom to come under the gospel. Consequently, he emphasizes Christ's royal lineage, inherited through Israel:

> Thou art, my Lord, the King of Glory bright.
>   A glory't is unto the Angells flame
> To be thy Harauld publishing thy Light
>   Unto the Sons of Men: and thy rich Name.
>   They are thy Subjects. Yea thy realm is faire.
>   Ore Jacobs House thou reignest: they declare.
>
> Their brightest glory lies in thee their king.
>   My Glory is that thou my king maist bee.
> That I may be thy Subject thee to sing
>   And thou may'st have thy kingdoms reign in mee.
>   (II.16.1–10)

From Luke's account of the annunciation, Taylor evolves a reading consistent with his previous themes in the sermons and meditations on personal types. Descended from the ancient house of Jacob (Israel), Christ assumes his kingship – to reign not literally on earth but spiritually enthroned in believers' hearts. Just as Taylor had praised the Son's glorious kingship adumbrated by Old Testament individuals (David, Solomon) and by ranks in Meditation II.14, he again recalls the messianic promise and its substantial accomplishment through Christ's incarnation. Christ is predestined to redeem men, indeed Taylor himself, from "Sins mutiny," "tawny Pride, and Gall," and "base Hypocrisy" which infect the "rotten heart" (II.16.17, 23, 30). Through Christ's sacrifice, alienated sinners become grafted into "thy Olive tree/ The house of Jacob," a spiritual implantation which enables a thorny human "Bramble bush" to bear instead "sweet Roses then for thee" (II.16.37–8, 41, 42). Taylor often assimilates material from the Bible and preceding expositions, as in his repeated use of Mather's configurations, details, and themes, but he also far surpasses his teachers with innovative realignments of the figural categories and imagistic recreations of traditional themes.

Originality was not a quality highly valued by Puritan theologians, since the mandate to read the Bible literally led to standardly acceptable glosses. Although expositors might vary in style and manner of presentation, nonetheless, the basic scriptural matter and Puritan exegetical approach to figural persons and ranks remained much the same. Thomas Taylor, Samuel Mather, and Edward Taylor held steady to the Christological focus or, as Mather stated the criterion, "an aptness to restrain all the Types to the *Person* of Christ," although with an Abraham or Moses they would countenance the prefiguring of a broader "Gospel Truth or Mystery" (*FT,* p. 81). For most personal figures, the typological accounts are strikingly congruous, even though each exegete builds upon preceding versions by adding biblical details, reorganizing categories, adopting a new framework, or as in Edward Taylor's case creating evocative images and metaphors for his meditations. For example, Thomas Taylor arranges his explication of "Sampson *a type of Christ"* according to four traditional groupings, (1) by "person and condition," (2) "in three especiall actions," (3) in "passion and suffering," and (4) in "victory and fortitude" (*CR,* pp. 55, 56, 57). Mather, who frequently adapts Taylor's renderings, likewise specifies Samson's traits according to the "Circumstances of his Birth," "in some special Actions of his Life," "in his Strength and Victories over his Enemies," and "in the Victoriousness of his Sufferings" (*FT,* p. 104). Mather reorders the last two aspects, heightens the emotional affect of Samson's achievements, and sets the active life against the victorious sufferings of death. Somewhat unusually, he condenses rather than expands Taylor's details, although he adds a special note on Samson's name, which "imports שמשון *Soliculus* or *Solparvus"* or "little Sun" to announce the "dawnings of the Day," as later Christ does spiritually for Jews "under the yoke of the *Romans"* (*FT,* p. 104). For the myriad details of Samson's life, both exegetes emphasize his miraculous birth foretold by an angel and his being made a Nazarite from the womb; Samson's marriage with a Philistine and putting forth his mind in parables and riddles; his victorious slaying of a thousand men with the jawbone of an ass; and finally the mockery of a trial, during which sold for money Samson is led away bound and blinded to a feast, yet reigns victorious by slaying more enemies in his death than in his life. Both treatises pair Samson's qualities with Christ's, or as Mather proclaims in one proof, "they were both *Nazarites* from the Womb. *Sampson* by the Law of *Nazarites, Numb.* 6. 2. *Christ* by special *Sanctity* fulfilling that Type" (*FT,* p. 104). Mather's account of Samson is among the briefest, most strikingly homogeneous of all such borrowings from *Christ Revealed,* and it illustrates how scriptural readings would pass from exegete to exegete, creating thereby a repertoire of conventional Puritan interpretations.

Edward Taylor adds his own flourishes when he redacts these parallels in Sermon and Meditation II.11. He responds first with a long exordium on objections against Samson as a type, because of his wickedness in "marrying with a Canaanite" and "his Slaughtering of the Philistins," in which he defends all such actions as providentially guided (*UTOT,* pp. 196, 197). He then positively establishes the ways "Wherein was Samson a Type of Christ," reviewing his birth (before and after), person (public and private), conquering actions which display wisdom, fortitude, and strength, and sufferings both in life and death (*UTOT,* p. 200). Although he appropriates Mather's order and fascination with the "Sun" (available in glosses as well), the sermon and poem reflect Taylor's extensive reliance upon both sources and the Bible (Judges 13–16), a procedure that dominates his meditations on the most popular types, such as Joseph, Moses, Joshua, Solomon, and the Nazarites. Taylor falls prey to a prosaic didacticism because he closely imitates the sources and paraphrases his own sermon, but he succeeds imagistically by lightening the exegesis with a few imaginative *divertissements:*

> Eternall Love burnisht in Glory thick,
>   Doth butt, and Center in thee, Lord, my joy.
> Thou portrai'd art in Colours bright, that stick
>   Their Glory on the Choicest Saints, Whereby
>   They are thy Pictures made. Samson Exceld
>   Herein thy Type, as he thy foes once queld.
>
> An Angell tells his mother of his birth.
>   An Angell telleth thine of thine. Ye two
> Both Males that ope the Womb in Wedlock Kerfe
>   Both Nazarited from the Womb up grew.
>   He after pitchy night a Sunshine grows
>   And thou the Sun of Righteousness up rose.

His Love did Court a Gentile spouse, and thine
    Espous'd a Gentile to bebride thyselfe.
His Gentile Bride apostatizd betime.
    Apostasy in thine grew full of Wealth.
    He sindgd the Authours of't with Foxes tails.
    And foxy men by thee on thine prevaile.

The Fret now rose. Thousands upon him poure.
    And asses Jaw his javling is, whereby
He slew a Thousand, heap by heap that hour.
    Thou by weake means makest many thousands fly.
    Thou ribbon like wast platted in his Locks
    And hence he thus his Enemies did box.

He's by his Friend betray'd, for money sold,
    Took, bound, blindfolded, made a May game Flout
Dies freely with great sinners, when they hold
    A Sacred Feast. With arms stretcht greatly out,
    Slew more by Death, than in his Life he slew.
    And all such things, my Lord, in thee are true.

Samson at Gaza went to bed to sleep.
    The Gazites watch him and the Soldiers thee.
He Champion stout, at midnight rose full deep.
    Took Gaza's Gate on's back away went hee.
    Thou rose didst from thy Grave and also tookst
    Deaths Doore away throwing it off o'th'hooks.
                    (II.11.1–36)

Taylor embellishes Mather's etymological discussion of Samson's name
with his own vision of Christ who "after pitchy night a Sunshine grows"
and as "the Sun of Righteousness up rose." In Sermon II.11 the germs
for these poetic images (and congruities with Mather) appear more clearly:
"Samson שִׁמְשׁוֹן Sol. or as Some Soliculus, a little Sun. He rose as a
Shining Sun Scattering abroad his lightsom beams in the morning after
a darksom night of affliction" (*UTOT,* p. 201). Drawing upon this basic
metaphor, Taylor also praises the illuminating insights into Christ derived
from types through which "Thou portrai'd art in Colours bright," since
"all the shine that Samson wore is thine" (II.11.3, 37). The image resurfaces three times in Taylor's final stanza (as it does in the homiletic uses),
in which he appeals to the "Lord, a Rising Sun,/ Of Righteousness" to
spout forth grace that he might be "set . . . in thy Sunshine" (II.11.49–
50, 53).

In Meditation II.11 Taylor digresses less into imagistic ornamentation,
preferring to remodel his sources and sermon only enough to coordinate
typal analogies with the demands of a six-line stanza and usual *a b a b c c*
rhyme. Constrained by the typological formulas, though momentarily
sparked into poetic variations by a fleeting image, Meditation II.11 epit-

omizes the unevenness of Edward Taylor's poetic achievement. Unwilling or unable to free himself from strict correlations, he falls into dulling regularity with line-by-line parallels, accentuated by comparative phrases and pronouns, such as "both," "and thou," "he and thou," "his and thine." Yet, despite this doctrinaire figuralism which smacks of the sermon, the lingering effect remains reverential. Judged as poetry, Meditation II.11 collapses beneath a mechanical didacticism, which reveals too much the disciplined exegete engaged in homiletic preparation, too little the religious visionary.[14] But as a meditation designed to portray Samson as a type of Christ and by illuminating the petitioner's understanding to stir his heart to prayer and imitation, the poem succeeds, though hardly with the provocative ecstasies of other, more original meditations.

The imagery makes Taylor's poetic version more colorful, but the format offers compelling evidence of the continuity of Puritan exegetical traditions and of the Christological import of Samson. In many things Samson's life prefigures Christ's, although the Son's salvation of man from sin's curse rather than Israel from the Philistines is a far superior endeavor. From the similarities in names to the victorious triumphs over enemies, Samson's historical exploits foreshadow Christ's more spiritual mission. Samson's heroics at Gaza pale before Christ's sacrifice, when in His battle for man's soul He takes "Deaths Doore away." Samson's release of Israel from Philistine bondage is a concrete event; but for all gospel saints liberation from eternal damnation constitutes a far more important spiritual victory for the Savior. Although Samson achieves renown in his own right, New Testament believers must rely on Christ's mediation, because man's strength alone has no supernatural dimension, no capacity to defeat the invisible foes and temptations of sin and Satan. In all his sermons and poems on personal types, Taylor makes clear the utter dependency of gospel saints upon the "Sun of Righteousness." Consequently, the dynamic of these meditations is not merely comparative, a two-step process which ends with Christ's fulfillment of the typical person or rank – neatly explicated, neatly abrogated. For as he contemplates these eminent figures, Taylor seeks in them models for his own deportment under the evangelical dispensation; but, even more, he acknowledges the sole agency of his redemption and *exemplum exemplorum,* Christ the antitype.

Though in strictest Puritan tradition Christ fulfills all prophecies and persons, from the ancient fathers to contemporary Protestants, the adopting of scriptural types as *exempla fidei* had become commonplace. An outgrowth of man's need to discover models for spiritual struggles and triumphs, the moral efficacy of typical persons appears trenchantly in the uses of Thomas Taylor's and Samuel Mather's sermons. Concluding his study of Samson, Taylor calls readers to emulate the type and Christ: "In both, learne to prepare for death approaching, by faithfull and fervent prayer. So did both these *Sampsons*. And the issue will bee comfortable as theirs" (*CR*, p. 62). Mather urges parishioners to take "Comfort and Support, *as to all the Conflicts and Enemies that God is pleased to exercise his People with,* whether particular Saints, or whole Churches," for *"Samson, David, Solomon* had Enemies; Christ had so"; yet, "these Conflicts will end in peace, and quiet Establishment," since *"Christ's* peace is a Peace after and out of trouble, by War and Victory over Sin and spiritual Enemies" (*FT,* p. 108). In accord with Puritan exegetical principles, neither Taylor nor Mather omits Christ from the figural schema, even while they recommend Samson's experience for the saint's imitation. Heeding these expositors, Edward Taylor in his Sermon II.11 also exhorts listeners to take comfort from Samson's and Christ's exemplary defiance of enemies and death in hope of ultimate spiritual triumph: "If Christ be your Samson, he hath delivered you from your Spirituall Enemies, From Sin, & Death. & from all the Powers of the Enemie. Hence your Love must needs be great, Syncere, & Stronge to him" (*UTOT,* p. 213). For Taylor and his colleagues, homiletic exegesis provided the foundation upon which to uplift parishioners to a further devotional contemplation of how to apply types and Christ to their lives. Primarily in the sermon uses these ministers glided over a thin line which differentiated exegesis from moral and devotional applications, a line clearly drawn between Taylor's sermons *Upon the Types of the Old Testament* and his *Preparatory Meditations.* Within the meditative tradition defined by Louis Martz, the sermons were to educate the understanding, so that in private diaries, prayers, or poems the meditator might then exercise his soul's affections and will to move closer to God.[15]

Taking his public instructions to heart in Meditation II.11, Edward Taylor abstracts from the rational analysis of Samson directives for his own spiritual life.[16] His private process of meditation usually begins with moaning evocations of human frailty, then applies the understanding to decipher typal truths, and ends with fervent prayers for divine guidance and/or ecstasies of renewed dedication. Delaying his grievances until after the typal correlations in Meditation II.11, Taylor only compounds his self-disgust by implicitly measuring his polluted heart against Samson's courageous one:

> But woe is me! my heart doth run out to
>   Poor bits of Clay: or dirty Gayes embrace.
> Doth leave thy Lovely Selfe for loveless show:
>   For lumps of Lust, nay sorrow and disgrace.
>   Alas, poore Soule! a Pardon, Lord, I crave.
>   I have dishonourd thee and all I have.
>   (II.11.43–8)

Steeped in vanity, lust, and disgrace, Taylor's "poore Soule" seems insufficient and self-loving by contrast with Samson's valiant self-abnegation at the "Sacred Feast" and Christ's on the cross. But this woeful humiliation makes all the clearer Taylor's personal need for divine grace, but more so for the patriarch's model and the Son's exemplary sacrifice and defiance of all foes:

> Thus all the shine that Samson wore is thine,
>   Thine in the Type. Oh. Glorious One, Rich glee.
> Gods Love hath made thee thus. Hence thy bright shine
>   Commands our Love to bow thereto the Knee.
>   Thy Glory chargeth us in Sacrifice
>   To make our Hearts and Love to thee to rise.
>
> . . . .
>
> Be thou my Samson, Lord, a Rising Sun,
>   Of Righteousness unto my Soule, I pray.
> Conquour my Foes. Let Graces Spouts all run
>   Upon my Soule O're which thy sunshine lay.
>   And set me in thy Sunshine, make each flower
>   Of Grace in me thy Praise perfum'd out poure.
>   (II.11.37–42, 49–54)

Taylor calls upon the Old Testament hero and Christ jointly as his personal *exempla fidei,* seeking in them spiritual guidance along the path to salvation. Recall, however, that before turning to soul-wrenching appeals, Taylor has meticulously extended parallels between a Samson, or Joseph, or Moses and Christ the antitype in both his sermons and meditations. What among medieval expositors is termed the tropological reading of figures becomes, therefore, ancillary, a moral abstraction or extension which follows upon literal and spiritual analogies with the Savior.[17] Commanded by the example of Samson's deeds, but inspired more by the perfect fulfillment in Christ's life, Taylor's "poore Soule" receives the charge to "bow thereto the Knee" in reverence and through imitative self-denial to "make our Hearts and Love to thee to rise." Having absorbed the figural truths, henceforth, Taylor as the faithful, aspiring saint must pattern his life on these moral precepts. He draws comfort and strength from Samson's triumphs, but the true power for victory over his "Clay" and "Lust" derives from Christ's spouting grace and "sunshine," beneath which he may "flower."

As with Samson, so also with other personal types, Taylor pleads, "That blazing Star in Joshua's but a Beam/ Of thy Bright Sun, my Lord, fix such in mee" (II.10.49–50), or more pointedly,

> Pare off, my Lord, from mee I pray, my pelfe.
> Make mee thy Nazarite by imitation

> Not of the Ceremony, but thy selfe,
>   In Holiness of Heart, and Conversation.
>   Then I shall weare thy Nazarite like a Crown
>   In Glory bright with Songs of thy Renown.
>   (II.15.37–42)

This example makes clear Taylor's distinctions with respect to two important tenets of devotional typology. First, the Nazarite (Num. 6:1–21) foreshadows Christ, as the previous six stanzas of Meditation II.15 detail. Even though shadowy, the Nazarite points toward Christ's asceticism, His fortitude, and His passionate commitment (vow) to the covenant of redemption made with God. By denying continuing efficacy to Nazarite ceremonies, Taylor acknowledges Christ's superior spiritual embodiments, since the "letter of the Law of Nazarites/ Concerns thee not," rather "The Spirit oft is meet/ For thee alone" (II.15.19–20, 20–1). Never threatened by defilement from the "Dead" as the Nazarites of old, Christ himself represents the very essence of life, since "Thy Thoughts, Words, Works are lively, frim, do still/ Out Spirituall Life" (II.15.31, 35–6). Hence, the Christological emphasis of Puritan exegesis remains foremost throughout this meditation, with the constant reminders that Christ is "A Nazarite indeed. Not such another," that His is the "Head that wares a Nazaritick Crown/ Of Holiness" and was "Dide in the Blood" of His crucifixion (II.15.1, 25–6, 27). By accentuating Christ's antipal supremacy and repeatedly using the term "Nazarite" as an epithet for Jesus, Taylor remains within bounds of conservative exegetical interpretation. Although imitation of Nazarene asceticism might be desirable in itself, Taylor affirms that a gospel commitment to inward sanctity is infinitely preferable, since it conforms with Christ's newer "Nazarite-like" instructions.

Second, the word "imitation" evidences Taylor's concept of modeling one's life on Christ and through him on the Nazarite code, spiritually reinterpreted for the gospel saint. He makes the *imitatio Christi* primary, since man must pattern his life after Christ's New Testament precepts for the spirit rather than the Old Testament letter of the law. In the *Christographia* Taylor exhorts:

> If therefore we attende not this Pattern and Example, we dishonour him. We were made, and formed with an Imitating Principle in our Nature, which cannot be Suffocated, or Stifled, but will act in Imitating Some Example; God to prevent us from taking wrong Patterns to follow, hath presented us with a perfect Pattern of right practice in our own nature in Christ, which is most Examplary, being a most Exact Coppy, written by the Deity of the Son of God, with the Pen of the Humanity, on the milk white sheet of an Holy Life. Hence our Imitation of him is His due, and our Duty. (*CHR*, p. 34)

Taylor thus employs a system best termed "Christomimetic," because he seeks to make biblical figures relevant in spiritual, not ceremonial or legalistic, ways to his experiences as a seventeenth-century Puritan saint. He nowhere in the *Preparatory Meditations* falls prey to the fallacy of a recapitulative typology whereby some New England historians declare their leaders as veritable antitypes of Moses, Joshua, or Nehemiah and ignore or merely imply Christ's centrality in the figural scheme.[18] Imitation does not mean (to Edward Taylor) adopting a Moses or Joshua to exalt contemporary men; rather, imitation means modeling one's spiritual life on those moral qualities and spiritual deeds adumbrated by Old Testament types, but fulfilled in all truth and light by Jesus himself. Taylor may plead to partake of Solomon's wisdom or Samson's courage or a Nazarite's asceticism, only because such qualities are shadowy versions, human manifestations, of Christ's infinite, less accessible, less visible attributes. Taylor does not, however, identify with the kingliness of Solomon, perceiving that role as reserved for Christ alone. Not so circumscribed by historical period, geographical locale, or the leadership of cultural heroes, Taylor chooses to align himself within a totally spiritual, inward realm of experience. Specifics of history, landscape, or culture have little relevance to the spiritual progress of individual souls, since all men are engaged in fundamentally the same journey through this earthly wilderness to the New Canaan of heaven. When Taylor chooses personal types as guides to the inner way of faith, as paradigms for the moral life, as humans in God's service, he grants them a due, but a more modest role than the historians do. Less concerned with inspiring parishioners with august visions of their cultural destiny, Taylor preaches *Upon the Types of the Old Testament* as instructions in the spiritual destiny of each saint, as do Thomas Taylor and Samuel Mather. Likewise, the meditations reflect his intimate psychic needs for spiritual exempla in the Old Testament figures, but more so for a pattern from Christ who perfectly fulfills and supersedes all types. Engaged doubly in a process of *imitatio figura* and Christomimesis, Taylor applies the personal types to the private soul, not to the public arena of history.

Such a distinction between the historical and spiritual plots of salvation may well account for discrepancies between New England historians and stricter typological expositors. Transitions to a new physical territory, an abandonment of homes for the sake of religious liberty are visible tasks – those that require inward courage, but that manifest themselves in journeys, settlements, and buildings. In praising the leaders of such a mission, he can more easily associate the heroism of an Old Testament type with the New England errand. Human and fallible, these types provide models in historical ways, spurring men to accomplishments within reach of mortal beings. But to identify with the feats of Christ is to set up a perfect ideal – to call forth a vision of heroism beyond the scope of human achievement. In histories and elegies, the elimination of Christ from the typological equation allows the contemporary Christian to emulate the *exemplum fidei* without feeling self-defeated by the *exemplum exemplorum* of Christ Himself. Even Edward Taylor in the previously noted "Elegie upon the Death of . . . Mr. Sims," calls upon the type of Samson to portray the thinning ranks of stalwart defenders of New Israel against Philistine assaults by Roman or episcopal opponents or by second generation apostates:

> [Ou]r Nazarites grow thin; which always stoode
> [As] Objects hatefull to Philistick brude.
> [W]ho could not stroy them: for like Sampson they
> [Bor]e on their backs proud Gaza's Gates away,
> [Their s]trength was such . . .
> [Philis]tick Gates thus blown up by the aire
> [Are] bussles in a Nazarits bush of haire!
> [Conquer]'d Philistia, (Revenge is Sweet)
> [To] give it vent, in Convocation meet
>
> . . . .
>
> Altho' the Doors be firm, & would abide
> Rift off the bars, & down the boards will Slide
> When Posts do faile, the Pales & Rales down fall
>
> . . . .
>
> Hereby our Israels glory waxeth thin;
> Compared now to what it once hath bin.
>
> . . . .
>
> He did What God said do, &'s gone away
> His day thus ore, to meet his Masters pay.
> Like to a Shock of Wheate thats fully ripe,
> God inned hath this aged Nazarite.[19]

Modeled upon Samson's triumphs at Gaza, Taylor's images are conflated to emblemize both the Philistine bondage of English Anglicanism which staunch Puritan "Nazarites" such as Zecharia Symmes opposed, and the crumbling within New England–Israel when the posts and bars fail to uphold the temple. The loss of this "aged Nazarite" leaves the ministerial ranks thinner and weaker just when new attacks from disgruntled colonists most require a Samson-like strength, a Nazarite-like dedication to God's work in New England. How different this elegy is from the meditation on Samson, because the recapitulative use of typology entirely omits the figure of Christ; indeed, this poem invokes God as the omnipotent "Master," but draws no typological analogies with the spiritual strength from Christ upon which New England saints should rely in their time of trouble.

Within the realm of devotional typology, the landscape is neither literal nor historical, for it is the soul and salvation that become primary. In this schema Christ becomes paramount – not merely for His human perfections, but for the divine accomplishments that excel the human. Not only the Christocentric focus of the *Preparatory Meditations,* but also the recurring pleadings which include both type and antitype testify to Taylor's greater concern with spiritual than with secular history. The differing emphasis appears if we juxtapose Benjamin Woodbridge's elegy on John Cotton with Taylor's Meditation II.10. Woodbridge writes from the perspective of temporal history, equating Cotton with Moses and Norton with Joshua:

> But Let his Mourning Flock be Comforted,
>   Though *Moses* be, yet *Joshua* is not Dead:
> I mean Renowned *Norton;* worthy he,
>   Successor to our *Moses,* is to be.
> O Happy *Israel* in *America,*
>   In such a *Moses,* such a *Joshua.*[20]

Edward Taylor portrays this patriarchal succession within the framework of scriptural history, as a prefiguration of gospel fulfillments in Christ – antitype to both Moses and Joshua:

> Moses farewell. I with a mournfull teare.
>   Will wash thy Marble Vault, and leave thy Shine
> To follow Josuah to Jordan where
>   He weares a Type, of Jesus Christ, divine.
> Did by the Priests bearing the Arke off Cut
>   Her Stream, that Isr'el through it drieshod foot.
>   (II.10.1–6)

Christ's fulfillment within the *Heilsgeschichte* becomes critical because it institutes a new gospel dispensation and ultimately the millennium. Although the "Mourning Flock" in New England may find momentary comfort in the elegiac tear shed by Woodbridge and the promise of continued leadership for *"Israel* in *America,"* that relief bears little weight compared to the solace of Christ, who as divine successor to both Moses and Joshua promises eternal joy within the heavenly New Canaan. As the antitype, only Christ transcends all types. Only Christ as Son/Sun to His Father can perfect the prophetic role, the priestly sacrifices that redeem from sin, and the kingly functions in earth and heaven.

Edward Taylor does not look to New England–Israel for his heroic leader, either as pastor or as petitioner. Not journeyer to the New Canaan, as in Bradford's *Of Plymouth Plantation* (written 1630, 1645–6) or John Cotton's *God's Promise to His Plantations* (1630), or a Jeremiah of the declension, as in Increase Mather's *The Day of Trouble is Near* (1674), or millennial historian like Cotton Mather in *The Wonders of the Invisible World* (1692) and the *Magnalia Christi Americana* (1702), he upholds devotional rather than recapitulative uses of types. Although acknowledging God's providential designs, he avoids historical applications of personal (as opposed to ceremonial) types to suit partisan English politics or to bolster New England's nationalistic fervor. Scriptural history takes priority over contemporary upheavals. Old Testament figures find surpassing fulfillment in Christ and His gospel mission, not in the cultural heroes of the New Israel's errand. Edward Taylor models his spiritual strivings after the *exempla fidei* of Old Testament types but trusts only Christ's guarantee of eternal liberty from sin's bondage. He anticipates an ascension into a paradise, which is not to be found in the wilderness of the Connecticut Valley, but in the mansions of God's Holy City. Historians glorify their ancestors with metaphoric exempla from the ancient patriarchs to immortalize the New Canaan and Jerusalem of this world. But devotional typologists, such as Edward Taylor, glorify the Son, who more perfectly brings the elect saints into His Father's eschatological kingdom and the church into *the* New Jerusalem in spiritual perpetuity.

4

Edward Taylor's Puritan "Worship-mould"

That I might not receive this mould in vain
Thy Son, My Lord, my Tabernacle he
Shall be: me run into thy mould again.
Then in this Temple I will Worship thee.
(II.20.7–10)

In the New England wilderness, the Puritan preacher not only turned to biblical patriarchs as models for his prophetic and priestly functions in the New Israel, he also looked to Old Testament types and New Testament fulfillments in order to defend Puritan worship. Although Calvinist covenant theology originated as an offshoot of the Protestant Reformation, by the later seventeenth century lines among European Roman Catholics, English Anglicans, and New England Puritans were narrowly drawn. Reformers had called into question the perpetuation of idolatrous ceremonies adapted from the Old Testament or "hatched" by human imaginations and urged instead a purified worship based upon strict New Testament instructions. They perceived a conflict between the primacy of man's relationship with God mediated through Christ alone and the elaborate Catholic system of priestly mediations, purchased pardons, and ceremonial worship. To resolve these issues, Anglicans offered a compromise still grounded in a hierarchical paradigm of power by substituting kings and archbishops for Roman popes and priests. Although they discarded many ceremonies that had generated the grossest abuses among the Catholic priesthood, Anglicans still reserved their surplices, altars, rites of worship, and church music. Originally covenant theologians comprised a splinter faction; ultimately these Puritans became radical revisionists of church polity and worship. Scorning all remnants of an episcopacy, Puritans called forth the covenanting church of elect saints, militant in its denunciation of still prevailing abuses within the Anglican Church. More fervently committed to reading Scripture literally, Puritan theologians used typological arguments to preach the abrogation of *all* Mosaic ceremonies and Christ's institution of a new evangelical worship. To strict covenanters, the Church of England retained too many Old Testament observances, too much ornamentation in priestly garments and temple furnishings, and too fully a gradated prelacy; thus, they remained contaminated with a residue from Roman Catholicism. By 1662 when Charles II imposed the Act of Uniformity, the political climate had become intolerable, and covenanting ministers sought escape from Anglican civil and religious persecutions. These Puritan struggles, however, yielded an enduring legacy, as covenanting preachers, delivered from the latter-day "Egyptian bondage" of English Anglicanism, immigrated to New England, often by way of the Netherlands, where Dutch Calvinism continued to flourish.

Within this volatile political atmosphere, Thomas Taylor, Samuel Mather, and Edward Taylor advocated a conservative exegesis of types, but one dedicated to the service of a radical Puritanism. Though standing "as a brazen wall against popery," Thomas Taylor published the remarkably restrained devotional exposition, *Christ Revealed,* largely on personal types and ranks but also including noncontroversial purifications, events from Israel's wilderness journey, and circumcision and Passover.[1] More embroiled in late-century schisms, Samuel Mather launched a sermon series (1666–8), published posthumously as *The Figures or Types* (1683), in which he denounced all continuances of legal ceremonies by English Anglicans, who were merely Catholic wolves in sheep's clothing. For Edward Taylor, preaching the law in New England posed a challenge as potent as Samuel Mather's crusade from Dublin against the Anglicans. Disrupted by schismatic Quakers and Socinians, Westfield existed tenuously on the western reaches of civilized New England. Cotton Mather's *Magnalia Christi Americana* in 1702 would lament second- and third-generation spiritual backslidings, which threatened the cohesiveness of the Puritan community as surely as materialism and territorial dispersion. By preaching typal interpretations of ceremonial law (1696–8) and God's providential guidances (1703–4), Edward Taylor sought to revitalize the purity of covenant theology and worship within this New Canaan. Not simply reiterating platitudes from the Puritan tradition of figuralism, Edward Taylor's *Upon the Types of the Old Testament* and his *Preparatory Meditations* turn typology into a potent weapon to combat apostasies in New England's wilderness and to defend a new gospel worship that would supplant old ceremonial laws.

By the seventeenth century, it was commonplace in such treatises as *Christ Revealed* and *The Figures or Types* both to decry the Jews' blindness in denying Christ as the Messiah and in holding Old Testament ceremonies as legally binding and to condemn the Catholic use of rites to warrant remission of sin. Thomas Taylor, for example, argued the primary function of Mosaic rituals typically to shadow forth God's Cove-

nant of Grace, in which faith, rather than works or ceremonial observances, becomes the prerequisite for receiving benefits from Christ. Jewish
"Ceremonies," he proclaims,

> were not given to merit remission of sinnes by them, nor to appease
> Gods anger, nor to bee an acceptable worship by the worth of the worke
> done, nor to justifie the observer: but to shew justification by Iesus
> Christ, the truth and substance of them; to bee types of him, pointing
> at him in whom the Father is pleased; to bee Allegories and resem-
> blances of the benefits of Christ, exhibited in the new Testament; to
> bee testimonies of the promise and Covenant on Gods part; to be Sac-
> raments and seales of faith on the part of the beleeving Iew, exciting
> and confirming his faith in the Messiah. (CR, pp. 4–5)

Although he briefly mentions various Hebrew ceremonies, Thomas Taylor
dedicates 41 percent of *Christ Revealed* to a sacramental explication of
ordinary and extraordinary types (Appendix 2).[2] The "ordinary or standing" types of circumcision and Passover are God's ordained seals for the
old covenant with Israel, but they are superseded when Christ inaugurates the "speciall seales" of Baptism and the Lord's Supper (CR, p. 204).
To amplify his sacramental interpretation, Taylor also includes the
"Extraordinary and occasionall" figures by paralleling the "Sacraments
of the Cloud and the red Sea" with "Circumcision and Baptisme" and
the "Mannah from heaven and water out of the Rock" with the "Passeover and the Lords Supper" (CR, pp. 204, 205). He eventually adds
the brazen serpent lifted up by Moses in the wilderness as a figure for
Christ's sacrificial cure of man's sin. Despite a few outraged jibes against
popish idolatries and Roman teachers, Thomas Taylor remains, at least
in *Christ Revealed,* largely detached from contemporary disputes over
ecclesiastical polity and ceremonial worship, which even by 1635 threatened to splinter Protestant sects and renew animosities among Puritans,
Anglicans, and Catholics.

In the wake of Cromwell's defeat, with Charles II restored to the throne
and a Catholic queen in England, the Anglican Church once more resumed
its ceremonial worship and pressured dissenting clergy to sign the Act of
Uniformity (1662). It was most likely this act that drove Edward Taylor
from England to America to pursue training as a covenanting minister at
Harvard and eventually to preach his typological sermons in Westfield.
Samuel Mather, descended from the illustrious Mathers of Massachusetts
and graduated from Harvard, crossed the Atlantic in reverse, returning
to England in 1650 and subsequently traveling to Ireland for his ministry.
Dismayed by Anglican and popish perpetuations of Jewish ceremonies,
he preached two sermons in 1660 in Dublin, published as *A Testimony
from the Scripture against Idolatry and superstition* (1670?).[3] In his later *apologia* for Puritan polity and doctrine, *The Figures or Types,* Mather again

attacks the instituting of false ceremonies to imitate Old Testament observances and denounces Anglican compromises:

> So now, when the Church of God under the New Testament is coming forth out of Spiritual *Babylon:* There is a mongrel Generation risen up, whom some have fitly called *Calvino-Papistas, Calvinian Papists,* who are *for the Protestant Doctrine, and for Popish Worship.* I refer it to every ones Conscience, to judge, whether it may not be fitly applied to our late Innovators, who are for a Linsey-woolsey Religion, a mixture of sound and wholsome Doctrine, with Antichristian Popish Worship; their Wine is mixt with Water; the Protestant Faith, with Popish Ceremonies and Superstitions: *They build Hay and Stubble upon the Foundation.* The Foundation of our Church is right, which is *Jesus Christ,* and *Justification by Faith in his Blood:* But the Superstructure, they build upon it, is Humane Inventions and Superstitions. (*FT,* p. 161)[4]

Monarchical support for Anglican worship and an episcopacy could only be perceived by Mather as political appeasement of the Catholics and a dangerous backsliding from reformed Protestantism. To decorate temples with ornate furnishings, permit organ music, clothe priests in ostentatious vestments, keep holy and feast days, nominate their own saints and bishops, and imitate ancient rites in contemporary services is idolatrous. Having indicted the "Papists and Semi-Protestants" for grave misreadings of Scripture, Mather argues instead that although Jewish ceremonies retain some power as moral examples, they were fulfilled and abrogated by Christ. A proper typological reading of Mosaic rituals is the cornerstone of Mather's Puritan theology.

Although Mather treats the "occasional" types from Israel's Exodus and wilderness trek, unlike Thomas Taylor he minimizes sacramental applications and emphasizes instead God's providential deliverances of His people. Moreover, he differentiates these "extraordinary" types as occurring before God's settling of the "ordinary" or *"Perpetual Statutes,"* which Moses "received from the Mouth of God" in three forms: the moral law as ten commandments, ceremonial law, and judicial laws for worship and civil obedience (*FT,* pp. 166, 168). These perpetual statutes, to which Mather devotes 70 percent of his treatise, constitute the fiber and framework of his *Figures or Types* (Appendix 3), through which he guides readers by delineating five major divisions: the "initiating Seal" or "Circumcision"; the "Sacrifices and Purifications of Sin"; the "Temple and Tabernacle"; the "Priesthood"; and the "Festivals or legal Times and Seasons" (*FT,* p. 170).[5] Mather's distinctions may seem as legalistic as the Hebrew ordinances, but he never loses sight of the evangelical message, as his paraphrase of a key text from Colossians 2:16–17 indicates: "That *Moses* delivered *Law* that is, *Shadows* and *Ceremonies,* which were but legal, and dark and rigorous: But Christ brought in *Grace* and

Truth, that is, the real and sweet *Accomplishment* and *Performance,* of all the good, that *Moses* had promised in that dark and low and legal way" (*FT,* p. 167). Mather chides the Jews' "Weakness and Folly" for preferring *"meer Law"* and denying Christ and the prefigurative function of Mosaic ordinances, while he also condemns Anglicans and Catholics who err by imitating Old Testament rites, as if the mere display of temple worship would pass for genuine service originating in the heart's tabernacle (*FT,* pp. 166, 172).

Intolerant of idolatrous worship, Mather offers his own corrective canons for interpreting the Old Testament ceremonial law. First, without explicit gospel inauguration, all practices modeled upon Mosaic rituals or invented by man's ingenuity, whether holy days, indulgences, or cathedral choirs, defy God's will and word. *"Hath the Lord commanded it,"* Mather teaches, must be "your great Enquiry in all Things, that concern the Worship of God" (*FT,* p. 193). Second, he distinguishes moral laws still in effect, such as the ten commandments, from ceremonial laws. For Puritans statutes governing temple sacrifices, priests, and altars exist perpetually *only as types* and lose their legalistic efficacy as forms of worship when superseded by Christ's spiritual covenant with man. Third, because of their typical signification, ceremonies can, however, shadow forth truths which Christ and His church under the new dispensation fully illuminate. For instance, Aaron foreshadows "no other High Priest . . . or chief Shepherd of our Souls under the Gospel, but only *Jesus Christ,"* and hence the minister within a Puritan congregational polity exercises his functions as a disciple equal to all other saints (*FT,* p. 530). In contrast, Mather condemns the "judaizing antichristian Wickedness" of "the Bishop of *Rome. . . .* And all other such Archbishops, and Primates, and Prelates," for exalting themselves as high priests like Aaron, thereby upholding the episcopacy, but failing to acknowledge the singular efficacy of Christ's fulfillment and evangelical ministry (*FT,* p. 530). Fourth, the abrogation of *all* Old Testament ordinances, given Christ's fulfilling and excelling of them, undergirds Mather's exegesis. Mather finds "manifest Intimations in the Old Testament, that these Ceremonial Laws were *not to continue always, but to cease and be abolished in the fulness of Time"* (*FT,* p. 167). *"Not according to the Covenant that I made with their Fathers,"* Jeremiah writes in 31:31–3, *"but this shall be the Covenant, I will put my Law in their inward Parts, and write it in their Hearts"* (*FT,* p. 167). Whether applied to Jewish feasts and holy days, purifications, priestly garments, temple furnishings, sacrifices, or music, Christ's New Testament covenant expressly summons believers to turn from ceremonial evidences of grace to search their hearts for inward salvation. By clarifying standards for interpreting ceremonial types, Mather established the clear link between Puritan hermeneutics and refutations of Anglican and Catholic worship and ecclesiology, and he provided the theoretical framework within which Edward Taylor composed his *Upon the Types of the Old Testament* and *Preparatory Meditations*.

Much as Mather felt in Dublin, congregationalist Edward Taylor felt in Westfield that orthodox Puritans were crusaders engaged in a holy war to preserve the purity of doctrine, polity, and worship against Anglican compromisers and radical New England revisionists. Though free from direct pressures under the Church of England, Taylor continued to justify an evangelical worship through strict typological readings of Hebrew rites. In *Upon the Types* and *Christographia*, Taylor regularly devotes his uses by way of conviction or reproof to castigating "such as Carry on a Ceremoniall Worship under the Gospell dispensation. As the Papists, and Prelates" (*CHR*, p. 290). He sometimes calls forth authorities, here Bellarmine and Tertullian, before ridiculing the presumption in false imitations:

> The Papist . . . draw arguments tingd with the poison of the old Serpent out of the Sides of the brazen Serpent to Support the Idolatry of the Old Serpent in worshipping of Images. . . . And this is the very answer that our Doctrine presents us against this Abomination . . . that the Brazen Serpent was not erected to be an Object of Worship . . . But to be a Type of the Lord Christ held out to be remedy against the poison of the old Serpent. applied by Faith. (*UTOT*, pp. 719–20).

To worship brazen images is to challenge Christ's abrogation of Old Testament laws by trusting in visible signs rather than in a spiritual covenant and "Cure" through "Faith in Christ Crucified" (*UTOT*, p. 702). Catholics and Anglicans, according to Taylor, blaspheme not merely by imitating profane and now abrogated rituals but also by creating *ex nihilo* idolatrous practices. Papists know Christ to be the only mediator, yet deliberately "in all their Prayers . . . poure out to Saints, & Angells to mediate for them to God" as surrogate advocates and "erect Altars of their own, & hence they have not their prayers Sanctified" (*UTOT*, p. 417). More frequently at "their Masses which they assert to be propitiatory," Taylor scoffs, they adulate "a foolish invention of their own brains," thus betraying a lack of faith in Christ's "propitiatory Sacrifice" as *the* medium of all gospel worship (*UTOT*, pp. 417, 381).

Moreover, Catholics undermine not only Christ's mediatorial power, but also his preeminence as priest and King. Taylor compares papists to an "Apostate bruide of Antichrist" who like the devil's procuress seduces susceptible men with illusory promises of heavenly delights obtained by purchasing pardons and merits (*CHR*, p. 357). Only Jesus shedding his blood in obedience to God's law gains pardon for mankind and only faith, not bartered forgiveness or good works, merits salvation. Priests who dispense grace as if it were a commodity to be bought and sold or a probation warrantable by good behavior falsely usurp "Christs Right and Authority as a Priest" (*CHR*, p. 360). Anglican archbishops, bishops, and more particularly the pope who claims earthly "Headship over the Universall Church," heretically imitate Christ's divine kingship (*CHR*, p. 391). Like other covenant theologians, Taylor thus denies efficacy to external ceremonies or ecclesiastical hierarchies sponsored by papists and prelates, viewing them all as abominable condescensions to weak-willed men who must cling to a visible, legal worship. By rejecting these so-called idolatries, man-made rituals, and surrogate intercessors in order to worship Christ as sole mediator, high priest, and head of the gospel church, the Puritan receives direct access to God and His saving grace.

Further removed from religious factionalism in England, Edward Taylor found that threats to New England's fabric of covenant worship came increasingly from local heresies spawned by Quakers, latter-day Socinians, and Solomon Stoddard's liberalizing of the Lord's Supper in neighboring Northampton. Since the trial and banishment of Antinomian Anne Hutchinson (1637), the virulent persecutions of 1656–61, and organization of the Society of Friends in 1666, Quakers epitomized the dangerous sectarian threat to the covenant community.[6] They externalized deep-seated Puritan fears of religious enthusiasms unrestrained by reason or church discipline. These "filthy Spawn of Jesuitism abiding in the rotten Eggs of Quakery" (*UTOT*, p. 523) hatch into "Subverters of the Gospell," a "Strong and reason deserted rout" ruled by passion (*CHR*, p. 163). Or as Taylor dramatizes in Sermon II.25, while they "plead in appearance for Spirituall Worship, in truth they are most unspirituall, & Carnall," for Quakers "are so saddly drownd in the Sea of Errour, so besotted, & drunken with Divelish Delusions, as to oppose & gain say all Divine Instituted Worship, & Ordinances" (*UTOT*, p. 522). By asserting that God "requires a Spirituall, heart Worship onely," Quakers negate the framework of typical and gospel worship (*UTOT*, p. 522). Against this "Divelish Delusion," Taylor defends the ideal of a self-disciplining covenant society which demands "Dayly, and Weekly Worshiping God in Christ with a Visible Holy, & Spirituall Worship" (*UTOT*, p. 522). At one extreme, Catholic and Anglican ceremonies encouraged presumptuous faith in external, humanly designed rites, albeit justified as extensions of Old Testament law. At the other extreme, Quakers urged a personal search for Christ immanent within each individual, a process that slighted the historical efficacy of both Old and New Testament instructions for worship. Under attack by this heretical "broode of men" (*UTOT*, p. 694) of marauding "Wolves in Sheeps woole" (*CHR*, p. 354) masquerading as true Christians, the Puritan community might disintegrate and itself succumb to religous enthuasiasm, as it did later during the Great Awakening.

Disturbed by this dangerous sectarianism, Edward Taylor also refutes Quaker beliefs that run counter to stricter Puritan definitions of Christ's nature and typological readings of Scripture. Although in actuality Quakers denied neither the Trinity, Christ as Savior, nor the divine inspiration of Scripture, they acknowledged not the historical Jesus, but instead affirmed Christ as an immanent light within each soul. Taylor mocks the insubstantial mysticism of these "Worst of Men, the Quakers, that advance a Light within, (that is onely *Lumen Naturae*) actuated as an *Ignis Fatuus* by the Spirit of darkness" (*CHR,* p. 295). By granting man power to discover Christ as a spiritual truth within, "this Pest of the Christian Religion, the Quakers," according to Taylor in Sermon II.58, "Vilify Christ & slight him as being the Man born in Judea," and by "Comparison to the light Within, & the Christ within them, they make a triviall Matter of him" (*UTOT,* p. 693). Central to Puritan doctrine, of course, is Christ's historical reality; *as a man* he suffers death to satisfy the ceremonial law and God's justice through His perfectly obedient sacrifice. In Quaker dismissals of Jesus' historical humanity, Taylor thus spied a heresy that threatened Puritan belief in gospel authority, antitypal fulfillments of messianic prophecy, and Christ's human nature. The pursuit of inner light "leads them into all false wayes, and durty boggs, and brambly thickets of notorious Vilany even against the law of nature, as Well as against the Gospell of Christ, and Christ himselfe" (*CHR,* p. 296). To escape this landscape of heretical horrors, Taylor counseled parishioners to travel a purer pathway and "Rest our Faith upon" Christ alone "Whom God had & hath such an utterable Love for as he hath been pointing of him out in all the Ages of the Church with Sparkling Emblems and Types" (*UTOT,* pp. 693–4).

Though more a doctrinal than political threat to Puritanism, the Socinian heresy originated in sixteenth-century Europe, spreading from Poland through Holland and England to the New World.[7] Locally, William Pynchon, founder of Springfield, as early as 1650 espoused Socinian beliefs in *The Meritorious Price of Our Redemption* and initiated a movement that later gave rise to American Unitarianism.[8] Taylor also directly indicts "Mr William Sherlock," who "hath had the Impudency boldly to plead in this present age" for this "later dated Heresy" (*UTOT,* p. 381).[9] It was not so much overt acts, but rather challenges to Puritan belief in Christ's conjoined divine and human nature within the Trinity that aroused the antagonism of Taylor as it had that of John Owen and of strict Calvinists earlier: "The Socinians deny the Personall Subsistence of Christ in the Divine Nature" and "make Sin but a light matter, as easily remooved and got clear from, Whereas nothing below the Godhead of Christ is Sufficient to deliver from it" (*CHR*, pp. 68, 69).[10] By emphasizing man's free will and reason as sufficient to achieve redemption, Socinians further reduce the "Excellency of Christ as God Eternall . . . and the necessity of Such an Excellent Mediator" (*CHR*, pp. 68–9). Contrarily, for Taylor and Puritans man's reason is fallible, his sinfulness perpetual, and separation from God a torment, making mandatory divine mediation by a Savior who personally subsists in the Trinity.

Having renounced Christ's divine nature, Socinians further strip away His earthly powers and antitypal fulfillments. They "deny Christs Priesthood" and seeing

> him so oft in Scripture Styled a Priest they . . . bring their Sun in their own account to lay its Shining beams upon these glimmering Star lights, thus, that these descriptions of Christ are not proper but metaphoricall. He is said to be a Priest, not that he was Properly a Priest, but because Something done by him bore upon it some likeness unto what was done by the Priests of old. (*UTOT*, p. 415)

Such a dismissal of the New Testament as merely a repository of metaphors horrifies Puritans, including Taylor, who affirm Scripture's recording of Christ's historical fulfillment of types. Foreshadowed by Aaron and Melchizedek who administered ceremonial offerings of old, Christ becomes both "a Priest Properly" and a "Gospell Altar," making "Satisfaction to Gods Justice for the Sins of Gods people"; hence, "this Socinian dotage is exploded by our Doctrine" of types (*UTOT*, pp. 415–16). Christ's divinity incarnate enables Him not just as a priest, but as King and mediator, perfectly to atone for mankind's sin. The "Socinian litter . . . shamefully deny Christs Mediatory Worke," but Taylor praises His "Power in Heaven, and Earth" to prescribe a new evangelical salvation and worship (*CHR*, pp. 427–8). Beset by vivid memories of Anglican and Catholic extravagances and assailed at home by chronic Quaker and Socinian heresies, Edward Taylor seeks to smother sectarian controversy by refortifying typological readings of the law. Rather than circumvent the Old and New Testament historical record of ceremonial rites, as Quakers and Socinians do, Taylor uses Scripture to defend a purified gospel worship against ultra-enthusiasts and rationalists. Acceptance of Scripture's historicity and Christ's mediatorial and sacerdotal fulfillments remain unshakable tenets upon which Puritans base their figural readings of ceremonial law and doctrine of redemption.

Although preached against this background of controversy, Taylor's *Upon the Types of the Old Testament* neither bristles with the virulent polemic of Mather's *Figures or Type* nor subsides into the low-key devotionalism of *Christ Revealed*. By training and temperament, Edward Taylor seems both more scholastic and more dedicated to edifying his parishioners. He designs his series on Old Testament persons and ceremonies to illuminate Christ's antitypal excellence and the New Testament worship and to strengthen the congregational solidarity among Westfield's Elect. Unlike Cotton Mather's *Magnalia Christi Americana* or other chronicles, he draws no wholesale parallels to contemporary history, but instead directs jeremiads toward individual sinners rather than a declining nation of New England Canaanites. Taylor's scholasticism appears in his frequent recourse to authorities, most often Origen's homilies, numerical symbolism, ecclesiastical calendars, rhetorical proofs, and in the prescribed sermon format which explicates the scriptural text, argues the doctrine, then applies it. The sermons abound with numbered points and ramistic bilateralisms, as with holy days universal or particular, feasts lunar or septinary, uncleanness moral or ceremonial, and sacraments either initiatory (Baptism) or confirmatory (Lord's Supper). Yet contrasted with Samuel Mather's equally erudite *apologia, Upon the Types of the Old Testament* seems enlivened by the intimacy of communication, as if we hear Taylor in his uses by way of information, conviction, reproof, and exhortation earnestly lecturing his congregation to stimulate each mind with gospel truths, to enflame each heart with spiritual ardor for Christ. Preaching for a smaller audience, perhaps less with an eye toward publication, Taylor devotes fewer sermons to figural theory and ceremonial intricacies than Mather, yet he maintains the richness of doctrine and organization of his predecessor.

Methodical and with a passion for architectonics, Taylor superimposes his own taxonomy upon structures borrowed from *Christ Revealed* and *The Figures or Types*. From March 1696 (Sermon II.16) to February 1698/9 (Sermon II.29), at irregular intervals, he preached on the Old Testament ceremonies (Appendixes 1 and 4). To signal his shift from the "Personall" to the "Reall Types," he selects the figure of Jacob's house in Sermon II.16: "the Old Testament Church was the House of Jacob typicall & literall. The New Testament Church is the House of Jacob typified, & Spirituall," within which all further types of worship and discipline must be practiced (*UTOT*, p. 328). He gathers these rites under three major headings: the "Greate Mediums of Worship," including sacrifices, altars, and the holy temple (II.17–20); "Circumstances appertaining to Worship," specifically the new moon, anniversary feasts, and sabbaths (II.21–25); and "Typicall Discipline" (II.26–28) or purifications (*UTOT*, pp. 453, 578). Taylor eliminates the priesthood, partly because he collapses it together with the ranks of prophets, priests, and kings (II.14) and Aaron's atonement (II.23), and possibly because he felt further removed from the direct confrontations with Anglican authorities that had spurred Mather to expound so fully on priestly duties and apparel. With Sermon II.29 on

Noah's ark and the flood, Taylor moves to a study of occasional deliverances which he recommences in 1703–4 with Israel's release from
Egyptian bondage (II.58) and the remaining extraordinary types – pillar
of cloud and fire (II.59), manna from heaven (II.60A), water from the
rock (II.60B), and the brazen serpent (II.61). By linking Noah's ark with
Israel's deliverance, Taylor effectively bridges the gap between habitual
purifications and God's occasional miracles to protect his chosen people.
He defends this arrangement by declaring that "the Doctrine appertaining to Discipline [Purifications], standes in need of Confirmation by Divine
Operation," that is, by miraculous providences ("Signa. Extra ordinary") and covenantal seals ("Sigilla. Ordinary") respectively (UTOT,
p. 647). Taylor thus treats all ceremonial worship (II.17–25) and purifications (II.26–28) before extraordinary confirmations (II.29, 58–61) of
God's covenant with Israel. Two years later, in 1706, he concludes *Upon
the Types* by preaching on circumcision and Passover, those types of "an
Ordinary & Standing Nature" or "Sigilla" which clearly emblemize the
New Testament sacraments of Baptism and the Lord's Supper (UTOT,
p. 801).[11]

More often logical than eloquent, Taylor's sermons clarify the ceremonial law by systematically exposing figural truths. Preaching approx-
imately every eight weeks (II.1–30) a series that eventually stretches over
thirteen years (1693–1706), Taylor must repeatedly job sluggish memories, reminding his parishioners "as we have considered" and "having
gone over," so "now I am come to." Commonplace in seventeenth-
century treatises, the elaborate schemata and directives not only serve
pedagogical aims, they also illuminate the doctrine of Puritan typology.
Mimetically, *Upon the Types* redrafts God's laws for ritual worship delivered to Moses at Sinai, but the essential truths prefigured remain entirely
spiritual: "the Ceremoniall Law being accomplisht in the thing typified,
. . . Ceremony is to be laid aside," for "Spirituall attendence . . . is the
Service of Evangelicall obedience unto the Law of the Spirit of Life, that
is in Christ Jesus" (UTOT, p. 500). Christ calls for evangelical obedience, not prescribed by law but inscribed within each believer's heart.
Hence, in Sermon II.16 Taylor challenges each of Westfield's Elect to
cultivate an inward temple worship:

> All thy Service, & Offerings which indeed are Spirituall . . . were typ-
> ified by the Ceremoniall Sacrifices, Priests, & Altars used in the Old
> Testament Church. . . . Now here is thy Work: dost thou bring thy
> offering unto this Priest? dost thou offer the Same upon the Altar of the
> Lord Christ? . . . Is all thy Service, Worship, Prayers, Confessions,
> thanks giving etc presented to God by & in Christ? Dost thou make
> him thine atturnie? Dost thou offer Christ to the Father as thy Sin offer-
> ing? what sayst to this? (UTOT, p. 350)

In contrast to ancient rites and Anglican and Catholic perpetuations, Puritan worship reduces to a few spiritual observances: the profession of faith and baptism into the church; regular sabbath attendance to hear God's Word; offerings of prayers, praise, and thanksgiving; coming to the Lord's Supper with a prepared heart; and partaking of the Sacrament to memorialize Christ's sacrifice and reconfirm the new covenant bond between saint and Savior. Taylor aptly portrays Mosaic rituals as external adjuncts to a legalistic covenant under which atonement is obtained through burnt offerings and temple worship. But he teaches that faith alone gains entree into the new covenant, wherein man's sins are absolved by Christ's crucifixion and election manifest through an evangelical worship.

Not solely as Puritan apologist in *Upon the Types of the Old Testament* and *Christographia,* but also as heart-searching contemplative in the *Preparatory Meditations,* Edward Taylor yearns to participate in a new gospel worship. As a dedicated Puritan preacher, he constantly monitors his soul to scourge manifold sins and to strengthen the "Worship-mould" within his heart's temple. For how could the Puritan pastor better testify to man's need for evangelical worship to replace Old Testament ceremonies than by personal example? Whereas *Upon the Types* documents the minutiae of figural analogies or maps overarching schemata, the *Preparatory Meditations* pursues the quintessential comfort of Christ's promise to forgive sins and grant eternal life. Rather than the vigilant pedagogue who lectures recalcitrant pupils on their moral duties, Taylor condemns himself as a dissolute reprobate, a "guilded Cask of tawny Pride, and Gall,/ With Veans of Venom o're my Spirits sprawle" (II.16.23–4). A starving soul, he cleanses the heart to receive grace, seeks admittance as "thy Guest too at this Feast" of Christ's body and blood, and vows always to "live/ Up to thy Gospell Law" (II.22.68, 68–9). In his meditations as in the sermons, Taylor explains spiritual analogies for ancient legal types, but he also more personally deplores his soul's corruption and seeks Christ's salving grace. These psalms become an integral part of his inward worship, a private means of beseeching and praising Christ's mediation. In this transforming of homiletic into meditative praxis, Edward Taylor crosses the boundary from rational exegete to poetic worshiper and singer.

At times in these poems, though less often than we might wish, Taylor eschews typal parallels for provocative conceits as one means of translating analytic doctrine into fiery pledges of devout service. In Sermon II.16, for example, he proclaims "the Old Testament Church is a Type of the Church of Christ in the New Testament times," as he adopts the typical "House of Jacob" to begin his study of ceremonial law (*UTOT,* p. 329). Detached and doctrinaire, Taylor cites scriptural authority, examines the church's "Constitution" by "Matter" and "Form," its priests as "Organizing Officers," and preaches its "Use" and "Circumstances" under the old dispensation. He also takes this occasion to confirm the cardinal principles of a Puritan reading of legal worship. Instituted after Adam's fall, renewed by covenant with Abraham and Moses, "the Fabrick of the Old Testament Worship was raised, & founded in Types. This none can deny," he declares unequivocably (*UTOT,* p. 334). He further distinguishes "Ceremoniall Worship" from that "Divine Worship of a morall nature . . . as Prayer, Singing Psalms, Preaching the Word," which though "not properly types, but Examples" yet counsels New Testament converts in a continuing "Morall Duty" (*UTOT,* pp. 334, 336). By contrast, all tabernacle sacrifices, altars, feasts, and purifications that manifested Israel's visible covenant with Yahweh, "were not durable" but "perishing," destined to cease under a gospel dispensation (*UTOT,* p. 334). Such legal ceremonies might temporarily sustain Israel's belief in God's divine protection, but they function more significantly as "typicall of the Gospell Church," and "did Speake out good to come," the promised Messiah (*UTOT,* p. 334). Fulfilled and abrogated by this prophesied Savior, they give way to a "Gospell Worship" without external ceremony, though not without the same "Spirit" of "Hope," "Grace," and "Salvation" that ancient rites anticipated. While instructing his congregation in the differing "Manner of the Dispensation," Taylor also concludes by extolling "how much the Antitype doth excell the type" and "how the Grace of God doth Shine out upon you more abundantly" (*UTOT,* pp. 346, 348). These truths must be apprehended by the Westfield Elect, but Taylor's myriad proofs and principles rarely rise above dry didacticism. Even the curious mystery of "sevens" and "twelves" or fleeting images of the sun and moon only momentarily enliven the sermon's otherwise labored prose, tough meat even for the well-honed minds of Puritan churchgoers.

The seemingly intractable nature of the doctrine makes more impressive the imagistic ingenuity and personalism of the companion Meditation II.16. Ignoring unwieldy proofs, Taylor takes his poetic cue from Luke's prophecy in 1:33, "He shall reign over the house of Jacob forever," and from Paul's parable of the olive tree in Romans 11:16–24. The sermon starkly designates this "House of Jacob" as the "Whole Posterity of Jacob incorporated into one Body politick & otherwise Styled the Common Wealth of Israel," which prefigures that "Evangelicall Kingdom," over which "as the Virgins Son" Christ shall reign "after his Incarnation" (*UTOT,* p. 328). Rather than delineate Israel's political theory, however, the meditation revisualizes the glorious annunciation from Luke, as "Angells flame/ To be thy [Christ's] Harauld publishing thy Light" unto Mary and the "Sons of Men" (II.16.2–3, 4). The sermon's rational correspondences between an old and new church disappear, as

Taylor affirms instead the "King of Glory bright" come to reign evangelically "Ore Jacobs House" (II.16.1, 6). A servant kneeling in awed obeisance, he dedicates himself to his liege lord and King: "My Glory is that thou my king maist bee./ That I may be thy Subject thee to sing/ And thou may'st have thy kingdoms reign in mee" (II.16.8–10). He perhaps alludes back to the sermon in which "Rich Reason, and Religion Good thus cry,/ Be Subject, Soule," as if heeding dogma alone might gain entry into this kingdom (II.16.13–14). But beneath a flaunted certitude, doubts fester. Am I worthy to serve in Christ's kingdom? Am I one of the blessed Elect whose "Lips" may "thy Scepter Kiss"? (II.16.11) Though he treasures an illusion of courtly attendance, self-examination reveals decadence within, as "Unheartiness hatcht in my heart doth hiss," while "Sins mutiny" and "Pray'res grow Dead" (II.16.12, 17, 18).

The call for a clean heart from those who desire admittance to the Lord's Supper takes on special urgency for Taylor as priestly administrator. Could he be a hypocrite who mouths God's truths like pious platitudes, yet conceals within a "rotten heart," rife with "Pride, and Gall"? (II.16.30, 23) Taylor's fear that he may pose as a saintly preacher only to harbor a rebel's "base Hypocrisy" within escalates, as he generates a tumbling series of antitheses. Am I a "lowly Vine" or "Humble Olive" rich with fruit or oil, or merely a "fiery Bramble" crackling with "an empty Sound"? (II.16.19, 20, 21, 22) Am I like the fabled jack "Daugh all glorious made when dresst/ In feathers borrowed of other birds," who preens his irridescent black plumage to "be King of birds"? (II.16.25–7) Or am I a gentle "Turtle Dove ore laid/ With golden feathers," a "Cooing" songster rather than a cackling crow? (II.16.44–5, 47) An ingenious variety of botanical and ornithological images, these self-portraitures convey Taylor's anxiety over his own hypocrisy and pride, sins that would exclude him forever from Jacob's house, whether the evangelical church or heavenly kingdom.

Having witnessed his corruption, Taylor begs for Christ's "golden Sword" of justice to "Sheath . . . in the bowells of my Sin" and rejuvenating grace to "Implant" him anew in "Gods true vine" (II.16.31, 32, 35). Matching each previous caricature of iniquity with a plea for conversion, he calls the "Blesst Lord, my King" to "Slay my Rebellion, make thy Law my Word," "Lord make my Bramble bush thy rosie tree," and "make my Daugh thy Turtle Dove" (II.16.31, 33, 41, 44). The allusion to "thy Law my Word" anticipates Taylor's forthcoming preoccupation with ceremonial law and the antitypal message to heed Christ's superior word of spirit and life. It is, however, his desire for acceptance into Jacob's house that inspires the provocative genealogical and horticultural conceit of "grafting." Whether he notes Mather's commentary (*FT*, pp. 179–80) or finds Romans 11:16–17 apt, the parable in Sermon

II.16 proves the common inheritance of Jews and Gentiles under the New Testament dispensation:

> The Apostle doth not make the Gentile Churches New Olive Trees: but Branches brought off from the Wild Olive tree, & planted into the True Olive Tree Rom.11.16.17. The Olive Tree is the Old Testament Church. . . . The Lord called thee a Green Olive tree, faire, & of Goodly Fruite. Now this Olive tree [Israel] is not rooted up saith Paul, but the unfruitfull branches broken off: & you [Gentiles] are taken & Graffted in. (*UTOT*, p. 346)

Even though Taylor's miniature fable usefully instructs parishioners, it remains coldly analytic in contrast to the lively particularity of his poetic appeal, as he seeks to rectify his own "Bramble" state:

> Shall I now grafted in thy Olive tree
>   The house of Jacob, bramble berries beare?
> This burdens me to thinke of, much more thee.
>   Breake off my black brire Claws: mee scrape, and pare.
>   Lord make my Bramble bush thy rosie tree.
>   And it will beare sweet Roses then for thee.
>   (II.16.37–42)

In this personalized allegory, Taylor desires to be grafted into the olive tree, typifying Christ who is born of David's lineage to reign over the New Israel. But fearing his profligate nature, he conceives a mis-implanting which yields a monstrous hybrid, an olive branch bearing "bramble berries" instead of goodly fruit. Only after stripping off the "black brire Claws," that is, his thorny sins, will grafting tame the prickly "fiery Bramble" bush into a primrose bearing tree. Hovering behind this horticultural parable is the image of a genealogical tree, an emblem of Taylor's desire through Christ to inherit Jacob's royal kingdom, open now gospelly to all men who profess faith and fruitfully serve.

Taylor's poetic style in Meditation II.16 seems characteristic of other meditations in which he explores images growing almost haphazardly (like an oddly branching tree) one out of the other, even as his tense questioning plunges toward a crescendo of imperative pleas for release from pain: "Slay my Rebellion, make thy Law my Word./ Against thine Enemies Without within" and "Kill my Hypocrisie, Pride Poison, Gall./ And make my Daugh thy Turtle Dove" (II.16.33–4, 43–4). The tortured and confined spirit thus expresses itself in cumulative similes, metaphors, exclamations, and imperatives ("Sheath," "Slay," "Breake," "scrape, and pare," "Kill") that become increasingly violent, as if pruning the "Bramble bush" of its thorns will allow the "rosie tree" to thrive and bloom. Taylor frequently resorts in his poems to the muscularity of verbs, fragmented lists of nouns or adjectives ("Hypocrisie, Pride Poison, Gall"), self-castigating epithets ("Oh! rotten heart!"), and caesuras that abruptly break lines, or even feet ("The lowly Vine Grows fruitfull clusters, Rich./ . . . / But I like to the fiery Bramble, Which"), as if to signal his disintegration, a body and soul too thorny with "black brire Claws" of sin to produce "sweet Roses" or smooth verse (II. 16.43, 30, 19–20, 40, 42). Later, in Meditation II. 18's similarly scathing self-denunciation, Taylor includes the "Bryer prickle" in a syllabically packed catalog that invokes images from country harvests and village games to capture the sin-riddled soul's empty frivolities:

> A Bran, a Chaff, a very Barly yawn,
>   An Husk, a Shell, a Nothing, nay yet Worse,
> A Thistle, Bryer prickle, pricking Thorn
>   A Lump of Lewdeness, Pouch of Sin, a purse
>   Of Naughtiness, I am, yea what not Lord?
>   And wilt thou be mine Altar? and my bord?
>
> Mine Heart's a Park or Chase of sins: Mine Head
>   'S a Bowling Alley. Sins play Ninehole here.
> Phansy's a Green: sin Barly breaks in't led.
>   Judgment's a pingle. Blindeman's Buff's plaid there.
>   Sin playes at Coursey Parke within my Minde.
>   My Wills a Walke in which it aires what's blinde.
>
> (II. 18. 1–12)

Noun stumbling over noun, epithet upon epithet, a near chiasmus ("Thistle, Bryer prickle, pricking Thorn") contribute to Taylor's litany of devil-driven games, by which sin wreaks havoc with his head and heart.

The signature of an Edward Taylor poem may well be as much its lack of poetic fluidity as (ironically) his persistent pursuit of God's grace and of harmonious verse. Having left himself no room for experimentation with form by imposing a uniform six-line stanza, rhyming *a b a b c c,* he seeks his effects through harsh, homely, idiosyncratic diction, cumulative images drawn from multiple realms, overloaded and elaborated narratives or allegories, syntactic variations, and curious (or perhaps merely unskilled) uses of meter and slant rhymes. The effect is a dramatically heightened, though distinctively personal voice, as if Taylor composes each meditation out of a feverish need, or at other times as a dutiful (if futile) exercise. A verbal flagellant, he seems to relish the self-inflicted degradation, the stretching of language's boundaries to the depths of abasement and the contrasting heights of hyperbolic praise for God. Taylor thus creates a style that insists upon remaining "Cabbin'd" and cribbed by an unrelenting stanza, yet just as insistently seeks to break bondages. His poetry symptomatically reflects the soul's longing to burst free of the body, and hence the poet's desire to transcend linguistic limits, to speak not with a serpent's tongue that "Unheartiness hatcht in my heart doth *hiss,"* but to "coo" dovelike with ineffable, angelic hymns of perfected praise (II.16.12).

Whereas Taylor's homiletic uses mention sacrifices and altars to anticipate the ceremonial types, Meditation II.16 illuminates the psychic issue that afflicts Taylor's heart. To be within the house of Jacob under the Old Testament means to be one of God's participants in tabernacle feasts and purifications, recipient of providential signs in the desert, and celebrator of the covenant sealed with Abraham through circumcision and with Moses through Passover. But to be chosen for Christ's evangelical community, whether the visible Puritan church or spiritual kingdom, demands more exacting self-appraisals and deeper faith. If one is not admitted to the Elect, all Taylor's preachments and meditations remain basest hypocrisies; but if one is a saint, all his "Cooing then shall be thy Musick in,/ The House of Jacob, tun'de to thee, my King" (II.16.47–8). As he embarks, therefore, on his study of Mosaic ritual, Taylor more brutally castigates his own hypocrisy and pride, prepares his heart, and ensures that his grafting has taken, bearing roses and fruits for Christ. Not many of Taylor's subsequent ceremonial meditations so dramatically depart from formal parallels in the sermons. But here in Sermon and Meditation II.16 Taylor poses the fundamental questions for which he seeks divine reassurance: Do I possess the sinner's rotten heart or saint's fruit-bearing soul? Can Christ's sacrifice transform my heart into a sacred altar and temple? Am I worthy to receive evangelical grace and to serve in thy kingdom? Are my meditations and ministry acceptable offerings?

Not only in *Upon the Types of the Old Testament* but also in the *Christographia,* which often synthesizes typological theory, Taylor acknowledges that "if we cast an Eye upon this Ceremoniall Constitution, one would think the Same a poore, weake, beggarly, Inefficacious and foolish thing," for "some parts of this Service one would rather deem a Charm, than a Divine Ordinance of God" (*CHR,* p. 123). Having rhetorically admitted the ineffectuality of the Jewish rites (except to instruct and restrain Israel from man-made idolatries), Taylor then defends their ultimate significance:

> But if we Seriously Observe them delineating out Christ and Containing Christ in them in dark draughts, and resemblances, we may see Christ the Wisdom of them all. . . . So that as for Revelation He is the Marrow of Prophesy; as for Righteousness, he is the End and Wisdom of the Morall Law Rom. 10. 4; and as to Design, and Truth, he is the Substance, Body, and the Whole Wisdom of the Ceremoniall institution Col. 2. 10. 17. (*CHR,* p. 123)

By reaffirming Puritan premises of Scripture's historicity and the primary function of ceremonial law to foreshadow Christ, Taylor establishes a worthy rationale for both his extensive homiletic and meditative series. The saint comes to Christ first through rational understandings of prefigurative laws; but evangelical fellowship also demands the passion of belief. Hence, homilies and meditations alike bring Taylor closer to Christ, Who becomes man's eternal mediator with a wrathful Father, a high priest to accept all sacrifices, a tabernacle for worship, host and meat at the Lord's Supper, and divine King. Exploring Christ's multifaceted fulfillment of ceremonial law and, thereby, man's many avenues of grace, Taylor creates in the *Preparatory Meditations* (II.17–28) a diversity of typal metaphors. Yet the ambivalent doubt and hope, the leitmotifs of sin and salvation, the appeal to Old Testament figures for insights into gospel truths, and man's need for evangelical worship and service – these key-notes remain constant.

Taylor justifies his entry into ceremonial law (*Res Ecclesia* or Church Adjuncts) in chronological terms, that "Offerings" and "Altars" (II.17–18) were "Instituted by God from the Beginning of the World" before "any Confirming Ordinances whether Miracles [II.29, 58–61] or Sacraments [II.70–71]" (*UTOT*, pp. 354–5). His entrance strikingly resembles George Herbert's opening of *The Temple* with "The Sacrifice" and "The Altar." Taylor refrains, however, from transforming the temple as an architectural structure into a controlling metaphor for his poetic series, an *imitatio* too emblematic of Herbert's Anglican ritualism. Yet one cannot dismiss the implicit patterning, since like the Israelite who approaches through the temple courtyard to the brazen altar for burnt offerings Taylor as evangelical worshiper focuses first on Christ's redemptive sacrifice. A son of Adam as much as an inheritor of Jacob, Taylor perceives in his own failures of sanctity and service the sins that make such a sacrifice necessary. Since Adam first transgressed God's rule of obedience, all men suffer beneath a wrathful judgment, dooming them to sin's wages in death and demanding an ultimate atonement. In Meditation II.17 Taylor recapitulates this transgression as a personal saga, adopting the conceits of abused service and a broken fiscal contract to convey the old covenant's essential legalism:

> Thou Greate Supream, thou Infinite first One:
>   Thy Being Being gave to all that be
> Yea to the best of Beings thee alone
>   To serve with Service best for best of fee.
>   But man the best servd thee the Worst of all
>   And so the Worst of incomes on him falls.
>
> Hence I who'me Capable to serve thee best
>   Of all the ranks of Beings here below
> And best of Wages win, have been a pest
>   And done the Worst, earn'd thus the Worst of Woe.

> Sin that imploys mee findes mee worke indeed
> Me qualifies, ill qualities doth breed.
>
> This is an hell indeed thus to be held
> From that which nature holdst her chiefe delights
> To that that is her horrour and refelld
> Ev'n by the Law God in her Essence writes.
>
> (II. 17. 1–16)

Recasting this perverse saga of man's downfall, Taylor bemoans the earthly "hell" in which man is "held," self-condemned to "breed" further "ill qualities" and worse deeds in sin's employ. For his repeated failure to "serve with Service best," man is denied both his promised "fee" of eternal life and union with God which "nature holdst her chiefe delights." Forfeiting the original contract's "best of Wages" by his rebellious disservice, man is sentenced to receive the "Worst of incomes" and "Worst of Woe" in worldly labor, death, and alienation from God. Man's only hope for restitution of his status as "best of Beings" rests with Christ, Who comes as God's agent of grace: "But for reliefe Grace in her tender would/ Massiah cast all Sacrifices told" (II.17.17–18).[12]

Taylor's metaphor from judicial proceedings in Sermon and Meditation II.17 makes clear man's predicament, subjected to God's legalistic judgments with appeal only to the forthcoming Messiah. But whereas Sermon II.17 enumerates the efficacies of Christ's sacrifice, Meditation II.17 abstracts and synthesizes these figural truths into a dramatically condensed narrative. Momentarily bailed out, because the Son offers himself as "Bondsman, & Surety" (*UTOT*, p. 378), man must wait upon Christ's later incarnation to obtain full pardon:

> I sin'd. Christ, bailes. Grace takes him Surety,
> Translates my Sin upon his sinless Shine.
> He's guilty thus, and Justice thus doth eye
> And sues the band, and brings on him the fine.
> All Sacrifices burn but yet their blood
> Can't quench the fire, When laid upon the Wood.
>
> The type thy Veane phlebotomizd must bee
> To quench this Fire: no other blood nor thing
> Can do't. Hence thou alone art made for mee
> Burnt, Meat, Peace Sin, and Trespass Offering.
> Thy blood must fall: thy life must go or I
> Under the Wrath of God must ever fry.
>
> (II. 17. 19–30)

Both *Upon the Types* and other meditations on ceremonies portray man under the ancient dispensation as a seeker of temporary atonement through external sacrifices, feasts, and purifications. Images of "fire" and "fry" point graphically to earlier burnt offerings and to the Puritan terror of the fiery "Wrath of God" and hell. But Taylor exposes them as not "Sufficient to appease Gods anger of themselves. Hence they as used are used as types & Shaddows prefiguring the Atonement that should be made by the Blood of one Sufficient to make amends for mans sin. . . . And thus they are types of Christ" (*UTOT*, p. 377). Like placebos which allay but cannot cure, sacrifices "burn but yet their blood/ Can't quench the fire" of God's anger which consumes man's soul, assaulting it with feverish visions of sinful alienation from divine solace. Taylor transforms these Hebraic ceremonies of fire into trenchant types of Christ's shedding of blood, a spilling forth from his wounded side of the only effective medicine – divine grace. Whereas under ceremonial law, the blood of the slain sacrifice was sprinkled about the altar, Taylor writes in Sermon II.17 "that our attonement for Sin, & the Sanctification of our persons is wholy by the blood of Christ . . . applied us to us. Hence the blood of Christ is said to cleanse us from all Sin" (*UTOT*, pp. 363–4). Thus, Taylor exults, "thou alone art made for mee/ Burnt, Meat, Peace Sin, and Trespass Offering," since all those types grouped as "fire" offerings are inferior to the Savior's single act of sacrifice. Christ's crucifixion negates the need for legalistic sacrifices and promises eternal relief from God's punishing rage: "So shall this Wrath from mee be retrograde./ No Fire shall sindge my rags nor on them stay" (II.17.33–4).

Unable to countenance Quaker dismissals of Jesus' humanity or Socinian denials of His divine personhood, Taylor also repeatedly defends Christ as God-man, or as "Jacob's golden Ladder" emblemizes, the mystery of "THEANTHROPIE," by which "The Godhead personated in Gods Son/ Assum'd the Manhood to its Person known" (II.44.9, 10, 19–20). Without this foundation in the Savior's conjoined human and divine natures, the whole edifice of Puritan covenant theology and typology would crumble. To appease God's wrath, Christ voluntarily assumed a human body to become an innocent scapegoat and expiate man's sin. But though His suffering within the "Humane tent/ Of Humane frailty" satisfies the transgressed law, only Christ's divinity makes this offering infinitely propitiating (II.43.35–6). In both Sermons II.17 and II.18 Taylor, therefore, emphasizes the conjunction of typal sacrifices and altars: "Now the Altar being a type of the Divine Nature, & the Offering of the Humane, did typify the Divine & Humane Nature in Union together in one person, & the Efficacy of the Whole person making attonement, & propitiating in the Offering of Christ" (*UTOT*, p. 360). Similarly, to complement Meditation II.17 on Christ's mortal fulfillment of ancient sacrifices, Meditation II.18 draws upon the brazen and incense altars to typify Christ's divine nature and priestly mediation:

Sure then I lack Atonement. Lord me help.
  Thy Shittim Wood ore laid With Wealthy brass
Was an Atoning altar, and sweet smelt:
    But if ore laid with pure pure gold it was
    It was an Incense Altar, all perfum'd
    With Odours, wherein Lord thou thus was bloom'd.

Did this ere during Wood when thus orespread
  With these erelasting Metalls altarwise
Type thy Eternall Plank of Godhead, Wed
    Unto our Mortall Chip, its sacrifice?
    Thy Deity mine Altar. Manhood thine.
    Mine Offring on't for all men's Sins, and mine?

This Golden Altar puts such weight into
  The sacrifices offer'd on't, that it
Ore weighs the Weight of all the sins that flow
    In thine Elect. This Wedge, and beetle split
    The knotty Logs of Vengeance too to shivers:
    And from their Guilt and shame them cleare delivers.

This Holy Altar by its Heavenly fire
  Refines our Offerings: casts out their dross
And sanctifies their Gold by its rich 'tire
    And all their steams with Holy Odours boss.
    Pillars of Frankincense and rich Perfume
    They 'tone Gods nosthrills with, off from this Loom.
                         (II.18.13–36)

Whereas Meditation II.17 extols Christ's shedding of blood as a counterpart to the Old Testament slaying of beasts for burnt offerings, this poem correlates the temple altars with His sanctity. Comparable to the "ere during Wood" and "erelasting Metalls" of the altars, the Savior's "Eternall Plank of Godhead" is hypostatically "Wed/ Unto our Mortall Chip, its sacrifice." Mankind's perpetual disobedience requires an atonement with double potency. Hence, Christ's human offering is insufficient unless His divinity, emblemized by the golden altar, "puts such weight into/ The sacrifices" that it "Ore weighs the Weight of all the sins." Through His filial divinity, Jesus wields an omnipotent "beetle" to "Wedge," hammer, and "split/ The knotty Logs" of God's implacable "Vengeance," as Taylor's metaphor implies. Having cleft His Father's wrath into reverberating "shivers" or "slivers" of disapproval, Jesus with divine compassion delivers men from their trembling beneath the weighty load of "Guilt and shame." Taylor thus reinforces Christ's mystical hypostatical union which brings man full redemption, since "by Altar . . . we are to understand the Person of Christ . . . for the Humane was the Offering he offered up in Sacrifice . . . & the Consideration of this as Sanctified by, & offered upon the Altar of the Divine Nature un to God," more "so that thô the Heart, & Soule felt the burning intollerable, yet the Divine Nature supported the Whole to sustain it to the full Satisfaction of Divine Justice" (*UTOT*, pp. 387, 399).

By deliberately linking Sermons and Meditations II.17 and II.18, Taylor mimetically recreates Christ's unique duality, the wedded humanity and divinity that enables Him antitypally to supersede all legal sacrifices and altars. He also translates pedagogy and polemic into dynamic poetry. Sometimes that creative transmutation involves simply a paraphrase with a personal pronoun: "This Holy Altar by its Heavenly fire/ Refines *our* Offerings: casts out their dross/ And sanctifies their Gold by its rich 'tire" (II.18.31–3). Or just as often, Taylor chooses a verb, as in "Godhead, *Wed/* Unto our Mortall Chip" which resonates with the intimacy of Christ's two natures made one. Or implicitly a new metaphor, as the New England farmer's earth-clearing with "beetle" and "Wedge" wielded against "knotty Logs" suddenly melds together with Christ's divine clearing of "Logs" (the biblical "motes" in one's eye) of sin's "Guilt and shame." Or, the figural analogy once proclaimed, Taylor accumulates detail upon detail of the ceremonial sacrifice, from the altar's very construction to the wafting "Holy Odours" of "Frankincense and rich Perfume." Having distilled the essential figural truth from his homiletic analysis, Taylor then casts his meditation in the personal voice: not all men, but "*I* lack Atonement. Lord *me* help," not the impersonal injunction but the tentative query, "And shall mine Offering by thine Altars fire/ Refin'd, and sanctifi'd to God aspire?" (II.18.13, 47–8). Invigorated by these imagistic variations and ardent personalism, Meditation II.18 conveys a passionate sense of dramatic monologue quite unlike the sermon's pedantic rationalism.

For Taylor the Savior's functions as divinity extend beyond the sanctification of His human sacrifice, as foreshadowed by the brazen altar. Fulfilling the ancient symbolism of incense altars and offerings, Christ also becomes man's omnipresent intercessor, conveying New Testament "perfumes" or prayers from man to God. As Sermon II.18 records, the golden altar was located "within the Tabernacle before the Vaile, Holy of Holies," and was designed "to burn Incense upon to make Sweet perfume that should go up as a Cloud into the Holy of Holies, & also to make an atonement upon its Horns with the blood of the Sin Offering" (*UTOT*, p. 406).[13] Whereas the brazen altar typifies Christ's oblation and satisfaction, the golden altar signifies His "Advocateship, or Mediation" with God, made more potent by His "Propitiation," "obedience," and "Excellent Natures" (*UTOT*, p. 406). Taylor translates these typal ideas into poetic images by explicitly invoking distinctions between a brazen altar of "Shittim Wood ore laid With Wealthy brass" suitable for "Atoning" and the "Incense Altar, all perfum'd" and "ore laid with pure

pure gold" which "Refines our Offerings: casts out their dross" (II.18.14, 15, 17, 16, 32). Disguising, if not dispelling, the stench of sin, signified by the burnt offering, the "Pillars of Frankincense and rich Perfume" (II.18.35) typify the need for the gospel believer's "best of our Services even our Prayers" to "be offered upon the Golden Altar, in the Name of Christ," for "there is but onely one way of Mediation for Sinners to walk in unto Heaven" (UTOT, p. 407). Tendering his prayers "stufft with thy Altars blooms" and "Praise in Melody" as appeals for God's forgiveness, Taylor like all men relies upon Christ to be his divine intermediary (II.18.63, 64). To underscore the Son's intercession, he frames his typal analysis of the incense altar between the personal pleadings of one who lacks "Atonement" and calls out "Lord me help" and God whose "nosthrills" inhale the "Holy Odours" of human prayers and breathe forth far sweeter grace. In both sermon and meditation, Taylor pledges, "My Morn, and Evning Offerings I'le bring/ And on this Golden Altar Incense fling," and he pleads for God to accept his poetic gifts, the "tunes" which "as fume,/ From off this Altar rise to thee Most High" as a substitute for incense offerings of old (II.18.53–4, 61–2). Displacing the "Heavenly fire" of the ancient golden altar, Christ as evangelical interlocutor refines these imperfect human offerings. Thus, Taylor exalts Christ's divine nature which sanctifies His human sacrifice and empowers Him to intercede with God, obtaining for the Elect remission of sins and a new breathing forth from God's "nosthrills" of life, grace, and glory.

Meditation II.19 has often seemed incongruous among the legalistic ceremonies, both for its text from Canticles 1:12 and for its sensuous indulgence in the aromatic "Lavender" and "Oyle of Spike most sweet" which "muskify thy [God's] Palace with their Reeke" (II.19.9, 11–12). Apparently Taylor also reconsidered its suitability, since Upon the Types lacks pages 427–60, located between II.18 and II.20, where a sermon corresponding with Meditation II.19 and preached on December 7, 1696, might reasonably have appeared.[14] Having briefly defined incense in II.18 as a "Perfume made of a Composition of many Choice Spices," Taylor may have elaborated upon this ambrosial offering which wafts from the golden altar into the holy of holies (UTOT, p. 407). A homiletic analysis of "spicknard" would complete his architectural progress from the temple courtyard's brazen altar (II.17) to the sanctuary's golden altar (II.18) into the holy of holies and prepare for an overview of the whole tabernacle (II.20). Based upon just such a progress in Sermon II.20, Taylor typically argues that "as the High Priest in the Celebration of his Office went thrô the body of the Tabernacle, or Temple with the blood of Bulls, & Goats into the Holy of Holies. So did Christ in his Office work pass thrô this his Tabernacle with his own Blood into the most holy Place"

(*UTOT,* p. 421). Embellished by poetic metaphors in II.19, Christ becomes as much King as priest, who reigns in a "Palace" where "at thy Circuite Table sitst," bespeaking "Thine Ordinances, Lord, to greet poor hearts" (II.19.12, 19–20). Taylor transmutes the Old Testament figural scene of God's enthronement on the mercy seat in the tabernacle's holy of holies into a sacramental fresco in which "at thy Table sitst to feast/ Thy Guests there at, Thy Supper, Lord, well drest" (II.19.25–6). A sensuous evocation of Taylor's spiritual yearnings, Meditation II.19 seems more eucharistic than typological because it lacks the strict figural analogies that characterize his other meditations on ceremonial worship. Nonetheless, Taylor implicitly suggests that the Lord's Supper and eschatological King's banquet fulfill ancient services of worship and culminate the saint's entrance into the temple. Furthermore, he correlates the incense "Odour-Oyle rich bright" with his evangelical preachings and poetic prayers, and the ark (in Hebrew "chest" or "box") of the covenant with Christ's temple within the heart. With a "sweet Spicknard breath," Taylor then pledges to "advance thy Glory best" and make his "heart thine Alabaster Box" from which ascend "Songs of Praise" to "scale" the King's "Eares in Spicknardisick Tune" (II.19.27, 28, 29, 35, 36).

Because Taylor posits Christ as sole mediator, concomitantly he denounces Anglican and Catholic reliance upon false intercessors and artificial perpetuations of now defunct ceremonies. He inveighs against "Papists" and "Prelaticall Divines," for instance, who justify their crosses and "Communion Table" or "high Altar" by appealing to ancient types (*UTOT,* p. 387). Because "Altars were not an Humane Invention but a Divine Institution" now fulfilled, they cease, since "all Evangelical Worship" and "Service is to be carried on in this day in the Name & Mediation of Christ," the gospel altar (*UTOT,* pp. 408, 405). Although he eschews overt indictments in Meditation II.18, Taylor offers his services not before a man-made shrine of wood and plaster but upon the only altar with sovereign power:

> Lord let thy Deity mine Altar bee
>   And make thy Manhood, on't my sacrifice.
> For mine Atonement: make them both for mee
>   My Altar t'sanctify my gifts likewise
>   That so myselfe and service on't may bring
>   Its worth along with them to thee my king.
> (II.18.55–60)

By substantiating Christ's omnipotent fulfillment of an altar's atoning functions, Taylor gives the lie to decorative excesses and continuing papist homage to an inanimate type. Furthermore, for Catholics then to deck out priests in lavish array encourages idolatry by glorifying surrogates when the true advocate has come in Jesus. Or as Taylor later rails: "Hence this is to pull Christs Sacerdotall Robe, and Mitre away from him, and also his Ephod, and Office, and to array Saints, and Angells with the Same. And What abuse is this to Christ's Priestly Right, and Power?" (*CHR*, p. 359). By cataloging the symbolic accouterments here or spiritualizing Aaron's "Rich attire" in Meditation II.23, Taylor affirms that Christ alone performs the sacerdotal office and, therefore, abrogates other visible signs of authority. Not "Humane Inventions" or imitations but only enlightened preaching upon Mosaic rites as shadows of the Messiah's satisfaction and intercession, His conjoined humanity and divinity, stirs men to heed the call for a new evangelical obedience.

Heeded rightly, the New Testament altogether abrogates ceremonial laws and heralds Christ as medium of a superior gospel worship: "But the Ceremoniall Law being accomplisht in the thing typified, the Spirituality of the Ceremoniall Law is to be attended, & the Ceremony is to be laid aside. & the Morall Dutie of the Morall Law being Carried on with the Spirituall attendence of the other is the Service of Evangelicall obedience unto the Law of the Spirit of Life, that is in Christ Jesus" (*UTOT*, p. 500). To smother any resuscitation of bygone rites, Taylor certifies the "death" of all Old Testament statutes with Latinate finality: "And hence Ceremonies go no further. . . . they were all in their own Nature *Mortalia*. Such things as should vanish. John Baptists Axe at the Root of the tree rendred them *Mortificata*, mortified, mortaly wounded. Christ's Death rendered them *Mortua*, Stark dead" (*CHR*, p. 290). Taylor's image of a tree causally links the ever burgeoning Jewish rituals to Christ's single, redeeming sacrifice on the cross. That Christ's death should render "Stark dead" all Mosaic ceremonies epitomizes the condign rigor of God's justice. Hence Taylor almost morbidly delights in John the Baptist's ax and Christ's deadly stroke, because the crucifixion signals the passing away of Old Testament offerings and altars and advent of a new spiritual worship.

Reviving his metaphors of the "Draught" and "grafting" from the typological sermons in the later *Christographia*, Taylor cogently synthesizes the paradox of redemption by which Christ's death weeds out legal services, while implanting new evangelical obedience:

> Hence Christ in his Compact with his Father in the Covenant of Redemption . . . came and assumed our nature to glory his law in, and fulfill it Isai. 42. 21, and having done this gives out a renewall of his holy Image on man again in the Work of Regeneration, afresh upon his Soule in Evangelicall Colours according to the eternall purpose of God Rom. 8. 29. He gives him a new Stock of Grace to improove in Obe-

dience to the Holy law of God . . . but changeth the Nature of the Obedience from Legall, to Evangelicall, because the Qualifications fitting and inabling thereunto, are wholy New-Covenant Guifts: and the Condition, Nature and Use of the Same Wholy Evangelicall. (*CHR,* pp. 314–15)

Christ's fulfillment liberates man from Old Testament visible sacrifices, festivals, and purifications administered by priests; but released from contractual or legalistic bonds, man must still adhere to the inner law of righteousness. Christ's "renewall of his holy Image on man" and "Work of Regeneration" empower man to cultivate his "new Stock of Grace to improove in Obedience to the Holy law of God." Freshly blooming with "Evangelicall Colours," the penitent "Soule" concomitantly adopts new modes of obedience and worship, offering up prayers and praises direct from the regenerate heart to the antitypal high priest – Christ. Compared to the prolific legalities of ancient ceremonies, Christ's message appears deceptively simple: "Nay the Gospell is the Doctrine of Salvation, which Christ hath Delivered unto his Church to live up unto. If you live up unto this Doctrine, you cannot miss of Salvation" (*CHR,* p. 295). One creed to displace multiple ceremonies, one eternal rule of salvation for ephemeral constraints under Mosaic institutions, seems a miraculous boon to hard-pressed reprobates. Yet this single rule of evangelical obedience sets standards of perfection unobtainable by fallen mankind – without Christ's example of moral courage and God's grace.

But how does one grow in spiritual purity? cultivate an inwardly cleansed heart? practice outwardly perfected service? Unable to rely upon priestly mediations or propitiations, the new covenant petitioner must begin by scouring his heart for sin, harkening to the preaching of God's Word, and reconfirming his faith. God as Old Testament judge no longer requires ritualized offerings; instead, Christ becomes the "Heart Searcher" Who attempts to "Scoure" the "Heart" which harbors "all Sin, and Iniquity" (*CHR,* pp. 61, 60). The magnitude of man's new duties under an evangelical dispensation casts Edward Taylor into despair when he probes his own heart and discovers only iniquitous putrefactions:

> Guilty, my Lord, What can I more declare?
>   Thou knowst the Case, and Cases of my Soule.
> A Box of tinder: Sparks that falling o're
>   Set all on fire, and worke me all in Shoals.
>   A Pouch of Passion is my Pericarde.
>   Sparks fly when ere my Flint and Steele strike hard.
>
> I am a Dish of Dumps: yea ponderous dross,
>   Black blood all clotted, burdening my heart,
> That Anger's anvill, and my bark bears moss.

My Spirits soakt are drunke with blackish Art.
If any Vertue stir, it is but feeble.
Th'Earth Magnet is, my heart's the trembling needle.
My Mannah breedeth Worms: Thoughts fly blow'd are.
My heart's the Temple of the God of Flies.
My Tongue's an Altar of forbidden Weare
    Fansy a foolish fire enflam'd by toys
    Perfum'de with reeching Offerings of Sins
    Whose steaming reeches delight hobgoblings.
                                    (II.25.1–18)

Magnetically tempted and enflamed by explosive human desires, clotted with ponderous dross, and drunk with blackish (brackish?) arts of sin, Taylor finds only a feeble "Vertue" in that "Pouch of Passion," his "Pericarde." The guilty heart that should be man's sacred temple to worship God becomes the "Temple of the God of Flies." More desecrating even than temple furnishings of old, Taylor's own tongue seems an "Altar of forbidden Weare" spewing forth "reeching [rancid] Offerings of Sins" (not incense's sweet perfume) to be consumed in a mock, "foolish fire" of "Fansy." Densely alliterative, acatalectic in the extreme, end-stopped, and punctuated by itemized self-diagnoses ("Mannah," "Thoughts," "heart's," "Tongue's," "Fansy"), Taylor's plodding dissection ultimately compounds into multiple counts of a judicial indictment – the verdict is "Guilty." The passage seems almost to reflect on the poverty of his own poetic offerings, so often riddled with sin's tortures, yet fancy's seductive allure. Perhaps at times these Meditations seem to Taylor "forbidden Weare," one man's secret vanity, "toys" or playthings rather than genuine psalms of devout praise. By contrast with such heart-searching and debilitating self-doubts, even tabernacle rituals may seem a preferable form of worship. But only when believers turn toward Christ as "King of his Church" does the promised salvation become an obtainable reality, for "this Kingdom is wholy Spirituall: and it is universall, set up in the hearts of Every individuall person from the beginning to the end of the World, that Shall be Saved: and it consist[s] in the Uniting the Soule to the King, whereby the Soul is matriculated, Implanted into Christ, and Swears allegience to Him" (*CHR*, p. 61). Having united with Christ, the sinner gathers sufficient strength to cleanse his heart of "Dumps" and "dross," "Passion" and "Worms," and to purge his heart as a spiritually virtuous temple or "Kingdom" within, dedicated to worshiping and serving Christ as King.

Forbidden to perpetuate ceremonial laws and Jewish sanctuaries as formulas and places for obtaining redemption, nevertheless initially faint-hearted believers take comfort from evangelical designs for new processes and mediums of worship. Just as fallen man no longer seeks merely outward signs of sin or regeneration but plumbs his heart for roots of iniquity and new stocks of grace, so also under New Testament teachings he shifts from idolatrous, external rites to inward spiritual adorations. Drawing upon typal analogies with the tabernacle and temple, Taylor in Meditation II.20 captures his own human confusion. As a dismayed, puzzled persona, he initiates a dialogue with Christ, seeking for some rationale in his fated fall, then pleading for a rejuvenated "Worship-mould":

> Didst thou, Lord, Cast mee in a Worship-mould
>   That I might Worship thee immediatly?
> Hath Sin blurd all thy Print, that so I should
>   Be made in vain unto this End? and Why?
>   Lord print me ore again. Begon, begon,
>   Yee Fly blows all of hell: I'le harbour none.
>
> That I might not receive this mould in vain
>   Thy Son, my Lord, my Tabernacle he
> Shall be: me run into thy mould again.
>   Then in this Temple I will Worship thee.
>   If he the Medium of my Worship stand
>   Mee, and my Worship he will to thee hand.
>   (II.20.1–12)

First printed or "cast" with pristine capacities to worship God, man is polluted by sin, leaving original patterns of obedience smudged and indecipherable. Although he adheres to ceremonial laws and moral commandments engraved on Moses' tablets of stone, man under the old dispensation often strays into self-generated idolatries. As Taylor imagines the metamorphosis under an evangelical era, however, Christ's advent sculpturally recasts man's inward "Worship-mould" and orthographically re-engraves the "print." He prays for the "Temples Influences" to "stick on mee" and Christ's "Holiness" to "guild Every part" that "I in Holy Love may stow my heart/ Upon thyselfe, and on my God in thee" (II.20.55, 58, 56–7). Hence, Christ repatterns the heart to pursue spiritual services internally and to wage holy wars outwardly against wickedness.

Neither individual nor communal obedience to an evangelical rule of righteousness becomes conceivable, however, without the "medium" of Christ, as Taylor's Sermon and Meditation II.20 on Solomon's temple proclaim. Although "run into thy mould again" of spiritual service, the still reluctant soul searches for a visible "house of Worship":

> I can't thee Worship now without an House.
>   An house of Worship here will do no good,
> Unless it type my Woe, in which I douse,
>   And Remedy in deifyed Blood.

> Thy Tabernacle, and thy Temple they
> Such Types arose. Christ is their Sun, and Ray.
>   (II.20.13–18)

Accustomed to external temples, even the redeemed believer skeptically questions the "invisible" conduit to God. Not just a prophet to replace Moses and his legal institutions, nor merely a high priest to outshine Aaron's ministrations, Christ supplants the very habitations, tabernacle and temple, where Israel practiced their ceremonies. As Sermon II.20 teaches, "the Lord Christ is the Gospell Tabernacle or Temple for Gospell Worship," through which, like the high priest of old, He passes "with his own Blood into the most holy Place," which some consider heaven (*UTOT*, pp. 423, 427). Instituted when "Moses, & the Israelites came out of Egypt" to form a distinct "Politicall body Ecclesiastical," the tabernacle provided a visible channel for divine worship sufficient to impress errant souls with Yahweh's superiority to heathen idols (*UTOT*, p. 465). But just as Christ's new dispensing of grace inaugurates a more intimate communion between man and God, so also the "medium" of worship becomes personalized:

> Thou art my Tabernacle, Temple right,
>   My Cleansing, Holiness, Atonement, Food,
> My Righteousness, My Guide of Temple Light
>   In to the Holy Holies, (as is shewd)
>   My Oracle, Arke, Mercy Seat: the place
>   Of Cherubims amazde at such rich grace.
>
> Thou art my Medium to God, thou art
>   My Medium of Worship done to thee,
> And of Divine Communion, Sweet heart!
>   Oh Heavenly intercourse! Yee Angells see!
>   Art thou my Temple, Lord? Then thou Most Choice
>   Art Angells Play-House, and Saints Paradise.
>   (II.20.43–54)

Holiness of place loses all significance when Christ in "his Person in its respect to the Humane Nature, & as to his Church as his Mysticall Selfe" fulfills the ancient typical habitations (*UTOT*, p. 448). Even Solomon's resplendent temple fades into mere shadow as Christ the "Sun, and Ray" eclipses it with his surpassing radiancy of "rich grace." To dramatize the new intimacy between man and God, Taylor extols the "Divine Communion" and "Heavenly intercourse" and with piquant humor transmutes Solomon's revered temple into an antitypal "Angells Play-House." Centrally though, he lauds the surpassing New Testament "Medium of Worship" through Christ, Who to evangelical saints dispenses an immediate "Paradise" within the remolded heart and promises an eternal "Paradise" in heaven.

Wary of encouraging a rampant spiritualism, such as Quakers espoused, Taylor interprets the "Temple" not just as a type of the individual soul and of the Savior, but also as a shadow of the gospel church: "the Person of Christ the Head & the Church of Christ the Body consisting of many Members make up one Mysticall Man . . . Now the Tabernacle, or Temple is a Type of . . . the Mysticall Body of Christ, the Church" (*UTOT*, p. 438). Even though Christ ushers in a spiritual worship, man's innate weakness requires that Christ's kingdom "Internall in the Soul" be manifest visibly in an external "Rule, and Practice" drawn out in "Holy Worship: and holy Societies waring therein against Sin and Satan" (*CHR*, pp. 61–2). Interpreted mystically, the temple and tabernacle thus foreshadow the "holy society" of all believers who profess faith in Christ's redemption. While he urges that Christ is "the Onely Medium or Mediatour wherein our approach is, & onely can be, made acceptably, in our Persons, & Services unto God," Taylor also stresses that "we when in Covenant must be cleansed, & Sanctified . . . visibly in order to our visible Communion with God in his Instituted Worship" (*UTOT*, pp. 433, 434). He then analyzes the various courts of the Old Testament temple in order to differentiate classes of believers. The "Outward" or "people's court" is "a Suitable representation of the Catholick Church under the Gospell in the largest sense, as it contains good & bad," and the "Sanctuary . . . seems to be an Emblem of the Gospell Church consisting in its visible Societies Celebrating the Holy Ordinances of God, in the Preaching the Word, & Celebrating the Lords Supper" (*UTOT*, pp. 438, 439). Only those cleansed, ceremonially under the old rites and through a saving relation under the new, can enter this church estate. Just as "under the Old Testament Ceremoniall Uncleaness Secluded from Divine Ordinances . . . So under the Gospell Dispensation Morall Uncleaness visible Secludes from Divine Fellowship in Gospell Sacraments" (*UTOT*, p. 442). Such distinctions prove crucial to Taylor's refutations of Solomon Stoddard's criteria by which all church members, professed or not, cleansed or not, might be admitted to the Lord's Supper. In Sermon II.20 he completes his typal progression by correlating the "Lords Court" where the incense altar stands outside the holy of holies with "the Invisible Church of Christ contain'd in the Visible. . . . And so these are the true Worshippers that worship God in Spirit," those Elect destined for heavenly fellowship (*UTOT*, p. 439). Because there is a "totall Cessation of Temple, & Templeworship, in the world of a Ceremoniall Stamp," evangelical believers must cultivate a "Worship-mould" within and manifest their obedience through Christ as the spiritual medium and through the church (*UTOT*, p. 428). Only within this church which is Christ's mystical body do individual saints receive strength to obey stringent evangelical ordinances and to exercise their recast hearts in appropriate worship.

Left to their own inventions with no biblical or homiletic guidance for "Holy Worship" and "holy Societies," men too easily regress to heathen forms, papist and prelatical imitations, or to sectarian enthusiasms. Preaching a typological reading of Old Testament law, Taylor advocates instead spiritual proceedings within a purified meetinghouse, such as the visible church at Westfield. Ordained by Christ's own instructions to his disciples, true New Testament churches possess no intrinsic holiness, display no ornate furnishings, nor reproduce Old Testament temples as Catholic cathedrals did. Only the presence of covenanting believers, gathered to hear the preaching of God's Word, to offer prayers and psalms, and to receive the sacraments, gives to any visible church its significance as a "house of Worship." Erring in the opposite extreme from Catholic and Anglican retentions of Mosaic rites, Quaker reliances on intuition and Socinian rationalism pose equally serious threats to Puritan ecclesiology. When religion becomes too individual and inward a seeking for grace or a reasoned pursuit of the single God (Unitarian), it becomes less dependent upon rigorous church discipline. Against both sects Taylor cites the New Testament which positively institutes church societies and evangelical worship. Taylor urges parishioners to "Strive to get a Saving Relation to Christ. Then thou wilt have access to this House, & to Carry on the Worship of God in this Gospell Tabernacle," and to "Live Up to the Laws of the Tabernacle" (*UTOT*, p. 451). Countering Quaker spiritualism, Taylor culls the gospel to justify communal worship. Against Socinian rationalism, he cites Christ's calling for faith in his salvation and Word (the matter), as preached within sanctioned churches of worship (the manner). To rely too much on externals in worship (as Anglicans and papists) or too little (as Quakers and Socinians) is to stumble from the middle road of Puritan worship for which the Bible provides ample guidelines. Grounded in fundamental typological doctrine which teaches the abrogation of Old Testament altars, temples, and priestly services, Taylor's *Upon the Types of the Old Testament* and meditations on ceremonial law, like Mather's treatise earlier, champion the Puritan gospel church and worship.

Under the old dispensation Israel worshiped God through feasts and festivals, according to the days, weeks, and years of the Jewish calendar. In *Upon the Types of the Old Testament,* Taylor opens Sermon II.25 by reviewing his previous topics and forecasting his new subjects: "We have heard of the Substantialls of the Typicall Worship, as it Consists in Sacrifices; & the Places of Sacrificing, viz, the Altar, & the Tabernacle, or Temple. Now I am come to the Adjuncts of this Worship," which are the "Seasons" and "Discipline" (*UTOT*, p. 501). The "Seasons" include the "Universall: which are to be attended alwayes, & thrô all other: as that of the Continuall Burnt Offering. Or (if you please) the Morning, & Evening Sacrifice," and the "Particular," among which he cites the

"Ordinary" or "Weekly, & Monthly Seasons" (*UTOT*, pp. 501–2). "At
this time," he proclaims, "I shall Consider the Continuall Burnt Offering: & the Weekly or Sabbath Sacrifices" (*UTOT*, p. 502). Despite problems with Sermon II.25's placement, Taylor's directive suggests that daily
and sabbath sacrifices were to form a bridge from "Mediums of Worship" (II.17–20) to major feasts (II.21–24).[15] That Taylor believed the
"Continuall Burnt Offerings" universal took precedence over "Particular" festivals is confirmed by a chart in which he tabulates the number of
beasts slaughtered yearly, beginning with the "Mornings & Evenings"
then "Weekly Sabbaths" before enumerating in chronological order the
lunar and anniversary feasts (*UTOT*, p. 521). Developing a strict Puritan
reading, Taylor carefully distinguishes the burnt, meat, and drink offerings which as "Ceremonies cease" from "the Creede/ Contained therein"
which "continues gospelly," for these types usefully foreshadow the moral
duties of evangelical worshipers (II.25.45–6). As preacher in Sermon II.25
he exhorts his flock to "attend, the Evening, Morning, & Sabbath Days
Sacrifices. Evangelicall Sacrifices. Pray, Read the Word, Worship God
with the Sacrifice of Praise" (*UTOT*, p. 524). As preparationist and poet,
he slants the figural analogy in a more sacramental direction. Under Mosaic
ordinances God required "Two Lambs, a Meat, and Drinke offering,"
which typify the "Gospell Sabbaths" on which days the New Testament
chosen are invited to taste "Spirituall Wine/ Pourd out to God: and Sanctified Bread" commemorating Christ's "Atonement" (II.25.34, 36, 37–
8). Celebrated continuously throughout all other Jewish feasts, the daily
and sabbath services teach new covenant saints a moral lesson: Worship
God without ceasing through prayer, praise, and partaking of the Lord's
Supper.

Taylor's fascination with numerology and the Hebraic calendar dominates the sermons on seasonal or "particular" feasts, and the companion
meditations primarily extol Christ's miraculous fulfillments as antitype.
Proclaiming these "Sacred Seasons" of "Holy Worship" to be "either
Lunary. as New Moons" or "Septinary" in his sermon (*UTOT*, p. 454),
Meditation II.21 then lauds these "Rich Festivalls" made "to entertain
thy Guests most dresst/ In dishes up by SEVENS," even paraphrasing a
catalog from the sermon (II.21.1, 2–3).[16] As he then navigates through
the "Septinary Solemnities" either "Anniversary" or "Annual," he faith-
fully heeds the Scripture's Judaic chronology and annotates each anniversary feast's date and duration (*UTOT*, p. 468). Passover is "Celebrated
upon the 14:[th] day at Even of the first Month" (Nisan/March–April) and
linked with the "Feast of Unleavened bread consisting of the Seven following Dayes" (II.22), then succeeded by Pentecost (II.22A) "just Seven
complete Weeks after the Passover" (*UTOT*, p. 494).[17] Concluding the
holy seasons, the Feast of Atonement (II.23) on the tenth and of Tabernacles (II.24) on the fifteenth–twenty-third take place in the seventh month

(Tishri/September–October). In an addendum to Sermon II.24 (Feast of Tabernacles) Taylor pronounces resolutely that "having thus gone over the Anniversary Feasts as they are Types, I am now come to consider the Annual Feasts typicall as

the $\begin{cases} \text{Sabbaticall Yeare every seventh} \\ \\ \text{The Yeare of Jubilee every fiftieth} \end{cases}$ " (*UTOT*, p. 573). A homily on

sabbatical and jubilee years would seem a likely culmination of Taylor's chronometric escalation from holy days (new moons) to weeks (Passover and Pentecost) to months (Atonement and Tabernacles). But the following pages between 613 and 637 have been cut from the manuscript, leaving Taylor's actual composition unknown.[18]

Abrogated under the New Testament, Jewish festivals find their counterparts only in Christological fulfillments, not through literal or imitative performance. In Sermon II.22 Taylor bemoans the contemporary "human inventions in worship" that would perpetuate a Passover through Easter celebrations: "If Christ be the Gospell Passover, then the Type Ceaseth in Christ, as all other types did in their Antitype. Hence Celebration of the Easter Week is altogether unwarrantable, it is to make that time & not Christ our Gospell Passover" (*UTOT*, pp. 488, 486). Christ becomes Passover's "Paschall Lamb" and Pentecost's giver of "Gospell Law of Spirit and Life" (II.22.26, 58); the new "Aaron" to officiate and "Scape Goate" to atone for man's sin (II.23.34); the Savior incarnate, whose "Tent cloath of a Humane Quilt" canopies His "Person all Divine" (II.24.22, 27). By casting Jesus in these luminous guises as foreshadowed by typical feasts, Taylor dramatizes the paradox that Christ's expiatory death to appease an angry Father turns the tide of history and of each believer's spiritual life. Prefigured by the ancient Feast of Weeks which commemorates that "Isra'l a fift'th day from Egypt broke,/ Gave Sinai's Law, and Crown'd the mount with Smoke," Pentecost signifies that Christ also "in fiery guise" and "Tongues" gave "Mount Zions Law from graces store" unto the disciples, empowering them to preach a new covenant between man and God (II.22.53–4, 56, 59, 57). Henceforth, man feeds upon the Lord's Supper's paschal lamb, obeys "Zions Law" of grace (II.22.57), receives "Heate and Spirits all divine" from Christ's "Gracious hand" (II.23.69, 67), and transforms his heart's "Tabernacle" into Christ's "Tenement" (II.24.48).

Christ accomplishes the evangelical salvation only by assuming man's mortal flesh, a marvelous incarnation which Taylor finds adumbrated by Israel's Feast of Tabernacles. Initially, he accumulates a series of brief metaphysical conceits, which conjoin God's divine, macrocosmic omnipotence with homely, earthbound objects, to evoke the miracle of

Christ's "Theanthropy" (II.24.61). Comparable to the "burning Sun, with'ts golden locks . . . buttond up in a Tobacco box," Christ the Son must enclose His radiant warmth and immensity within a stained body (II.24.2, 4). Or in similar fashion Taylor portrays Christ the creator who "hast the Heavens bright/ Pav'd with the Sun, and Moon, with Stars o're pinckt," descending to earth to become a "Heavens Filler housd in Clay" and to assume a "Tent cloath of a Humane Quilt" (II.24.7–8, 12, 22). These cumulative comparisons that repeatedly shrink Christ's all-powerful divinity into the smallest human spaces underscore the ideas of confinement, the housing of infinite grandeur in finite flesh, and of clothing or donning the human form like a robe or shroud. But Taylor finds yet more apt the prefigurations in the Feast of Tabernacles or Booths, during which Israel tented in booths made of leafy boughs to commemorate their forty years of nomadic wandering:

> Thy Godhead Cabbin'd in a Myrtle bowre,
>   A Palm branch tent, an Olive Tabernacle,
> A Pine bough Booth, An Osier House or tower
>   A mortall bitt of Manhood, where the Staple
> Doth fixt, uniting of thy natures, hold,
> And hold our marvels more than can be told.
>
> . . . .
>
> Wonders! my Lord, Thy Nature all With Mine
>   Doth by the Feast of Booths Conjoyned appeare
> Together in thy Person all Divine
>   Stand House, and House holder. What Wonder's here?
> Thy Person infinite, without compare
> Cloaths made of a Carnation leafe doth ware.
>   (II.24.13–18, 25–30)

By blending secular and scriptural images, such words as "tabernacle," "housd," "buttond," "Cabbin'd," and "Tent," recreate the mystery of Christ's incarnation, an emwombing and embodying within mortal flesh. And the pun on "Carnation leafe" and "Incarnation" succinctly links Christ's assumed humanity to the motivating cause, for when Adam and Eve fell into shameful disgrace before God's eyes, they clothed themselves with leaves. Taylor substitutes tobacco, pine, palm, and olive branches (connoting victory and peace) for fig leaves, but the implicit reminders of Adam's fall and Israel's desert journey make clear that only through Christ's mediation does each saint receive a new clothing in evangelical grace, a new habitation within Christ's tabernacle, and a paradisiacal Canaan. Taylor concludes his meditation by rejoicing in the reciprocal covenant that Christ offers, pleading that "Thy Tenent, and thy Teniment I'le live" and "Ile be thy Tabernacle: thou shalt bee/ My Tabernacle. Lord thus mutuall wee" (II.24.57, 59–60). Because Christ takes on the human form, like a tenant he pays "Rent of Celestiall Wealth," ransoming His divinity in order to pay off mankind's debt (II.24.58). But through this sacrifice, He becomes the evangelical tabernacle within which all men may lodge, paying "thee rent of Reverent fear" (II.24.51). As in Meditation II.20 in which Taylor's heart becomes a temple for gospel worship, in Meditation II.24 he also stresses how Christ's incarnation miraculously enables man himself to become a living "Tabernacle" and "Tenement." Christ as the divine "Landlord" sets the terms (repentance and faith) by which man's heart becomes a fit habitation, but so too as a "Tenent" He promises (through grace) to abide forever within the saint's purified heart or tabernacle. By mingling typal analogies with worldly images, Taylor imitates in his poetic technique the very mystery of "Theanthropy," the conjoining of divine and human natures, that he praises with "Palmifer'd Hosannah Songs" (II.24.65).

Meditation II.24 also illustrates that Taylor need not depart from biblical images in order to generate complicated and engaging poems. Because the rough-hewn diction so idiosyncratically adorns other poems, startling the reader into appreciation of Taylor's often cranky independence and tortured honesty, we may overly esteem those moments when he tumbles images upon images from disparate realms of human experience – architecture, horticulture, cabinetry, farming, medicine, law, games, astronomy, nature, cooking, writing. But in the figural meditations, poetic inspiration frequently springs from the abundant repertoire of biblical images, metaphors, and stories, as in the use of "Tent," "Tabernacle," and "Booth" in Meditation II.24. Starting with the "Feast of Booths," he need only spin out, phrase by phrase, the ceremonial details and spiritual fulfillments. Like the delicate variations derived from a single musical melody, the modest tent becomes replayed as a "Myrtle bowre,/ A Palm branch tent, an Olive Tabernacle,/ A Pine bough Booth, An Osier House, or tower," designed like Christ's "mortall bitt of Manhood" to "hold out marvels more than can be told" (II.24.13–15, 16, 17). The rhetorical exercise in the sermon and meditation is precisely "to tell out" the marvels in a series of questions, exclamations, assertions, and hyperboles. The labored conceit may at times stretch our patience, but the meditative process itself demands such a search for universal truths grounded in particularities, just as the spiritual meaning or kernel of truth must be extracted from the literalism of types. Taylor creates as well a sense of dramatic reciprocity in Meditation II.24 (and elsewhere), when he seems virtually to barter with God, for "Thou wilst mee thy, and thee, my tent to bee./ Thou wilt, if I my heart will to thee rent" (II.24.46–7). "Rent mutuall" and "Lord thus mutuall wee" culminates the seeming divorce of Taylor's "I" and "me" from God's "thee," "thy," and "thou" to underscore how Christ's mediatory grace effects the desired reconciliation between man and God. Furthermore, Taylor displays his penchant for playfully manipulating words and images, pleading on the one hand for Christ to "lease thyselfe to mee," and pledging on the other to "give/ A Leafe unto thy Lordship of myselfe" (II.24.55–6). By blending the biblically inspired type of leafy tents from the Festival of Booths with the language of tenements and rents, Taylor both reinforces the legalism of the old covenant ceremonies and concretely renders the new covenant fulfillment by which saints inhabit Christ's spiritual tabernacle and Christ in turn resides within the temple of human hearts.

When Christ becomes the tabernacle within which man worships, he also assumes His role as the high priest of all New Testament worship, antitypally fulfilling Aaron's officiating at the Feast of Atonement. More perfectly than what the inferior priests "did, but in the Shadow, he did in the very Substance of the thing . . . and Priesthood Consisting in the office, that attended upon rituall attonement, hath breathed out its last gasp: leaving the office Wholy unto Christ" (*CHR*, p. 349). In Meditation II.23 Taylor virtually reenacts each stage of the atonement, while simultaneously exalting Christ's superiority as both sacrifice and intermediary between God and His people. Though Sermon II.23 nowhere mentions Aaron, Taylor here casts him as the exemplary priest of Levi, officiating at the yearly feast of expiation (Lev. 16:2–28). Even dressed in celebratory finery, Aaron no more than adumbrates the human purity of Christ's priestly service.

> A'ron as he atonement made did ware
>   His milke white linen Robes, to typify
> Christ cloath'd in human flesh pure White, all fair,
>   And undefild, atoneing God most High.
>   Two Goates he took, and lots to know Gods will,
>   Which he should send away: and Which, should kill.
>
> Dear Christ, thy Natures two are typ't thereby
>   Making one Sacrifice, Humane, Divine
> The Manhood is Gods Lot, and this must dy.
>   The Godhead as the Scape Goate death declines.
>   One Goat atones, one bares all Sin away.
>   Thy natures do this work, each as they lay.
>   . . . .
>
>   Thus done with God Aaron aside did lay
>   His Linen Robes, and put on's Golden Ray.
>
> And in this Rich attire he doth apply
>   Himselfe before the peoples very eyes,
> Unto the other Service, richly high
>   To typify the gracious properties

> Wherewith Christs human nature was bedight
> In which he mediates within Gods Sight.
>   (II.23.25–36, 53–60)

The efficacy of Christ's sacerdotal office and "Scape Goate" sacrifice crystallizes here, because Taylor highlights the primary typal truth from among abundant homiletic details. Taylor heeds Levitical prefigurations about Christ's dual nature when he distinguishes between the "Linen Robes" and those of "Golden Ray." Donning his "pure White Raiment Lev. 16.4 calld Linen Garments," Aaron foreshadows "the Undefiled, unspotted, & Milk White Righteousness of Christ even of the Humane Nature of Christ, in which he carries on the Work of Atonement with God for our Sins" (*UTOT*, p. 534). Through mortification of this "human flesh pure White, all fair," by which His "Garments" are "Died with his Blood," Jesus renders satisfaction for transgressions against the law. Attired in more opulent "Glorious golden Garments," Aaron officiates "in the Sight of the people" and enacts his second service by mediating for sinners who themselves cannot offer sacrifices. Comparably, these "glorious Robes Broidered with Gold, & Studded with precious Stones" signify "Christs Glorious accomplishments with Divine Grace," as he pleads before His Father on behalf of mankind (*UTOT*, p. 540). Just as the altars of brass and gold typified Christ's blood sacrifice and intercession, so also Aaron's linen and golden vestments prefigure His double efficacy as high priest – both to satisfy God's justice through a perfect sin offering and to mediate for man's salvation. Clearly a variation of this same duality, the two scapegoats symbolize the Savior "renderd dead by the dying of the Human Nature," but "made a live his Divine Nature" (*UTOT*, p. 535). Through His unique nature as incarnate deity, whether as atoning beast or priest, the Son secures forever that longed-for reconciliation between mankind and God.

Though Meditation II.23 lacks metaphoric ingenuity and soul-searching anguish, it exemplifies Taylor's definitional use of a typological conceit, in which he catalogs figural analogies to gloss homiletic doctrines. Sermon II.23 engulfs one with intricacies – an opening discourse on atonement's symbolic date, the priest's preparations (materials and garments), the burnt and incense offerings, rites exercised within the holy of holies or before the congregation, and a polemical reproof against papists, Socinians, and other historical heretics. Rather than integrate his personal fears with figural reassurances as in Meditation II.16 on the house of Jacob, in Meditation II.23 Taylor frames his doctrine with personal pleas. He diminishes himself, "I'm small and Naught" like an "Ant" or "Emmets Egge," while he magnifies God as "Greatest Lord of Lords," "King of Kings," the "Almighty" who dispenses grace as largess (II.23.11,

5, 8, 1, 2, 9). By compacting prefigurative acts, he attempts to recreate the momentum of a pageant, as if the propitiation regally proceeds before one's eyes. First, "Aaron must in a Censar all of Gold/ Sweet incense burn with Altars fire Divine," before going "unto the Holy place/ With blood of Sprinkling" to atone "the Tabernacle, Altars face/ And Congregation, for defild all were" (II.23.39–40, 43–4, 45–6). He "then burns the Goat without the Camp/ And Bullock too whose blood went in the Vaile" to complete the ceremony of atonement (II.23.49–50). But rationalism dominates over experience, as Taylor immediately translates all ceremonial acts into spiritual emblems for Christ's nature and priesthood. Hence "Sweet Incense" does "Typify the Incense of thy Prayer," "Christ with his proper blood did enter in/ The Heavens bright, propitiates for Sin," and like goat and bullock, "Christ sufferd so without the Gate Deaths Cramp" (II.23.40, 41, 47–8, 51). Distinguished by its logic, Meditation II.23 gains in controlled perfection but loses the spontaneity of personal monologue, psychic pain, or miraculous conversion which often vitalizes other poems. Though it assists the understanding, it barely kindles the holy affections; Meditation II.23 adheres to the forms of meditative exercise, but it lacks passionate engagement. Whatever the diverse manners of these meditations on sacrifices (II.17), altars (II.18), tabernacles (II.24), and atonement (II.23), however, the themes remain consistent. Taylor spies Christ's dual nature emblemized in all guises – as antitype to the burnt offerings, brazen and incense altars, palm branch tent, Aaronic priest, and scapegoat. As he seeks spiritual illuminations about the means of man's salvation, one pathway looms preeminently – belief in Christ's incarnation. Providentially determined by God, set in motion by an angelic annunciation, the advent of Jesus as God's divine Son, man born of woman, the promised seed out of the house of Jacob, changes the covenant from a legal contract into an evangelical worship.

Having rejected visible rituals, whether in sacrificial offerings, feasts, or priestly atonements, Puritans advocate even more zealously the preaching of God's Word by an enlightened ministry. As a preacher, Taylor thus fulfills an essential role in New Testament processes of salvation, because Christ entrusts to anointed disciples power to interpret and spread His Word. Within the new covenant Church, enlightened exegesis of Old Testament shadows, such as ceremonial law and temple furnishings, and new gospel truths set forth in reasoned sermons must attend affectionate professions of faith, for if uncurbed by rational exegesis of God's Word, faith rebelliously breaks away into unbridled and self-willed enthusiasm. Gravitating toward an imagistic presentation, as is often his habit in applications, Taylor substitutes a use "By way of Light" rather than "Information" in Sermon II.20. From his study of "Christ Jesus" as "Gospell Tabernacle, & Temple," he finds that the

"Holy Truth of God Shines as a Glorious Beam of the Sun of Righteousness in the Firmament of the Church to enlighten our Eyes" (*UTOT*, p.
443). He interprets the "Golden Candlesticks mentaind by the Holy Oyle"
here "as a cleare intimation that by the Light of the Word the Graces of
the Spirit are Communicated. . . . So that this is for the expelling of all
darkness out of our Understanding, & filling it with Light & all pervers-
ness in our Will, & Affections & Stowing them with Grace" (*UTOT*, p.
445). Just as Mather had argued that "A Church without a Minister, is a
Candlestick without a Light" (*FT*, p. 391), so also Taylor acknowledges
that "the Ministers" are the "Golden Candlesticks," who must illuminate the light of God's word (*UTOT*, p. 433). In a later poetic variation
on this figure, Taylor also prays, "my Reason make thy Candle/ And
light it with thy Wisdom's flames that spangle" (II.45.11–12). More needy
than other men, the preacher requires within his "Soule a lamp to light
that place/ That so these beames let in, may generate/ Grace in my Soule,
and so an Holy State" (II.45.46–8). Endowed with radiant beams of vision,
wisdom, and grace from Christ, the pastor shines incandescently in his
church and illumines the divine gospel for his benighted flock.

Taylor repeatedly calls Jesus the "Sun of Righteousness" Who radiates
truth into earth's gloom, but in Meditation II.21 he generates a more
original metaphysical conceit for his own ministering role:

> Make mee thy Lunar Body to be filld
>   In full Conjunction, with thy Shining Selfe
> The Sun of Righteousness: whose beams let guild
>   My Face turnd up to heaven, on which high Shelfe
>   I shall thy Glorys in my face that shine,
>   Set in Reflected Rayes. Hence thou hast thine.
>
> (II.21.31–6)

Whether stellar or lunar, Taylor imagines himself as a diminished light,
but possessed of sufficient insight to reflect Christ's holy rays to men
shrouded in ignorance and earthly wickedness. As an enlightened exegete, he rejects Old Testament ceremonialism and priestly pretensions to
preach instead the simplicities of evangelical worship – reading the Bible,
practicing self-examination of the soul, and attending the Sacrament. And
he instructs parishioners accordingly "to trim our Lamps that Stand in
the Candlesticks of our Souls the Temple of the Holy Ghost 1 Cor. 6.16.
& light them with the Heavenly Fire of the Word by reading Some portion thereof Morning, & Evening. & so to keep this Heavenly fire alive
upon the Altar. & to be addressing the Oracle & the Mercy Seate dayly"
(*UTOT*, p. 447). As a disciple, Taylor labors not only to illuminate the
understanding of Old Testament temple types, he seeks also ultimately
to recast each parishioner's heart into a mold imprinted by Christ's New
Testament ordinances.

The motif of service which recurs in both homilies and ceremonial meditations accentuates Taylor's ministerial dedication, whether in his role as an outspoken covenant theologian in Westfield or in his private search for a perfected inner worship. In the *Christographia* he elaborates on Christ's "Spirituall Constraints" which press the "Soule out upon his Service" to create an allegory in which Jesus, the marshaling general, armors a ragged recruit for a holy crusade.

> And then accomplish it with all accomplishments for his Service: Give it a new heart, a New Spirit, a Spiritualized frame, and raised Disposi-tion for God, and his Cause: then put the Press mony into its hand: inrich it with all Grace, put upon it all the Armor of God: and then Call it out to the Spirituall Exercise in holiness, and Righteousness before God, in Holy Meditations, Examinations, applications, Reformations, Ejaculations, Admirations, Faith, Love, Repentance, and Praise: and also into the Spirituall Warfar against Spirituall Wickednesses, and the darkness of this World, by Repentance, resistance of Evill, plucking down Strong hold, High imaginations, and every thought into obedi-ence to Christ. (*CHR*, p. 61)

Not merely a passive shepherd for a fearful flock, Taylor becomes a more militant crusader. Once armored with God's grace, he launches "Spiri-tuall Warfar against Spirituall Wickednesses, and the darkness of this World," by forging his sermons into polemical weapons to repudiate erring sects and papist perpetuations of ceremonial law. Retaliating against their heretical sallies with his own typological attacks, he vindicates the Puritan ecclesiology and vows that his "feeble Spirits will grow frim" so that "My Vespers, and my Mattins Ile attend:/ My Sabbath Service carry on I will" (II.25.47, 49–50). In both *Upon the Types* and *Christographia,* Taylor thus champions an evangelical worship to muster his parishioners for distinctly spiritual battles. Strengthened by his readings of all Mosaic law as types of Christ and the church, he leads his small regiment of the Westfield church militant in sabbath service, exhorting his flock to enter a new evangelical fellowship under Christ's banner.

Though Taylor embraces his public office as evangelical preacher with crusading zeal, he inwardly suffers from excruciating doubts when he contemplates the "Cases of my Soule" (II.25.2). Because he is more gifted with vision, he flagellates himself the more severely for rebellious explo-sions from that "Pouch of Passion," his "Pericarde" (II.25.5). Unable to exercise pastoral service without perpetual chastening of his inward loathsomeness, he commits his revitalized "Will" to the most strenuous heart-searching through regular meditation. Repeatedly in his poetic examinations of self, Taylor cries out for Christ's rejuvenating touch, so that he can pursue his ministerial-and personal services to the King. In Meditation II.23, he prays for healing from the Lord's "Gracious hand"

to "chafe, and rub/ Till my numbd joynts be quickn'd and compleat"
(II.23.67–8). Delivered from enervating sin and imbued instead "With
Heate and Spirits all divine, and good," Taylor energetically limbers once
flaccid muscles into "nimble . . . Service Greate" (II.23.69, 70).

The *Preparatory Meditations* on Mosaic law (II.16–25) capture Taylor in
the midst of an intimate "Spirituall Exercise," as he personally obeys
Christ's calling of transgressing souls to "Holy Meditations, Examinations, applications, Reformations, Ejaculations, Admirations, Faith, Love,
Repentance, and Praise" (*CHR,* p. 61). Having rejected Old Testament
and Catholic rituals as idolatries which delude men, Taylor must discover new molds compatible with personalized, inward belief. Bemoaning Adam's original lapse from perfect service, he inaugurates a quest for
an evangelical worship to supersede Old Testament ceremonies. Fulfilling Christ's command to examine and reform the heart within, Taylor's
poetic meditations become his unique offerings of spiritual service. In
outbursts of "Faith, Love, Repentance, and Praise," he brings to God a
new "Temple Musick" (II.20.60) and the "Sacrifice of Praise in Melody"
as his homage (II.18.64). Being cast into a new "Worship–mould,"
therefore, becomes not simply the message of his ceremonial meditations
but the very process of each poem. Having mourned originally in Meditation II.17 that "man the best servd thee the Worst of all," Taylor ends
his poem with renewed prayers and pledges to Christ (II.17.5):

> Then own thine own. Be thou my Sacrifice,
>   Thy Father too, that he may father mee,
> And I may be his Child, and thy blood prize,
>   That thy attonement may my clearing bee.
>   In hope of Which I in thy Service sing
>   Unto thy Praise upon my Harp within.
>   (II.17.49–54)

Renewed in his faith, Taylor, like a newborn child, offers his evangelical
services to the divine Father, both by preaching the necessary purification and deliverance from sin's bondage to his Westfield congregation
and by meditating within his heart's temple on his personal need for
Christ's sacrifice and atonement.

5

New England's Saints Delivered

But Isra'ls coming out of Egypt thus,
  Is Such a Coppy that doth well Descry
Not onely Christ in person unto us.
  But Spirituall Christ, and Egypt Spiritually.
  Egyptian Bondage whence gates Israel shows
  That Spirituall Bondage whence Christs children goe.
                                        (II.58.31–6)

During the seventeenth century in England, poets as well as theologians split along religious lines, yet both Anglicans and Puritans incorporated typological metaphors into their poetry, as George Herbert did in *The Temple* (1633) and John Milton in *Paradise Lost* (1667), *Samson Agonistes* (1671), and *Paradise Regained* (1671).[1] Part of the traditional reservoir of biblical exempla and literary images, Old Testament figures could be manipulated to serve the purposes of either religious disputation or poetic meditation. Drawing upon the commingled strains of this double heritage, Edward Taylor was a latecomer when he composed his homilies *Upon the Types of the Old Testament* and *Preparatory Meditations*. Although he applied typological analogies with doctrinaire clarity, his sermons and meditations reflect the potential dangers of coming late to figural exegesis. He relies often uncritically upon Thomas Taylor and Samuel Mather, adopting structures, details, and theories from their well-stocked compendiums, and he occasionally reverts in the meditative lyrics to simple lists of parallelisms. In many respects Taylor worked under unavoidable restraints on his poetic creativity, since the Puritan theory of typology restricted spiritual analyses and applications and condemned as heretical the ingenuities of human imagination. Even given these momentary artistic lapses and theological constraints, Taylor's use of typology, like Herbert's and Milton's, frequently strikes us as uniquely creative. Like George Herbert, Taylor lets loose the rebellious soul, mourns his unworthiness, and yet finally requests the "collar" from Christ that will fit him to bear his ministerial duty of preaching the gospel in New England. Although a "priesthood" of a different order than Herbert's Anglicanism, Taylor's

Puritan ministry was equally grounded in the personal meditative exercise of poetry.

The need to defend the church's purity and its covenant worship from backsliders and schismatics was also an imperative for Taylor in the Westfield wilderness. Like the historians, though more implicitly, he perceived this particular band of Elect, like others scattered throughout New England, as God's newly chosen people, providentially guided to America to become, as John Winthrop had declared, "a Citty vpon a Hill," set before "the eies of all people." Though the recapitulation of Israel's flight from Egypt's bondage seems to us such a defining mythology for the New England settlers, within the context of *Upon the Types of the Old Testament* and *Preparatory Meditations* the journey remains a spiritual one, reenacted within the soul of every Christian pilgrim and, more particularly, within the heart of Edward Taylor. In political terms purification and deliverance meant purifying the Church of England of its recalcitrant commitment to external worship forms and delivering parishioners from an enforced episcopal polity, if necessary by a mass removal to the New World. But for Taylor and conservative typologists like him, purification and deliverance also retained their primary sense of cleansing the soul from sin and delivering it from the tyranny of law into a celebration of Christ's evangelical promises of a new spiritual life. Taylor too followed the path of many dissenters by fleeing the Act of Uniformity to establish a reformed worship in New England, but his preachments to the Westfield congregation speak to the inward status of the sin-infested heart, "Black Blew" with "Purple Spots of Horrid guilt" (II.28.13). For the Puritans outward worship, particularly in condemned ceremonial forms, lacked efficacy without the transmutation of the soul, prepared through a calling, the conviction of sin, and justification for entrance into the church, where the sacraments might seal this newly made covenant with God. Despite Taylor's apparent surety about his election, in the *Preparatory Meditations* he repeatedly castigates his own backslidings into sin, using the poems as one way of achieving repentance and new faith in Christ's cleansing and curative powers. And he seeks throughout a lifetime for deliverance from the "Bondage State to Sin and Satan," so that he may not only participate as a bona fide member of the church, but may as its ordained pastor administer the sacraments of Baptism and the Lord's Supper (II.58.37).

Edward Taylor diverges, though not radically, in his order and focus from both *Christ Revealed* and *The Figures or Types*. In *Upon the Types* he rigorously justifies his own transitions and succeeds remarkably in uniting Thomas Taylor's sacramental focus with Samuel Mather's emphasis on ceremonial worship and God's providences. Having "considerd the Worship as typicall" within the "Res Ecclesia," Taylor announces in Sermon II.26, "now I am come to the Typicall Discipline of the Church under the Typicall Administration," thereby initiating his three sermons on purifications (*UTOT,* p. 577). Calvinist doctrine began by assuming man's innate depravity, a legacy that Taylor attributes in Meditation II.28 to Adam's original fall, which leaves all men with "their Glory . . . benighted/ Their Beauty blasted, and their Bliss befrighted" (II.28.11–12). Within Puritan typological tradition, both Thomas Taylor and Samuel Mather had extensively detailed the varieties of uncleanness and ritual purifications. Though Mather adopted the same texts from Hebrews 9:13–14 and Leviticus 13 and 14 to discourse on excommunication and popish superstitions, Edward Taylor assumes a less political stance, defining the putrefactions which corrupt all men, while encouraging diseased souls to seek Christ as the "Holy Fountain" to "lavor off (all sapt/ With Sin) their Sins and Sinfulness away" (II.26.26, 27–8). Ceremonial uncleanness permitted Taylor not only to examine man's sinful state which only Christ can cleanse, but as well to reflect on the purifying preparations necessary for entering into church fellowship. Sermon II.26 thus enunciates the doctrine that circumscribes the intricate explications to follow: "That that Discipline enacted by God to fit Such as were Ceremonially unclean, for Church Fellowship under the Legall Dispensation, was typicall of Christ's Evangelicall preparing Such as are Spiritually unclean, for Church Fellowship in the Gospell day" (*UTOT,* p. 577). To support his doctrine Taylor carefully exposes the Old Testament types of ceremonial uncleanness "Ab Extra" by touching (II.26), "Ab Intra" by issues and leprosy (II.27), and moral impurity (II.28).

Taylor delights in minutely distinguishing kinds of impurity, designs for "Ablusion" and "Oblation," sacrificial animals (heifer, lamb, doves) and herbs, and the numerology of ritual cleansings (*UTOT,* pp. 581ff.). But his analyses inevitably circle back to several key motifs, primarily oppositions between legal prefigurations and man's evangelical status, filth and cleanliness, disease and cure, exclusion or inclusion in church fellowship. Defending the typical properties of these Old Testament ceremonies, for instance, Taylor correlates the fleshly uncleanness contracted from "touching the Dead, or a Dead karkass, etc, or purely Physicall Imbicillities, as the Gonorrhea, or Leprosie" with the "Object of the Antitype," which is "the Spiritually Unclean calld by a Synecdochee our Conscience" or "the Soule" (*UTOT,* p. 576). Condensed into the self-castigations of Meditation II.26, Taylor's images saliently portray his own soul's "Defild" status, "a bag of botches, Lump of Loathsomeness:/ Defild by Touch, by Issue: Leproust flesh" (II.26.5–6). "Not fit for holy Soile,/ Nor for Communion of Saints below," Taylor recognizes that "all that enter do thy fold" must be "Pure, Cleane, and bright, Whiter than whitest Snow/ Better refin'd than most refined Gold" (II.26.3–4, 7, 8–9).

Since evangelical fulfillments represent a superior dispensation, in Sermon II.26 Taylor argues that legal purifications merely foreshadow Christ's greater purgative powers: "If the ashes of an heifer Sprinkling the unclean Sanctify for the purifying of the Flesh, i,e, for Church fellowship. how much more doth the blood of Christ purge the Conscience from dead works to serve the Living God" (*UTOT*, p. 577). Even though his sermon addresses this doctrine to parishioners, the truths equally apply to Taylor's own condition. In Meditation II.26, he rejects the "Brisk Red heifer's Ashes" as "too Weake/ To wash away my Filth" and the "Dooves assign'd/ Burnt, and Sin Offerings" which "neer do the feate" (II.26.19, 20–1, 21–2). No matter their efficacy in Hebrew times, the washings and offerings do primarily "Emblemize" Christ's "Rich Veans" which sluice forth a "bright Chrystall Crimson Fountain" that "washeth whiter, than the Swan or Rose" (II.26.23, 25, 29, 30).

The paradox of red blood (like the red heifer) that rinses white the soul captures Taylor's poetic fancy, and he plays a few homely variations as well on the notion of soap and water: a divine "Niter bright/ And Sope" will "wash me White," and "running Water" will metamorphose into a "Holy Fountain (boundless Sea)," an implicit reference perhaps to the Red Sea (II.26.17–18, 20, 26). And Taylor's ingeniously multiple use of "lavor" recalls the everyday cisterns or basins for washing, the large basin used for ceremonial ablutions in ancient Judaism, and the body of Christ as a vessel whose blood bathes white the soul. For the filthy soul, "tumbled thus in mire," the "running Water" or sluggish "current" in a riverbed remains an insufficient cleansing agent; hence, he escalates the image, appealing repeatedly to Christ's "Blood" as a "Fountain Spring," "this Holy Fountain (boundless Sea)," and "this bright Chrystall Crimson Fountain," that sluice-like floods the soul with purifying grace (II.26.15, 20, 16, 24, 23, 26, 29). Taylor's intricate oppositions initially capture the very condition of his leprous soul that requires a cure, cleansing, and (paradoxically) a crystal crimson fount. But the extended, superimposed images also vivify two different processes of purification, the inferior Old Testament rituals of ashes cast upon the waters and the superior eternal cleansing through cathartic grace, streaming boundlessly from Christ's "Rich Veans" to lave "Sins and Sinfulness away" (II.26.25, 28).

Like the sermon, Meditation II.26 begins and ends with the question of due preparation for inclusion among the "Communion of Saints." To lack a requisite holiness is to be, in Old Testament terms, sent outside the camp for purification, whereas under the New Testament covenant Taylor fearfully questions, "Shall thy Church Doors be shut, and shut out mee?/ Shall not Church fellowship my portion bee?" (II.26.11–12). The answer preached to his congregation is that indeed "Spirituall uncleanness will debar the Soule" from the "holy Ordinances of Church

Fellowship," specifically from "Admittance nto & partaking in the Holy
Table of the Lord" (*UTOT*, pp. 580, 579). Cleansing the soul is an essential
part of Puritan preparation, leading to justification (awareness of one's
unworthiness, mortifying of sin, and reliance on faith) and to sanctification (admittance to the church, partaking of the Sacrament, and living a
holy life). Taylor finds in Sermon II.27 that the "Cleansing Work, & the
Sanctifying Work of the Spirit . . . go both together," because the "Blood
of Christ" not only purges man from sin, but it also bathes "the Soule"
in "the Sanctifying Graces of the Spirit in the Work of Conversion,"
which qualifies one for church fellowship (*UTOT*, pp. 607, 582). Ever
vigilant about his own holy estate, Taylor ends Meditation II.26 by
requesting reentry into the camp of the saints:

> Oh! wash mee, Lord, in this Choice Fountain, White
> That I may enter, and not sully here
> Thy Church, whose floore is pav'de with Graces bright
> And hold Church fellowship with Saints most cleare.
> (II.26.31–4)

Taylor perceives this fellowship to be both an earthly and heavenly
membership, because the soul's lifetime preparation for glory is as much
an antitype to the Old Testament ceremonies as the evangelical entry into
Westfield's church of the Elect (cf. *UTOT*, p. 593). As with many other
meditations, II.26 reflects in miniature the homiletic themes and images.
But the common plight of mankind's uncleanness here finds a more personal, poignant statement because Taylor castigates his own loathsomely
defiled conscience and seeks a process by which he can emerge spiritually
cleansed and holy for admittance to the saint's communion. The poem
both records the need for such a cleansing process and in itself, as a meditative self-examination and application of the Word preached, becomes
part of the process of justification.

Meditation II.27 picks up where II.26 leaves off, as Taylor's "mentall
Eye" spies the "sparkling Fold/ Bedeckt" that "doth out do all Broideries of Gold," as Christ's gown skims Heaven's "Pavements of Rich Pearles,
and Precious Stone" (II.27.1–2, 3, 4). But he turns the visionary "Beams"
back from that radiant glory to undertake an "inward Search" for the
putrefactions of his soul's "Issues and Leprosies" (II.27.5, 6, 8). He condenses the catalog of leprous symptoms from the companion sermon
into a few stanzas, viscerally evoking man's spiritual disease, "Lungs all
Corrupted, Skin all botch't and scabd/ A Feeble Voice, a Stinking Breath,"
and "Scurfy Skale," in short a "Nature Poysond" (II.26.14–15, 16, 13).
Rather than accumulate images of filth and cleanliness (from II.26), here
Taylor compounds metaphors of sickness and cure, for "Without a Miracle there is no Cure," since "Worse than the Elephantick Mange I spie/

My Sickness is" (II.27.20, 21–2). To counteract the debilitating leprosy (which emblemizes man's hereditary sin), the soul needs a miraculous gift of grace, a "wonder working" antidote (II.27.24). The miracle cure derives from "Two Curious pritty pure Birds, types most sure/ Of thy two Natures," the one shedding "its blood in running waters pure/ Held in an Earthen Panchin," the other a "Living Turtle" dipped in this blood to sprinkle the leper (II.27.26–7, 28–9, 32). According to Sermon II.27, in which Taylor acknowledges that "Doctor Taylor on the Types is full in this Sense" (UTOT, p. 600), the two birds prefigure Christ's two natures:

> . . . the Lord Jesus as our Great High Priest by his Eternall Spirit offer'd himselfe in his Humane Nature, whose blood, as of the Slain Bird, falling upon the Living Water of the Holy Spirit poured out into the Earthen Vessels, of the Church is by the Sweet dispensation of the Means of Grace Sprinkled upon the Sinners Soule for its Sacred Cleansing. & so he is made Cleane in order for Church Fellowship. But the Divine Nature appropriating this blood to its selfe is Such as Stands cleare from Suffering. as the Living Bird let loose into the open field. & doth restore the humane nature that was Buried, to life & liberty again after death. (UTOT, p. 601)

Christ, who dies for our offenses and rises "again for our justification" (UTOT, p. 600), provides the means for "Grace" to be "applide/ To Sinners vile, and then they're purifide" (II.27.35–6). What had turned putrid before is sweetened, and the diseased soul once "Undone! Undone!" is healed (II.27.19).

For the sermon's comprehensive detailing of leprosy and the purifying rites, Taylor draws repeatedly on Origen, Mather, Taylor, Ainsworth, and Jackson, but he also relies directly on the Bible for Meditations II.27 (UTOT, p. 600 and passim).[2] He paraphrases Leviticus 13:45–6 to describe the tell-tale signs of a leper ("Robes rent: Head bare, Lips Coverd too, I cry,/ Unclean, Unclean, and from thy Camp do fly"), Leviticus 14:4–7 to specify the first ablution ("dipted" in blood, "Ceder, Scarlet twine/ And Hysop"), and chapter 14 for further washings and oblations (II.27.17–18, 32–3). From these biblical directives, he not only extrapolates figural parallels between the old and Christ's new priestly cleansing, but also creates powerful typological conceits which shape his meditation. For example, in stanza seven Taylor's appeal to be washed in Shiloam's Pool and shaven of head follows the ancient purification's second step of bathing, shaving, living seven days in the camp, but outside the tent, shaving the head again, then bathing and making sacrifices eight days later (Lev. 14:8–9). Whereas Sermon II.27 delves into the hair-splitting numerology of sevens and eights, the meditation makes an imaginative leap from a ritual shaving to a provocative conceit: "and shave mee bare/ With Gospells Razer. Though the Roots of Sin/ Bud up again, again shave off its hair" (II.27.38–40). Likewise, in stanzas eight and nine the poet draws his images of various sacrifices and applications of the atoning blood from Leviticus 14:12–32. However, in this poetic elaboration a blood drop metaphorically becomes a "jewell," "Gem," or "Gold-Ring-like," and Taylor's response is acutely personal: "And put it [thy Blood] Gold-Ring-like on my Right Thumbe/ And on my Right Greate toe as a Rich Gem" (II.27.49–50). Brilliantly perfect and pure, these drops and later the "Holy Oyle," accepted as guilt offerings to purify man from spiritual leprosy, signify Christ's "Rich Bloods Sweet Shower" and "Sanctifying Grace" respectively (II.27.53, 61, 58). No longer a skeletal beggar, "Corrupted" by "Scurfy Skale," Taylor now in "thy Holy Blood atonement" finds, sufficient to bedeck him like a King with grace's jewels, though they are but shadows of Christ's "sparkling Fold" and "Broideries of Gold" glimpsed earlier (II.27.14, 16, 46, 1, 3).

In the Old Testament such purifications restore the leper to the camp; here Taylor seeks to enter the holy estate of church fellowship. Because the sermon speaks to his congregation, Taylor invariably brings the analysis back to the preparations essential for the Puritan saint, for "the Soule that is prepared for Church-fellowship must have his Eare Cleansed by the Blood of Christ, & Sanctified by the Grace of the Spirit, thrô the ministry of the Gospell, to give a due attendence upon the Dispensation of Grace. and must have his hand & foot Sanctified by the Same Blood, & Oyle, for the Carrying on a Life & Conversation in the practice of Piety" (*UTOT*, p. 607). Livelier and more personalized than the sermon, Meditation II.27 highlights Taylor's fascination with the ceremonial applications to "Fingers Ends, and Toes" and captures the lifesaving holiness newly infused into his resanctified soul, whose "hearing, Working, Walking here" outwardly manifest the "Breath of Sanctifying Grace" (II.27.56, 57, 58). It is not sufficient to mortify stinking sins and receive cleansing grace; Puritan preachers as well as parishioners must exhibit the new estate in visible holiness, "Perfuming all these Actions, and my life" (II.27.59). Before stripped naked with "robes rent," Taylor by the meditation's end beseeches the Lord to "cloathe my heart and Life with Sanctity" (II.27.64). Once excluded, like the leper forced to fly "from thy Camp," Taylor concludes Meditation II.27 by promising that "If thus besprinkled" with "thy Rich Bloods Sweet Shower" and "Holy Oyle," he will "Encamp thy Wayes" (II.27.18, 66, 61, 63, 66). The marvelous image of "encamping" suggests the way in which Christ's sanctifying grace resides inwardly in the heart, yet becomes visibly manifest by bringing the soul into the church fellowship. Mimetically, the poem itself brings Taylor back from the position of an exiled leper to safety within Christ's fold, from which (as at the poem's opening) he can once more glimpse heaven, the ultimate antitype of the Israelite camp, where the redeemed saints eternally commune.

Meditation II.27 is one of the finest examples of Taylor's poetic craft, particularly his creation of what we might term "typological conceits." Although often acclaimed as an American counterpart of Donne or Herbert, Taylor adopts poetic methods that fundamentally differ from the classic definition of a metaphysical conceit as a *discordia concors* in which "the most heterogeneous ideas are yoked by violence together" in order to discover "occult resemblances" or "likeness in things unlike."[3] In some meditations Taylor may adopt cosmological comparisons (II.21) or terms from business, trade, and law (II.17), forcibly yoke the earthly with the divine, as in metaphors for Christ's incarnation (II.24), or contrast his soul's dissipate animalism with God's divinity (II.20). But in the figural meditations, it is typological correspondences rather than metaphysical discordances that predominate. To the metaphysical poet the universe seems rife with hidden, potentially shocking, correspondences between disparate elements.[4] For Taylor God's preordained spiritual history of salvation is singular, manifest in historical events and recorded in Scripture. Whereas metaphysical conceits, therefore, link images and ideas from heterogeneous realms, often disregarding space and time, typological conceits develop analogies between types and antitypes, both drawn from the homogeneous sphere of sacred history. Types differ from the antitype only because Old Testament persons, events, and objects predate and spiritually prefigure Christ and his New Testament teachings. This difference in perceiving the fundamental repository of ideas and images explains why Taylor so consistently relies upon the Bible, typological treatises, or general theological commentaries for his basic comparisons. In Meditation II.27 he draws upon the Bible, Mather and Thomas Taylor, and also Origen's and Ainsworth's glosses on Levitical purifications. Taylor thus derives his poetic images from a realm that is coextensive with and restricted by the same criteria that define acceptable Puritan types, since ultimately the Bible is the single authoritative account of historical events and figural correlations.

In Donne's famous metaphysical conceit, the compass and lovers seem initially divergent, and the esthetic pleasure derives from the intellectual perception of similarity drawn out of such apparent disparity. We credit the poet with the ingenuity of art. By contrast, in a typological conceit the basic elements are an Old Testament type (as vehicle) and the antitype (tenor) Christ, His nature, roles, and gospel message. Because God (the ultimate poet) predetermines the relationship between type and antitype, Taylor's function is to decipher (not create) the truths, revealing how figure and fulfillment jointly participate in salvation history. We credit the expositor with spiritual insight. Rather than react with surprise or shock, the reader is called upon to reverence God's revelations, which Taylor interprets through scriptural signs. As we have seen, figural treatises, including Taylor's own *Upon the Types of the Old Testament,* commonly catalog similarities between types and the antitype. Comparably, Taylor's meditations frequently summarize the congruities between ancient persons or ceremonies, such as the purification from leprosy, and Christ, the infinitely various, yet unvarying fulfillment. Whereas in many meditations Taylor interjects a variant of "so also Christ" or creates strict parallel lines, in Meditation II.27 he proclaims the "Two Curious pritty pure Birds, types most sure/ Of thy two Natures" or the ablutions "That typify Christs Blood by Grace applide," seeking to ground his conceit on the firm foundation of resemblances (II.27.26–7, 35). Taylor's technique inverts, therefore, the progression of metaphysical conceits from discordia to concordia. Instead, typological conceits originate with documented similarities between type and antitype, then proceed to disparities that prove Christ's superiority. By offering himself as human and divine sacrifice and cleansing with "Rich Bloods Sweet Shower," Christ inaugurates a purification superior to legal atonements and makes possible man's receipt of evangelical grace. Just as the exegetical method itself so also the poetic conceits make Taylor (and the reader) aware of Christ's supreme difference – without negating the context of similarities and reciprocity between Christ and the types.

As exemplified by Meditation II.27 and many of Taylor's other figural meditations, the typological conceit possesses the following characteristics: (1) the homogeneity of the sphere of experience, the sacred history of salvation, from which all images and ideas ultimately derive; (2) the Bible as the original source of imagery with overlays from typological treatises and theological commentaries; (3) the nature of the core poetic analogy as coexistent with a type–antitype relationship; (4) the evolution of the conceit so that similarities between the Old Testament image and New Testament idea (vehicle and tenor) form a framework within which disparity may be explored; (5) the convergence, in terms of the homogeneity of images and progress of the analogy, toward a focus in Christ or New Testament teachings, and a pervading sense of congruity despite the exaltation of Christ's superiority over all images or types; and (6) the response of awe and reverence both for the spiritual truth and the poet's skillful unveiling of God-ordained, though Puritan-restricted, correspondences. By making the typological conceit his primary poetic device, Taylor thus maintains his primary commitment to searching for theological truths through private meditation, yet he also creates viable poetic metaphors.

The underlying premise that "to typify" is synonymous with "to signify something else" in the sense that literary critics define analogy, similitude, metaphor, and conceit may, however, betray us into a fallacy. As Stephen Manning cautions, "Typology, then, is not properly a literary technique, nor can it be reduced to one. But it is a mode of spiritual perception and can affect literary techniques and can resemble literary modes."[5] Certainly Taylor and other Puritan exegetes would agree that metaphors and types are not synonymous, nor is typology itself a creative literary method. Typology is, nevertheless, a method of comparative exegesis, and as such resembles metaphor and simile because it characterizes one object or idea (Christ and gospel worship) by reference to another (Mosaic rites), relates an abstract idea (grace) to some more concrete ritual (atonement) or image (holy oil and water), and defines similarities and differences. Even though typology is *not equivalent* to metaphor, similitude, or conceit, it does substantially influence Edward Taylor's choice of poetic technique. In Taylor's meditations a conceit becomes a complex of metaphors or similitudes in which a basic or core typological analogy is extended by analysis of similarities and disparities or amplified by the accumulation of metaphors (usually biblically derived) to illuminate a single main idea.[6] The creation of typological conceits constitutes, therefore, Taylor's major innovation in poetic craft because he unites theology with poetics, making spiritual meditation coterminus with poetry.

Taylor's meditations often begin with a basic typal identification ("Doth Joseph type out thee?"), then explicate the historical person or ceremony and parallels with Christ ("Josephs bright shine th'Eleven Tribes must preach./ And thine Apostles now Eleven, thine"), and conclude with appeals to apply this figural truth to his personal condition, "Lord, lay thy brightsome Colours on me thine," like Joseph's coat of many colors (II.7.7, 31–2, 39). The mode of definition dominates Taylor's first fifteen figural meditations on ancient persons and ranks, for example, in Meditations II.9 through II.13 on Moses, Joshua, Samson, David, and Solomon respectively. And definition lends itself to Taylor's penchant for a meticulous accretion of details, a process that reflects the method of his sermons. In such definitional uses of typological conceits, images may offer momentary variations yet never seem to coalesce into anything more than suggestive annotations. In Meditation II.7, for instance, Taylor adopts the commonplace images of "shine," "bright," and the penciled sketch from typal theory to query, "How hast thou pensild out, my Lord, most bright/ Thy glorious Image here, on Josephs Light" (II.7.34–6). A few references to food ("Sweet apples mellow," "Famine," "Bread of Life," "Corn," and "Benjamin like messe") might have yielded a consistent pattern leading from the apple's reminder of original sin to the Lord's Supper feast, but Taylor does not exploit these resonant possibilities. Structurally, the meditation also reveals its limits, since the versified doctrine seems artificially inserted between framing stanzas of personal angst,

"Oh! Screw mee up and make my Spirits bed/ Thy quickening vertue
For my inke is dim,/ My pensill blunt," and a final pleading to "Scoure
thou my pipes then play thy tunes therein" (II.7.3–5, 40). In short, when
left without a firmer framework of existential, soul-wrenching conflict,
sustained images or metaphors, or the crabbed, multileveled diction that
often jolts our sensibilities, Taylor's definitional poems and figural conceits settle into flatness, their meditative clarity the only redemption from
poetic dullness.

But Meditation II.27 blends definition with dialectic, since its reasoned
argument by way of typological correspondences enables Taylor to resolve
a spiritual dilemma.[7] The vibrancy stems in part from Taylor's characteristic technique, a virtual wallowing in images that degrade and dimin-
ish his worthiness, making vivid the "Sickness" of soul as well as body,
"Worse than the Elephantick Mange," for which only miracles of grace
provide a cure:

> Issues and Leprosies all ore mee streame.
> Such have not Enterance. I am beguild:
>   My Seate, Bed, Saddle, Spittle too's uncleane.
>   My Issue Running Leprosy doth spread:
>   My upper Lip is Covered: not my Head.
>
> Hence all ore ugly, Nature Poysond stands,
>   Lungs all Corrupted, Skin all botch't and scabd
> A Feeble Voice, a Stinking Breath out fand
>   And with a Scurfy Skale I'me all ore clagd.
>   Robes rent: Head bare, Lips Coverd too, I cry,
>   Unclean, Unclean, and from thy Camp do fly.
>
> Woe's mee. Undone! Undone! my Leprosy!
>   (II.27.8–19)

Catalog nouns describing body parts, accentuated by repulsively foul
adjectives ("ugly," "Poysond," "Corrupted," "Stinking," "Scurfy"), by
rough, virulent verbs ("botch't," "scabd," "ore clagd"), or ones that
stress rapidly corrosive infection ("ore mee streame," "spread") culminate in the iambically punctuated outbursts of anguish. In addition to the
imagistic heightening of these biblically derived symptoms of leprosy,
Taylor personalizes the meditation still further by claiming to undertake
an "inward Search," in which he will discover not simply a poisoned
soul within, but the "wonder working" purification adumbrated in Leviticus, fulfilled in Christ. The metaphors of disease and soul-searching
that consistently attend the typological analysis thus complicate and
transform an otherwise dry versification of figural doctrine into a vibrantly
conceived, imaginatively powerful meditation, one that satisfies the
demands of both religious praxis and poetic art. Initially naked, leprous,
and excluded, he uses the meditation to reconfirm his sanctification, so

that newly clothed and purified he may enter the saints' fellowship. Similarly, in Meditation II.23 Taylor poses the problem of lacking atonement, in Meditation II.20 he fears his inability to worship in the proper gospel mold, and in II.58 he seeks deliverance from sin's bondage. By using typological analysis (and conceits) to resolve these dilemmas, Taylor creates a dialectic that is more dramatic, less a merely descriptive rehearsal of figural parallels. Meditation II.27 also exhibits the multiple levels that make typological conceits so characteristically Taylorian. Literally, Taylor explicates the purification rites for lepers, echoing Leviticus. Typologically, he reasons that Hebraic priestly ablutions and oblations prefigure Christ's eternal spiritual cleansing of man's sin. He then transmutes the spiritual into poetic insights, transforming strict figural correspondences into artistic flourishes, as when the "Gospells Razer" shaves off the "Roots of Sin" and blood drops become "Rich Gem[s]." In this layering of Old Testament literalism, figural analogy, and poetic metaphor, Taylor reveals his successful transmutation of rationalism into spiritual illumination, typology into typological conceit, theology into art. By meditation's end, Taylor speaks as Puritan typologist, as saintly recipient of Christ's cleansing grace, and ultimately as a poet who presents a theologio-poetic resolution of spiritual conflict.

In Sermons and Meditations II.26 and II.27, Taylor traces the diseased soul's progress through the stages of mortification and justification (via the cleansing with Christ's blood) to the receipt of sanctifying grace which permits due entrance into church fellowship. Whereas Thomas Taylor and Samuel Mather restrict themselves to purifications of ceremonial uncleanness, Edward Taylor elaborates further in II.28 on the "Ecclesiastical cleansing of Such, as were morally uncleane" (*UTOT*, p. 627). What may seem initially an idiosyncratic departure in Meditation II.28 from the figural series, upon examination of the sermon integrally melds into Taylor's meticulous organization. Sermon II.28 aptly summarizes Taylor's concern with sin and purity, but it also appears fragmented perhaps because Taylor collapses together diverse Old Testament

instructions about "Morall, Sins $\left\{\begin{array}{l}\text{Not Capitall} \\ \\ \text{Capitall}\end{array}\right.$ " (*UTOT*, p. 627).

It may shock modern sensibilities to discover how readily he accepts a Hebraic definition of capital crimes that equates the severity of "Supposed Lewdness in a mans Wife" with murder, though he makes no comparable claim for a husband's adultery (*UTOT*, p. 629). He dwells without demurrer in the Old Testament trial of a supposed adulteress who must "drinke the bitter Water," proving herself a "harlot" by primitive magic, for if "the Water . . . enter into her bowells" doth "cause her thigh to Rot, & her belly to Swell . . . she shall die quickly before the Congregation" (*UTOT*, p. 629). Taylor interprets the bitter water as a type of the "Dust of the Humane Body of Christ. . . . put to the Kathartick of Christ blood," which "doth Constitute that Spirituall Elixer, or Panacea for Sinners to take" (*UTOT*, p. 632). Depending upon his inward pollution or holiness, the gospel partaker of the Lord's Supper, comparable to the lewd woman, will be either refreshed or cursed, subject to "Eternall Salvation, or Damnation" (*UTOT*, p. 632).

Were it not for the second half which explicates the cities of refuge (perhaps inspired by Mather's brief paragraph in *FT*, p. 326), Sermon II.28 would still seem to have little discernible connection with Meditation II.28. However, set within the context of Taylor's examination of moral sin, which includes the capital crime of manslaughter, Meditation II.28 becomes a foreshortened allegory of the way in which all men, as descendants of Adam, historically participate in moral evil and require Christ as a spiritual city of refuge. Taylor recalls the creation story when he depicts Eden's bower "pollished most gay" in which "every ranck/ Of Creatures in't shone bright" and over which "Man then bore the Bell:/ Shone like a Carbuncle in Glories Shell" (II.28.2–3, 5–6). Recollecting how Adam disobeyed God's command, Taylor turns collective guilt into personal denigration: "How brave, and bright was I then, Lord, myselfe?/ But woe is mee! I have transgresst thy Law,/ Undone, defild, Disgrac'd, destroy'd my Wealth" (II.28.7–9). Although the Old Testament speaks literally to the plight of the accused "Manslayer," under the gospel he denotes the "dead man . . . cut short of eternal Glory," or "every one in a State of Sin. For Sin is murder, it slayes the Image & the Life of God in man. It is Selfe murder, it murders the person Sinning," for "So it did Adam, & all his posterity" (*UTOT*, pp. 635, 638). As inheritor of Adam's curse, Taylor also participates in Christ's death, for "Ive by my Sin a man, the Son of man/ Slain, and myselfe, Selfe Murderer, I slew" (II.28.25–6). With his bright inward "Glory" now "benighted," his outward "Beauty blasted," and a conscience infected with "Purple Spots of Horrid guilt," he flees the "Venger's hand," much as Adam departed the garden "Persu'de by flaming Vengeance" under God's edict and Michael's sword (II.28.11, 12, 13, 17, 10).

Cities of refuge, denoting in Hebrew a "gathering" or referring to the one "Decurted, or Cut Short off from his very life without it," protected accused murderers against self-appointed blood avengers in the Old Testament (*UTOT*, p. 635). By figural analogy, Taylor seeks Christ, the evangelical "Refuge City," whose "Blood" will "Disgrace my Guilt, and grace me with thy Wealth" (II.28.21, 33, 34). Introducing another variant of the earlier motif of exclusion, Taylor worries in Meditation

II.28 (much as he sought to enter the camp and church fellowship before) that he will "fall . . . before/ I get within the Refuge Citie's doore" (II.28.17–18). Predictably, it is "Renouncing all my Sins, and Vanity" and faith in Christ's "Refuge and thy Blood" (II.28.29, 33) that will substitute grace for God's "Red hot firy Vengeance of Divine Justice," bringing Taylor safely into the church of the saints (*UTOT*, p. 642). By eliding figure into fulfillment, Taylor also cleverly transmutes the manslayer's need to fly from one city to refuge in another into a brief conceit: "Golden Wings of Faith which fan/ The Gospell Aire" will give the sinner Taylor "Angells Wings" or "Sailes," so that he may "swiftly sayle unto thyselfe," that is, Christ as a spiritual refuge in heaven (II.28.27, 19, 31, 32). Though Meditation II.28 seems less polished than the perfected typological conceit in II.27, the images of defilement, sin, and Christ's redeeming blood look back to Taylor's accounts of uncleanness and purification. The repetition of phrases, such as "woe is mee," alliterative "Undone, defild, Disgrac'd, destroy'd," and invoking of various images of exclusions and inclusion ("Church Doors be shut," "from thy Camp do fly," "Encamp thy Wayes," "Refuge Citie's doore") illustrate the ways in which Taylor sustains motifs poem to poem, slowly building more extended patterns of meaning that unify whole sequences within the *Preparatory Meditations*. Simultaneously the new images of vengeance from which the sinner must seek protection and the melding of personal with collective experience anticipate Taylor's shift to the miraculous deliverances effected by God for Noah and the Israelites.

Upon the Types of the Old Testament deliberately emphasizes (as is Taylor's habit) the categorical transition from II.28 to II.29, for "the Doctrine appertaining to Discipline, standes in need of Confirmation by Divine Operation" by way of types extraordinary and ordinary (*UTOT*, p. 647). The "Signa" or "Extra ordinary Types," according to Taylor's taxonomy, include the "Deliverances . . . whereby God hath in a wonderfull way delivered his people From Desolating judgments" and "Such Types as have respect to the Sacraments," specifically God's dispensation of the cloudy and fiery pillar, manna, and Horeb's water during Israel's wilderness journey (*UTOT*, pp. 647, 725). Taylor acknowledges that he diverges from "Systamatick Divinity," then dismisses it as of "greate indifference . . . Whether the Tractate about Discipline Lead in the Seales, or that of the Seales usher in that of Discipline" (*UTOT*, p. 647). Despite this peculiarly blithe dismissal in Sermon II.29, Taylor apparently has in mind the alternate organizations of *Christ Revealed* and *The Figures or Types*. Thomas Taylor, we may recall, placed purifications within the typical ranks of persons, proceeded immediately to the "ordinary" sacraments of circumcision and Passover, then omitted deliverances and spoke only of extraordinary things prefiguring New Testament sacraments (Appendix 2). Samuel Mather passed from the personal types directly to the "occasional" (or extraordinary) things and deliverance out of Egypt, then to the covenant seal of circumcision (leaving Passover for the festivals later), and ended with purifications within the ceremonial law (Appendix 3). By comparison, Edward Taylor's structuring appears uniquely his own (Appendix 4), and he rationalizes that because historically the "Exercise" of disciplinary purifying "takes place in Practice, before the Seales are to be dispensed, I conclude, the Same will pleade an excuse for my so doing" (*UTOT*, p. 647). Consequently, Taylor's own figural movement from purifications (II.26–28) to extraordinary deliverances (II.29, 58, 61), to things prefiguring the sacraments (II.58–60B), and finally to circumcision and Passover as ordinary seals (II.70–71) parallels the sinner's requisite preparation for entry into full church communion. In spite of the curiously half hearted excuse, his rationale remains entirely consistent with the previous theme of Sermons II.26–28, in which he repeatedly enjoins parishioners to obey the gospel discipline for cleansing and deliverance from sin in order to partake of the Lord's Supper. Though decidedly his own configuration, nevertheless Taylor's interpretations and organization of the extraordinary types also blend together Thomas Taylor's sacramental thrust with Mather's focus on Israel's deliverance from Egyptian bondage and ceremonialism.

Taylor opens Sermon II.29 by distinguishing God's deliverances as either "Universall" or "Particular," the universal being Noah's ark and Israel's liberation and the particular the brazen serpent (*UTOT*, p. 647). The sermon underscores the categorical shift from disciplines to deliverances, but Meditation II.29 highlights instead the underlying paradigm of collective and personal experience. Old Testament events often prefiguratively enact man's sin, suffering beneath onslaughts of vengeance, and miraculous salvation through Christ, whether as antitypal fountain, dove, refuge city, golden ark, or liberator from bondage. In II.29 Taylor flees a cosmic holocaust, in which "Floodgates of Firy Vengeance open fly/ And Smoakie Clouds of Wrath darken the Skie," while "The Fountains of the Deep up broken are" (II.29.5–6, 7). Noah's experience becomes paradigmatic of Taylor's fear that such "Immence Profaneness Wormholes ery part" that "the World is saddlebackt with Loads of Sin," a state of such pervasive corruption that hell's deluges "drownd the World" with fire, while simultaneously God's wrathful "Thunder, and Lightenings tare/ Spouts out of Heaven" itself (II.29.2, 3, 11, 9–10). That "Sea of Fiery Wrath" unleashed in Noah's time prefigures "that Flood of fire that, at the End of the World, shall drownd the World of ungodly men" (*UTOT*, pp. 668, 651). Hell's floods and heavens "Cataracts," as Taylor portrays the prophecies of 2 Peter 3:6–7 and Revelation 16, allow no escape from divine vengeance and judgment, since the elements of fire

and water do not cancel one another but instead mutually fuel the cata-
clysm. Rather than the intense personalism of sin signified by fleshly and
moral uncleanness in Meditations II.26–28, Taylor's figural reading of
Noah draws attention to the world's collective iniquity and need for salvation.

Noah also brings the consolation of redemption, since he built "An
Ark of Gopher Wood" to "swim upon the fiery flood" in olden times
(II.29.13, 25). Perhaps, Taylor pleads, he too can safely harbor in Christ's
"golden Ark," that he "May dance upon these drownding Waves with
joye," implicitly reenacting the story from Matthew 14:22–36 in which
Peter, buoyed up by his faith in Christ, walks across the stormy waves
(II.29.36). Noah's deliverance had not appeared among Thomas Taylor's or Mather's extraordinary types, but both exegetes had detailed Noah
as a personal type, a patriarch to whom Edward Taylor only briefly alludes
in Sermon and Meditation II.3. Noah's importance becomes plain in II.29,
however, not by virtue of his personal qualities but because the ark enabled
Noah, exemplar of the faithful man, and his family to escape God's vengeance. A seaworthy vessel made of "Choice Timber Rich," the ark typifies
Christ's "Humane Nature . . . / Bituminated ore within, and out/ With
Dressing of the Holy Spirits pitch," so that with "Propitiatory Grace"
He can appease God's wrath and effect mankind's salvation (II.29.19, 19–
21, 22). Not only a "famous Type of Christ" personally, the ark also
foreshadows "Christ Mysticall i,e, of Christ & his Church, considered
as a Body consisting of Head & Members. & so the whole as Spiritually
related together is calld by the Name Christ" (*UTOT*, pp. 649, 656).
Addressing both parishioners and himself, Taylor warns that

> All that would not be drownded must be in't
>   Be Arkd in Christ, or else the Cursed rout
> Of Crimson Sins their Cargoe will them sinke
>   And Suffocate in Hell. . . .
>   (II.29.31–4)

Once secure, however, within the mystical Christ and His church, the
Elect discover "Concord sweetend" among all creatures, escape hell's
"streams of Flames" and heaven's "Storms of burning Coals," and "swim
safe ore all" to heaven (II.29.37, 45, 46). Taylor also identifies the floods
as a possible type of Baptism, but he defends this typal reading only "by
relation that they stand in unto the Ark," that is, Christ who institutes
the sacrament (*UTOT*, p. 659). For those who would enter the church,
Baptism becomes "a teaching Sign, that Such as are Saved by Christ
must be holy. washt with the Waters from above, the grace of Gods
Spirit poured on them, – drowned in the Waters below, the old man, &
his Lusts in which the old world lived" (*UTOT*, p. 657). Perhaps fore-

shadowing the later extraordinary types of Baptism in the Red Sea and pillar of cloud and fire, Taylor recognizes here that Baptism signals entry into the secure "Ark" of church membership. Nevertheless, his primary focus in II.29 falls upon the ark as a "Type of Christ, who is the Means of all this Deliverance," who founds "his Church anew, upon a New & better Covenant . . . New Laws, New Promises, New People," and "makes the World an Habitation of Holiness" (*UTOT,* p. 656). Reminiscent of the images of "encamping" and a "refuge city" in preceding sermons and meditations, the ark foreshadows the embracing of the saints, individually and collectively, within a new habitation of worship, the church as instituted by Christ's new covenant. Through Christ's miraculous intervention mankind progresses from old laws of divine vengeance to new covenant promises of sweet concord, from the old man beset with crimson sins to new men clothed in sanctity, from wormholes of profane wickedness to a holy habitation. Though Taylor seeks personally to be "Arkd in Christ," newborn in the Covenant of Grace, and walk upon the waters in absolute faith, his sermon and meditation address the larger communal needs of all elect saints who quake at the coming of Armageddon.

In the meditative series, Jonah might seem a plausible sequel to the seafaring saga and salvation of Noah. However, composed just two months later, in April 1699, Sermon II.30 treats Jonah entirely as a personal type and makes no mention of the universal deliverances upon which Taylor embarked so deliberately with Noah's ark. Despite the meditation's echoes of vengeful tempests, sinking vessels, and Christ the turtle dove's atoning death and ressurection, Taylor reveals how self-consciously he plans his homiletic treatise by replacing Jonah as the last typical personage after Solomon (II.13). Then, in Sermon and Meditation II.58, written almost five years later, in December 1703, he picks up again the theme of universal deliverances and the extraordinary types which he had so carefully orchestrated in Sermon II.29. Indicating his resumption of the figural series after this hiatus, Taylor opens II.58 by requesting a new "Eye Salve" to "Christen mine Eyeballs," so that "Mine Eyes will spy how Isra'ls journeying/ Into, and out of Egypt's bondage Den/ A Glass thy vissage was imbellisht in" (II.58.13, 14–16). More than merely an imaginative appeal for a baptismal ointment to clarify the eye's clouded lens, Taylor's request also signifies the expositor's need for a divine Muse (God) who will dispense spiritual insight. As an image for the typological relationship, the "Glass" or ancient mirror of brass, enables the illuminated exegete to perceive in Israel's journeying the embellished visage of Christ. An immigrant himself, whose arduous Atlantic voyage and trek into the wilderness (like Noah's and Israel's) may have seemed a miraculous deliverance, Taylor might be expected to follow the chroniclers in making New England's Israelites a recapitulative antitype of the Old Testament tribe, fleeing Catholic and Anglican persecutions much as the Hebrews had fled Pharaoh's legions. But within Taylor's conservative typology, each soul's spiritual journey from sin to salvation and the church's collective progress toward celestial Canaan remain far more prominent issues than the vagaries of temporal history. In developing his figural analogies Taylor, therefore, leaves behind Mather's overt attacks on *"Calvino-Papistas"* and Romish Protestantism to focus instead on the Puritan morphology of conversion in which every saint must travel from sin's Egyptian bondage to the promised land of glory (*FT,* p. 161).

Serving as one of the "Miraculous Confirmations of the Faith of Gods Covenant people," Israel's deliverance prefigures Christ both "Personally" and "Spiritually" or "Mysticall" (*UTOT,* p. 671). Fulfilling the Old Testament prophecies, Joseph's flight into Egypt, wherefrom "God calls his Son" to the gospel ministry, and "Christ 40 days in Wilderness tride" parallel the ancient Jewish pilgrimage (II.58.26, 28). But it is not "Christ in person" that preoccupies Taylor in the sermon and meditation so much as "Spirituall Christ, and Egypt Spiritually" (II.58.33, 34) to which he attributes a twofold significance:

> And Pareus on Hosea 11.1. saith that it is accommodated most aptly to Christ in the name of a double type, 1. that the deliverance from Egypt imports & is a type of Spirituall deliverance from Sins no godly man over doubts. The other, is this, that what ever in former time fell out in the Church belongs to Christ as the Head of the Church, & indeed Christ politically taken doth most aptly answer the type. (*UTOT,* p. 671)

Though the sermon also interprets the "Ecclesiasticall" triumph and destruction of enemies by the covenant church, as in the escape from Babylonian captivity and Roman slavery, Meditation II.58 highlights everyman's paradigmatic "Spirituall deliverance from Sins" typified by Israel's journey. One of Taylor's more extended definitional uses of a conceit, Meditation II.58 offers a veritable travelogue of Israel's way stations and wanderings. Bidding "Farewell Goshen; Farewell Rameses," Israel flees "Egypts Bondage" to "Succoth" under God's "Cloude and firy pillard," and "thus bannerd Hiroths mouth attempt," where "Moses his rod divides the red Sea" (II.58.51, 40, 55, 57, 67, 71). In the desert they encounter Marah's bitter waters, Elim's oasis of "Twelve Springs of Water" and "Seventy Palm trees fruitfull," return back to the Red Sea and wilderness, and finally arrive at "Sinai where/ By open Covenant God Israel takes/ His onely Church" (II.58.86, 87, 100–2). Although Taylor's topographical details may seem to contrast sharply with the saint's ineffable conversion that they prefigure, they make concretely visual the soul's interchanging trials of doubt and faith that normally mark progress toward a covenant estate.

Taylor establishes clear correlates with the saint's progress in Sermon II.58, where Israel constitutes "Gods Children by Election," who heed "the Effectuall Call from God" and endure wilderness temptations, while they are "prepared by a probationary triall" in order to "receive the Covenant of Churchhood" and "Divine Communion" (*UTOT*, pp. 675, 676, 683, 684). In the meditation Taylor captures the parallels with the saint's journey from calling to glorification by repeatedly declaring, "So here the Soule attends Gods Call," or "So here the Soule in Christ at twelve wells, drinks/ Of Living waters, twelve Apostles shewd" (II.58.53, 91–2). Taylor's pairings recall the exegetical catalogs of figural treatises, but they do dramatically serve to equate Israel's trek with the pilgrim's progress. Elected by God, the soul must first heed the "Effectuall Call" to come forth from the "Bondage State to Sin and Satan" and dare to combat (as Israel did "Pharo's Wrath") "Satan red mad" with "rage" (II.58.37, 50, 48). In struggling to defeat sin, the soul must next "attend their Duties; fall upon the practicall journey to the land of Promise Mortify the deeds of the Flesh, put off the Old man, Forsake the World & its prosperity, frown upon its glaring Smiles," and "betake themselves to Gods Tabernacles" (*UTOT*, p. 680). According to Taylor's meditation, the "Soul Call'd to Effect" cannot passively embark on this spiritual quest, but must actively renounce the world, the flesh, and the devil, go forth searchingly "To Succoth, to Gods tabernacles" for instruction, and seek protection beneath God's "firy flag" (II.58.61, 62, 63). But the nomadic convert reaches a crossroads when, like the Israelites driven into the Red Sea, the "Soule on goes into the jaws/ Of Worldly rage with mountains him do round," finally crying in extremity for divine help (II.58.73–4). Like the miracle by which "Moses his rod divides the red Sea," allowing Israel to pass safely, while "Hells armies" drown in the "red Sea of Gods wrath," so too "Christs Cross divides the Sea whereby" the soul "passeth safe, and it his foes doth stroy" (II.58.71, 75, 76, 77, 78). In his sermon Taylor interprets this miraculous passage as a "Cleare portraiture of Gods proceeding with his Effectually Called ones. When they are arrived thro' the blood of Christ into a State of Grace & the red Sea passt over Separates their two States," the old "Power of Pharaoh, & Egyptian Bondage" from the new "State of Spirituall Freedom" (*UTOT*, pp. 683, 681). Despite this justifying through Christ's blood and free grace, the soul still requires further preparation before fully engaging in the sanctified life within a church covenant, under which God ordains worship and divine laws.

The saint's progress may thus far seem deceptively straightforward from election to vocation to justification, but Taylor continually stresses how perilously this pilgrimage to Canaan's glory is fraught with temptations. Under the Old Testament, Israel passes beyond the Red Sea into a desert, where the people murmur against Moses, but God provides the refreshing springs of Elim's oasis, dates from palm trees, "Quails & Mannah" to sustain them (*UTOT*, p. 683). Comparably, even "now in a State of Grace," the soul remains "yet in a Wilderness State" and "must be 1. Prepared by a probationary triall for Communion with God in Church Ordinances, & Instituted Worship before they are dignified therewith" (*UTOT*, p. 683). Under the gospel dispensation, therefore, the "Soul sings praise in Christ, yet shall/ The wilderness work griefe," until Christ's "tree" or cross sweetens the bitter waters, until the saint "drinks/ Of Living waters," that is, the "twelve Apostles," and until they receive the "Holy Scriptures, and Christs Doctrine" which are "Waters these Wells, and Dates these Palm trees bare" (II.58.83–4, 91–2, 92, 95, 96). As if heeding a Puritan pastor who would advise the probationary saint, the soul here gains strength from singing praises, reading Scripture, and studying holy doctrine – all essential preparations for entering into a visible covenant state. Then sanctified by purifying the "Flesh, & Spirit, the Washing of the Word, & renewall of the Holy Ghost by faith in Christ, the Soule humbly is to come & receive the Covenant of Churchhood," just as Israel returned to the Red Sea and ceremonially cleansed itself at the foot of Mount Sinai before Moses received the law (*UTOT*, p. 684).

Brought ultimately by God into "open Covenant" to be "His onely Church: and select peoples," Israel collectively receives the "Laws and ordinances just" for worship, designed to unite this nomadic Elect during their forty years of wilderness wanderings "Untill they Come to keep in Canaans land" (II.58.101, 102, 103, 108). Engaged in a lifetime spiritual journey, gospel saints must similarly "rise/ In Covenant on Zion mount like wise," where "enricht with Holy Oracles," they enter into visible church "fellowship in holy worship," until "here within Celestiall Canaan sings" (II.58.113–14, 115, 116, 120). Church membership may seem the *terminus ad quem* of the saint's long journey, but Taylor finds that seemingly irreconcilable tensions between sin and grace, Satan and God, so tormenting in the earlier preparatory stages, continue to afflict even the sanctified Elect. Caught up in the "interchangeable Providences in the Wilderness" of this world, both Israel and the gospel saint suffer beneath conflicting dispensations, "Some most Sweet Some most bitter: Some most pleasent, Some most grievous: Some, Sinfull, and Sorrowful on their part. Some judiciary & Some most gracious on Gods part. till they come into the land of Promise" (*UTOT*, pp. 682–3). For Israel Canaan literally fulfilled God's promise to exchange bondage for liberty, a desert for fruitful fields flowing with milk and honey. For Puritan immigrants, New England appeared as a promised land, abundant with fertile forests and pastures but even more bountiful in the spiritual freedom to worship within God's covenant church free from religious persecutions. Yet for Edward Taylor, Canaan typologically signifies glorification *within* the soul, now secure in the knowledge and peace of its election. Even assured inwardly, however, the saint aspires to rise "Through [an] interchanging Course . . . Of Providences, Honycombs and Stings," which mark man's temporal ascent to the "Celestiall Canaan" (II.58.117–19, 120). Earthly life, at least for the Puritan pilgrim, is consumed by wilderness perils from sin's perpetual assaults, but strength derives from faith in Christ and the promised reward of heaven's eternal glory.

Meditation II.58 consistently reflects the rational analysis of its accompanying sermon, in part because Taylor adopts the typological conceit to define the Puritan morphology of conversion by which the soul effectually prepares for sainthood. Unlike the dialectical engagement of Meditation II.27, in which Taylor heeds his own uses by spiritually seeking a cure for leprous sin, in II.58 the personal applications, when they occur, refer less to Taylor's spiritual angst than to his artistic frustrations and goals that frame the meditation. Whether these frustrations are read as a formulaic depreciation of his talent or a literal comment on a particular encounter with the muse, Taylor bitterly complains "my Quills too dry,/ My Inke too thick and naught," and "My Standish . . . is empty, Paper loose/ That drains all blotches from my inkie Sluce" (II.58.3–4, 5–6). "What shall I then, Lord, doe? Desist thy praise?" he queries in a rare fit of defiance (II.58.7). Relief comes swiftly, however, when he turns to Christ to "Steep my Stubborn Quill/ In Zions Wine fat," to "mend my pen, and raise/ Thy right arms Vean, a drop of'ts blood distill/ Into mine inkhorn," and "to make my paper tite/ That it mayn't blot," so that "In Sacred Text I write" (II.58.8–12). For the archetypal convert of the meditation proper, salvation flows from "the Red Sea deare/ Of Christ's rich blood," whereas that same "drop" of "Zions Wine fat" inspires Taylor as poet to interpret sacred texts while he simultaneously creates his own sacred lyric (II.58.110–11, 9). In fact, the progress that Taylor envisions for himself by the poem's end becomes an artistic conversion, inspired implicitly by an inward spiritual reformation. Buoyed by his hope that "thou my Soule with this Rich trade" will "delight/ And bring mee thus into thy promisd aire," he imagines himself transported to heaven "Wherein my Virginalls shall play for joy/ Thy Praise with Zions virgins Company" (II.58.123, 123–4, 125–6). Relying upon Revelation 14:1–5, which prophesies the Lamb enthroned on Mount Zion surrounded by virgin harpists, Taylor anticipates his glory as an inspired musician. Compared with the detached impersonalism of the eighteen central stanzas that define Israel's communal deliverance, only these embracing glimpses of artistic trial and transcendence exhibit Taylor's deeply personal need for spiritual deliverance.

Sermon and Meditation II.58 provide a comprehensive overview of the preparatory purification and deliverance necessary for entry into the covenant church – themes that permeate Taylor's series on ceremonial cleansings and extraordinary types. Certainly Noah's voyage and Israel's journey aptly serve as metaphors for the collective redemption of the church and Elect. But as he turns to those "Miraculous Providences" by which God assists Israel during its forty-year quest, Taylor focuses more singly on particular agents of deliverance (brazen serpent) and on the seals initiating (cloudy and fiery pillar) and confirming (manna and Horeb's waters) God's covenant with Israel. In both Mather's and Thomas Taylor's treatises, the brazen serpent originally appears as the last of these extraordinary types, but uniquely for Edward Taylor it becomes a type of "Deliverances" with respect to "Particular persons" (*UTOT*, p. 702). Taylor apparently changed his mind about its placement, first lodging the brazen serpent (II.61) after the covenantal seals (II.59–60B), then later inserting a slip of paper after Sermon II.58 which specified:

> Miraculous Deliverances
> of a Particular Nature
> I have not Spooke to: & for this
> So that of the Brazen Serpent. &
> Place it here.
>   (*UTOT*, insert at p. 725)

He did little more than cancel "the Seale of the Covenant" and "the Seales" from his original text, before making interlinear substitutions to amend the doctrine:

> I have touched upon Such as respect [Deliverances of a generall Nature]. & passing from them, I am come to Such as have an Eye upon [Particular persons]. . . . Here is the Redeemer typified, Christ, by the Brazen Serpent healing. The Manner of his Redeeming how he Effected it. & this is by his being lift up upon the Cross. And the manner how it is applied: & this is by Faith in Christ Crucified: looking unto the Brazen Serpent wrought the Cure. So doth faith in Christ Crucified Save the Soule unto Eternal Life. (*UTOT*, p. 702; interlinear substitutions bracketed)

Sermon and Meditation II.61 thus extend the theme of deliverance to each man's individual redemption through Christ's healing crucifixion, a theme that Taylor had universally applied with Noah's ark and Israel's journey.

Though replete with typological parallels, Meditation II.61 also exploits the paradox of a deadly "naturall Serpent" defeated by a lifesaving "brazen Serpent's Sight," the metaphors of the venomous "Serpents Sting" and "Sovereign Counter Poison" or antidote, and the power of "A Spirituall Sight of Christ" to penetrate the poisoned soul (II.61.26, 6, 12, 36, 27). The paradox of the brazen serpent turns, of course, on identifying the "Fiery Serpents," whose "bites poisonous, & deadly . . . unto our Naturall Happiness, & life," with Satan and his fiery legions of seraphim whose sting is mortal "to all Holiness of Life & eternall Happiness" (*UTOT,* p. 706). Whereas Satan's sting dooms mankind to certain death by poisoning his nature, Christ, prefigured in the brazen serpent, supplies the spiritual antidote. "Th'Artificiall Serpent" made of brass may seem a peculiarly idolatrous figure, but for Moses and the Hebrews it formed the "Banner Standard of the Camp," where by God's decree it beamed forth "a Healing vertue to the Serpents Cramp" (II.61.25, 14, 16). Shaped like an aesculapius, the Greco-Roman symbol for the physician, this brazen serpent foreshadows the very manner by which Christ heals mankind: "Christ in this Snake shapt brass/ Raist on the Standard, Crucified was" and his "humanity with sharp thorns Crownd," as he suffered death in order to gain life eternal (II.58.17–18, 30).

To capture the superiority of Christ's antidote, Taylor accumulates image upon image of "Healing vertue," "Sovereign Salve," and physic "plaster 'plide," to counteract the "poison Serpentine," the "burning bite," and "venom wound the naturall Serpent made" (II.61.16, 33, 23, 4, 20, 26). Yet more clever juxtapositions, accented by rhymed feet and couplets, underscore the oppositions between the "Serpents Bite" and "Serpents Sight," "th'golden Coach of th'eyes" that the "Serpents Sting defies," and "fiery Serpents burning bite" countered by a "Beam Divine of Grace's might" (II.61.5–6, 11–12, 20, 22). Can it be happenstance or sheer wit that reminds us of the demonic "hiss" when Taylor lards this meditation with "s" sounds, both alliteratively and consonantly used, as in "Serpentine," "Sight," "Standard," "Snake shapt," "Shelfe," "Sovereign Salve," "Sore," "Spirituall," and "Springhead," or the "brass the bosoms poison" set against the "Christ . . . Raist on the Standard, Crucified was," a "Physick" and "plaster" of "Grace" to counteract the brazen "Serpents Flesh"? In a virtuoso display of sound effects, he also accumulates clusters of "c" words, so that "Christ," "Crucified," "Crownd," on the cross engenders in the "golden Charet cleare" of the eyes the "Counter poison" that will "Countermand" and "Cure" the "Serpents Cramp." Though the imagery of bites and sights, sores and cures, poisons and plasters itself carries the message, Taylor spares no ounce of ingenuity in

creating intricate effects of sound, rhyme, and meter, even concluding
his poem with a flourish:

> I by the fiery Serpent bitt be here.
>   Be thou my brazen Serpent me to *Cure*.
> My Sight, Lord, make thy golden Charet cleare
>   To bring thy remedy unto my *Sore*.
>   If this thou dost I shall be heald: My *wound*
>   Shall sing thy praises: and thy glory *sound*.
>   (II.61.37–42; italics added)

What Christ brings is a spiritual remedy transcending the natural susceptibility of mankind to earthly wounds, a healing sight that synesthetically
manifests itself in song and sound.

But the efficacy of redemption depends upon the soul's "Spirituall Sight
of Christ" and "Faith in Christs blood di'de" (II.61.27, 24). Taylor's
imagery recalls his earlier request in II.58 for an "Eye Salve" to "Christen mine Eyeballs," when in II.61 he repeatedly calls for "a Beam Divine
of Grace's might," which will pierce the eye, just as the brazen serpent's
"Vertue rode in th'golden Coach of th'eyes/ Into the Soule, and Serpents
Sting defies" (II.61.22, 11–12). Taylor's sermon emphasizes not only the
"Direct Act" of beholding the serpent, but also the "Reflect Act" by
which "the Sight of the Soule from the Brazen Serpent" turns "its thoughts
back upon its Sore with the Medicinall virtue of the Brazen Serpent,
empregnated. . . . And this holds out the reflect act of Faith turning in
upon the Soule with the blood of Christ, with which it besprinkles the
Soule, for its Spirituall Cure" (*UTOT*, p. 708). By beholding the crucified Son with "Eyebeames" that "do bring/ The Sovereign Counter poison" of faith into the soul, the sinner once mortally wounded rises beyond
the threat of death (II.61.35, 36). Once transported (as if by golden chariot) to eternity, the saint's new vision becomes light suffused because
"Eternall Life is the Life of Grace in its full glory Shined upon with the
Sun of Righteousness in his Splendent reviving beams, & With the Bea-
tifying Vision of the glorifying face of God" (*UTOT*, p. 710). Both
Sermon and Meditation II.61 gain their effects from Taylor's embellish-
ment of basic typological metaphors. Though it lacks Meditation II.58's
scope and narrative flow, the microscopic intensity of II.61 successfully
works to rivet Taylor's personal vision on the psychomachic battle between
Satan's wounding and Christ's healing. By adding a homely vignette of
the brazen serpent as a "Doctors Shop/ On ev'ry Shelfe's a Sovereign
remedy," which recreates a visit to the local apothecary (or pastor within
the church), Taylor further humanizes the meditation (II.61.31–2). His
personal need for transfiguring vision also dominates the final stanza, in
which he confesses that he too has been "by the fiery Serpent bitt," and

calls for Christ to "be thou my brazen Serpent me to Cure," for "My Sight, Lord, make thy golden Charet cleare/ To bring thy remedy unto my Sore" (II.61.37, 38, 39–40). It is the pleading of a man who finds miracles in God's extraordinary deliverances of His church and each saint therein and who believes in the promised eternal life through faith in Christ crucified.

When he makes the transition to the pillar of cloud and fire, Taylor overtly proclaims a more sacramental approach to the remaining "Miraculous Providences" by focusing on those wilderness events "as have upon them a typicall aspect unto Sacraments" (*UTOT*, p. 725). Having already incorporated "the Passage through the Red Sea . . . under the Head of Miraculous deliverances" in II.58, he proposes "this Pillar of the Cloude, & Fire" as his primary type of Baptism in II.59 (*UTOT*, p. 725). As "Initiatory Seals of the Covenant," the pillar foreshadows the baptismal regeneration through water and the spirit, whereas the later

"confirmatory Seals as the $\left\{\begin{array}{l} \text{Manna} \\ \\ \text{Water of the Rock} \end{array}\right.$ " (II.60A–60B)

prefigure the New Testament Lord's Supper, which commemorates man's salvation through Christ's body and blood (*UTOT*, p. 751). Taylor's declared sacramentalism reflects the similar emphasis in *Christ Revealed,* more so than Mather's focus in *The Figures or Types,* in which Israel's deliverance and the extraordinary things as types of Christ play a more prominent part. The predicated sacramental interpretation recedes quickly, however, in Taylor's Sermon II.59, as he undertakes a more straightforward correlation with Christ as leader of the gospel church: "But yet there is more in this Type. For as the Act of baptism, & the Elementary Instrument Water, & the Spirituall Efficacy Regeneration are typified thereby. So the Object unto which the Soule is Sealed thereby is by it typified," and consequently "the Pillar of the Cloude & of the Fire upon the Camp of Israel is a Type of Christ Conducting his Church into Eternall Glory" (*UTOT*, p. 726). Though clearly Baptism signals the saint's entry into church membership, Taylor's sermon and meditation heighten the theme of a longer journey to eternal glory, along which the church and individual saints must be guided by Christ, as Israel had been by the "Pillar strange," whose "Spire/ Doth kiss the Heavens, leading Israel on" (II.59.7, 9–10). To be cleansed of sin (II.26–28) and delivered from vengeance into grace (II.29, 58, 61), as we have seen, represent only steps along an "interchanging Course," on which each saint marches under Christ's banner and covenant.

Stocked like a Pandora's box with mixed metaphors, which frequently echo other sermons and meditations in this series, Meditation II. 59 seems more haphazardly constructed, less controlled than many of Taylor's poems, an example perhaps of an abundant imagination with little esthetic judgment. Echoing the appeal of II. 58 and traditional images for the types, Taylor initially pleads for "enoculate[d]" sight, so that the "Cloudy-Firy Pillar high" might become a "Tabernacles Looking-Glass Divine," in which to discern figural truths (II. 59. 3, 4). But by line and stanza, this banner staff takes on kaleidoscopic shapes and functions, first sitting on the "Stoole" of "Israels Camp," then billowing its "Skirts" to "Canopy that Camp," while its "Spire/ Doth kiss the Heavens," then transforming suddenly into "Christ's Charret drawn by Angells high" (II. 59. 8, 9, 9–10, 11). Although in fact the pillar protects Israel and provides one channel for divine guidance (Exod. 13:21–2), the peculiar pictorial mélange leaves one wondering whether it squats or flies, canopies or points. In a brief image of the "Humane jacket, typ'te, of's Deity" (II. 59. 12), Taylor also fails to convey his sermon's more precise delineation of the pillar as a type of "The Godhead & Manhood natures of Christ pesonally United," wherein some theologians do "looke upon the Cloude to typify the Manhood Nature, & the Fire the Godhead" (*UTOT*, p. 727). Perhaps recollecting Noah's seafaring ark, in stanza three Taylor transmutes the pillar into "The Churches Pilot," "Her Quarter Master," "Christ's Watch tower," and finally the "Tent of the Holy Ghost," images successful only to the extent that they annotate Christ's watchful guidance of the "Churches Host" (II. 59. 15, 16, 17, 18, 17). The meditation lacks skillful elaboration of paradoxes (as in II. 61); the inserted mention of "A Sun by night, to Dayify the dark./ A Shade by Day, Sunbeames to mollify" captures the pillar's essential dualism, but it fails to connect poetically with the images of pilots and watch towers, except perhaps as an oblique reference to heavenly stars that guide ships aright (II. 59. 13–14). Summarizing the sermon's breakdowns of Christ's mediatorial functions, Taylor resorts to a catalog in which Christ becomes "The Churches King, to guid, support, Defend," the "Priest to Cleanse her: in the Cloud to baptize./ And Reconcile with Incense that ascends," and finally "Her Prophet too that Lights her in her way/ By Night With Lanthorn Fire. With Cloud by day" (II. 59. 26, 27–8, 29–30). Clearer, though no less compounded than other stanzas, Taylor's summary highlights Christ's fulfillment of the type, but it cannot redeem an already shattered poem. An unusually staccato poem for a type so concerned with directing and guiding, Meditation II. 59 recycles rather than shapes the various metaphors into a cohesive conceit. Taylor apparently finds no controlling poetic device or structure to meld pieces into a polished whole, no sea saga as with Noah's ark, no topographical journey to Canaan, no dialectic use of paradox as with the brazen serpent. In this context of imagistic hyperkinesis, Taylor's final prayer becomes curiously ironic, as he pleads, "Then lead me, Lord, through all this Wilderness/ By this Choice shining Pillar Cloud and Fire" and "I shall not then digress," a request fulfilled more satisfactorily in Israel's journey to Canaan or Taylor's spiritual progress than in his poetic venture (II.59.31–2, 33).

Where Meditation II.59 fails, however, Meditation II.60A and 60B succeed, both in capturing the joint sacramental and Christological focus on manna and Horeb's waters and in forging figural images into more pleasing esthetic unities. Meditation II.60A, somewhat less convincingly, reflects Taylor's dialectical use of a typological conceit, and Meditation II.60B displays his ability to create associative patterns in which Christ appears centrally amid imaginatively varied figural metaphors. Already anticipating the Lord's Supper toward which the "Manna" as a type for Christ Jesus as the bread of life points, Taylor opens Meditation II.60A with complaints of soul sickness and starvation. Like a hungry Israelite, he murmurs, "Ist die of Famine, Lord, My Stomach's weak," for "I'm sick; my sickness is mortality/ And Sin both Complicate" (II.60A.5, 7–8). Visions of health-restoring food consume his fantasies, as he seeks "Angells bread of Heavens wheate . . . bakt in Heavens backhouse for our meate," for the mortally ill soul finds "No cure . . . Save Manna" which the "Queasy Stomach this alone doth Crave" (II.60A.2–4, 9–10, 11). As recorded in Exodus 16, Israel received physical nourishment from a dewlike grain which descended daily from heaven, but for gospel saints, according to John 6:31–5, only an eternally sustaining manna will satiate the spiritual craving. Drawing upon the sermon's complex definitions, Taylor devotes whole stanzas to depicting the "Dew" in all "its beauty bright/ Like pearly Bdellium White and Cleare" and God's bountiful provision on all days except the Sabbath (II.60A.22–3). But the conceit turns in the central stanzas on the expressly declared supremacy of Christ:

> This is a Shining Glass, wherein thy face
>   My Lord, as Bread of Life, is clearly seen.
> The Bread of Life, and Life of lively Grace
>   Of such as live upon't do flowrish Green.
>   That makes their lives that on it live ascend
>   In heav'nly rayes to heaven that have none end.
>
> Refresh my Sight, Lord, with thy Manna's eye.
>   Delight my tast with this sweet Honied Cake.
> Enrich my Stomach with this Cake bread high.
>   And with this Angells bread me recreate.
>   Lord, make my Soule thy Manna's Golden Pot
>   Within thine Arke: and never more forgot.
>   (II.60A.25–36)

Had Taylor rearranged his poem to culminate with these stanzas, Meditation II.60A would have gained in dramatic momentum; nonetheless, the images effectively heighten Christ's superiority as the richest source of spiritual revitalization. Shining more beauteously than pearly bdellium, Christ's face refreshes the "Sight," and rather than descend about the camp like Manna, this "Angells bread" resurrects so that all those "lives that on it live ascend" to eternal glory. Where before the stomach was queasy, now Christ the "Bread of Life" stirs a ravenous appetite, content no longer with plain meal ground from Israel's manna, but hungering instead for a "sweet Honied Cake" risen high to satisfy a gourmet's taste. Although Taylor's elevated images evoke man's sensual needs (sight, taste, kinesis), they do so only to emphasize Christ's supremacy, because He provides no ordinary fare but instead the pure essence of a "Life of lively Grace," which reinvigorates the famished soul to "flowrish Green." That sustaining power continues within the gospel church, where Christ supplies a perpetual dew "in the beauty of his Holy ordinances upon the Souls of his people in the Word of his Grace full of his Holy Spirit" and himself as the "bread of Life for them to feed upon" (*UTOT*, p. 757). By recreating the disparity between type and antitype, Taylor in part achieves a resolution of his earlier dilemma of soul-sickness, because feasting upon Christ and His Word (as in preaching and meditation) brings restorative grace to the hungry, mortally stricken saint.

The repeated mention of angels in this sermon and meditation lofts the figural interpretation several strains higher, since when Taylor anticipates the "Angells delight, attending on this table" and "this Angell fare I'm fed," he refers both to the Lord's Supper and heaven's feast (II.60A.46, 47). More prominently than in II.59, Taylor clearly pursues a sacramental analysis, for his second major argument in Sermon II.60A proclaims that "Manna . . . typifies Christ . . . in Such wise that it held him forth to come as a Seale of the Covenant; of like use as the Lords Supper Seale is, holding forth Christ to us in

like Manner but already Come. & this as Spirituall $\left\{\begin{array}{l}\text{Meate} \\ \\ \text{Memorandum}\end{array}\right.$ " (*UTOT*, p. 762).

Only those within the covenant might partake of this God-given meat, much as Taylor later argues that only lawfully admitted church members may come to the Lord's Supper. Under the old dispensation, a "Homer of the Manna" was also "put up in a golden Pot, & kept in it in the Tabernacle" for a "memoriall" of God's miraculous provision in feeding his chosen people (*UTOT*, pp. 763, 764). Similarly, Taylor preaches that under an evangelical dispensation the Lord Jesus is "to be kept in the Tabernacle of this body in the Golden pot of the Soule, the Temple of the Holy Ghost, till Death destroy the Tabernacle. And he is to be kept in the Golden Pot in the Ark of the Church a Divine Testimony of this bread that came down from heaven, in the Lords Table. Here is the Memoriall of this Favour Celebrated" (*UTOT*, p. 764). Beyond the immediate anticipation of administering the Lord's Supper to the West-field Elect, Taylor looks further to "the Eternall Commemoration of Christ the Living bread preserved for ever in Eternall Glory before Glo-rious Angells, & glorified Saints to the Glory of Gods unsearchable Grace" (*UTOT*, p. 764). Though he reserves elaborations of the heavenly feast for later meditations on the Sacrament (II.71, 102–111), Taylor does sug-gest the multilayered fulfillment of the ancient manna. Meditation II.60A illustrates a less rigidly parallel structuring of the typological conceit than appears in many meditations on the personal types and, regrettably, a less perfected dialectical use than in Meditation II.27 on leprosy and II.24 on the Feast of Tabernacles. But the heightened images exemplify the way in which Taylor exalts Christ's superior fulfillment of all earlier, shadowy types and keeps Christ the central figure in man's redemption. His poetic effects frequently derive from this imaginative ability to embellish gospel fulfillments with colors that excel the Old Testament prefigurations, so that the "Shining Glass" of his figural and poetic ren-derings more brilliantly reflect the face of Christ, the living grace, and the eternal glory to come.

Meditation II.60A also points to Taylor's growing preoccupation with sacramental themes, which he pursues with more impressive artistry in Meditation II.60B in which the associative development of images of water, blood, and aqua vitae arouses the meditator's desire for the eucha-ristic wine. Rather than rely on the sermon's analysis for his main inspi-ration (as in II.60A), Taylor takes his meditative cue in II.60B from the uses; he links together "Aqua Purgans," "Aqua Vitae," "Aqua Caeles-tis," "Aqua Benedicta," and the "Elizer Salutis of Heavens Alimbeck," as if relishing the various epithets for Christ's rejuvenating blood, adum-brated by the fountain flowing from Horeb's rock (*UTOT*, pp. 788, 789). Meditation II.60B similarly accumulates epithets, adjectives, and metaphors to contrast common waters with Christ's blood which pos-sesses purgative, heavenly, and life-giving powers. Even "Sea water straind through Mineralls, Rocks, and Sands/ Well Clarifi'de by Sunbeams, Dulcifi'de" as "Insipid, Sordid, Swill, Dishwater stands," compared with the "beere" and "Nectar" that Moses lets flow from "A Fountain opte, to wash off Sin and Fall," which like "A River down out runs through ages all" (II.60B.13–14, 15, 21, 22, 24, 23). In a series of rapid transmutations, this prefigurative water, destined to refresh Israel by flowing continuously throughout their wilderness sojourn, becomes fulfilled in Christ's blood and the sacramental wine:

> Christ is this Horebs Rock, the streames that slide
>   A River is of Aqua Vitae Deare
> Yet costs us nothing, gushing from his side.
>   Celestiall Wine our Sinsunk souls to cheare.
>   This Rock and Water, Sacramentall Cup
>   Are made, Lords Supper Wine for us to sup.
>
> This Rock's the Grape that Zions Vineyard bore
>   Which Moses Rod did smiting pound, and press
> Until its blood, the brooke of Life, run ore.
>   All Glorious Grace, and Gracious Righteousness.
>   We in this brook must bath; and with faiths quill
>   Suck Grace, and Life out of this Rock our fill.
>   (II.60B.25–36)

In "Solid Substantialness," "Strength," "Weightiness," and "durableness," Christ becomes the "Horebs Rock" or "good foundation" upon which the church is built (*UTOT*, p. 755). But Taylor passes quickly beyond this figural fulfillment to a dazzling array of metaphors that display how the "Water of the Rock" was a "Sacred thing of Divine Ordinance holding out Some Spirituall blessing of the Covenant of Grace, to be received by the hand of Faith . . . & So had a Speciall eye unto the blood of Christ. & unto the Wine in the Lords Supper as a Seale of the Covenant of Grace" (*UTOT*, p. 782).

The adjectives and metaphors recreate Christ's crucifixion when blood "gushing from his side" replicates the miracle at Horeb (Exod. 17:1–7), where "Moses Rod did smiting pound, and press/ Untill its blood, the brooke of Life, run ore." Although some expositors view it as "an Emblem of the Cross," according to Taylor the rod signifies "the Stroke of Justice" and "Speare point of the Law," which having smitten Jesus lets flow "the River of Living Waters, the Aqua Vita from Grace her Stillatory" (*UTOT*, pp. 777, 789). By transforming the "Rock" into the "Grape," Taylor also implicitly recalls that Christ, the "root and offspring of David" (Rev. 22:16) sprang forth from "Zions Vineyard," bearing the perfect fruit of grace. For Israel too, the brook and grapes of Eschol (Num. 13:23) symbolize the lush vineyards of Canaan and foreshadow Zion's paradise where the saints will reside after Christ's Second Coming. The grape pounded and pressed into wine recalls yet another metaphor for Christ, not only as the vine, but also the winepress, a figure common in Renaissance emblem books, Vertue's *Christ and the Church: Or Parallels,* and Keach's *Tropologia*.[8] Drawn from Isaiah 63:3, a parable in Matthew 21:33–46, and Revelation 14:19 and 19:15, the winepress emblemizes God's wrath, the same wrath that crushes Christ until by bringing forth blood he redeems Israel into "Glorious Grace, and Gracious Righteousness." What the "Lords Supper Wine" commemorates is, therefore, Christ's willing submission to God's sword of justice and law. Horeb's waters prefigure what the "Sacramentall Cup" later spiritually signifies, the "blood of Christ Shed for his own people onely for their Renovation, & that both as to justification, in its cleansing them from filth by Washing & making them Cleane. & also as to their Sanctification, and Holiness of Life in its refreshing of them: & giving them new Spirits, & life" (*UTOT*, p. 781). Into these densely associated images, Taylor conflates the key sacrificial act in salvation history, whereby Christ crucified liberates the eternal flood of purifying and sanctifying grace, becomes the rock upon which the church rises, and forecasts the Second Coming. Though in a pattern unlike the elongated rational structures of his definitional and dialectical conceits, Taylor superbly weaves around the core analogy between Horeb's waters and Christ's blood and sacramental wine other biblically derived metaphors to make this typological conceit as powerful as it is brief.

He frames the typological conceit with personal pleadings for the water that cleanses, blood that redeems, and wine that seals the Covenant of Grace, as well as for the "Eye" that "righter may describe" the "Drink Drawn from the Rock, tapt by/ The Rod of God, in Horeb, typickly" (II.60B.7, 11–12). But as in Meditation II.58, Taylor appeals as much for artistic as spiritual recreation, since without divine inspiration "My muddy Inke, and Cloudy fancy dark,/ Will dull its glory, lacking highest Art" (II.60B.5–6). Recalling God's heavenly banquet, he entreats "Ye Angells bright, pluck from your Wings a Quill./ Make me a pen thereof that best will write" and "Lende me your fancy, and Angellick skill/ To treate this Theme, more rich than Rubies bright" (II.60B.1–2, 3–4). In the sermon uses, Horeb's rock appears similarly bejeweled with "Precious Pearle. Rubies, & Carbuncles, Agats, and Amathysts, Corall, & Cristall," but Taylor selects rubies in his Meditation to foreshadow the blood and wine yet to flow from the smitten Christ (*UTOT*, p. 787). He concludes the meditation with a series of imperative requests, "Lord, oynt me with this Petro oyle," "Make mee drinke Water of the Rock," "Me in this fountain wash," "give Aqua Vitae or I dy," aptly summarizing the capacity of Christ's blood to heal the sick, quench the thirsty (in the desert and Supper), cleanse filth, and restore the faint and dying (II.60B.37, 38, 39, 40). Justified and sanctified by the *aqua coelestis* from Christ the rock *(Petra)*, Taylor may then preach, as Peter *(petros)* the anointed disciple did in 1 Corinthians 10:4, on the Lord's Supper, administer it, and himself partake of the sacramental cup. What makes his personal entreaty yet more ingeniously integrated with the typological conceit, however, is Taylor's reference to the "Quill," which he also defines in the homiletic applications, urging parishioners to "refresheth thee at this River. Faith is the Quill whereby thou Suckest in this Water of the Rock. Believing in Christ is drinking of this Water" (*UTOT*, p. 793). In Meditation II.60B this quill signifies in one sense everyman's rod, a symbol of both the stricken Christ in whose death all men share and also the necessity of faith drinking His blood, for each soul will "with faiths quill/ Suck Grace, and Life out of this Rock our fill" (II.60B.35–6). But Taylor also seeks a more uniquely artistic revival, for "If in this stream thou cleanse and Chearish mee/ My Heart thy Hallelujahs Pipe shall bee" (II.60B.41–2). In this final associative transmutation, in a poem filled with such, the quill as smiting rod and pen becomes a pipe, an angelic musical instrument releasing floods of psalms and hallelujahs from within a once petrified heart.

In the earliest *Preparatory Meditations* on personal types, Taylor's poetic technique frequently resembled the cataloged parallels of typological expositions, including his own *Upon the Types of the Old Testament*. But that impression perhaps obscures the ways in which Taylor does, progressively more so as his figural series continues, variously employ typological conceits. At times, the conceit becomes absorbed into an allegory (II.17), saga (II.30), or history of salvation (II.50), as in Meditation II.28 in which Taylor touches upon man's fall from Edenic grace and consequent need for a refuge city in Christ, or in Meditation II.29's story of Noah's deliverance from cosmic destruction to salvation, uplifted by Christ the antitypal ark. In its purest form, as in Meditation II.58, the typological conceit elaborates parallels between Israel's deliverance and Christ's fulfillment or the soul's spiritual progress, often sounding like a rational synopsis of the sermon's doctrine, though framed with Taylor's personal pleadings as devout saint and poet. In more complicated and personalized uses, Taylor moves beyond definition to a dialectic proposition in which the conceit resolves the saint's internal struggle, whether the spiritual leprosy that corrodes the soul as in Meditation II.27 or the desperate need to "Countermand all poison Serpentine" as in Meditation II.61 on the brazen serpent (II.61.4). Taylor also breaks free of a strict definitional format in those few poems in which he surrounds the core typal analogy with associated metaphors, allowing the imaginative flow of imagery to establish the miraculous supremacy of Christ's fulfillment. In Meditation II.59 this method falters, when Taylor's attempted associations for the pillar of cloud and fire dissipate into fragmented images. But in Meditation II.60B, the associative pattern succeeds because the evocatively conceived metaphors capture Taylor's desire for an evangelical Horeb's rock from which gushes Christ's blood, so that as poet and preacher he may commemorate Christ's crucifixion, receive the revitalizing of grace, and go forth to celebrate the Lord's Supper with sacramental wine. Though by no means exclusive models, the meditations on disciplinary purifications and extraordinary types display Taylor's artistry in molding the typological conceit into an effective poetic device.

Thematically, the morphology of conversion by which saints progress from calling to glorification, from Egyptian slavery and wilderness wanderings to heaven's Canaan, forms the backbone for many of Taylor's sermons and meditations. Within that journey he perceives always the soul's need for purification. Sin, which infects the soul with leprosy, murderous desires, or the serpent's mortal venom, requires a supreme antidote in Christ's sacrifice as the "Living Turtle" dove or brazen serpent crucified. Taylor looks also to the sacramental elements that spiritually memorialize the means by which Christ died, in the breaking of his body on the cross (II.61), smote by God's sword of justice, and in shedding his blood (II.26–27), like a fountain of living water spewing forth from the rock (II.60B). Throughout this journey from mortifying sin to sanctification, Taylor also emphasizes the saint's need to belong within the camp (II.26–29, II.58–59), so that he may be led (as by a pillar of cloud and fire) by Christ the supreme guide as well as deliverer. Commensurate with his earlier stress upon appropriate gospel worship, he applies these ceremonial and extraordinary types to both individual saints and the collective church. Redemptive grace brings the saint into the church, where membership is sealed by the Lord's Supper, the celebration toward which all Taylor's meditations ultimately point.

Within the typological sermons and meditations, Taylor also gradually moves toward a more concerted focus on sacramental themes. Without purification of sins (II.26–28), the saint cannot partake of the Sacrament, nor is entry into the church sanctified without the holy ordinance of Baptism, as foreshadowed by the Red Sea (II.58) and pillar of cloud and fire (II.59). Taylor's analysis of extraordinary types also proceeds from Israel's deliverance (II.58), which the Supper like its predecessor Passover commemorates, to the precise elements of manna and water from the rock (II.60A–60B), which prefigure Christ the bread of life and His blood, elements spiritually signified by the Supper's bread and wine. As he concludes the miraculous providences, Taylor already anticipates the transition to those "ordinary" seals of the covenant in circumcision and the Passover. Meditations II.70–71 and the later sacramental series (II.102–111), as we shall discover, must be set against the background of controversy in New England in which Taylor employed his typological readings of Scripture to combat the liberal reformism of Solomon Stoddard, a reformism that rocked the Connecticut Valley and threatened to split the camp of latter-day saints. Much as George Herbert struggled with his soul and Anglican ministry through the medium of *The Temple* and as John Milton defended the Puritan reading of providential history in

Paradise Lost and *Paradise Regained,* so also Edward Taylor brought to his *Preparatory Meditations* a personal need to explicate Puritan typology, to prepare for his ministry, and to defend the purity of the Lord's Supper. In order to worship gospelly Taylor prepared his own soul through the private meditations, which strengthened his doctrinal understanding, roused his holy affections, and offered to God angelic psalms, so that he might in all purity administer the Lord's Supper to the faithful Elect.

6

Sacramental Types: Seals to the Covenant

Now Types good night, with Ceremonies strict,
The Glorious Sun is risen, its broad day.
Now Passover farewell, and leave thy Place.
Lords Supper seales the Covenant of Grace.
(II.103.33–6)

For Edward Taylor the *Preparatory Meditations* becomes his means of inner worship – an extension of and preparation for his preaching of God's Word and administering the Lord's Supper. These searching examinations comprise Taylor's offerings to Christ – a laying upon the divine altar of his oblation of praise. Seeking through his poetry for Christ as the temple within which the gospel saint worships, Taylor expresses the inner spiritual life. The meditations recreate his search for God Who as an indwelling principle illuminates or confirms his election. Purification signifies no longer an ancient ceremony but the ongoing process by which man seeks to cleanse the leprosy of sin. And spiritual purification is, after all, merely an earthly preparation for the consummate purity of heaven where the newly clothed Elect are admitted into the Savior's radiant presence to partake of the living bread and choicest wine of Christ's blood at the angelic banquet. As his *Upon the Types of the Old Testament, Christographia,* and *Preparatory Meditations* on the ceremonial law illustrate, Taylor firmly espoused a purified evangelical worship, not pursued through any external medium of idolatrous rites and altars, but cultivated within the heart's temple where faith flourishes.

Taylor's prose writings and typal meditations testify to the importance of Baptism and the Lord's Supper within this new evangelical worship. In well-reasoned homilies, doctrinal refutations, and private meditations, Taylor advocated a fundamentally conservative doctrine rooted in a Calvinist theory of the covenant and supported by typological exegesis of circumcision and Passover. Preaching in the wake of New England's 1662 adoption of the Half-Way Covenant, Taylor found it progressively more difficult to protect the exclusivity of church fellowship from con-

165

tamination by unprofessed and unconfirmed, though baptized, members. In response to Solomon Stoddard's campaign for the Lord's Supper as a converting ordinance, he denounced such liberalism because it undercut the need to prepare a "festival frame of spirit" and demoted the Supper from an eminent sacrament to an ordinance preliminary to, not signifying the receipt of, grace. Rebutting Stoddard's erroneous typological readings of the Passover in a private letter, unpublished treatises, and in his meditative practice, Taylor sought to maintain the purity of sacramental worship. Beginning with his Foundation Day Sermon in 1679, later revised as "A Particular Church is Gods House" (1692–3), then more trenchantly with the homiletic *Treatise Concerning the Lord's Supper* of 1693–4, and ultimately in an unpublished refutation of Stoddard, "The *Appeale* Tried" (1710–11), he attempted to dissuade his Northhampton neighbor from his schismatic beliefs and to heal the dangerous breach in New England's theocracy. In those meditations particularly devoted to circumcision (II.70), the Passover (II.22, 71), and the Supper (II.102–111), Taylor also defined this feast as a "Signet" or "Seale to the Covenant of Grace" (II.108.35, 36), providing "food for those Regenerate that are" (II.104.60). Together with his prose writings, these poetic meditations cogently establish Taylor's sacramental theory and his reliance upon the typology of circumcision and the Passover to defend his conservative ideals against the inroads of Solomon Stoddard's liberalism.

In the Puritan struggle against papist and prelatical abuses of ceremonies, debate naturally centered on the major sacraments of Baptism and the Lord's Supper. Puritans accepted only these two sacraments as legitimately ordained under the New Testament to seal the Covenant of Grace. However, their exclusivity in admitting only those who showed visible signs of inward salvation (attested by confessions of faith, church membership, perseverance in mortifying sins, and hearing of the Word) set them at cross-purposes with more inclusive administerings by Catholics and Anglicans. Samuel Mather challenged the indiscriminateness with which papists and prelates gathered souls into church fellowship by proclaiming it "a common Mistake in our Times, that many think that Baptism doth *make* a Person a Member of the Church of God," when "it doth *Seal* Membership," for like circumcision, "they have no right to the Seals of the Covenant, who are not first in the Covenant" (*FT,* p. 181). Mather's caveat of 1666 not only responded to traditional enemies outside Puritanism, it also issued a veiled warning to American Puritans, who at the Synod of 1662 had adopted the controversial Half-Way Covenant.[1] Infants of baptized parents (though not necessarily practicing church members) might be baptismally initiated into the church, but not confirmed in covenant fellowship until a later time, when a mature sign of saving grace and a public relation of conversion would admit them to the Lord's Supper. Any halfway measure blurred Baptism's original purpose which was *to seal*, not *to confer* or to proselytize for, membership. A harbinger of the later Solomon Stoddard controversy, the Half-Way Covenant threatened to unravel the close-knit Puritan community by creating a schizophrenic constituency of nonpartaking, though baptized saints – neither decisively in nor out of the church.[2]

The Lord's Supper called forth even more abundant cautions than Baptism. Saddened by the profanations, Thomas Taylor in his typal explication of Passover (1635), beshrewed those "Papists, who thinke it insufficient to ratifie the Covenant unto them without other additions and supplies from themselves" and "yea ascribe as much to the blood of *Thomas Becket* and other traytors, as to this blood" (*CR*, p. 228). Writing in his *Treatise* nearly sixty years later, Edward Taylor cites these blasphemous desecrations of the Supper as sufficient motivation for the Puritan flight from England to establish the Massachusetts Bay Colony:

> It is one of the main things on the account of which the old and new Nonconformists have deserted Episcopal government, and suffered persecution, loss of their public ministry, poverty, imprisonment, and to avoid such mixt administrations of the Lord's Supper, and to enjoy an holy administrating of it to the visibly worthy was that that brought this people from all things near and dear to them in their native country to encounter with the sorrows and difficulties of the wilderness. (*TCLS*, p. 126)

Although the admittance to and proper administration of the Lord's Supper became the most heated controversy during Edward Taylor's ministry in Westfield, basic tenets that separated Puritans from papists and from other reforming sects also remained prominent issues. In his later meditations on the Lord's Supper (II.102–111), Taylor attempts to refute Lutheran ideas of consubstantiation and Catholic doctrines of transubstantiation:

> It Consubstantiation too Confounds.
>   Bread still is bread, Wine still is wine its sure.
> It Transubstantiation deadly wounds.
>   Your touch, Tast, Sight say true. The Pope's a whore.
>   Can Bread and Wine by words be Carnifide?
>   And manifestly bread and Wine abide?
>   (II.108.13–18)

He rejects consubstantiation, by which Christ's body is actually present with the bread and wine, by stressing their material reality. Sufficiently outraged to curse the pope as a whore, Taylor also ridicules transubstantiation, the Catholic belief that at their consecration in the Mass the eucharistic elements change from the substance of bread and wine into the substance of the body and blood of Christ, with only the accidents of taste, color, shape, and smell remaining. In contrast, Taylor articulates the contravening Puritan stance:

> Its Sabbath Entertainment, spirituall fare.
>   It's Churches banquet, Spirituall Bread and Wine.
>   It is the Signet of the Kings right hande,
>   Seale to the Covenant of Grace Gods bande.
>
> The Sign, bread, made of th'kidnies of Wheate
>   That grew in Zions field: And th'juyce we sup
> Presst from the grape of Zions Vine sweet, great
>   Doth make the Signall Wine within the Cup.
>   Those Signals Bread and Wine are food that bear
>   Christ in them Crucified, as spirituall fare.
>   (II.108.33–42)

Emphasizing the "spirituall fare" and the Supper as a "Seale" and "Sign" of the Covenant of Grace, Taylor outlines the Puritan belief, one that involves no magically "Con-, or Trans-Substantiated" elements (II.108.24). Affirming the reality of the elements, yet Christ's spiritual presence in the Supper, Taylor thoroughly agrees with Calvin's *Institutes* and *The Westminster Confession,* the latter of which sets forth orthodox Puritan doctrine with "the Body and Blood of Christ being then not corporally or carnally, in, with, or under the Bread or Wine; yet as really, but spiritually present to the Faith of Believers in that Ordinance, as the Elements themselves are to their outward senses."[3]

Under the more imminently disruptive threat from Solomon Stoddard, who preached the Sacrament as a converting ordinance, Taylor retaliated with his *Treatise Concerning the Lord's Supper,* typologically interpreted God's providences to Israel (II.58–61), Passover (II.22, 71), and circumcision (II.70) in *Upon the Types of the Old Testament,* and composed meditations on the Lord's Supper (II.102–111), most likely to accompany a sermon series now lost. As with those broader disputes that divorced Puritans from Catholics, Lutherans, and Anglicans with respect to all ceremonial laws and evangelical worship, so too with the local theological debate Taylor turned to typology for polemical ammunition to defuse Stoddard's conversionism. Both Samuel Mather and Thomas Taylor, the latter more so than the former, had related the extraordinary events from Israel's wilderness pilgrimage to Baptism and the Lord's Supper, as did Edward Taylor in his sacramental interpretations of these divine signs. The Red Sea and pillar of cloud and fire, according to ancient and modern exegetes, typified Baptism, whereas the manna and water from the rock foreshadowed Christ commemorated in the bread and wine. God's covenant with Israel was sealed in the Old Testament with the outwardly visible signs of circumcision and the Passover. But with Christ's fulfillment of messianic prophecies, salvation became a spiritual actuality, ratified by New Testament special seals which confirmed the soul's intimate covenant with the church and Christ.

In *Upon the Types of the Old Testament*, Edward Taylor differentiates circumcision and Passover as "Ordinary & Standing" seals of the covenant from those extraordinary signs during Israel's wilderness trek (*UTOT*, p. 799). And he proclaims the double function of circumcision as a "Type of Christ and an Emblem of Baptism" (*UTOT*, p. 799). As a type of Christ, circumcision forecasts His human nature, His descent as Abraham's seed, mediation between God and man, necessary shedding of blood in order to redeem our sins, and His maleness. Compared with previous expositors, however, Taylor gives short shrift to these analogies, preferring instead to elaborate on the sacramental emblemizing of Baptism. He cites the commonplace doctrine that both circumcision and Baptism function as seals "Initiatory of the New Covenant," signifying one's "Visible Entrance into Covenant with God" and the church (*UTOT*, p. 803). He differentiates the "Covenant of Works" made with Adam from the "Covenant of Grace & Salvation, the Gospell Covenant given forth in typicall Ordinances, & the Morall Law as a Rule of Morall Obedience," for it is only the Covenant of Grace that is sealed by circumcision under Abraham and by Baptism under an evangelical dispensation (*UTOT*, p. 803). Though the seals may differ, the one initiating by cutting, the other by water, the Covenant of Grace remains the same, promising man redemption through faith in Christ's sacrifice for our sins. Furthermore, the spiritual purposes of both ceremonies are similar – to put off the "Filthy defiled & Damnable State that the Soul is in" and to renounce those fleshly sins through "Mortification"; both ceremonies "import the Regeneration or Renovation of the Soule" in its new "State of Grace" (*UTOT*, p. 804). On the question of infant Baptism, Taylor firmly and repeatedly sanctions it: "Hence the infant seed was to be Circumcised, if a male, on the eighth day. So likewise are the Infants of Believers to be baptised under the Gospell. They are incovenant hence holy I Cor. 7.14. Hence the Promise belongs to them . . . & therefore they have a right to the Seale of Baptism" (*UTOT*, p. 806). He makes clear his typological defense of the Half-Way Covenant by arguing that "Infants of Covenanting Parents are to be Baptised now, as well as Infants of Covenanting Parents were Circumcised then," for God offers a "gracious acceptation" to the second-generation babes of New England–Israel, who possess "Covenant Qualifications" by bloodline, if not by a holy profession (*UTOT*, pp. 816, 814). But like many other colonial theologians, Taylor deplored the recalcitrance and hypocrisy of those who, once baptized in the church, then failed to partake of the confirmatory seal in the Lord's Supper, lacking either a profession of faith or moral worthiness.

Though Sermon II.70 recalls the many parallels of *Christ Revealed* and

The Figures or Types, Meditation II.70 heightens images that seem muted by the homily's intense rationalism. Perhaps unable to encompass the extended analogies within one short poem, Taylor often collapses whole concepts into brief evocative images. For instance, the complicated proof by which the Covenant of Works to Adam is differentiated from the Covenant of Grace to Abraham, becomes condensed into a single query. Since "Thy first Free Covenant, Calld not for this," shall "Thy Covenant of Graces Quilting kinde" then "require a Seale that Cutting is?" (II.70.7, 8, 9). Taylor affirms man's need for circumcision under the old dispensation, because "The Infant male must lose its Foreskin first,/ Before Gods Spirit Workes as Pulse," thereby "To sanctify it from the Sin in't nurst,/ And make't in Graces Covenant to spring" (II.70.25–8). He implicitly alludes to man's original sin, which babes imbibe like milk from the nursing mother's breast. But by forfeiting the foreskin which emblemizes sin, the child receives in its place the vivifying "Pulse" of God's spirit which initiates the newborn soul into "Graces Covenant." Not by works, and not without circumcision or Baptism, can any man hope to participate in Christ's saving grace.

Heeding his own homiletic admonition to attend upon the covenant duties, Taylor voices in the meditation a tortured impatience with his own "Callous" which "doth the Heart Disspiritualize/ Till Gilgal's Razer doth it Circumcise" (II.70.5–6). He echoes his public warnings to those in a corrupt condition by mournfully querying, "Hath Sin encrusted thus my heart? Sad! Sad!/ And latcht my Lips? And Eares made deafe, and ditcht?" (II.70.13–14). Desperately, he appeals to Christ for an abscission: "O! Lord! pare off, I pray, what ere is bad:/ And Circumcise my Heart, mine Eares and Lips," for "This in thy Circumcisions heart doth bed./ The Same in baptism is bosomed" (II.70.15–18). So "encrusted" with sin's filth that it incapacitates his speech and hearing, Taylor seeks the tandem remedies of fleshly mortification and faith in Christ's curative blood:

> What must Christs Circumcision pacify
>   Gods Wrath? And's Blood of's Circumcision sore,
> Bring Righteousness, Purge Sin, and Mortify
>   Proude Naughtiness? And wash with Grace mee o'er?
>   And my Uncircumcisedness all slay?
>   That I might walke in glorious Graces way?
>
> . . . .
>
> Hence me implant in Christ, that I may have
>   And His Blood to wash away the filth in mee.
> And finde his Wounds that are so deep, the grave
>   Wherein my Sins ly dead and buri'de bee.
>   (II.70.19–24, 37–40)

Taylor self-prescribes an antidote for original sin, a requirement to "Mortify/ Proude Naughtiness," but it is ultimately Christ's descent into the "grave" that obliterates sin's power. Like the blood shed from "Circumcision sore," Christ's "Blood to wash away the filth in mee" stems from the crucifixion's "Wounds that are so deep," a far more significant cutting than the removal of the infant's foreskin. Christ's "Covenantall blood" not only fulfills circumcision's prefigurings, it also promises a gospel cure for all sins and a less onerous initiation into the Covenant of Grace. New Testament converts will enter the church through Baptism, which seals a believer's faith in Christ's righteousness.

In Taylor's poem the images of cutting and cleansing suggestively intertwine. The cutting "sharp" knife of circumcision in ancient times "fleys the Skin off, that the heart doth rinde," but Baptism which is "Circumcision's Rightfull Heir" does more gently "wash with Grace," "scoure off guilt," and the heart's "wounds bathe with New Covenantall blood" (II.70.32, 10, 35, 22, 45, 44). Stricken initially with tremors over circumcision, that "Seale so keen and Cutting sharp," Taylor eventually takes comfort from Baptism which "is a better marke" and salves the heart's callous "Naughtiness" (II.70.32, 34). He selects an apt head text from Colossians 2:11–12, "In whom also ye are circumcised with the circumcision made without hands, in putting off the body of the sins of the flesh by the circumcision of Christ, buried with him in baptism, in which also ye are risen with *him* through the faith of the operation of God," which pronounces Baptism's superiority to the old ritual, because it calls for a spiritual, not merely physical, slaying of "sins of the flesh." The crafted interweaving of the painful bodily circumcision with the antitypal fulfillment in Baptism's soothing spiritual ministrations thus imagistically sustains Taylor's dialectical development of the typological conceit, in which he once again seeks a cleansing cure for original sin ("filth," "defilde"). One of Taylor's more controlled meditations, II.70 closes by recapitulating the infected body parts (and earlier poetic images), as he prays for Christ to "bed mee in thy Circumcisions Quilt./ My wounds bathe with New Covenantall blood," and "My ears with Grace Lord syringe . . . / My Tongue With holy tasled Languague Dub," that "then these parts, baptisde thine Organs keep" (II.70.43–7). The triple sense of "Organs" as body parts, the organs of sense and speech in particular, and a musical instrument allows Taylor a parting stab of wit in pledging "To tune thy Praise, run forth on golden *feet*" (II.70.48). Taylor thus invests the dry sacramental analogies from preceding typologists and his own sermon with an inward-looking sensitivity, as he conveys his human vulnerability for which the sacraments of Baptism and the Lord's Supper provide religious strengthening. Within Puritan worship these two visible sacraments like buoys mark out the covenantal channel through which each saint voyages toward the heavenly Canaan, even as it was promised to Abraham and his seed.

Edward Taylor appealed to the ceremonial types with an urgency provoked by theological disputes peculiar to late seventeenth-century New England. Not even Socinian and Quaker enthusiasms threatened so seriously to rend the fabric of New England's theocracy as those inward schisms that devalued God's two covenant seals by permitting unregenerate souls to commune equally with visibly sanctified church members. Just as the Half-Way Covenant of 1662 enflamed the ire of conservative Puritans, so later Solomon Stoddard's defense of the Lord's Supper as a converting ordinance ignited new controversies (see Appendix 5).[4] Between 1677 and 1709 in nearby Northampton, Stoddard preached and published his liberalizing, if not heretical, doctrine. Just as genuinely dismayed by the decline in New England's piety as his more conservative brethren, Stoddard attributed the problem to an increasing rigidity under the Half-Way Covenant.[5] Rigorously enforced, the covenant requirement that baptized members manifest a certain knowledge of salvation by publicly relating a work of conversion before coming to the Supper discouraged uncertain or timorous believers. Known for his reformist views earlier, Stoddard at the Synod of September 1679 put the question "Whether all such as do make a solemn profession of faith and repentance, and are of a godly conversation, having knowledge, to examine themselves, and discern the Lords body, are to be admitted to the Lords Supper."[6] As Increase Mather's "Confutation of the Rev. Mr Stoddard's Observations respecting the Lords Supper 1680" clarifies, Stoddard's proposition would have immediately admitted to the Supper doctrinally orthodox believers *"without any examination . . . concerning a work of grace upon their souls"* (p. 45). Recalling the synod twenty years later, Stoddard writes of his success after heated debate in getting the synod to blot out the clause, "That persons should make a Relation of the work of Gods Spirit upon their hearts, in order to coming into full Communion" and "put in the room of it, *The Making a Profession of their Faith and Repentance.*"[7] Rather than requiring the communicant to offer visible signs of achieved conversion in a public relation, such loosening of standards for admission would, as Mather feared, ultimately open the door to all half-way members, for "inasmuch as my brother amongst all his qualification [of who is] fitting to partake at the Lords Supper, saith not a word about regeneration, one would think that he looketh upon the *sacrament* as a *converting ordinance*" (p. 56).[8]

Stoddard's more extreme formulation of the Supper as a converting ordinance and translation of principles into practice were still another decade off in 1679, but his advocacy of admitting half-way members to the Lord's Supper without a public relation was already known in the

Connecticut Valley. Fearful that such a democratizing extension of this covenantal seal would corrupt both church and Sacrament, Edward Taylor, in his August 1679 Foundation Day Sermon, with Stoddard present, takes up the gauntlet.[9] Delivering this sermon at the formal organization of the church at Westfield, Taylor supports the Half-Way Covenant but denounces Stoddard's innovations: "It is necessary that the Person seeking with any Church of Christ to have Communion, give an account of the workings of Gods Spirit upon his heart" (*CRRS*, p. 128). Mandated for full entry into church fellowship, an account of saving grace is also an essential preliminary to the Lord's Supper, which seals the believer's new covenanting. Educing "Divine arguments" from Scripture, Taylor shows his proclivity for typological proofs, when he asserts that "in the Old Testament are Scattered up & down such testimonies as point out this truth, some in Ceremonies . . . as they hold fourth the publick Confession of Gods working upon the soule . . . & as they hold it out to be made upon the Souls Covenanting with God & his people, i.e., when it enters into a Church State" (*CRRS*, p. 129). Together with the temple which he adopted to define the Westfield church as Christ's habitation, he also draws upon the types of Israel and Solomon to defend the strict mandates for Puritan church covenanting and the sacraments. Rather than perceive the testimony of saving grace as cause for discouragement, Taylor envisions it as an encouragement: "For when the Soule sees that an account of Gods working upon his Soule is of such weight as that he must make it manifest in some measure, as a Sign of his preparation for, before he be admitted into, Full-Communion how intent will it make him in observing the motions of the spirit of God upon his Soule & hating Sin" (*CRRS*, p. 137). Due preparation ideally gives rise to a visible, jewel-like "Holiness that is the Essentiall Qualification," for (to use Taylor's analogy) the "stones" or church members "are fetcht out of the Quarry, or Stone pit of Mankind, & hewen, & Squared by the Axe of the Spirit till they are rightly pollisht & fitted for this building: & so made living stones, Eph. 21, for this Spirituall Temple, I Pet. 2.5" (*CRRS*, p. 125). Taylor's note in the "Church Records" that Stoddard's ceremonial words offering the "Right hand of Fellowship" were "not altogether approved on" by the attending elders hints perhaps at Stoddard's frosty reception of Taylor's implicitly rebuking preachment (*CRRS*, p. 159).

Some eight years later in his first published work, *The Safety of Appearing* (1687), Stoddard catalogs the Lord's Supper with reading Scripture, hearing the Word preached, and praying as means to bring souls to *"live a life of Faith upon Christ's Righteousness, and not be discouraged"* and as "a special help to those that are in the dark."[10] Previously unsuccessful in getting the Northampton church to assent to his practice, he renews his efforts, pushing in this same year, as Taylor's letter records, "to cast off Relations, & to bring all above 14 years of age, that live morally, & having Cathechisticall knowledge of the Principalls of Religion, to the Lords Supper" (*ETSS*, p. 63).[11] No doubt apprised of *The Safety of Appearing*, but more distressed by Stoddard's local attempts to put theory into practice, Taylor writes in a conciliatory tone and in "Friend ship" a letter dated February 13, 1687/88. He requests Stoddard to desist from his controversy which could only generate a "greate Commotion, & Disturbance of their Peace" and incite "malevolent persons" to grow "audacious" at this loosening of restraints to their communing (*ETSS*, pp. 63, 64). Deliberately hinting at Stoddard's heresy, yet only gently accusing in his rhetoric, Taylor appeals to his neighbor's sense of a New England heritage. To argue for an open administration of the Lord's Supper (comparable to Anglicans and Catholics) "seems to turn the Stream, & swim the Interest of Christ, that the Church, & those Eminent ones, that brought it hitherto, & hither in this Wilderness, just back again, & this is not pleasant, either yours or their motions are *Flumina contra mare*" (*ETSS*, p. 64). Exercising his vigilance over the Westfield church, Taylor assumes Jeremiah's guise to prophesy the shattering of the New World covenant community: "Nay in a Word Gods faithfull Ones in following ages will be ready to date the begining of New Englands Apostacy in Mr. Stoddard's Motion, the which *Deus Prohibeat*" (*ETSS*, p. 65).

Neither Taylor's gentle persuasion nor Increase Mather's vociferous public denunciations dissuaded Stoddard from his mission, which he termed a "Cause of God" in his polite, yet unswayed reply to Taylor in June 1688 (*ETSS*, p. 66). Ironically, both Taylor and Stoddard sought to preserve New England from a dangerous declension; but, in attempting to cure the same malaise of spirit, they prescribed utterly different remedies. Whereas Taylor reaffirms the sacramental strictures as instituted by the founding fathers and reconfirmed under the Half-Way Covenant, Stoddard argues for an easement to encourage new converts.[12] Taylor seeks to preserve the Lord's Supper by keeping it sacred and exclusive only to those suitably prepared through a relation of saving grace; Stoddard aims to strengthen the church by making it pluralistic and by admitting all professed, nonscandalous members. Since human psychology indicates that men more frequently choose the easier path and since historical currents in eighteenth-century New England favored a broadening of church membership, the time coincided with Stoddard's liberalism. Hence, by 1728 when Nehemiah Bull replaced an aged and senile Edward Taylor in the pulpit at Westfield, he could call for and get an affirmative vote upon the proposition "that those who enter full communion, may have liberty to give an account of a work of saving conversion or not. *It shall be regarded by the church as a matter of indifference.*"[13] Within a short six weeks, the Westfield congregation overturned sacra-

mental standards that Edward Taylor had stalwartly upheld for fifty years
of his ministry. Administration of the Lord's Supper based upon a
profession of saving grace slipped over to admission based merely upon
the fact of church membership.

As debate raged back and forth in the Connecticut Valley, both Stoddard and Taylor turned to Old Testament types to substantiate their
respective definitions of proper standards for admission. Increase Mather's "Confutation" documents Stoddard's use of Passover during the 1679
Synod to argue against a prior examination or relation: "And whereas,
my brother alledgeth that all adult persons whom the Jews did admitt to
circumcision, were received to the passover, therefore all baptised persons should be admitted to the Lord's Supper; Both the assertion, and
the consequence from it (supposing it to be true) is to be denied" (p.
54).[14] In "Arguments for the Proposition" (probably a revised version of
the "Observations" provided to Mather in 1679), obtained by Taylor
sometime in 1689–90, Stoddard argues typologically that qualifications
"sufficient" for all adults "in order to Communion in all ordinances in
the Jewish Church," are likewise sufficient "to such Communion in the
Gospell Church," though evanglical saints must be able also "to examine
themselves, & discern the Lords Body" (*ETSS*, p. 70).[15] He supports his
contention by alluding briefly to "Manna, & the Water that Came out of
the Rock" and "Paschall Lamb" as types of Christ and more often to
circumcision and Passover as precursors of the new covenant seals of
Baptism and the Supper (*ETSS*, p. 71). More polemicist than exegete,
Stoddard haphazardly cites the types in his early documents and, indeed,
throughout the dispute, whereas his opponents, most notably Edward
Taylor, marshal rigorous figural analyses to contravene the increasingly
liberal doctrines and practices.

Though never published or circulated, Taylor's "Animadversions"
(1690) point by point rebut Stoddard's propositions and offer sound exegetical correctives to Stoddard's looser use of types.[16] Taylor criticizes
him for ignoring the difference between the Old and New Testament
dispensations which make conclusions drawn strictly from Jewish ordinances and covenant seals suspect when applied indiscriminately to the
Lord's Supper. For instance, he argues that "Jewish Sacraments" had
"Speciall Carnall, & Politicall" ends, so that circumcision "was a Seale
of the Covenant" with Abraham, Passover was designed to "Celebrate
Gods bringing Israel out of Egypt," and "Mannah, & the Water of the
Rock" to serve as "meat & Drink to the Whole host in the Wilderness"
(*ETSS*, p. 98). By "Birth Right" all Israelites were "Members of that
Civill Body of People, as a Civill Corporation" and "must of necessity
attend upon the Sacraments of the Church" (*ETSS*, pp. 97, 98). But for
gospel saints under a congregational, not national polity, the "Case is

Quite otherwise. . . . For the Qualifications under it, have a necessary Relation unto Sanctifying Grace, that give the Person an Intrest Right unto the Seales of the Covenant" (*ETSS*, p. 98). Moreover, insofar as the ancient providences and seals are types, "they are all antiquated with the Typicall Worship," and hence "Cessasion of Ceremoniall Holiness" under the Old Testament dispensation "must infer Spirituall Holiness the typified Qualifications of the New Testament Communicant," that is, a sanctifying grace attested to by a public relation (*ETSS*, p. 99). According to Taylor, to reason thus wholesale from qualifications for Old Testament sacraments to those for the "Lords Supper is Egregiously to impose upon Gods people with Sophiticall pleas" (*ETSS*, p. 98). A harbinger of his later treatises, Taylor's refutations are founded upon scrupulous typological readings of Scripture. Still, the reference to Passover and the Jewish ceremonies remain relatively sparse, perhaps reflecting the limited focus of this first phase of debate upon the pressing contemporary question of a saving relation.

Gradually escalating in the 1680s, then erupting between 1690 and 1710, the controversy ultimately spawned more sophisticated theological proofs, including more frequent appeals to types. The basis for the dispute also changed after 1690, when Solomon Stoddard began openly to enunciate and to implement his doctrine that the Lord's Supper was a converting ordinance, a point of theology more threatening to the fabric of Calvinist doctrine than collegial disagreements about qualifications for admission. The question was no longer simply who might come to the table, but the nature of the Lord's Supper itself, whether it was initiatory or confirmatory, whether it was a sacrament or an ordinance comparable with prayer and preaching, whether it was efficacious for converting sinners or for nourishing growth in an already exhibited grace. According to Edward Taylor's "Commonplace Book," in the winter of 1690 Stoddard preached a sermon on Galatians 3:1 to call his "Church to New Covenanting" and to urge acceptance of an "Article to bring all to the Lords Supper that had a knowledge of Principles of Religion, & not scandalous by open Sinfull Living."[17] Arguing his case for the Supper as an agency "for the begetting of Grace as Well as for the Strengthning of Grace," Stoddard invokes the Passover: "As the Passover of old was, the Lords Supper now is appointed for Conversion. Sometimes it is blessed by God for this end: & its design'd by God for this end," that is, to stimulate a saving faith in those who still lack spiritual assurance (*ETSS*, p. 131).[18] With a far different construing than Edward Taylor's later delineating in Sermons and Meditations II.60A–60B, Stoddard interprets the extraordinary types to defend his open admissions policy, for "The Lord gave the same Supper Spirituall meat, & Drinck unto the Whole Church of Israel in the Wilderness, I Cor. 10.3,4 . . . & the Lords Supper is to be administred to the whole Church that are of age, & without offence, I Cor. 10.17" (*ETSS,* p. 132). Seeking to comfort discouraged church members, Stoddard recalls both the New Testament example in which "all that were converted unto the christian religion, were admitted to it by the Apostles" and the Old Testament in which "persons of such qualifications, were admitted to the passover"; hence, "it was not forbidden to such as were in their naturall condition" (*ETSS,* p. 144). Thus, during 1690 Stoddard employs this typological analogy with the Passover to defend his motion to open the Lord's Supper to all nonscandalous members, even those lacking a state of grace and unable or unwilling publicly to relate their conversions. As a testimony to Stoddard's persuasive oratory in this Galatians sermon, the Northampton congregation soon adopted his theories into ceremonial practice.[19]

No doubt set forth in other homilies as Stoddard pursued his "harvests" of souls, arguments from Old Testament types noticeably proliferated in his public pamphlet war with Increase Mather and provoked as well Edward Taylor's unpublished rebuttals in the *Treatise* and *Upon the Types of the Old Testament.* Mather diametrically opposed Stoddard's nascent liberalism, although emotional objections rather than logic prevail in much of his hastily composed *A Dissertation, wherein The Strange Doctrine Lately Published in a Sermon, The Tendency of which, is, to Encourage Unsanctified Persons (while such) to Approach the Holy Table of the Lord, is Examined and Confuted* (1708).[20] He does, however, recapitulate typal correlations between Passover and the Supper from his brother Samuel Mather's *The Figures or Types* before concluding that ancient restrictions foreshadow contemporary prohibitings of unsanctified persons from the table.[21] Since "no Uncircumcised Person might Eat the Passover. Thus no Unbaptised Person nor any who are Uncircumcised in Heart have a Right to the Lords Supper, nor may such as are apparently Unregenerate be received to that Holy Ordinance" (pp. 17–18). Mather clearly argues that, because the Jews required a circumcised state and purging of ceremonial impurities in order to partake in the sacrifices, temple worship, or Passover, the Lord's Supper properly demands a corresponding Baptism of the heart and morally pure or regenerate soul. To countermand Stoddard's plea for admitting just such "unregenerate Persons," Mather further distinguishes between Old and New Testament churches: "Altho' Gospel Mysteries were Typified by the Passover, Nevertheless, it was Instituted in Special to be a Commemoration of a wonderful *Deliverance to that Nation,* on which account the whole Nation were to observe it. But to reason from thence, that therefore all who are called Christians, should come to the Lords Supper, is inconsequent Argumentation" (p. 74). The inconsequence, according to Mather, stems from mistakenly identifying the national church of Israel with all Christians. Instead, he correlates the select Israelite nation with the likewise circumscribed "Church under the Gospel" which is *"Congregational"* and substitutes his own acceptable typal analogy (p. 74). As a commemoration of the nation's deliverance, the Passover rightfully commands observance by all Israelites; analogously, as a spiritual memorial to Christ's deliverance of his *chosen saints* from sin, the Lord's Supper becomes sacred only to that "holy Nation of true Believers, being the Peculiar People, who are the Subjects of the Redemption of Christ" (p. 75). Under this new dispensation of congregational churches, "Real Saints [who] are Christs Guests," having made a saving relation of grace, may be admitted to the holy banquet (p. 79).

Mather thus transforms a spurious typological proof for an inclusive administering into a sound rationale for Puritan exclusivity in restricting the Sacrament to professed "Real Saints." When he resorts to scare tactics, prophesying that Stoddard's application of the Passover will unleash an influx of "Adulterers, Thieves, Liars, Slanderers, and Perjured Persons," he also reveals the depth of his own fears (p. 75). Threatened by Stoddard's push for a Presbyterian church in New England, Mather, like his colleague Edward Taylor, envisions the crumbling of all congregational authority to enforce sacramental standards originated by Calvin and the Puritan founding fathers. Bemoaning the second generation's decline and yet holding out an eschatological vision of a purified church worthy of entering the heavenly New Jerusalem, he calls in his earlier 1680 "Confutation" for stalwart resistance to Stoddard's corruptions: "To use all lawful means to keep churches pure is a duty, and most eminently, our duty," for "it is well known that purity in churches and church-administrations was designed by our fathers when they followed the Lord into this wilderness" and that "unregenerate persons shall not enter within the gates of the New Jerusalem, Rev. 21. 27" (pp. 63–4). Drawing upon Israel as a historical example and Passover as a prefiguration of sacramental practices under the New Testament, and thus under the New England dispensation, Mather stood firm in opening full church communion and the Holy Table only to professed and examined regenerate members.

In his 1709 *An Appeal to the Learned*, Stoddard easily ridiculed Mather's dire allegations and attacked the typological assertions with well-reasoned erudition. Stoddard's final sally in this explosive pamphlet war, this *Vindication of the Right of Visible Saints to the Lords Supper, Though they be destitute of a Saving Work of God's Spirit on their Hearts: Against the Exceptions of Mr. Increase Mather*, recapitulates his tenacious commitment to sacramental liberalism. Ground finer in the mills of three decades of disputation, the doctrines in Stoddard's *Appeal* represent his theological synthesis, even while their reiteration betrays his weary impatience.

However, in attempting to refute Mather's inconsistent (because hurried) treatise, Stoddard himself falls prey to a self-contradiction on the matter of types. Initially, he reaffirms his "former Answer" against types as guides to New Testament sacraments:

> A Type properly is some instituted resemblance of some Gospel Truth; and the Ordinances of the Jewish Church were not instituted to be resemblances of the Ordinances of the New-Testament: they did not instruct the Church of the Jews in Gospel Ordinances. Was Circumcision instituted to instruct the Church of the Jews for above *two thousand* years, that Baptism should be appointed in the Christian Church, and that it must be administred with such and such circumstances? The like I may say of the Passover and the Sacrifices, Ec. neither were they instituted to teach us Gospel Ordinances; we may receive some Edification from them: but we are under better Ordinances, & a more glorious dispensation. (p. 13)[22]

Whether Stoddard bases his rejection on a quibble between ordinances and truths, hair-splitting between instructions and edification, or a disparity between old and new rituals, he highhandedly discards centuries of exegesis by challenging the figural premise of "instituted resemblances." Perhaps enflamed by the intellectual warfare, he seems more defensively intent upon destroying Mather's contention that *"such as were unclean might not eat the Passover"* which doth *"typifie, that they who are unclean . . . should not come to the Lords Supper"* than constructing his own flawlessly logical *apologia* (p. 12).

Moreover, the wholesale dismissal of the epistemology of types seems curiously shortsighted, since Stoddard later employs figural analogies to justify his own sacramental beliefs. He holds fast to his concepts of even the unregenerate man's right to the covenant seals, the Lord's Supper as a converting ordinance, and the necessary admission of all visible saints to the table, even if unsanctified. Having scattered appeals to Baptism and the Passover throughout, Stoddard climaxes his *Appeal* with a summary, ironically typological in method:

> If the want of Sanctification, did not make it unlawful for men to come to the Passover: Then it don't make it unlawful for men to come to the Lords Supper. The Passover is a Sacrament as well as the Lords Supper, therefore *Christ is called our Passover,* I Cor. 5.7. *Christ our Passover is Sacrificed or [sic] us.* In the Passover Christ is represented, and it is as well as Circumcision a Seal of the righteousness of faith. If it be unlawful for Unsanctifyed persons to partake of the Lords Supper, because that is a sign of Christ Crucifyed, it would on the same account have been unlawful to have partook of the Passover, for that likewise was a sign of Christ Crucifyed. If it were unlawful, because it is an holy Ordi-

nance; then they might not have come to the Passover, for that was an holy Ordinance also. If it be unlawful because therein saints have communion with Christ, it would upon the same account have been unlawful to have come to the Passover; for Saints therein had communion with Christ. If it were unlawful, because the Sacrament of the Lords Supper is a Sacrament of confirmation, then it would have been unlawful to have pertook of the Passover, on the same account: the Passover & the Lords Supper are like figures, one of Christ to come, the other of Christ already come: and when Christ abolished one, he instituted the other in the room thereof. (pp. 52–3)

Despite Stoddard's previous denial, this barrage of instituted resemblances bristles with the language of types. Designed to obliterate Mather's exceptions, the catalog of figural parallels falls into a curiously post-figurative format. Stoddard reasons backward from his own sacramental beliefs, thereby investing the Passover in retrospect with attributes that will legitimize his practices. For example, to demolish Mather's claim that it is unlawful for unsanctified persons to partake of the Supper because it is a particularly holy ordinance, Stoddard argues that if so, such admissions would have been similarly illegal under the Old Testament. Reversing the assumption, he instead makes Passover a holy ordinance to which unsanctified Israelites might come; consequently, his admittance of unregenerate persons to the Lord's Supper fully conforms with the typological instruction. The ease with which exegetes manipulated the typology to prove their theological biases becomes clear when, drawing upon the same type of the Passover, Mather's *Dissertation* and Stoddard's *Appeal* arrive at totally antithetical principles for administering the Lord's Supper.

The antipodal readings of Passover which so clearly separate the conversative camp of Increase Mather and Edward Taylor from Solomon Stoddard ultimately revolve around four issues which appear prominently in *An Appeal to the Learned*. First, Stoddard claims that as Passover seals the "truth" of God's covenant pledge to Israel of an eventual release from sin, so also the Lord's Supper seals a "promise" of redemption made possible by Christ's sacrifice. Since the Sacrament does not "Seal up Pardon and Salvation," but only signifies "the truth of the Covenant," all visible members, just as all Israelites, qualify for receiving the bread and wine (pp. 22, 23). By contrast, because Mather and Taylor perceive the Sacrament as sealing man's entry into a state of grace, as testified by a saving work of conversion, they would exclude all other visible covenanting members who lack regeneracy.

Second, just as Passover is a converting ordinance in which all Israel engages, the Lord's Supper also provides an "affecting offer of Christ crucifyed" to all, even uncertain or spiritually destitute souls (p. 25). Stoddard's open admittance to Passover and the Supper convinces wavering believers of the "safety in coming to Christ" and thus could induce conversions (p. 25). Mather and Taylor unequivocally reject this position by denying either Passover or the Lord's Table any converting efficacy, while they uphold the Supper as a celebratory seal of the communicant's prior conversion.

Third, Stoddard not only admits unsanctified, nonscandalous persons to the Supper, but he likewise warns that anyone who *"forbeareth to keep the Passover . . . shall be cut off from his People"* (p. 51). He makes nonattendance almost a sin of omission, if the unsanctified communicant neglects his sacramental service. In opposition, Mather and Taylor condemn unsanctified participants as sinners by commission, who pollute the Supper with their unworthiness. Clearly Stoddard's philosophy allows for the realistic dilemma of Puritans who may have sufficient but not an absolutely certifiable knowledge of grace. By deemphasizing the seemingly punitive barriers, Stoddard allays a waverer's insecurities and encourages sacramental participation.

Fourth, Stoddard claims that just as Passover belongs among Old Testament ordinances, the Supper joins other gospel measures designed by God to bring men to His grace. With this view both Mather and Taylor violently disagree because they distinguish between merely preparatory acts, such as hearing the Word and prayer, and the exalted feast. Stoddard's argument makes the banquet less a culminating celebration of man's achieved assurance of salvation and more an inducement to the pursuit of it. The conservative doctrine "blesses" a soul's entrance into sainthood, whereas Stoddard's liberal practice seems almost to "bribe" the participant with promises. The former vision succors a believer with strengthening grace, the latter sells the Eucharist on the speculation of "begetting" grace.

The question of congruity between the Lord's Supper and contemporary ordinances aroused virulent accusations of popishness from both parties. In the *Dissertation* Mather castigated his adversary, because "as Mr. S. his Notions are against the stream of the most Eminent, and Orthodox Divines, so they agree with those who are in other Points very Heterodox in their Judgments. Popish writers say as he does. They are mighty sticklers for the Sacraments being Converting Ordinances" (p. 52). Similarly, in his revised Foundation Day Sermon Edward Taylor scoffs at Stoddard's audacity, since "non-Converted persons admission to the Lords Table, as to a Converting Ordinance" is tantamount to "a Popish Doctrine" (*CRRS*, p. 343). In stinging rebuttal, Stoddard accuses his opponents of superstitious idolatry in seeking to glorify the Supper:

> Many Persons do make an idol of the Lords Supper; crying it up above
> all Ordinances both of the Old & New Testament, as if it were as pecu-
> liar to Saints as heavenly glory, and to be attended with more reverence
> than all other Ordinances. It may be this is some of the relicks of Popish
> Idolatry, in making the Bread & Wine to be the natural Body & Blood
> of Christ. (*Appeal,* p. 53).

Perhaps as an ironic tribute to the triumph of his reformism, Stoddard
became remembered as "Pope" of the Connecticut Valley. But the acri-
monious split among Puritan theologians over administering the Lord's
Supper signaled major schisms in New England's theocracy. Furthermore, in these disputes the danger that typology itself would deteriorate
into merely a useful weapon in a warfare of words also seemed imminent. Indeed, those Puritan ministers who almost succumbed to distort-
ing figural analogies to win ecclesiastical struggles came to resemble the
medieval and Renaissance typologists who, with similar motives, created
divergent and often idiosyncratic expositions. As subsequent American
writings prove, Mather's and Taylor's fight to sustain pure readings and
applications of types failed – as did their sacramental conservatism.
Transmuted into providential signs of contemporary historical events,
emblems of God in nature, metaphors for millennial visions, or literary
symbols, biblical types became more secularized and politicized than early
Calvinist exegetes ever envisioned.[23]

An advocate of stringent sacramental requirements, Edward Taylor
played an important, though unpublished and unpublicized role in the
Connecticut Valley upheavals. Sufficiently alarmed by Stoddard's Galatians sermon and his successful 1690 motion to admit all nonscandalous
members to the Lord's Table, Taylor privately recorded his disagreements in a variety of writings over the next twenty years. During the
1690s, as we have seen, he sketched out thirty-four pages of "Animadversions," recorded six new syllogisms in his "Commonplace Book"
(ca. 1693) and added twenty-four manuscript pages to his Foundation
Day Sermon, now titled "A Particular Church is Gods House" (1692–
3). Enraged by Stoddard's incendiary practices as well as preachments,
from fall 1693 through spring 1694, Taylor penned eight sermons in a
Treatise Concerning the Lord's Supper, to which the earlier materials contribute.[24] Although he may have shared his manuscript with Increase
Mather, as congruities with the *Dissertation* (1709) and a longstanding
Harvard friendship and correspondence suggest, no evidence confirms
the speculation. That the *Treatise* never appeared in print represents a
decided loss to the debates, since the coherent logic of his arguments
often surpasses the scattered musings and defensive posturings of the
other contemporary disputants. Responding to Stoddard before the

eruption of printed animosities, yet privy at first hand to the burgeoning apostasy, Taylor seems remarkably prescient and comprehensive in his *Treatise*. He sets his refutation within the framework of a broader thesis that makes partaking of the Supper conditional upon a believer's professed conversion and inward preparation and, therefore, celebratory rather than proselytizing in function.

Among other proofs from the Church Fathers and Protestant Reformers, Scripture, and ramistic logic, Taylor deploys an impressive array of typological points, specifically to counter Stoddard's contention that Passover warrants admitting all visible church members, except those who lead blatantly sinful lives. Unlike his adversary, who later purports to reject, yet conveniently uses Passover as a type, Taylor consistently accepts this ceremonial foreshadowing. He first placates his opponent by conceding that "the Passover, sacrifices, offerings, etc: as to their natures duly considered . . . may be blessed unto the conversion of sinners: the like is granted as touching the Lord's Supper" (*TCLS*, p. 73). But he hastens to append a qualifying distinction: "The reason is because God hath ordained *consideration* a duty in order to conversion, a suitable object of which *consideration* are these ordinances, as well as other things. And not in that they are ordained to be means of conversion in their *celebration*" (*TCLS*, p. 73; my italics). While encouraging the study of ceremonial types as an enrichment, Taylor still renounces their celebration as a legitimate inducement to conversion. Considering the joys of the Lord's Supper may stimulate an aspiring believer to cultivate a state of grace, but attending the banquet remains reserved only for those communicants already blessed in their conversion.

Second, by reaffirming a traditional Puritan concept of the sacraments as signs that seal man's covenant with God, Taylor reduces Stoddard's theory to a logical absurdity. "The signifying of the *signatum* or thing signified, is the reason of the *signum*, or sign; and therefore the *signatum* is *prius natura*, the first in being, for it must be before it can be signified. Hence the sign and seal . . . cannot beget the thing it signifies and seals" (*TCLS*, p. 74). In fact, Stoddard's doctrine precisely reverses the relationship between the sacramental sign and covenant it signifies by making the Lord's Supper precede and procure faith rather than follow upon and ratify it. In contrast, Taylor claims that Passover and "all sacrifices were . . . signs and seals of our reconciliation to God in Christ, and of our . . . living upon Christ by faith in Christ typified" (*TCLS*, p. 74). By typological analogy, just as Passover was "not ordained to beget the first grace, but for the exercise of grace begot," so also the Supper nourishes a believer after the begetting of faith and entry into full churchhood (*TCLS*, p. 74). By emphasizing the intimate jointure between the sign and grace signified, Taylor does not limit this Sacrament only to sealing the truth of covenant promises, but accepts it as a genuine sign of man's achieved conversion and grace – the promises fulfilled. Hence, it seems heretical even to suggest splitting the sign from the experience of salvation thereby signified: "The nature of the Lord's Supper is such as is above the capacity of an unconverted person to celebrate: and this is clear. For the sign and the thing signified must go together in its celebration. If they be torn asunder, there is but a shell and not the kirnel of the sacrament. He that cannot receive both receives neither" (*TCLS*, p. 86). From Taylor's viewpoint, Stoddard's admittance of unconverted communicants makes the Supper a mockery by which the "shell" of ritualism flourishes whereas the signified "kirnel" of true grace withers away.

Third, Taylor decisively rejects the attributing of any "converting efficacy" to any other "seals, whether types or antitypes," as a rationale for so using the Lord's Supper (*TCLS*, pp. 97–8). He refers to the exact texts that Samuel Mather and Thomas Taylor had cited earlier, when he pronounces that "Circumcision, the sign (Gen. 17:11) and seal (Rom. 4:11) of God's covenant was no converting ordinance; neither is baptism" (*TCLS*, p. 98). In *The Safety of Appearing* and Galatians sermon, Stoddard had also cited Romans to declare circumcision and Baptism as covenant seals; but, from the very same postulate, he derives conclusions totally inimical to Edward Taylor. Stoddard concludes in his sermon that all such ordinances as circumcision, Baptism, the Passover, and the Lord's Supper "are for the begetting of grace as well as the strengthning of it . . . for the conversion of Sinners, as well as for the edification of Saints" (*ETSS*, p. 136). After reviewing celebratory customs at length in the *Treatise*, Taylor contradicts Stoddard by classifying Passover, like all other seals, as "very unlikely to be a converting ordinance" (*TCLS*, p. 100). Furthermore, he agrees with Increase Mather's and Stoddard's premise that Passover serves as a "memorandum of that deliverance" and as "a famous type of Christ, and redemption from sin" (*TCLS*, p. 100). But contrary to Stoddard's unequivocal stance that service as a memorial does not preclude an ordinance's converting power, Taylor retorts that neither Jewish rabbis nor Puritan exegetes envisioned Passover as a "means of conversion" (*TCLS*, p. 100). For Taylor the word "memorandum" embodies a key concept, since it allows for the typal analogy between Passover as a memorial of Israel's release from Egyptian bondage and the Lord's Supper as commemorating Christ's sacrifice to redeem man from sin. However, as sealing celebrations which strengthen grace, neither Passover nor the Lord's Supper by definition can serve as converting ordinances to *engender* salvation. Both Passover and the Lord's Supper memorialize deliverances, but cannot deliver; both seal a state of grace, but cannot beget it.

Even if one supposes Passover to be a stimulus to conversion, Taylor finally argues, differences between the legal and evangelical dispensations establish the Supper's superiority. The Old Testament rituals consist of "worldly and carnal things" which function as "shadows and types" of the spiritual blessings under a gospel church (*TCLS*, p. 128). The slain lamb roasted, the lintels and posts sprinkled with hyssop dipped in blood, and the paschal lamb eaten with unleavened bread and bitter herbs – these acts memorialize God's earthly deliverance of Israel, but also seal His promise of a greater salvation to come. Under the New Testament, partaking of the bread and wine spiritually commemorates Christ's body and blood. Slain in the flesh, yet unlike the paschal lamb, the Messiah accomplishes through His sacrifice man's eternal redemption. Such disparities between figure and fulfillment apply, however, not just to differing manners or meanings of these two sacraments, but also to the stringent requirements for admittance, a point that Taylor resolutely affirms against Stoddard:

> As then the shadow or type accepted of a ceremonial or typical holiness, as sufficient for the constitution of its visible church state, and so to churchhood, calling to no higher holiness as absolutely necessary; the seal of the covenant, or Passover, acquiesseth in such a qualified subject. So now, the substance, or thing typified, a typified or real holiness, is essential to the constituting of a visible church state. . . . Hence it's rational to conclude, that the cleanness required in the subject of the typical Passover was a type of the real holiness in the subject of the typified Passover, the Lord's Supper. (*TCLS*, p. 128)

Calling for an inwardly "real" as opposed to outward holiness under the ancient law, the Lord's Supper charges believers to come prepared – visibly clean, professed in their conversion, ready to renew their covenant with God. Taylor thus upholds the typal premise of a superior dispensation under the gospel which grants the Lord's Supper special eminence among all ceremonies. Stoddard, on the other hand, almost annuls the antitype's superiority by making the Eucharist distinct from the Old Testament Passover only by its newness and elements. It is, therefore, not necessarily superior in nature (both are seals to the covenant), in requirements (both permit unregenerates to partake), or in function (both strengthen grace *and* convert sinners). Moreover, by clustering the Supper with other ordinances, Stoddard does not grant it due preeminence as the foremost of New Testament rituals. Through his reversals of Stoddard's appeals to the Passover, Edward Taylor succeeds in generating his own antithetical arguments for a traditionalist view of the Supper as a specially ordained seal or sign of, not merely a convenient means toward, the soul's conversion.

The *Treatise* remains Taylor's most tightly woven rebuttal to Stoddard, even during the fifteen subsequent years of intense pamphlet warfare and Taylor's preaching on the types. To examine *Upon the Types of the Old Testament* for evidences of Taylor's attitudes toward Stoddard and the sacramental controversy is, however, to discover a surprising – or perhaps not so – lack of direct references. As Taylor's extant corpus testifies, his habit was to devote a separate sermon series to distinct critical issues, whether the Lord's Supper, Christ's nature, or the types. Having responded in the *Treatise* so extensively to Stoddard's apostasy, Taylor apparently felt less compelled to reexplore the terrain in a series devoted exclusively to Old Testament types. He nowhere mentions Stoddard by name, nor does he treat any type primarily as a basis for arguing against the Supper as a converting ordinance. In inverse proportion to the *Treatise,* the exegesis of divine figures dominates *Upon the Types,* with only intermittent excursions into sacramental doctrine or attacks upon those who err in administering the Supper. Predictably, the discussions of fit admission to the church, required holiness, and eating of the bread and wine repeat arguments elaborated elsewhere in greater detail. Even in the Sermons and Meditations II.22 and 71 on the Passover (to be discussed fully in Chapter 7) and on the extraordinary types II.58–61, in which Taylor imitates Thomas Taylor's sacramental interpretations in *Christ Revealed,* the modicum of direct engagement in controversial debate with Stoddard is notable. The lacunas in Taylor's exposition may occur because these sequences (1703–6) were written ten years after the *Treatise* and before the publication of Mather's *Dissertation* (1708) and Stoddard's *Appeal* (1709). Although Thomas Davis has suggested that the controversy stimulated Taylor to undertake a concentrated study of types, it is rather more likely that he conceived of *Upon the Types of the Old Testament* as independent of his refutations of Stoddard. However, finding the types useful in disputing Stoddard's claims, he adopted them in his *Treatise,* as he had done briefly in the Foundation Day Sermon and more extensively in the revision, "A Particular Church is Gods House."[25]

When Taylor engages the issue of the criteria for admission to the church and Supper, he frequently does so in brief digressions or in his exhortations to his congregation to purify themselves before partaking of the sacred feast. For example, in one such reference from *Upon the Types,* he reasons typologically from Israel's exclusivity in requiring a visible covenant and ceremonial cleansing prior to worship. Sermon and Meditation II.20 on the tabernacle reaffirm the Puritan premise that "before any one might approach un to God in Tabernacle Worship, he must be in Visible Covenant with God & his people" and "So it is with our Gospell Temple," within which all saints "must be cleansed, & Sanctified, by Christ Jesus visibly in order to our visible Communion with God in his Instituted Worship" (*UTOT,* pp. 433, 434). Because visible communion requires a prior saving relation, Taylor exhorts his parishioners in the sermon's uses to "Strive to get a Saving Relation to Christ. Then thou wilt have access to this House, & to Carry on the Worship of God in this Gospell Tabernacle" (*UTOT*, p. 451). Perhaps as an implicit rebuttal to Stoddard's claims, Taylor also analyzes the tabernacle's three courts in order to discriminate among the variety of believers. The "Camp of Israel" during the wanderings or temple's "Outward Court" represents the "Catholick Church under the Gospel in the largest sense, as it contains good & bad," whereas the "Inward Court" of the brazen altar emblemizes the "Gospell Church consisting in its visible Societies Celebrating the Holy Ordinances of God, in the Preaching the Word, & Celebrating the Lords Supper," unto which none but the consecrated and cleansed might approach (*UTOT*, pp. 438, 439). Located within the third or "Lords Court," God's innermost sanctum, the temple's holy of holies, prefigures the "Invisible Church of Christ contained in the Visible" and "the true Worshippers that worship God in Spirit" (*UTOT*, p. 439). Charged with administering church discipline as well as worship, Puritan ministers, like the Old Testament priests, must oversee the qualifications of those who partake of the ordinances and Sacrament. They must separate "Good & Bad Christians, Holy, & Prophane Tares & Wheate," those scandalous ones remanded to the outer camp from holy worshipers permitted to enter into full communion, as into Israel's inward court, where they present themselves not only as visible covenanters, but also as saints spiritually cleansed (invisibly) to worship God truly (*UTOT*, p. 440).

The mandate that only "the Visibly, & Spiritually Cleane, & not Unholy; & Unregenerate, are persons to have admittance into the Communion of Gospell Churches" finds reaffirmation in Sermon II.27 on disciplinary purifications, in which Taylor also comes closest to attacking Solomon Stoddard outright (*UTOT*, p. 623). By way of reproof, he singles out those

> that Suck up like a Spunge the Dirty Pudle Water of Popish, & Erastian fopperies: asserting all Divine Ordinances, yea, the Sacraments themselves, to be ordained of God for the Conversion of Sinners . . . & hence they mentain, that unregenerate persons are to be admitted to the Lords Table, & so Condemn the judgment of the Holy Church of God thrô all ages in holding the Contrary. (*UTOT*, p. 624)

"Our doctrine," he warns, "comes with a Scourge to Whip them, for their Conclusion. For that they boldly give the Type the Ly," as he brings forward Old Testament ceremonial purifications to argue figurally that "Such as are not Spiritually Cleane, but Uncleane, have no right to the Holy Things of Gods House or Church fellowship" (*UTOT*, p. 624). By metaphorically identifying Israel's tabernacle courts with the gospel church as both a fellowship and a sacred habitation, Taylor mournfully rages against those who not simply in principle but also in practice "throw the Doore of Gospell Discipline off of its hinges, or pull the lock off of the Doore," allowing persons who labor not for saving grace but instead "all to come thô never so uncleane" (*UTOT*, p. 624). Hence, Taylor predicts that "dogs shall have Childrens bread. Pearls shall be for Swine . . . thô he [Christ] saith, the Dogs are to be without; they open, & let them in. Oh! what a thing is this? How Contrary is it to the very Ordinance of Discipline" (*UTOT*, p. 624). Even as he seeks to reassure his Westfield parishioners, Taylor's heightened rhetoric betrays his fears about Stoddard's open admissions and advocacy of the Supper as a converting ordinance. In his subsequent assault against "Erastian Presbyterians, in there warping from our Congregationall Discipline," Taylor also recognizes the potential danger of Stoddard's appeals to English Erastians and to a Presbyterian polity (*UTOT*, p. 627).[26]

Edward Taylor also takes serious exception to Stoddard's appeal to the extraordinary types of the manna and water from the rock in his figural Sermon II.60B. Both theologians might agree that the waters from Horeb's rock typified "the Blood of Christ our Spirituall Rock as the Wine in the Lords Supper Signified," but the issue of who could properly nourish themselves from this fount was not so easily resolved (*UTOT*, p. 780). Echoing Stoddard's doctrinal contention, though he does not attribute it as such, Taylor posits the key objection:

> Queried it may be thus. If the Water of the Rock in Horeb typify the Same things in Christ as are Signified by the Wine in the Lords Supper . . . then how is it, that all under the means of Grace may not receive the Lords Supper: but onely Such as are under higher qualifications than Commonly which are universall Seing all the Camp of Israel, yea, & Strangers . . . did drink this Water. (*UTOT*, p. 782)

Taylor's three solutions constitute one of his clearest rebuttals to Stoddard in *Upon the Types*. First, he condemns the analogy with Israel's *camp* as nonsensical, since it would countenance "not onely the giving the Lords Supper to infants, & Children, that Cannot examine themselves. contrary to the Qualifications to be Exercised preparatory to the receiving. . . . But also unto beasts & Cattle," for so they all "dranke of this Water" (*UTOT*, p. 783). Second, he distinguishes the "two fold Design & End" of this type, on the one hand to provide a necessary relief "Common to all the Camp," and on the other hand "for a Sacred end to point out unto their Faith Some Sacred & Spirituall good thing" (*UTOT*, p. 783). Contrary to the twofold significance of these ancient waters, however, the Supper's wine "hath the Stamp of Christs blood upon it, & it is a Sacred thing; yet it hath no Common Design at all" (*UTOT*, p. 783). Though Horeb's water has a "typicall Relation" which "in no wise remoove[s] from it the Common use," Taylor argues in his third solution that its gospel antitype "the Sacramentall wine . . . passeth under a Compleate Consecration, that Separates it from all Common Use . . . hence none but Truely Qualified persons may pertake thereof" (*UTOT*, p. 783). In short, Taylor validates the New Testament's superiority which requires sacramental participants to examine and spiritually to cleanse themselves before coming to the Sacrament to confirm the operation of saving grace upon their souls. The methodical *reductio ad absurdum* of Stoddard's contentions is unusual in *Upon the Types,* though perhaps nowhere more appropriately so than with a type that clearly prefigures the eucharistic wine. The figural rebuttal enables Taylor to exhort his Westfield congregation not only to attend the Lord's Supper but also to prepare for this Sacrament by rejecting the dominion of sin, uniting with Christ, and living a life of visible holiness.

Primarily in Sermons II.22 and II.71, Taylor interprets Passover as a commemoration of God's deliverance of Israel from Egypt and seal of the covenant, foreshadowing Christ's deliverance of mankind from sin and the Lord's Supper as a superseding evangelical seal. Rather than redefine the Lord's Table as an initiatory ordinance, as Stoddard proposed, Taylor reiterates its divinely instituted function as a confirming "Seale of Growth in the Covenant of Grace, administer'd onely in a Church State, unto Such onely as are Visibly Holy as to judgment of Charity" (*UTOT*, p. 480). Sermon II.71 abounds with variants of the verbs to "grow," "nourish," and "strengthen," as if sheer repetition might resurrect the proper end of this much disputed Sacrament to stimulate "Spirituall nourishment," "to Strengthen, & give Growth to the Grace" of God's faithful Elect (*UTOT*, pp. 824, 833). Taylor vehemently rejects any more liberal practices, for "we admit not to the Lords Table upon bare baptism or Covenantall relation," as he summarizes his prior defense of church fellowship, ceremonial cleanness, and holy preparations before receipt of the Passover or Supper (*UTOT*, p. 837). Though he attacks the Quakers and papists, the latter for their belief in transubstantiation and extreme unction, he refrains from any direct indictment of Stoddard. Thus, in the broader scheme of *Upon the Types of the Old Testament,* the nearly overt, occasionally vehement, but always unattributed rebuttals of Stoddard are a minor strand or lingering leitmotif. They do suggest, however, that in the period 1696–1706 (II.20–71), Stoddard's controversial administration in Northampton was always on Taylor's mind as in Westfield he sought to maintain the Sacrament's purity, church discipline, and his own flock from the contamination of reformist doctrines of church covenanting and the Lord's Supper.

Spurred to further refutations after Stoddard published his *Appeal to the Learned* and initiated his fifth harvest of souls in Northampton, Taylor retaliates with "The *Appeale* Tried" (ca. 1710–11), an unpublished pamphlet which clearly denigrates Stoddard's logical fallacies.[27] "The *Appeale* Tried" is divided into three books to correspond with Stoddard's units and a fourth to "evidence the Lords Supper nott Ordaind to Convert Sinners," so that Taylor's "trial" ostensibly permits him to judge the validity of each side's arguments (*ETSS*, p. 211). In reality, he takes the opportunity to exonerate Increase Mather's injudicious *Dissertation*. Accordingly, he repudiates Stoddard's admission of "unsyncere persons & Hypocrites" to the Supper; "no Unregenerate man can do the Duty Called to by this Examination," since he lacks sanctifying grace (*ETSS*, p. 200). Responding spottily to Stoddard's use of Passover, he steadfastly asserts that "Bread & Wine give nourishment to the Living & do not give Life to the Dead" (*ETSS*, p. 178). Because the "Sacramentall eating & drinking signify feeding on Christ," consequently they also "signify not begetting faith, but a Living faith in Being" (*ETSS*, p. 179). Moreover, he reaffirms the Lord's Supper's preeminence as a confirming seal to which a man must come initiated through Baptism, nurtured through hearing the Word, and robed in inward sanctification:

> The Dispensing of the Gospell to them, is the Calling them to the Wedden. The Sanctifying & Justifying Grace of Christ the Wedden Garment: the Gathering of them together the bringing of them into a Church State, συναγωγόν, the ensynagoguing of them & so bringing them into Christs house, & so the Feast to import all the Gracious administrations there of Divine Comunion & Fellowship in Gods Ordinances, where of the Lords Supper is an Eminent one, Calld a Feast or Supper. (*ETSS*, p. 154)

Unswerving in its support of Mather and attacks upon Stoddard, "The *Appeale* Tried"exudes the mustiness of litigious scholasticism. More polemical than polished, it lacks the coherent metaphoric structure that lightens the *Treatise* and the comprehensive, systematic logic of *Upon the Types of the Old Testament*.

Similarly, Meditations II.102–111 on Christ's instituting of the Supper from Matthew 26:26–30 often lapse into disputatious and compressed outlines of doctrine. But here the poetic metaphors of festal joy and "Sabbath Entertainment," which hark back to the earlier *Treatise*, often alleviate the doctrinal tedium. Probably related to a sermon series preached from June 1711 through December 1712, Taylor's meditations communicate the intensity of his anti-Stoddard sentiments.[28] Furthermore, these poems epitomize Taylor's fascination with the wedding feast not merely as a thorny public issue in New England but as the glorious celebration that confirms his personal salvation and intimacy with God. Thus, when Taylor meditates upon the nature, reasons, and benefits of this "Choice Feast," he cogently synthesizes the fundamental concepts of the Lord's

Supper which he had disputed for over thirty years in his unpublished writings, the *Treatise,* and *Upon the Types.* In Meditation II.103, for example, he draws out typological parallels with Passover to portray the Supper as God's spiritual seal of new covenant grace:

> New Covenant worship Wisdom first proclaims
>   Deckt up in Types and Ceremonies gay.
> Rich Metaphors the first Edition gains.
>   A Divine key unlocks these trunks to lay
>   All spirituall treasures in them open Cleare.
>   The Ark and Mannah, in't, Christ and Good Cheere.
>
> This first Edition did the Cov'nant tend
>   With Typick Seales and Rites and Ceremonie
> That till the Typick Dispensations end
>   Should ratify it as Gods Testimony.
>   'Mong which the Passover (whose Kirnell's Christ)
>   Tooke place with all its Rites, graciously spic't.
>
> But when the Pay day came their kirnells Pickt.
>   The Shell is cast out hence. Cloudes flew away.
> Now Types good night, with Ceremonies strict,
>   The Glorious Sun is risen, its broad day.
>   Now Passover farewell, and leave thy Place.
>   Lords Supper seales the Covenant of Grace.
>
> But though the Passover is passt away.
>   And Ceremonies that belong'd to it,
> Yet doth its kirnell and their Kirnell stay
>   Attending on the Seale succeeding it.
>   The Ceremony parting leaves behinde
>   Its Spirit to attend this Seale designd.
>
> As it passt off, it passt its place o're to
>   The Supper of the Lord (Choice Feast) to seale
> The Covenant of Grace thus, even so
>   The Ceremoniall Cleaness did reveale
>   A Spirituall Cleaness qualifying all
>   That have a Right to tend this Festivall.
>
> All must grant Ceremonies must have Sense,
>   Or Ceremonies are but senseless things.
> Had God no reason when, for to dispense
>   His Grace, he ope'd all Ceremoniall Springs?
>   The reason why God deckt his sacred Shrine
>   With Senseless Ceremonies, here Divine.
>
> A Typick Ceremony well attends
>   A Typick Ordinance, these harmonize.
> A Spirituall Ordinance the Type suspendes
>   And Onely owneth Spirituall Qualities

> To have a right thereto. And this the Will
> The dying Ceremony made, stands still.
>
> Morall, and Ceremoniall cleaness, which
>   The Pascall Lamb requir'd Foreshow the Guests
> Must at the Supper Seale with Spoiles be rich
>   Of Sin and be with Saving Grace up dresst.
>   God Chose no Ceremonies for their sake
>   But for Signification did them take.
>
> Give me true Grace that I may grace thy Feast.
>   My Gracious Lord, and so sit at thy Table.
> Thy Spirituall Dainties this Rich Dress at least
>   Will have the Guests have. Nothing less is able
>   To prove their right to't. This therefore bestow.
>   Then as I eate, my lips with Grace shall flow.
>
>   (II. 103. 19–72)

As the prefiguring seal, Passover remains surrounded by "Cloudes" of mystery, commensurate with the nightlike darkness that shrouds the entire Old Testament dispensation. By contrast, in the "broad day" with the "Glorious Sun" of Christ now "risen" to enlighten the world and reveal the "Kirnell" of divine truth, the Lord's Supper takes over Passover's sealing function. Or depicted by another Taylorian metaphor, Passover is the "Typick" seal to the "first Edition" of God's "Wisdom" on earth, an edition composed of prefigurative rites. Just as the Supper supplants Passover to become the seal to a second edition of "the Covenant of Grace," so too man learns to read the typal ceremonies merely as fore-shadowings of the new worship. Taylor captures the dramatic change that makes this inward "Spirituall" confirming of man's covenant state superior to the old "Ceremoniall," which is merely an external legal rat-ification. He similarly marks the fine gradation from "Ceremoniall Clea-ness" to "Spirituall Cleaness" as the new qualification for "all/ That have a Right to tend this Festivall." In much the way he had countered Stod-dard's eroding laxness toward preparation by calling for "real holiness," Taylor here charges communicants to be rid of the "Spoiles" of "Sin and be with Saving Grace up dresst." The wedding guest's need for the "Rich Dress" of inward and "Morall," not an inferior "Ceremoniall," fashion is underscored by Taylor's repeated pleadings for "true Grace" with which to "grace thy Feast./ My Gracious Lord." "Nothing less" than sanctify-ing righteousness proves the appellant's "right" to "sit at thy Table."

  The images of "Deckt up" ceremonies in "gay" apparel, of divine keys to unlock treasure-laden trunks, and of the kernel within a shell momen-tarily vary the language of strict typological exegesis. But the first four stanzas go yet further toward incorporating this elaborately drawn out definitional use of a typological conceit within a more compelling allegorical framework. In a monarchical trial the "Deity did call a Parliament" of His "Properties Divine," allowing the case for "mankinde" to be argued by the prosecutor "Justice," who sentences man to the rigors of "Law," while "Grace gave band securing Gods Elect" (II.103.1, 2, 3, 5). In exaggerated legal language Taylor sets the stage on which the pageant of humanity plays, when "Justice offended, Grace to worke doth Fall," tracing out "New Cov'nant worship suited to/ His present State to save him from all Woe" (II.103.8, 11–12). The interjection of monetary terms, grace's "Credits Good" and justice "Rests in her Bill," prepares for Taylor's later use of "ratify" and "Pay Day" (II.103.15, 16, 28, 31). Just as typology traces the progression from an Old Testament judicial to a New Testament spiritual dispensation, so too predictably Taylor poetically imitates the shift, moving from court legalisms and contracts to images of a festal celebration, specifically the Lord's Supper to which Christ, the "Gracious Lord," bids "Guests" arrayed in "Rich Dress" (II.103.68, 70, 69). Thus, as a poetic synopsis of his quarrel with Stoddard, this meditation draws upon the same figural analogies with which Taylor earlier defended the right of only regenerate church members to partake of the wedding feast's "SpiritualDainties."

Consistent with his conservative sacramentalism, Taylor concludes in Meditation II.104 that "This Feast is no Regenerating fare./ But food for those Regenerate that are" (II.104.59–60). Hence, the Sacrament provides nourishment only for those who have achieved faith in Christ's redeeming grace. Reiterating his fiat that "spiritualfood doth spirituall life require" (II.106.52) in Meditation II.106, Taylor may even borrow his poetic images from Mather's *Dissertation,* in which Mather himself quotes from "Mr. *Vines* . . . a Learned Presbyterian . . . in his Treatise of the Lords Supper":

> But the Conversion of a Sinner is not signified in the Sacrament, or Sealed. . . . Bread, and Wine speak Nourishment, but not the giving Life. Does Bread and Wine give life to one that is Dead; Meat is not set before Dead Folks. . . . This Sacrament by the Institution of it, Presupposeth those that reap the benefits of it to be Converts, and in Grace, to have Faith in Christ, and to be living Members, And if this is presupposed by this Ordinance, then it is not first wrought by it. They are Children whose Bread this is: Living Members, and not Wooden Legs that are capable of this benefit. (pp. 44–5)[29]

Not only does Taylor annotate this same argument in "The *Appeale* Tried," he also virtually redacts the passage from Vines in his poetic meditation:

> Food is for Living Limbs, not Wooden legs:
>   Life's necessary, unto nourishment.
> Dead limbs must be cut off: the Addle Eggs
>   Rot by the heat the dam upon them spent.

> A State of Sin that takes this bread and Wine
> From the Signatum tareth off the Signe.
>
> A Principle of Life, to eate implies,
> And of such life that sutes the Foods desire.
> Food naturall doth naturall Life supply.
> And spirituall food doth spirituall life require.
> The Dead don't eate. Though Folly childish dotes
> In th'Child that gives his Hobby horses oates.
>
> (II.106.43–54)

Taylor upholds the unity of the sacramental signs with the "spirituall life" of grace signified thereby. And by cleverly evoking the "Wooden" qualities of unconverted applicants, he ridicules the "Folly childish" of giving "oates" to "Hobby horses" or "Food" to "Dead limbs." While excluding those dead souls who lack regeneration from the Holy Table, Taylor conversely invites those "Living Limbs" who have a saving grace to come, to be nourished, to be strengthened by supping on the spiritual bread and wine.

Because Meditations II.103 and 106 treat Taylor's doctrine of the Lord's Supper so overtly, they fulfill in classic fashion his exhortation in the *Treatise,* challenging parishioners to "Meditate upon the feast: its causes, its nature, its guests, its dainties, its reason and ends, and its benefits, etc." (*TCLS*, p. 203). Recall also Taylor's hearty endorsement of "Passover, sacrifices, offerings," or in short, those Old Testament rituals that foreshadow New Testament sacraments, as viable subjects for "consideration." As both a polemicist and a minister who anticipates his sacramental duty, Taylor no doubt feels acutely the need to examine himself for signs of saving grace before tasting the "Rich spirituall fare Soul-Food, Faiths nourishment" (II.105.39). As a man who then practices what he preaches, he makes his meditations personal reflections upon the Sacrament's nature and benefits in order to achieve that heightened state of affections suitable for approaching the wedding feast. Moreover, as he rouses his soul into the proper "festival frame of spirit" (*TCLS*, p. 199), Taylor also envisions his preaching and administering of the Supper, at which time his "lips with Grace shall flow" (II.103.72).

Meditation II.103 exemplifies Taylor's persistent reference to typology in order to defend his conservative sacramental ideals. He carefully encloses all the fine points of doctrine within broader typological distinctions between a ceremonial or "Typick" dispensation and an evangelical or "spirituall" one. As the type most crucial to the pamphlet debates with Stoddard, Passover prominently resurfaces in the poetic meditations as well. Taylor's bonding together of sacramental theories with typological arguments in the *Treatise* and manuscript refutations owes much to his conversance with Thomas Taylor's and Samuel Mather's earlier expositions, to his own *Upon the Types of the Old Testament,* and to an intimate knowledge of Increase Mather's campaign against Stoddard. At the turn of the eighteenth century in New England, Taylor could only perceive Solomon Stoddard as an ominous herald whose liberal ideas and enthusiastic sentiments augured the toppling of a strict Puritan discipline and the sullying of the church's polity. Stoddard's doctrine too easily blurred the boundary between unworthy persons who merely through church affiliation hypocritically came to the Sacrament and those virtuous guests who, like Taylor in his poetic meditations, inwardly prepared for the Lord's wedding feast.

7

Preparing for the Wedding Feast

The Wedden garment of Christs Righteousness
  And Holy Cloathes of Sanctity most pure,
Are their atire, their Festivall rich dress:
  Faith feeds upon the Paschall Lamb its sure.
  That on God's Porslain Dish is disht for them
  And drinks the Cup studded with graces Gem.
                                    (II.71.25–30)

Edward Taylor's meditations on Passover (II.22 and II.71) and the Lord's Supper (II.102–111) occasionally sound more like a preacher's instructions than a soul's affectionate monologues with Christ. They are replete with rational arguments that echo the *Treatise Concerning the Lord's Supper,* documents from the sacramental controversy, and the major typological expositions. With the ministerial voice often rising above personal pleas, these meditations exhort wayward Puritans to return to the purity of Calvinist tenets, to come back to the New England Way. The jeremiad tone derives no doubt from Taylor's vehement opposition to Stoddard's preachings, perceived by him as part of the third-generation decline from the fervor that had originally united the New World community. If Taylor, like his Anglican counterpart George Herbert in *The Temple,* had chosen to publish these poems, they could well stand as a comparable Puritan model for wandering believers. Yet, suppressed from publication under Taylor's directive, the sacramental, like all the other *Preparatory Meditations,* remain private rather than public inspirations. They function not only as miniature discourses on Puritan sacramental theory but also as poetic paradigms for the art of meditation – personal testimonials to the necessity of the prepared heart.

Although we cannot date his affixing of the title, we may well speculate that Taylor conceived of his meditative preparation as essential to administering the Lord's Supper. Whether or not he literally composed his poems prior to delivering sacrament Sunday sermons, as most critics maintain, the title *Preparatory Meditations before my Approach to the Lords Supper* points to his conceptual linking of the act of poetic meditation with Puritan preparation for the eucharistic feast.[1] Surpassing the ancient

Passover, the Lord's Supper spiritually rather than legally seals God's Covenant of Grace. As the most glorious sign of man's inward salvation, the Supper, according to Taylor, requires communicants to assume a "Wedden Robe" (II.106.41) splendid enough for this "Royall Feast Magnificent" of "Spirituall Bread and Wine" (II.108.1, 34). But much as the "Worship-mould" in general springs from a continuous monitoring through self-examination, reading of Scripture, and prayers to Christ, so too the wedding robe constitutes a cultivated inner state of virtue, not a mere fashionable adornment for the wedding guest. Moreover, not just a service necessitated by each discrete celebration of the Lord's Supper, ever-vigilant preparation becomes a lifelong endeavor for the elect saint. The Sacrament may initially motivate Taylor's earthly practice of meditation, but it is the eschatological hope that sustains him in his habit of poetic preparation throughout forty-three years. Hence, as overt arguments for and mimetic demonstrations of one soul's searching contemplations before partaking of the Supper's dainties, these religious lyrics make clear Taylor's commitment to preparatory meditation in practice as well as theory. What begins as the contemplative exercise of a public preacher and private sinner, and consequently of a man who seeks to discover and nourish his sainthood, ends as the creation of a visionary singer.

The Passover as the preeminent Old Testament celebration became a cherished Puritan type, used by theologians of varying persuasions to solidify their arguments respecting the Lord's Supper, criteria for admission, and its benefits. Although purporting opposite doctrines, both Solomon Stoddard and Increase Mather drew heavily upon Passover as a memorial of Israel's deliverance from Egyptian bondage and as a seal to the covenant promises by which God guarantees immediate protection and ultimate redemption to His chosen people. Similarly, as a controversialist in his prose manuscripts ("The *Appeale* Tried") and *Treatise* sermons, Edward Taylor centered on Passover as a covenant seal and prefiguration of the Lord's Supper and, therefore, on necessary restrictions for admitting communicants. However, it is not merely as a weapon for polemical debates and counterattacks, whether with Anglicans and Catholics or against Stoddard's schismatic doctrine in New England, that Taylor seeks typal truths in Passover's ancient ritualism. Though doctrinal applications remain prominent in the *Preparatory Meditations,* as exemplified by the specialized sacramental grouping (II.102–111), Taylor's contemplations also betray personal fascinations at once more focused on the literal elements of paschal lamb, unleavened bread, and shed blood, and yet more compulsively drawn toward spiritual meanings of Passover and the Supper for the individual saint's life. Sermons and Meditations II.22 and II.71 leave behind the political rhetoric that characterizes the extended

series, in part because Taylor turns to the devotional typologists Thomas
Taylor and Samuel Mather for his inspirations. Engaged less by issues of
the Supper's converting efficacy than by its power to nourish the already
regenerate, Taylor explores in these two poems the basic typological parallels. He invokes Passover not so much as a prefiguring seal of the covenant but as a guide to the material elements that foreshadow Christ, as
with the paschal lamb whose bones must not be broken though it must
be slain as an atoning sacrifice. Passover's typal promises of man's deliverance from sin and of Christ as the divine sacrifice who becomes mediator of that redemption are more compelling mysteries for contemplation.
In the ceremonial regulations, Taylor finds numerous "Shaddows" of
the spiritual celebration that Christ inaugurates with his disciples and that
later gospel saints perpetuate by repeatedly partaking of the Supper. By
leavening the doctrinaire polemics of his preaching with the personal
sensitivity of his meditations, Taylor integrates his passionate responses
to Christ's redeeming act with the intellectual debates surrounding the
administration. He cultivates his affections in brief poetic arias to har-
monize with the orchestrated rational arguments of the sermons.

Taylor's bonding of typology with sacramentalism probably owes as
much to Thomas Taylor's example in *Christ Revealed* and Samuel Mather's in *The Figures or Types* as to the contemporary theological disputes
or the intrinsic symbolisms of Scripture. In keeping with traditional exegesis, as in William Guild's *Moses Unvailed,* both exegetes emphasized
Passover's prefiguration of Christ as the Messiah and true lamb whose
sacrifice delivers man forever from sin and God's accompanying wrath.[2]
Likewise, they viewed this sacred type as, according to Mather, "the
Commemoration of their Deliverance and Redemption out of Egypt, *and from
the destroying Angel there"* (*FT,* p. 417). Details of the lamb's selection, its
preparation, the shedding of blood, and eating of the feast became the
foundation for establishing extensive parallels with Christ as the New
Testament's paschal sacrifice. Writing well before New England's controversy over the Supper, neither Taylor nor Mather questioned the need
for circumcision, or the comparable Baptism and "Circumcision of the
heart" under the gospel, before partaking of the feast. Moreover, both
works sanctioned the concept of the Lord's feast as a *"Communion"* that
brings together all regenerate members of the church as "being one Body,
one spiritual Family" within which participants personally and jointly
"feed upon Christ" (*FT,* pp. 421, 422). Fine discriminations for excluding or including church members which so wracked the consciences of
later New England theologians are set forth unequivocally as bedrock
truths. According to Passover, the typal shadow, and Christ's gospel
enlightenment and ordaining, the Lord's Supper unites those saints who

shun souring malice, lust, hypocrisy, and false doctrine, while it steadfastly affirms their faith and heart's regeneracy.

Although Thomas Taylor and Samuel Mather agree in theory and
interpretation, their frameworks differ substantially. Taylor allies Passover with circumcision, finding both to be foreshadowings of the companion New Testament rites of Baptism and the Lord's Supper. Mather,
however, divorces Passover from circumcision, relocates it under the
"Gospel of the Jewish Festivals," and treats it broadly as a festal observance, not narrowly a sacramental one, since it looks as well toward
Christ's crucifixion and resurrection that the Supper commemorates. These
distinctions in turn account for Edward Taylor's two separate sermons
and meditations on Passover. Acknowledging the double function of
Passover as a type, in Sermon II.71 Taylor claims "That the Passover is
a type of Christ. & this hath been made out in our treating upon the
Typicall Feasts. & therefore not to be Spoken to now," referring back to
II.22 among seasonal festivals, while he also anticipates II.71's doctrine
"That the Passover is an Emblem of Lords Supper & this is now to be
Spoken to" (*UTOT*, p. 882).

Consider Meditation II.22 in which Taylor adapts the framework from *The
Figures or Types*. He locates the poem (as he had the sermon) among other
Mosaic feasts, preceding it with Meditation II.21 on the New Moon, attaching four stanzas on Pentecost to Meditation II.22 itself, and then following with Meditation II.23 on the Feast of Atonement and II.24 on the Feast of
Tabernacles (Appendixes 1 and 4).[3] Although he draws images from both
sources and his own sermon, Taylor's meditative format and focus on
the soul's deliverance emphasize the fulfillment of ceremonial law:

> I from the New Moon of the first month high
>   Unto its fourteenth day When she is Full
> Of Light the Which the Shining Sun let fly
>   And when the Sun's all black to see Sins pull
>   The Sun of Righteousness from Heaven down
>   Into the Grave and weare a Pascall Crown.
>
> A Bond Slave in Egyptick Slavery
>   This Noble Stem, Angellick Bud, this Seed
> Of Heavenly Birth, my Soul, doth groaning ly.
>   When shall its Passo're come? When shall't be Freed?
>   The Lamb is slaine upon the fourteenth day
>   Of Month the first, my Doore posts do display.
>
> Send out thy Slaughter Angell, Lord, and slay
>   All my Enslaving 'Gypsies Sins, while I
> Eate this rost Mutten, Paschall Lamb, Display
>   Thy Grace herein, while I from Egypt high.

> I'le feed upon thy Roast meat here updresst,
> With Bitter hearbs, unleaven'd bread the best.
>
> I'le banish Leaven from my very Soule
>   And from its Leanetoe tent: and search out all
> With Candles lest a Crum thereof should rowle
>   Into its Corners or in mouseholes fall,
>   Which when I finde I'le burn up, and will sweep
>   From every Corner all, and all cleane keep.
>
> My Bunch of Hyssop, Faith, dipt in thy blood
>   My Paschall Lamb, held in thy Bason bright
> Baptize my Doore Posts shall, make Crimson good.
>   Let nothing off this Varnish from them wipe,
>   And while they weare thy Crimson painted dy,
>   No Slaughter Angell shall mine house annoy.
>
> Lord, purge my Leaven out: my Tast make quick:
>   My Souls strong Posts baptize with this rich blood
> By bunch of Hyssop, then I'le also Lick
>   Thy Dripping Pan: and eat thy Roast Lamb good,
>   With Staff in hand, Loins Girt, and Feet well shod
>   With Gospell ware as walking to my God.
>
> I'le Goshen's Ramesis now leave apace.
>   Thy Flag I'le follow to thy Succoth tent.
> Thy sprinkled blood being my lintells grace
>   Thy Flesh my Food With bitter herbs attent
>   To minde me of my bitter bondage State
>   And my Deliverance from all such fate.
>   (II.22.1–42)

Taylor's images remain virtually indistinguishable from the parallels in *Christ Revealed* and *The Figures or Types,* and they reflect his knowledge of the biblical directives (Exod. 12:2–42, 13:3) for slaying the lamb on the fourteenth day, sprinkling the lintels and posts with blood, eating the unleavened bread with bitter herbs, and for the pilgrim posture of the recipients with staves in hand, loins girt, and feet well shod for the journey ahead. Taylor's lunar fascination appears with the "New Moon" of the "first month high" (our March–April), and Passover on the "fourteenth day When she is Full" looks back to his previous Sermon and Meditation II.21 on the "New Moon feast."

Unlike Thomas Taylor who divorces Passover from any consideration of other ceremonial feasts, Edward Taylor deliberately stresses (as Mather had done) the connections. He attaches Pentecost to Passover in *Upon the Types of the Old Testament* and designates its purposes to be a "thankfull remembrance of Gods gratious deliverance," to be "a Solemn thanksgiving unto God for the Wheate Harvest," and most important to celebrate

Israel's "Solemn Covenanting With God to be his holy People" (*UTOT*, p. 495). Reminding us of the alternate title for Pentecost as the feast of first fruits (Lev. 23:10–21) that testifies to Israel's thankfulness unto God for the fruitful land of Canaan, Taylor's meditation also marks the transition from one feast to another:

> I'le at this Feast my First Sheafe bring, and Wave
>> Before thee, Lord, my Crop to sanctify
> That in my first Fruits I my harvest have
>> May blest unto by Cyckle Constantly.
>> So at this Feast my harp shall Tunes advance
>> Upon thy Lamb, and my Deliverance.
>
> But now I from the Passover do pass.
>> Easter farewell, rich jewells thou did shew,
> And come to Whitsuntide; and turn the Glass
>> To search her Sands for pearles therin anew.
>> For Isra'l a fift'th day from Egypt broke,
>> Gave Sinai's Law, and Crown'd the mount with Smoke.
>>   (II.22.43–54)

The Israelites' wilderness trek begins with the passing over of God's avenging angel to liberate them from Egyptian bondage and peaks fifty days later with God's transmitting of the law to Moses on Mount Sinai. These events prefigure Christ's resurrection from the grave on Easter and his decree fifty days later on Pentecost of "Mount Zions Law from graces store./ The Gospell Law of Spirit and Life" as the "fiery Tongues" descend upon his disciples (II.22.57–8, 59). By accentuating Israel's history and placing Passover within the context of Hebraic festal celebrations, Taylor thus gives his meditation a decidedly narrative cast.

By discarding as well a sterile cataloging of parallels, Taylor heightens those elements which most immediately touch upon his spiritual life. In his sermon Taylor had delineated spiritual applications for Passover because as the memorial for Israel's flight it figures forth man's eventual redemption, but he internalizes this *Heilgeschichte* in the meditation, making it the viable drama of his own life. The Israelites who flee from "Egyptick Slavery" are no longer impersonal; Taylor adopts personal pronouns to translate the communal into the individual "my Soul" which "doth groaning ly," a "Bond Slave" longing to be "Freed" and yearning for the "Passo're" to liberate him from "my Enslaving 'Gypsies Sins" (II.22.7, 9, 7, 10, 14). As the "passing over" unfolds, he utters personal promises: "while I from Egypt high./ I'le feed upon thy Roast meat here updresst" and "I'le banish Leaven from my very Soule" (II.22.16–17, 19). For every material element of the ancient ceremony, he substitutes its spiritual counterpart for the gospel saint. Thus, the "rost Mutten, Paschall Lamb" becomes Christ upon whom all men feed, just as "My Bunch of Hys-

sop" is "Faith, dipt in thy blood" of His crucifixion (II.22.15, 25). Furthermore, Passover signifies the continuing spiritual journey. Like a pilgrim "With Staff in hand, Loins Girt, and Feet well shod/ With Gospell
ware as walking to my God," Taylor hopes by sustaining faith in Christ's
atonement to enter a land of eternal grace (II.22.35–6).

The concepts of journey and deliverance, the first a metaphor for the
saint's earthly life in search of heaven and the second a metaphor for
man's need to be released from inner as well as worldly corruptions,
thematically unify this meditative narrative. Though far more imperson-
ally proclaimed, these concepts also govern Sermon II.22's doctrine, as
Taylor clearly avows:

> The Passover was an Holy Ordinance instituted by God to be Cele-
> brated every yeare in his Old Church of Israel by way of Remembrance
> of Gods gracious deliverance of the Children of Israel out of their bond-
> age in Egypt to Carry on his holy Service in a polliticall Church State
> in Canaan, as a Sacred Type of Gods gracious deliverance of his people
> by the blood of Christ from under the bondage State of Sin into the
> Liberty & Service of Gods Children in a State [of] Grace & Glory.
> (*UTOT*, p. 470)

Having escaped sin's bondage, however, man still requires Christ, foreshadowed by "the Flesh or Body of our Paschall Lamb" in Passover, but
come now evangelically "to Nourish, & Support our Spirituall Life in
our Walke from our Spirituall Egypt towards our Heavenly Canaan"
(*UTOT*, p. 477). Curiously less Christological than his own sermon,
Taylor's meditation gains, however, in dramatic intensity by its departure from strict parallelism and its greater personalization of Passover's
typal meanings. Remaining implicit are, of course, associations that link
the lamb's blood sprinkled on lintel and posts with Christ's blood, sprinkled upon men's consciences to turn away God's wrath, and with sacramental wine. Similarly, the "rost Mutten" prefigures Christ's agonies as
the crucified "Paschall Lamb" memorialized in the bread as a token of
Christ's body broken for mankind's sins. Although Taylor clearly composes both sermon and meditation with the sacramental administration
in mind, it is the concept of man's spiritual journey toward redemption
that takes priority over narrowly sacramental applications of Passover.

Writing nine years after his series on ceremonial feasts (1706), Taylor
coordinates his second poem on Passover with Meditation II.70 on circumcision, a pairing that looks back to Thomas Taylor's bonding of
these ordinances as prefigurations of Baptism and the Lord's Supper.
Taylor even refers to "Doctor Taylor on the Types" twice, echoing his
directive that men must come to the Supper with a "Sin mortifying Sense,
of the bitterness of Sin" (comparable to Passover's bitter herbs) and having purged the "Smelling Spreading Corruption . . . & the Leaven of

Sin" from our lives (*UTOT*, p. 831). Though ceremonial details (the lamb's slaughter and roasting, eating and consecration) recur in this sermon, Taylor offers a drier analysis of Passover and the Lord's Supper, the old and new "Seale of the New Covenant . . . of Grace for the Spirituall nourishment & growth in grace" (*UTOT*, p. 824). He outlines the duties of the "Officers" to prepare the people and the Passover and focuses on the sacramental requirements – membership in the church, the cleanliness and moral worthiness of communicants, and abuses of the elements and administering. Although he seems to shadowbox with a theological opponent, he nowhere mentions the likely combatant Solomon Stoddard, preferring to confine polemics to the earlier *Treatise Concerning the Lord's Supper* or the later sermons correlated with Meditations II.102–111. A rigorously rational exposition of doctrine, with arguments clearly derived from the *Treatise,* Sermon II.71 remains less inspiring than Taylor's initial homily on the Passover.

Ironically, although Sermon II.71 seems lethargic, even mechanical, the complementary meditation sparkles with "gourmet" images, as if Taylor lets loose the spiritual delight in the Supper that lurks beneath but never erupts in the disciplined preachment:

> Oh! Dove most innocent. O Lamb, most White.
>   A spotless Male in prime. Whose blood's the Dier
> That dies the Doore posts of the Soule most bright.
>   Whose body all is rost at justice's fire
>   And yet no bone is broken, though the Spit
>   Whereon its rost runs speare like, thorow it.
>
> This Choicest Cookery is made the Feast
>   Where glories king doth entertain his Guests.
> Where Pastie past is Godhead, filld at least
>   With Venison, of Paschall Lamb the best.
>   All spic'd and Plumb'd with Grace and disht up right
>   Upon Gods Table Plate Divinely bright.
>
> This Spirituall Fare in Ordinances, and
>   The Wine bled from the Holy Grape, and Vine,
> Thats on the Table orderd by God's hand
>   The Supper of the Lord, the feast Divine
>   God's Gospel Priests this to that Table beare
>   Where Saints are Guests and Angells waiters are.
>
> . . . .
>
> Let at this Table, Lord, thy Servant sit,
>   And load my trencher with thy Paschall Lamb.
> My Doore posts dy with the red blood of it.
>   The stroying angells weapon therewith sham
>   And let my Faith on thy rost mutton feed
>   And Drinke the Wine thy holy grape doth bleed.

> Lord make my Faith feed on it heartily.
>   Let holy Charity my heart Cement
> Unto thy Saints: and for a Cordiall high
>   Make mee partaker of thy Sacrament:
>   When with this Paschall bread and Wine I'm brisk
>   I in sweet Tunes thy sweetest praise will twist.
>   (II.71.7–24, 31–42)

More imagistically provocative, Meditation II.71 picks up the typological thread where Meditation II.22 leaves off. Old Testament details, which saturate the previous poem, establish the network of ceremonial observances by which Passover foretells Christ's future passion and man's redemption. But although the "spotless Male in prime," "blood" which "dies the Doore posts," and "Paschall Lamb" with "no bone . . . broken" reemerge in Meditation II.71, the referent for these metaphors substantially alters. The incarnate Christ merely hovers in the background of his first poem, but here Taylor's deliberate word choices carve out the Messiah's crucifixion in bold relief. He addresses Christ more directly not only as the "Lamb, most White," but also as the turtle "Dove most innocent," reminding one of His sterling human qualities. The gentle humanization gives way, however, to a startling miniature evocation of Christ's bodily agony on the cross, as "the Spit/ Whereon its rost runs speare like, thorow it" (II.71.11–12). Rather than obliquely allude to the typical lamb's precious blood shed in a basin, Taylor here puns morbidly upon the Messiah's "blood," the "Dier/ That dies the Doore posts of the Soule most bright" (II.71.8–9). The allusions to the "body," "speare," "posts," and "dies" starkly animate Christ's sacrifice on the cross. Taylor thus depicts this shameful spectacle of human cruelty while he ironically acknowledges that Christ dies "spotless" of any crimes and willingly endures "justice's fire" to rescue mankind. Rapidly shifting between the ancient rites and their agonizing fulfillment, Taylor makes Christological applications of Passover more central to this meditation than Israel's liberating flight. Reversing the emphasis in Meditation II.22, Old Testament types in II.71 suggestively linger in the wings, while gospel truths take center stage.

Consistent with this Christocentric focus, Taylor also elaborates more exuberantly on the Lord's Supper, ordained as the gospel commemoration to supersede Passover. Sacramental imagery remains subdued in Meditation II.22. However, Taylor's Meditation II.71 not only specifies the connections between Christ's passion and the bread and wine, it also glorifies them with highly original images. Surpassing the "rost Mutten," unleavened bread, and blood sprinkled with hyssop with which Jews memorialized their temporal deliverance from Egypt, the "Spirituall Fare in Ordinances," newly betokens an eternal deliverance from sin, Satan, and death. This "Wine bled from *the* Holy Grape, and Vine" and this unique "Paschall Lamb" excel in preciousness because they remind communicants of Christ's human reality as blood and body. Taylor captures the gospel dispensation's superiority with his lavish superlatives – "this Choicest Cookery," "Paschall Lamb the best," and the "feast Divine" – and he delights in God's gourmet preparations for a luxurious feast. He opens with a tantalizing vision of God's "Cookroom" and whiff of "Heavens Cookery" and concludes with the assembled faithful servants feasting on the banquet's delicacies. Not pausing to debate the virtues of roasted rather than raw or sodden meat, he launches with culinary gusto into describing the "Paschall Lamb" which is "All spic'd and Plumb'd with Grace" and the "Pastie past" of "Godhead, filld at least/ With Venison" all served "Upon Gods Table Plate Divinely bright" (II.71.16, 17, 15–16, 18). The sheer splendor of these images illuminates the single difference that makes this gospel sacrament superior to Passover – the divinity of God the banquet master and Christ the sacrificial lamb. Gazing with imagination's eye beyond even the forthcoming celebration of the Supper in his church at Westfield, Taylor envisions the heavenly banquet "Where Saints are Guests and Angells waiters are" (II.71.24). Thus, rather than identify with the Israelites and their shadowy types, human rituals, and uneasy expectations of a future kingdom, Taylor in Meditation II.71 participates immediately in Christ's truth, His divinely ordained spiritual ceremony, and His certain promise of heavenly reward.

Comparable to the changed perspective on his typological matter, Taylor's poetic mode also shifts in Meditation II.71 from II.22. In his earlier poem the narrative format appropriately conveyed his feeling for Israel's and every man's plodding journey as a pilgrim in this world with faint hope for redemption and a distant vision of a heavenly destination. But Meditation II.71's lyrical ecstasies sensitively communicate his assurances as a gospel saint who has internally arrived at faith in Christ's incarnate sacrifice, partakes of the memorial Supper, and yearns only for attendance at the transcendent banquet. Such changes in themes and format are mirrored also by Taylor's different handling of basic typological images. Meditation II.22's elements remain commonplace, the setting domestic: "thy Roast meat here updresst/ With Bitter hearbs, unleaven'd bread the best" is served within the house where partakers search diligently for leaven with "Candles lest a Crum thereof should rowle/ Into its Corners or in mouseholes fall" (II.22.17–18, 21–2). By contrast, in Meditation II.71 God's divine touch transmutes homely fare and humble abodes into an elegant "Paschall Lamb" which is "All spic'd and Plumb'd with Grace and disht up right/ Upon Gods Table Plate Divinely bright" at the "feast Divine" where "glories king doth entertain his Guests" (II.71.15, 17–18, 22, 14). Together Meditations II.22 and II.71 thus make apparent Taylor's threefold concept of Passover as a type. As a feast to commemorate the Jews' deliverance from Egypt, Passover foreshadows first our spiritual redemption from sin's bondage, second Christ's crucifixion and paschal resurrection, and third the Lord's Supper. As the gospel's spiritual ordinance, the newer feast perpetually reminds man of his indebtedness to the Messiah who undergoes a human death to fulfill those Old Testament promises. But as Taylor's imagery intimates, this earthly banquet is itself a mere shadow of the gloriously transcendent feast in heaven. Although he begins his poetic process by seeking plainly to unveil typal truths and to prepare for the Sacrament, Taylor's poetic syntheses, whether the meditative narratives of personal salvation or the lyrical raptures, imaginatively animate and personalize the often flat rationalism of his *Treatise* and *Upon the Types of the Old Testament*.

Although the imagery and themes of Meditations II.22 and II.71 primarily derive from Taylor's knowledge of earlier typological guides, his motives for composing poems on Passover and the Lord's Supper (II.102–111) cannot be divorced from the contemporary pressures of the Stoddard controversy in New England. As we examined in the previous chapter, the figural parallels between Old and New Testament seals to the covenant became a cause for debate between the New England conservatives Increase Mather and Edward Taylor and the liberalizer Solomon Stoddard. Resonances of those doctrinal antagonisms remain muted in Edward Taylor's early typal Sermons and Meditations II.1–30 and 58–61, in which he develops a highly personalized devotional approach to individual and ceremonial types. Even those poems written concurrently with the *Treatise Concerning the Lord's Supper* in 1694 studiously trace out the typology of Abraham (II.4) and Isaac (II.5), but betray nothing of the heated sacramental controversies. However, as the pamphlet war pitting Increase Mather against Stoddard escalated during the late 1690s and early 1700s, so too Edward Taylor's stance shifted from the temperate persuasions of his 1687/88 letter to the rigorously logical defense of sacramental practices in the *Treatise,* and eventually to the disputatious counterattacks in "The *Appeale* Tried" (ca. 1710–11). Similarly, the tenor of Taylor's meditations also subtly shifts, beginning with the bonded poems on circumcision and Passover in 1706 and culminating with the forthrightly combative series II.102–111 on the Lord's Supper. Unlike the adaptation of Passover into an internalized spiritual narrative as in II.22 or a lyrical encomium in II.71, Meditation II.103, for example, rationally documents the suspension of this "Typick Ceremony" by the excelling "Spirituall Ordinance" (II.103.55, 57). Often viewed as the poetic counterparts of the earlier prose *Treatise* and, no doubt, of a later sermon series, these sacramental meditations most clearly exhibit Taylor in his double role. Defending the sacramental policy of admitting only sanctified souls, he assumes the strident, argumentative tone of a confirmed polemicist: "This Feast is no Regenerating fare./ But food for those Regenerate that are" (II.104.59–60). Yearning for his own acceptance at the Lord's Table, he whets his appetite and raises his affections to feast upon the bread and wine which are "Thyselfe, my Lord, Celestiall Food indeed,/ Rich spirituall fare Soul-Food, Faiths nourishment" (II.105.38–9). Polemicist and poet, rationalist and spiritualist – the two facets of Taylor's personality coexist in these meditations, illuminated by his twofold use of typology to serve controversial and devotional aims. The metaphors for the saint's preparation which link the *Treatise* with these sacramental meditations reveal Taylor's fluidity as he moves between a need to justify Puritan sacramental theories and his personal desires to participate spiritually in Christ's glorious feast.

Earlier theologians had viewed as pro forma the admitting of only circumcised Israelites to the Passover and by analogy only baptized and regenerate saints to the Lord's Supper. But the issue of the communicant's spiritual status and, therefore, of his preparation for receiving the Sacrament cleaved the widest split in New England Puritanism of the late seventeenth century. As we examined in the prose pamphlets and sermons of Increase Mather, Solomon Stoddard, and Edward Taylor, criteria for judging aspiring participants ranged from extreme conservative demands for conversion attested by public examination and professions of faith to Stoddard's liberal invitation to all nonscandalous church members. The controversy, most scholars claim, gave rise to Edward Taylor's peculiar fascination with the concept of a "Wedden robe," which became his preferred metaphor in both the *Treatise* and *Preparatory Meditations* for the soul qualified for the wedding feast. Certainly disputants before and after Taylor also mentioned the "Wedding garment" and the parable from Matthew 22:1–14 of the marriage feast, with both factions calling for the communicants' preparation but offering widely varying rationales. Thus, responding to Stoddard's attacks at the 1679 Synod, Increase Mather's 1680 "Confutation" warns: "But no persons are fitt to come unto the Lords Supper excepting as have experienced a saving work of grace. They that have not the wedding garment (which implyeth faith and sanctification) are unworthy guests. Math. 22. 11, 12" (p. 61). Although Mather does not elaborate on this metaphor here or later in his *Dissertation,* he plainly associates the wedding garment with a candidate's possession of faith and sanctification so that he may come a spiritually regenerate or "living" man to feast upon sabbath nourishment.[4]

Exhorting his readers to beware "the *great day* of the Lord," when multitudes that have made a profession of religion "will miserably fail of their expectations," because they "want the *Wedding Garment,*" Stoddard as early as *The Safety of Appearing* (1687) adopts the same allusion (p.

173). But rather than pursue any sacramental application, he generally calls men away from the pretense to the reality of faith in Christ. Using this specter of the disowned "wedding guest" in his Galatians sermon of 1690, Stoddard specifically addresses profane men who outwardly have "been reckoned among the Saints & have eat the same spirituall meat, & drunk the same spirituall drink," but resist conversion after admittance to the Supper: "What will you say when you shall be picked out from among the guests & for want of a wedding garment bee bound hand & foot & be cast into utter darkness, Matt. 22.11, 12, 13, there will be wayling & gnashing of teeth" (*ETSS*, p. 142). Antithetical to applications by Mather and Edward Taylor, Stoddard presumes the inclusion of unconverted souls at the earthly wedding supper and predicts only their expulsion on the Day of Judgment if they remain in a profane state. Even in his later *Appeal to the Learned* (1709) in which he rebuts his opponent's argument from Matthew 22:11–12, Stoddard unequivocally claims that "Christ Jesus, and Pardon & Salvation are the Feast, that they were invited to, & not the Sacrament of the Lords Supper. . . . By this it does appear that here is a representation of the Day of Judgment, and that such Persons as come for Salvation without a Wedding Garment shall be rejected in that day" (pp. 3–5).[5] Thus, he steadfastly refrains from identifying the wedding garment with a "work of Saving Conversion," dismissing both the metaphor and parable which Mather and Taylor find essential scriptural proofs for their sacramental criteria. Whereas Stoddard includes the Lord's Supper itself as an ordinance to persuade the unregenerate to convert, Increase Mather regards the fitting of this wedding garb as entirely a priori to any enjoyment of festal dainties. To come without the garment of inward righteousness is to desecrate the Supper, to imitate that guest, according to Matthew's exemplum, who must be expelled from this celebration.

If allusions to the wedding garment occur erratically in the controversial literature, it is not until later writings that the contrary catalogs of the "Scandalous" surface noticeably. In his 1708 *Dissertation,* Mather recoils from the threat of an admissions policy so radical as to welcome notoriously unregenerate sinners. According to Mather, Stoddard's analogy with Israel's Passover "Proves that Scandalous, as well as Non-Scandalous Unregenerates, should be admitted to the Lords Table," since "very many of them were Adulterers, Thieves, Liars, Slanderers, and Perjured Persons" (p. 75). Although a biased exaggeration of Stoddard's position and one that the *Appeal to the Learned* derides, Mather's accusation exemplifies the disputants' heated attempts to discriminate among the openly reprobate, the hypocrites who claim outward church membership but lack inward sanctity, and the regenerate righteous who alone are worthy of the Lord's "Soul-Food."[6]

Despite the later emergence of these distinctions, Edward Taylor predates Mather in denouncing ineligible petitioners and in fully developing the definition of evangelically clad "wedding guests" in the *Treatise*. If we look only to New England writings prior to 1693/4 for Edward Taylor's inspiration in his sermons, we find few instances mentioning wedding garments and cloaked hypocrites. And although Taylor certainly knew Stoddard's Galatians sermon of 1690, no sound evidence confirms his reading of Mather's unpublished "Confutation" (1680) or Stoddard's published *Safety of Appearing* (1687). However, George Gillespie in his 1646 *Aarons Rod Blossoming* (cited by Taylor in the revised Foundation Day Sermon, the *Treatise*, and "The *Appeale* Tried") had listed the wedding garment as one among twenty arguments proving that the Lord's Supper was not a converting ordinance (pp. 510–11). Furthermore, the wedding garment specifically opposed to a list of scandalous offenders had appeared in Thomas Taylor's *Christ Revealed* and perhaps provided one possible stimulus for Edward Taylor's polemical and subsequent poetic depictions. When concluding his lengthy discourse on Passover, Thomas Taylor condones the admission of "reverent professed Christian[s]" but scathingly excludes those "notorious evill men" who "thrust into the presence chamber of the great King, yea sit downe at the Lords Table, and like swine swill in his cup without controll, or any rebuke" (*CR*, p. 236). "Open blasphemers, common-drunkards, scoffing Ishmaels, noted adulterers, obstinate sinners," all pollute and profane God's holy Supper, since "as hee must bee circumcised that must eate the Passeover: so must hee be baptized that must be admitted to the Supper" (*CR*, p. 236). Sharing his predecessor's alarm and biblical models from 1 Corinthians 5:11 and 11:27, Edward Taylor draws a similar analogy and list, for just as the "ceremonially unclean was to abide from the Passover," so also "the visibly unclean are not to have the Lord's Supper administered unto" (*TCLS*, pp. 73, 74).[7] Taylor condemns a motley crowd of pretended saints who seek to desecrate the wedding feast: "The visibly unclean are such. Hence the covetous, the railler, extortioner, the liar as well as the drunkard, adulterer, idolater, etc., are not to partake or to eat here. The uncircumcised in heart hath no right hereunto: and hence if visible, is to be debarred" (*TCLS*, p. 74). Although the unbaptized and visibly unclean comprise an easily discernible group of nonadmissible persons, professed church members who disguise their lack of inward holiness provoke greater consternation. Thomas Taylor describes plumed hypocrites whose "common preparation is, to put on our best clothes, and to cover our bodily nakednesse in most curious manner," while "mens owne consciences witnesse against them, how naked their soules lie, and filthily discovered" (*CR*, p. 237). Consequently, he warns all men to beware God's wrath against such misarrayed guests: "What a fearefull thing is it to come as most men doe, not considering the Lords body? How miserable was the sentence of that guest, that sate down at the Kings table without his *wedding garment?*" (*CR*, p. 237).

Whereas Thomas Taylor marginally alludes to it, some sixty years later Edward Taylor opens his *Treatise* with a full exegesis of the parable from Matthew 22:1–14. In fact, this exemplum supplies not only the metaphoric core, but the argumentative structure for Taylor's most comprehensive refutation of Stoddard's conversionism.[8] As doctrines for his initial four *Treatise* sermons, Taylor preaches respectively on God's bidding of all men to the *"gospel wedden supper,"* the "absolutely necessary" donning of a "gospel wedden garment," God's "strict account" if it is lacking, and the inexcusability of "approaching unto the wedden supper without the wedden garment" (*TCLS*, p. 7). Elaborating the case of the unwelcome guest, Taylor condemns him as a man who by Stoddard's standards might "discern the Lords body" and thereby gain admission, but by conservative criteria lacks an essential righteousness. Though this guest possesses the "ornament of a doctrinal profession," resulting from "historical faith," he lacks, according to Taylor, the inwardly "sanctifying work of the spirit upon the soul," which constitutes the only acceptable "wedden garment" (*TCLS*, pp. 28, 29). Thus, outwardly to adorn one's person with church attendance or ostentatious belief may bring a man to the Lord's feast, but external garb without an inner sanctifying grace will not guarantee him eventual celebration. As the debates over preparation escalated, Edward Taylor not only took up the typology of the Passover to document prerequisites for attending the Lord's Supper, but he also developed the leitmotif of the "wedding supper" and "wedding garment" into the controlling metaphor for man's prepared and receptive state of grace.

Not merely in the *Treatise* sermons, but also in the sacramental meditations, Taylor embellishes his distinctions between hypocrites or scandalous aspirants and the worthily qualified, who come robed in "evangelical righteousness constituting the soul complete in the sight of God" (*TCLS*, p. 29). He draws his first poetic sketch in Meditation II.71 on Passover; having tantalized his soul's appetite with aromas from "Heavens Cookery" and enviously gazed upon the divine banquet hall, he prescribes the "Wedden garment of Christs Righteousness/ And Holy Cloathes of Sanctity most pure" as mandatory "atire, their Festivall rich dress" for God's welcome guests (II.71.5, 25–6, 27). Taylor immediately modifies the concrete references to "garment," "Cloathes," "atire," and "dress" with their spiritual equivalents – Christ's imputed and implanted "Righteousness," inward holiness, and "Sanctity" – which attest to the communicant's "Festivall" readiness. Taylor stands more as the observer who longingly peers at the guests, and who retains doubts about his own entree into this sacred communion of saints. Even though he most likely feels in 1706 the rumblings of another erupting controversy, his tone throughout Meditation II.71 conveys a gentle self-chiding and awed appreciation of the Passover as a figure for the Lord's feast. Prose references to the wedding garment had begun as early as Taylor's casual mention in the Foundation Day Sermon (1679) to "remember . . . the man without the Wedden garment," increased substantially in his revised version of 1692–3, and expanded tenfold into the dominating metaphor and concept of the *Treatise* (*CRRS*, p. 149).[9] But the twin notions of a wedding feast and wedding robes momentarily enter in Meditation II.71, not at all in Sermon II.71, and then prominently only among the later meditations on the sacraments and Canticles.

The reasons for such a delayed inclusion of these provocative metaphors for the prepared saint and the Supper, ones so apparently congenial to a poet's imagination, seem both political and personal. In the period between Meditation II.71 and his subsequent series on the Sacrament (II.102–111) of 1711–12, Taylor again confronted the threat from Stoddard, whose harvests of souls in the Connecticut Valley seemed to thrive in the face of conservative opposition. Hard upon the publication of Increase Mather's *A Dissertation, wherein The Strange Doctrine Lately Published in a Sermon . . . is Examined and Confuted* (1708) and Stoddard's rebuttal in *An Appeal to the Learned* (1709), Taylor himself composed a counterattack in "The *Appeale* Tried" (ca. 1710–11). Throughout this notably argumentative retaliation, Taylor bolsters Mather's occasionally weak evidences and contrarily reduces Stoddard's contentions to absurdities. Immediately plunging into Stoddard's misreading of the wedding parable, he blatantly accuses his opponent: "altho' the *Appeale* saith its abundantly manifest that Christ, Pardon, & Righteousness is the Feast it must be returnd that its easier said so, than manifested so to be" (*ETSS*, p. 154). Summarizing his own "abundantly manifest" interpretation from the *Treatise*, Taylor correlates spiritual applications with each happening in Matthew's parable:

> I am perswaded that . . . the servants are the Apostles & Faithful Ministers of the Word: the Persons under their Ministry are those they are sent to of all Sorts & Conditions. The Dispensing of the Gospell to them, is the Calling them to the Wedden. The Sanctifying & Justifying Grace of Christ the Wedden Garment: the Gathering of them together the bringing of them into a Church State . . . & so the Feast to import all the Gracious administrations there of Divine Comunion & Fellowship in Gods Ordinances, where of the Lords Supper is an Eminent one, Calld a Feast or Supper. (*ETSS*, p. 154)

Not content with a synopsis, he appends five proofs to substantiate that "the Circumstances of the man without the Wedden Garment agrees to nothing else fittly as to the Lords Supper" (*ETSS,* p. 155). Although "The *Appeale* Tried" lacks both the graceful coherence of the more finely wrought *Treatise,* its very manner captures Taylor's mood during 1710–11. Testy, occasionally bellicose, often disgusted with Stoddard's irrational tenacity, Taylor tackles each controversial point with pugnacity; he rationally convinces but does not imaginatively persuade.

Not unpredictably, the subsequently composed *Preparatory Meditations* II.102–111 often manifest tightly knit argumentative structures, reminiscent of Taylor's sermons and of "The *Appeale* Tried." Doctrinal distinctions from the controversy and the *Treatise* intermingle with recurrent strains from Taylor's poetic imagery. Simultaneously, he generates an astute rational defense of Puritan principles and an ecstatic response to the Sacrament's spirituality. For example, Meditation II.106 rehearses, with slight imagistic variations, previous discriminations between hypocrites and worthily robed partakers:

> Lord make thy Vitall Principall in mee
> In Gospellwise to eate and drinke on thee.
>
> These acts of mine that from thy Vitall Spark
> In mee being to thyself, my Lord, my Deare,
> As formative in touching thee their marke
> Of this thy Sacrament, my Spirituall Cheere.
> Life first doth Act and Faith that's lifes First-born
> Receiving gives the Sacramentall form.
>
> Hence its as needfull as the forme unto
> This Choice formation Hypocrites beg on.
> Elfes Vizzarded, and Lambskinde Woolves hence goe.
> Your Counterfeted Coine is worse than none.
> Your gilding though it may the Schoole beguile
> The Court will Cast and all your gilt off file.
>
> Morality is here no market ware,
> Although it in the Outward Court is free.
> A State of Sin this Banquet cannot beare.
> Old and New Cov'nant Guests here don't agree.
> The Wedden Robe is Welcome, but the back
> This Supper cloaths not with, that doth it lack.
>   (II.106.23–42)

Although he collapses complex arguments into a poetic synthesis so dense as to be obscure, Taylor delineates one basis for rejecting Stoddard's admissions policies. In *An Appeal to the Learned* Stoddard explicitly sanctions the inclusion of all visible church members in the sacramental feast:

> The Church by the Ordinances of God is bound to admit many Unconverted persons to the Lords-Supper; they are Ecclesiastically qualified

having knowledge and a good conversation; they are Saints to a judgment of Charity, walking orderly; and therefore the Church is to accept
them into their communion; the Church is to act upon what is visible,
so that according to the Ordinance of God they are to be received to
communion. (p. 73)

From Taylor's perspective, however, such external qualities as holy conversation, a nonscandalous life, and doctrinal knowledge are meritorious, but not sufficient to distinguish false hypocrites from welcome
guests. "Morality" is common "market ware" which all covenant members possess; the "gilding" of a doctrinal profession may "beguile" scho-
lastics and Stoddard alike, who envision the Sacrament as an ordinance
to teach conversion. Taylor's diverse epithets for hypocrites as "Elfes
Vizzarded," "Lambskinde Woolves," and "Counterfeted Coine" heighten
the discrepancy between those benificent appearances and corrupt realities. Caught up in the mask or pretense of worship, hypocrites may temporarily pass for saints by virtue of outward morality; but once the gilt
is filed off, the guilty conscience appears naked beneath. Taylor's images
look back to the *Treatise*'s earlier depiction of the cloaked wedding guest
who becomes the prototypal hypocrite. With the "ornament" of "common profession" of "historical faith" and the "web of a civil and sober
life and conversation," this man beguiles even the king's servants, "they
not being able to discern counterfeit coin from the king's mint" (*TCLS*,
pp. 28, 29). Thus, "acts" in the double sense of deeds and role-playing
may create an illusion of righteousness convincing enough to gain church
membership, but without the "Vitall Principall" of faith which derives
from saving grace; no self-generated actions gain man a seat at the King's
wedding feast.

To accentuate the futility of pretenses and conversely a need for genuine preparation, Taylor also borrows Samuel Mather's typal correlations of the Temple's "*outward* and the *inward* Court" of the "People"
and "Priests" respectively and his instruction to "*Leave out the outer Court
. . .* that is, nominal Christians . . . take heed of Extreams, and of admitting Persons visibly unfit," a distinction that Taylor adopts in *Upon the
Types of the Old Testament*, Sermon II.20 (*FT*, pp. 341, 342). But Taylor
draws even finer boundaries by relegating visible members who lack
inward grace to the "Outward Court" where the people exist in a "State
of Sin"; only those who have striven to "get a Saving Relation to Christ"
and made their public relation of conversion may enter the "Inward Court"
(*UTOT*, pp. 438, 451). Like Israelites who offer sacrifices through the
priest's mediation, so too duly examined and welcomed gospel saints
may savor Christ's sacrifice in the Supper, administered by "Faithfull
Ministers of the Word." Moreover, by partaking of this feast, each believer
submits himself to a higher court, not merely to judgments by God's

appointed disciples. These apostles may mistake signs of outward morality for saving grace and grant entrance to crafty hypocrites, but God's court hands down infallible verdicts upon each man's inner spiritual state. In "The *Appeale* Tried" Taylor repeatedly accosts Stoddard for his blithe assertion "that Visible Saints, tho' they are Hypocrites are fit matter for Church-membership" and hence for sacramental attendance (*ETSS*, p. 163). Quite the contrary, Taylor concedes that "the Church is to proceed by Visible Holiness. . . . But God accepts according to the heart, & hence when Hypocrisy is discovered, the heart appears not right before God, & so Such are Cast out" (*ETSS*, p. 163). Thus, nominal Christians who listen to Stoddard run a risk of double deception, beguiled first by the lax nature of his sacramental requirements and second by a foolish hope that mere forms of sacramental piety will pass muster under God's scrutiny.

Whereas Stoddard also justifies his admissions by analogy with the Old Testament Passover which all Israel might attend, Edward Taylor differentiates "Old and New Cov'nant Guests," the latter falling under a more stringent spiritual dispensation.[10] As he reaffirms in "The *Appeale* Tried" this "Wedden Garment, or Saving Grace is Such a Preparation of the Soule for some Speciall Ordinance of Gospell Communion without which it is not lawfull in the sight of God to appeare, tho' it may be lawfull in the sight of men" (*ETSS*, pp. 155–6). Poetically in Meditation II.106 as well, he reiterates this "Wedden Robe is Welcome" because it manifests symbolically the guest's inward readiness. Once infused with the "Vitall Spark" of Christ's life-giving grace, which converts the receptive soul, then man's "Faith" enables him to act appropriately in receiving the Lord's Supper. Unlike a cloaking "Vizzard" to gloss inward decadence, the evangelical "Wedden Robe" seems virtually an organic outgrowth, because it clothes the outer man with behavioral holiness genuinely congruent with his inward grace. The "Vitall Principall" engendered by God's saving grace gives birth to faith, which then guarantees the guest a suitable "Sacramentall form." However, Taylor goes one step further in conceiving a necessary reciprocity between guest and feast, since only the communicant's sanctity invests the sacramental fare with meaning. He prays: "Then form mee Lord, a former here to bee/ Of this thy Sacrament receiving here" (II.106.61–2). As he cogently explains in "The *Appeale* Tried," only persons with the "Spirituall Discerning . . . Eye of true Faith" can comprehend that "the Sacramentall Bread & Wine are Signs Signifying Christ's Body Crucified & his blood shead as Standing in my stead to sustain the Curse of the Law" (*ETSS*, p. 159). To partake as a natural rather than spiritually revitalized man dishonors the feast, reducing its elements to mere bread and wine. Thus, if "nominal Christians" and hypocrites who persist in their natural decadence, near "Dead" from sin's rot, partake of the Supper, they "From the Signatum tareth off the Signe" (II.106.48). By contrast, the saint who finds "Spirituall Life renewd" by eating "this Bread and Wine" not only observes the "Signe" of the covenant but also benefits from the strengthening nourishment signified by Christ's body and blood (II.106.59, 63).

Filled with intricate arguments, theological paradoxes, implicit attacks on Stoddard, and manifold puns, Meditation II.106 exemplifies the disputatiousness of the sacramental meditations, a carry-over from the drier logic of "The *Appeale* Tried." Although relieved by bursts of imagery and apt metaphors, this tightly constructed, almost elliptical meditation epitomizes Taylor as the New England polemicist. Motivated undoubtedly by Stoddard's doctrinal intransigence, Taylor probably preached a sermon series on sacramental theory with which Meditations II.102–111 correspond; consequently, the poems betray the mannerisms of his pulpit oratory, as if Taylor only half-turns from ramistic proofs and controversial debate to personal contemplations. Thus, the convoluted distinctions between hypocrites and wedding guests seem a curious amalgam of doctrinal terms ("Sacramentall form," "Vitall Principall," "acts," "forms, formative, formation," "Signatum," and "Signe") and private images ("Spirituall Cheere," "Elfes Vizzarded, and Lambskinde Woolves," "Wedden Robe," and "Supper cloaths"). Other sacramental reflections display a similarly double mode of defining the communicant's state. Linking the technicality of "Adjuncts" with a metaphor of divine tailoring in Meditation II.108, Taylor praises "These Robes of Adjuncts shining round about/ Christs golden Sheers did cut exactly out," that is, those spiritual qualities which Christ instills in the prepared guest (II.108.5–6). The combining of theological abstractions with striking metaphors from biblical parables or his own imagination corresponds with Taylor's double status as both preacher and private saint, as the man of intellect and feeling. As a theologian who instructs his parishioners, Taylor doctrinally defines the invisible state of being suitable to approaching the Lord's Supper. For any Puritan minister, the concepts of evangelical righteousness imputed and implanted by Christ and the principles of sanctification arise automatically. Though they are conceptual terms denoting spiritual realities, nonetheless the rhetoric reverberates with the logic of pulpit and pamphlet. But abstractions convey little of the splendor of this "Royall Feast Magnificent" (II.108.1), the "richest Dainties Cookery can Dress/ Thy Table with," or the wedding "Cloaths" which "trim thy Soule" when "adorned . . . in Spirituall State" (II.104.9–10, 63, 65). Based upon biblical metaphors, the images of wedding robes and wedding feast create vivid impressions of the saint's ecstasy in supping on Christ's "Celestiall Mannah" and "Royall Wine in Zion's Sacred bowles" (II.104.24, 29). As a minister who wants to inspire as well as instruct communicants in the "festival frame of spirit" and as a private meditator who yearns to don wedding robes, Taylor gravitates toward metaphoric evocation.[11]

In the *Preparatory Meditations* as in the *Treatise,* logical definitions appeal to the intellect's "discerning Eye" to induce a doctrinal acuity, but metaphoric illuminations pierce the inwardly discerning heart to rouse the will and sacramental affections. Not just discrete choices of imagery or language reflect Taylor's bifurcated vision, but even whole meditations adopt different moods, responsive to his fluctuating needs to defend or delight in the Sacrament. For instance, the basic metaphor of "robing" prominently emerges in both Meditations II.106 and II.109. But whereas the first somberly denounces hypocrites whose counterfeiting morality warrants exclusion from the Supper, the latter portrays the attending wedding guests in their radiant splendor:

> Thou sittest at the table head in Glory,
>   With thy brave guests With grace adornd and drest.
> No Table e're was set like thine, in Story,
>   Or with such guests as thine was ever blesst,
>   That linings have embroider'd as with gold,
>   And upper robes all glorious to behold.
> They'r Gods Elect, and thy Selected Ones,
>   Whose Inward man doth ware rich robes of Grace,
> Tongues tipt with Zion Languague, Precious Stones.
>   Their Robes are quilted ore with graces lace.
>   Their Lives are Checker work of th'Holy Ghost.
>   Their 'ffections journy unto Heavens Coast.
>   (II.109.43–54)

Unlike hypocrites who come cloaked, vizzarded, and gilt with ostentatious displays of piety, God's "Selected Ones" arrive at his banquet well "drest" in "rich robes" neither presumptuous, nor understated for the occasion. Robes "quilted ore with graces lace," "linings . . . embroider'd as with gold," and "Spiritual apparell whitend white" tastefully manifest the Elect's sanctity (II.109.64). Not flaunting outward "forms" of "market" morality, these welcome guests genuinely possess "Tongues tipt with Zion Languague," "Lives" that "are Checker work of th'Holy Ghost," and " 'ffections" which "journy unto Heavens Coast." With poetic subtlety, Taylor transmutes the staid doctrinal requirements for holy conversation and nonscandalous lives into an arresting vignette.

However, the finery remains less important than its symbolic bodying forth of the heart's purity. By modifying each action and article of clothing with the adjectives "grace" and "spiritual," Taylor portrays the manner in which converting grace irradiates the soul. Whereas Meditation II.106 denigrates those who put on deceitful facades, in II.109 the poet glorifies the fluid integration of inner being and outer acts when the "Inward man doth ware rich robes of Grace." Just as formerly he turned to Matthew's parable for his model of the excluded impostor, he now takes a contrary New Testament "sample" from Christ's "faithfull Disciples" (II. 109. 56). Their attending of the Last Supper and ministry make the apostles perfect *exempla fidei* for newly "Qualifide Disciples," the succeeding gospel servants to imitate (II. 109. 63). Casting aside polemical rhetoric, Taylor substitutes lavish praises and "embroider'd" images and metaphors. "Sacramentall form[s]" become "gracious frames," "acts" and "Principall[s]" become "Lives" and "[a]ffections," "gilt" becomes "gold" to underscore the distinctions between "Elfes Vizzarded, and Lambskinde Woolves" and "brave guests With grace adornd and drest." By minimizing technical theology while heightening his ornate imagery, Taylor reveals himself as a contemplator who finds grace's truth superior to intellectual rationales. Transcending doctrinal disputation, he discovers his own ecstatic response to this wedding feast. Far less densely argumentative than II. 106, Meditation II. 109 epitomizes Taylor in his visionary mode, looking not simply for an earthly ideal of the Lord's Supper but projecting beyond to the heavenly banquet where only "Elect" guests will be enthroned "in Glory" with the "faithfull Disciples."

The sacramental meditations betray Taylor's firm commitment to defending limited admissions against Stoddard's conversionism, so much so that some poems assume disputatious qualities better suited to the homiletic *Treatise* or "The *Appeale* Tried." However, as Meditation II. 109 illustrates, not only as synopses of eucharistic theory, but also as lyric celebrations to rouse festal affections, these poems serve distinctly private needs. The oft-debated issue of distinguishing scandalous sinners or hypocrites from worthy communicants deeply touches Taylor both as the Westfield preacher who administers the Supper and as a Puritan believer who hopes to partake. As he denounces hypocritical shows of morality, Taylor externalizes his private fears that he too might possess the outward signs of saving grace, but lack the essential wedding "robes all glorious to behold" of inward sanctification. Similarly, when he lauds the "brave guests" enthroned in heaven's banquet hall, he confesses his inner longings for sainthood. Both Taylor's prose writings and *Preparatory Meditations* thus discriminate between impostors who are remanded to the outer "People's" court and the "grace adornd" guests admitted to the inner court where temple priests offer eucharistic rites. Despite the clarity of the categories, however, implicit questions remain that bear upon Taylor's poetic theory and practice. By what means does an aspiring participant judge his state of grace? Through what preparatory ministrations can a doubting soul cultivate the proper eucharistic spirit? In short, how does one fashion a wedding robe? And it is precisely the

Puritan concept of preparation that not only constitutes a *locus classicus* of Taylor's *Treatise* but also motivates the eucharistic content and process of his poetic meditations.

Solomon Stoddard's theory virtually eliminated the need for preparation, since the Sacrament itself might initiate a participant into "first grace." By contrast, Increase Mather and Edward Taylor demanded conscientious preparation leading to a "festival frame of spirit" (*TCLS*, p. 199). Lacking this festival frame, otherwise known as the "wedden garment," one is unsuited for attending the Lord's Supper, which is not grace inducing but a "grace strengthening ordinance" (*TCLS*, p. 41). In his revised Foundation Day Sermon, Taylor declares "an Evangelicall Preparation" for the Supper as "absolutely necessary not onely to the Benefits thereof but also to the Escaping the guilt of the blood of Christ" (*CRRS*, p. 320). And in the *Treatise*, he calls all communicants to hear the Word preached, receive "baptism" which "initiates the soul into its visible covenant state," and join in a "church state . . . without which there is no entrance into the feast" (*TCLS*, p. 41). Under Stoddard's philosophy these actions alone would be sufficient both to grant church membership and condone sacramental attendance by which a believer might then experience converting grace.[12] But for Edward Taylor, who requires more substantial evidences of converting grace prior to a coming to the Lord's Table, these ordinances are mere preliminaries.[13] They must be enriched by rigorous practices of "prayer, meditation, and self-examination" which "are of special use to prepare the soul for this feast," since only such duties enable one to ascertain his spiritual worthiness (*TCLS*, p. 41). Self-examination brings "the soul under trial of itself" to prove its rectitude "in the judgment of conscience and to God Himself" (*TCLS*, pp. 200–1). Assisted by the "work of the Spirit of grace," self-examination induces a conviction first of sin from which "springs sorrow, and loathing thyself" and second of the "righteousness of sanctification, consisting in all the holy graces of the Spirit of God in the soul" (*TCLS*, pp. 201, 202). Thus converted from sin to a "love, longing, esteem, hungering and thirsting after God, Christ, grace, holiness," the soul worthily dons the wedding garment (*TCLS*, p. 202). As a complement to examining the soul, Taylor also recommends contemplation of the feast's mystery, which produces a discerning spiritual knowledge. Summoning would-be partakers, he exhorts: "Meditate upon the feast: its causes, its nature, its guests, its dainties, its reason and ends, and its benefits, etc. For it carries in its nature and circumstance an umbrage, or epitomized draught of the whole grace of the gospel. For here our Savior is set out in lively colors" (*TCLS*, p. 203). Thus, in countermanding Stoddard's "lowering the Esteem of, & the preparation for, this Ordinance," Taylor outlines a double-faceted preparatory process (*ETSS*, p. 160).[14] Meditation embraces both the examining the heart for signs of corruption or righteousness and the contemplation of the feast's benefits, mainly its nature as a covenant seal and commemoration of Christ's sacrifice.

Obedient to his own instructions, Taylor composes the *Preparatory Meditations* as personal exercises. As minister to the Westfield congregation, he no doubt felt acutely the need to set an example. Though these poems never became known to his parishioners, the habitual practice of meditation was integral to Taylor's private preparations for administering the Lord's Supper. Over forty-three years in 216 poems, he conscientiously set himself the task of heart-searching examinations and contemplations of Scripture, if not always of the Eucharist itself.[15] Through this preparatory process, he sought signs of his conversion from sin to sanctification, insights for the understanding, and a rousing of his holy will and affections suitable for the "Royall Feast Magnificent." In many ways the sacramental cluster II.102–111 epitomizes Taylor's motives and manner in the more extensive series. By submitting himself to a self-examination that reveals inward disease, he takes an essential first step. Sorrow and loathing often open his meditations, as he confesses sinful failings, doubts about his state of grace, and dread of potential hypocrisy. Frequently he apologizes for his inadequate poetic skills, as in Meditation II.106, in which the insufficiency of human language corresponds to his feelings of spiritual worthlessness:

> I fain would Prize, and Praise thee, Lord, but finde
>   My Prizing Faculty imprison'd lyes.
> That its Appreciation is confinde
>   Within its prison walls and small doth rise.
>   Its Prizing Act it would mount up so high
>   That might oremount its possibility.
>
> I fain would praise thee, but want words to do't:
>   And searching ore the realm of thoughts finde none
> Significant enough and therefore vote
>   For a new set of Words and thoughts hereon
>   And leap beyond the line such words to gain
>   In other Realms, to praise thee: but in vain.
>
> Me pitty, parden mee and Lord accept
>   My Penny Prize, and penny worth of Praise.
> Words and their Sense within thy bounds are kept
>   And richer Fruits my Vintage cannot raise.
>   I can no better bring, do what I can:
>   Accept thereof and make me better man.
>   (II.106.1–18)

Bereft of inward grace, Taylor perceives his creation of poetry as equivalently shabby, stumbling, limited by "Words and thoughts" which yield only a "penny worth of Praise." Monetarily and qualitatively inferior, human speech cannot generate "richer Fruits" of imagery commensurate with Christ's glorious "Sabbath Entertainment" (II.108.33). Languishing in this earthly prison, Taylor's words like his prostrate soul are unable, without God's saving grace, to "rise," "leap," or "mount" into a spiritual realm and, thereby, join in partaking of "richest Dainties Cookery." Just as Israel must sweep away all crumbs of leaven before the Passover, so gospel saints must search out their malicious iniquities, whether in word or deed. Once convinced of his natural unworthiness, paradoxically Taylor acknowledges his need for Christ's implanted righteousness ("parden mee" and "make me better man"). This diligent bringing forth of repentance ("Me pitty") and desires for reformation must take place before Taylor as priest administers the Sacrament, as guest eats the festal dainties, or as poet hymns this "Soul-Food, Faiths nourishment" (II.105.39). Meticulous self-scourging examination which readies the heart to receive Christ's saving grace is the believer's first act in donning the wedding garb.

Following upon confessions of inadequacy, Taylor's meditative subjects may vary from Old Testament types, to Christ's gospel sacrifice and salvation, to eschatological visions of heaven's banquet and union with the Bridegroom. All such contemplations enhance Taylor's readiness for the Lord's Supper. In Meditations II.102–111 definitions or lavish praises of the Sacrament itself transform the meditative goal into an immediate poetic subject. Moreover, these poems exemplify two of Taylor's frequent contemplative modes – both compatible with aims set by the *Treatise,* both contributing to the inward man's rich robing in grace. Through rational arguments or intricate definitions, Taylor explores the nature of this "Spirituall Ordinance" which supersedes all "Typick Seales and Rites and Ceremonie" to confirm "New Covenant worship" (II.103.57, 26, 19). Working still in the logical vein, he distinguishes hypocrites from wedding guests (II.106), articulates the "Mystery" of Christ's "Union" in this bread and wine (II.105), or specifies the "End, Efficient, Matter and the Form" of the Lord's Supper (II.107.32). At other times, however, metaphoric raptures whet the appetite for "Gods Temple bread; the fine Flower Cake./ The pure Shew Bread on th'golden Table set" and "wine too of brave State./ The Blood, the pure red blood of Zions Grape" (II.104.19–20, 25–6). Such ecstatic portrayals of the feast's "Cordialls rich," which "do Comfort bring./ Make Sanctifying Grace thrive ery day," appeal less to the intellect than to the holy affections (II.104.69–70). In reality, appeals to the intellect's discerning eye cannot be so easily divorced from evocations touching the heart's affections, because contemplation must stimulate both faculties. Both insights and holy sympathies rejuvenate the spiritual man, exciting the will to seek "Faiths

nourishment" in the Lord's Supper. In tandem, therefore, self-examination cauterizes the natural man's sin-infected wounds, while contemplation of scriptural or sacramental mysteries nurtures the spiritual life within.
Having raised his affections and stimulated the will, Taylor often ends
his poems with prayers of heightened desire:

> Lord, feed me with th'Bread of thy Sacrament:
> And make me drinke thy Sacramentall Wine:
> That I may Grow by Graces nourishment
> Wash't in thy Vinall liquour till I shine,
> And rai'd in Sparkling Grace unto thy Glory,
> That so my Life may be a gracious story.
>
> (II.104.73–8)

Never efficacious without God's grace, nonetheless meditation inwardly
prepares and splendidly arrays the saint for the wedding feast. The partaking of sacramental food and drink then nourishes the saint's growth
in grace, infusing his natural life with spiritual vitality.

The climax of preparatory meditation for most saints would be attending the eucharistic feast, but Edward Taylor often requests another more
unique transformation. Invested with power to administer and sanctity
to partake, he yet desires lyrical inspiration with which to hymn the
banquet in poetry. In contrast to mere words, which betray the natural
man's limitations, he yearns for spiritual grace potent enough to "tune
thee Hymns melodiously" (II.110.36). Meditation II.110, for example,
concludes not by anticipating pastoral duties, but with Taylor's pleas to
become God's designated instrument as a poet. "Oh! make my heart thy
Pipe: the Holy Ghost/ The Breath that fills the same and Spiritually," he
pleads, for "Worn out with piping tunes of Vanity," he now longs to
become the pipe upon which God will tune the hymn of eternal salvation
(II.110.37–8, 40). Other men might sit contentedly among the wedding
guests; not Taylor who conceives of himself not only as a Puritan saint
robed in evangelical righteousness, but also as a divinely inspired singer,
capable of offering "heart enravishing Hymns with Sweetest Voice" to
God (II.110.45). Just as the first cause for robing in wedding finery originates from God's grace, here too Taylor carefully subordinates himself
as the mere pipe, trumpet, or cittern upon which the Lord orchestrates
anthems. Only God's holy dispensation enables him to become "thy
Golden Trumpet Choice" or his "Soul" a "Cittern, and its wyers" his
"affections," harmoniously "screwed" with grace to "tune thy praise
most Just" and "close thy Supper then with Hymns, most sweet/ Bur-
r'ing thy Grave in thy Sepulcher's reech" (II.110.43, 49–50, 52, 53–4).
He finds no fitter subject for "enravishing Hymns" than Christ Himself,
whose descent into the grave and resurrection into heaven, where the
saints come as guests to the banquet, is commemorated by the Lord's

Supper. In concert with his spiritual motives for all his *Preparatory Meditations,* Taylor clearly equates poetic inspiration with the "Breath" of the "Holy Ghost" or an influx of "bright Grace" (II.110. 38, 37, 51). Grace transforms the poet from a "penny worth" praiser in human "Words and thoughts," a "piper" of vanities, and a lyricist with rusty affections into a "Cittern" with "Strings up higher."

Even though his poetry may be less than perfectly melodic, the connection that Taylor draws between celebrating the Supper and singing hymns suggests the double nature of his poems. As meditations in keeping with the tradition of Puritan preparationism, these lyrics become equivalent to the wedding garb, woven of Taylor's self-examinings, intellectual reflections, and rapturous praises. With the warp and woof of faith, he weaves each poem from the fine thread of holy words into the whole cloth of sanctified anthems. The meditations are products of a saint's life, remnants that provide insights into his theology and his spiritual desire to unite with Christ, as signified and celebrated by the wedding Supper. In keeping with traditions of religious lyrics, the meditations take form as prayers or hymns. Thus, when he praises Christ's institution of the Lord's Supper, he reveals a double perception of himself as both saint and singer: "To entertain thy Guests, thou callst, and place/ Allowst, with welcome," for the saints, "And with these Guests I am invited to't/ And this rich banquet makes me thus a Poet" (II.110.21–2, 23–4). Because these songs extol the Passover, Lord's Supper, or wedding feast, they become Taylor's poetic offerings in God's service. Inspirited originally by grace, Taylor as God's poetic instrument dedicates all sacramental hymns to the divine Host.

Because Taylor's vision often remains fixed on an immediate preparation for administering this earthly Supper, the poems exhibit an episodic disjunction. Each poem exists as a discrete act of meditation, moving habitually from self-examination to scriptural contemplations to ecstasies of holy affections. As moments in a lifetime, they reflect the Puritan saint's persistent doubts, for which repeated mortifying of sins and soul-probings for signs of saving grace provide a soothing antidote. Each self-contained introspective act also anticipates a literal action beyond, when the Lord's Supper visibly confirms the soul's communion among the Elect. Arrayed inwardly in evangelical graces, Taylor therefore comes as a worthy guest to partake of the "Sabbath Entertainment, spirituall fare" (II.108.33). From the "bread, made of th'kidnies of Wheate/ That grew in Zions field: And th'juyce we sup/ Presst from the grape of Zions Vine sweet," he imbibes nourishment to grow in grace here on earth (II.108.37–9). Discrete and episodic as they are, Taylor's meditations nevertheless still yield a continuous narrative of his inner life over forty-two years. Furthermore, the vision embodied in the full *Preparatory Meditations* does not end with Taylor's religio-poetic offerings rendered to God through personal introspections or with his communion Sunday service. Perpetually seeking divine guidance, nourishment, and curing, Taylor cultivates his inward sanctity not merely for the earthly Supper, but in preparation for the heavenly wedding feast. The poems may begin as independent exercises, each geared toward administering the Sacrament, each coordinated with homiletic doctrine, each one a unique robing of the soul for memorial celebration of Christ's sacrifice, all paeans to God's beneficent grace. But as a cohesive *series* of meditations, these poems map out Taylor's inward journey – one paradigmatic of every Puritan saint's aspiration for spiritual transcendence.

Just as the sacramental meditations capsulize Taylor's earthly preparationism, so too Meditation II.109 sets out in liveliest colors the eschatological wedding feast for which Taylor yearns in his most visionary moments:

> A Feast is said to be for Laughter made.
>   Belshazzars Feast was made for Luxury.
> Ahashueru's feast for pomp's displayde.
>   George Nevill's Feast at Yorks, for gluttony.
>   But thou my Lord a Spirituall Feast hast dresst
>   Whereat the Angells gaze. And Saints are Guests.
>
> Suppose a Feast in such a Room is kept
>   Thats deckt in flaming Guildings every where,
> And richest Fare in China Chargers deckt
>   And set on golden Tables. Waiters there
>   In flaming robes waite pouring Royall wine
>   In Jasper Cups out. Oh! what glories shine?
>
> But all this Glorious Feast seems but a Cloud,
>   My Lord, unto the Feast thou makst for thine.
> Although the matters thou hast thine allowd,
>   Plain as a pike Staffe bee, as Bread and Wine,
>   This feast doth fall below thine, Lord, as far
>   As the bright Sun excells a painted Star.
>
> Thine is a Feast, the Funerall feast to prize
>   The Death, Oh! my Redeemer, of the Son
> Of God Almighty King of Heaven and'ts joys,
>   Where spirituall food disht on thy Table comes.
>   All Heavenly Bread and Spirituall Wine, rich rare,
>   Almighty gives, here's Mannah, Angells Fare.
>
> This Feast indeed yields gracious Laughing ripe
>   Wherein its Authour laugheth Hell to Scorn:

Lifts up the Soule that drowns in tears, a wipe
 To give th'old Serpent. Now his head piece's torn.
 Thou art, my Lord, the Authour, and beside
 The Good Cheer of this Feast, as Crucifide.

The Palace where thou this dost Celebrate
 Is New Jerusalem with Precious Stones
Walld in: all pavde with Gold: and Every Gate,
 A precious pearle: An Angell keeps each one.
 And at the Table head, more rich than gold,
 Dost sit thyselfe, and thy rich fare unfold.

Thy Table's set with fare that doth Excell
 The richest Bread, and Wine that ever were
Squeezd out of Corn or Vines: and Cookt up well.
 Its Mannah, Angells food. Yea, Heavens Good Cheer.
 Thou are the Authour, and the Feast itselfe.
 Thy Table Feast hence doth excell all wealth.
      (II. 109. 1–42)

To the easily deluded viewer, renowned pagan and contemporary feasts, such as "Belshazzars," "Ahashueru's," or "George Nevill's," might appear epitomes of glamour.[16] But these grandiose entertainments are contaminated by pretentious "Luxury," decadent "Laughter," "pomp's displayde," and "gluttony" which signal the celebrants' corrupt estates. So too, those dazzling feasts projected with imagination's eye, bedecked with "flaming Guildings," "richest Fare," "golden Tables," and "Royall wine/ In Jasper Cups," deceive the observer, if he judges inner wealth by opulent facades. By comparison with such resplendent worldly banquets, the "Bread and Wine" of God's "Spirituall Feast" may seem "Plain as a pike Staffe" and the "Death" of Christ a maudlin cause for a "Funerall feast." Paradoxically, however, this spartan celebration initiates the sainted guests into a spiritual realm where "God Almighty King of Heaven" and Christ His "Redeemer . . . Son" reign with unparalleled glory. By emphasizing the "spirituall food," "Heavenly Bread," and "Angells Fare," Taylor clarifies the reasons for the Eucharist's superiority. Instituted in heaven through Christ, the Lord's Supper commemorates the most momentous event in mankind's spiritual history. Because of his crucifixion, Christ "laugheth Hell to Scorn," and treads upon "th'old Serpent," whose "head piece's torn," thus fulfilling God's ancient promise. More significantly, Christ's death "Lifts up the Soule that drowns in tears" and opens for repentant saints the gates of the eternal "New Jerusalem." Because of its spiritual import, the eucharistic feast, whether earthly or heavenly, excels all testimonials to worldly delights and decadence. Hence, in this poem Taylor revisualizes the panorama of Christian salvation, but he focuses upon Christ's sacrifice which honors God's ancient pledge of redemption. In the divine scenario, the Lord's Supper memorializes Christ's death, seals the Covenant of Grace, and points toward the faithful saints' eschatological communion.

Meditation II.109 simultaneously culminates Taylor's typological study of Passover and signals a new realm for his visionary poetry. As he delineates in Meditations II.22, II.71, and II.103, Passover as a "Typick Ceremony" is the preeminent Old Testament feast, for which all Israel prepares by purging out old leaven, separating from Egyptians to commune within the house, and dyeing the doorposts to ward off the avenging angel. Feasting upon the paschal lamb and sprinkling sacrificial blood with hyssop (faith), ancient Israelites perform their obligatory services to God. In after years the eating of the roasted lamb with unleavened bread and drinking of wine memorialize their safe deliverance from Egypt's bondage under God's direction. With "Staff in hand, Loins Girt, and Feet well shod" the Jews embark upon their journey to the promised land of Canaan (II.22.35). Moreover, Passover seals their covenant with God, by which He promises a future Savior to release the inward bondages of sin. Overtly in the sacramental series and in Meditations II.22 and II.71, Taylor portrays the New Testament accomplishment of Passover's foreshadowings. Under the gospel Christ the antitype becomes the Messiah, sacrificed like a lamb through His crucifixion and shedding of blood. Christ's deed of self-abnegating love satisfies God's wrath, which like the avenging angel hovers over sinners to demand justice. The Son's atonement reconciles man with the Father, bringing within human reach divine forgiveness and promises of celestial rewards. Instituted to commemorate this supreme redemptive act, the Lord's Supper bread and wine signify Christ's deliverance of man from sin's bondage, an effect comparable to Israel's liberation. And like the Jews, gospel saints must also prepare for this Supper by examining the heart for crumbs of malice, hypocrisy, or sin, then meditating on this Sacrament. Once assured of inward grace, testified by an open profession of faith and conversion, the saint joins other select communicants. Robed in wedding finery, all sanctified guests not only come to the earthly feast, but also embark on a journey to the New Jerusalem. Preparing the heart or donning the garment of evangelical righteousness are more strenuous, but each practice is superior to outward rituals under Mosaic law.

In Meditation II.109, this typological schema extends beyond temporal history, beyond earthly celebrations of Passover or the Lord's Supper. When Taylor postulates the Supper itself as a figure for the celestial wedding feast, he envisions an eschatological fulfillment, which brings man to the essence of all divine shadows. Like the figure of the temple that also adumbrates God's kingdom or the threefold application of the "Looking Glass" to define figural progressions, so also through Passover, as a type for the gospel feast, he seeks revelations of heavenly truths. The *Treatise* illuminates the origin and end of this nuptial feast and its link with the Supper:

> Consider the nature of the feast, and you shall find it is the marriage feast of the King's Son. The King of Glory, King of Kings, the King Immortal and Invisible and Eternal herein celebrates the espousals made between His own and only begotten Son, and heir of all things, and the souls of His elect drawn up in an holy contract at the time of their particular conversions. Wherein He entertains them with the royalest dainties, and the richest provision that heaven itself affords: with that miraculous water out of the rock, and Manna, the breads of heaven, angels' bread. (*TCLS*, pp. 168–9)

Man's espousal with Christ originates when God institutes the new covenant of redemption and grace, which the Savior seals with his pledged self-sacrifice. Both the promises of salvation and ultimate nuptial union are reaffirmed by the Old Testament Passover and gospel seal of the Lord's Supper. Thus, as each convert enters the covenant, he obtains a right to participate in the sacramental feast, which celebrates his espousal to Christ.

Yet old and new feasts alike are shadows compared with the soul's subsequent union with the Bridegroom in eternal wedlock. That celestial wedding feast which Taylor envisions in the *Treatise* and Meditation II.109 signifies each saint's and the church's everlasting marriage with the King's Son. To come properly garbed as a guest or Bride to this ultimate feast requires lifetime examination and contemplation, just as Taylor pursues in his *Preparatory Meditations*. Not vizzarded hypocrites or sinners still seeking regeneration, the guests at this earthly and eschatological banquet are antitypes of Christ's original disciples:

> They'r Gods Elect, and thy Selected Ones,
>> Whose Inward man doth ware rich robes of Grace,
> Tongues tipt with Zion Languague, Precious Stones.
>> Their Robes are quilted ore with graces lace.
>> Their Lives are Checker work of th'Holy Ghost.
>> Their 'ffections journy unto Heavens Coast.
>
> The Subjects that at first sat at this feast
>> With Christ himselfe, faithfull Disciples were
> Whose gracious frames 'fore this time so increast
>> Into Apostleship that brought them here.
>> Who when Christ comes in Glory, saith, they shall
>> Sit with him on twelve thrones in's Judgment hall.
>
> These sample out the Subjects and the Guests
>> That Welcome are unto this Table bright,
> As Qualifide Disciples up well drest

In Spiritual apparell whitend white
Else Spot there's in this feast. They cannot thrive
For none can eate, or ere he be alive.
                    (II.109.49–66)

Taylor reminds liberal proponents who would echo Stoddard that even
Christ's own "faithfull Disciples" were increased in grace before they
came to the Supper, an example to be imitated by latter-day Puritans.
To come with "Spot" is to desecrate the Sacrament, for one must be
"alive" spiritually in order to partake of the feast. Robed in grace inwardly,
the Elect must also manifest their new covenant sanctification in "Languague," "Lives," and " 'ffections," much as Taylor seeks to make his
preached and poetic words, his self-examined life, and his holy affections
(expressed in poetry) acceptable for both the Lord's Supper here and the
final journey "unto Heavens Coast." Hence, Taylor envisions himself
under several aspects: a ministerial disciple, comparable to Christ's apostles, who must preach the Word and administer the Sacrament; an elect
saint who like all other "Subjects" and "Guests" must come to the Supper "drest/ In Spiritual apparell whitend white"; and a betrothed saint
who anticipates the heavenly nuptials for which all earthly meditations
and robings in the "Wedden garment" are mere preliminaries. No longer
journeying through a wilderness and delivered from the serpent sin, the
elect saint enters the promised kingdom of New Jerusalem. Ironically,
the "Funerall feast" that Christ celebrated in the Last Supper becomes
the vehicle by which redeemed souls enter into not only the heavenly
kingdom, but also into a living spiritual "Marriage" with Christ, also
commemorated and adumbrated by the Lord's Supper. At the celestial
feast angels are waiters, guests "ware rich robes of Grace," the "Table"
is laid with "richest Bread, and Wine," "Mannah, Angells food," and all
inhabit the "Palace," walled in "with Precious Stones" and "all pavde
with Gold." For his images Taylor looks in part to Revelation's apocalyptic visions. But he also magnifies and irradiates the typal elements
from Passover and the reflected shine in the gospel Supper. Emerging
out of shadowy figuralism, the explosion of light and glory, "bright
Sun" and "flaming Grace" attend this revelation of divine Truth. Without the medium of filtering types or veiled gospel truths, through Christ
incarnate, the saint perceives God directly in his essential wisdom and
glory.

Even within his sacramental series, Taylor traces a figural progression,
as Meditation II.103 portrays Passover as the "Typick Ceremony" for
the gospel's "Spirituall Ordinance," and Meditation II.109 anticipates
heavenly abrogations of this "Funerall feast." In these meditations then
the dialectic of hypocrisy and sainthood, vizzarded depravity and luminous inner grace, the worldly and the spiritual eventually give way to a

vision of transcendence. Taylor not only maps out his individual saga of salvation against the backdrop of a fallen world, he also projects the grandiose spectacle of God's providential drama which exists beyond the human realm. In keeping with his meditative poses, he concludes II. 109 by pledging service triply as the robed saint seeking nuptial union with the Bridegroom, as a guest at the celestial banquet, and as a poetic singer who dedicates heart and hymns to heaven:

> Lord Deck my Soule with thy bright Grace I pray:
>   That I may at thy Table Welcome bee,
> Thy hand Let take my heart its Captive prey
>   In Chains of Grace that it ne're slip from thee
>   When that thy Grace hath set my heart in trim
>   My Heart shall end thy Supper with an Hymn.
>   (II. 109.73–8)

8

The Artistry of Types

Then my Beloved your beloved shall bee
  And both make him one Spouse enriched with Grace
And when dresst up in glory and bright glee
  Shall sing together fore his blessed face
  Our Weddin Songs with Angells mild * * * * *
  In ravishing notes throughout Eternity.
                    (II.133.41–6)

Can saints be singers? Critical opinion seems to argue against it, since Puritan demands for a plain style rhetoric appear to preclude the ornaments normally associated with poetry. In the American tradition of literature, colonial poetry is often dismissed as a "little *Recreation,"* hardly essential to the wilderness trials or spiritual life of the New Israel.[1] But can we continue to dismiss the plethora of elegies, the meditations of Bradstreet, and the epic of Wigglesworth as aberrations that place their authors beyond the pale of strait-laced Puritanism? How do we evaluate the *Preparatory Meditations* of Edward Taylor except as the idiosyncratic creations of an unusually fertile Puritan imagination?

One step toward reenvisioning American Puritan poetry should be to recall the Bible as a poetic model and stimulus. It was common for English clerics of varying persuasions to compose poetic paraphrases of the Bible, especially of those books, such as the lamentations of Job, the Psalms, and Canticles, which were by nature poetic. Moreover, as exemplified by English ecclesiastics, including Donne, Herbert, and Milton, meditation on scriptural mysteries, including the Old Testament types, was widely practiced as a means of tutoring the spiritual understanding and affections. That such meditations might take the form of poems would be only a logical extension of the inspired contemplator's desire to offer prayers and hymns of praise to God. Although perhaps unique in his concentration upon personal and ceremonial types, nonetheless, Edward Taylor participated in well-established traditions of scriptural exegesis with his *Upon the Types of the Old Testament* and *Christographia* and of meditation through poetry. To become a singer in his *Preparatory Meditations* made him no less a Puritan saint, as he sought his own pathway to spiritual truths through a divinely sanctioned medium. In his personal search for assurances of grace and revelations of divine wisdom, Old Testament figures provided one "Looking Glass" through which to visualize the patterns of his own spiritual life.

Three metaphors dominate the second series of Edward Taylor's *Preparatory Meditations,* all reflecting his central motives and goals: 1) the journey from Egypt to Canaan as a pattern for spiritual deliverance from sin; 2) the image of the heart as a temple within which gospel saints worship Christ; and 3) the metaphor of the "Wedden garment," robing the saint not only for the earthly Lord's Supper, but also for the celestial banquet. Examined closely, however, each metaphor has its roots in a broader typological framework and providential schema of history to which Taylor like other seventeenth-century Puritans adhered with unshaken faith. These metaphors, grounded in Puritan typological readings of Scripture, point to the spiritual crises, and consequently the poetic themes, that preoccupy Taylor in his meditations.

The theme of man's spiritual journey derives from the typological deliverance of Israel from Egypt (II.58), that land emblematic of bondage and sin in the Old Testament. The extraordinary types of Israel's wilderness wanderings (II.58–61) in part foretold the Puritans' escape from religious oppression, as the founding fathers sought a New Canaan or New Jerusalem in the New World. Fleeing from the Babylon of Anglican England, Taylor also braved the wilderness when he preached on the frontier in Westfield. But Israel's trek signified as well a spiritual journey, one that led New Testament saints into battle against sin, while it promised eventual transcendence into a heavenly paradise. Despite those figuralists who envisioned New England as the lush paradise rather than a wilderness, the ardent Puritan perceived any earthly locale as an imperfect way station in a journey that was not temporal, but a timeless traveling of the spirit. Often Puritan aspirations on a social level turned toward millennial predictions, a looking toward the apocalypse when the church would unite eternally with God. But personally, this journey became a process of spiritual purification. In the types of the cloudy and fiery pillar (II.59), manna (II.60A), water from Horeb's rock (II.60B), and brazen serpent (II.61), Taylor perceives the soul on earth searching for Christ's guidance, nourishment, and curing. The journey of the inward consciousness stretches from original sin to a final state of saving grace. Consequently, Taylor's *Preparatory Meditations* becomes his autobiography of one saint's spiritual quest. In each meditation and the entire series, the goal is not immediate gratification within a worldly Canaan. Instead, the persona turns inward and ahead to find an eschatological reward. The New Jerusalem in heaven lies beyond the grave and beyond the physical torments of this corrupt wilderness, whether in New England or the mind.

As a second dominant metaphor, Taylor turns repeatedly to the concept of the heart as a temple, in which the struggle for man's soul originates. Adumbrated by the opulent temple that Solomon constructs to
house Hebrew worshipers, the New Testament fulfillment becomes the
superior inward temple of each saint's heart (II.20). New covenant worship focuses upon a state of being, not upon the glories of golden furnishings, the priestly intermediaries, or the rituals of ceremonial worship
(II.21–24). Neigther does the gospel preach reliance on easy crutches,
such as papists and Anglicans provide with lavish altars, soothing music,
or exalted priests and saints. For Taylor the heart's temple only reaches
perfection through perpetual recleansings (II.26–28), self-sacrifices to atone
for sin (II.17–18, 25), and a purging of inward filthiness through an infusion of Christ's redeeming grace. Only in coming to Christ as High Priest
(II.14, 23), does the worshiper discover an effective mediator.

Within the social sphere, this temple metaphor corresponds with the
strict purity existing within New England's congregational churches,
devoid of ornamentation or elaborate rituals. Puritan worship emphasized preaching and hearing of the Word, the study of Scripture, and
inward prayer – each petitioner seeking Christ and not a priest for his
confession. The solitary quest (emblemized by the journey) finds its
counterpart in the individualism of Puritan worship. Without distrac-
tions from external ceremony, which made so clear the Old Testament's
legalism, the gospel worshiper concentrates upon his inward spiritual
state. The soul weeping over its innate sinfulness, the mortifying of
naughtiness within, the internal search for evangelical righteousness, the
praying for salvation – the essence of gospel worship is personal and
internal. Like other Puritan sojourners, Taylor turns toward self-examination and contemplations of Scripture to find his way to God. And his
poetic series becomes again autobiographical, a putting into the form of
psalms and poetic meditations a saint's personal worship, not a minister's
public preachings as in *Upon the Types of the Old Testament*. Each poem
initially uncovers the petitioner's unworthiness, but just as often it concludes by praising Christ as the fount of cleansing grace. Hence, the process of each discrete poem is one of regaining faith. And the entire sequence
becomes a lifelong revisualization and reassurance of Christ's presence as
the Savior who hovers in watchful care over His saints. That temple
toward which Taylor ultimately aspires is not made with hands, but is
the spiritual palace in heaven. In divine bliss, saints remain eternally purified, sing perpetual hymns of praise excelling all human meditations,
and thrive in their union with the radiant Son.

The third metaphor, which expresses most clearly the intimate relationship between the redeemed saint and Christ, is that of the wedding
garment and nuptial feast. Taylor abstracts this metaphor not so much
from a type of the Old Testament as from the allegorical Canticles. In

the wedding between the Bride and Bridegroom Taylor perceives the promise of an eschatological marriage between Christ and each saint or the church. Thus, every preparatory act on earth becomes part of the soul's robing in evangelical righteousness, readying himself to celebrate his espousal with Christ. By professing an experience of saving grace, saints don the wedding finery and come as welcome guests to the sabbath entertainment, the Lord's Supper (II.102–111). Prefigured by Israel's Passover (II.22, 71), the Lord's Supper sacramentally seals the covenant between God and His redeemed saint. Thus, Taylor's meditations become an integral part of robing himself, not only to administer the Supper, but also to partake among the other saints of the spiritual bread and wine (II.22, 60A–60B, 71). But a wedding gown assumed for sacrament Sundays is not garb to be easily discarded as fashion dictates or worldly demands intrude. In Taylor's mind, preparing the soul for the celestial feast and nuptials is a continual process of cultivating inward sanctity. Comparable to the other two metaphoric concepts, this ideal of the wedding garment alludes not merely to an earthly activity, nor to an eternal one. Instead, the design and weaving of the wedding array, cut with God's golden shears to fit only the saint prepared by grace – that tailoring prepares Taylor for a heavenly wedding which unites him eternally with Christ as the Bridegroom. Not surprisingly, the last sequence in the *Preparatory Meditations* II.115–165 forms an epithalamium based upon Canticles. In these meditations of his old age, Taylor anticipates a consummation of his nuptial relationship with Christ.

In adapting these metaphors, Taylor follows a tradition at once theological and literary. The sources of his typology reach as far back as the New Testament and Church Fathers yet derive more immediately from Puritan exegetes, such as Thomas Taylor and Samuel Mather, all of whom inform his treatise *Upon the Types of the Old Testament*. But Taylor claims and deserves a place in a literary tradition as well. Much like the Catholic Dante or the Puritan Bunyan, who similarly rely on biblical types, Taylor also adopts the journey as his central conceit (or figure) for the Christian's spiritual progress through this world into the next. Like George Herbert, who entitles his poems *The Temple* (1633), so also Taylor in his *Preparatory Meditations* unveils the temple of his heart where he privately searches and worships.[2] Like Herbert as well, who progresses from the stony heart remolded into an altar for God to the vision of Christ's loving gathering of saints at the eucharistic feast, Taylor discovers his need for divine compassion to redeem him from hardhearted sinfulness. Although alone in New England in writing so extensively on Canticles, Taylor also looks back to another group of poetic ancestors from Théodore Bèza to Francis Quarles, John Mason, and Henry Ainsworth, who paraphrased these nuptial lyrics.[3]

Although Taylor belongs to a tradition of religious poets as much as to a lineage of biblical exegetes, his uniquely Puritan typology and conceits make these poems decidedly different from Richard Crashaw's baroque Catholic ecstasies, Henry Vaughan's mysticism, or the worship of the church as artifact and architectural emblem in George Herbert's Anglican devotions.[4] Clearly not on the epic scale of Milton's *Paradise Lost* or in the dramatic form of *Samson Agonistes,* Taylor's meditations belong to a tradition of religious lyrics, as Barbara Lewalski has shown in *Protestant Poetics and the Seventeenth-Century Religious Lyric.* He looks not to the panorama of mankind's history but to the innermost history of a single penitent believer's repeated falls and redemptions. Taylor participates in this literary tradition because he conceives of himself as not just a sinner and saint but a singer as well. Fascinated even on earth by images, metaphors, and typological conceits that coalesce into poems, Taylor also envisions himself in heaven in a unique position. He arrives not merely as a guest at the wedding banquet, nor as Bride for the Bridegroom, nor even as a weary journeyer seeking eternal rest or a heart-worshiper seeking a beatific temple. Rather, Taylor portrays himself in heaven as on earth as a singer or psalmist who praises Christ and salvation in all-admiring style. But he longs for the transcendent poetry of divine hymns that will surpass his imperfect rhymes and fumbling verse.

Edward Taylor finds no theoretical confinement, beyond the limitations of his own ability and humanity, in the Puritan esthetic of a plain style because the Bible provides sufficient metaphors, themes, and models for poetry, particularly in the types of Davidic psalms and Solomon's nuptial canticles that foreshadow angelic hymns. The medium of human language itself, however, can never be equivalent to God's Word, either in its manifestation as Scripture or in its ineffable expression through Christ as Word made flesh; consequently Taylor must refine his "Metaphors" of "ragged Non-Sense" in order to "serve thy Sacred selfe with Sacred art" (II.36.31, 32, 40). As critics, we must question how, and how successfully, he creates poetry within these more stringent standards, some imposed by human failings of perception or skill, some by the Puritan demands for reasoned clarity and order rather than ornamental effusions and rhetoric, some by Taylor's own determination to make his poems meditations to prepare his soul for the Lord's Supper, some by the sheer strictures of form imposed by an unvaried six-line stave, in iambic pentameter, rhyming *a b a b c c.*[5] Meditation upon homiletic doctrine preached before his administration of the Sacrament sets the boundaries for Taylor's subject matter, and doubts about his own creativity in generating images and metaphors adequatè to the spiritual themes pose the challenge for his art. Taylor constantly treads a fine line between the fear of an overly enthusiastic style that may too mightily exalt the human fancy and the ebullient desire to praise God in a poetic language decorously perfected for the Deity. The study of the types made Taylor yet more conscious of the excruciating limits of human perception. If even the Bible, as God's divine Word, can only prefigure in shadowy and coded language, but never fully capture the spiritual essence or the scope of God's providential signs and Christ's theanthropic fulfillment, then how can human skill so presume to perceive and praise? Typology thus made Taylor far more sensitive to his inherently flawed status as seer and poet, granted interpretive insights and poetic inspiration only through Christ's divine mediation as Savior and Muse.

But what is the impact of Puritan theology, or more specifically typology, on Edward Taylor's poetics? What are the stylistic traits that can be traced, in part if not fully, to his theory and practice of an exegetical and devotional typology? Taylor's poetry abounds with antitheses, particularly with his soul's sinful degradation set in contrast to God's and Christ's glorious omnipotence. Nouns, adjectives, epithets, all compounded, cataloged, tumbled in cumulative disarray often capture the shredded, piecemeal quality of the sin-wracked soul, "Halfe Dead," "rotten at the Coare," "Consumptive," with "Wasted lungs," that "Scarce draw a Breath of aire," a "Heart" that is "Fistulate," a body a mere "Shell," a man reduced to beast, wallowing in "Guilt and Filth . . . Sent and Smell" (II.14.1–6). Taylor's graphically particled autopsy of humanity contrasts with the hyperbolic abstractions and "Sparkling Colours bright,/ Most bright indeed, and soul enamoring" with which he habitually decks portraitures of Christ (II.12.7–8). In Meditation II.14, "Cloathd with the Glory/ Of Prophets, Priests, and Kings," Christ radiates "glorious Beams of Wisdom," "shining Holiness," and "rich Grace" (II.14.31–2, 38, 45, 47). Fascinated with types again later in Meditation II.54, Taylor combines the metaphor of Christ as the sun of righteousness with the same threefold figuralism to laud "My Gracious-Glorious Lord," whose "brightest brightness, and the mighti'st Might/ Is lodg'd in each one of these Balls of Light" (II.54.49, 29–30). The rhetoric of divine glory (superlative, abstract, hyperbolic) contrasts with the rhetoric of human defilement (diminutive, concrete, meiotic), eschatology with scatology.[6]

This penchant for rhetorical and thematic antitheses can be traced in part to typological reasoning, in which the old and new Covenant of Grace appear disparate by virtue of the manner of their dispensations, and in which Christ, divine and eternal, supersedes the types, bound in historical time and space. For the Old Testament relies upon the visual, concrete, external ceremonies that manifest man's old covenant worship of God. The personal figures are mere human approximations of Christ, who dimly shadow only a portion of His glorious roles, whether as first-born seed of the Father (Adam, Isaac), Israel's savior (Abraham, Jacob,

Joseph), divine guide (Joshua), prophet (Moses), priest (Aaron), king (David, Solomon), Nazarite (Samson), or crucified redeemer (Jonah). In the typological conceits, therefore, this nearly pictorial dimension of Old Testament ceremonies, life sagas for prophetic persons, and of sea journeys and topographical landscapes gives a concrete, earthbound quality to Taylor's poetic images. But the New Testament sets forth Christ in evangelical colors, because the message of fulfillment is one of spirit triumphing over literalism, grace over legalism, light over shadow, heart's worship over temple rites. Precisely this need to see the Old and New Testaments as different in *manner* of dispensation, to seek in typology a method of making the literal text (even its encoded signs) yield up spiritual truths, and to laud the superiority of what cannot be seen to that which can be, provides Taylor with a theological rationale for the antitheses that characterize his poetry.

Although typology acknowledges the differing manners of dispensation, it also maintains a continuity between the Old and New Testaments, since both speak forth the same *matter* – Christ, His benefits of grace and salvation, and the church – whether in shadowy prophecy or brilliant fulfillment, in pencil sketch or colored portrait, in shell or kernel. Typology as an exegetical method makes it possible to reconcile Old Testament messianic predictions with Christ's New Testament accomplishments. Consequently, in the very premises of typology reside the means for resolving the antitheses that seem theologically to separate sinful man from an exalted God and that poetically threaten to dissolve all poems into rigid oppositions. Taylor thus seeks parallels between the Old Testament adumbrations and New Testament illuminations as part of a conjoined theologio-poetic process that resolves his ever recurrent dilemma as a corrupt man fallen away from an Almighty God. Consequently the figural meditations often open with anguished outbursts of despair, as Taylor expresses his acute distance from God and then in mid-poem establishes typological parallels to reaffirm Christ's intervention.

Consider, for example, Meditation II.23 in which Taylor acknowledges not only his spiritual but also his poetic alienation:

> Greate Lord, yea Greatest Lord of Lords thou art,
>   And King of Kings, may my poor Creaking Pipe
> Salute thine Eare; This thought doth sink my heart
>   Ore burdened with over sweet Delight.
>   An Ant bears more proportion to the World
>   Than doth my piping to thine eare thus hurld.
>   (II.23.1–6)

The disparate images of size between an "Ant," nay an "Emmets Egge" or "Nit," and the "Greatest Lord of Lords," exalting epithets, a comparison of proportions, and pronoun oppositions ("thous" and "thine" versus "my") capture the soul's dilemma (II.23.8, 12). But Taylor also belittles his poetic skill. His pen or cacophonous voice, a "poor Creaking Pipe" or single instrument, lacks sufficient orchestral power to salute the King's "Eare" attuned to sweet seraphic symphonies. He turns next to the typological "meat" of his poem, proclaiming the grace of Christ, Who is "The marrow of the matter choice that Clings/ Unto the Service of Atonment's day," for "This was his Type, He is its Treasure rich/ That Reconciles for Sin that doth us ditch" (II.23.15–16, 17–18). The center, as in so many of Taylor's figural meditations, lays out precise parallels by which Christ, like the high priest Aaron, performs the atonement. This dialectical use of the conceit leads Taylor to a three-stanza conclusion that recalls the dichotomies of the initial plea: "What wonder's here? Shall such a sorry thing/ As I have such rich Cost laid down for mee/ Whose best at best as mine's not worth a Wing./ Of one poore Fly" (II.23.61–4). The resolution is both spiritual and poetic. In the penultimate stanza Taylor prays for "thy Gracious hand me chafe, and rub/ . . . / With Heate and Spirits all divine, and good,/ To make them nimble in thy Service Greate," a clear emblem of achieved sanctification, Taylor's ministerial recommitment, and his anticipation of the sacramental service that will commemorate Christ's atonement through His sacrificial body and blood (II.23.67–70). But the resolution is also poetic. Taylor pledges his "gift," which is "but a Wooden toole," trusting that if Christ receives it, "thou wilt it enrich/ With Grace, thats better than Apollo's Stoole" (II.23.73, 74–5). Reformed by atoning grace from a "poor Creaking Pipe" and better inspired than with counsels from Apollo's Delphic oracle, "Thy Oracles 'twill utter out the which/ Will make my Spirits thy bright golden Wyers,/ ALTASCHAT Michtam tune in Angells Quires" (II.23.76–8). What begin as poetic antitheses frequently end with metamorphoses in which lowliness becomes exalted, the bestial turns angelic, rusty wires or creaking pipes transform into angelic harps, and the life of spirit supplants the natural life – but only through Christ's mediation. Structurally in Meditation II.23, both as the matter *and* the method of the poem, typological parallels (or conceits) resolve the alienation of the unworthy sinner. They do so by reinforcing the continuity between the old and new Covenant of Grace, in which Christ is preached first in promises of prophetic types, then in the evangelical gospel lessons. Christ, adumbrated in persons and ceremonies (Aaron and Atonement), intercedes to bring man once again into at-one-ment with God.

Taylor does not, as I have shown earlier, create metaphysical conceits in which oppositions disappear into extended *discordia concors*. Instead, by drawing upon figural parallels from the Bible and theological guides (including his own *Upon the Types of the Old Testament*), he emphasizes inherent similarities between Old Testament persons, events, and things and Christ's antitypal fulfillments. The poetic version of typological exegesis appears in the elaborated conceits, whether developed in strictly definitional ways (II.5, 7, 9, 10, 11, 58), dialectically (II.17, 18, 20, 22, 23, 24, 27, 61), or in associative accumulations of images (II.16, 21, 26, 59, 60A, 60B, 71). The hallmarks of typological conceits are the repeated use of "type" or "to typify," linking, as in Meditation II.23, Aaron's "milke white linen Robes, to typify/ Christ cloath'd in human flesh pure White, all fair" (II.23.26–7) and the phrase-by-phrase, line-by-line, stanza-by-stanza balancing of type with antitype: "Aaron the blood must catch in's Vessell to hold./ Lord let my Soule the Vessell be of thine," and "Aaron must in a Censar all of Gold/ Sweet incense burn with Altars fire Divine," thus "To Typify the Incense of thy Prayer/ Perfuming of thy Service thou didst beare" (II.23.37–42). Whether Taylor recreates the ceremonial rites, the figure's life (by way of birth, qualities, actions, and death), maps out Israel's journey in the wilderness, or pairs Passover with the Lord's Supper, the parallelisms remain a constant, not only echoing the exegetical tradition upon which he draws so heavily, but also defining a unique poetic method grounded in biblical models.[7]

The underlying assurance of a world governed by an all-knowing God Who providentially provides for mankind's redemption and Who embeds in history and in a text the signs of and the key to reading that promised salvation differentiates Taylor's conceits from metaphysical and baroque tropes spun out by human ingenuity. Writing in his "Introduction" to Jonathan Edwards's *Images or Shadows of Divine Things*, Perry Miller distinguishes types from tropes:

> In the type there must be evidence of the one eternal intention; in the trope there can be evidence only of the intention of one writer. The type exists in history and its meaning is factual. . . . By contrast, the allegory, the simile, and the metaphor have been made according to the fancy of men, and they mean whatever the brain of the begetter is pleased they should mean. In the type there is a rigorous correspondence, which is not a chance resemblance, between the representation and the antitype; in the trope there is correspondence only between the thing and the associations it happens to excite in the impressionable . . . senses of men.[8]

Both as method and matter in Taylor's sermons and meditations, typology enables the exegete to read, decipher, penetrate the resident significance that makes temporal events and persons in the Old Testament dispensation predictive of Christ and His church yet to come, and who once come spiritually fulfills all the promises of adumbrative types. The very reciprocity of typology with its emphasis on God-created meanings and

parallels leads, therefore, to the shaping of Taylor's characteristic typological conceits, ones that differ substantially from mere metaphor, simile, allegory, or the metaphysical conceits of other seventeenth-century
poets. But in moving from preached text in which exegetical typology
dominates to the devotional applications in his poetic meditations, Taylor creates, as Albert Gelpi argues in *The Tenth Muse,* a "highly tropological style [that] rests on a typological vision which is the heart of the
miscellaneous pieces as well as the sequences."[9] Edward Taylor always
values more highly the "seeing" into God's truths than the creation of
poetry itself, which is among the lowlier skills that human imagination
possesses, insufficient without divine mediation to pierce either figural
meanings or to render them in poetic tropes. Nevertheless, he moves
from type to trope in the very process of writing his meditations because
(flawed as they may be) he creates complex images, similes, conceits,
and allegories that turn figural exegesis into the poetry of types. Consequently Taylor must establish himself as both seer and singer, and his
metaphors in pleading for the requisite craft constantly resort to images
of vision, "Wilt thou enoculate within mine Eye/ Thy Image bright, My
Lord" (II.59.1–2), and of singing or writing, "Steep my Stubborn Quill/
In Zions Wine fat, mend my pen," for "In Sacred Text I write" (II.58.8–
9, 12), suitable for the creation of angelic poems and hymns: "My Voice
all sweet, with their melodious layes/ Shall make sweet Musick blossom'd with thy praise" (II.26.35–6).

One way (beyond creating typological conceits) in which Taylor frequently expands a typological vision into a tropological style for his
meditations is to employ various narrative structures, whether miniature
sagas, allegories, or trials of the soul, to capture the *Heilsgeschichte.* In
meditations such as II.8, 17, 20, 22, 29, 30, 50, 58, and 103, in which he
traces out mankind's history from the fall to ultimate salvation, from
God's parliament of deities to Christ's crucifixion, from creation to the
heavenly paradise, we apprehend God's providential plan within which
biblical typology becomes a cipher to be deciphered. Meditation II.30,
for instance, sketches out the ancient time when "man was the miror of
thy Works/ In happy state, adorn'd with Glory's Wealth," only to be
deceived by the "serpent" who "lurks/ Under an apple paring, and by
stealth/ Destroy'd her Glory" (II.30.7–8, 9–11). Memories of Eden and
Adam, the original fallen man, merely set the stage for the adventures of
Jonah, another archetypal sinful man, whose sea sufferings and near death
in the whale's belly yield final salvation. Taylor's sea saga depends upon
the figural relationship to unravel the riddle because only through Christ
do all men, from Adam to Jonah to Puritan saints, discover "rich Atonement in thy Death" (II.30.67). A brief infusion of allegorical language
elevates the moral of this tale into a more comprehensive vision of God's

redemptive plan: "Oh! Happy Message squandering Curst foes," for "Grace in her glorious Charriot here rides deckt./ Wrath's Fire is quencht. And Graces sun out shines./ Death on her deathbed lies, Consumes and pines" (II.30.63, 64–6). The personification of grace recalls not only biblical chariots but also the chariot in which Helios, Greek god of the sun, travels the skies. Taylor here weaves together these allusions with his previous evocations of tempestuous rains, which punitively drench Jonah and the seamen, to suggest that the Son's coming, like sunshine after storm, brings "Grace" that quenches God's fiery torrents of wrath. Taylor does not parse out literal meanings, as I have done, but merely hints at multiple resonances. Instead, the personification of "Grace" and "Death" to the brink of allegory universalizes Christ's triumph over the deadly curse laid upon Adam and all mankind thereafter. A sustained narrative, graphic images, such as those that vivify Jonah's travails and Christ's descent to the grave, and multileveled meanings characterize these meditations, in which Taylor condenses human history into a miniature, thirteen-stanza epic.

Allegories appear more elaborately in Meditations II.50 and II.103, both of which take as their explicit themes the function of types within God's divine scheme. In Meditation II.50 Taylor imagines God as an "Artist," who shapes successive boxes (dispensations or covenants), the first of which "of Pearle Fell, Broke, undone" signals man's "lost Smaragdine Glory" and consequent legacy of "Falshood" and "Boxes teemd of Sory" (II.50.10, 11, 12). But "The Artist puts his glorious hand again/ Out to the Worke" (perhaps a reminder of the Covenant of Works) to refashion a new "Choice pearle-made-Box," one (note the pun on inlay) first "lay'd in inke Divine/ Of Promises, of a Prophetick Shade,/ And in embellishments of Types that shine" (II.50.13–14, 23, 20–22). The choice "Smaragdine Box where Truth doth ly," is the Messiah incarnate (another emboxing of divinity within a human or "made" form), in whom men, once fallen, can now "Embox" their faith (II.50.27). The evocation of a vast time span ("four thousand yeares") and of God as the "Artist" with transcendent power to create what He wills when He wills it, together with the elaborate play on the metaphor of boxes to signify man's fall and faith, the types, and Christ incarnate, makes this allegory a powerful rendition of Christian providential history. Taylor draws upon his fertile repertoire again in Meditation II.103, in which the same story is retold through images of God as a monarch whose "Parliament" of "all the Properties Divine" (justice, grace, wisdom) legislates the fate of "man's life" (II.103.1, 2, 4). The prevailing metaphors are contractual, either of the "Covenant" in its first and second "Edition," either "Deckt up in Types and Ceremonies gay" or certified by the New Testament Lord's Supper, and financial, since "Grace" must pay the "Bill" that "Justice" demands (II.103.20). The accumulated metaphors retell man's saga from the point of view of divinely instituted dispensations, a heritage or history in which "Typick Seales and Rites and Ceremonie" first "ratify" the Covenant "as Gods Testimony," until Christ's "Glorious Sun is risen" and "Lords Supper seales the Covenant of Grace" (II.103.26, 28, 34, 36). Notably, all of these meditations have their roots in commonly accepted biblical metaphors, stories, and typal parallels, from the concept of God as a divine Creator or Artist, to the account of Jonah, to the vision of God as a wrathful King imposing ceremonial rites only as preludes to the more glorious gospel dispensation. The embracing of the typological vision within a poetic context of tropological narratives and allegories makes us more conscious that types and antitypes exist within the encompassing pattern of providential history itself.

Providential history becomes, however, only a macrocosmic pattern for the microcosmic journey of each soul, a journey through which Taylor repeatedly travels, meditation by meditation, and one made poetic through figural narratives, personal applications, and recurrent images that signal the soul's transport from sin to salvation. Meditation II.58, which traces Israel's wilderness wanderings in geographical detail, makes plain typology's potential for defining not only the collective experience of God's Elect but also the intimate morphology of conversion for each Christian soul. "Egyptian Bondage whence gates Israel shows/ The Spirituall bondage whence Christs children goe," but this communal type merely adumbrates the process by which individually "God calls the Soule," out of "The Bondage State to Sin and Satan" and into the Covenant of "His onely Church" and "Of Christ's rich blood" (II.58.35–6, 42, 37, 102, 111). Here type and trope, Israel's wilderness travails and the metaphor of a journey, both of which signify (in different senses of that word) the soul's conversion, remain so congruent as to disappear one into the other. Recall Miller's distinction that in the type there is evidence of "eternal intention," "factual" or historical reality, and a "rigorous correspondence, which is not a chance resemblance." Such is the epistemological basis that Taylor presumes in declaring that Israel's trek *signi*fies the soul's conversion. In the trope of traveling a journey, however, the "fancy" or "intention of one writer" may prevail. Dante, Herbert, and Taylor, all adopt the journey because of its traditional resonance as a metaphor for spiritual experience, but each poet's style differs as does the theological interpretation each derives. In Taylor's case, he barely (if at all) separates the type from that which we call the vehicle of the metaphor (Israel's wanderings/journey), or the antitype from the tenor (soul's conversion), though we sense the change as he moves from exegesis to poetry. For Taylor, modern theorists might assert, the semiotics of types through which God speaks takes priority over a semiotics of artifically constructed tropes that constitute poetic language through which one man speaks.[10] Taylor thus chooses to create typological conceits, in which the figurative style remains within the bounds of his self-imposed decorum of worshiping God in an all-admiring but plain style, one rooted in the literal text of the Bible, capable of illuminating spiritual truths, but devoid of the tainted excesses of human fancy.

Meditation II.58 suggests how Israel's collective experience has its counterpart in personal history, though the morphology of conversion is still represented by the archetypal "Soule," meaning Everyman's soul. In Meditation II.22, however, the Passover that begins Israel's journey provides Taylor with a way of comprehending the trials of his own soul. "A Bond Slave in Egyptick Slavery," his "Soul, doth groaning ly," and like the Israelites, he too must "banish Leaven," dip *"My* Bunch of Hyssop, Faith . . . in thy blood/ *My* Paschall Lamb," and "With Staff in hand, Loins Girt, and Feet well shod/ With Gospell ware" walk "to *my* God" (II.22.7, 9, 19, 25–6, 35–6). Here Taylor's personal progress becomes paramount, in part because the first-person pronouns "I" and "my" abound. He also envisions a unique way of celebrating his sanctification, for "at this Feast my harp shall Tunes advance/ Upon thy Lamb, and my Deliverance," a declaration neatly entwining his exegesis of types, a need to meditate upon his soul's deliverance, sacramental preparation for administering the Supper, and a desire to worship Christ through poetic "Tunes" (II.22.47–8). If the church (through exegesis and preaching) gains a clearer understanding through adumbrative types of Christ's mediation, so also for Taylor as an individual saint, tropologically heightened types offer him a poetic idiom by which to praise the supremacy of Christ's grace in his own spiritual life. Allegories that embrace typal parallels as signs within a grander providential scheme that affects all time and all men create an explosion of reference or telescopic perspective, so that one seems to share an omniscient vision comparable to God's. When Taylor creates highly personalized salvation narratives, the field of reference implodes, generating a more intensely microscopic focus. As one saint, he delves into his own heart's needs and the ways in which types apply directly to his spiritual progress. In either case, whether through tropes that expand the visionary context or intensify the personalism, Taylor blends a typological vision with a figurative style, the latter marking the difference between the more purely rational exegesis, as in *Upon the Types of the Old Testament,* and poetic art, the medium of the *Preparatory Meditations.*

Taylor's meditations illustrate two ways in which the concept of "tropology" intersects with his poetics, the first drawn from rhetorical convention, the second from exegetical practice. First, in the rhetorical sense of "trope" from the Greek τρόπος, meaning a turn, or Latin *tropus,* a figure of speech, his poems abound with metaphors, similes, allegories, and conceits. In Taylor's poetics, however, tropes are not merely ornaments ingeniously woven by the human fancy but rather natural elaborations or spiritual associations drawn from the vast repository of biblical images, metaphors, and sacred types. As a Calvinist exegete and poet, he can envision no other approach when composing poetry than as a seer to "read" what God has "written" in sacred metaphors and types and as a singer to create tropically enhanced types to worship God in a style that seeks to imitate, but can never supplant, the divine poet's craft. Benjamin Keach, we may recall, titled his 1681 compendium *Tropologia: A Key To Open Scripture-Metaphors. Wherein the most Significant Tropes, (As Metaphors, &c) And Express Similitudes, Respecting the Father, Son, & Holy-Spirit, As also such as respect the Sacred Word of God, Are opened, and Parallel-wise applied, together with the Disparities.* Keach's title itself betrays a mounting confusion during the seventeenth century that elided sacred types with "Scripture-Metaphors" with tropes, although his treatise includes primarily biblical types and metaphors, as had Henry Vertue's 1659 *Christ and the Church: Or Parallels.* Drawing upon Salomon Glass's *Philologia Sacra* (1623), Keach's guide abounds in rhetorical terms (metonymy, prosopopoeia, synecdoche, catachresis, anthropopathia, hyperbole, allegory, paronomasia, et al.), and it extensively examines metaphors, ones derived not only from Scripture but also from minerals, plants, and living creatures, including man and what belongs to him. Topical headings would seem to distinguish types from metaphors: in fact the copious catalogs belie his assertion that "there is a great difference between *Metaphorical* or *Allegorical*, and *Typical* Scriptures" by indiscriminately mingling them together.[11] For example, under the all-inclusive heading, "Metaphors, Allegories, Similes, Types . . . Respecting the Lord Jesus Christ," Keach includes types (brazen serpent, prophet, priest, king, altar, manna), scriptural metaphors (sun of righteousness, root of David, true vine, bright and morning star, saints' wedding garment), and less definitively biblical metaphors (door, lion, compassion to sinners under the similitude of a hen, captain of our salvation, ambassador, eagle). Henry Vertue distinctly separates the personal and real types from metaphors, though his list of resemblances for Christ contains a grain of mustard seed, word, worm, city on a hill, moon, threshing floor, winepress, house, hill, and mother that even vary from Keach's later collection. In short, the seventeenth-century theological tradition that feeds into Edward Taylor's poetry encompassed not simply acceptable types, which constitute the substance of *Upon the Types of the Old Testament* and the correlated *Preparatory Meditations,* but also numerous metaphors, sanctioned by their biblical origins or by repeated usage in sermons, treatises, and guides as illuminating "tropes" for Christ, God the Father, and the Holy Spirit.

Mather's *The Figures or Types of the Old Testament,* Guild's *Moses Unvailed,* and Thomas Taylor's *Christ Revealed* as well as Edward Taylor's sermons all hew a strict line in setting aside metaphors to study exclusively sacred types. Mather scrupulously differentiates parables and similes from types, or as he terms them *"Typus arbitrarius* and *Typus fixus & institutus,"* the former meaning "a similitude or comparison," for so "Riders on white Horses are *resemblances* used in Scripture to set out Christ and the Angels; but yet not properly *Types* of them" (*FT,* p. 58). He not only separates types expressly instituted as such by God from arbitrary parables and similitudes but also advocates a strict reading of Scripture in two senses, the literal and spiritual, the latter meaning typological resemblances between the Old and New Testaments. Sacred metaphors and rhetorical tropes lie distinctly outside the province of Mather's *Figures or Types* and Taylor's *Christ Revealed.* In *Upon the Types of the Old Testament,* Edward Taylor certainly endorses Mather's distinction, but in the *Christographia* he more enthusiastically praises Scripture's metaphorical content:

> For Words are used onely to import the intent in the minde of the Speaker. And all Languages admit of Metaphoricall forms of Speech, and the Spirit of God abounds in this manner of Speech in the Scripture and did foreshew that Christ Should abound in this Sort of Speech Ps. 78. 2. Matt. 13. 35, and this Sort of Speech never was expected to be literally true, nor Charged to be a lying form of Speech, but a neate Rhetoricall, and Wise manner of Speaking. Hence saith Gods Spirit in the Psalmist Ps. 49. 3. 4: I will open my mouth in Wisdom: the meditation of my heart shall be of understanding. I will encline mine eare to a Parable and open my dark Saying upon my harp. Hence then this form of Speech is a truth Speaking form, Convaying the thoughts of the heart of the Speaker unto the hearers in Such words as are apt to do it metaphorically and wisely. (*CHR,* p. 273)

This dictum grants Taylor the authority to utilize scriptural metaphors liberally in his sermons and poetry, for they issue from no less than the spirit of God and Christ Himself. It inspires him as well to create his own images and metaphors, recognizing always their inferiority as humanly contrived or mere rhetorical tropes, for "My tatter'd Fancy; and my Ragged Rymes/ Teeme leaden Metaphors: which yet might serve/ To hum a little touching terrene Shines" (II.82.1–3).

In the *Preparatory Meditations,* therefore, Taylor employs a broad spectrum of similitudes and metaphors, ranging from divinely instituted types to biblical metaphors to invented tropes. The types require no further elaboration here, but images and metaphors that extrapolate from the types also regularly appear in the figural meditations. For example, in Meditation II.24, the passage from John 1:14 ("Tabernacled amongst us") generates a splendid array of structures, "Thy Godhead Cabbin'd in a Myrtle bowre,/ A Palm branch tent, an Olive Tabernacle,/ A Pine bough Booth, An Osier House or tower," all variants of the tents and booths from the Jewish Feast of Tabernacles, all signifying Christ's incarnation to come, when "through this leafy Tent" of human nature, "the glory cleare/ Of thy Rich Godhead shineth very much" (II.24.13–15, 37, 37–8). In Meditation II.60B, Taylor pours forth a torrent of epithets to describe Christ's blood flowing like Horeb's water from the rock, outdoing himself in both sermon and poem in accumulating associative metaphors, some biblical, some purely of his own invention: "here's a River in a Rock up tun'd/ Not of Sea Water nor of Swill. Its beere./ No Nectar like it," "Christ is this Horebs Rock, the streames that slide/ A River is of Aqua Vitae Deare," and "This Rock's the Grape that Zions Vineyard bore/ Which Moses Rod did smiting pound, and press/ Untill its blood, the brooke of Life, run ore" (II.60B.20–2, 25–6, 31–3). Such metaphoric extensions and compounding of resemblances characterize Taylor's figural series.

But the types and derivative metaphors, by a process that makes all of Taylor's poems cross-referential, provide him with a new repository to be plumbed in later poems. Types become central in some meditations in which Christ appears as the "First born from the Dead" (II.39.21), whose "Preheminence" is magnified over all other offices, including "Priest, Prophet-King-Hood" (II.40.31, 32). Full of the truth "Of promises, of Prophesies, and Types" (II.50.38), this sovereign "Sun" outshines the "three fold glory, Prophet's, Priest's and King's" that with "Trible Authority bestud thy Crown" (II.54.37, 38), and His body and blood are celebrated in figural and festal terms throughout Taylor's series on the Sacrament (II.102–111). Echoes of the types linger as well in passing references to "Pillars of Perfumeing Incense" (II.42.11), "Jacob's golden Ladder," holding forth Christ's "THEANTHROPIE" (II.44.9, 10), to the altar (II.52) and "coale" (II.73, 82, 86, 92) that cleanses the lips of new prophets, as it did Isaiah's in the Old Testament, and to fountains, wells, and floods of life-giving waters and blood in abundance. In Meditation II.78, for example, having triggered a train of figural associations, Taylor not only portrays himself fallen helplessly into "a Springless Well./ Like Josephs Pit" but then reverts to Meditation II.50's allegory to seek relief, for "in the upper room of Paradise/ An Artist anvill'd out Reliefe sure, Good" via an appropriately fashioned "Golden Coarde, and bucket of Grace Choice/ Let down top full of Covenantall blood" (II.78.7–8, 19–20, 21–2). Exuberant over the thirst-quenching release, Taylor compounds his images of "boundless Grace," like "a Spring of Liquour," whose "Streams oreflow these banks," whose "Spring head's Godhead, and its Chan-nells" are "Manhood veans that Christ keeps Chase," thus with a "Springtide Flood" drowning the hellish pit "with Covenantall blood" (II.78.25–30). The epithets recall Meditation II.60B, but in addition Tay-lor invokes the Israelites as models, for once freed from "Sins Filthy Dungeon State," these "Pris'ners" too "on this Red Sea swim/ In Zions Barke: and in their Cabbins sing" and "sayling in the Arke of Grace that flies/ Drove sweetly by Gailes of the Holy Ghost" find rescue (II.78.13, 41–2, 34–5). Certainly Meditation II.78 draws imagistically and themat-ically from the same vein that inspires Taylor earlier to study Joseph's bondage in a pit (II.7), or the deliverance of God's chosen people under the types of Israel's crossing of the Red Sea (II.58), the water flowing from Horeb's rock (II.60B), and the ark of the covenant and Noah's ark (II.29). Characteristically, many of Taylor's later poems develop figural images or metaphors that evoke resonances rather than retrace minutely detailed definitions, dialectical arguments, or associations as in the typo-logical meditations themselves.

Like his exegetical predecessors, Taylor also mines the golden array of scriptural metaphors, particularly in those meditations (II.31–114) that bridge from the series on types to the final series on Canticles (II.115–165) and in which he focuses primarily on Christ as the New Testament fulfillment. In the very first page of *Upon the Types of the Old Testament,* he acknowledges "the many methods attended on by the Spirit of God to set before us the Loveliness of the Lord Jesus," noting not only the "Prophesies" and "Types," but also "Certain of the Choicest of things in the Whole Creation, by their Excellency to paint out some of the Excellency of Christ; & that Metaphorically in Parables, as Chiefly in the New Testament as the Pearle of Great Price Matt. 13. A Vine Joh. 15. a King's Son Matt. 22 etc" (*UTOT,* p. 1). Taylor takes his inspiration, if not clearly from the compendiums, then assuredly from the Bible and the tradition of "Scripture-Metaphors." He devotes whole poems or stanzas to the tree of life (held by some exegetes to be a type) in II.31, 33, 47, 52, and 56, Christ as head of the church (II.36, 37, 38), the sun of righ-teousness (II.54, 67B, 68A), King in glory (II.62) and in Zion (II.100), Christ as superior to the sun and moon (II.99, 101), and most notably as the vine (II.98), the "Root and Offspring of David" (II.113), and the "bright and morning Star" (II.114).[12] The last three poems reflect both Taylor's figural parallels and Keach's cataloging in the *Tropologia.* In lan-guage reminiscent of the figural terminology, Taylor praises the "Choic-est Vine, the royallst grape that rose, / Or ere in Cana'ns Vinyard did take Root" as a powerful metaphor that "Did *Emblemize* [Christ] thy selfe the True Vine" (II.98.7–8, 9). Replete with imagistic associations,

Meditation II.98 then translates the vine into the Savior's "Wine thy Love bleeds from thy grape," so potent with "spirituall reech" that like a medicinal "Cordiall" it transfuses the "Chilly person" with life-reviving "blood and Spirits of the gracious heart," a heart in turn prepared to partake of the Sacrament (II.98.25, 27, 30, 29, 28). Taylor delightfully manipulates the consonantal proximity and orthographic interchangeability of *v* and *w* and multiplies exact end rhymes to capture mimetically the transformative mystery of Christ's blood: "thy rich Love its Wine" will "my heart and blood refine," and in the Supper "I" will "drinke the juyce of this true Vine," then joyfully "sing thy Love better than Wine" (II.98.43, 45, 47, 48). Rather predictably, Meditation II.113 begins with Taylor's plea to "anoint mine Eyes" and claim to find Christ as the "Root, and Offspring too/ Of David" a riddle "harder far to read than Sampsons Riddle," progresses to the "key" that shows that "Thy Deity, my Lord, is Davids root" and "Thy Humane nature is its Offspring-Sute," an analysis that enables Taylor to request, "Make me thy branch, be thou my root thyselfe,/ And let thy Grace root in my heart, I Crave" (II.113.1, 11–12, 16, 32, 34, 50–1). Perhaps these are the most overt Scripture metaphors, but they are not the only ones, since from Keach's list alone we might also find the following scattered throughout the *Preparatory Meditations*: Christ as the rose of sharon, lily of the valley, bundle of myrrh, and Bridegroom (poems primarily on Canticles); as an advocate, surety, witness, testator, and judge (poems with legal themes); as heir, express image of the father, foundation, cornerstone, and mediator (inheritance and atonement poems); as the bread of life, true manna, lamb, garment of sanctification, saints' wedding dress (meditations on the Sacrament); and as a physician, fountain, pearl of great price, and refiner, the all in all.

As if the biblical array of types and metaphors were not sufficient for the inventive imagination of even the lowliest poet, Taylor also draws upon a third repertoire – the faculties of his own mind and perceptions, metaphors drawn from homely New England crafts and arts, and esoteric references from the mental library of a learned minister. Taylor's poems abound with tropes of disease, putrefactions, scatalogy, of rivers, gardens, farming, wine casking, weaving, games, cookery, birds, beasts, insects, journeys, and ones drawn from law, history, astronomy, astrology, ancient myth, music, angelography, jewels, castles, wars, and oratory – to mention only a few categories. By and large, such metaphors describe the human condition or inferior creations that are eclipsed by the supremacy of the Godhead whose glory requires the elevated language of scriptural metaphors and types. The metaphors that spring from Taylor's own imagination are often the ones in which we hear most distinctively his voice, only because their oddity or curiosity strikes us so forcibly, often intruding into otherwise soundly scriptural or figural evocations.

These three varieties, however, constitute not totally exclusive categories, but more accurately a spectrum that takes us gradually from types that are signs instituted by God to be read, to those Scripture metaphors that bear no seal of institution, yet nonetheless illuminate the Godhead and spiritual truths, to those tropes that are fully of human design, in which, as Miller suggests, the appeal is to "the associations it happens to excite in the impressionable . . . senses of men." Although human inventions of poesy bespeak the intention of a single imagination, not the divine imagination, Taylor attempts to hold forth the model of divine speech, as recorded in the Bible. Whatever the source, Taylor's *Preparatory Meditations* abounds with types and tropes and fundamentally reveals an imagination so tutored in finding similarities and disparities that metaphors and conceits become the cornerstone upon which his poetic style rests. Neither in metrical form nor lyrical variety does Taylor venture so bravely as he does in creating typological conceits, scriptural metaphors, and his own tropes. When one speaks of the tropological, meaning the rhetoric of Taylor's poetry, it is apparent that he remains thoroughly steeped in the Bible and exegetical traditions, though the predictability does not detract from our appreciation of the distinctive voice with which he translates this rich inheritance of types and tropes.

In the second sense, from the Greek τροπολογία (Justin Martyr, 160) and Latin *tropologia* (Jerome, 400), "tropological" derives from an exegetical tradition that spans from the Church Fathers through medieval exegetes into the Renaissance and advocates a fourfold reading of Scripture according to the *sensus literalis, tropologicus, allegoricus,* and *anagogicus.* In hermeneutics, tropology designates a moral discourse, or more precisely a second sense or interpretation of Scripture relating or applied to conduct or morals. In both Mather's *The Figures or Types* and Taylor's *Upon the Types of the Old Testament,* the sermon uses lend themselves, if not to a tropological reading in the strict exegetical sense, then at least to its remnants as a moral application of Scripture, whereby the readers or congregation are enjoined to go forth and apply to their own conduct spiritual truths and moral guidance abstracted from the figural analysis. Samuel Mather allows that the *"occasional Types"* were *"Instructions in Moral Duties, as indeed all Providences are,"* and acknowledges that the ancient *"moral Laws,"* as in the Ten Commandments, are *"still in force and binding unto all Men in all Ages"* (*FT,* pp. 129, 168). And as Taylor asserts, although "The Ceremonies cease" with Christ's coming, "yet the Creede/ Contained therein, continues gospelly," counseling men to worship inwardly with the heart and, in Puritan theology, to manifest their sanctification in an upright and moral life (II.25.45–6). In Edward Taylor's case, the deliberate act of regularly meditating upon the homiletic doctrine constitutes a form of moral application, a mandated self-examination of his life's conduct, and a means to reestablish the heart's proper "Worship-mould."

What makes Taylor's tropological applications of figural truths so compelling a part of his Puritan poetics is that he seeks to insert himself humbly, nimbly, even wittily into the figural equation, or seeks to turn the *figura* into exemplar by invoking the *imitatio Christi*. Recall his direct pleadings, "Be thou my Samson, Lord, a Rising Sun,/ Of Righteousness unto my Soule" (II.11.49–50), "Make mee thy Nazarite by imitation/ Not of the Ceremony, but thy selfe,/ In Holiness of Heart, and Conversation" (II.15.37–9), or "Be thou my brazen Serpent me to Cure" (II.61.38). Taylor clearly finds in Old Testament types models for the moral conduct of his own life, but these exemplars gain their efficacy only in and through Christ's fulfillment. Christ comes, through this Christomimetic process, to reside within the soul as a spiritual guide governing moral behavior, or in other words, the soul's embedded desire to imitate Christ directly or through exemplary *figura is* the process of living a sanctified life. Taylor also uses other metaphors derived from typology to lodge his request, as in "Unite my Soule, Lord, to thyselfe, and stamp/ Thy holy print on my unholy heart," an imprinting that recalls the Greek τύπος, meaning an imprint or impression (II.44.49–50). Or as he explains in *Upon the Types* Sermon 1, "Type . . . coming from Τύπτω . . . notes to smite . . . to import any thing bearing an impression of an agent upon it, & hence is Sometimes read Ensample. I Cor. 10.11 . . . [or] used for a Sacred rite, or Ceremony, bearing a Divine Significant Stamp on it" (*UTOT,* p. 3). If the Old Testament types provide a glimpse through prophetic, yet vague outlines of Christ, once time gives way to the *eschaton* Taylor hopes to find himself reflecting back the perfect image of his Maker: "My person make thy Lookinglass Lord, clear/ And in my Looking Glass cast thou thine Eye./ Thy Image view that standeth shining there" (II.92.38–40). As prophesied in 1 Corinthians 13:12, "for now we see through a glass darkly; but then, face to face," in the final days the image of God once thought to reside outside and beyond the faculty of human sight will become the image within the soul in a transparent reflection that virtually dissolves the boundaries between self and other, saint and Savior.[13] In the meantime, Taylor can only plead, "Lord, make me with thy *likeness like* to thee./ Upon my Soule thy Shining Image place./ And let thy glorious grace shine bright in mee./ Enlay my thoughts, my words, and Works with Grace" (II.99.49–52). Not only does Taylor employ the language of typology to express his deep-seated need for this *imitatio Christi,* but as well he dedicates each poem to the very process of stamping within his soul that divine image that will morally guide his conversation, deeds, and life. Meditating in poetic form becomes his personal process for imprinting spiritual images within his soul in a repeated act of autobiographical self-reflexiveness that reminds him constantly of his need for the Savior and reassures him of his status as an elect saint. Metatextually, the meditations "robe" him with the garment of sanctification necessary to attend the Sacrament and nuptial feast, so that the clothing without reflects the radiance of the spiritual image within inspired by the antitypal Christ.

Taylor never forgets Christ's centrality in the typological equation, but he feels his unworthiness so acutely that he must wheedle, often cleverly, his way into the divine cosmology. Almost invariably, such appeals to be brought within the grand scheme of salvation follow after the figural analysis, usually in a final stanza or two, as if prayer will secure his membership in the camp of God's Elect. Not only are these petitions the high point of Taylor's preparation for the Sacrament, they also reflect his poetic ingenuity in grafting personal pleas into the meditation's figural and/or metaphoric progress. As Karl Keller observes, "Taylor is for the most part attracted to types into which he can slip himself without in any way changing the nature of the original type-antitype relationship, thereby sneaking himself into the plan of salvation by means of the vehicle of language."[14] The startling variety of his inclusions ranges from the bold to the subtle, almost self-effacing. He may baldly appeal to be Abraham's preferred son, "let not the Bondmaids type/ Take place in mee. But thy blesst Promisd Seed" (II.4.25–6) implore Christ to "lay thy brightsome Colours on me" (II.7.39) as with Joseph, or pledge, "I'le be thy Tabernacle: thou shalt bee/ My Tabernacle. Lord thus mutuall wee" (II.24.59–60). Such outright imperatives make Taylor seem virtually the antitype, but the appeal is always directed toward Christ, the "Lord" who can effect the new gospel relationship. His desire may be so intense that he skirts the boundaries of presumptuous pride, seeking even to become God's adopted son, "Make mee thy Babe, and him my Elder Brother./ A Right, Lord grant me in his Birth Right high./ His Grace, my Treasure make above all other:/ His Life my Sampler" a paternity that he reclaims in Meditations II.17 and II.111 (II.2.37–40). In more dejected moments, Taylor diminishes his size, identifying with the humblest creatures, for whom a mere scrap of redeeming grace will suffice: "Yet let my Titimouses Quill suck in/ Thy Graces milk Pails some small drop" he supplicates (II.3.31–2). If transformed into "thy little Linet," he "Will/ Upon thy Nut tree sit and sweetly sing" (II.63.56–7), or huddle "Under the healing wings of this bright Sun/ Of Righteousness, as Chicken Chearping wise/ Under its Dam" (II.68B.14–16), or in eternity "bee one of these Crumbs of thine," a mere speck of "dust" once "flect with Sin," now radiant with "Grace may shine" (II.95.43, 44, 45). Taylor's vision of himself thus ranges from the mighty to the minute, as through types and metaphors he seeks inclusion in the New Testament dispensation.

The need to personalize the salvation process leads Taylor into this fertile profusion of images and metaphors, a devotional use of tropological language to satisfy the tropological (moral) needs of his soul that goes beyond the often dryly depersonalized exegesis of his predecessors. But a sin-riddled soul does not transform into saintly Bride at the mere turn of a pun or rhyme, though Taylor uses both, but instead undergoes a *process* of spiritual regeneration. Hence, the metaphors and typological conceits emphasize the *in-process achieving* of a state of grace, whether as a cleansing, transfusing, refining, distillation, photosynthesis, cultivation, purging, grafting, journeying, dying and dyeing, weaving, bathing, robing, or irradiation. Many such evangelical processes look back to Old Testament types in which altars refine, purge, and waft distilled odors heavenward, in which holy oils cleanse leprosy and brazen serpents cure the sight, in which Israelites journey to Canaan, and in which sacrifices, atonements, and tabernacle rites occur as daily, monthly, and yearly festivals. In Canticles too the garden emblemizes Christ and the church wherein the soul must be rooted, nourished by fructifying rains and sunshine, cultivated into a blossoming tree, fruit, or flower. All of the meditations are evangelical preparations, robing the Bride for the nuptials with Christ, sanctifying the guest to feast upon Christ's body and blood. Such reconstructions of the soul, readied to partake of the Sacrament, to serve God wisely, and to sing divine hymns become the thematic and metaphoric content of Taylor's meditations.

Perhaps the most subtle poetic device, one too easily overlooked, yet used by Taylor at his pertinacious best, is the possessive pronoun "my." Taylor himself recognizes its disproportionately immense claim of relationship:

> My Blessed Lord, that Golden Linck that joyns
> My Soule, and thee, out blossoms on't this Spruice
> Peart Pronown MY more spiritous than wines,
> Rooted in Rich Relation, Graces Sluce.
> This little Voice feasts mee with fatter Sweets
> Than all the Stars that pave the Heavens Streets.
>
> It hands me All, my heart, and hand to thee
> And up doth lodge them in thy persons Lodge
> And as a Golden bridg ore it to mee
> Thee, and thine All to me, and never dodge.
> In this small Ship a mutuall Intrest sayles
> From Heaven and Earth, by th'holy Spirits gales.
>   (II.35.1–12)

The "my" with which Taylor first claims responsibility for the unworthy self, as in "My Stains . . . sinke so deep" (II.1.7), "My Heart is Fistulate" (II.14.5), and "My Soile is sandy," "My Stock is stunted," "My Garden weed" (II.4.3, 4, 5), through the intervening process of salvation also signals the saint's renewed relationship with Christ, in which He becomes "my Tabernacle," "my Altar," "my Samson," and "my Lord." This "Golden Linck" or "bridg" of "Rich Relation" expresses the personal commitment to which a proper interpretation of biblical typology brings all saints. Each inspired seer must acknowledge "the existential claim, and demand," as Allan Charity phrases it, implied by the "proposition 'Jesus Christ is history's fulfillment . . . in as much as in him it finds its norm, its perfector, and judge' " by "affirming also 'Christ is my perfector and my judge.' "[15] The "little Voice" of "my" places Taylor within the schema of providential history, but it does so though the paradoxically simple, yet grandest affirmation of Christ as "my" perfect antitypal redeemer. Consequently, types as well as Scripture metaphors may provide Taylor with his themes, but it is the process of devotional meditation and application that motivates him to transform exegesis into poetic art. Typological analysis, covenant theology, conversion morphology, meditative self-examination, sacramental preparation cannot be divorced one from the other in a Calvinist vision of man's place within the *Heilsgeschichte* or within the temporality of daily life, nor should they be. Preaching becomes poetry precisely when Taylor's typological vision becomes tropological – in the dual sense of a rhetorical style that depends upon Scripture metaphors, conceits, allegories, and other tropes and as a devotional medium that applies spiritual truths to moral conduct. Taylor translates figural exegesis into personal praxis, doctrine preached into a life lived as evangelical saint and singer.

Though Taylor's personalism may provide glimmers of a later Emersonian individualism, it remains far closer to the Calvinist awareness of the totally undeserving soul, whose election depends entirely upon Christ's mediation.[16] Man, imprisoned in a corrupt body, possesses no inherent power to change, but instead must look to the Savior, whose omnipotence redirects all history and all men's spiritual lives. Christ's supremacy, first signified by types of a prophetic shade, then manifest in the substantial antitype, the Messiah who accomplishes all types – this Christocentricity influences Taylor's poetics in another way, by transforming what seems to be a spiritual autobiography from one perspective into a lifelong panegyric or rich "Love Letter" to God, both Father and Son, from another. Christ's ability to redeem sinners stems from His paradoxical nature, that is, the hypostatic union of Godhead with humanity through the divine incarnation, and it is this most profound mystery that Taylor celebrates in the *Preparatory Meditations,* because Christ provides the only avenue through which man's spirit may also transcend his nature.

In Sermon 1 of *Upon the Types of the Old Testament,* Taylor inscribes this theme of the Christological fulfillment:

> . . . The Excellency of Christ . . . doth as far transcend the Excellency of the type, as the Glorious body of the Sun Exceeds the Sign of the Sun upon the Signpost. . . . Because Christ Jesus is the Accomplishment of the Type unto the Full. there is a twofold fulfilling of the Type. or as to many types: as for Instance, the Temple in which Gods presence did reside did Type out Christs Humane nature in Union to his divine, or Christ Jesus as His Divine, & Humane Nature are United in one person. John. 2.19.21. & as to the reason of the thing why it is so: & this is various; in Speciall as a medium of Divine access rendering the approach unto God acceptable. & thus Christ is the onely medium to the Father. Joh. 14.6: I Tim. 2.5. So that Christ accomplisheth the type in both respects. (*UTOT,* pp. 5, 8)

By entering into human time and space, Christ surpasses all lowly shells in creation, because He comes infused with transcendent divinity, a Son/Sun of God Who irradiates types from within. Taylor never exhausts the pun on Sun/Son that so truly figures Christ's brilliance, yet exalts Him beyond the brightest objects in the natural universe. The excellency of the antitype, Christ incarnate, so exceeds human comprehension, for "This Union, that it is, wee clearely see/ But se not How, or What it is: although/ We stande and gaze on't, at't amazed bee," that he can only reiterate his awe in terms of comparatives and superlatives (II.105.13–15). Thus, through types and poetic metaphors, Taylor seeks to express the inexpressible, to approximate Christ as nearly as possible by that which is known to the human senses, while acknowledging that He can never be fully apprehended. "The Moon and Sun the Worlds bright Candle's light/ . . . / These Candle flames lighting the World as tapers,/ Set in thy Sunshine seem like smokie vapors," and "The Glory bright of Glorified Saints/ And brightest Glory sparkling out with grace/ Comparde with thine my Lord is but as Paint," a "weak reflection" on "Walls not to compare with thine" (II.101.39–42, 43–5, 47, 48). Even the incandescence of the heaven's brightest orbs or the saint's inward spiritual shine are dark illusions compared with Christ's divine radiance, even momentarily shrouded in the human form.

In all his *Preparatory Meditations,* Taylor attempts through the medium of language to capture the mysterious paradox of the incarnation, because it not only provides the key to fully interpreting the adumbrative figures but it also establishes Christ as the conduit through which man requests salvation and through which in turn God dispenses grace. Opening his poetic sequence on types, Taylor finds even the "Excellency in Created Shells" inadequate, for mankind's "leather Coate" remains indelibly stained, nature's most "Choise things" are "a Shaddow," and types merely dull shades compared wtih the Lord's dazzling glory (II.1.8, 10, 14, 16). Christ excels, according to the companion Meditation II.2, by birthright, His incarnation aptly conveyed by images both sexual and spiritual. "Gods onely Son begot," "a Lump of Love/ Son of Eternall Father, Chambered/ Once in a Virgins Womb, dropt from above./ All Humane royalty hereby Divin'de./ The First Born's Antitype: in whom they're shrin'de" possesses the redemptive power to transform the first Adam's sin into salvation, leather shells into saints' robes, universal nature into an eternal paradise, and all types into one antitype (II.2.8, 32–6). The miracle that makes all possible and that brings us back to the sublime paradox is Christ's very Being as spirit housed within human flesh, the theanthropy to which Taylor returns time and again in his figural poems. And the Old Testament types present readily accessible scriptural signs in which to divine this duality. "Isaac, and the Ram," for example, "fore shew by typick laws/ Christs Person, all Divine, joynd whereto's made/ Unperson'd Manhood" (II.5.9, 10–12), the "Altar" prefigures "thy Eternall Plank of Godhead, Wed/ Unto our Mortall Chip, its sacrifice" (II.18.21–2), and the Hebrew Feast of Booths displays Christ's donning "of a Humane Quilt," His "Person" made "a bit of flesh of mee/ Thy Tabernacle, and its Canopee" (II.24.22, 23–4). Taylor accepts that the Godhead exists in some otherworldly dimension, a glorious circumference beyond mankind's control or apprehension. But Christ's incarnation holds forth the promise that spirit may inhabit flesh, that God's divine grace can become the palpable core and center of human existence.

Christ's theanthropy is unique, yet it sets forth the likeness toward which mankind aspires, as we have seen in the *imitatio Christi*. In the recurrent imagery of containment, whether as treasure chests, wombs, boxes, cabinets, kernels within shells, temples and tabernacles, Taylor finds the poetic metaphors to vivify not only Christ's dual nature but also man's need to receive the spirit within. Metaphors drawn from the reservoir of types frequently inspire him, as in Meditation II.24, in which his "Soul would gazing all amazed stand,/ To see the burning Sun, with'ts golden locks/ . . . / Ly buttond up in a Tobacco box" and in which Christ's antitypal "Nature all With Mine/ Doth by the Feast of Booths Conjoynd appeare," the very "Godhead Cabbin'd in a Myrtle bowre" (II.24.1–4, 25–6, 13). This miraculous incarnation sparks Taylor's imagination into a tumbling array of suppositions, similes, metaphors, and hyperbolic comparisons in Meditation II.34's playful extrapolation from the concept of Christ as the kernel within the shell, a commonplace metaphor for the relationship between antitype and type. In a series of rapidly transmuting metaphors, Taylor first supposes "this Earthy globe a Cocoe Nut/ Whose Shell most bright, and hard out challenge should/ The richest Carbunckle in gold ring put/ How rich would proove the kirnell it should hold" (II.34.1–4). But, in a second supposition, were this same "World a sparking pearle, 't would bee/ Worse than a dot of Dung," or "a worm eat nut" when compared with Christ Whose "worth as far excell[s]" (II.34.11–12, 10, 9). We may hear echoes of Keach's "Scripture-Metaphors" when Taylor then asserts that "to finde a Pearle in Oister Shells's not strange," but to discover the "Rich Gem" of Deity "Encabbineting Jewell wise" within "Humane Natures grange" defies mankind's power to imagine (II.34.19, 21, 15, 21). In exuberant delight at this gift from God, Taylor further extends his images into a cardio-vascular dissection: "This bit of Humane Flesh Divinizd in/ The Person of the Son of God" is like "the Cell/ Of Soule, and Blood, where Love Divine doth swim/ Through veans, through Arteries, Heart flesh, and fell" that "Doth with its Circkling Arms about entwinde/ A Portion of its kindred choice, Mankinde" (II.34.25–30).

Taylor's multilayered images so tightly interwoven into cumulative comparisons create an intricate representation of the incarnation, but Taylor also frequently invokes discrete images in other poems. In Meditation II.45 Christ's "Person's Wisdoms Sparkling Treasury" unites "blest infinity" with "a Locker of a Humane frame/ With richer than Corinthian Amber tills/ And Shelves of Emralds," or shines "Like to a Sparkling Carbuncle up Caskt/ Within a Globe of Chrystall glass most cleare" (II.45.13, 15, 19–21, 25–6). Christ becomes the "Choice pearle-made-Box" in Meditation II.50.23 and in II.99 a "China Dish" and "Golden Viol full of gracious Grace/ Whose flashing Shine out shines the Angells face" (II.99.25, 35–6). The repeated use of gems as a variant of the kernel recalls Revelation's unhewn palace walls studded so brilliantly and circling the Deity's throne in heaven, but here the particled essence resides in a human body, nay even descends into the darkness of a mortal grave. In the macrocosmos beyond man's ken God reigns so supreme that the very notion of His immense circumference ("All-Might," "Canopie," "Circkling Arms") contracting to the size of a "Mite," "Pearle," or kernel, much less embedded within earthbound globes, treasuries, cabinets, shells, nuts, boxes excites Taylor's wonder at God's omnipresence without and within the universe, the world, and the soul and at Christ's humility in descending to take on a human body and reside within this fallen garden.

Having accepted, though never fully comprehended, Christ's para-doxical incarnation, Taylor himself longs to be nucleated with a spark from the divine spirit. As Albert Gelpi concludes, "once God had become flesh, the duality which is the law of matter and of human sexuality could be resolved, by His own design, only in our integration and perfection as human beings."[17] But human transmutation is not easily accomplished. Unlike Christ's mystical assumption of a human form, the innately

corrupt body remains too sinful to receive a new spirit without mediation. Taylor conceives of his own body (and soul) as "A Bran, a Chaff,
a very Barly yawn,/ An Husk, a Shell, a Nothing," a "Pouch of Sin, a
purse/ Of Naughtiness" (II.18.1–2, 4–5), a "Mudwall tent, whose Mat-
ters are/ Dead Elements," "A varnisht pot of putrid excrements," a "Vile
Bodie" and diseased soul (II.75.13–14, 25). The emptiness that requires
filling, the vessel that needs a revitalizing liquor, the shell that needs
again a seed within can receive invigoration from nothing other than the
gracious spirit that flows from Christ. Hence, Taylor repeatedly calls
upon Christ to quicken him through an impregnation that finds its
closest analogy in sexual fertilization:

> The Soule's the Womb. Christ is the Spermodote
>   And Saving Grace the seed cast thereinto
> This Life's the principall in Graces Coate,
>   Making vitality in all things flow,
>   In Heavenly verdure brisking holily
>   With sharp ey'de peartness of Vivacity.
>   (II.80.31–6)

The processes by which such invigoration occurs, however, reflect the
diverse types and metaphors for Christ Himself, since it is in His image
that the seemingly irredeemable soul becomes once more refigure. If Christ
shines as the "Sun of Righteousness," then man becomes "thy Lunar
Body to be filld" (II.21.33, 31); if He spews forth "lovely streams of
Love," Taylor's receptive being becomes "my Viall, and my Vessell" to
contain it (II.32.49, 51); or when with "Graces stoute" Christ erects a
"garison against my foes and thine," thereafter the "Soul" becomes
"Walled around about/ With Orient Pearle fetcht out of holy Mine/ And
made a Castle" (II.42.15, 16, 13–15). Whether as a sacramental "Cask"
to receive "thy rich Love its Wine" or a "heart" to be "Impregnate[d]
with its Spirits" (II.98.43, 44), Taylor becomes transfigured through this
infusion of divine grace, love, and truth that emanates from Christ. That
grace, metaphorically expressed as rays, beams, streams, fountains, wine,
sparks, heat, and light, flows through pipes, channels, gutters, veins,
spouts, sluices, limbs, or roots and can be drawn up in buckets from
Christ the "Well of Living Water" (II.47.25). Once "faith" becomes the
"Key" to "back the Wards" on the imprisoned soul, Christ enters in to
"Set in my Soule a lamp to light that place/ That so these beames let in,
may generate/ Grace in my Soule, and so an Holy State" (II.45.37, 38,
46–8). By portraying grace suffusing and irradiating from within his being,
Taylor seeks obsessively to recreate himself in the image of Christ incar-
nate.

Images of grace flowing from the all-vitalizing source to a parched, begrimed receptacle implicitly recall humanity's original separation from the Godhead, a divorce and resulting dichotomy between flesh and spirit that Taylor further seeks to dissolve through poetic metaphors of mutual habitation, interchange, and mediation. To possess divine grace within is not only to contain God, but also to be contained by Him, to receive the circling arms of His embrace, to enter into the habitations of the Lord. As early as 1679 in his Foundation Day Sermon, Taylor had chosen his text from Ephesians 2:22, *"In whom you are also builded (up) together, for an Habitation of God through the Spirit,"* which he interpreted to apply to the whole church of the Elect, specifically to the new Westfield congregation, and to all saints who individually must become habitations of the spirit before entering worthily into membership (*CRRS,* p. 118). He also cautioned that the *"Modus Habitandi"* of "Gods presence . . . is by his Spirit, not in a visible but in a Spirituall way," an inhabiting that Taylor repeatedly attempts to express through his later poetic metaphors and conceits (*CRRS,* p. 142). In a complicated series of reciprocal images and pronouns, Taylor in Meditation II.24 finds that Christ "wilst mee thy, and thee, my tent to bee./ Thou wilt, if I my heart will to thee rent,/ My Tabernacle make thy Tenement," for "I'le be thy Tabernacle: thou shalt bee/ My Tabernacle. Lord thus mutuall wee" (II.24.46–8, 59–60). In this poem both Christ and the saint become virtual antitypes to the Old Testament tabernacle, since each possesses a human frame (tent) within which divinity harbors (like the ark of the covenant within the holy of holies). The mutuality, expressed in the contractual terms of tenancy, stems from Taylor's recognition that Christ both motivates the worship from within the heart's tabernacle *and* becomes the medium or tabernacle through which each saint offers praises to God: "Thou art my Medium to God, thou art/ My Medium of Worship done to thee,/ And of Divine Communion, Sweet heart!/ Oh Heavenly intercourse!" (II.20.49–52). Christ serves first as the obedient Son Who mediates on mankind's behalf with the Father, then through the incarnation becomes God's medium to dispense grace, funneling it into "Fistulate," yet receptive hearts. In return, each soul renewed by grace offers back to God through the medium of Christ praises, whether in the form of church membership, holy worship, life, and conversation, partaking of the Supper, or poetic meditations. New England Puritans found no need for ornamented chapels, votary candles, or priestly mediations, because under an evangelical dispensation the heart's temple becomes the Lord's habitation and reciprocally the Lord becomes the holiest of holy tabernacles (a perfect antitype) within which all saints live and worship. Possessive pronouns and echoes of the wedding ceremony rather than a figural conceit convey the essence of Taylor's understanding in Meditation II.79: "I'm Thine, Thou Mine! Mutuall propriety:/ Thou giv'st thyselfe. And for this gift takst mee/ To be thine own. I give myselfe (poore toy)/ And take thee for myne own, and so to bee" (II.79.19–22). Only Christ's theanthropic union that weds flesh with spirit makes possible this subsequent "mutuall claim" that conjoins divine God with human sinner in an eternal "weddenwise" embrace (II.79.31, 30).

Throughout the typological meditations and the later Christological ones (II.31–114), Taylor struggles to convey the rich significance of the new evangelical relationship, often resorting to attenuated analyses of paradoxes or verbal sleight of hand by which "Mine, thine" become "Predicates unto us both" (II.79.32). But with increasing regularity he also turns in the *Preparatory Meditations* to the scriptural metaphor of marriage, most beautifully rendered in the allegorical Song of Solomon, to express his desire for a union in which the "mee" and "thee" of humanity and divinity become wed eternally into a "mutuall wee" (II.24.60). Canticles abounds with spiritualized sexual images of the Bride and Bridegroom (who in theological tradition stand for the church or soul and Christ respectively), wedded bliss, gems, and gardens, the very metaphors that weave together fine threads of imagery from Taylor's previous meditations. He inaugurates the final sequence (II.115–165), almost entirely on Canticles, with a tone of astonished wonder and passionate commitment: "What art thou mine? Am I espousd to thee?" for if so, then "Oh! make my Heart loaded with Love ascend/ Up to thyselfe, its bridegroom, bright, and Friend" (II.115.1, 5–6). When he possessed a husk for a heart, a "Pouch of Sin," he hardly dared believe in Christ's promises of spiritual union; here he ecstatically embraces the full and fulfilling meaning of evangelical marriage, though a marriage yet to be consummated at the eternal nuptial feast. Whereas before he yearned for a divine spark and "blesst Bellows" to strike his soul's "Coale" into "Loves hottest Steams" (II.6.49, 50), now he bursts forth with unrestrained ardor, for "The ripest Fruits that my affections beare/ I offer, thee. Oh! my Beloved faire," and "The Stories/ Within my Soul can hold refinde most pure/ In flaming bundles polishd all with Grace/ Most sparklingly about thyselfe t'imbrace" (II.115.17–18, 21–4). Once the soul remained closed against Christ, here the "Holy Word" becomes the "golden Key" that opens the heart to be filled "with Grace refining Love" in an eternal reciprocity that need only be affirmed, not rationalized or dissected. "Be thou my onely Well-Belov'd I pray," Taylor prays, "And make my Heart with all its Love right move/ Unto thyselfe, and all her Love display," for "My Love is then right well bestow'd, alone/ When it obtains thyselfe her Lovely One" (II.115.44–8).

Drawing upon the long tradition of Protestant spiritual interpretations of Canticles as an allegory for the church's and soul's marriage to Christ, Taylor clearly discovers the most effective scriptural text through which to express both his desire and satisfaction.[18] By identifying himself with the Bride, Taylor becomes the female vessel seeking to be filled with grace and love and finds all-fullness in the Bridegroom, who embraces, impregnates, and satiates the spiritual appetite. As the Bride, the soul finds its greatest happiness in reflecting the glory of the Beloved, but more so in relinquishing twoness (body and soul, male and female, flesh and spirit, human and divine) for oneness, a spiritual union only partially emblemized by human sexual consummation. Though Taylor may seem to echo the eroticism of Canticles and Renaissance love sonnets, he clearly adhered to Puritan theories of spiritual interpretation, as articulated by exegetes, such as James Durham in *Clavis Cantici*.[19] Marriage for Taylor, as for other poets, provided the metaphor most analogous to that union that remains inexpressible, the eternal joining/wedding in which pure spirit mates with spirit, in which flesh drops away. No matter the ardency of physical desire nor the ecstasy of consummation, the human expression of eros remains merely a metaphoric and conceptual approximation to the reality of *agape*.[20]

In typology, as we have seen, Christ's dual nature fulfills all types, but presents mankind with the impenetrable paradox of divinity conjoined with a human form. In turn, that miraculous union of spirit and flesh opens up the potential that all redeemed saints might one day share in this jointure – through faith in Christ, an infusion of grace, and in the eternal marriage. Hence, Taylor's Christocentric typology leads almost inevitably to his final poetic epithalamium, one gloriously rich in its poetic artistry as Taylor seeks to render metaphorically, and thereby to apprehend, the hoped for eschatological state of transcendence in which the dichotomies of body and soul, human and divine dissolve. Albert Gelpi correctly asserts that "Taylor's poems represent his attempt to pitch himself beyond the paradoxes and divisions of our natural experience, epitomized in the sexual polarity, into a transpolar, transsexual, androgynous wholeness of mind and heart and soul posited in the images of God husbanding human nature and manhood brided to Godhead."[21] Typology's Christocentric fulfillment and the saint's union with Christ as Bride and Bridegroom, portrayed in the Canticles poems, turn the *Preparatory Meditations* not merely into tortured examinations of Taylor's own soul and his journey toward salvation but as well into an extended "Love Letter," one continuous series of psalms of praise in which cumulative metaphors, images, conceits, types, and allegories gradually turn his vision from the earthbound to the eschatological.

Typology further predicated not simply a fulfillment in historical time with Christ's advent, but also the setting in motion of a new schema of prophecy that looks from the New Testament to the *eschaton*. This developmental assumption provided the basis for seventeenth-century attempts to see in successive dispensations the closer approach to the millennium, an interpretation that among colonial chroniclers led to the emergence of a distinctively American mythology of historical progressivism.[22] But this schema also takes on a faintly Neoplatonic cast by envisioning the Old Testament as a repository of literal, external rituals and personal types, or in short, a world bounded by nature and time. When under the evangelical dispensation Christ chooses to enter nature, He does so to illuminate the superiority of a spiritual fulfillment and, hence, of the life of grace for the would-be saint. That spiritual life in turn finds its ultimate completion only in the heavenly realm where God and His redeemed live forever. We may also recall in the commonplace metaphors used to define typology, the distinctions among the artist's rude draft or "smutty lineaments" of the Messiah yet to come, the portrait in "evangelicall colours" of Christ incarnate, and the reality of a gloriously transcendent Christ invisible to mortal sight. Correspondingly, the exegete reads with ever increasing clarity the "signs" first of Christ adumbrated in Old Testament shadows, then spiritually manifest in the New Testament records of His life, yet he can only imagine, as through a glass darkly, the full radiant glory to be unveiled when the saints will "see" Christ face to face. In Taylor's *Preparatory Meditations* the assumption of progressively clearer revelations underlies imagistic and structural patterns in the second series and also illuminates the ways in which Taylor defines the limits and ambitions of the poet and poetic language.

Taylor's metaphors remain too imaginatively varied to fall into neatly prescribed patterns, but through repeated usage they often gather a resonance that underscores the movement from Old Testament types to eschatological visions. In addition to an increasing use of sexual metaphors from the Song of Solomon, Taylor invokes the related images of gardens and feasts that cumulate into dominant leitmotifs in the second series. Drawing upon the Bible, he portrays gardens, beginning with Eden's fall and ending with the paradisaical garden, and feasts derived from the Old Testament Passover that foreshadows the evangelical Lord's Supper, which in turn anticipates the heavenly nuptial feast. Both figures, developed over a lifetime, mirror the progress of Taylor's soul, and as metaphoric strands lead him inevitably toward the capstone series on Canticles in his old age. Though glimmers of "That Bowre" of Eden "pollished most gay" in which Adam together with "every ranck/ Of Creatures in't shone bright" hover at the edges of the early typological poems, this once Edenic state falls rapidly into the decay of "Beauty blasted" and "Bliss befrighted" (II.28.1, 2–3, 12), for so "poor" a "keeper hee/ Was of himselfe" that man "lost God, and lost his Glee" (II.30.11–12). Descended from the original Adam, Taylor characterizes himself as a "Garden over grown with weeds," whose "Soile is sandy," "Stock is stunted," and "branch no good Fruits breeds" (II.4.2, 3, 4). A "fiery Bramble," thorny with "Hypocrisie, Pride Poison, Gall," he requires an implanting in "Gods true vine" or "Olive tree" in order to bear "sweet Roses" and fruit once again (II.16.21, 43, 35, 37, 42). Under the New Testament dispensation Christ creates a new garden, doubly defined, to receive the evangelical saints: "This Garden, Lord," is both "thy Church, this Paradise" and also "the Soule, of thy Redeem'd" (II.83.19, 20, 21, 25). With the shift from the types of fallen nature to the Christological promises of regeneration, Taylor bemoans loss less and envisions with greater hope his soul as "thy Garden" and "thy Vineyard, and my plants thy Vine" (II.83.31, 32) in which he will thrive beneath Christ's sunshine (II.54), suck "In Aromatick aire of blesst perfume" (II.63.52), blossom like a lily (II.69), feast on "bitter Myrrh" and "Sweet Spices" (II.84.23, 22), and nurture an herb garden set with "True Love. Herb of Grace with Rosie Sheds" (II.86.33). Under the new Covenant of Grace, Christ's garden spiritually signifies not only His church and redeemed souls, but also His very Being in which the saints implant and thus harvest the abundance that outdoes any earthly or Old Testament counterpart, even the "Vines of Lebanon," "Engedi's Vineyard," or "Mount Olivet" (II.65.1, 7, 13). But this evangelical cornucopia still remains inferior to that new Edenic paradise that Taylor anticipates in heaven, the "Zions Paradise, Christs Garden Deare/ His Church, enwalld, with Heavenly Crystall fine/ Hath every Bed beset with Pearle all Clear/ And Allies Opald with Gold, and Silver Shrine," in which "The Sparkling Plants, Sweet Spices, Herbs and Trees,/ The glorious Shews of aromatick Flowers" flourish beneath Christ's eternally "Sweet Showers of Grace" (II.63.25–8, 31–2, 35). In that garden, most fittingly emblemized by the *hortus conclusus* of Canticles overlaid with visions of jeweled castles from Revelation, the "Elect Lillies gather" (II.131.38), saints who "with Gusts of Spirituall Odors" (II.130.33) are sustained by Christ as both garden and "my Gardener" (II.85.37). Just as Taylor's pronouns and other images of containment reinforce the concept of a reciprocal union, so too the garden signifies the "Soule Christs Spouse" *and* Christ's being within which mankind newly plants his roots.

In similar fashion Taylor also progresses throughout the second series of *Preparatory Meditations* from the multiple Jewish feasts (atonement, tabernacles, Passover) to the singular New Testament Lord's Supper (II.102–111), which merely adumbrates the heavenly nuptial feast. Rife with echoes from earlier meditations on old and new feasts, Meditation II.157B gloriously praises "Christs Banquet's all of Sugar Cake": the "Meate and Drink is best ten thousand fold/ Of th'Paschall Mutton," the "Banquits Fare, it's Christ himself, the Rock," the "Drinke here drunk is Zions water red/ It is the Blood of the Grape that" bled from the "true

true Vine" out of Christ's side, and the "Saints are its Guests" attended by "Angells the servitors" in a festal display in which "All things hereof" are "super superlative" (II.157B.24, 25–6, 28, 37–8, 40, 43, 44, 47). More poignant because Taylor's old age confronts him with his own inescapable mortality, this meditation also reminds us that every preceding meditation has been a preparation not simply for the Lord's Supper administered to the church at Westfield, but also for the eschatological wedding feast. Many of Taylor's last poems resound with echoes, as in Meditation II.157B, from his decades of sustained poetic meditation leading from the typological to the Christological to the eschatological visions derived from Canticles. Structurally he deliberately inaugurates his second series of meditations with the concentrated analysis of biblical types (1693–99), sporadically returning to them again in 1703–4 (II.58–61) and 1706 (II.70–71). From 1699 to 1713 he settles into a varied exploration of Christ's nature, occasionally in longer consecutive sequences to accompany the *Christographia* sermons (II.42–56) or on the Lord's Supper (II.102–111). More frequently, shorter clusters topically and/or textually delimited focus upon Christ as, for example, the head of the body which is the church from Colossians 1:18 (II.36–40) or the sun of righteousness (II.67A, 67B, 68A, 68B), whereas apparently unlinked single poems explore other scriptural metaphors, among them Christ as the true vine (II.98), root and offspring of David (II.113), and bright and morning star (II.114). Taylor devotes forty-nine of his later meditations (from 1713 to 1725), with only four exclusions (II.154–155, 158–159), to the study of the allegorical Canticles, and hence his anticipation of death and the eschatological wedding with the Bridegroom.[23] In Canticles, Taylor perhaps finds at last the emblems of heaven eternal, his journey's destination, that he repeatedly seeks throughout the *Preparatory Meditations,* the garden Paradise in which the saints bloom, the wedding with the Bridegroom that binds him forever to Christ, and a feast that satisfies the hungry soul with angels' banquets and with the elixir of immortal life that transcends all material substance and nature.

Because typology presumes superior dispensations progressing from the Old Testament to the New Testament to the *eschaton,* Taylor readily discovers in it the paradigm for portraying the parallel needs of the soul to move beyond the natural life (Adam's fallen estate) to Christ's evangelical revelations of a new spiritual life, to the eternal life consummating the saint's earthly betrothal. He envisions that progress explicitly in Meditations II.87–90 (lacking II.88) on John 10:10, "I am come that they might have life, and that they might have it more abundantly." In a metaphor both intimate and cosmic, Meditation II.89 captures the natural world's birth from nonentity into being. "What Birth of Wonders from thy Fingers ends/ Dropt, when the World, Lord, dropt out of the

Womb/ Of its Non-Entity for to attende/ Thy Will its Cradle," Taylor
exclaims, "And its Midwife Strong./ Non-Entity in Travail full did bare/
The World, big belli'd with all Wonders rare" (II.89.1–6). Hardly an
attempt to deify nature that anticipates nineteenth-century transcendentalism, this depiction instead lauds God the Creator, whose "Vitall Heate"
not only sparks the world into miraculous life, but whose "Fingers" (calling
to mind Michelangelo's Sistine Chapel) also "freely dropt into/ The
Humane shaped Elements and made" man "Excell the Rest and nobler
goe" (II.89.11, 19–20, 21). But this metaphoric evocation of *natura creata*
merely sets off Christ's supreme transcending of nature with spirit, a feat
necessitated ever since "man by Sin hath lost all life, and marr'd/ Himselfe eternally," reaping "Death" as "his reward" (II.89.23–4). Christ,
the second Adam, provides the only recourse for man who seeks spiritually to recreate himself in God's image, for "Life Naturall indeed is in
the Bill/ Thou with thy Father drewst up, it to buy./ Life Spirituall much
more; which ever Will/ As Heaven doth Earth, all Naturall Life out Vie"
(II.89.31–4). According to Taylor's strict Puritan reading of typology
and a morphology of conversion, the "Spirituall Life" outwardly gilds
"Saints Souls and Conversation" with "Godlike Glory of a Gracious
Shine," transforms the human backbone into a "Superstructure" of "Holy
Life Divine," and rekindles the soul's vital spark, the "Richest Jewell in
the Cabinet/ Of Nature made" (II.89.43, 44, 45, 46, 47–8). But in the
saint's "Pilgrimage" spiritual life is merely a way station, since only death
releases man from the natural life and opens the way back to the eternal
source, the ineffable "Spring of Life, and Life of bliss" (II.90.34, 33). The
Puritan typologist remains literally worlds apart from the Emersonian
transcendentalist, for only the resurrected Christ, not the indwelling Holy
Spirit, and a translation from this world to heaven delivers the saint into
"Eternall Life." Taylor succinctly defines that life "in a right Sense" as
"this./ That All things blissful do to it belong/ Life Naturall, and Spiri-
tuall Life's in bliss/ Eternizde in Eternall Joyes that throng" (II.90.19–
22). Any attempt at further rational definition dissolves into superlatives:
"Oh! richest gift ere gi'n!/ Worth more than thousands Worlds: all Heaven
above,/ Whole Heavens of Love," wherein saints enjoy forever "Ripe
Grace in all its Orient Blossoms bright/ Ripe Glory in its flower of brightest
Shine,/ Ripe joy upon the highest branch full ripe" (II.90.50–2, 43–5).
This ecstatic vision of eternal life, transcending both man's and the world's
inherently fallen nature and also the spiritual life rational creatures can
achieve, is the goal of Taylor's pilgrimage as a Puritan saint, expressed
in both his theological writings and *Preparatory Meditations*. The desired
progress from natural to spiritual to eternal life applies to all the Elect.
But Taylor is not only saint but also singer. And the attainment of a
human language spiritualized that approximates the eternal, or even its

near echo in God's Holy Scripture, and that prepares the way for divine hymns of glory becomes the goal of his poetics: an "Eternall Life" will "gild my Harp O're very gloriously" and "spiritualize my Strings thy tunes to play," for "Life Naturall's the Base: the Spirituall is/ The Meane: the Tenour is Eternall Bliss" (II.90.56, 57, 58, 59–60).

Taylor's pursuit of the spiritual life preparatory to the eternal is thus the substance of each individual meditation and shapes as well his lengthy autobiographical series. The purposes of typology may sometimes seem to end with the fulfillment and, consequently, with exegetical readings that extrapolate correspondences between the Old and New Testaments, as Taylor does in *Upon the Types of the Old Testament*. But rational analysis has no effect without its devotional extension into the very lives of Puritan saints, a tropological application that Taylor achieves through his meditative lyrics. An integral part of the process by which Christ's grace abides within the heart, governing moral behavior and preparing the soul for eternity, Taylor's poetics become not simply an exercise but a spiritual necessity. Often a task more than an overflow of spontaneous feeling, the composition of the *Preparatory Meditations* is a self-imposed discipline, for even when his "leane Muses garden thwarts the spring," still "duty raps upon her doore for Verse./ That makes her bleed a poem through her searce [strainer]" (II.30.3, 5–6). In the *Treatise Concerning the Lord's Supper,* Taylor includes meditation as an essential part of the saint's preparation, a wedding garment to be assumed for the immediate festival of the Sacrament *and* for the eventual divine nuptials in heaven. As a devout Puritan Taylor recognizes that election is not guaranteed nor sanctification an end in itself. He must, therefore, through poetry constantly feed his soul with spiritual nourishment, keeping it vital by calling for Christ's implanting, by approximating the divine image, or by seeking to insert himself in a nearer relationship with Christ via the types, Christomimetic imitations, or the allegorical roles of Canticles.

It may seem simplistic, but nonetheless true, to affirm that Taylor uses homiletic analyses in the meditations to appeal to his reason and derivative tropes to rouse the affections, because the meditative process, as Louis Martz and Norman Grabo suggest, requires that the understanding give rise to holy affections, thence moving the will (or heart) to pursue more ardently a state of grace and sanctification.[24] Repeatedly Taylor acknowledges the limitations of reason alone: "Nay Speeches Bloomery can't from the Ore/ Of Reasons mine, melt words for to define/ Thy Deity, nor t'deck the reeches that sore/ From Loves rich Vales, sweeter than hony rhimes" and "Words though the finest twine of reason, are/ Too Course a web for Deity to ware" (II.43.7–10, 11–12). Similarly, the "stund affections all with Cinders clag'd" (II.36.33), or like "the Lake/ . . . frozen ore with ice/ And Spirits Crampt" seem initially recalcitrant and unaspiring (II.53.1–3). But the act/art of meditating itself can transform the "Heart" into a musical "Harp: and mine Affections brac'de/ With gracious Grace thy Golden Strings to shake/ With Quavers of thy glory well begrac'de," that once so "tun'de by thy Spirits Skill" (II.54.8–10, 12), he can "Chime my affections in/ To serve thy Sacred selfe with Sacred art" (II.36.39–40). For Taylor habitual, disciplined meditation is the *raison d'être* for his poetics. Within his poetics types, Christ's fulfillment, and eschatological visions provide the matter; figural conceits and Scripture metaphors the manner; and "tropological" poesy a fitting worship mold for the soul. As rational exegesis and as poetic hymns, Taylor's meditations serve a dual purpose, both to foster understanding through sequential proofs and narratives and also to provoke insight and inspiration through flights of metaphor and conceit. Hence, Taylor's poems reflect the same fusion of literal scriptural text and spiritual interpretation that undergirds the Puritan exegesis of biblical types and allegories. The divinely ordained figures, literal and timebound albeit prophetic, point always toward a superior spiritual truth, the shell to the kernel, typal persons to Christ incarnate and risen. Poetry in its literalism as text, even when echoing the Scripture itself or at its most metaphoric, remains always an approximation, a mere outward form, a dark glass or sketch, in which nuggets of illumination lurk, ever unrevealed in their fullest splendor – until language is no more and spirit reigns eternal.

Even in turning to the Old Testament types, gospel fulfillments, and the allegory of Canticles for his themes and metaphors, Taylor ultimately confronts the cul-de-sac of language and of human imagination. No matter the ardency of his desire or his poetic skill, "Things styld Transcendent, do transcende the Stile/ Of Reason," and that transcendent style and voice continually elude him (II.44.7–8). The meditations themselves testify to the nature of human limitations because they are formally restricted by a six-line stanza, the confines of one poet's imagination, and by the inescapable medium of words. And Taylor deplores the limitations of language as a corollary of human sin:

> Words Mentall are syllabicated thoughts:
>   Words Orall but thoughts Whiffld in the Winde.
> Words Writ, are incky, Goose quill-slabbred draughts,
>   Although the fairest blossoms of the minde.
>   Then can such glasses cleare enough descry
>   My Love to thee, or thy rich Deity?
>
> Words are befould, Thoughts filthy fumes that smoake,
>   From Smutty Huts, like Will-a-Wisps that rise
> From Quaugmires, run ore bogs where frogs do Croake,
>   Lead all astray led by them by the eyes.

My muddy Words so dark thy Deity,
And cloude thy Sun-Shine, and its Shining Sky.
(II.43.13–24)

"Whiffld in the Winde," "Goose quill-slabbred," "filthy fumes," words are after all merely signs, not things or objective realities, surely not transcendent ones. Language approximates, but it does not realize transcendent truths. Even as he traces the spiritual life, hoping to make his poems habitations of divine grace, Taylor surrenders to imperfection: "My choisest words when spoke are then/ Articulated Breath, soon disappeare./ If wrote are but the Drivle of my pen/ Beblackt with my inke, soon torn worn out" (II.142.2–5). Imperfection will never yield to perfection of spirit or poetry, fallenness can never be overcome in the temporal world, and transcendent felicity is beyond the power of language to express, or so Taylor believes.[25] Hence, he bitterly deprecates his own "Metaphors" as "but dull Tacklings tag'd/ With ragged Non-Sense" (II.36.31–2) and his "tatter'd Fancy; and my Ragged Rymes" that "Teeme leaden Metaphors," when the "Spirituall Life doth better fare deserve" (II.82.1, 2, 4). All images, metaphors, conceits are part of poetry's innate imperfection, though Taylor still attempts by imitating the biblical Psalms to express the essence of Christ's divinity. Within the context of Puritan theology, all human language, poetry included, remains an uneasy fusion of spiritual matter imprisoned within inky letters, syllables, and words.

In Taylor's postlapsarian world, poetic language is by definition misshapen, syntactically tortured, cacophonous, filled with slant rhymes, caged within rigidly inflexible stanzas.[26] This inherent linguistic crudity appears in the cranky peculiarities of Taylor's diction, the "rags, and jags: so snicksnarld to the thrum" (II.56.6), crafted by a "jarring Pen" that "makes but a ragged line" (II.132.11). "Feeble terms I use/ Whose Selvedge, Hem, and Web weare Sorry Shews" (II.122.5–6), Taylor proclaims, words blurted from the "lisping tongue" that "can but stut and blur what I/ Do go about and so indeed much marre" (II.138.3, 7–8). Taylor's rough-hewn New England colloquialisms capture the insufficiency of human speech and of self-generated metaphors to capture God's divine essence created or increate. The curious, by now obsolete, jargon of rural life adds an antiquated primitivism to Taylor's poems: "pingle," "frim," "spangle," "sprindge," "gudgeons," "tantarrow'd," "womble-Crops," "glout," "rence wring," "frindge," "saddlebackt," "peckled," "quorns," "searcde," "bibble," and "simnill." But his diction also ranges from the eccentric and homely to the erudite and esoteric, from the technical precision of figural exegesis to flights of fancy and tumbles of metaphoric flourishes, from the rational to the emotional and spiritual, the scatological to the eschatological. At times diction alone suggests Taylor's struggle between an earthbound sinner's lot in which "dung," "sickness," "putrefaction," and "vomit" persist and the saint's aspirations to be lofted into heaven's air, where "sweet Spice Showers of Precious grace" waft fragrantly amid God's "Spicey Garden green," far removed from the unplanted wilderness of New England's frostbitten clime (II.131.27, 17). But no matter how saliently the diction renders these oppositions between human and godly realms, a sinner's life and saint's longings, it also continually reminds Taylor of the fallenness of language and his ineffectual efforts to break the bonds of all human speech.

Despite its feeble inadequacy, language is the best man has to offer. It is the only medium given to rational creatures to speak of spiritual truths, to express visions of Christ, and to convey God's splendor or the anticipated eschatological union. "The words my pen doth teem are far too Faint/ And not significant enough to shew/ Thy Famous fame or mine affection paint," Taylor bemoans with one breath, "But thus I force myselfe to speake of thee./ If I had better thou shouldst better have" (II.132.7–9, 13–14). For a poet steeped in theology, scholastic proofs, and ramistic logic, the vocabulary of reason offers one option, certainly more acceptable than the vocabulary of scatalogy, that constantly reminds Taylor of man's undeserving bestiality. And Taylor turns to the rational, orderly discourse in his poetry as a vehicle for overcoming sin and searching for grace. What seems an imposed order, a predictable patterning in many poems in the *Preparatory Meditations* is his attempt to control the chaotic aberrations of the animal and natural life, human desire and despair. Hence, typology's methodical exegesis yields spiritual insights, reveals Christ as human preacher and antitype, yet God's Son and heaven's King, and allows Taylor to puzzle out the parallels with the "mentall Eye" and "Visive Spirits of the Holy Ghost" (II.72.1, 2). Yet Taylor recognizes the crude formulations of purely rational discourse, for "Reason stands for it, moving to persue't./ But Flesh and Blood, are Elementall things./ That sink me down, dulling my Spirits fruit./ Life Animall a Spirituall Sparke ne'er springs" (II.82.7–10). In the pursuit of transcendent truths he must develop another language:

> I fain would praise thee, but want words to do't:
>   And searching ore the realm of thoughts finde none
> Significant enough and therefore vote
>   For a new set of Words and thoughts hereon
>   And leap beyond the line such words to gain
>   In other Realms, to praise thee: but in vain.
>   (II.106.7–12)

Though in an inevitably vain pursuit of divinely transcendent language, Taylor still seeks a new vocabulary for his "Sacred art," composed of

Scripture metaphors and types elaborated into conceits, albeit still the products of a limited human imagination that only approximates God's creative power. The impossibility does not, however, detract from the search, a relentless one, for higher inspiration, for a purified tongue, for more adequate tropes. And in that search, Taylor turns to Christ as his Muse and to Old Testament types as his models.

Christ, who is the Word made flesh and fulfills the Old Testament's prophecies, sanctions the Bible as God's repository of words, images, types, metaphors, and allegories, all of which convey the message and are the medium of communication between God and his elect saints.[27] According to Taylor, the poet's task resembles the typologist's, because both require an inspired sight with which to read the signs within biblical texts: "Its the internall Eye Sight takes this thing/ This glorious light the Sin blind Eye doth miss./ Th'Internall Eye with Christ's Eye Salve annointed/ Is on this beauteous face alone well pointed," Taylor exclaims in a familiar plea, echoed often in requests for spectacles, glasses, eye-salves, and for sparkling rays that pierce and refine the sight (II.147.33–6). Fitted with "Spectacles . . . / Made of a pair of Stars" (II.21.29–30) with which to peer into the "Looking-glass" of types, Taylor needs only the "Spirit" to "wipe my Watry eyes/ That I may see his flashing glory darte/ Like Lightening quick till it infire my heart" and ignite the poetic flame (II.9.51, 52–4). There are poets who read signs and those who create them. Taylor is of the first camp, perceiving himself as a conduit and amanuensis for the spirit that writes in and through him. His spiritual insight, imagination, and poetic language are all gifts from God. The "Spirit" is Christ, His infused grace, and the Holy Spirit that rouses the soul's affections and moves the will to religious meditation and poetic creation. Albert Gelpi draws a useful distinction; he asserts:

> All poets employ tropes, but only some see types. . . . The poet who has little or no typological sense will have to order experience into art through the innate, unaided powers of his craft and his imaginative scope; the form and meaning of the poem are a matter of mind moving tongue. The poet who has a strong and operative sense of types will respond to the sign and speak as a medium or seer. Taylor and Edwards would have identified such a vessel with the elected man of grace.[28]

Edward Taylor surely equates the poet with the religious medium and seer. For him the eyes, ears, and other sensing faculties become inlets to the soul, within which divine sparks of grace fuel the imaginative fires, thereby stimulating the expression of the spiritual life through poetic art.

In defining the nature of his poetic power, however, Taylor betrays a not uncommon medieval and Renaissance fusion of the terms "fancy" from the Greek *phantasia* and "imagination" from the Latin *imaginatio,* used interchangeably to designate the faculty or processes by which images are received (passively) and also formed or invented (actively). Taylor clearly acknowledges God as the source or archetype of divine imagination, echoing the sixteenth-centry rhetorician George Puttenham, who compared the poet to God, the Creator " 'who without any travail to his Divine Imagination made all the world of nought.' "[29] In its healthy, ordered state, imagination serves the rational soul by transmitting accurate images of sense data and by creating or inventing them, and in its highest capacity imagination mirrors divinely revealed truths (or beauty) through an imitative art. But potentially uncontrolled, immoral, and susceptible to onslaughts of passion (love or worldly vanities), the imagination can also be distorted, thereby falsely reporting and inventing images, as happens so delightfully and instructively in the lovers' fantasies of Shakespeare's *A Midsummer Night's Dream*.[30] Defenders of poetic imagination countered the accusations against this deluded, often irrational power, but the mistrust of the "lesser" fancy remained intense among the Neoplatonists, Stoics, and Church Fathers, including Augustine. Other theorists, such as the Neoplatonist Plotinus, distinguished a fantasy reflective of ideas "higher" because a function of the rational soul. As William Rossky concludes about English Renaissance views, "There evolves a concept of poetic feigning: that poetic feigning is a glorious compounding of images beyond life, of distortions which are yet verisimilar imitations, expressing a truth to reality and yet a higher truth also, controlled by the practical purpose, the molding power, and, in almost every aspect, by the reason and morality of the poet."[31]

Taylor denigrates the decadent fancy as a product of the sin-wracked sensual life that infects the human vision and voice. He variously depicts the fancy as a "foolish fire enflam'd by toys," the world's vanities (II.25.16), as "stagnate" with "Spirits Crampt" (II.53.1, 3), as "Chilly" (II.64), "rusty" (II.92), and "Dull, Dull" (II.131). He closely allies the "frozen" state of this poetic faculty with the frostbitten spirit and affections that require Christ's revivifying fires: "My Muses Hermetage is grown so old/ Her Spirits shiver doe, her Phancy's Laws/ Are much transgresst. She sits so Crampt with cold," but Christ's "Hands" may "my Chil'd Spirits into raptures put/ Of right delight of an Extatick Cut" (II.122.8–10, 23–4). Or if the "Fancy's rusty" and dull, he pleads for the Lord to "rub/ And brighten't on an Angels Rubston sharp./ Furbish it with thy Spirits File," that so to "Quicken my Fancy Lord; and mend my Pen," he will "Flowerish up the same, as brightest Gem" (II.92.1–3, 11–12). Taylor thus pursues the "higher" poetic imagination, conceiving of it as virtually synonymous with God-given spiritual insight and creative power, an imagination that is an aspect of transcendent reason. Hence, he yearns for "Ye Angells bright" to "pluck from your Wings a Quill./ Make me a pen thereof that best will write./ Lende me your fancy, and Angellick skill/ To treate this Theme, more rich than Rubies bright," for lacking that transcendent inspiration and example, "My muddy Inke, and Cloudy fancy dark,/ Will dull its glory, lacking highest Art" (II.60B.1–4, 5–6). According to Taylor's poetics, the meditative poet (like the typologist) reads biblical images, metaphors, types, and allegories as expressions of God's divine imagination, interpreting them rightly through an understanding sharpened by the spectacles of spiritual faith. But imagination in its actively inventive rather than passively receptive aspect can fail or succeed. It threatens always to sink into mere dullness by piecing together sense images and impressions distorted by earthly passions, or it can rise to become an exalted "Phansy" that communicates higher spiritual understandings because, though still a shadowy approximation, it nonetheless is an inspired imitation of the divine imagination. A "Phansy" enriched with "Seraphick Life,/ Enquicknd nimbly to catch the Beams/ Thy Honour flurs abroad," it enables the elect poet to "make sweet Musick on such Happy Themes./ That in such Raptures, and Transports of joy,/ To Honour kings I may my Phansy 'ploy" (II.72.7–9, 10–12).

Taylor draws one of his primary metaphors for the process of "inspiriting" that leads to prophetic insight and thence to poetic art from the Old Testament type of Isaiah (6:1–8), who also initially shrinks from God's calling. Isaiah, whose name means salvation of the Lord and who ranks among the foremost Hebrew prophets of Christ's advent, ministry, and future millennial reign, recoils from his vision of the Lord enthroned, crying "Woe is me! For I am undone, because I am a man of unclean lips." But a seraphim, one of the six-winged angels of fiery light who guard God's throne and sing in the celestial choir, "having a live coal in his hand, which he had taken with the tongs from off the altar," lays it upon Isaiah's lips to purge his sin. When called by the "voice of the Lord, saying Whom shall I send," Isaiah then responds, "Here am I; send me." Though Taylor only passingly refers to Isaiah among the ranks of prophets in *Upon the Types of the Old Testament,* he implicitly elevates this ancient figure into a symbol for the poet throughout the *Preparatory Meditations,* though he most frequently addresses his appeals to Christ the antitype (see passim II.6, 49, 52, 73, 82, 86, 92). Cleverly recasting the biblical story in Meditation II.49, he takes upon himself Isaiah's role, crying "woe is mee. Unclean I am: my Slips!/ Lord, let a Seraphim a live Coale take/ Off of thine Altar, with it touch my lips./ And purge away my Sins for mercys sake" (II.49.25–8). Often peppered with allusions to bellows, coals, sparks, fires, the tongue, altars, and seraphim, the meditations enable Taylor to confess his slothful dullness, while trusting in a miraculous cure: "That mine Affections, (O! their sluggish growth)/ Might with Seraphick Wings, Lord, swiftly fly,/ Unto thine Altar for an Holy Cure/ Produced by a Coale thence took most pure" (II.52.27–30). Fanned by flames of spiritual love, Taylor dedicates "this Blesst Life my Soule" to "be thy Sparke," a spark of "new Kindled Life" (II.82.12, 18) that readies him for administering the Lord's Supper, but also gives rise to "sweetest melody," the "Tunes" that "with thy praises frisk and skip," setting forth Christ's glory in meditative verse (II.86.9, 10). In one sense then, Taylor conceives of himself as a prophetic seer, like Isaiah. Predicting through types, metaphors, and allegories the Messiah's coming, yet possessing the spiritual vision of an elect saint under the gospel dispensation, he can preach and meditate not only upon the prophecy but also upon the Christological fulfillment and millennium yet to come.

The frustrations of poetic art vent themselves in the symbol of the rebellious quill, or associated instruments for writing, and in the distinction Taylor ultimately draws between writing poetry and singing hymns.[32] Seeking "from Rhetorick gardens" the "Spangled Flowers of sweet-breathd Eloquence" (II.44.1, 2), Taylor often finds instead the recalcitrance of a labored quill:

> When in Italian flourisht hand I would
>   Lord, flourish up thy praise, my Quills too dry,
> My Inke too thick and naught (though liquid Gold)
>   That will not write, this will not run, nay I
>   My Standish finde is empty, Paper loose
>   That drains all blotches from my inkie Sluce.
>
> What shall I then, Lord, doe? Desist thy praise?
>   Thou Canst amend it. Steep my Stubborn Quill
> In Zions Wine fat, mend my pen, and raise
>   Thy right arms Vean, a drop of 'ts blood distill
>   Into mine inkhorn, make my paper tite
>   That it mayn't blot. In Sacred Text I write.
>   (II.58.1–12)

Far more than the petulant complaints of a harried minister, brought once again to his meditative task, Taylor's frustrations betray the existential angst of a poet with limited skill, but glorious ambitions. Besotted with sin, he will always find the "pensill blunt" (II.7.5), a "Pen . . . workd to the very Stumps," a mere "Drumb Stick thin of Dogtree Wood" (II.155.2, 5), the ink dry, faint, or blotchy, the "Speeche's Organs . . . so transcifide" that "My words stand startld, can't thy praises stride" (II.43.5, 6), and the fancy cramped and cold. Parched and empty, Taylor calls upon Christ to stir the creative juices, to "Ope to thy Blood a passage through my veans" (II.1.33), to "let my Titimouses Quill suck in/ Thy Graces milk Pails some small drop" (II.3.31–2), and to "Distill thy Spirit through thy royall Pipe/ Into my Soule, and so my Spirits feed" (II.4.27–8). A variant of other pipes and channels that spill grace from a divine source into the soul, its receptacle, the quill becomes Taylor's

uniquely personal vessel for receiving spiritual inspiration, necessary to
rejuvenate the soul and stimulate the fancy, and an instrument capable of
both receiving grace from and returning praise back to God. He even
imagines a metamorphosis by which the "Stubborn Quill" transmutes
into "my Faith thy golden Quill where through/ I vitall Spirits from thy
[Christ's] blood may suck" (II.82.43–4). The Savior's blood becomes the
liquid form of grace celebrated in all of these sacramental meditations,
but Taylor envisions it too as an agent that transforms into the very ink
with which he writes. Without the sacrifice of the Son's blood that brings
"My Heart in kilter, and my Spirits oyle," he finds that his "Theme is
rich: my Skill is poore untill/ Thy Spirit makes my hand its holy quill"
(II.6.4, 5–6). Finding only chasms of despair between his skill and his
visions, Taylor must settle repeatedly for a lesser offering, rather than
none at all, for "I do humbly stand, and humbly pray,/ Thee to accept
my homely Style" (II.141.13–14); in truth he yearns to "weave with an
angelick skill/ A Damask Web of Velvet Verse" (II.56.3–4). An amanuensis for the divine spirit, Taylor crafts his verse as a discipline for his
reasoning faculties, but the arousal of his heart's affections through Christ's
infusion of divine grace turns mere words into writing, writing into
homely poetry, poetry into hymns of praises, meditative praxis into poetic
art.

Despite his artistic frustrations and self-deprecating humility, Edward
Taylor holds forth an ideal of poetry toward which he strives, only
approaching the transcendent style of "Sacred art" on earth, while anticipating its perfection in heaven. Like many seventeenth-century poets,
he conceives of poetry in terms of music. As a Puritan he takes his primary model from the Davidic Psalms, widely disseminated first in the
Sternhold-Hopkins psalter in England, then reparaphrased for New
England settlers in the often republished *The Whole Booke of Psalms,* pop-
ularly called the Massachusetts Bay Psalm Book. As preceding English
clerics had done, Taylor also undertook as an early poetic exercise the
paraphrases of both the Psalms (1674–5, 1680s) and the Book of Job
(1690–1700), an endeavor that overlapped from the 1680s onward with
the composing and transcribing of his *Preparatory Meditations.* Although
Taylor never included Job (nor had his exegetical sources) among the
strict Old Testament types, Job stood as the archetype for the suffering
man and doubting sinner, restored ultimately to God's blessing. And
Taylor echoes this prototype by frequently lamenting his own corrupt
estate, yet celebrating in the meditations the emergence time and again
into final affirmations of submission and sainthood. In addition to Job,
the Psalms, Proverbs, Ecclesiastes, Song of Solomon, and Lamentations,
as well as several "songs" from the Old Testament were routinely class-
ified as "poetical" books. The Psalms, from the Greek *psalmos,* meaning

a poem sung to the accompaniment of musical instruments or in Hebrew *Sepher Tehillim,* meaning Book of Praises, celebrate God's power in past events, predict what He will do in the future, and express the longing for God in the present, while exalting His sovereignty and goodness. Thus, the Psalms set the Puritan standard for poetry within which Taylor conceives of his own voice and verse. Thomas Davis concludes:

> The Psalm paraphrases direct Taylor toward the meditative voice. He discovered for himself what Calvin had claimed: "There is no other book [than the *Psalms*] in which we are more perfectly taught the right manner of praising God, or in which we are more powerfully stirred up to the performance of this religious exercise." By providing a means of fashioning his own experience in the framework of biblical *and* historical precedent, the paraphrases invite the poet to make poetry a central concern in his life. Combined with Taylor's knowledge of meditative traditions, the paraphrases point directly toward the *Preparatory Meditations.*[33]

In the meditations Taylor often complains about the tuneless voice, the "instrument" with which he seeks to create his personal psalms: "I fain would praise thee, Lord, but finde black Sin,/ To stain my Tunes my Virginalls to spoile," he laments, choosing on this occasion the spinet as his metaphor (II.6.1–2). But just as often the musical instrument that signifies his voice is a "poor Creaking Pipe" (II.23.2), or he compares his minuscule sound to the "Lady Bee" who "Doth tune her Musick in her mudd wall Cell," for so his "Humming so, no musick makes to thee:/ Nor can my bagpipes play thy glory well" (II.51.13, 14, 15–16). Just as he requires the "Spirit's eye-salve" to purify the sight, the coal to ignite the fancy, and Christ's grace to oil the quill, so also he needs the divine breath *(spiritus)* to transform a cacophonous voice into a melodious instrument capable of praising the Lord in all-admiring style. Frequently, Taylor marks his progress from rational analysis to raised affections by appealing to God and solemnly pledging praise in return, as he does in Meditation II.110, which epitomizes his use of music to symbolize poetry written in God's service:

> Oh! make my heart thy Pipe: the Holy Ghost
>   The Breath that fills the same and Spiritually.
> Then play on mee thy pipe that is almost
>   Worn out with piping tunes of Vanity.
>   Winde musick is the best if thou delight
>   To play the same thyselfe, upon my pipe.
>
> Hence make me, Lord, thy Golden Trumpet Choice
>   And trumpet thou thyselfe upon the same
> Thy heart enravishing Hymns with Sweetest Voice.
>   When thou thy Trumpet soundst, thy tunes will flame.

My heart shall then sing forth thy praises sweet
When sounded thus with thy Sepulcher reech.

Make too my Soul thy Cittern, and its wyers
Make my affections: and rub off their rust
With thy bright Grace. And screw my Strings up higher
And tune the same to tune thy praise most Just.
Ile close thy Supper then with Hymns, most sweet
Burr'ing thy Grave in thy Sepulcher's reech.

(II.110.37–54)

Whether in the guise of a pipe, trumpet, virginal, organ, harp, cittern, bells, or bagpipes, Taylor conceives of himself as an instrument upon whom God tunes the melodies. And his poetics enables him at once to acknowledge the limitations of his skill, to remain within the Puritan tradition of an esthetic dictated by biblical language and example, and yet to find fitting lyric expression for the affections that take root in the soul, flight in divine song.

Taylor knows that poetry exists as a flawed, inadequate form of speech, despite his polishings and strivings for perfection. For all types merely approximate the divine; all tropes only approach spiritual truth – they do not reveal its essence, nor *are* its essence. In the painful recognition of language's innate fallenness, Taylor seems curiously modern, but he inhabits a linguistic universe in which speech remains secondary to spirit – and spirit expressed will only take its proper form in heaven. Hence, the prayers that conclude many poems in the *Preparatory Meditations* promise hymns employed in God's service here on earth, a fitting complement to his meditation upon and administration of the Lord's Supper, yet progressively throughout his lifetime the anticipation of spiritual as well as poetic perfection assumes an eschatological dimension.[34] Hence, Taylor casts his pledges in the future tense, allying himself more and more with angelic hosts that sing eternal psalms at the nuptial banquet, for he offers "My Sacrifice of Praise in Melody," and pleads, "Let thy bright Angells catch my tune, and sing't./ That Equalls Davids Michtam which is in't" (II.18.64, 65–6). In the Song of Solomon and Revelation, he finds justification for his anticipated role as a saint who sings eternally, for once elevated to the state of bliss, "Then on my Spirituall Wiars harmoniously/ Thy Sweetest Tunes shall ring Eternall Joy" in never-ending paeans for Christ and the Father (II.90.65–6). Within the eschatological *hortus conclusus* that fulfills the garden visions of Canticles, Taylor can envision himself as nothing other than a bird or the Bride. "If, Lord, thou opst, and in thy garden bring/ Mee," he petitions, "then thy little Linet sweetly Will/ Upon thy Nut tree sit and sweetly sing," and "My Lungs and Breath ensweetend thus shall raise/ The Glory of thy garden in its praise" (II.63.55–7, 65–6). If not a cooing songster, then as Christ's Beloved, he will lavish his poetic notes: "My Best love then shall on Shoshannim play,/ Like David her Sweet Musick, and thy praise/ Inspire her Songs, that Glory ever may/ In Sweetest tunes thy Excellency Glaze," for "thou shalt be that burden of her Song/ Loaded with Praise that to thyselfe belong" (II.115.49–52, 53–4). From the wilderness to heaven's divine garden, from the Lord's Supper to the nuptial banquet, from earthly saint to Christ's Bride, Taylor journeys toward an eschatological fulfillment. Both saint and singer, he envisions himself among the angelic choirs, where "my Beloved your beloved shall bee/ And both make him one Spouse enriched with Grace," and "when dresst up in glory and bright glee/ Shall sing together fore his blessed face/ Our Weddin Songs with Angells mild * * * * * / In ravishing notes throughout Eternity" (II.133.41–2, 43–6).

Taylor wants to fulfill the type of the biblical poets and in Solomon and the epithalamic Canticles, composed in the later sixteen years of his life, he finds the transcendent language and a voice for "Sacred art." That voice is, however, decidedly Puritan, biblical, exegetical, and yet distinctively Taylor's – taut, muscular, constructed, probing, ecstatic, hyperbolic, tumbling from salvation to sin, from sin to grace, from doubt to certainty, assurance into despair in a never-ending cycle of one man's fall and hope of redemption. Without the conceits, the allegorical narratives, the imagistic associations, and the tortured outbursts or colloquial diction, Taylor's poems might well remain merely versified exegesis or paraphrases, as were his earlier versions of Job and the Psalms. But the recognition that meditative poetry presents a vehicle for understanding is insufficient for the poetic visionary, who must translate homiletic assurances into imaginative visions of sainthood. Shadowy and ill-formed at times, Taylor's figural meditations are his personal "glass darkly" in which he struggles to "see" Christ face to face, so that the antitype can become part of a personal prophecy directed to him as an elect saint and singer. Without Christ's efficacious intervention under the New Testament dispensation, Taylor, however, sees no possibility of either the perfection of grace or of poesy. When in his final poem he offers up the *Preparatory Meditations* as a "Hidebound gift," an emblem for the actual binding and for his sinner's "leather Coate" with which he began the second series, he humbly hopes that "there's Something in't will please thee well./ Hence Lord Accept of this, reject the rest," for "Had I but better thou shouldst better have" (II.165.8, 22–3, 25).[35] His poetics disavows worldly models to seek in typological conceits and the allegory of Canticles a language that will prefigure the ineffable praises of angelic hymns. Hence, David's harp and Solomon's lyre signify for Taylor the very heartstrings on which he plays his tunes, expecting and hoping that grace will transform inharmonious numbers and feet into melodious psalms of praise.

For Edward Taylor both David and Solomon emerge from all the personal figures of the Old Testament as those patriarchs or *exempla fidei* peculiarly relevant to his own self-concept. He does not adopt them as a Puritan historian would, perceiving David and Solomon as prototypal builders of the temple and, consequently, as models for the New England fathers, such as John Winthrop, John Cotton, and Increase Mather. Only covertly might we discover Taylor's affinity with this historical application. He too struggles as a preacher to sustain the temple of a congregational church in Westfield, having sailed across the Atlantic into the wilderness to arrive nearer the New Jerusalem. But, as we continually see in the typological sermons and meditations, Edward Taylor's arena is not so much the wilderness of the Connecticut Valley as the barrenness within the human soul. The temple he seeks to build is within his own heart, just as his meditations on ceremonial types portray his cultivation of the inward worship mold.

More important, it is the poetic endeavors of David and Solomon that attract Taylor to these two types. David, renowned as the psalmist, the Old Testament lyricist of prayer and praise, becomes an inspiration to Taylor in composing his wilderness lyrics. Solomon, the author of Canticles, becomes his model for the nuptial cantor. Just as Solomon in allegorical songs depicts the marriage of the Bride and Bridegroom, so also Edward Taylor in his meditations on Canticles envisions the individual saint's union with Christ. With a fervor increased by advancing age, he longs in Meditations II.115–165 for a heavenly marriage and apotheosis. Hence, both David and Solomon are biblically linked not only as typal kings but as figures for the poet. Taylor's modesty precludes his identifying with their kingship, which Christ so decisively supersedes; nevertheless, he finds their more human roles as poets viable archetypes for his own life. Both patriarchs excel as visionaries and singers, saints who not only wear angelic crowns but also sing in harmony with the heavenly hosts of other saints and seraphim. Lords attendant at the nuptial feast as well as participants, poets such as David, Solomon, and Edward Taylor fulfill a more unique function. Just as on earth Edward Taylor comes forth to administer the Lord's Supper fresh from the ecstasies of meditation and ready to worship with hymns in his heart's temple, so too he anticipates a perpetual feasting at the nuptial banquet. But he comes not only as a saintly guest robed in wedding finery but also as the singer who celebrates the harmonious union of Bride and Bridegroom.

Taylor belongs not just among the Samuel Mathers and Thomas Taylors who explicate and preach the types from the Old Testament but also among seventeenth-century poets. The combination of rationality and heightened affections so characteristic of Taylor's attempt to bring homiletic doctrine from *Upon the Types of the Old Testament* and *Christographia* into his meditations may have its roots in a far deeper schizophrenia in Taylor's own religious heritage, one that does not point toward a psychological dividedness, but rather to a potent integration of two human dimensions. In Taylor we discover the ascetic, preacher, and physical man concerned with his outward sinfulness; yet he also appears as the spiritual saint transported into realms of vision. He is both the rationalist who seeks new understandings and the sensualist who wants to *feel* his faith through his affections – to sense as well as know grace. Taylor views his religion in dichotomous terms – as a framework that disciplines the unruly and corrupt impulses of mankind and as a source of inspiration that promises man ineffable joys. His Puritanism embodies both suffering and salvation, excruciating self-degradations and grace-inspired ecstasies. Every man in some sense reflects Christ as the suffering martyr and as the resurrected Son; similarly, Taylor feels God's divine wrath *and* his forgiving love. As public preacher and private petitioner, Taylor reconciles the outer and inner beings into one prototypal Puritan, who hopes to take his place in heaven, not among eminent theologians or typologists but among the poets, where he will "sing/ New Psalms on Davids Harpe" (II.2.41–2). His gift for lyric meditation makes Edward Taylor both saint and singer.

> My Glorious Lord thy work upon my hand
>   A work so greate and doth so Ample grow
> Too larg to be by my Souls limits spand.
>   Lord let me to thy Angell Palace goe
>   To borrow thence Angelick Organs bright
>   To play thy praises with these pipes aright.
>
> You Holy Angells lend yee mee your Skill.
>   Your Organs set and fill them up well stuft
> With Christs rich praises whose lips do distill
>   Upon his Spouse such ravishing dews to gust
>   With Silver Metaphors and Tropes bedight.
>   How fair, how pleasant art, Love, for delight?
>
> Which Rhetorick of thine my Lord descry
>   Such influences from thy Spouses face
> That do upon me run and raise thy Joy
>   Above my narrow Fancy to uncase.
>   But yet demands my praise so high, so much
>   The which my narrow pipe can neer tune such.
>
> Hence I come to your doors bright Starrs on high
>   And beg you to imply your pipes herein.
> Winde musick makes the Sweetest Melody.
>   I'le with my little pipe thy praises sing.
>   Accept I pray and what for this I borrow,
>   I'le pay thee more when rise on heavens morrow.
>   (II.153.1–24)

Appendix 1. *Comparative Analysis of Edward Taylor's Typological Sermons and Meditations*

	Upon the Types of the Old Testament		Theme	Preparatory Meditations	
	Date	Text		Text	Date
Introduction					
II.1[a]	28 3m[May] 1693	Col. 2:17	Glory of all Types	Col. 2:17	[16]93
II.2	20 6m[Aug.] 1693	Collos. 1:15	Excellency of Christ First Born	Coll. 1:15	Undated
Personal Types: Before the Law					
II.3	15 8m[Oct.] 1693	Rom. 5:14	Adam and Noah Melchizedek[b]	Rom. 5:14	15 8m[Oct.] 1693
II.4	24 10m[Dec.] 1693	Gal. 4:24	Abraham	Gal. 4:24	24 10m[Dec.] 1693
II.5	4 1m[Mar.] 1693/4	Gal. 3:16	Isaac	Gal. 3:16	4 1m[Mar.] 1693/4
II.6	20 3m[May] 1694	Isai. 49:3	Jacob	Isai. 49:3	27 3m[May] 1694
II.7	5 6m[Aug.] 1694	Psa. 105	Joseph	Ps. 105:17	5 6m[Aug.] 1694
Personal Types: Under the Law					
II.8			Moses: Type of Law	Rom. 5:8	14 8m[Oct.] 1694
II.9	Undated	Deut. 18:15	Moses: Type of Christ	Deut. 18:[15]	16 10m[Dec.] 1694
II.10	10 12m[Feb.] 1694/5	Act. 7:45	Joshua	Acts 7:45	10 12m[Feb.] 1694
II.11	19 3m[May] 1695	Jud. 13:3.5	Samson	Jud. 13:3	19 3m[May] 1695
II.12	7 5m[July] 1695	Ezek. 37:24	David	Ezek. 37:24	7 5m[July] 1695
II.13	1 7m[Sept.] 1695	Ps. 72	Solomon	Ps. 72	1 7m[Sept.] 1695
II.30[c]	9 2m[Apr.] 1699	Math. 12:39.40	Jonah	Math. 12:40	9 2m[Apr.] 1699
Personal Types: Religious Ranks					
II.14	3 9m[Nov.] 1695	Collos. 2:3	Prophets, Priests, and	Col. 2:3	3 9m[Nov.] 1695

No.	Date	Scripture	Topic	Scripture	Date
II.15[d]	12 11m[Jan.] 1694/5	Matt. 2:23	Kings by Office / Nazarites by Vow	Mat. 2:23	12 10m[Dec.] 1695/6

Real Types: Old Testament Church and Ceremonial Worship

Old Testament Church

No.	Date	Scripture	Topic	Scripture	Date
II.16	9 1m[Mar.] 1695/6	Lu. 1:33	House of Jacob / Type of Gospel Church	Lu. 1:33	9 1m[Mar.] 1695/6

Mediums of Worship

Legal Sacrifices and Altars

No.	Date	Scripture	Topic	Scripture	Date
II.17	16 6m[Aug.] 1696	Ephe. 5:1	Burnt Offerings	Eph. 5:2	16 6[m] [Aug.] 1696
II.18	18 8m[Oct.] 1696	Heb. 13:10	Altars: Brazen and Golden Incense	Heb. 13:10	18 8m[Oct.] 1696
II.19		Can. 1:12	Spicknard	Can. 1:12	7 10m[Dec.] 1696

Holy Places: The Tabernacle and Temple

No.	Date	Scripture	Topic	Scripture	Date
II.20	7 12m[Feb.] 1696	Heb. 9:11	Tabernacle and Temple	Heb. 9:11	7 12m[Feb.] 1696

Sacred Seasons

Continual Worship Daily and Sabbath

No.	Date	Scripture	Topic	Scripture	Date
II.25[e]	6 1m[Mar.] 1697	Numb. 28:4	Morning, Evening, and Sabbath Offerings	Numb. 28:4.9	6 1m[Mar.] 1698

Lunar Festivals

No.	Date	Scripture	Topic	Scripture	Date
II.21	16 3m[May] 1697	Col. 2:16.17	New Moon Feasts	Col. 2:16.17	16 3m[May] 1697

Septinary or Anniversary Feasts

No.	Date	Scripture	Topic	Scripture	Date
II.22	4 4m[June] 1697	1 Cor. 5:7	Passover	1 Cor. 5:7	Undated
II.22A[f]	Undated	Act. 2:1.4	Pentecost		
II.23	17 8m[Oct.] 1697	1 Joh. 2:2	Feast of Atonement	1 Joh. 2:2	17 7m[Sept.] 1697
II.24[g]	26 10m[Dec.] 1697	Coloss. 2:16.17	Feast of Tabernacles	Joh. 1:14	25 10m[Dec.] 1697

Appendix 1 (Cont.)

Church Discipline in Purifications

Ceremonial Uncleanness

II.26	26 4m[June] 1698	Unclean Touchings	Heb. 9:13.14	26 4m[June] 1698
II.27	4 7m[Sept.] 1698	Unclean Issues and Leprosy	Heb. 9:13.14	4 7m[Sept.] 1698

Moral Uncleanness

II.28	11 10m[Dec.] 1698	Moral Sins and Cities of Refuge	Collos. 2:17	11 10m[Dec.] 1698

Extraordinary Providences Confirming of Faith

Miraculous Deliverances: Universal

II.29	5 12m[Feb.] 1698	Noah's Ark	1 Pet. 3:21	5 12m[Feb.] 1698
II.58	5 10m[Dec.] 1703	Israel's Deliverance from Egypt's Bondage	Math. 2:15	5 10m[Dec.] 1703

Miraculous Deliverances: Particular

II.61[h]	17 7m[Sept.] 1704	Brazen Serpent	John 3:14.15	17 7m[Sept.] 1704

Miraculous Providences: Initiatory Seal of the Covenant

II.59	6 12m[Feb.] 1703	Pillar of Cloud and Fire	1 Cor. 10:2	6 12m[Feb.] 1703

Miraculous Providences: Confirmatory Seals of the Covenant

II.60A	16 2m[Apr.] 1704	Manna from Heaven	Joh. 6:51	16 2m[Apr.] 1704
II.60B	30 5m[July] 1704	Water from the Rock	1 Cor. 10:4	30 5m[July] 1704

Ordinary Seals Confirming Faith

II.70[i]	25 9m[Nov.] 1706	Circumcision Initiatory Seal	Collos. 2:11.12	25 6m[Aug.] 1706
II.71	20 8m[Oct.] 1706	Passover Confirmatory Seal	1 Cor. 5:8	20 8m[Oct.] 1706

Notes:

[a] Numbers refer to the second series of *Preparatory Meditations*.

[b] Taylor explicates Melchizedek as a priest and king with mediatorial functions only in the sermon, omitting all mention of this type in Meditation II.3.

[c] Taylor locates this sermon on Jonah with other personal types under the law, even though in the poetic series, the subject appears in Meditation II.30 after the real type of Noah's miraculous deliverance from the flood (II.29).

[d] The dating of Sermon II.15 seems contradictory, since Taylor apparently dated it 12.11m.1694/5, then attached a small "10" to the right side and a question mark over the second "1" of "11," meaning composition in January or December respectively. A December (10m) date would correspond with Meditation II.15, although Taylor dates the sermon 1694/5 and the poem 1695/6, the latter consistent with dates of composition for surrounding sermons and meditations. Moreover, Taylor clearly identifies Nazarites as a typical order in his sermon.

[e] In the sermons Taylor lodges this analysis of morning, evening, and sabbath sacrifices after sermons II.22 and II.22A on Passover and Pentecost among the anniversary feasts, whereas in the *Preparatory Meditations* he locates it after Meditation II.24 on the Feast of Tabernacles. His exegetical directions, however, recommend placement after Sermon II.20 on the tabernacle and before all major feasts, since the "Continuall Burnt offering" for daily and sabbath worship is "Universall" and "to be attended alwayes, & thrô, all other" (*UTOT*, pp. 501–2). The sermon's date of composition, March 6, 1697, might also recommend its placement before II.21 on new moon feasts, dated May 1697. In calendar schemes, daily and weekly observances would naturally precede particular lunar and septinary feasts.

[f] This sermon on Pentecost has no separate correlate among the meditations, although it is clear that Taylor composes a four-stanza fragment on Pentecost, initially affixing it to Meditation II.21 on new moon feasts and the mystery of sevens, later attaching it to Meditation II.22 on Passover.

[g] Only items II.24 and II.28 have radically different biblical texts for the sermons and poems, though the subjects for typological analysis remain congruent.

[h] Although he composes Sermon and Meditation II.61 in September 1704, Taylor obviously reconsiders its placement, crossing out "the Seals of the Covenant" to declare instead, "I have touched upon Such as respect Deliverances of a generall Nature" (*UTOT*, p. 702). Furthermore, he inserts a slip of paper after II.58, which reads, "Miraculous Deliverances of a Particular Nature I have not Spooke to: & for this So that of the Brazen Serpent. & place it here" (*UTOT*, insert at p. 725).

[i] Sermon II.70 is clearly dated in the ninth month, denoting a November 1706 composition. However, the topic circumcision, the fact that this sermon precedes one on Passover dated in both sermon and poem as October, and the August composition of Meditation II.70 suggest that Taylor may well have reordered the homilies at a later date.

Appendix 2. *Thomas Taylor's* Christ Revealed: *Organization*

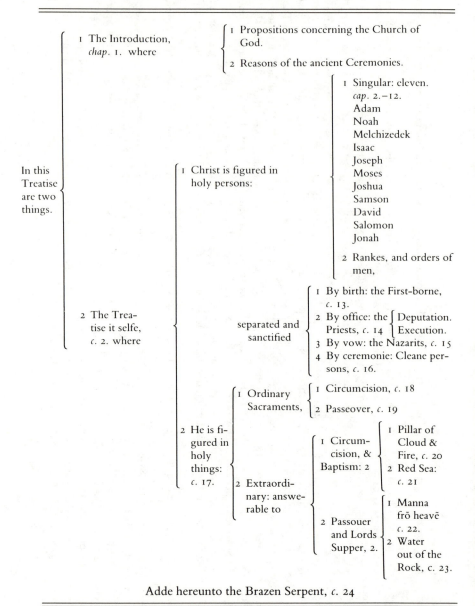

In this Treatise are two things.

1 The Introduction, *chap.* 1. where
- 1 Propositions concerning the Church of God.
- 2 Reasons of the ancient Ceremonies.

2 The Treatise it selfe, *c.* 2. where

1 Christ is figured in holy persons:
- 1 Singular: eleven. *cap.* 2.–12.
  Adam
  Noah
  Melchizedek
  Isaac
  Joseph
  Moses
  Joshua
  Samson
  David
  Salomon
  Jonah
- 2 Rankes, and orders of men, separated and sanctified
  - 1 By birth: the First-borne, *c.* 13.
  - 2 By office: the Priests, *c.* 14 — Deputation. Execution.
  - 3 By vow: the Nazarits, *c.* 15
  - 4 By ceremonie: Cleane persons, *c.* 16.

2 He is figured in holy things: *c.* 17.
- 1 Ordinary Sacraments,
  - 1 Circumcision, *c.* 18
  - 2 Passeover, *c.* 19
- 2 Extraordinary: answerable to
  - 1 Circumcision, & Baptism: 2
    - 1 Pillar of Cloud & Fire, *c.* 20
    - 2 Red Sea: *c.* 21
  - 2 Passouer and Lords Supper, 2.
    - 1 Manna frõ heavē *c.* 22.
    - 2 Water out of the Rock, *c.* 23.

Adde hereunto the Brazen Serpent, *c.* 24

Note: This chart is reproduced as it appears in the 1635 edition with the addition of the full list of singular types. ·

Appendix 3. *Samuel Mather's* The Figures or Types: *Organization*

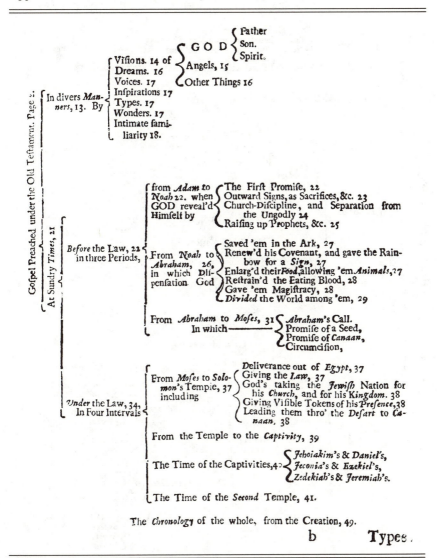

Appendix 3 *(Cont.)*

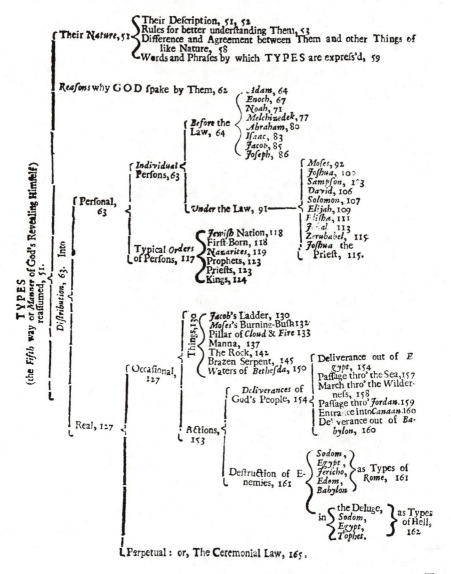

TYPES
(the *Fifth* way or *Manner of* God's *Revealing Himself*) reassumed, 51.

Their *Nature*, 51 {
- Their Description, 51, 52
- Rules for better understanding Them, 53
- Difference and Agreement between Them and other Things of like Nature, 58
- Words and Phrases by which TYPES are express'd, 59

Reasons why GOD spake by Them, 62

Distribution, 63; Into

Personal, 63
- *Individual* Persons, 63
  - *Before* the Law, 64 {
    - *Adam*, 64
    - *Enoch*, 67
    - *Noah*, 71
    - *Melchizedek*, 77
    - *Abraham*, 80
    - *Isaac*, 83
    - *Jacob*, 85
    - *Joseph*, 86
  - *Under* the Law, 91 {
    - *Moses*, 92
    - *Joshua*, 100
    - *Sampson*, 103
    - *David*, 106
    - *Solomon*, 107
    - *Elijah*, 109
    - *Elisha*, 111
    - *Joel*, 113
    - *Zerubabel*, 115
    - *Joshua* the Priest, 115.
- Typical *Orders* of Persons, 117 {
  - *Jewish* Nation, 118
  - First-Born, 118
  - *Nazarites*, 119
  - Prophets, 123
  - Priests, 123
  - Kings, 124

Real, 127
- Occasional, 127
  - Things, 130 {
    - *Jacob's* Ladder, 130
    - *Moses's* Burning-Bush 132
    - Pillar of *Cloud & Fire* 133
    - Manna, 137
    - The Rock, 142
    - Brazen Serpent, 145
    - Waters of *Bethesda*, 150
  - *Actions*, 153 {
    - *Deliverances* of God's People, 154 {
      - Deliverance out of *Egypt*, 154
      - Passage thro' the Sea, 157
      - March thro' the Wilderness, 158
      - Passage thro' *Jordan*. 159
      - Entrance into *Canaan*. 160
      - Deliverance out of *Babylon*, 160
    - Destruction of Enemies, 161 {
      - *Sodom*, *Egypt*, *Jericho*, *Edom*, *Babylon* } as Types of *Rome*, 161
      - in { the Deluge, *Sodom*, *Egypt*, *Tophet*. } as Types of Hell, 162
- Perpetual : or, The Ceremonial Law, 165.

Typ

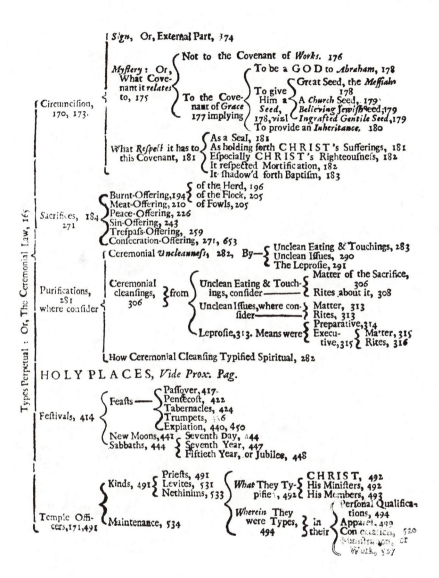

Types Perpetual : Or, The Ceremonial Law, 165

Circumcision, 170, 173.
- Sign, Or, External Part, 174
- Mystery: Or, What Covenant it relates to, 175
  - Not to the Covenant of *Works*. 176
  - To the Covenant of *Grace* 177 implying
    - To be a GOD to *Abraham*, 178
    - To give Him a Seed, 178, viz
      - Great Seed, the *Messiah* 178
      - A *Church* Seed, 179
      - Believing *Jewish* Seed, 179
      - Ingrafted *Gentile* Seed, 179
    - To provide an *Inheritance*. 180
- What *Respect* it has to this Covenant, 181
  - As a Seal, 181
  - As holding forth CHRIST's Sufferings, 181
  - Especially CHRIST's Righteousness, 182
  - It respected Mortification, 182
  - It shadow'd forth Baptism, 183

Sacrifices, 184, 271
- Burnt-Offering, 194
  - of the Herd, 196
  - of the Flock, 205
  - of Fowls, 205
- Meat-Offering, 210
- Peace-Offering, 226
- Sin-Offering, 243
- Trespass-Offering, 259
- Confecration-Offering, 271, 653

Purifications, 281 where confider
- Ceremonial *Uncleaness*, 282, By—
  - Unclean Eating & Touchings, 283
  - Unclean Iffues, 290
  - The Leprofie, 291
- Ceremonial cleanfings, 306 from
  - Unclean Eating & Touchings, confider
    - Matter of the Sacrifice, 306
    - Rites about it, 308
  - Unclean Iffues, where confider
    - Matter, 313
    - Rites, 313
  - Leprofie, 313. Means were
    - Preparative, 314
    - Executive, 315
      - Matter, 315
      - Rites, 316
- How Ceremonial Cleanfing Typified Spiritual, 282

HOLY PLACES, *Vide Prox. Pag.*

Festivals, 414
- Feafts
  - Paffover, 417
  - Pentecoft, 422
  - Tabernacles, 424
  - Trumpets, 436
  - Expiation, 440, 450
- New Moons, 441
- Sabbaths, 444
  - Seventh Day, 444
  - Seventh Year, 447
  - Fiftieth Year, or Jubilee, 448

Temple Officers, 171, 491
- Kinds, 491
  - Priefts, 491
  - Levites, 531
  - Nethinims, 533
- What They Typifie, 492
  - CHRIST, 492
  - His Minifters, 492
  - His Members, 493
- Wherein They were Types, 494
  - in their
    - Perfonal Qualifications, 494
    - Apparel, 499
    - Confecration, 520
    - Adminiftration, or Works, 527
- Maintenance, 534

Appendix 3 *(Cont.)*

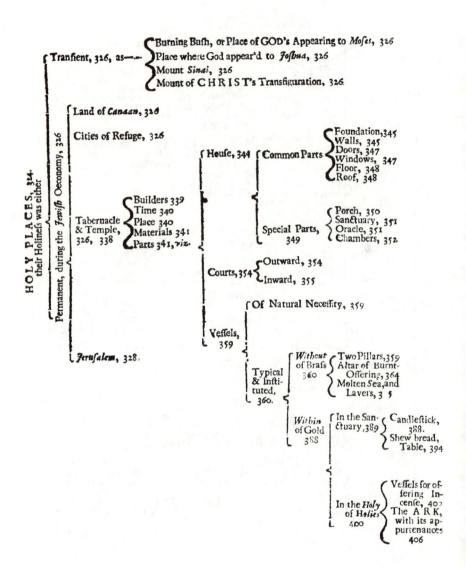

HOLY PLACES, 324. their Holiness was either

Transient, 326, as—
- Burning Bush, or Place of GOD's Appearing to *Moses*, 326
- Place where God appear'd to *Joshua*, 326
- Mount *Sinai*, 326
- Mount of CHRIST's Transfiguration, 326.

Permanent, during the *Jewish* Oeconomy, 326
- Land of *Canaan*, 326
- Cities of Refuge, 326
- Tabernacle & Temple, 326, 338
  - Builders 339
  - Time 340
  - Place 340
  - Materials 341
  - Parts 341, *viz.*
    - House, 344
      - Common Parts
        - Foundation, 345
        - Walls, 345
        - Doors, 347
        - Windows, 347
        - Floor, 348
        - Roof, 348
      - Special Parts, 349
        - Porch, 350
        - Sanctuary, 351
        - Oracle, 351
        - Chambers, 352.
    - Courts, 354
      - Outward, 354
      - Inward, 355
    - Vessels, 359
      - Of Natural Necessity, 359
      - Typical & Instituted, 360.
        - *Without* of Brass 360
          - Two Pillars, 359
          - Altar of Burnt-Offering, 364
          - Molten Sea, and Lavers, 3 5
        - *Within* of Gold 388
          - In the Sanctuary, 389
            - Candlestick, 388.
            - Shew bread, Table, 394
          - In the *Holy* of *Holies* 400
            - Vessels for offering Incense, 402
            - The ARK, with its appurtenances 406
- *Jerusalem*, 328.

Appendix 4. *Edward Taylor's* Preparatory Meditations *and* Upon the Types of the Old Testament: *Organization*

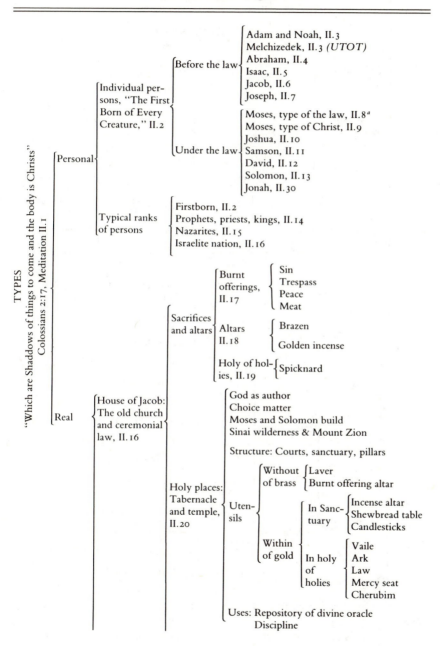

TYPES

"Which are Shaddows of things to come and the body is Christs" Colossians 2:17, Meditation II.1

Personal

  Individual persons, "The First Born of Every Creature," II.2

    Before the law
      Adam and Noah, II.3
      Melchizedek, II.3 *(UTOT)*
      Abraham, II.4
      Isaac, II.5
      Jacob, II.6
      Joseph, II.7

    Under the law
      Moses, type of the law, II.8[a]
      Moses, type of Christ, II.9
      Joshua, II.10
      Samson, II.11
      David, II.12
      Solomon, II.13
      Jonah, II.30

  Typical ranks of persons
    Firstborn, II.2
    Prophets, priests, kings, II.14
    Nazarites, II.15
    Israelite nation, II.16

Real

  House of Jacob: The old church and ceremonial law, II.16

    Sacrifices and altars
      Burnt offerings, II.17
        Sin
        Trespass
        Peace
        Meat
      Altars II.18
        Brazen
        Golden incense
      Holy of holies, II.19
        Spicknard

    Holy places: Tabernacle and temple, II.20
      God as author
      Choice matter
      Moses and Solomon build
      Sinai wilderness & Mount Zion

      Structure: Courts, sanctuary, pillars

      Utensils
        Without of brass
          Laver
          Burnt offering altar
        Within of gold
          In Sanctuary
            Incense altar
            Shewbread table
            Candlesticks
          In holy of holies
            Vaile
            Ark
            Law
            Mercy seat
            Cherubim

      Uses: Repository of divine oracle
      Discipline

Real
├─ Old Testament church and ceremonial law
│   ├─ Festivals
│   │   ├─ Daily and weekly, II.25
│   │   │   ├─ Morn and evening sacrifices
│   │   │   ├─ Burnt, meat, drink offerings
│   │   │   └─ Special sabbath offerings
│   │   ├─ Lunar, II.21
│   │   │   ├─ Mystery of sevens
│   │   │   └─ New moon feasts
│   │   └─ Septinary or anniversary feasts
│   │   ├─ Passover, II.22
│   │   ├─ Pentecost, II.22A
│   │   ├─ Atonement, II.23
│   │   └─ Tabernacles, II.24
│   └─ Disciplinary purifications
│   ├─ Ceremonial uncleanness
│   │   ├─ Unclean touchings, II.26
│   │   │   └─ Sacrifice of a red heifer; burnt & sin offerings
│   │   └─ Unclean issues, leprosy, II.27
│   │   └─ Separation, sacrifice of two birds & lambs, bathing, shaving, anointing; burnt, sin, trespass, meat offerings
│   └─ Moral uncleanness, II.28
│   ├─ Sins not capital, but scandalous
│   │   └─ Burnt, trespass, sin offerings
│   └─ Sins capital, as lewdness and manslaughter
│   └─ Burnt offerings, bitter waters, cities of refuge
└─ Extraordinary providences
    ├─ Deliverances
    │   ├─ Noah's ark, II.29 — God's people from the flood
    │   ├─ Out of Egypt, II.58
    │   │   ├─ God calls Jacob
    │   │   ├─ Israel flees out of Egypt
    │   │   ├─ Crossing the Red Sea
    │   │   ├─ March in the wilderness
    │   │   └─ Entrance into Canaan
    │   └─ Brazen serpent, II.61 — Individuals from sin's ruin
    └─ Providential seals of faith
        ├─ Initiating — Pillar of cloud and fire, II.59
        └─ Confirming
            ├─ Manna from heaven, II.60A
            └─ Water from the rock, II.60B

Ordinary seals of the covenant
    ├─ Initiating   Circumcision, II.70
    └─ Confirming   Passover, II.71

Note:
[a]In the sermons Moses as a type of the law appears in II.9. No extant sermon correlates with Meditation II.19.

Appendix 5. *The Stoddardean Controversy Concerning the Lord's Supper: A Calendar of Significant Events and Documents*

1677	Unable to accept the Half-Way Covenant (1662), Solomon Stoddard in Northampton advocates baptizing every adult who consents to the articles of faith and admitting them to the Lord's Supper without evidence of a conversion experience.
1677	Increase Mather, *A Discourse concerning the danger of apostasy*, in *A Call from heaven to the present and succeeding generations* (1679), warns against the new liberalism without, however, naming Stoddard.
1679 (Aug. 26)	Edward Taylor preaches his Foundation Day Sermon on Ephesians 2:22, recorded in "The Publick Records of the Church at Westfield" on the occasion of the Westfield church's formal organization, which Stoddard attended. Taylor upholds the Half-Way Covenant and affirms the need for a person to give a public "account of the workings of Gods Spirit upon his heart" in order to obtain "Church Fellowship" and to undertake an "Evangelicall Preparation" in order to receive the Supper (*CRRS*, p. 128).
1679 (Sept. 10–19)	At the Reforming Synod Mather and Stoddard first publicly espouse conflicting doctrines respecting the communicant's qualifications for celebrating the Supper, though with no disruptive hostilities. Stoddard would allow all half-way members to commune, whereas Mather requires examinations or relations concerning a work of saving grace before admitting one to the Lord's Supper. Stoddard prevails at the synod sufficiently to modify the requirement from making "a Relation of the work of Gods Spirit" to simply *"The Making a Profession of their Faith and Repentance"* (see Stoddard's *An Appeal to the Learned,* p. 94).
1680	Increase Mather, "Confutation of the Rev. Mr Stoddard's Observations respecting the Lords Supper 1680," an unpublished manuscript refuting Stoddard's arguments as presented at

	the 1679 Synod and in a manuscript of "Observations" composed shortly thereafter.
1680 (May 12–13)	The Reforming Synod's committee meets to draw up a *Confession of Faith* with no apparent friction between attending members Mather and Stoddard. Taylor does not attend.
1687	Stoddard, *The Safety of Appearing at the Day of Judgment, In the Righteousness of Christ: Opened and Applied.*
1687/8 (Feb. 13)	Taylor writes a conciliatory letter, entreating Stoddard to desist from his controversial doctrine. Contained in Taylor's "Commonplace Book," Massachusetts Historical Society (MHS).
1688 (June 4)	Stoddard responds evasively to Taylor's letter, while he politely affirms his commitment to this "Cause of God." See Taylor's "Commonplace Book" (MHS).
1689–90 (ca.)	Stoddard's "Arguments for the Proposition" revises somewhat his position and probably his "Observations" from the 1679 Synod. Transcribed in "Extracts, by Rev. Edward Taylor, Westfield," the Prince Collection, Boston Public Library (BPL).
1690	"Some notes of the said Mr. Stoddards touching the Lords Supper as a Converting Ordi-..ance preacht before he urged his Church to the Practice thereof which motion he urged them to Octob: 5. 1690." Stoddard preaches his "Sermon on Galatians 3:1," prior to calling the Northampton church to a new covenanting. See the only extant copy in Taylor's "Extracts" (BPL). According to Taylor's prefatory note to his syllogisms in the "Commonplace Book" (MHS), Stoddard draws up articles designed "to bring all to the Lords Supper that had a knowledge of Principles of Religion, & not scandalous by open Sinfull Living."
1690 (ca.)	Taylor, "These things thus laid down by this Worthie man, do call for some few Animad-

versions upon the same. & such thoughts as readilie tender themse[l]ves unto me as Serviceable to this matter fall upon his

Admittendi ad Caenam

."

Convertendae Naturam Caenae

Taylor probably transcribed the "Animadversions" in his "Extracts" volume (BPL) after he had received Stoddard's "Arguments for the Proposition," possibly with the Galatians sermon in hand, and before he revised Foundation Day Sermon.

1692/3	Taylor revises and appends twenty-four manuscript pages to his Foundation Day Sermon from 1679, now entitled "A Particular Church is Gods House," in the "Extracts" (BPL). The revisions address the issue of the Lord's Supper as a converting ordinance as detailed in Stoddard's Galatians sermon. The "Commonplace Book" and "Extracts" contain most of Taylor's anti-Stoddard manuscripts.
1693 (ca.)	Taylor adds six "Anti-Stoddard Syllogisms" in his "Commonplace Book," (MHS) as "further thoughts about this matter besides those laid down in my Manuscript on Eph. 2.22," the matter being Stoddard's successful implementing of his sacramental practices in Northampton.
1693 (Dec.) – 1694 (Apr.)	Taylor, *Treatise Concerning the Lord's Supper.* These eight sermons set forth Taylor's most comprehensive rebuttal to Stoddard's arguments for the Supper as a converting ordinance. Taylor defends instead the need for preparation and the concept of the wedding feast as a confirming seal of the covenant and, consequently, a grace nourishing, not begetting Sacrament. See "Extracts" (BPL).
1693 (May) – 1699 (Apr.)	Taylor, *Preparatory Meditations before my Approach to the Lords Supper. Chiefly upon the Doctrin preached upon the Day of administration,* II.1–30, and *Upon the Types of the Old Testament* on the personal types and ceremonial law, including

Sermon and Meditation II.22 on Passover. Manuscript at the Beinecke Library, Yale University.

1700   Increase Mather, *The Order of the Gospel.*

1700   Stoddard, *The Doctrine of Instituted Churches Explained and Proved from the Word of God.* The pamphlet war between Mather and Stoddard erupts publicly.

1703 (Dec.) – 1704 (Sept.)   Taylor, *Upon the Types* and *Preparatory Meditations* II.58–61 on the extraordinary types of Israel's deliverance from Egypt and wilderness wanderings. Includes meditations on manna (II.60A) and the water from Horeb's rock (II.60B) as types of the sacramental bread and wine.

1706 (Aug.–Oct.)   Taylor, *Upon the Types* and *Preparatory Meditations* II.70–71 on circumcision and Passover respectively.

1708   Stoddard, *The Inexcusableness of Neglecting the Worship of God, under A Pretence of being in an Unconverted Condition.* Civility gives way to outright hostility with this publication and Mather's subsequent refutation.

1708   Mather, *A Dissertation, wherein The Strange Doctrine Lately Published in a Sermon, The Tendency of which, is, to Encourage Unsanctified Persons (while such) to Approach the Holy Table of the Lord, is Examined and Confuted* (Boston).

1709   Stoddard, *An Appeal to the Learned. Being a Vindication of the Right of Visible Saints to the Lords Supper, though they be destitute of a Saving Work of God's Spirit on their Hearts: Against the Exceptions of Mr. Increase Mather.*

1709   Anon., *An Appeal, Of some of the Unlearned, both to the Learned and Unlearned; Containing some Queries on a Discourse Entituled, An Appeal to the Learned; Lately Published by Mr. S. Stoddard.* Composed by members of Mather's faction, this pamphlet summarizes both positions.

1710–11 (ca.)   Taylor, "The *Appeale* Tried," in "Extracts" (BPL). The printed controversy calls forth

	Taylor's additional prose refutation of Stoddard and defense of Mather's opinions.
1711 (June) – 1712 (Dec.)	Taylor, *Preparatory Meditations,* II.102–111. Taking Matthew 26:26–30 as his main text, Taylor composes ten meditations on the Lord's Supper, probably as companions to a homiletic series.
1728	One year before Taylor's death from old age and apparent senility, the Rev. Nehemiah Bull puts the following proposition to the church at Westfield, which then adopts Stoddard's practices on February 25: "Those who enter full communion, may have liberty to give an account of a work of saving conversion or not. *It shall be regarded by the church as a matter of indifference.*"
1750	Only four ministers in the Connecticut Valley hold out against Stoddard's tenets for administering the Lord's Supper.

Notes

1 THE HERITAGE OF PURITAN TYPOLOGY

1 Edward Taylor, *The Poems of Edward Taylor,* ed. Donald E. Stanford (New Haven: Yale Univ. Press, 1960), II. 59. 31–6. All subsequent references to Edward Taylor's *Preparatory Meditations* are to this edition and are incorporated in the text. The Roman numeral designates the first or second series of the *Preparatory Meditations* followed by the poem's number, then the specific lines.

2 Consult the annotated bibliography in *Typology and Early American Literature,* ed. Sacvan Bercovitch (Amherst: Univ. of Massachusetts Press, 1972), pp. 245–337, for an authoritative listing of primary and secondary studies that define the concept and exegetical history of typology.

3 Walther Eichrodt, "Is Typological Exegesis an Appropriate Method?" in *Essays on Old Testament Hermeneutics,* ed. Claus Westermann (Richmond, Va.: John Knox, 1963), p. 226.

4 Erich Auerbach, "Figura," *Scenes from the Drama of European Literature,* Eng. trans. (New York: Meridian Books, 1959), p. 53. Auerbach provides an etymological analysis of the term "figura" in his essay. For further lexical studies and definitions, see K.J. Woollcombe, "The Biblical Origins and Patristic Development of Typology," in *Essays on Typology,* Studies in Biblical Theology, no. 22 (London: SCM Press, 1957), pp. 39–75; and Ursula Brumm, *American Thought and Religious Typology,* trans. John Hoaglund (New Brunswick, N.J.: Rutgers Univ. Press, 1970).

5 In addition to Auerbach's essay, see also Allan C. Charity, *Events and Their Afterlife: The Dialectics of Christian Typology in the Bible and Dante* (Cambridge: Cambridge Univ. Press, 1966); and G.W.H. Lampe, "Hermeneutics and Typology," *London Quarterly and Holborn Review,* 6th ser. 34 (1965): 17–25, for analyses of typology's Christocentricity.

6 Charity, *Events and Their Afterlife,* p. 159.

7 My discussion of the Church Fathers is indebted to R.P.C. Hanson, *Allegory*

and Event: A Study of the Sources and Significance of Origen's Interpretation of Scripture (Richmond, Va.: John Knox, 1959); Jean Daniélou, *From Shadows to Reality: Studies in the Biblical Typology of the Fathers* (London: Burns & Oates, 1960); Thomas M. Davis, "The Traditions of Puritan Typology," in *Typology and Early American Literature,* pp. 11–45, and Woollcombe, "Biblical Origins and Patristic Development," pp. 39–75.

8 Charles Donahue, "Patristic Exegesis in the Criticism of Medieval Literature: Summation," in *Critical Approaches to Medieval Literature,* ed. Dorothy Bethurum (New York: Columbia Univ. Press, 1960), pp. 61–82.

9 Robert M. Grant, *A Short History of the Interpretation of the Bible,* rev. ed. (London: Adam & Charles Black, 1965), pp. 60–8; and Victor Harris, "Allegory to Analogy in the Interpretation of Scriptures," *Philological Quarterly* 45 (1966): 1–23.

10 Hanson, *Allegory and Event,* pp. 253, 257.

11 Harry Caplan, "The Four Senses of Scriptural Interpretation and the Medieval Theory of Preaching," *Speculum* 4 (1929): 282–90. Davis, "Traditions of Puritan Typology," pp. 22–8, concludes that, although Augustine insisted on the historicity of the literal text, his works demonstrate a dependence on the fourfold method traceable to Jerome and Origen.

12 Harris, "Allegory to Analogy," p. 4. Among theologians and literary critics, including Auerbach, "Figura," pp. 39–43, and Donahue, "Patristic Exegesis," pp. 68–72, there is considerable debate about Augustine's relative emphasis on the literal text and on allegorical interpretations.

13 See Beryl Smalley, *The Study of the Bible in the Middle Ages,* 2d ed. (Oxford: Blackwell, 1952; Notre Dame, Ind.: Univ. of Notre Dame Press, 1964); and Henri de Lubac, *Exégèse Médiévale: Les quatres sens de l'Ecriture,* 4 vols. (Paris: Aubier, 1959–64), the two authoritative studies of exegesis in the Middle Ages. For briefer surveys, consult Johan Chydenius, *The Theory of Medieval Symbolism,* Societas Scientiarum Fennica: Commentationes Humanarum Litterarum, vol. 27, no. 2 (Helsinki, 1960); idem, *Medieval Institutions and the Old Testament,* Societas Scientiarum Fennica: Commentationes Humanarum Litterarum, vol. 37, no. 2 (Helsinki, 1965).

14 See Emile Mâle, *The Gothic Image: Religious Art in France of the Thirteenth Century,* trans. Dora Nussey, 3d ed. (New York: Harper & Brothers, 1958).

15 Karlfried Froehlich, " 'Always to Keep the Literal Sense in Holy Scripture Means to Kill One's Soul': The State of Biblical Hermeneutics at the Beginning of the Fifteenth Century," in *Literary Uses of Typology from the Late Middle Ages to the Present,* ed. Earl Miner (Princeton: Princeton Univ. Press, 1977), pp. 20–48.

16 See Davis, "Traditions of Puritan Typology," pp. 25–43; Harris, "Allegory to Analogy," pp. 5–14; Woollcombe, "Biblical Origins and Patristic Development," pp. 72–5; Smalley, *Study of the Bible in the Middle Ages,* pp. 14–20; and Grant, *History of the Interpretation of the Bible,* pp. 69–79.

17 William Tyndale, "The Obedience of a Christian Man," *The Work of William Tyndale,* ed. G. E. Duffield (Appleford, Eng.: Sutton Courtenay, 1964), p. 343.

18 William Guild, *Moses Unvailed . . .* (London: G. Purslow for J. Budge, 1619 [part I]–1620 [part II]; Glasgow: Robert Sanders, 1701). A Scottish divine, Wil-

liam Guild (1586–1657) dedicated his *Moses Unvailed* to King James I and later became chaplain to Charles I. Initially supporting the episcopacy during his ministry in Aberdeen, he was persuaded to subscribe to the covenant, although he refused to condemn Episcopal government absolutely and reserved his duty to the king. After retreating to Holland to avoid unconditional subscription, he returned to offer communion according to the Presbyterian form on November 3, 1640, and was appointed principal of King's College, where he purged the cathedral and college chapel of ornaments. Displaced by Cromwell's military commissioners in 1651 because of his lukewarm covenanting, he died in 1657. Although labeled a "weak, time-serving man," he was respected for his philanthropy.

19 Thomas Taylor, *Christ Revealed: Or The Old Testament Explained. A Treatise of the Types and Shadowes of our Saviour contained throughout the whole Scripture,* ed. W. Jemmat (London: M. F. for R. Dawlman & L. Fawne, 1635), hereafter cited as *CR* for all textual references. Henry Vertue, *Christ and the Church: Or Parallels* (London: T. Roycroft, 1659). The second edition (London: For Nathaniel Hillier, 1705) of Mather's *The Figures or Types* altered the pagination but not the content of the earlier 1683 edition (Dublin: n.p., 1683), and it also included an index and a chart of the contents. All references are taken from Mather's 1705 edition (rpt. New York: Johnson, 1969), hereafter cited as *FT* in the text, and the old-style "S" spelling is modernized.

   Benjamin Keach, Τροπολογια: *A Key To Open Scripture-Metaphors. Wherein the most Significant Tropes, (As Metaphors, &c.) And Express Similitudes, Respecting the Father, Son, & Holy-Spirit, As also such as respect the Sacred Word of God, Are opened, and Parallel-wise applied, together with the Disparities . . .* (London: J. D. for Enoch Prosser, 1681). Because second title pages for each of two parts are both dated 1682, most scholars give this year for Keach's volume. Coming under the influence of Arminian Baptists around 1655, Keach (1640–1704) was persecuted in Buckinghamshire before removing in 1668 to London where he became a pastor and Calvinistic Baptist. His advocacy of congregational singing and issue of a collection of original hymns caused a break with the London general Baptist association in 1689–91. Keach was a versifier and prose controversialist with some fifty-four publications; most of his surviving works are expository, including the *Tropologia*.

20 See Mason Lowance's discussion of the moral equity of types in his introduction to the Johnson reprint edition of Mather's *The Figures or Types,* pp. ix–xxi.

21 Keach, "The Epistle To The Reader," *Tropologia,* Part 2, sig. A4ʳ. Keach borrows his distinctions verbatim from James Durham, *Clavis Cantici: or, an Exposition of the Song of Solomon* (Edinburgh: George Swintoun & James Glen, 1668), p. 22.

22 Mason I. Lowance, Jr., *The Language of Canaan: Metaphor and Symbol in New England from the Puritans to the Transcendentalists* (Cambridge: Harvard Univ. Press, 1980), p. 62, as quoted from J. Paul Hunter, *The Reluctant Pilgrim: Defoe's Emblematic Method and Quest for Form in Robinson Crusoe* (Baltimore: Johns Hopkins Univ. Press, 1966), pp. 100–1. Steven N. Zwicker, *Dryden's Political Poetry: The Typology of King and Nation* (Providence, R.I.: Brown Univ. Press, 1972), pp. 13–23, adopts the term "correlative typology" for identifications between Old Testament types and seventeenth-century persons and events. Since the term has been

used elsewhere, somewhat confusingly, to signify simply those correlations which typologically link the Old and New Testaments or the correspondences between literal events and spiritual fulfillments, it seems preferable to adopt Lowance's terms "developmental" and "recapitulative" for historical applications.

23 Lowance, *Language of Canaan,* p. 116.

24 Cotton Mather, *Magnalia Christi Americana: Or, The Ecclesiastical History of New-England . . . In Seven Books* (London: For Thomas Parkhurst, 1702; rpt. New York: Arno, 1972), 2:8–9. Each book is separately paginated.

25 See the discussions of Cotton Mather as historian and typologist in Lowance, *Language of Canaan,* pp. 160–77; Sacvan Bercovitch, *The Puritan Origins of the American Self* (New Haven: Yale Univ. Press, 1975); and Robert Middlekauff, *The Mathers: Three Generations of Puritan Intellectuals, 1596–1728* (New York: Oxford Univ. Press, 1971).

26 Thomas Hooker, *The Application of Redemption,* 2 vols. (London: Peter Cole, 1656), 9:5. Each of the ten books is separately paginated.

27 Richard Mather, *An Apologie of the Churches in New-England for Church-covenant* in *Church-Government And Church-Covenant* (London: R. O. & G. D. for Benjamin Allen, 1643), pp. 1–2. See also Bercovitch, *Puritan Origins of the American Self,* pp. 58–61, for a discussion of the soteriological use of types.

28 Cotton Mather, quoted in Emory Elliott, *Power and the Pulpit in Puritan New England* (Princeton: Princeton Univ. Press, 1975), p. 190; and Perry Miller, *The New England Mind: From Colony to Province* (1953; rpt. Cambridge: Harvard Univ. Press, 1967), p. 188.

29 See Emory Elliott, "From Father to Son: The Evolution of Typology in Puritan New England," in *Literary Uses of Typology,* ed. Miner, pp. 204–27; idem, *Power and the Pulpit,* in which Elliott displays how the choice of scriptural images in Puritan sermons shifts in response to generational conflicts, replacing visions of a wrathful God with a merciful Son to alleviate the psychic despair of second- and third-generation sons of the founding fathers.

30 Urian Oakes, *New–England Pleaded With, And pressed to consider the things which concern her peace . . .* (Cambridge: Samuel Green, 1673), pp. 17, 20. For studies of the wilderness metaphor, see Alan Heimert, "Puritanism, the Wilderness, and the Frontier," *New England Quarterly* 26 (1953): 361–82; Perry Miller, *Errand into the Wilderness* (Cambridge: Harvard Univ. Press, 1956); George H. Williams, *Wilderness and Paradise in Christian Thought* (New York: Harper & Brothers, 1962); Roderick Nash, *Wilderness and the American Mind* (New Haven: Yale Univ. Press, 1967); and Peter N. Carroll, *Puritanism and the Wilderness: The Intellectual Significance of the New England Frontier, 1629–1700* (New York: Columbia Univ. Press, 1969).

31 Sacvan Bercovitch, "Horologicals to Chronometricals: The Rhetoric of the Jeremiad," *Literary Monographs* 3, ed. Eric Rothstein (Madison: Univ. of Wisconsin Press, 1970), pp. 1–124, 187–215. In this seminal study as well as in his later revision *The American Jeremiad* (Madison: Univ. of Wisconsin Press, 1978), Bercovitch illuminates the impact of biblical types from the Babylonian captivity and return to Jerusalem upon Puritan histories, jeremiads, and millennial writings.

32 John Winthrop, "A Modell of Christian Charity," *Winthrop Papers,* ed. Stewart Mitchell, 5 vols. (Boston: Massachusetts Historical Society, 1929–47), 2:295.

33 Cotton Mather, *The Wonders of the Invisible World* (Boston: Benj. Harris for

Sm. Phillips, 1693; rpt. London: For John Dunton, 1693), pp. 34–5, 38–9. In both "Cotton Mather," *Major Writers of Early American Literature,* ed. Everett Emerson (Madison: Univ. of Wisconsin Press, 1972), pp. 93–149, and *Puritan Origins of the American Self,* Bercovitch studies how Cotton Mather's personal millennial eschatology intertwines with his vision of New England's destiny.

34 Cecelia Tichi, "The Puritan Historians and Their New Jerusalem," *Early American Literature* 6 (1971): 143–55; and Lowance, *Language of Canaan,* pp. 115–59, who draws upon a broad array of American millennialists.

35 Bercovitch, *The American Jeremiad,* pp. 33–47, traces two strains of thought from the English Reformation which together created the uniqueness of the Great Migration. From Luther, English Puritans derived their concept of national election which focuses on the revelation of providential favor through actual terrestrial affairs, whereas from Calvin English Congregationalists inherited a second concept – independent of human and historical cycles, each saint and the collective Elect participate in a spiritual progress toward redemption.

36 John Robinson, *A Justification of Separation from the Church of England,* in *The Works of John Robinson,* ed. Robert Ashton, 3 vols. (London: J. Snow, 1851), 2:304; originally published in Leiden or Amsterdam, 1610. See Jesper Rosenmeier, " 'With My Owne Eyes': William Bradford's *Of Plymouth Plantation,*" in *Typology and Early American Literature,* ed. Bercovitch, pp. 68–105.

37 Bercovitch, *The American Jeremiad,* pp. 67–73; idem, *Puritan Origins of the American Self,* pp. 35–71, in which he concludes that "it was not by chance, then, that Nehemiah became the favorite ministerial as well as magisterial *exemplum* of the colonial clergy. He stood for the succession of exoduses, at once repetitive and developmental, that would culminate in the exodus from history itself" (p. 63).

38 John Norton, *The Evangelical Worshipper, Subjecting to the Prescription and Soveraignty of Scripture-patern* (Cambridge: S[amuel] G[reen] & M[armaduke] I[ohnson] for Hezekiah Vsher of Boston, 1664), p. 37.

39 Ibid.

40 Ibid.

41 Cotton Mather, *Magnalia Christi Americana,* 1:4.

42 See also Zwicker, *Dryden's Political Poetry;* idem, "Politics and Panegyric: The Figural Mode from Marvell to Pope," in *Literary Uses of Typology,* ed. Miner, pp. 115–46; and Paul J. Korshin, "The Development of Abstracted Typology in England, 1650–1820," in *Literary Uses of Typology,* ed. Miner, pp. 147–203; idem, *Typologies in England 1650–1820* (Princeton: Princeton Univ. Press, 1982), all of which discuss English adaptations of biblical types for historical purposes. Korshin, *Typologies in England,* pp. 30–8, 70–132, distinguishes among three varieties of typology. *Conventional typology,* based upon the Gospels and Epistles to St. Paul and elaborations by patristic theologians, becomes the basis for the exegesis undertaken by Protestant Reformers and American Puritans, including Edward Taylor. When this analogizing extends to parallels between Old Testament figures and contemporary monarchs, statesmen, and other worthies (sometimes called correlative typology), it becomes what Korshin terms *applied typology,* since the context may be religious but the associations political and literary as well. This form includes a branch (also arising out of what Lowance calls developmental typology) of millennial prefiguration that becomes widespread in

late seventeenth- and eighteenth-century America. Korshin focuses most extensively upon the third form, *abstracted typology*, which retains overtones of its
Christian purpose, but appears in a wide variety of eighteenth-century English
adaptations in secular literature. Rather than decode or interpret past mysteries,
the practitioners of an *abstracted typology* fashion their own fictions (Richardson,
Fielding, Goldsmith, and others), but introduce typological schemas to provide
a key for interpretation, a secularization and application as a device of literary
style to which Edward Taylor would vehemently object.

43 For seminal discussions of covenant theology, consult Perry Miller, *The New
England Mind: The Seventeenth Century* (1939; rpt. Cambridge: Harvard Univ.
Press, 1967), pp. 365–462; Everett H. Emerson, "Calvin and Covenant Theol-
ogy," *Church History* 25 (1956): 136–44; Peter Y. De Jong, *The Covenant Idea in
New England Theology, 1620–1847* (Grand Rapids, Mich.: Eerdmans, 1945); and
Robert G. Pope, *The Half-Way Covenant: Church Membership in Puritan New England*
(Princeton: Princeton Univ. Press, 1969).

44 Cotton Mather, *Magnalia Christi Americana*, 5:9.

45 John Langdon Sibley, "Edward Taylor," in *Biographical Sketches of Graduates
of Harvard University* (Cambridge: Charles William Sever, 1881), 2:397–412, 534–
6. See also Norman S. Grabo, *Edward Taylor* (New York: Twayne, 1961); and
Karl Keller, *The Example of Edward Taylor* (Amherst: Univ. of Massachusetts
Press, 1975) for recent biographical and critical studies.

46 Edward Taylor, *The Diary of Edward Taylor,* ed. Francis Murphy (Springfield,
Mass.: Connecticut Valley Historical Museum, 1964), p. 39.

47 Oakes, *New-England Pleaded With*, p. 22.

2 PROPHETS AND POETS: TYPOLOGY AS ILLUMINATION

1 See Taylor's account in "The Publick Records of the Church at Westfield,"
in *Edward Taylor's "Church Records" and Related Sermons,* vol. 1 of *The Unpublished Writings of Edward Taylor,* ed. Thomas M. and Virginia L. Davis, 3 vols.
to date (Boston: Twayne, 1981), pp. 1–162; and the editors' "Introduction" to
the same, pp. xi–xl. Excerpts appear in John Hoyt Lockwood, *Westfield and Its
Historic Influences, 1669–1919,* 2 vols. (Springfield, Mass.: By the Author, 1922),
1:102–321 passim. Taylor's "Spiritual Relation" on this occasion has also been
discussed by Donald E. Stanford, "Edward Taylor's 'Spiritual Relation,' " *American
Literature* 35 (1964): 467–75; and Daniel B. Shea, Jr., *Spiritual Autobiography in
Early America* (Princeton: Princeton Univ. Press, 1968), pp. 92–100.

2 Consult Constance J. Gefvert, *Edward Taylor: An Annotated Bibliography, 1668–
1970* (Kent, Ohio: Kent State Univ. Press, 1971) for a listing of primary biographical materials. Authoritative biographies of Taylor appear in Donald Stanford, "An Edition of the Complete Poetical Works of Edward Taylor" (Ph.D.
diss., Stanford University, 1953), pp. v–lxxxiii; idem, "Introduction," *The Poems
of Edward Taylor* (New Haven: Yale Univ. Press, 1960), pp. xxxix–xlviii; idem,
Edward Taylor, University of Minnesota Pamphlets on American Writers, no. 52
(Minneapolis: Univ. of Minnesota Press, 1965); Norman S. Grabo, *Edward Taylor* (New York: Twayne, 1961); and Karl Keller, *The Example of Edward Taylor*
(Amherst: Univ. of Massachusetts Press, 1975). In a genealogical memoir, Henry
Wyllys Taylor (great-grandson of Edward) writes: "Rev. Edward Taylor. of

Westfield Massachusetts was educated for the ministry among the Dissenters in England. To this end he received an admirable education, having pursued his studies for seven years in the University of Cambridge; during which he became well instructed in all the learning of the age." See Deborah Koelling, "Taylor on Taylor: A Family Memoir of Edward Taylor," *Resources for American Literary Study* 12 (1982): 29–42.

3 *The Poetical Works of Edward Taylor,* ed. Thomas H. Johnson (1939; rpt. Princeton: Princeton Univ. Press, 1960), pp. 201–20. Johnson bases his listings upon the inventory of Taylor's estate on August 29, 1729, two months after Taylor's death.

4 Keller, *Example of Edward Taylor,* pp. 81–97, surveys Taylor's prolific writings and speculates on the reasons for his literary proclivity but reluctance to publish the meditations. Thomas M. Davis, the editor of Taylor's works, estimates that the extant prose and poetry will fill twelve volumes.

5 Thomas M. Davis, "Edward Taylor and the Traditions of Puritan Typology," *Early American Literature* 4 (1969–70): 27–47, asserts that Taylor translated both the *De Principiis* and *Contra Celsum,* and Donald Stanford, *Poems of Edward Taylor,* p. 512, notes that the title page of *De Principiis* suggests a previous translation by Rufinus.

6 The "Metallographia" (337 pp., many of them blank) and "Dispensatory" (500 pp.) are in the Beinecke Library, Yale University, New Haven, Conn.

7 Edward Taylor's "Commonplace Book" (400 pp.), Massachusetts Historical Society, Boston, Mass., is distinct from "China's Description and Commonplace Book" (335 pp.), Beinecke Library, Yale University, New Haven, Conn.

8 For Taylor's early experimentation with poetic forms, see *Edward Taylor's Minor Poetry,* vol. 3 of *The Unpublished Writings of Edward Taylor,* ed. Thomas M. and Virginia L. Davis, 3 vols. to date (Boston: Twayne, 1981). *Gods Determinations touching his Elect* appears in full in both Thomas Johnson's and Donald Stanford's editions of Taylor's poems. See also *A Transcript of Edward Taylor's Metrical History of Christianity,* ed. Donald E. Stanford (Cleveland, Ohio: Micro Photo, 1962).

9 Henry W. Taylor, "Edward Taylor," in *Annals of the American Pulpit,* ed. William B. Sprague, 9 vols. (New York: R. Carter & Brothers, 1857–9), 1:179. Judge Henry Taylor draws upon his manuscript copy of Ezra Stiles's short biographical memoir, in which Stiles asserts that his grandfather Edward Taylor "left about 100 volumes bound by himself, many of them folio, written with his own hand."

10 See Robert E. Reiter, "Poetry and Doctrine in Edward Taylor's *Preparatory Meditations,* Series II, 1–30," in *Typology and Early American Literature,* ed. Sacvan Bercovitch (Amherst: Univ. of Massachusetts Press, 1972), pp. 162–74; Robert M. Benton, "Edward Taylor's Use of His Text," *American Literature* 39 (1967): 31–41; Mason I. Lowance, Jr., *The Language of Canaan: Metaphor and Symbol in New England from the Puritans to the Transcendentalists* (Cambridge: Harvard Univ. Press, 1980), pp. 89–111; and Norman S. Grabo, "Introduction," *Edward Taylor's Christographia* (New Haven: Yale Univ. Press, 1962), pp. xi–xliv, hereafter cited in the text as *CHR.* These critics affirm the close interconnections of the administration of the Lord's Supper, the sermons preached on sacrament Sundays, and the *Preparatory Meditations.* Thomas M. Davis, "Edward Taylor's

'Occasional' Meditations," *Early American Literature* 5 (1970–1): 17–29, points to irregularities in Taylor's meditative practices and questions how consistently the meditations coincide with Taylor's administration of the Lord's Supper.

11 *Edward Taylor's Treatise Concerning the Lord's Supper*, ed. Norman S. Grabo (East Lansing: Michigan State Univ. Press, 1966), hereafter cited as *TCLS*.

12 Davis, "Edward Taylor and the Traditions of Puritan Typology," p. 35, finds "that the impetus for initiating a new series of Meditations came not from Mather's work or a similar study, but from the actions of Solomon Stoddard." Taylor's interest in types certainly exists concurrent with, and therefore influences his composition of, the *Treatise,* but the meditations and sermons *Upon the Types of the Old Testament* also clearly document Taylor's inspiration drawn from Thomas Taylor's *Christ Revealed* and Samuel Mather's *The Figures or Types.*

13 See Charles W. Mignon, "The Nebraska Edward Taylor Manuscript: 'Upon the Types of the Old Testament,' " *Early American Literature* 12 (1977–8): 296–301; I am indebted to his announcement of this discovery and discussion of the provenance. The genealogy is here reproduced and amended:

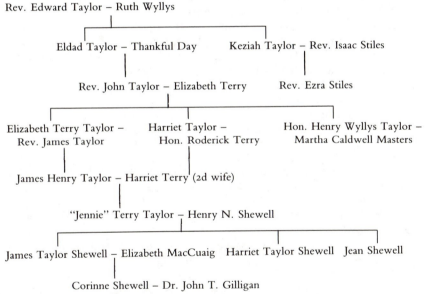

Taylor's sermons probably descended through his son-in-law Isaac Stiles to grandson Ezra, then to Judge Henry Wyllys Taylor, who donated both the "Poetical Works" and *Christographia* to Yale University in 1833. The manuscript most likely passed to the present owner through either of Henry's brothers-in-law, Rev. James Taylor or the Hon. Roderick Terry; the estate of the latter contributed *A Metrical History of Christianity*, the *Diary*, and "The Harmony of the Gospels" to the Redwood Athenaeum in 1951. Intermarriage of fifth-generation cousins James Henry Taylor and Harriet Terry may have consolidated the once dispersed library. *Upon the Types of the Old Testament* will be cited hereafter in the text as *UTOT*.

14 See Karen E. Rowe, "Puritan Typology and Allegory as Metaphor and Conceit in Edward Taylor's *Preparatory Meditations*" (Ph.D. diss., Indiana University, 1971), for the earliest claim that Meditations II.58, 59, 60A, 60B, 61, and II.70–71 also belonged within Taylor's exposition on types.

15 Born 1576 into a Yorkshire family sympathetic to Puritans and silenced ministers, Thomas Taylor graduated from Christ's College, Cambridge (B.A., 1594–5; M.A., 1598), became a fellow from 1599 to 1604, and eventually Wentworth Hebrew lecturer (1601–4). He preached at age twenty-five in St. Paul's Cross before Queen Elizabeth, but was later silenced for preaching at St. Mary's, Cambridge, against the severe treatment of Puritans. Living at Watford (perhaps as vicar) in 1612 and then removing to Reading, he gathered around him a "nursery of young preachers," including William Jemmat who later edited *Christ Revealed*. On January 22, 1625, he was chosen minister of St. Mary Aldermanbury, London, where he preached zealously until 1630, when failing health forced a retirement to Isleworth, where he died in 1633. Taylor's outspokenness in defense of Puritans apparently retarded his progress toward the doctor's degree at Cambridge (1628) and his belated receipt of the D.D. at Oxford (1630).

16 Samuel Mather, *A Testimony from the Scripture against Idolatry & superstition, in two sermons* (Cambridge, Mass.: Samuel Green, 1670?). Eldest son of Richard Mather and brother to Increase, Samuel Mather was born in England (1626), graduated M.A. from Harvard (1643), and became a fellow there before returning to become the chaplain at Magdalen College, Oxford, in 1650. Graduated M.A. first at Cambridge and then at Trinity College, Dublin (1654), where he was appointed a senior fellow, he was then ordained in St. Nicholas's Church, Dublin, on December 5, 1656, under the auspices of prominent congregationalists. He was suspended at the Restoration in October 1660 for the sermons preached against the revival of ceremonies and took over a curacy in Lancashire, England, only to be ejected under the Act of Uniformity in 1662. Back in Dublin, he gathered a congregation, but was imprisoned in 1664 for preaching at a private conventicle, then released. Before he died at age forty-six (1671), he was, according to Cotton Mather's *Magnalia Christi Americana* (London: For Thomas Parkhurst, 1702; rpt. New York: Arno, 1972), 5:152, urged by "the *Non-Conformist* Ministers, in the City of *Dublin,* to preach upon the *Types of Evangelical Mysteries, in the Dispensations of the Old Testament.*" His younger brother Nathanael subsequently edited these sermons for the 1683 posthumous publication of *The Figures or Types*.

17 See Mason I. Lowance's "Introduction" to Samuel Mather's *The Figures or Types of the Old Testament* (London: For Nathaniel Hillier, 1705; rpt. New York: Johnson, 1969), pp. v–xxiii, for information about the inception, writing, and publication of Samuel Mather's work. I have identified ten extant copies of the 1683 Dublin edition, four of the 1685 (London: H. Sawbridge & A. Churchill), two of the 1695 (London: For Nath. Hillier), and ten more of the 1705 second edition (London: Nath. Hillier), for a total of twenty-six copies in American libraries alone. Although none of the 1683 or 1685 volumes contains marginalia in Edward Taylor's hand, he probably used, even annotated, a copy now lost or still in family hands. The large number of extant copies (contrasting, for instance, to three of Thomas Taylor's *Christ Revealed* in American libraries) confirms the widespread popularity of Mather's *Figures or Types* among colonial theologians.

Edward Taylor's page references in *Upon the Types of the Old Testament* indicate that he used either a 1683 or 1685 edition of Mather's treatise.

18 Gordon E. Slethaug, "Edward Taylor's Copy of Thomas Taylor's *Types:* A New Taylor Document," *Early American Literature* 8 (1973): 132–9. In his "Itineraries and Memoirs. 1760," Beinecke Library, Yale University, New Haven, Conn., 1:63, Ezra Stiles lists this very volume of "Taylors Types" as among "Grandfathers Book apprizd in Fathers Lib." (Isaac Stiles, Taylor's son-in-law), lending credence to the supposition that Edward Taylor distributed much of his well-stocked library before his death. Further references to Thomas "Taylors Types" appear in "Itineraries and Memoirs," 1:60, and in a later "Account of Books I took out of Fathers Library Oct. 1 1761," 1:451.

19 In *Annals of the American Pulpit,* ed. Sprague (p. 179) Hon. Henry W. Taylor remarks of Edward Taylor:

> Unable, through the poverty alike of himself and his parishioners, to purchase his necessary professional books, all, or nearly all those used by him were in manuscript, which he had transcribed as he had found opportunity. . . . His manuscripts were all handsomely bound in parchment by himself, of which tradition says he left, at his death, more than a hundred volumes. Fourteen of these were in quarto. Many of the smaller ones were of his own composition.

Only fourteen are now extant. If we accept Judge Taylor's statements as reliable, then it is also possible that Taylor transcribed Mather's *Figures or Types* in a manuscript yet unrecovered.

20 To facilitate references in the following discussion I transcribe in full Edward Taylor's marginal comments on Adam from p. 10 of *Christ Revealed:*

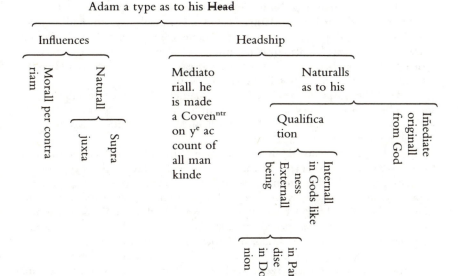

21 Outstripping his models in ramistic subdivisions, Edward Taylor Sermon II.3 reveals an organization more elaborate even than his own marginal sketch in *Christ Revealed*. Compare with note 20.

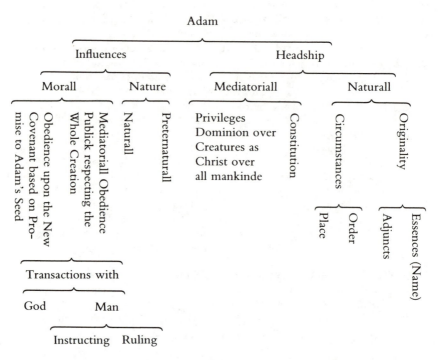

22 The key word "influences," as in "Such Influences on my Spirits light" (II.3.17), also links Meditation II.3 to Mather, Taylor's marginal diagram, and Sermon II.3. Meditation II.63 later develops the same concept that Adam's natural "Headship" and rule "in Paradise in Dominion" over other creatures typify, as earlier in Sermon II.3, "Zions Paradise, Christs Garden Deare/ His Church, enwalld, with Heavenly Crystall fine" (II.63.25–6).

23 Under "The Gospel of the Holy Places," Mather also characterizes the *"Types and Shadows* of the *Ceremonial Law"* as "hard Shells, but there are sweet Kernels within, if the Lord help us to break the Shell, and to understand the Mystery and Meaning of them" (*FT*, p. 324).

24 Several critics have noted but not extensively studied the influence of Samuel Mather's *The Figures or Types* on the structure of Edward Taylor's typological meditations. See Ursula Brumm, *American Thought and Religious Typology,* trans. John Hoaglund (New Brunswick, N.J.: Rutgers Univ. Press, 1970), p. 65; Karl Keller, " 'The World Slickt Up in Types': Edward Taylor as a Version of Emerson," in *Typology and Early American Literature,* ed. Bercovitch, p. 177; Davis, "Edward Taylor and the Traditions of Puritan Typology," p. 33; and Lowance, *Language of Canaan,* pp. 90, 98. Until Slethaug's recovery of the annotated copy of *Christ Revealed,* it too was overlooked as an important contributor to Edward

Taylor's *Preparatory Meditations* and, as we now recognize, to his sermons *Upon the Types of the Old Testament.*

25 Charles W. Mignon in "Christ the Glory of All Types: The Initial Sermon from Edward Taylor's 'Upon the Types of the Old Testament,' " *William and Mary Quarterly* 37 (1980): 286-301, provides a complete transcription of Sermon II.1, which sets the context for Taylor's examination of types in the remaining thirty-five sermons.

26 See Brumm, *American Thought and Religious Typology*, pp. 56-85; Keller, " 'The World Slickt Up in Types,' " in *Typology and Early American Literature*, ed. Bercovitch, pp. 175-90; idem, *Example of Edward Taylor*, pp. 177-88; Albert Gelpi, *The Tenth Muse: The Psyche of the American Poet* (Cambridge: Harvard Univ. Press, 1975), pp. 13-54. These critics place Edward Taylor in a lineage that leads directly to Jonathan Edwards and ultimately to the transcendentalism of Emerson, an approach that sometimes blurs the distinctions among types, tropes, and symbols and between biblical and natural typology. Both Reiter, "Edward Taylor's *Preparatory Meditations,* Series II, 1-30," in *Typology and Early American Literature,* ed. Bercovitch, pp. 165-6, and Peter White, "An Analysis of Edward Taylor's *Preparatory Meditation* 2.1," *Concerning Poetry* 11 (1978): 19-23, offer sound readings of Meditation II.1. Anthony Damico, "The Conceit of Dyeing in Edward Taylor's *Preparatory Meditations,* Second Series, Number One," *Early American Literature* 17 (1982-3): 227-38, challenges both readings with a convincing analysis of the typal images of dyeing and shells. See also discussions by Lowance, *Language of Canaan,* pp. 96-111; and Barbara Kiefer Lewalski, *Protestant Poetics and the Seventeenth-Century Religious Lyric* (Princeton: Princeton Univ. Press, 1979), pp. 388-426.

27 Marginal references from *Upon the Types of the Old Testament* and *Christographia* indicate Taylor's immense respect for Origen's homilies (even though later exegetes interpreted him controversially), Theophylact's erudite commentary on the evangelists, and Augustine's writings. The library inventory at his death lists *Origenis homiliae duae in cantica canticorum interprete divo Hieronymo,* Theophylact's *In quator Evangelia enarrationes,* and Augustine's ten-volume *Omnium Operum,* though references might as easily derive from Matthew Poole's five-volume *Synopsis criticorum aliorumque de scripturae interpretum,* the most widely consulted seventeenth-century collection of annotations and treatises on the Bible, also owned by Taylor. Recall too that he transcribed Origen's *Contra Celsum* and *De Principiis* into a manuscript book. See Johnson, ed. *Poetical Works,* pp. 204-5, 219.

28 Cited by Jean Daniélou, *From Shadows to Reality: Studies in the Biblical Typology of the Fathers* (London: Burns & Oates, 1960), p. 191.

29 Cited by Ronald S. Wallace, *Calvin's Doctrine of the Word and Sacrament* (Grand Rapids, Mich.: Eerdmans, 1957), p. 34. Thomas M. Davis, "The Traditions of Puritan Typology" (Ph.D. diss., University of Missouri, 1968), pp. 121-4, 282-3, also discusses these examples from Chrysostom and Calvin and illuminates the patristic heritage which informs all later exegeses and Puritan typology.

30 In the *Christographia* Taylor applies these images to Old Testament ceremonies of worship "delineating out Christ . . . in dark draughts, and resemblances" and other types through which "God doth as it were pensill out in fair Colours and [ingrave] and portray Christ and his Natures and Properties in him" (*CHR,*

pp. 123, 269). Once having assumed our human nature, the Son "gives out a renewall of his holy Image on man again in the Work of Regeneration, afresh upon his Soule in Evangelicall Colours" (*CHR*, p. 314). See *Christographia*, pp. 10, 288, 293 passim.

3 OF PROPHETS, PRIESTS, AND KINGS: PERSONALIZING THE TYPES

1 John Wilson, "A Song of Deliverance," in *Handkerchiefs from Paul*, ed. Kenneth B. Murdock (Cambridge: Harvard Univ. Press, 1927), p. 28.

2 Ibid., pp. 28, 27.

3 Cotton Mather, *Magnalia Christi Americana* (London: For Thomas Parkhurst, 1702; rpt. New York: Arno, 1972), 2:15. Sacvan Bercovitch, *The Puritan Origins of the American Self* (New Haven: Yale Univ. Press, 1975), uses Winthrop to show how Mather's adoption of the types, Nehemiah as well as David, Joseph, and Jacob, transforms this worthy divine into an exemplary Christian saint, one who participates heroically in the timeless schema of salvation as part of "the *communio praedestinarum*" (p. 43). Bercovitch argues:

> As the configuration comes to bear upon the New England magistrate – in *his* wilderness, providentially overcoming *his* trials, providing for *his* often ungrateful people – the *figura* that emerges bespeaks the furthest moral, spiritual, and eschatological reach of Winthrop as *exemplum fidei*. . . . the same hermeneutic which raises Winthrop beyond time locates him in time and place, as "Americanus"; the same technique which broadens our sense of Nehemiah as archetype deepens our sense of him as precedent, as a distinctive individual engaged in certain historical events that occurred some two millennia before the settlement of Massachusetts Bay. This is the second, larger reason for recognizing Mather's use of typology: it turns our attention to ordinary, temporal, geographical facts. (p. 39)

Rather than disjoint secular from sacred history (or biography), Mather interfuses the temporal with spiritual schemata, primarily by identifying contemporary Puritan ministers and magistrates with Old Testament types. See also Jesper Rosenmeier, "Bradford's *Of Plymouth Plantation*," in *Typology and Early American Literature*, ed. Sacvan Bercovitch (Amherst: Univ. of Massachusetts Press, 1972), pp. 68–105; and Mason I. Lowance, Jr., *The Language of Canaan: Metaphor and Symbol in New England from the Puritans to the Transcendentalists* (Cambridge: Harvard Univ. Press, 1980), pp. 160–77.

4 Edward Taylor, "An Elegie upon the Death of that holy man of God Mr. Sims, late Pastor of the Church of Christ at Charlestown in N. England who departed this life the 4th of 12m Ano Dni 1670/71," in *Edward Taylor's Minor Poetry*, vol. 3 of *The Unpublished Writings of Edward Taylor*, ed. Thomas M. and Virginia L. Davis, 3 vols. to date (Boston: Twayne, 1981), p. 21.

5 For earlier discussions of Edward Taylor's meditations on the personal types, see Ursula Brumm, *American Thought and Religious Typology*, trans. John Hoaglund (New Brunswick, N.J.: Rutgers Univ. Press, 1970), pp. 56–85; Robert E. Reiter, "Edward Taylor's *Preparatory Meditations*, Series II, 1–30," in *Typology*

and Early American Literature, ed. Bercovitch, pp. 162–74; Karl Keller, " 'The World Slickt Up in Types,' " in *Typology and Early American Literature*, ed. Bercovitch, pp. 175–90; Lowance, *Language of Canaan*, pp. 89–111; and Barbara Kiefer Lewalski, *Protestant Poetics and the Seventeenth-Century Religious Lyric* (Princeton: Princeton Univ. Press, 1979), pp. 405–9.

6 Emory Elliott, "From Father to Son: The Evolution of Typology in Puritan New England," in *Literary Uses of Typology from the Late Middle Ages to the Present*, ed. Earl Miner (Princeton: Princeton Univ. Press, 1977), pp. 204–27. Elliott argues that "his brother Increase may have been stunned" by the posthumous publication of Samuel Mather's *Figures or Types*, "which almost seemed to be a direct reprimand to those, like himself, who had gone to extremes to give meaning to modern history" by elaborating correspondences between Old Testament persons and events and New England's circumstances (p. 216).

7 Both Thomas Taylor and Samuel Mather argue that (in the latter's terms) "*Isaac* was the Seed of the Promise made to *Abraham, Ga.* 4.28. *in whom all the Nations of the Earth should be blessed:* But Christ was indeed the promised Seed, he was chiefly and principally intended in that Promise, see *Gal.* 3. 16" (*FT*, p. 83). Although Thomas Taylor neither cites Galatians 3:16, nor includes Abraham or Jacob in his treatise, his analysis of Isaac emphasizes the ram "caught . . . among the thornes" as a figure for "Christ our sacrifice" (*CR*, p. 27). This motif reappears in Edward Taylor's Sermon and Meditation II.5, in which he makes "This Isaac, and the Ram caught in the briars/ One Sacrifice" and asserts that "The full grown Ram" which is "Caught in the brambles by the horns, must bow,/ Under the Knife" (II.5.9–10, 13, 15–16). Diverging from both sources, Edward Taylor also stresses Christ's two natures, an interpretation that must have been commonplace, since Cotton Mather in his "Commentary on Genesis" from the unpublished "Biblia Americana" offers a similar reading:

> In the sacrifice offered by *Abraham*, wee must consider it was the *Ram* that felt the Knife. This admirably answers to the two natures of Our Lord Jesus Christ; both of which together contribute unto the Sacrifice of the New Covenant. The *Divine Nature* of Our Lord, suspending the Expressions of His Power & His Glory, was the Mystery of Isaac ty'd. The *Humane Nature* of Our Lord, crucify'd, was the mystery of the Ram slain. (p. 175)

See Lowance, *Language of Canaan*, pp. 169–77, in which he quotes further from Mather's "Biblia Americana," and pp. 107–9, for a discussion of Edward Taylor's meditation on Isaac.

8 Samuel Mather denies any arbitrariness in configurations of types by arguing that "the Nature of the Matter will not only *bear* it; but doth partly *lead unto it*" and, addressing his congregation or readers, he recommends that "the conjoyning or putting of them thus together will be some help both to your Understandings and Memories" (*FT*, p. 91).

9 In "Edward Taylor's *Preparatory Meditations*, Series II, 1–30," in *Typology and Early American Literature*, ed. Bercovitch, Reiter finds it puzzling that "Meditations 8, 19, and 28 lie, so far as I can presently determine, outside the series on types" and speculates that "if we had the accompanying sermons, their tenuous

connection with the rest of the series would probably become more apparent"
(pp. 164–5). As discussed later, Taylor in *Upon the Types of the Old Testament*
does omit II.19 on spicknard, but includes II.28 on moral sin and cities of refuge
as well as II.8.

10 Thomas Taylor also proclaims, but does not elaborate, Moses as a "Mediator
of the Old Testament, not a mediator of redemption, but of receiving the law
and delivering it to the people," and Christ as "our true *Moses*," who "not onely
receives the Law, but fulfils it" and becomes "Mediator of a new Covenant" of
grace (*CR*, p. 42).

11 Taylor's sermon on Jonah is one of the sections in *Upon the Types of the Old
Testament* that does not have page numbers, one indication that it may have been
added or relocated between Solomon and "All the Treasures of Wisdom" at a
later date.

12 Although Elisha and Elijah do not appear in Taylor's *Preparatory Meditations*
on personal types, they appear in two earlier poems, the first "An Acrostick
Chronogram," part of the "Elogy upon the Death of the Reverend & Learned
Man of God Mr. Charles Chauncey" (1672), an eminent president of Harvard
College to whom Taylor attributes Elijah's qualities:

> I – If this Elijahs Mantle, as he went
> V – Vnto the Kingdom filld with full Content,
> V – Vnto a man had fallen to inherit,
> V – With double Portion of Elijahs Spirit,
> V – Vnto Such Riches Sweet he should attain
> V – Which would inrich. . . .
> (*Edward Taylor's Minor Poetry*, p. 34)

In "The Lay-mans Lamentation upon the Civill Death of the late Labour[ers] in
the Lords vinyard, by way of Dialogue between a proud PRELATE, and a Poor
PROFESSOUR Silenced on Bartholomew day 1662," Taylor mourns the intrusion
of false ministers to supplant those Puritan preachers either dead or fled:

> Our lost Elijahs had they been succeded
> By choice Elisha's, wee noe more had needed.
> After our former Preachers Exterpation,
> Wee went t'our Churches, big with expectation
> Hoping to finde Elishas, but wee saw
> Onely Elijahs Mantle stuff'd with straw.
> Wee found our publicke places once a Bed
> Of fragrant Spices to perfume our head:
> Since, wee have gone, & walk'd the old bed round
> But for a David, have an image found.
> (*Edward Taylor's Minor Poetry*, p. 14)

In these lamentations Taylor attributes the characteristics of Old Testament prophets
to contemporary preachers, a practice that he eschews in the later *Preparatory
Meditations*.

13 See Barbara Kiefer Lewalski, *Milton's Brief Epic: The Genre, Meaning, and Art*

of Paradise Regained (Providence, R.I.: Brown Univ. Press, 1966), pp. 193–321, which examines Milton's use of prophets, priests, and kings to prefigure Christ.

14 William G. Madsen, *From Shadowy Types to Truth: Studies in Milton's Symbolism* (New Haven: Yale Univ. Press, 1968), pp. 181–202, explicates Milton's typological uses of Samson in *Samson Agonistes,* a dramatic portrayal far different from Edward Taylor's meditative style.

15 Louis L. Martz, *The Poetry of Meditation* (1954; rev. ed. New Haven: Yale Univ. Press, 1962); idem, "Foreword," *The Poems of Edward Taylor* (New Haven: Yale Univ. Press, 1960), pp. xiii–xxxvii.

16 Keller, " 'The World Slickt Up in Types,' " in *Typology and Early American Literature,* ed. Bercovitch, comments upon the subtlety with which Taylor personalizes the types, insinuating himself into the divine cosmology:

> Taylor accomplishes this self-inclusion by writing about Christ as a fulfillment of Old Testament foreshadowings in such a way that he is involved unobtrusively but noticeably in the relationship. . . . Taylor is for the most part attracted to types into which he can slip himself without in any way changing the nature of the original type-antitype relationship, thereby sneaking himself into the plan of salvation by means of the vehicle of language. (pp. 181–2)

Taylor's language has its subtleties, but his desire to identify with typical figures and Christ provokes notably overt requests in the meditations. For the Puritan saint, adopting types and the Savior as models for the spiritual progress toward salvation would not require linguistic trickery, since such applications found repeated sanction in figural studies and in the very practices of the Puritan sermon. As a conservative exegete, Taylor can respect the sacrosanct relationship between the patriarchal types and Christ's fulfillment, while simultaneously personalizing them.

17 Robert Hollander, "Typology and Secular Literature: Some Medieval Problems and Examples," in *Literary Uses of Typology,* ed. Miner, pp. 3–19, observes that in Prudentius's *Psychomachia,* "he reveals the basic allegorical stance of the entire work: We move from the Old Testament *figurae* through Christ to a tropological sense in our present lives – which is where the 'action' of this great conversionary poem takes place" (p. 13). I use the term "tropological" cautiously, recognizing that the medieval allegories which emphasize human moral struggles differ vastly from Edward Taylor's Puritan meditations, in which primary emphasis falls on the *littera-historia* of the type and antitype before any application of morals.

18 Sacvan Bercovitch's discussion of the suppression of Christ in biographical and historical uses of types should be recalled, since it differentiates the posture of a Cotton Mather from Edward Taylor's meditative stance:

> Seventeenth-century Protestant spiritual biographies repeatedly and insistently invoke the *imitatio* through parallels with "humane" precedents, rather than with Jesus Himself. The term "Nehemias Americanus" implies that the American is like Christ because he is like Nehemiah; the same formula applies to most of Mather's biographical

allusions, and to those of virtually all Puritans' Lives. It is as though the biographers, conscious of their enormous charge, felt that they could not trust the *imitatio Christi* alone, the direct correlation between the individual's experiences and Christ's, to carry its own message. . . . All evidence suggests a reluctance to equate the elect directly with Christ. . . . [because] a tremendous gulf separates exemplar from imitator. . . . [Thus] the biographers found the authority they sought in the Old Testament. By that authority they could reiterate the premises of the microchristus ("The Fathers before Christ had as truly the same *Spiritual Life* in Christ as we"), even while they stressed the difference between man and Christ: although "the Life of his Divine Nature neither of us have," we are equal with the Israelites in "proportion and resemblance of his life." (*Puritan Origins of the American Self,* pp. 25–7)

Such qualms, which motivate historians and biographers to adopt Old Testament figures as more human and accessible figures for contemporary men's actions, seem less operative in the devotional treatises and Taylor's meditations on types in which the *imitatio Christi* takes priority over *imitatio figura*. See also James W. Earl, "Typology and Iconographic Style in Early Medieval Hagiography," *Studies in the Literary Imagination* 8 (1975): 15–46, for a discussion of the imperative placed upon individuals, in the form of the *imitatio Christi,* to establish a right relationship (through the practice of a moral life) of self to the sweep of salvation history.
19 *Edward Taylor's Minor Poetry,* ed. Davis, pp. 20–2.
20 Cotton Mather, *Magnalia Christi Americana,* 3:31.

4 EDWARD TAYLOR'S PURITAN "WORSHIP–MOULD"
1 *Dictionary of National Biography,* s.v. "Taylor, Thomas." *Christ Revealed* was published two years after Taylor's death.
2 Ceremonial laws for priests and purifications, which Taylor locates under personal ranks, account for another 27 percent (91 pp.) of *Christ Revealed* (339 pp.), and persons and ranks (Nazarites and firstborn) constitute the remainder.
3 Samuel Mather's full title reads, *A Testimony from the Scripture against Idolatry & superstition, in two sermons; upon the example of that great reformer Hezekiah, 2 Kings 18:4. The first, witnessing in generall against all the idols and inventions of men in the worship of God. The second, more particularly against the ceremonies, and some other corruptions of the Church of England. Preached, the one September 27, the other Septemb. 30. 1660* (Cambridge, Mass.: Samuel Green, 1670?).
4 Literally a textile woven from a mixture of wool and flax, "linsey-woolsey" was also a common term of disapproval for a strange medley in talk or action, suggesting confusion or hypocrisy. Samuel Mather may use the term cleverly to refer to Cardinal Thomas Wolsey (1475?–1530) who fell into disgrace for resisting Henry VIII's attempts to establish the Church of England and to Bishop of Edinburgh, David Lindsay (d. 1641?) who supported the articles of King James VI at the Perth Assembly (1618), specifically on kneeling to the king. Mather indicts all men who uphold popish ceremonies, despite political involvement with or doctrinal commitments to Protestant principles of religion.

5 Mather's account of the occasional types (including Israel's deliverance), Passover, and circumcision amounts to only 11 percent (59 pp.) of *The Figures or Types* (1705 ed.; 540 pp.). Included among ceremonies, the purifications and priesthood account for 16 percent (89 pp.), whereas exegesis of Old Testament sacrifices, festivals, temple furnishings, and sermons against popish holy days and music form the remainder of the total 70 percent on ceremonial law (372 pp.).

6 See Cotton Mather, *Magnalia Christi Americana* (London: For Thomas Parkhurst, 1702), 7:14–29, 96–101, for the classic statement of Puritan attitudes toward Anne Hutchinson and the Quakers. For additional commentary on both topics, see also Norman S. Grabo's notes to his edition of *Edward Taylor's Christographia* (New Haven: Yale Univ. Press, 1962), pp. 478–9; Perry Miller, *The New England Mind: From Colony to Province* (1953; rpt. Cambridge: Harvard Univ. Press, 1967), pp. 57–63, 123–6; Larzer Ziff, *Puritanism in America: New Culture in a New World* (New York: Viking, 1973), pp. 63–77, 138–45; Ben Barker-Benfield, "Anne Hutchinson and the Puritan Attitude toward Women," *Feminist Studies* 1 (1972): 65–96; Emery Battis, *Saints and Sectaries: Anne Hutchinson and the Antinomian Controversy in the Massachusetts Bay Colony* (Chapel Hill: Univ. of North Carolina Press, 1962); Arnold Lloyd, *Quaker Social History, 1669–1738* (New York: Longmans, Green, 1950); Richard T. Vann, *The Social Development of English Quakerism, 1665–1755* (Cambridge: Harvard Univ. Press, 1969); Lyle Koehler, *A Search for Power: The "Weaker Sex" in Seventeenth Century New England* (Urbana: Univ. of Illinois Press, 1980); and Carla Gardina Pestana, "The City upon a Hill under Siege: The Puritan Perception of the Quaker Threat to Massachusetts Bay, 1656–1661," *New England Quarterly* 53 (1983): 323–53.

7 See Grabo, "Explanatory Notes," *Edward Taylor's Christographia*, pp. 478, 487.

8 William Pynchon, *The Meritorious Price of Our Redemption* (London: J. M. for George Whittington & James Moxon, 1650).

9 First as a nonjuror, then (having sworn the oath) as dean of St. Paul's (1691), William Sherlock (1641?–1707) threw himself into a renewed controversy over Socinianism (now called Unitarianism) by publishing his *Vindication of the . . . Trinity* (1690). Rather than defending Socinian dogma, Sherlock actually sought to denounce it, but went too far, his *Vindication* being accused of tritheism. In his later *Present State of the Socinian Controversy* (1698; most printed in 1696), he retreated from the impugned positions, leading Robert South to conclude, "There is hardly any one subject that he has wrote upon . . . but he has wrote for and against it too." Writing his Sermon II.17 in 1696, Taylor may have felt that Sherlock's retraction constituted an indirect support of Socinian doctrine or, out of touch in New England, he may have recalled only a very early (mid-1670s) false linkage of Sherlock with this heresy.

10 John Owen, *Diatriba de Justitia Divina. Seu justitiae vindicatricis vindiciae quibus . . .* (Oxford: T. Robinson, 1653); idem, *Vindiciae Evangelicae Or The Mystery of the Gospell Vindicated and Socinianisme Examined, In the Consideration, and Confutation of A Catechisme, called A Scripture Catechisme, Written by J. Biddle* (Oxford: L. Lichfield for T. Robinson, 1655). In both works Owen defends the Calvinist position against Socinian doctrines set forth in John Biddle's English translation

of *The Racovian Catechisme* (Amsterdam: B. Janz, 1652) and publication of *A Twofold Catechism: The One simply called A Scripture Catechism; The Other, A brief Scripture-Catechism for Children* (London: J. Cottrel for Ri. Moone, 1654). Biddle was known as the father of English Unitarianism. Works also listed by Grabo, ed., *Christographia*, p. 487.

11 Pagination of *Upon the Types of the Old Testament,* in Edward Taylor's hand through 540 and Henry Wyllys Taylor's thereafter, reaches 906, though the actual number of pages is 844. Although pagination is lacking between the continuous but separate leaves for 426^r and 461^v, no stubs of cut gatherings indicate Taylor's excising of a sermon. It is possible, however, that he had preached a sermon on spicknard or the holy of holies as a companion to Meditation II.19, yet chose not to include it in his reedited volume. However, he did cut out pages between 613 and 637, presumably removing a sermon between II.24 on the Feast of Tabernacles and II.26 on unclean touchings, possibly by deleting a sermon on annual feasts or relocating Sermon II.25 on morn and evening sacrifices elsewhere. Taylor devotes 37 percent (316 pp.) to ceremonial worship and purifications (II.16–28), 18 percent (150 pp.) to extraordinary deliverances and Israel's wilderness signs (II.29, 58–61), and only 6 percent (48 pp.) to the ordinary seals circumcision and Passover (II.70–71).

12 In the manuscript of Taylor's "Poetical Works" (Beinecke Library, Yale University), the actual line reads "But for reliefe Grace in her tender *m*ould/ Massiah cast all Sacrifices told," a reading that more closely coincides with his preoccupation with the "Worship-mould" in the poems on ceremonial law.

13 According to Exodus 26, 27, 35–8, the brazen altar stood in the priest's court of the tabernacle and was used for burnt offerings of animals and birds to expiate sins. The golden incense altar stood within the holy place and was used for daily and special incense offerings. Although located in the sanctuary, it became associated with the holy of holies, because the incense (signifying prayer) was wafted before the mercy seat, thus ascending to God. Once a year the golden altar was sprinkled with the blood of a sin offering to make atonement, foreshadowing that Christ would intercede by virtue of his own oblation or self-sacrifice (see Meditation II.23). Completing the typal symbolism, the mercy seat signified God's throne of grace, and the holy of holies prefigured heaven itself, toward which men aspire through lifelong prayer and mortification of sins and prayer. A diagram of the tabernacle follows:

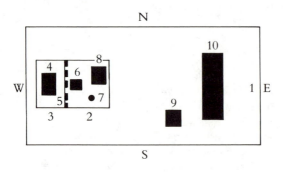

1. Court
2. Holy place
3. Holy of holies
4. Ark of the covenant (mercy seat is the golden lid)
5. Veil
6. Golden altar of incense
7. Candelabrum (Menorah)
8. Table of shewbread
9. Brazen laver
10. Brazen altar of burnt offering

14 The four-month interval between Sermon II.18 on altars (October 8, 1696) and II.20 on the tabernacle (February 7, 1696/7) and striking linkages between all the sermons and *Preparatory Meditations* on types make it plausible that Taylor originally composed a companion sermon to Meditation II.19 (December 7, 1696), perhaps on spicknard, priestly duties, and the holy of holies, only to eliminate it later from the collection.

15 Sermon II.25 (morn and evening sacrifices and sabbaths) presents one of the most puzzling problems in assessing Taylor's organization of *Upon the Types of the Old Testament*. In the *Types* manuscript, these twenty-four unnumbered pages are positioned after the sermons on Passover and Pentecost (II.22 and II.22A) and before the Feast of Atonement (II.23). In the *Preparatory Meditations* the corresponding poem (dated March 6, 1698) is located after the Feast of Tabernacles (II.24), the last of the annual feasts, and before Meditation II.26 on unclean touchings. In *Upon the Types* the twelve cut leaves between Sermons II.24 and II.26 *might* suggest that Taylor transcribed Sermon II.25 in its new position sometime after his initial composition. However, Taylor's written directives, as I have discussed in the text, would seem to recommend a third and different placement, one supported also by the affixed (and therefore *presumed*) date of composition. Sermon II.25 (morn and evening sacrifice and sabbaths) is dated March (1^m) 6, 1697, locating it chronologically between Sermon and Meditation II.20 on the temple and tabernacle (February 7, 1696) and II.21 on new moon feasts (May 16, 1697). Taylor's expressed design, I conclude, is to discuss the daily "Continuall Burnt Offering" (universal) and "the Weekly or Sabbath Sacrifices" before "More than Ordinary" (particular) lunar and septinary feasts, that is, prior to all Sermons and Meditations II.21–24 (*UTOT*, p. 502). The uncertainty about Sermon II.25, the sporadic numbering of pages after 540, and the cut leaves suggest that Taylor may not have put into place his final organization; consequently, the introductions to both II.21 and II.25 contain statements designed to make the transition from mediums of worship to seasonal feasts.

16 Meditation II.21 captures Taylor's fascination with the mystery of sevens; he recasts in the poem a catalog from *Upon the Types*, p. 455:

> Each Seventh Day a Sabbath Gracious Ware.
>   A Seventh Week a yearly Festivall.
> The Seventh Month a Feast nigh, all, rich fare.
>   The Seventh Yeare a Feast Sabbaticall.
>   And when seven years are seven times turnd about
>   A Jubilee. Now turn their inside out.
>
> What Secret Sweet Mysterie under the Wing
>   Of this so much Elected number lies?
> What Vean can e're Divine? Or Poet sing?
>   (II.21.7–15)

17 When he introduces a new text from Acts 2:1, 4 for that "next Great Anniversary Feast of Pentecost," Taylor apparently creates a separate sermon, beginning p. 484 and complete with independent uses which end abruptly on p. 500. Curiously lacking a date, this homily occupies a spare seven pages among sermons normally two to five times as long, and it may be a preaching rather than

elaborated version, or simply an unusually brief consideration of Pentecost. However, Pentecost's topical compatibility with Passover might also point to a continuous preaching rather than discrete sermons on these two anniversary feasts, a speculation strengthened by evidence from the meditations. Taylor places a four-stanza fragment on Pentecost initially after Meditation II.21, then reattaches a modified version to Meditation II.22. Fragment II.21A's opening, "But now I from the New Moon Feast do pass/ And pass the Passo're o're unto Gods Seales," suggests an original intent to withhold Passover entirely until the analysis of covenantal seals, a plan agreeing with Thomas Taylor's sacramental aims (II.21A.1–2). Instead, Taylor reappends the fragment to Meditation II.22 and alters the transitional lines: "But now I *from* the Passover do pass./ . . . And come to Whitsuntide" (II.22.49–51). By lodging both Passover and Pentecost among anniversary feasts, Taylor imitates Mather's treatment of the ceremonial feasts, though he returns later to a sacramental interpretation of Passover as a seal in Sermon II.71. Taylor may have preached with inordinate brevity or composed the sermon only for his typological collection, but the revision and reattachment of this Pentecost fragment to the Passover meditation points as well to a possible corresponding unity in Sermon II.22.

18 The directive is inscribed below a fully drawn line at the end of Sermon II.24. Taylor may have preached on sabbatical and Jubilee celebrations between December 1697 (II.24) and June 1698 (II.26), eliminating this sermon later for reasons unknown. But it is also possible that he preached Sermon II.25 to correspond with the extant meditation dated March 6, 1698. See note 15 in this chapter.

5 NEW ENGLAND'S SAINTS DELIVERED

1 See Rosemond Tuve, *A Reading of George Herbert* (Chicago: Univ. of Chicago Press, 1952); William J. Scheick, "Typology and Allegory: A Comparative Study of George Herbert and Edward Taylor," *Essays in Literature* 2 (1975): 76–86; Northrop Frye, "The Typology of *Paradise Regained*," *Modern Philology* 53 (1956): 227–38; William G. Madsen, *From Shadowy Types to Truth: Studies in Milton's Symbolism* (New Haven: Yale Univ. Press, 1968); and Barbara Kiefer Lewalski, *Milton's Brief Epic: The Genre, Meaning, and Art of Paradise Regained* (Providence, R.I.: Brown Univ. Press, 1966); idem, "Typological Symbolism and the 'Progress of the Soul' in Seventeenth-Century Literature," in *Literary Uses of Typology*, ed. Earl Miner (Princeton: Princeton Univ. Press, 1977), pp. 79–114; Jonathan Goldberg, "*Virga Iesse:* Analogy, Typology, and Anagogy in a Miltonic Simile," *Milton Studies* 5 (1973): 177–90; and Mary Ann Radzinowicz, *Toward "Samson Agonistes": The Growth of Milton's Mind* (Princeton: Princeton Univ. Press, 1978), pp. 273–312.

2 Karen E. Rowe, "A Biblical Illumination of Taylorian Art," *American Literature* 40 (1968): 370–4.

3 Early critics who identified Taylor as an "American metaphysical" or an anti-Puritan "colonial baroque" include Martha Ballinger, "The Metaphysical Echo," *English Studies in Africa* 8 (1965): 71–80; Wallace C. Brown, "Edward Taylor: An American 'Metaphysical,' " *American Literature* 16 (1944): 186–97; Austin War-

ren, "Edward Taylor's Poetry: Colonial Baroque," *Kenyon Review* 3 (1941): 355–71; and Emma Louise Shepherd, "The Metaphysical Conceit in the Poetry of Edward Taylor" (Ph.D. diss., Univ. of North Carolina, 1960). For seminal discussions of the metaphysical conceit as the definitive criterion of a metaphysical style, consult Samuel Johnson, "Cowley," from *The Lives of the English Poets* in *The Works of Samuel Johnson* (Oxford: Talboys & Wheeler, 1825; rpt. New York: AMS, 1970), 7:1–56; T. S. Eliot, "The Metaphysical Poets," *Selected Essays,* rev. ed. (New York: Harcourt, Brace & World, 1964), pp. 241–50 (essay first published in 1921); and Helen Gardner, *The Metaphysical Poets,* 2d ed. (Oxford: Oxford Univ. Press, 1967). Quotations from Johnson, *Works,* 7:15–16; and Gardner, *Metaphysical Poets,* p. xxiii.

4 See Frank Kermode, "Introduction," ed. *The Metaphysical Poets: Key Essays on Metaphysical Poetry and the Major Metaphysical Poets* (Greenwich, Conn.: Fawcett, 1969), p. 21; Rosemond Tuve, *Elizabethan and Metaphysical Imagery: Renaissance Poetic and Twentieth-Century Critics* (Chicago: Univ. of Chicago Press, 1947), p. 161; and Joseph A. Mazzeo, "A Critique of Some Modern Theories of Metaphysical Poetry," *Modern Philology* 50 (1952): 89–90.

5 Stephen Manning, "Scriptural Exegesis and the Literary Critic," in *Typology and Early American Literature,* ed. Sacvan Bercovitch (Amherst: Univ. of Massachusetts Press, 1972), p. 58.

6 Conceit has become so synonymous with metaphysical that it is generally defined as an "ingenious and fanciful notion or conception, usually expressed through an elaborate analogy and pointing to a striking parallel between two seemingly dissimilar things," as in *A Handbook to Literature,* ed. William F. Thrall, Addison Hibbard, and C. Hugh Holman, rev. ed. (New York: Odyssey, 1960), p. 103. My amended definition returns to the original emphasis on concept, the intellectual perception of relationships between two ideas, objects, or images, but it does not insist upon initial dissimilarities between the elements. See the discussions by Frank J. Warnke, *European Metaphysical Poetry* (New Haven: Yale Univ. Press, 1961), pp. 5–7; and Mazzeo, "A Critique of Some Modern Theories," pp. 88–90.

7 Earl Miner, *The Metaphysical Mode from Donne to Cowley* (Princeton: Princeton Univ. Press, 1969). Miner's use of the terms "definition" and "dialectic" with reference to seventeenth-century English metaphysicals may be applied in modified ways to patterns in Edward Taylor's meditations.

8 In his *Tropologia: A Key To Open Scripture-Metaphors* (London: J. D. for Enoch Prosser, 1681), Keach cites not only the root of David and vine (Bk. 2, pp. 221–6) but also a rock and a fountain (Bk. 2, pp. 170–7) as metaphors for Christ, though not with special reference to Horeb. Henry Vertue, *Christ and the Church: Or Parallels* (London: Tho. Roycroft, 1659), pp. 312–26, 426–30, includes the vine, winepress, and threshing floor.

6 SACRAMENTAL TYPES: SEALS TO THE COVENANT

1 Samuel Mather preached his sermon on "The Gospel of Circumcision," dated October 30, 1666, five months before beginning his study of the types on March 23, 1666/67. In *The Figures or Types* he locates this homily immediately after the

inaugural sermon on the ceremonial law or "Perpetual Types" (June 4 and 7, 1668).

2 For fuller considerations of the Half-Way Covenant, see Perry Miller, *The New England Mind: From Colony to Province* (1953; rpt. Cambridge: Harvard Univ. Press, 1967), pp. 93–115; idem, "The Marrow of Puritan Divinity," in *Errand into the Wilderness* (Cambridge: Harvard Univ. Press, 1956), pp. 48–98; Peter Y. De Jong, *The Covenant Idea in New England Theology, 1620–1847* (Grand Rapids, Mich.: Eerdmans, 1945); and Robert G. Pope, *The Half-Way Covenant: Church Membership in Puritan New England* (Princeton: Princeton Univ. Press, 1969). Although the Synod of 1662 adopted the Half-Way Covenant, dissension flared in Hartford (1666) and Boston (1669) and literally split these churches in two over the issue of Baptism.

3 Donald E. Stanford, "Edward Taylor and the Lord's Supper," *American Literature* 27 (1955): 174. Stanford analyzes this same Meditation II.108 to prove Edward Taylor's Puritan orthodoxy regarding the Supper (pp. 172–8).

4 See Perry Miller's narration of Solomon Stoddard's life and works, first published as "Solomon Stoddard, 1643–1729," *Harvard Theological Review* 34 (1941): 277–330, and then elaborated in *The New England Mind: From Colony to Province*, pp. 226–87; Thomas A. Schafer, "Solomon Stoddard and the Theology of the Revival," in *A Miscellany of American Christianity*, ed. Stuart C. Henry (Durham, N.C.: Duke Univ. Press, 1963), pp. 328–61; E. Brooks Holifield, *The Covenant Sealed: The Development of Puritan Sacramental Theology in Old and New England, 1570–1720* (New Haven: Yale Univ. Press, 1974); Burley Gene Smith, "Edward Taylor and the Lord's Supper: The Controversy with Solomon Stoddard" (Ph.D. diss., Kent State University, 1975); and Ralph J. Coffman, *Solomon Stoddard* (Boston: Twayne, 1978). Graduated from Harvard M.A. in 1665, Stoddard acted briefly as university librarian in 1667, then he received a call in 1669 from Northampton, where he was ordained in 1672. His residence in Cambridge in 1669 overlapped with Edward Taylor's tenure at Harvard during 1668–71, at which time (December 1671) Taylor began his ministry in Westfield. After nearly sixty years as theological adversaries, although geographical neighbors, both men died in 1729.

5 On New England's decline from original covenant principles, see Perry Miller, "Declension in a Bible Commonwealth," *Proceedings of the American Antiquarian Society* 51 (1941): 37–94; idem, *The New England Mind: From Colony to Province*, pp. 19–146; Robert G. Pope, "New England Versus the New England Mind: The Myth of Declension," *Journal of Social History* 3 (1969–70): 301–18; and Emory Elliott, *Power and the Pulpit in Puritan New England* (Princeton: Princeton Univ. Press, 1975). Many of the key documents for understanding the sacramental controversy now appear in *Edward Taylor vs. Solomon Stoddard: The Nature of the Lord's Supper*, vol. 2 of *The Unpublished Writings of Edward Taylor*, ed. Thomas M. and Virginia L. Davis, 3 vols. to date (Boston: Twayne, 1981), hereafter cited as *ETSS* in the text. My chapter emphasizes the uses of typological exegesis in the sacramental controversy and was substantially completed before the publication of Thomas Davis's "Introduction." I am indebted to his edition and commentary for clarifying the theological issues and relationships among the various documents. Davis persuasively argues that Stoddard initially proposed admitting

church members to the Lord's Supper without a saving relation as a response to the failure of the Half-Way Covenant in Northampton. Concerned that so few members had been admitted to full communion during his early ministry, Stoddard sought for a practical and principled extension of half-way provisions to the Lord's Supper, hoping thereby to encourage more communicants and to stem the declension. Preaching in 1690 on Galatians 3:1, he declares:

> The Lord's Supper is so much neglected, if you will not use all meanes God may righteously deny his blessing to the means that are used: wee have had some spetiall tokens of the presence of God: but the Country is greatly departed from God, in this little time, since the land has bin planted, wee may well suspect this to be one cause of it; that this meanes is so much neglected. (*ETSS,* p. 143)

6 Since no original Stoddard manuscript for the Synod of 1679 remains, we must rely on "Mather's Confutation of the Rev. Mr Stoddard's Observations respecting the Lords Supper 1680," ed. Everett Emerson and Mason I. Lowance, *Proceedings of the American Antiquarian Society* 83 (1973): 44, pages cited hereafter in the text. No evidence records the publication of either Stoddard's "Observations" or Mather's "Confutations," but Thomas Davis speculates (*ETSS,* p. 8) that, within a month or so of the synod debate on September 19, 1679, Stoddard must have supplied Mather with a detailed defense of his proposal, containing at least nine arguments that Mather attributes to Stoddard. For a fuller discussion of the 1679 Reforming Synod, see Williston Walker, *The Creeds and Platforms of Congregationalism* (New York: Charles Scribner's Sons, 1893), pp. 409–39.

7 Solomon Stoddard, *An Appeal to the Learned* (Boston: B. Green for Samuel Phillips, 1709), p. 94, cited hereafter in the text.

8 In retrospect, Mather did not take seriously enough his own prophecy in the "Confutation" about the result of Stoddard's "opinion which hath been maintained by papists, Erastians, and some prelatical men, but is abundantly refuted, not only by those of the Congregational persuasion, but by godly learned presbytereans; especially by Mr *Gelaspy* in his Aarons Rod, and by Dr *Drake* against Mr *Humphrey*. And by Mr *Vines* in his Treatise of the Lords Supper" (p. 56). He brushes aside the potential danger, "so that I shall not need to vindicate the truth in that controversy, others having done it so fully," before providing a glimpse of "one argument" that he will develop extensively in later denunciations of Stoddard: "If the sacrament were a converting ordinance, then scandalous persons, yea, very heathens should have it administered to them, for wee may not withold from them converting ordinances" (p. 56).

9 The Foundation Day Sermon exists in two manuscript versions, both now available in *Edward Taylor's "Church Records" and Related Sermons,* vol. 1 of *The Unpublished Writings of Edward Taylor,* ed. Thomas M. and Virginia L. Davis, 3 vols. to date (Boston: Twayne, 1981), pp. 118–58, 283–373, cited hereafter as *CRRS*. Recorded initially by Taylor in "The Publick Records of the Church at Westfield Together With a briefe account of our proceeding in order to our entrance into that State," Westfield Athenaeum, pp. 87–100, the first version, identified as the Foundation Day Sermon, accompanies Taylor's letters of invitation, "Profession of Faith," and "The Public Relations" of six foundation men on the .

occasion of his ordination and organization of the church. The second version, titled "A Particular Church is Gods House," appears in Taylor's "Extracts" volume in the Boston Public Library, and includes twenty-four manuscript pages added in 1692–3, in which he aggressively rebuts Stoddard's Galatians sermon of 1690 and espousal of the Supper as a converting ordinance. See Norman S. Grabo, "Edward Taylor on the Lord's Supper," *Boston Public Library Quarterly* 12 (1960): 22–36; Dean Hall and Thomas M. Davis, "The Two Versions of Edward Taylor's Foundation Day Sermon," *Resources for American Literary Study* 5 (1975): 199–216; and Thomas M. Davis's "Introduction" to *Edward Taylor's "Church Records" and Related Sermons* and to *Edward Taylor vs. Solomon Stoddard*.

10 Solomon Stoddard, *The Safety of Appearing at the Day of Judgment, In the Righteousness of Christ: Opened and Applied* (Boston: Samuel Green for Samuel Phillips, 1687). I quote from the 3d ed. (Boston: D. Henchman, 1742), pp. 282, 285, which is based upon Stoddard's corrections and additions for the 2d ed. (Boston: D. Henchman, 1729).

11 "A Letter sent to the Rev. Mr. Solomon Stoddard Past[or of the] Church of Christ at Northampton . . . Westfield 13: 12:ᵐ 1687/8," and Stoddard's reply to Taylor June 4, 1688, appear in Taylor's "Commonplace Book," Massachusetts Historical Society. Norman S. Grabo first transcribed these letters in "The Poet to the Pope: Edward Taylor to Solomon Stoddard," *American Literature* 32 (1960): 197–201. Parenthetical references are to the letters as they appear in *ETSS*.

12 Michael J. Colacurcio, "Gods Determinations Touching Half-Way Membership: Occasion and Audience in Edward Taylor," *American Literature* 39 (1967): 298–314, places *Gods Determinations touching his Elect* in the context of the religious upheavals of the 1680s by arguing that Taylor's audience is the half-way members whom he urges to search their hearts more diligently for signs of converting grace that they might come into full communion.

13 Williston Walker, "A Historical Sketch of Stoddardeanism, with some account of its effect upon the churches in Old Hampshire County, Mass.," *The New Englander* 4 (1846): 354, and cited by Grabo, "Edward Taylor on the Lord's Supper," p. 36.

14 Passover appears only briefly in Stoddard's *The Safety of Appearing* (1687) as a "commemoration" of God's mercy in "delivering of *Israel* out of *Egypt*" and as an instruction in *"their deliverance from eternal destruction,* and their *spiritual redemption by Jesus Christ"* (p. 57).

15 First edited by Thomas M. Davis and Jeff Jeske, "Solomon Stoddard's 'Arguments' Concerning Admission to the Lord's Supper," *Proceedings of the American Antiquarian Society* 86 (1976): 75–111, the version cited textually is from *ETSS*, pp. 67–86.

16 According to Thomas Davis, the "Animadversions" were transcribed after Taylor received Stoddard's "Arguments for the Proposition" (1689–90) and probably before he revised the Foundation Sermon (ca. 1692). Davis convincingly argues that "by the time Taylor had begun the 'Animadversions,' he had apparently received a copy of Stoddard's sermon on the converting nature of the Lord's Supper" and recognized in it the "much greater threat" to Protestant doctrine (*ETSS*, p. 34). The manuscript is contained in Taylor's "Extracts," Boston Public Library, and the version cited in the text is from *ETTS*, pp. 87–128.

17 I quote from the headnote to six "Anti-Stoddard Syllogisms" from Taylor's "Commonplace Book," Massachusetts Historical Society, which appear in *ETSS*, pp. 149–51. The full explanatory note summarizes Stoddard's actions in the winter of 1690:

> Mr. Stoddard having preached up from Ga[l.] 3.1. that the Lords Supper was a Converting Ordinance (Some Animadversions on which Sermon See among my Manuscrips) & urged till on an Occasion of the Ruling Elders absence by reason of Sickness, & many if not almost all the Ancient members of the Church were dead then he calls his Church to New Covenanting & among other Articles presented gains a major part to this Article to bring all to the Lords Supper that had a knowledge of Principles of Religion, & not scandalous by open Sinfull Living. This done in the Winter 1690. (*ETSS*, p. 149)

Michael Schuldiner, "Solomon Stoddard and the Process of Conversion," *Early American Literature* 17 (1982–3): 215–26, offers an analysis with which I essentially agree, concluding that "Stoddard's adoption of the converting ordinance doctrine in 1690. . . . represents a culminating stage in the shift in Stoddard's focus from admission requirements for the Lord's Supper to conversion" (p. 223).

18 Thomas M. Davis first transcribed "Solomon Stoddard's Sermon on the Lord's Supper as a Converting Ordinance," *Resources for American Literary Study* 4 (1974): 205–24, from the only extant manuscript in Taylor's "Extracts," Boston Public Library. I cite textually from *ETSS*, pp. 129–47. In *The Faithful Shepherd: A History of the New England Ministry in the Seventeenth Century* (Chapel Hill: Univ. of North Carolina Press, 1972), David Hall argues that Stoddard like the Mathers "attempted to accommodate older preaching forms to the needs of a second-generation audience," but "to avoid both the slackness . . . in the Mathers' strategy and the hyperscrupulosity their arguments could lead to," Stoddard elected to sever "the connections between conversion and the sacraments, or, indeed, between conversion and church membership" (p. 256).

19 Norman Grabo, "Poet to the Pope," p. 201, verifies Northampton's adoption of Stoddard's motions. As Thomas Davis argues in his "Introduction" to *ETSS*, despite Stoddard's agitation since the late 1670s, the Northampton church resisted his sacramental propositions until 1690. But, once having embraced the principle of more liberal admissions to the Lord's Supper and, thereby, countenanced the Sacrament as a converting ordinance, this congregation inaugurated an irreversible expansion of New England's covenant community. Williston Walker, "Historical Sketch of Stoddardeanism," records that by 1750 "there were not more than three [ministers] in the county, with the exception of his [Jonathan Edwards] young brother-in-law, Moses Tuttle, that were decidedly anti-Stoddardean" (p. 353).

20 Increase Mather, *A Dissertation* . . . (Boston: B. Green for Benj. Eliot, 1708), cited hereafter in the text. The sermon to which Mather's title alludes is Solomon Stoddard's *The Inexcusableness of Neglecting the Worship of God, under A Pretence of being in an Unconverted Condition* (Boston: B. Green for Samuel Phillips, 1708). Thomas H. Johnson, ed., *The Poetical Works of Edward Taylor* (1939; rpt. Prince-

ton: Princeton Univ. Press, 1960), pp. 201–20, reprints an inventory of Edward Taylor's library at his death, which does not list a single work by Stoddard, though it lists several works by Increase Mather, including his *Dissertation*. See Robert Middlekauff, *The Mathers: Three Generations of Puritan Intellectuals, 1596–1728* (New York: Oxford Univ. Press, 1971); James A. Goulding, "The Controversy between Solomon Stoddard and the Mathers: Western Versus Eastern Massachusetts Congregationalism" (Ph.D. diss., Claremont Graduate School, 1971); James P. Walsh, "Solomon Stoddard's Open Communion: A Reexamination," *New England Quarterly* 43 (1970): 97–114; E. Brooks Holifield, "The Renaissance of Sacramental Piety in Colonial New England," *William and Mary Quarterly*, 3d ser. 29 (1972): 33–48; idem, "The Intellectual Sources of Stoddardeanism," *New England Quarterly* 45 (1972): 373–92; Mason I. Lowance, Jr., *Increase Mather* (New York: Twayne, 1974); and Karl Keller, *The Example of Edward Taylor* (Amherst: Univ. of Massachusetts Press, 1975).

21 In *A Discourse concerning the danger of apostasy*, second title and part of *A Call from heaven to the present and succeeding generations* . . . (Boston: John Foster, 1679), Increase Mather stretches figural exegesis by erecting parallels between New England's religious declension during the 1670s and the tribulations of third-generation Israelites. Perhaps rebuked by his brother's conservatism in *The Figures or Types* (1683), Mather gradually modulates the extravagances of his historical analogies and reemphasizes New Testament fulfillments. In the *Dissertation* he directs the reader to *"see my Brother Samuel Mather of the Types.* p. 528, 529 *in the first Edition"* after he has summarized Samuel's major typal correspondences to prove that "the Israelites Eating the Paschal-Lamb, Typified our feeding upon Christ by Faith in the Lords Supper" (p. 17). Emory Elliott, "From Father to Son: The Evolution of Typology in Puritan New England," in *Literary Uses of Typology*, ed. Earl Miner (Princeton: Princeton Univ. Press, 1977), pp. 204–27, considers Mather's evolution as an example of seventeenth-century tensions between the "officially stated version of Puritan hermeneutics" which "insisted upon the strict and literal interpretation of the Old Testament," and the socially utilitarian interpretation of "modern historical events as fulfillments of the scriptural prophesies" (p. 205).

22 Thomas Davis also finds that "Stoddard's position on the significance of typology completely changes during the course of his publications," from his initial use of it in the "Arguments" to his apparent denial of figuralism in the *Appeal* (*ETSS*, p. 56). See Davis's discussion, *ETSS*, pp. 31–2, 56, 227. In "The Appeale Tried" Edward Taylor scornfully refutes Stoddard first by asserting "The Answer is against Scripture which calls Gospell Ordinances by the Names of the Old Types as the Gospell Feast the Paschall Feast, I Cor. 5.8. & Baptism the Circumcision of Christ, Col. 2.11," then by questioning Stoddard's rejection of authoritative divines, "What is this Slighting of the Testimonies of Learned & Holy Men for? is it of any good report?" and finally by reaffirming that Passover "was a Church Ordinance, & therefore a Sign & type that Unclean persons were not to have Fellowship with Gospell Churches" (*ETSS*, pp. 161, 162).

23 See Mason I. Lowance, Jr., "Typology and Millennial Eschatology in Early New England," *Literary Uses of Typology*, ed. Miner, pp. 228–73; idem, *The*

Language of Canaan: Metaphor and Symbol in New England from the Puritans to the Transcendentalists (Cambridge: Harvard Univ. Press, 1980).

24 In his "Introduction" to the edition of *Edward Taylor's Treatise Concerning the Lord's Supper* (East Lansing: Michigan State Univ. Press, 1966), pp. ix–li, Norman S. Grabo perceptively comments on the backgrounds, intention, and images of these anti-Stoddard homilies.

25 Davis, *ETSS*, p. 56, speculates that "Taylor's long unit of typological Meditations . . . begins shortly after this interchange [in the "Animadversions"] with Stoddard, and may have been prompted by his use of types to controvert Stoddard's view."

26 Davis, *ETSS*, p. 24, briefly illuminates the links between "Stoddard's view of the converting nature of the Supper" and the "Erastian controversy in England during the early decades of the seventeenth century, particularly in the works of such authors as William Prynne, John Humfrey, and John Timson, and their opponents George Gillespie, Richard Baxter, and Richard Vines." Both Edward Taylor and Increase Mather rely heavily on Gillespie's *Aarons Rod Blossoming, or, The Divine Ordinance of Church-Government Vindicated* (London: E. G. for Richard Whitaker, 1646) and Richard Vines, *A Treatise of the Institution, Right Administration, and Receiving of the Sacrament of the Lords-Supper* (London: A. M. for Thomas Underhill, 1657). In "A Particular Church is Gods House," Taylor explicitly recommends "Mr. Gillespy against the Erastians in his *Aarons Rod blossoming*, Reciting the Protestants in Generall against the Papist in this matter, & then he confirms by 20 Argument[s] the Lords Supper to be no Converting Ordinance, Book 3. Cap. 12 & 13" (*CRRS*, p. 338). Stoddard aligns himself with theologians of the Presbyterian fold, whereas Edward Taylor remains staunchly congregational in his polity, despite his use of notable Presbyterians Vines and Gillespie.

27 "The *Appeale* Tried," which appears in Taylor's "Extracts," Boston Public Library, was first identified by Norman S. Grabo, " 'The Appeale Tried': Another Edward Taylor Manuscript," *American Literature* 34 (1962): 394–400. The transcription by Thomas Davis in *ETSS*, pp. 153–216, is cited hereafter in the text. James W. Barbour discusses the sacramental imagery that links "The *Appeale* Tried" to the poems in "The Prose Context of Edward Taylor's Anti-Stoddard Meditations," *Early American Literature* 10 (1975): 144–57.

28 Donald E. Stanford, "*Sacramental Meditations* by Edward Taylor," *Yale University Library Gazette* 31 (1956): 61–75, first published Meditations II.104–109 and 111.

29 Stanford, "Edward Taylor and the Lord's Supper," p. 177, also annotates Taylor's dependency on Mather's *Dissertation* and Vines's *Treatise*, which Taylor may quote directly.

7 PREPARING FOR THE WEDDING FEAST

1 Thomas M. Davis, "Edward Taylor's 'Occasional' Meditations," *Early American Literature* 5 (1970–1): 17–29, argues that Taylor did not initially conceive of his poems and sermons as a united preparation for the sacramental administration. In *ETSS*, p. 56, Davis repeats his case, based upon an analysis of handwriting, the recopying of the first forty meditations in the fall of 1690, and a

suggestion that "Taylor's decision to identify his Meditations with the administration of the Sacrament may have been made within the context of his recognition of the enormous implications of Stoddard's doctrine," specifically after Stoddard's preaching of the Galatians sermon.

2 William Guild's *Moses Unvailed* (London: G. Purslow for J. Budge, 1619 [part I]–1620 [part II]; Glasgow: Robert Sanders, 1701) contains ten pages and thirty-four parallels on Passover, though we have no confirmation that Edward Taylor used Guild's work, except by way of the adaptations in Thomas Taylor's *Christ Revealed* and Mather's *The Figures or Types*.

3 The last four stanzas of Taylor's Meditation II.22, beginning with "But now I from the Passover do pass," appear crossed out after the conclusion of Meditation II.21 on new moons and sabbaths, then reappear with slight revision attached to this poem on Passover. Samuel Mather had broken down the "Jewish Festivals" into three sermons, the first treating Passover, Pentecost, and the Feast of Tabernacles, the second explicating the Feast of Trumpets, new moons, sabbaths, and Jubilee, and the third detailing the Feast of Expiation, also called the Great Day of Atonement (*FT*, pp. 414–59).

4 Reiterating the need for the wedding garment in his *Dissertation* (1708), Mather defines it simply: "Now by the Wedding Garment, Faith in the Righteousness of Christ, and Inherent Sanctification also, is doubtless intended" (p. 5).

5 Stoddard, *An Appeal to the Learned,* also offers a different reading of St. Matthew's parable:

> The Messengers of God are sent to invite men to this Feast: and I think he will not say, that the great errand of the Ministry is to invite men to the Lords Supper: besides this is a Feast that the Jews were invited to from Generation to Generation, long before the Lords-Supper was Instituted. . . . First he sent the Prophets and then the Apostles, after this the Gentiles were invited to the same Feast, *v. 9. Go ye into the highways, & as many as ye shall find, bid unto the Marriage.* Besides this man that had not the Wedding Garment was not suffered to partake of this Feast, but such persons are suffered to partake of the Lords Supper; besides this person that was objected against for not having a Wedding Garment was a Reprobate, v. 14 *Many are called, but few are chosen.* (p. 4)

6 Stoddard, *An Appeal to the Learned,* pp. 57–8, replies directly to Mather's

> Exception. *That Scandalous Persons might come to the Passover but not to the Lords Supper.* He saith, *Adulterers, Thieves, Liars, Slanderers, Perjured persons, might come to the Passover, and I must admit such Scandalous persons to the Lords Supper, or let go my argument from the Passover.* And he teaches me what to answer, *viz. That more positive fruits of Regeneration are required in the Church Members of the New Testament than the Old.* But I dare not give that answer, because of the absurdity of it: for the persons, that he speaks of wanted the Negative fruits of Regeneration.

Stoddard makes no claim that scandalous Israelites, except inadvertently, might celebrate the Passover, since "how to reconcile such practices with heart circumcision is quite beyond me" (p. 11). Likewise, he would not admit the visibly scandalous to the Lord's Supper, despite Mather's exaggerated accusations. The real issue revolves around those persons leading nonscandalous lives as church members, who may not have experienced a work of saving conversion or confessed their faith. Mather would exclude such members from communing; Stoddard would admit them.

7 In writing to the Corinthians (5:11), Paul warns: "But now I have written unto you not to keep company, if any man that is called a brother be a fornicator, or covetous, or an idolater, or a railer, or a drunkard, or an extortioner; with such an one, no, not to eat." In 1 Corinthians 11:27, he further enjoins: "Wherefore, whosover shall eat this bread, and drink *this* cup of the Lord, unworthily, shall be guilty of the body and blood of the Lord." This text and surrounding passages figure prominently in both early and later disputes over the Lord's Supper. See Dean Hall and Thomas M. Davis, "The Two Versions of Edward Taylor's Foundation Day Sermon," *Resources for American Literary Study* 5 (1975): 199–216, which discusses Taylor's rebuttal in the revised sermon (1692–3) to Stoddard's "Galatians" sermon (1690) on the issue of unworthy partaking. Similarly, the issue and biblical text reappear prominently in Mather's *Dissertation*, Stoddard's *An Appeal to the Learned*, and Edward Taylor's "The *Appeale* Tried."

8 See Norman S. Grabo's "Introduction," to *Edward Taylor's Treatise Concerning the Lord's Supper* (East Lansing: Michigan State Univ. Press, 1966), pp. ix–li, in which he discusses Taylor's use of this parable to structure his work and relates the concept of the wedding garment to the poem "Huswifery."

9 Cited also by James W. Barbour, "The Prose Context of Edward Taylor's Anti-Stoddard Meditations," *Early American Literature* 10 (1975): 145; Barbour relates Taylor's poetic images to their prose counterparts in the Foundation Day sermons (both versions), the *Treatise*, and "The *Appeale* Tried," including his usages of the wedding garment.

10 In the third book of "The *Appeale* Tried," Taylor directly counters Stoddard's assertion in *An Appeal to the Learned* that "If Unsanctifyed Persons might lawfully come to the Passover, then they may lawfully partake of the Lords Supper: But they might lawfully come to the Passover" (p. 50). As his proof, Taylor reiterates typological parallels between Passover and the Lord's Supper, based largely upon *Christ Revealed* and *The Figures or Types,* similar to his usages in the *Treatise, Upon the Types,* and Meditations II.22 and II.71. Displaying the Lord's Supper's superior institution to Passover, he argues, for example:

> The Passover had all *** of the Israelites, the first, for its Subjects, Good & Bad, Uncircumcised & Unclean, & under a necessity to Celebrate itt, & that upon the Perill of their lives. & after Passovers in the Wilderness all the Males Ceremonially Clean tho' Uncircumcised & not under insuperable Circumstances impending, were the Qualified Subjects of it. & when in the Land of Canaan all males were subject to it, if Circumcised, Ceremonially Cleane, not under too difficult Circumstances, & if morally unclean & they not revealing it if secret, they were to attend it tho' not by Gods allowance. . . . [However,] the Institution of the Lords Supper admits of no Such persons. The First Celebration

of it. Onely Eminent Disciples received it, afterward manifest sinners are excluded from it, I Cor. 5, all leaven is to be purgd away, v. 7,8,11. & this Leaven of mallice & wickedness, & the Old Leaven, yea & Covetousness, what are they but inward Sins, thatt all persons are to purge away before they approach this Ordinance. (*ETSS*, p. 188)

Recall Meditation II.103 in which Taylor also argues for the "Spirituall Cleaness qualifying all/ That have a Right to tend this Festival" of the Lord's Supper as opposed to Passover's merely "Ceremoniall Cleaness" (II.103.47–8, 46).

11 See Kathleen Blake, "Edward Taylor's Protestant Poetic: Nontransubstantiating Metaphor," *American Literature* 43 (1971): 1–24. Blake astutely relates Taylor's use of metaphor to the Puritan concept of the Lord's Supper as a partaking of the physical bread and wine, though these elements spiritually signify the body and blood of Christ. She summarizes, "under the aspect of metaphor Taylor conceives and expresses a key metaphysical relationship, namely, the link between concrete and abstract, physical and spiritual, vehicle and tenor, what he calls Signe and Signatum. . . . Specifically, he forwards the remarkably suggestive idea that the Lord's Supper works like a metaphor" (pp. 1–2). See also Michael North, "Edward Taylor's Metaphors of Promise," *American Literature* 51 (1979): 1–16.

12 In his Galatians sermon, Stoddard specifically exhorts "such unconverted persons, as doe come to the Lords Supper to use this ordinance for your conversion; improve this ordinance for that end, that you may be savingly brought home to God" (*ETSS*, p. 145). Moreover, he urges men "in the way of preparation for this ordinance to examine themselves, I Cor. 11.28 . . . whether they be converted or no . . . the depth of the corruption of their heart . . . & how unworthy they are, what need they have of the grace & mercy & power of Christ Jesus" (*ETSS*, pp. 146–7). However, he views the Lord's Supper as a "speciall opportunity" to stimulate such self-examination, yet does not make such preparations or prior conversion mandatory for partaking (*ETSS*, p. 146). According to the apostle Paul in Corinthians, he argues, "hee doth not say that they should examine themselves whether they should come or no, but they must examine themselves & so come" (*ETSS*, p. 136). Consequently, preparation through self-examination becomes a useful adjunct, but not an absolute requirement for celebrating the Supper.

13 In agreement with Edward Taylor's position as opposed to Stoddard's, Increase Mather in his "Confutation" declares: "[N]amely, that though it be true, that wee may and should hope that those whom wee administer baptism unto, are beleevers on Christ, yett a greater visibility of faith, or more satisfactory evidence concerning the regeneration of one that is admitted to the Lords Supper, is necessary, then can be affirmed of one that is admitted to baptism only" (p. 55). Thus, he makes the ascertaining of a "saving work of regeneration" mandatory: "And therefore examination concerning that qualification is no less requisite then examination concerning their knowledge, or orthodoxy" (p. 55). Likewise, Edward Taylor in "The *Appeale* Tried" takes issue with Stoddard's lax notion of self-examination to see whether one discerns merely the nature of the Lord's Supper rather than one's inward regeneration:

> If onely a Discerning the Lords Body was all that the Apostle aimed at
> in order for this Ordinance by the Duty preparatory of Examination,
> then the Apostles Plaster was too little for the Sore. Other sins were
> not repented of, nor reformed. But in truth the Apostle applieth a tho-
> row, & Full remedy, when he puts them on Self Examination, Saying
> Let a man Examine himself. . . . [I]t puts us on such duties, as render
> us approoved, & that for fellowship with God, & Christ, whereby we
> become Approoved to the Church, approoved of our own Consciences,
> & Approoved of God: & hence lies in the Exercise of Repentance on the
> discovery of Sin, & of Reformation in life & Faith in Christ. & this
> answers the Case of the Corinthians, & sets them right for the Lords
> Supper. (*ETSS*, p. 159)

Self-examination must lead not simply to doctrinal professions of faith but also
to the confession of a saving work of grace upon the soul, which then enables
one to come to the Lord's Supper.

14 See also David L. Parker, "Edward Taylor's Preparationism: A New Perspective on the Taylor-Stoddard Controversy," *Early American Literature* 11 (1976–
7): 259–78.

15 Neither the concept nor use of meditation to separate hypocrites from sincere
guests was original with Taylor, since eminent seventeenth-century divines, such
as Richard Baxter in *The Saints Everlasting Rest* (1650) and Thomas Shepard in
The Sincere Convert (1640) and *The Parable of the Ten Virgins* (1660), also demanded
soul-searching examinations. Puritan theologians would certainly applaud the
meditative ends that Taylor sets – to illuminate the understanding, excite the
holy affections, and move the will to acts of reformation or worship. See the
following studies of seventeenth-century meditative traditions and/or New England
preparationism: Louis L. Martz, *The Poetry of Meditation* (1954; rev. ed. New
Haven: Yale Univ. Press, 1962); Norman Pettit, *The Heart Prepared: Grace and
Conversion in Puritan Spiritual Life* (New Haven: Yale Univ. Press, 1966); William
Halewood, *The Poetry of Grace: Reformation Themes and Structures in English Seventeenth-Century Poetry* (New Haven: Yale Univ. Press, 1970); and Robert Daly,
God's Altar: The World and the Flesh in Puritan Poetry (Berkeley: Univ. of California Press, 1978). Louis L. Martz's prefatory comments to *The Poems of Edward
Taylor* and Norman S. Grabo's discussion in *Edward Taylor's Treatise Concerning
the Lord's Supper* directly connect Taylor with the seventeenth-century English
and American traditions of preparatory meditation.

16 See the *Treatise*, p. 169, in which Taylor lauds the Lord's Supper with comparable images, as for example:

> It is the richest and royalest feast that ever was made. George Neville's
> feast at York was nothing to this for costliness. Nor was King Ahasu-
> erus his feast (Esth. 1) to be mentioned with this. This feast for the
> provision of it in signs, and things signified, is an epitome of all gospel
> grace, or all the grace of the gospel. Now then think of it. Hence how
> can it be that the soul dressed up in the wedden garment should not
> have an high esteem and an unspeakable love unto it?

8 THE ARTISTRY OF TYPES

1 The phrase "a little *Recreation of Poetry*" originated with Cotton Mather and provides the basis for a seminal discussion of Puritan attitudes toward poetry, literary style, and aesthetics in Kenneth B. Murdock's *Literature & Theology in Colonial New England* (Cambridge: Harvard Univ. Press, 1949; rpt. New York: Harper & Row, 1963), pp. 137–72. The discussion has continued in works such as Norman S. Grabo's "The Veiled Vision: The Role of Aesthetics in Early American Intellectual History," *William and Mary Quarterly* 19 (1962): 493–510; Roy Harvey Pearce, *The Continuity of American Poetry* (Princeton: Princeton Univ. Press, 1961); Hyatt H. Waggoner, "Puritan Poetry," *Criticism* 6 (1964): 291–312; Michael McGiffert, "American Puritan Studies in the 1960s," *William and Mary Quarterly* 27 (1970): 36–67; Russell Fraser, *The War against Poetry* (Princeton: Princeton Univ. Press, 1970); Robert Daly, *God's Altar: The World and the Flesh in Puritan Poetry* (Berkeley: Univ. of California Press, 1978); David Leverenz, *The Language of Puritan Feeling: An Exploration in Literature, Psychology, and Social History* (New Brunswick, N.J.: Rutgers Univ. Press, 1980); and *Puritan Poets and Poetics*, ed. Peter White (University Park: Pennsylvania State Univ. Press, 1985).

2 For studies of Taylor's poetry in relationship to George Herbert's, see not only Barbara Kiefer Lewalski, *Protestant Poetics and the Seventeenth-Century Religious Lyric* (Princeton: Princeton Univ. Press, 1979), pp. 111–44, 283–316, 388–426, but also Samuel Eliot Morison, *The Intellectual Life of Colonial New England*, 2d ed. (New York: New York Univ. Press, 1956), pp. 235–40; Christopher Grose, "To the American Strand: A Study of the Poetry of George Herbert and Edward Taylor" (B.A. Honors Thesis, Amherst, 1961); Ursula Brumm, "Edward Taylor and the Poetic Use of Religious Imagery," in *Typology and Early American Literature*, ed. Sacvan Bercovitch (Amherst: Univ. of Massachusetts Press, 1972), pp. 191–206; Albert Gelpi, *The Tenth Muse: The Psyche of the American Poet* (Cambridge: Harvard Univ. Press, 1975), pp. 22–8; and William J. Scheick, "Typology and Allegory: A Comparative Study of George Herbert and Edward Taylor," *Essays in Literature* 2 (1975): 76–86.

3 Henry Ainsworth, *Solomons Song of Songs in English Metre* (Amsterdam: Bourne & Bellamy, 1623); Théodore de Bèze, *Canticum Canticorum Salomonis versibus et commentariis illustratum, Gilb. Genebrardo auctore. Adversus trochaicam Theodori Beza paraphrasim* (Paris: Gordinum, 1585); John Mason, *Spiritual Songs, or, Songs of Praise . . . Together with The Song of Songs Which is Solomons. First Turn'd, then Peraphrased in English Verse* (London: Northcott, 1683); and Francis Quarles, *Sions Sonets. Sung By Solomon the King, And Periphras'd By Fra. Quarles* (London: W. Stansby for Thomas Dewe, 1625). These works are only a sampling of the more than forty expositions and poetic paraphrases on Canticles composed during the sixteenth and seventeenth centuries.

4 Early studies that discuss Taylor's relationship to the traditions of English and continental poetry include the following: Thomas H. Johnson, "Edward Taylor: A Puritan 'Sacred Poet,' " *New England Quarterly* 10 (1937): 290–322; Austin Warren, "Edward Taylor's Poetry: Colonial Baroque," *Kenyon Review* 3 (1941): 355–71; Wallace C. Brown, "Edward Taylor: An American 'Metaphysical,' " *American Literature* 16 (1944): 186–97; Mindele Black, "Edward Taylor: Heavens

Sugar Cake," *New England Quarterly* 29 (1956): 159–81; Norman S. Grabo, "Catholic Tradition, Puritan Literature, and Edward Taylor," *Papers of the Michigan Academy of Science, Arts and Letters* 45 (1960): 395–402; Martha Ballinger, "The Metaphysical Echo," *English Studies in Africa* 8 (1965):71–80; Karl Keller, *The Example of Edward Taylor* (Amherst: Univ. of Massachusetts Press, 1975), pp. 163–88.

5 A variety of stimulating essays have examined the relationship of Taylor's Puritanism to his poetic structures and images. See E. F. Carlisle, "The Puritan Structure of Edward Taylor's Poetry," *American Quarterly* 20 (1968): 147–63; Joseph M. Garrison, Jr., "The 'Worship-Mould': A Note on Edward Taylor's *Preparatory Meditations*," *Early American Literature* 3 (1968): 127–31; Clark Griffith, "Edward Taylor and the Momentum of Metaphor," *English Literary History* 33 (1966): 448–60; Alan B. Howard, "The World as Emblem: Language and Vision in the Poetry of Edward Taylor," *American Literature* 44 (1972): 359–84; Donald Junkins, "Edward Taylor's Creative Process," *Early American Literature* 4 (1969–70): 67–78; idem, " 'Should Stars Wooe Lobster Claws?': A Study of Edward Taylor's Poetic Practice and Theory," *Early American Literature* 3 (1968): 88–117; Keller, *Example of Edward Taylor;* Charles W. Mignon, "Edward Taylor's *Preparatory Meditations:* A Decorum of Imperfection," *PMLA* 83 (1968): 1423–28; Peter Nicolaisen, *Die Bildlichkeit in der Dichtung Edward Taylors* (Neumünster: Karl Wachholtz, 1966); Evan Prosser, "Edward Taylor's Poetry," *New England Quarterly* 40 (1967): 375–98; Michael D. Reed, "Edward Taylor's Poetry: Puritan Structure and Form," *American Literature* 46 (1974): 304–12; and William J. Scheick, *The Will and the Word: The Poetry of Edward Taylor* (Athens: Univ. of Georgia Press, 1974).

6 See also Kenneth R. Ball, "Rhetoric in Edward Taylor's *Preparatory Meditations*," *Early American Literature* 4 (1969–70): 79–88, on Taylor's use of the rhetorical figures of amplification and meiosis.

7 Parker H. Johnson, "Poetry and Praise in Edward Taylor's *Preparatory Meditations*," *American Literature* 52 (1980): 84–96. Johnson defines the problem of Taylor's Puritan poetics as the need "to move from the depravity of human rhetoric to a vision of the perfected, transfigured rhetoric of heavenly praise," and the resolution of that dilemma in Taylor's discovery of "a divinely sanctioned language of correspondence," specifically "analogies . . . reasonably derived from the Bible's metaphorical, typological, and allegorical patterns" (pp. 89, 90). As the remainder of this chapter details, I agree with the emphasis on the essentially analogical strategies of Taylor's poetics, a poetics based upon biblical models.

8 Jonathan Edwards, *Images or Shadows of Divine Things,* ed. Perry Miller (New Haven: Yale Univ. Press, 1948), pp. 6–7. Everett Emerson, "Perry Miller and the Puritans: A Literary Scholar's Assessment," *The History Teacher* 14 (1981): 459–67, discusses Miller's apparent ignoring of the widespread uses of typology among New England theologians and historians, a lapse only partially overcome by his study of Edwards.

9 Gelpi, *Tenth Muse,* p. 50.

10 For a provocative study of Puritan semiology, see Michael Clark, " 'The Crucified Phrase': Sign and Desire in Puritan Semiology," *Early American Literature* 13 (1978–9): 278–93.

11 Keach, "The Epistle to the Reader," *Tropologia: A Key To Open Scripture-Metaphors* (London: J. D. for Enoch Prosser, 1681), 2, sig. A3ʳ. Lewalski, *Protestant Poetics,* pp. 82–3, also discusses Keach's adaptation of Salomon Glass's earlier work.

12 Though not included as a type by seventeenth-century exegetes, such as William Guild, Thomas Taylor, Samuel Mather, and Edward Taylor, and only obliquely rendered under the similitude of the apple tree for Christ in Benjamin Keach's *Tropologia,* the tree of life in the *Preparatory Meditations* has been rather extensively debated. See, for example, Ursula Brumm, "The 'Tree of Life' in Edward Taylor's Meditations," *Early American Literature* 3 (1968): 72–87; Carlisle, "The Puritan Structure of Edward Taylor's Poetry," pp. 147–63; Cecelia L. Halbert, "Tree of Life Imagery in the Poetry of Edward Taylor," *American Literature* 38 (1966): 22–34; Johannes Hedberg, "Meditations Linguistic and Literary on 'Meditation Twenty-Nine' by Edward Taylor," *Moderna Språk* 54 (1960): 253–70; Thomas Werge, "The Tree of Life in Edward Taylor's Poetry: The Sources of a Puritan Image," *Early American Literature* 3 (1968–9): 199–204.

13 Michael North, "Edward Taylor's Metaphors of Promise," *American Literature* 51 (1979): 10–13, also analyzes the "looking-glass metaphor" as an indicator of Taylor's desire through meditative self-examination to "discover which type his life is attached to in a metaphorical relation" and as a "perfect physical image of the mutual propriety" he seeks with Christ (pp. 10, 11).

14 Karl Keller, " 'The World Slickt Up in Types,' " *Typology and Early American Literature,* ed. Bercovitch, p. 182.

15 Allan C. Charity, *Events and Their Afterlife: The Dialectics of Christian Typology in the Bible and Dante* (Cambridge: Cambridge Univ. Press, 1966), p. 159.

16 Several critics place Taylor in the American tradition that descends to Emerson and the transcendentalists. See Hyatt H. Waggoner, "Edward Taylor," in *American Poets: From the Puritans to the Present* (Boston: Houghton-Mifflin, 1968), pp. 16–24; Keller, " 'The World Slickt Up in Types,' " *Typology and Early American Literature,* ed. Bercovitch, pp. 183–90; Gelpi, *Tenth Muse,* p. 53; and Mason I. Lowance, Jr., *The Language of Canaan: Metaphor and Symbol in New England from the Puritans to the Transcendentalists* (Cambridge: Harvard Univ. Press, 1980), pp. 277–95.

17 Gelpi, *Tenth Muse,* p. 35. Gelpi's study offers astute insights into the paradoxes of Christ's nature and the imagery of containing and being contained through which Taylor sought to express the soul's relationship with the Savior.

18 The collected lyrics or "canticles" celebrate pure marital love as ordained by God in creation and vindicate that love in opposition to both asceticism and lust. According to most interpretations of it as an allegory, the Song of Solomon unfolds Solomon's love for a Shulamite maiden, but it serves figuratively to reveal God's love for Israel as His covenant people and prophesies Christ's love for His heavenly church and redeemed souls under the guise of the Beloved or Bride. For more extensive discussions of Taylor's use of the Song of Solomon and the traditions of seventeenth-century exegesis, consult John Clendenning, "Piety and Imagery in Edward Taylor's 'The Reflexion,' " *American Quarterly* 16 (1964): 203–11; Stanley Stewart, *The Enclosed Garden: The Tradition and the Image in Seventeenth-Century Poetry* (Madison: Univ. of Wisconsin Press, 1966); Nico-

laisen, *Die Bildlichkeit in der Dichtung Edward Taylors,* pp. 131–37; Phillip E. Pierpont, " 'Oh! Angells, Stand Agastard At My Song': Edward Taylor's Meditations on Canticles" (Ph.D. diss., Southern Illinois Univ., 1972); Karen E. Rowe, "Sacred or Profane?: Edward Taylor's Meditations on Canticles," *Modern Philology* 72 (1974): 123–38; George L. Scheper, "Reformation Attitudes toward Allegory and the Song of Songs," *PMLA* 89 (1974): 551–62; Jeffrey A. Hammond, "Songs from the Garden: Edward Taylor and the Canticles" (Ph.D. diss., Kent State Univ., 1979); Lowance, *Language of Canaan,* pp. 41–54, 91–6; Lewalski, *Protestant Poetics,* pp. 59–69, 416–25; and Jeffrey A. Hammond, "A Puritan *Ars Moriendi:* Edward Taylor's Late Meditations on the Song of Songs," *Early American Literature* 17 (1982–3): 191–214.

19 Rowe, "Sacred or Profane?" pp. 127–30, delineates Taylor's reliance upon Durham's *Clavis Cantici* (1668), which was listed in Taylor's library at the time of his death in 1729. See Keller, *Example of Edward Taylor,* pp. 206–20, for an analysis of Taylor's choice of erotic imagery to signify salvation and the symbolic love-relation between God and man.

20 A late Greek word, found in the Septuagint, *agape* was adopted by the New Testament writers to express the distinctive character of Christian love, which includes God's fatherly love for man, man's adoration of God, and brotherly love for others. In the early church it denoted manifestations of such brotherly love among believers, particularly certain meals taken in common, such as rites, occasionally called "love feasts," that preceded celebration of the Lord's Supper. Christ himself, in his attitudes and life, best exemplifies the principles of *agape,* a love that transcends *eros* (sexual love).

21 Gelpi, *Tenth Muse,* p. 42.

22 See Lowance, *Language of Canaan,* pp. 115–59, for an analysis of the ways in which a developmental and recapitulative typology supported the emergence of American millennialism, a historical application of biblical prophecy quite different from Taylor's yearning for the soul's eschatological reward in heaven.

23 Ursula Brumm, *American Thought and Religious Typology,* trans. John Hoaglund (New Brunswick, N.J.: Rutgers Univ. Press, 1970), p. 80, envisioned this progress as one from "historically fixed types" to a "typological metaphorical interpretation of the Lord's Supper" and "from there . . . to a purely metaphorical, allegorical interpretation of the Song of Solomon." Hammond, "Edward Taylor's Late Meditations on the Song of Songs," pp. 191–214, argues persuasively, and I believe correctly, that Canticles "achieves a special significance for Taylor as a Puritan *ars moriendi,*" made more poignant by his identification with Solomon, the aging king, "penman for the Holy Spirit," who "became a model for those who, ripe in years and impatient with their earthly state, longed for the consummation of their union with Christ," as Taylor surely did when in later years his frail health gave urgency to his preparation for impending death (pp. 203, 206).

24 Louis L. Martz, "Foreword," *The Poems of Edward Taylor,* ed. Donald E. Stanford (New Haven: Yale Univ. Press, 1960), pp. xiii–xxxvii, first placed Taylor in the tradition of meditative poets, which he had defined in *The Poetry of Meditation* (1954; rev. ed. New Haven: Yale Univ. Press, 1962). See also Norman S. Grabo, "Introduction," *Edward Taylor's Christographia* (New Haven: Yale Univ.

Press, 1962), pp. xi–xliv; U. Milo Kaufmann, *"The Pilgrim's Progress" and Traditions in Puritan Meditation* (New Haven: Yale Univ. Press, 1966); Erdmute Lang, " 'Meditation 42' von Edward Taylor," *Jahrbuch für Amerikastudien* 12 (1967): 92–108; Scheick, *Will and the Word,* pp. 3–26, 49–90, on reason and the will; and Lewalski, *Protestant Poetics,* pp. 147–78.

25 The fallenness of language and imperfection of poetry are major topics for discussion in Mignon, "A Decorum of Imperfection," pp. 1423–28.

26 See Gelpi, *Tenth Muse,* pp. 23–32; Donald Junkins, "Edward Taylor's Revisions," *American Literature* 37 (1965): 135–52; Keller, *Example of Edward Taylor,* pp. 101–12, 223–59; Charles W. Mignon, "Diction in Edward Taylor's *Preparatory Meditations,*" *American Speech* 41 (1966): 243–53; and Peter Thorpe, "Edward Taylor as Poet," *New England Quarterly* 39 (1966): 356–72. Taylor's skepticism about the capacities of language and his use of obscure or rough diction do not preclude his attempts to "craft" his poetry through repeated revisions or to seek always the "artistic polish" that will make his poems worthy gifts to God. Serious explorations of Taylor's poetics have replaced the earlier dismissals of his poetic crudity as a mere byproduct of his Puritanism and status as a "wilderness" poet in New England and superseded also discussions of his injunction against publication, sometimes attributed to his self-consciousness of lapses in his art.

27 Scheick, *Will and the Word,* pp. 117–68, provides the fullest treatment to date of Taylor's concept of the Word and words.

28 Gelpi, *Tenth Muse,* pp. 51, 52.

29 As quoted by A. S. P. Woodhouse, "Imagination," *Princeton Encyclopedia of Poetry and Poetics,* ed. Alex Preminger, Frank J. Warnke, and O. B. Hardison, Jr., enlarged ed. (Princeton: Princeton Univ. Press, 1974), p. 372, on which my discussion of fancy and the imagination is in part based.

30 See Robert W. Dent, "Imagination in *A Midsummer Night's Dream,*" *Shakespeare Quarterly* 15 (1964): 115–29.

31 William Rossky, "Imagination in the English Renaissance: Psychology and Poetic," *Studies in the Renaissance* 5 (1958): 49–73.

32 Scheick, *Will and the Word,* pp. 124–9; and Gelpi, *Tenth Muse,* pp. 40–1, note the transformation of the pipe or the quill into a conduit for grace and instrument for writing.

33 Thomas M. and Virginia L. Davis, eds. "Introduction," *Edward Taylor's Minor Poetry,* vol. 3 of *The Unpublished Writings of Edward Taylor,* 3 vols. to date (Boston: Twayne, 1981), p. xiv. My preceding discussion of Taylor's paraphrases of the Psalms is indebted to this "Introduction," pp. xi–xx, 44–5, and to Thomas M. and Virginia L. Davis, "Edward Taylor's Metrical Paraphrases of the Psalms," *American Literature* 48 (1977): 455–70.

34 Johnson, "Poetry and Praise in Edward Taylor's *Preparatory Meditations,*" pp. 84–96, argues convincingly that despite Taylor's self-deprecation, he attempts "to perfect a language of praise" by imitating the biblical texts. Johnson cites as evidence 46 percent of the meditations that use "praise" or its variants in the final three lines, the familiar instruments and mentions of Psalms that end 66 percent of the poems, and the 40 percent that contain references to both praise and singing or music in the final lines. Reed, "Edward Taylor's Poetry: Puritan Structure and Form," pp. 311–12, also notes the conditional nature of Taylor's pledges.

35 Hammond, "A Puritan *Ars Moriendi*," pp. 208–9, 214, also conceives of the final Meditation II.165 as a poem deliberately composed to culminate Taylor's sequence on Canticles and his *Preparatory Meditations*, since Taylor stops just shy of Canticles 2:6 which contains the embrace of Christ and His Bride. Shortly after writing Meditation II.165 in 1725, he apparently bound the "Poetical Works" manuscript, making the image of "Hidebound gift" an allusion both to the literal volume and to his humble offering of a poesy limited by its human imperfections which he yields up to God. From 1720 to his death in 1729 Taylor suffered from increasingly frail health that hampered his composition of the meditations.

Index

Aaron, 5, 73, 94, 98, 99, 114, 118, 125–6, 127, 235, 236
Abel, 56
Abraham, 4, 19, 54, 57, 58, 64–5, 67, 71, 79, 102, 106, 169, 170, 172, 175, 206, 234, 249; as a type of Christ, 60–4
Act of Uniformity, xi, 91, 92, 132
Acts of the Apostles, 59
Adam, xii, 18–19, 27, 28, 29, 35, 55, 56, 57, 58, 68, 69, 71, 102, 107, 123, 130, 133, 143, 169, 170, 234, 238–9, 259, 261; as a type of Christ, 303 n20, 304 n21, 22
Ahasuerus, 223, 224
Ainsworth, Henry, 27, 136, 138, 232
allegory: Alexandrian, 5, 6, 8, 12; criticism of, 8–12; development of, 5–8; distinguished from allegorical scripture, 11–12; in Middle Ages, 7, 63; Taylor's poetic use of, 238–40
Ames, William, 27
Anglicanism, xii, 20, 21, 25, 28, 31, 78, 90–1, 92–4, 95, 96, 98, 101, 107, 113, 120, 131, 132, 168, 174, 196, 197, 231
Antinomian heresy, 18
Antiochenes, 6, 8, 27, 43
Apostles, the, 66
Arians, 41
Arminian heresy, 18
Auerbach, Erich, 3
Augustine, Saint, 6–7, 27, 32, 42, 65, 268, 295 n11, n12

Contra Faustum, 6
De Doctrina Christiana, 6

Babylon, 9, 13–16, 19, 54, 93, 230
Baptism, 146–7, 155, 163, 165–7, 168–71, 175, 198, 199
Barack, 57
Barlow, Joel, x
Basil, Saint, 8
Belshazzar, 223, 224
Benjamin, 140
Bercovitch, Sacvan, ix, 297 n31, 297–8 n33, 298 n35, n37, 306 n3, 309–10 n18
Bèze, Théodore de, 8, 27, 232
Bonaventure, Saint, 7, 12
Bradford, William, ix
    Of Plymouth Plantation, 89
Bradstreet, Anne, xi, 229
Brumm, Ursula, ix
Bull, Nehemiah, 74

Calvin, John, 8, 27, 44, 51, 61
    Commentary on Colossians, 43
    Institutes, 43, 168
Calvinism, 17–18, 97, 133, 165, 176, 178, 196; vs. Anglicanism, 90–1; vs. Catholicism, 90–1
Canaan, 1, 3, 14, 21, 36, 54, 71, 150, 151, 157, 160, 201, 202, 230, 245, 250
Canticles, xii, xiv, 11, 25, 112, 211, 229, 231–2, 245, 250, 257–8, 259–60, 261,

Canticles (*Cont.*)
263, 264, 271, 273–4, 275, 328–9 n18;
Taylor's meditations on, 329 n23, 331
n35
Catholicism, xii, 2, 8, 9, 11–12, 20, 25, 27,
28, 31, 36, 56, 58, 78, 90–1, 92, 93,
98, 101, 120, 174, 181, 182, 197, 231;
Taylor's denunciations of, 32, 33–4,
95–6, 113–14, 130, 167–8, 189
Cassian, 6
ceremonial law, 32–4, 68–70, 91–2, 95–7,
99–102, 106–7, 113–15
Charity, Allan C., 4–5, 64, 251
Charles II, 91, 92
Christographia (Edward Taylor), x, xiii,
25, 26, 76, 77, 101, 106, 165, 229,
261, 275
Sermon I, 85–6
Sermon II, 76, 97–8, 115, 116, 119,
129, 130
Sermon IV, 50, 76, 305–6 n3
Sermon V, 96
Sermon IX, 31–2, 33, 34, 49, 95, 97,
114, 115, 243, 305–6 n3
Sermon X, 32, 114–15, 306 n3
Sermon XI, 95–6, 114, 125
Sermon XII, 77, 96
Sermon XIII, 33, 98
Chronicles, Book of, 16
Chrysostom, Saint, 8, 43, 46, 61
Church Fathers, 2, 5, 7, 27, 32, 42, 56,
58, 62, 183, 232, 268
circumcision, 27, 36, 144, 168–71, 175,
198, 199
cities of refuge, 143–4
Colossians, Epistle to, 10, 30, 37, 41, 44,
75, 76, 106, 171, 261
Congregational Way, 17
consubstantiation, 167–8
Corinthians, First Epistle to, 9, 43, 51,
128, 161, 169, 176, 179, 209, 248, 323
n7; Second Epistle to, 20, 51
Cotton, John, 53, 88, 275
God's Promise to His Plantations, 89
Covenant of Grace, 22, 57, 62, 63, 147,
161, 166, 168, 169, 170, 191, 197; and
abrogation of Covenant of Law, 19–
20; Old Testament dispensation, 18–
19; Puritan concepts of, 17–21; relation to typology, 20–1
Covenant of Law, 19–20

Covenant of Works, 18, 57, 62, 67, 169,
170
Crashaw, Richard, 233
Cromwell, Oliver, 92
Cyril of Jerusalem, 8

Danforth, John, 55
David, xiii, 16–17, 27, 28, 54, 55, 57, 58,
71, 73, 79, 83, 104, 140, 235, 245,
246, 261, 271, 273, 274, 276; as a
type of the poet, 274–5
Davis, Thomas M., x, 186, 272
Davis, Virginia L., x
Deuteronomy, Book of, 14, 71, 76
Donne, John, x, xiv, 138, 229
Durham, James
Clavis Cantici, 258

Ecclesiastes, 271
Edwards, Jonathan, x, xi
Images or Shadows of Divine Things, ix,
39, 237
Egypt, xiii, 9, 27, 35, 66, 73, 118, 122,
131, 132, 145, 147, 148, 175, 189,
197, 201, 202, 204, 225, 230
Eichrodt, Walther, 2
Elijah, 57, 73, 308 n12
Elisha, 57, 73, 308 n12
Enoch, 56, 71
Ephesians, Epistle to, 256
Erastians, 188, 321 n26
Eusebius of Caesarea, 8
Evangelical worship, 120, 129–30, 165–6
Eve, 18, 123
exempla fidei, 87, 89, 217
Exodus, 2, 4, 11, 14, 16, 27, 93
Exodus, Book of, 51, 156, 157, 160, 200

fancy, 267–9
feasts, 259, 260–1

Galatians, Epistle to, 51, 58, 60, 62, 64
Gelpi, Albert, xiv, 238, 254, 258, 267
Genesis, Book of, 18, 19, 184
Gideon, 57
Gillespie, George
Aarons Rod Blossoming, 209, 321 n26
Glass Salomon
Philologia Sacra, 242
Grabo, Norman S., x, 263
Great Awakening, 97
Great Migration, 12, 15, 18, 298 n35

Guild, William, 60; career of, 295–6 n18
    Moses Unvailed, xi, 8, 27, 30, 51, 198

Hagar, 57, 58, 60, 62–4, 65
Half-Way Covenant, 165, 166–7, 169,
    172–3, 174
Hebrews, Book of, 3, 9, 43, 59, 60, 70,
    133
Herbert, George, xi, 138, 229, 240
    Temple, The, xiv, 107, 131, 163, 196,
    232–3
Hooker, Thomas
    Application of Redemption, The, 13
Hosea, Book of, 148
House of Jacob, 77–9, 99, 101–2, 106
Hunter, Paul, 12
Hutchinson, Anne, 96

imitatio Christi, 85–6, 248–9, 309–10 n18
Isaac, 57, 58, 59, 63, 64, 67, 71, 206, 234;
    as a type of Christ, 64–6, 307 n7
Isaiah, 73, 244; as a type of the poet, 269–
    70
Isaiah, Book of, 14, 59, 160, 269
Ishmael, 58

Jackson, Arthur, 136
Jacob, 54, 57, 63, 64, 71, 102, 107, 109,
    234; as a type of Christ, 65–7
Jehoshua, 73
Jeremiah, Book of, 59, 94
Jerome, Saint, 6, 247
Jewish ceremonies, 30–1, 32–4
Job, 57, 66
Job, Book of, 25, 229, 271, 274
John, Gospel of, 157, 244, 245, 252, 261
John the Baptist, 114
Johnson, Thomas H., x
Jonah, xii, 27, 35, 57, 71, 147, 235, 238–
    9, 240; as a type of Christ, 72–3
Joseph, 28, 45, 57, 66, 71, 80, 84, 140,
    148, 235, 245
Josephus, 54
Joshua, 3, 53, 54, 55, 57, 59, 71, 80, 84,
    86, 88, 140, 235
Judges, Book of, 80
Justin Martyr, 247

Keach, Benjamin, 60, 246; on allegory vs.
    allegorical scripture, 11; career of, 296
    n19
    Tropologia, 8–9, 11, 27, 58, 160, 242

Keller, Karl, x, 249, 309 n16
Korshin, Paul J., x; definition of typol-
    ogy, 298–9 n42

Lamech, 56
Lamentations, 271
Leviticus, Book of, 125, 126, 133, 136,
    142, 201
Lewalski, Barbara K., x, xiv, 233
Lord's Supper (*see also* Solomon Stoddard
    and Increase Mather), 159–61, 165–9,
    260–1; debate over admission to,
    172–8, 186–8, 322–3 n6; foreshadows
    heavenly feast, 223–8, 325 n16; prep-
    aration for, 196–7, 216–19, 325 n16;
    Taylor's meditations on, 190–5, 212–
    15
Lowance, Mason I., Jr., ix, x, 12
Luke, Gospel of, 78, 102
Luther, Martin, 8, 9, 27
Lutheranism, 167, 168

Manning, Stephen, 140
Martz, Louis, 83, 263
Mason, John, 232
Mather, Cotton, ix, xi, 14, 56, 64; on
    providential history of New England,
    13, 15, 17
    Confession of Faith, A, 19
    Magnalia Christi Americans, 13, 19, 54,
    89, 91, 99
    Wonders of the Invisible World, 15, 89
Mather, Increase, xiii, 55, 184, 195, 197,
    206, 275; attacks Stoddard, 174, 175,
    177–8, 181, 207–8, 211; on Lord's
    Supper, 324 n13; on sacramental
    preparation, 207–8, 218; on uses of
    types, 320 n21
    "Confutation of the Rev. Mr Stod-
    dard's Observations," 172, 175, 178,
    207, 209, 317 n6, n8, 324 n13
    Day of Trouble is Near, The, 89
    Dissertation, A, 177–8, 180, 181, 182,
    186, 190, 193, 207, 208, 211
Mather, Richard
    Apologie of the Churches, An, 13–14
Mather, Samuel, xv, 13, 22, 25, 31, 32,
    33, 36, 38, 39, 40, 42, 43, 57, 65, 66,
    72, 81, 86, 131, 133, 136, 138, 142,
    145, 152, 168, 184, 194, 232, 275; and
    allegory, 9; career of, 302 n16; on

Mather, Samuel (*Cont.*)
  ceremonial law, 92–5; on church
  membership, 166; on criteria for
  types, 9–10; on typological terms,
  10–11
  Figures or Types, The, xi, xii, 8–11, 19–
  20, 27, 28–30, 35–6, 37, 44, 50–2,
  55, 57, 58, 59–60, 67, 68, 70, 71, 73–
  4, 76, 77–8, 79–80, 82–3, 91, 92–5,
  98, 99, 103, 128, 132, 143, 144–5,
  148, 155, 170, 177, 198–9, 200, 213,
  243, 247, 296 n19, 307 n6; organization of, 283–6; Taylor's use of, 302–3
  n17
  Testimony from the Scripture, A, 28, 92
Matthew, Gospel of, 146, 160, 190, 207,
  208, 210, 211, 243, 245
meditation: in relation to Taylor's poetics,
  263–4; Taylor's practice of, 218–21
Melancthon (Philipp Schwarzert), 8
Melchizedek, 57, 58–60, 59, 71, 98
metaphysical conceit, 138–9, 236–8, 315
  n6
Methuselah, 56
Michael, 143
Middle Ages, 7, 63
Mignon, Charles W., xv–xvi, 26
millennialism, 12, 13, 258–9; in New
  England, 14–15, 17
Miller, Perry, ix, 237, 240, 247
Milton, John, x, 163, 229
  Samson Agonistes, 131, 233
  Paradise Lost, 131, 164, 233
  Paradise Regained, 131, 164
Miner, Earl, ix
morphology of conversion, 148–52, 163–
  4, 241
Moses, ix, 2, 3, 5, 10, 13, 14–15, 16–17,
  19, 33, 36, 49, 50, 53, 54–5, 57, 58,
  73, 76, 79, 80, 84, 86, 88, 92, 93–4,
  100, 101, 106, 118, 140, 148, 149,
  150, 153, 159, 160, 201, 235, 244;
  typal function of, 67–72

Nazarite, 86, 87, 235; as a type of Christ,
  84–5
Nehemiah, 16, 53, 86, 298 n37, 306 n3,
  309–10 n18
Nehemiah, Book of, 59
Neoplatonists, 268
Nevill, George, 223, 224

New Canaan, ix, 2, 13, 22, 31, 86, 88, 89,
  91, 230
New England history, ix–x, 12–17, 53–5,
  88–9
New Jerusalem, 13–17, 54, 89, 178, 224,
  225, 227, 230, 275
Noah, xiii, 5, 19, 57, 58, 71, 73, 100,
  145–7, 152, 156
Norton, John, 88
  Evangelical Worshipper, The, 16–17
Numbers, Book of, 80, 85, 160

Oakes, Urian
  New-England Pleaded With, 14, 21
Origen, 6–7, 11, 12, 27, 42, 61, 65, 99,
  136, 138
  Contra Celsum, 6, 24
  De Principiis, 6, 24
Owen, John, 97

Passover, xiii, 27, 36, 106, 122, 144, 145,
  163, 165, 166, 167, 168, 169, 175,
  186, 196, 197, 200–1, 209, 210, 227,
  232, 241, 260; correlation to the
  Lord's Supper, 177–81, 183–5, 206–
  7; Samuel Mather on, 199; Edward
  Taylor on, 199–207; Thomas Taylor
  on, 199; typal functions of, 189–95,
  197–9, 206–7, 225–6, 323 n10
Paul, Saint, xv, 2, 3, 27, 30, 31, 32, 36,
  37, 40, 41, 42, 43, 60, 62, 63, 102,
  323 n7
Pentecost, 313–14 n17, 322 n3
personal types: criteria for, 58–60; Taylor's definition of, 56–9; Taylor's
  organization of, 35, 55, 56–8, 162;
  under the law, 71
Peter, Saint, 146, 161
Peter, Second Epistle of, 145
Philo Judeaus, 5–6, 12
Platonism, 5, 6, 7, 44, 63
Plotinus, 268
Preparatory Meditations (Edward Taylor),
  x, xi, xiii, 2, 22, 25–6, 29, 36–7, 45,
  52, 55, 71, 74, 83, 86, 88, 91, 95,
  101, 107, 130, 131–2, 144, 162, 164,
  165, 196–7, 207, 212, 216, 217, 222,
  223, 226, 229, 230–2, 241–3, 246,
  247, 251, 252, 257–63, 266, 269, 271,
  273–4; and administration of the
  Lord's Supper, 321–2 n1; and Her-

bert, xiv; and music, 271–4; organization of, 26–7, 34–6, 261, 278–81; 287–8; and personal types, 55–8; as spiritual autobiography, 231; and *Upon the Types,* 26–7

First Series:
I. 11, 25
I. 12, 25
I. 13, 25, 75
I. 14/15, 25, 74
I. 16, 25, 74
I. 17, 25, 74

Second Series:
II. 1 (Glory of all Types), 24, 26, 37–42, 49, 58, 251, 252–3, 270
II. 2 (First Born), 41–2, 58, 78, 249, 253, 276
II. 3 (Adam, Noah, Melchizedek), 29, 57, 58, 146, 249, 270, 304 n22
II. 4 (Abraham), 58, 60–4, 65, 206, 249, 251, 260, 270
II. 5 (Isaac), 57, 59, 64–5, 206, 253, 307 n7
II. 6 (Jacob), 65–7, 257, 271, 272
II. 7 (Joseph), 45, 140–1, 245, 249, 270
II. 8 (Law), 67–71, 73
II. 9 (Moses), 36, 49–51, 68, 71, 73, 267
II. 10 (Joshua), 59, 71, 84, 88
II. 11 (Samson), 45, 71, 80–2, 83–4, 248
II. 12 (David), 51, 71, 234
II. 13 (Solomon), 72
II. 14 (Prophets, Priests, and Kings), 35, 74–7, 78, 79, 231, 234, 251
II. 15 (Nazarites), 35, 53, 78, 84–5, 248
II. 16 (House of Jacob), xii, 78–9, 101–5, 106, 126, 260
II. 17 (Burnt Offerings), 107–11, 127, 130, 138, 162, 249
II. 18 (Altars), xiv, 105, 109–12, 113, 127, 130, 253, 255, 273
II. 19 (Spicknard), 112–13
II. 20 (Temple), xiv, 35, 90, 117–18, 124, 130, 138, 142, 186, 231, 256
II. 21 (New Moon Feasts), 121, 128, 138, 199, 200, 255, 267, 313–14 n17
II. 22 (Passover), xiii, 101, 122, 166, 168, 186, 196, 197–8, 199–202,

204, 205–6, 225, 232, 241, 314 n17
II. 23 (Feast of Atonement), 78, 114, 122, 125–7, 129–30, 142, 199, 231, 235–6, 237, 272
II. 24 (Feast of Tabernacles), 122–5, 127, 138, 159, 199, 244, 249, 253, 256, 257
II. 25 (Morning, Evening, Sabbath Offerings), 115–16, 121, 129, 231, 247–8, 268
II. 26 (Unclean Touchings), 133–5, 142, 238
II. 27 (Leprosy), 135–9, 141–2, 144, 151, 159, 162
II. 28 (Cities of Refuge), 132, 142–4, 162, 259
II. 29 (Noah's Ark), xiii, 35, 73, 145–7, 162, 245
II. (Jonah), 55, 57, 72–3, 162, 238–9, 259, 263
II. 31, 245
II. 32, 255
II. 33, 245
II. 34, 253–4
II. 35, 250
II. 36, 233, 245, 263, 264, 265
II. 37, 245
II. 38, 245
II. 39, 244
II. 40, 244
II. 42, 244, 255
II. 43, 109, 263, 264–5, 270
II. 44, 109, 244, 248, 264, 270
II. 45, 75–7, 128, 254, 255
II. 47, 245, 255
II. 49, 269
II. 50, 46–9, 239, 244, 254
II. 51, 272
II. 52, 244, 245, 269
II. 53, 263–4, 268
II. 54, 234, 244, 245, 260, 264
II. 56, 245, 265, 271
II. 58 (Israel's Deliverance), xii, 35, 49, 73, 131, 132, 142, 147–52, 154, 156, 161, 162, 230, 240, 241, 245, 270
II. 59 (Pillar of Cloud and Fire), 1, 21–2, 35, 49, 155–7, 162, 230, 238
II. 60A (Manna), 35, 50–1, 157–9, 163, 230, 232
II. 60B (Horeb's Rock), 35, 157, 159–62, 163, 230, 232, 244, 245, 269

Preparatory Meditations (Cont.)
    II. 61 (Brazen Serpent), 35, 152–5,
        156, 162, 163, 230, 248
    II. 62, 245
    II. 63, 249, 260, 273, 304 n22
    II. 64, 268
    II. 65, 260
    II. 67B, 245
    II. 68A, 245
    II. 68B, 249
    II. 69, 260
    II. 70 (Circumcision), xiii, 166, 168,
        169–72, 202
    II. 71 (Passover), xiii, 166, 168, 186,
        196, 197–8, 203–6, 210–11, 225,
        232
    II. 72, 51–2, 266, 269
    II. 75, 255
    II. 78, 244–5
    II. 79, 256–7
    II. 80, 255
    II. 82, 243, 265, 266, 270, 271
    II. 83, 260
    II. 84, 260
    II. 85, 260
    II. 86, 260, 270
    II. 89, 261–2
    II. 90, 262–3, 273
    II. 92, 248, 268
    II. 95, 249–50
    II. 98, 245–6, 255, 261
    II. 99, 245, 248, 254
    II. 100, 245
    II. 101, 245, 252
    II. 103, 165, 191–3, 194, 206, 220,
        225, 227, 239–40, 324 n10
    II. 104, 193, 207, 215, 220–1
    II. 105, 194, 207, 220, 252
    II. 106, 193–4, 197, 212–13, 215–16,
        219–20, 266
    II. 107, 220
    II. 108, 167–8, 197, 215, 220, 222
    II. 109, 216–17, 223–8
    II. 110, 221–2, 272–3
    II. 111, 249
    II. 113, 245, 246, 261
    II. 114, 245, 261
    II. 115, 257, 274
    II. 122, 265, 268
    II. 130, 260
    II. 131, 260, 266, 268
    II. 132, 265, 266

    II. 133, 229, 274
    II. 138, 265
    II. 141, 271
    II. 142, 265
    II. 147, 267
    II. 153, 276
    II. 155, 270
    II. 157B, 260–1
    II. 165, 274, 331 n35
Presbyterianism, 17, 18, 21, 178, 188,
    193, 321 n26
Proverbs, Book of, 271
Prudentius
    Psychomachia, 309 n17
Psalms, xiv, 21, 25, 229, 233, 243, 265,
    274; and Puritan poetry, 271–2
Puttenham, George, 268
Pynchon, William
    Meritorious Price of Our Redemption, The,
    97

Quakers, 91, 98, 109, 172, 189; Taylor's
    attacks on, 96–7, 119, 120
Quarles, Francis, 232

Ramus, Petrus, 8
Reformation, x, 8, 27, 90
Restoration, 28
Revelation, 11, 14, 145, 151, 160, 178,
    227, 273
Robinson, John
    *Justification of Separation from the Church
    of England, A,* 16
Romans, Epistle to, 9, 58, 68, 69, 102,
    103, 106, 184
Rosenmeier, Jesper, ix
Rossky, William, 268

Sabellians, 41
Samson, 45, 57, 60, 71, 84, 86, 87, 140,
    235; as a type of Christ, 79–84
Samuel, 5, 57
Sarah, 57, 58, 60, 62–4
Second Coming, the, ix, 12, 14, 16, 17,
    160
Seth, 56
Shakespeare, William
    Midsummer Night's Dream, A, 268
Sherlock, William, 97; career of, 311 n9
Slethaug, Gordon, 28

Socinian heresy, xii, 41, 91, 96, 97–8,
    109, 120, 126, 172
Solomon, xiii, 16–17, 35, 54, 55, 57, 60,
    71, 72, 73, 79, 80, 83, 86, 117, 118,
    140, 147, 173, 231, 233, 235; as a
    type of the poet, 274–5
Stanford, Donald E., x
Stiles, Ezra, 26
Stoddard, Solomon, xi, xiii, 25, 26, 36,
    96, 119, 163, 166, 167, 168, 187,
    194–5, 196, 197, 203, 206, 207, 211,
    214, 215, 227; career of, 316 n4; on
    the Lord's Supper, 324 n12; on sacra-
    mental qualifications, 207–8, 218; and
    use of types, 175, 179–80
  Appeal to the Learned, An, 178–82, 186,
    189, 208, 211, 212–13, 322–3 n5, n6
  "Arguments for the Proposition," 175
  Galatians sermon, 176–7, 182, 184, 208,
    209, 316–17 n5, 319 n17, n18, n19,
    324 n12
  Safety of Appearing, The, 173, 174, 184,
    207–8, 209
Stoddardean controversy: chronology of,
    289–93; Increase Mather's participa-
    tion in, 175, 177–8, 181, 207–8, 211;
    Stoddard's liberalizing views, 172–4,
    176–7, 208, 218; Stoddard's response
    to attacks, 178–82, 211; Taylor's par-
    ticipation in, 165–6, 174, 175–6, 182–
    5, 189–90, 206–7, 209, 211–12
Stoicism, 6, 268
Symmes, Zecharia, 54, 87
Synod of 1662, 166
Synod of 1679, 172, 175, 207

Taylor, Edward: biography of 21; critical
    reaction to, x–xi; education of 24,
    299–300 n2; and English metyaphysi-
    cals, xi, xiv, 233; on evangelical wor-
    ship, 130, 165–6, 167–9, 196–7; fam-
    ily genealogy, 301 n13; library of, 24,
    25, 28–9, 303 n19, 305 n27; and the
    Lord's Supper, 169, 173–4, 182–5,
    186–95, 209–19; metaphors, 37–40,
    230–2, 243–7, 250; ministerial ser-
    vice, 127–30; and poetic language,
    264–7, 270–4; poetic style, 104–6,
    111, 124–5, 126–7, 138–40, 151,
    215–16, 238–41, 248–51, 264–6; and
    poetry as meditation, 36–7, 219–23,
    263–4; and Puritan poetics, 221–3,

233–4, 266–9, 271–6, 327 n7, 330
    n26, n34; on sacramental preparation,
    194–5, 209–19, 226–8
  "Animadversions," 175–6, 182, 318 n16
  "Anti-Stoddard Syllogisms," 176, 319
    n17
  "Appeale Tried, The," xiii, 166, 190,
    193, 197, 206, 209, 211–12, 214, 215,
    217, 323–4 n10, 324–5 n13
  "China's Description and Common-
    place Book," 24–5
  "Commonplace Book," 24, 176, 182
  "Dispensatory," 24
  "Elegie upon the Death of . . . Mr.
    Sims," 54–5, 87–8
  "Elogie upon the Death of . . . Mr.
    Charles Chauncey," 308 n12
  Foundation Day Sermon, 166, 173, 186,
    209, 211, 256, 317–8, n9
  Gods Determinations touching his Elect, x,
    25
  "Harmony of the Gospels," 24
  Letter to Stoddard of 1687/88, 174, 206
  "Lay-man's Lamentation, The," 308
    n12
  "Metallographia," 24
  Metrical History of Christianity, A, 25
  "Particular Church is Gods House, A,"
    166, 181, 182, 186, 209, 218
  Sacramental Meditations, x
  Treatise Concerning the Lord's Supper, x,
    xiii, 25, 166, 168, 177, 182–5, 186,
    190, 191, 194, 196, 197, 203, 206,
    207, 209, 210–13, 216, 217, 218, 220,
    226, 263, 325 n16; and typology, 26
  See also Christographia; Preparatory Medi-
    tations; and Upon the Types of the Old
    Testament
Taylor, Henry Wyllys, 25, 26
Taylor, Thomas, 22, 36, 37, 38, 42, 43–4,
    51, 57, 72, 86, 93, 131, 133, 136, 138,
    142, 145, 152, 168, 194, 232, 275;
    career of, 302 n15; and Catholicism,
    167; on Lord's Supper, 167; on sacra-
    mental preparation, 209–10
  Christ Revealed, xi, xii, 8, 27–30, 35,
    37, 38, 40, 43–4, 55, 57, 58, 60, 73,
    77, 79, 80, 82–3, 91–2, 98, 99, 132,
    144, 155, 169, 186, 198, 199, 200,
    209–10, 243; organization of, 92, 282;
    Taylor's copy of, 28–9, 303 n18, n19;
    Taylor's use of, 202–3

theanthropy, 39–40, 47–8, 109, 244, 251–4

Theophylact, 42

Thomas Aquinas, Saint, 7, 12

Thompson, Benjamin, 55

Timothy, Epistle of, 252

Traherne, Thomas, xiv

Transcendentalism, x

transubstantiation, 167–8

tropes, definition of, 241–2

tropology, 11, 84, 241–3, 309 n17; and Puritan exegesis, 247–8

types (see also ceremonial law, personal types, Preparatory Meditations and Upon the Types of the Old Testament): Christ's fulfillment of, 4–5, 20, 31–3, 38–42, 58–60; criteria for defining, 9–11, 248–9; exempla fidei, xii, 82–3, 84; extraordinary, 92, 93, 144, 145, 146, 152, 155, 163, 186, 230; of the firstborn, 40–2; Israel's deliverance, 13, 14, 71, 144–5, 147–52, 155, 162–3, 230, 240–1, 245; Jewish festivals, 120–4; and metaphors, 242–3; metaphors for, 37–9, 50–1; ordinary, 92, 93; prophets, priests, and kings, xi, xii, 35, 74–8, 244; Taylor's definition of, 30–3; Taylor's organization of, 99–100, 278–81, 287–8; Taylor's personalization of, 249–51; temple, 117–19, 186–7, 213, 231, 244, 256, 312 n13; terms used, 10; and tropes, 237–8; typical ranks, 73–5, 77–9,

typology: abstracted, 298–9 n42; and allegory, 5–8; in American Puritan historiography, ix–x, 12–17, 86; bipolarity of, 3; and Christocentricity, 3–5, 251–2; and covenant theology, 17–21, 31–6; definitions of, 2–5, 140; devotional, 86–9; and faith, 4–5; and historicity of types, 2–3; literary studies of, ix–x; metaphor of-artist's sketch, 43–9; Pauline, 5–6; and providential history, 2–3; and Puritan exegesis, 9–12; recapitulative (or developmental), 12–17, 53–5, 258–9, 296–7 n22; seventeenth-century treatises on, xi, 8, 27; typologist as inspired seer, 49–52

typological conceit, 138–40, 142, 144, 148, 156, 157, 161, 162–3, 236–8; def-

initional use of, 140–2; dialectic use of, 141–2, 171

Tyndale, William, 8, 11, 27

Upon the Types of the Old Testament (Edward Taylor), 2, 22, 25, 36, 42, 52, 55–7, 67, 77, 83, 86, 91, 95, 98–101, 106, 112, 129, 131, 132, 139, 162, 165, 168, 177, 189, 190, 191, 195, 200, 206, 213, 229, 231–2, 237, 241–3, 245, 247–8, 252, 263, 269, 275; and ceremonial types, xii–xiii; organization of, 26–7, 34–6, 99–100, 120–2, 132–3, 144–5, 152–3, 155, 169, 199, 278–81, 287–8, 312 n11; and personal types, xii, 35; provenance of, xi–xii, 26, 301 n13; sources of, xii, 27–30; and Stoddardean controversy, 185–9

II. 1 (Glory of all Types), 30–1, 32, 37–42, 44–5, 47, 58, 252

II. 2 (First Born), 40–2, 58

II. 3 (Adam, Noah, and Melchizedek), 29, 35, 57, 59, 146, 304 n21

II. 4 (Abraham), 57, 58, 60–4

II. 5 (Isaac), 64–5, 307 n7

II. 6 (Jacob), 57, 65–6

II. 9 (Moses), 50, 68–71

II. 10 (Joshua), 59

II. 11 (Samson), 80–3

II. 13 (Solomon), 57, 71

II. 14 (Prophets, Priests, and Kings), 35, 77, 78, 99

II. 15 (Nazarites), 35, 77, 78

II. 16 (House of Jacob), 57, 77–9, 99, 100, 101–2, 104, 106

II. 17 (Burnt Offerings), 107–9, 111

II. 18 (Altars), 109, 111–12

II. 20 (Temple), 25, 112, 117–20, 127–8, 186–7

II. 21 (New Moon Feasts), 121, 200, 313 n16

II. 22 (Passover), 121, 122, 186, 189, 197–8, 202, 313–4 n17

II. 22A (Pentecost), 121, 313–4 n17

II. 23 (Feast of Atonement), 99, 121, 126

II. 24 (Feast of Tabernacles), 121–2

II. 25 (Morning, Evening, Sabbath Offerings), 96, 120–2, 313 n15

II. 26 (Unclean Touchings), 132, 142